# Lecture Notes in Artificial Intelligence 1720

Subseries of Lecture Notes in Computer Science
Edited by J. G. Carbonell and J. Siekmann

## Lecture Notes in Computer Science

Edited by G. Goos, J. Hartmanis and J. van Leeuwen

# Springer

*Berlin*
*Heidelberg*
*New York*
*Barcelona*
*Hong Kong*
*London*
*Milan*
*Paris*
*Singapore*
*Tokyo*

Osamu Watanabe  Takashi Yokomori (Eds.)

# Algorithmic Learning Theory

10th International Conference, ALT'99
Tokyo, Japan, December 6-8, 1999
Proceedings

Springer

Series Editors

Jaime G. Carbonell, Carnegie Mellon University, Pittsburgh, PA, USA
Jörg Siekmann, University of Saarland, Saarbrücken, Germany


Volume Editors

Osamu Watanabe
Tokyo Institute of Technology
Department of Mathematical and Computing Sciences
Tokyo 152-8552, Japan
E-mail: watanabe@is.titech.ac.jp

Takashi Yokomori
Waseda University
Department of Mathematics, School of Education
1-6-1 Nishiwaseda, Shinjuku-ku, Tokyo 169-8050, Japan
E-mail: yokomori@mn.waseda.ac.jp

Cataloging-in-Publication data applied for

Die Deutsche Bibliothek - CIP-Einheitsaufnahme

**Algorithmic learning theory** : 10th international conference ;
proceedings / ALT '99, Tokyo, Japan, December 6 - 8, 1999. Osamu
Watanabe ; Takashi Yokomori (ed.). - Berlin ; Heidelberg ; New York
; Barcelona ; Hong Kong ; London ; Milan ; Paris ; Singapore ;
Tokyo : Springer, 1999
  (Lecture notes in computer science ; Vol. 1720 : Lecture notes in
  artificial intelligence)
  ISBN 3-540-66748-2


CR Subject Classification (1998): I.2.6, I.2.3, F.4.1, I.7

ISBN 3-540-66748-2 Springer-Verlag Berlin Heidelberg New York

© Springer-Verlag Berlin Heidelberg 1999
Printed in Germany

Typesetting: Camera-ready by author
SPIN 10705377   06/3142 – 5 4 3 2 1 0     Printed on acid-free paper

# Preface

This volume contains all the papers presented at the International Conference on Algorithmic Learning Theory 1999 (ALT'99), held at Waseda University International Conference Center, Tokyo, Japan, December 6–8, 1999. The conference was sponsored by the Japanese Society for Artificial Intelligence (JSAI).

In response to the call for papers, 51 papers on all aspects of algorithmic learning theory and related areas were submitted, of which 26 papers were selected for presentation by the program committee based on their originality, quality, and relevance to the theory of machine learning. In addition to these regular papers, this volume contains three papers of invited lectures presented by Katharina Morik of the University of Dortmund, Robert E. Schapire of AT&T Labs, Shannon Lab., and Kenji Yamanishi of NEC, C&C Media Research Lab.

ALT'99 is not just one of the ALT conference series, but this conference marks the *tenth anniversary* in the series that was launched in Tokyo, in October 1990, for the discussion of research topics on all areas related to algorithmic learning theory. The ALT series was renamed last year from "ALT workshop" to "ALT conference", expressing its wider goal of providing an ideal forum to bring together researchers from both theoretical and practical learning communities, producing novel concepts and criteria that would benefit both. This movement was reflected in the papers presented at ALT'99, where there were several papers motivated by application oriented problems such as noise, data precision, etc. Furthermore, ALT'99 benefited from being held jointly with the 2nd International Conference on Discovery Science (DS'99), the conference for discussing, among other things, more applied aspects of machine learning. Also, we could celebrate the tenth anniversary of the ALT series with researchers from both theoretical and practical communities.

This year we started the **E Mark Gold Award** for the most outstanding paper by a student author, selected by the program committee of the conference. This year's award was given to **Yuri Kalnishkan** for his paper "General Linear Relations among Different Types of Predictive Complexity".

We wish to thank all who made this conference possible, first of all, the authors for submitting papers and the three invited speakers for their excellent presentations and their contributions of papers to this volume.

We are indebted to all members of the program committee: Nader Bshouty (Technion, Israel), Satoshi Kobayashi (Tokyo Denki Univ., Japan), Gabor Lugosi (Pompeu Fabra Univ., Spain), Masayuki Numao (Tokyo Inst. of Tech., Japan), Robert Schapire (ATT Shannon Lab., USA), Arun Sharma (New South Wales, Australia), John Shawe-Taylor (Univ. of London, UK), Ayumi Shinohara (Kyushu Univ., Japan), Prasad Tadepalli (Oregon State Univ., USA), Junichi Takeuchi (NEC C&C Media Research Lab., Japan), Akihiro Yamamoto (Hokkaido Univ., Japan), Rolf Wiehagen (Univ. Kaiserslautern, Germany), and Thomas Zeugmann (Kyushu Univ., Japan). They and the subreferees (listed separately) put a huge amount of work into reviewing the submissions and judging their importance and significance.

We also gratefully acknowledge the work of all those who did important jobs behind the scenes to make this volume as well as the conference possible. We thank Akira Maruoka for providing valuable suggestions, Shigeki Goto for the initial arrangement of a conference place, Naoki Abe for arranging an invited speaker, Shinichi Shimozono for producing the ALT99 logo, Isao Saito for drawing the ALT99 posters, and Springer-Verlag for their excellent support in preparing this volume.

Last but not least, we are very grateful to all the members of the local arrangement committee: Taisuke Sato (chair), Satoru Miyano, Ayumi Shinohara, without whose efforts this conference would not have been successful.

Tokyo, August 1999                                         Osamu Watanabe
                                                          Takashi Yokomori

# List of Referees

Hiroki Arimura
Sanghamitra Bandyopadhyay
Jonathan Baxter
Nicolo Cesa-Bianchi
Nello Cristianini
Stuart Flockton
Ryutaro Ichise
Kimihito Ito
Michael Kearns
Pascal Koiran
Eric Martin
Llew Mason
Ujjwal Maulik

Eric McCreath
Andrew Mitchell
Koichi Moriyama
Atsuyoshi Nakamura
Thomas R. Amoth
Mark Reid
Yasubumi Sakakibara
Hiroshi Sakamoto
Bernhard Schoelkopf
Rich Sutton
Noriyuki Tanida
Chris Watkins
Kenji Yamanishi
Takashi Yokomori

# Table of Contents

## INVITED LECTURES

Tailoring Representations to Different Requirements . . . . . . . . . . . . . . . . . . . . . 1
  Katharina Morik

Theoretical Views of Boosting and Applications . . . . . . . . . . . . . . . . . . . . . . . . 13
  Robert E. Schapire

Extended Stochastic Complexity and Minimax Relative Loss Analysis . . . . 26
  Kenji Yamanishi

## REGULAR CONTRIBUTIONS

### Neural Networks

Algebraic Analysis for Singular Statistical Estimation . . . . . . . . . . . . . . . . . . 39
  Sumio Watanabe

Generalization Error of Linear Neural Networks in Unidentifiable Cases . . . 51
  Kenji Fukumizu

The Computational Limits to the Cognitive Power of the Neuroidal Tabula
Rasa . . . . . . . . . . . . . . . . . . . . . . . . . . . . . . . . . . . . . . . . . . . . . . . . . . . . . . . . . . . . . 63
  Jiří Wiedermann

### Learning Dimension

The Consistency Dimension and Distribution-Dependent Learning from
Queries . . . . . . . . . . . . . . . . . . . . . . . . . . . . . . . . . . . . . . . . . . . . . . . . . . . . . . . . . . 77
  José L. Balcázar, Jorge Castro, David Guijarro, and
  Hans-Ulrich Simon

The VC-Dimension of Subclasses of Pattern Languages . . . . . . . . . . . . . . . . 93
  Andrew Mitchell, Tobias Scheffer, Arun Sharma, and Frank Stephan

On the $V_\gamma$ Dimension for Regression in Reproducing Kernel Hilbert
Spaces . . . . . . . . . . . . . . . . . . . . . . . . . . . . . . . . . . . . . . . . . . . . . . . . . . . . . . . . . . . 106
  Theodoros Evgeniou and Massimiliano Pontil

# Inductive Inference

On the Strength of Incremental Learning.............................. 118
  Steffen Lange and Gunter Grieser

Learning from Random Text ........................................ 132
  Peter Rossmanith

Inductive Learning with Corroboration ............................. 145
  Phil Watson

# Inductive Logic Programming

Flattening and Implication ......................................... 157
  Kouichi Hirata

Induction of Logic Programs Based on $\psi$-Terms...................... 169
  Yutaka Sasaki

Complexity in the Case Against Accuracy: When Building One
Function-Free Horn Clause Is as Hard as Any ....................... 182
  Richard Nock

A Method of Similarity-Driven Knowledge Revision for Type
Specifications..................................................... 194
  Nobuhiro Morita, Makoto Haraguchi, and Yoshiaki Okubo

# PAC Learning

PAC Learning with Nasty Noise .................................... 206
  Nader H. Bshouty, Nadav Eiron, and Eyal Kushilevitz

Positive and Unlabeled Examples Help Learning ..................... 219
  Francesco De Comité, François Denis, Rémi Gilleron, and
  Fabien Letouzey

Learning Real Polynomials with a Turing Machine ................... 231
  Dennis Cheung

# Mathematical Tools for Learning

Faster Near-Optimal Reinforcement Learning: Adding Adaptiveness to
the $E^3$ Algorithm ............................................... 241
  Carlos Domingo

A Note on Support Vector Machine Degeneracy....................... 252
  Ryan Rifkin, Massimiliano Pontil, and Alessandro Verri

## Learning Recursive Functions

Learnability of Enumerable Classes of Recursive Functions from "Typical"
Examples ...................................................... 264
*Jochen Nessel*

On the Uniform Learnability of Approximations to Non-recursive
Functions ...................................................... 276
*Frank Stephan and Thomas Zeugmann*

## Query Learning

Learning Minimal Covers of Functional Dependencies with Queries ....... 291
*Montserrat Hermo and Víctor Lavín*

Boolean Formulas Are Hard to Learn for Most Gate Bases .............. 301
*Víctor Dalmau*

Finding Relevant Variables in PAC Model with Membership Queries ..... 313
*David Guijarro, Jun Tarui, and Tatsuie Tsukiji*

## On-Line Learning

General Linear Relations among Different Types of Predictive
Complexity ...................................................... 323
*Yuri Kalnishkan*

Predicting Nearly as Well as the Best Pruning of a Planar Decision
Graph .......................................................... 335
*Eiji Takimoto and Manfred K. Warmuth*

On Learning Unions of Pattern Languages and Tree Patterns ............ 347
*Sally A. Goldman and Stephen S. Kwek*

## Author Index ................................................. 365

# Tailoring Representations to Different Requirements

Katharina Morik

Univ. Dortmund, Computer Science VIII,
D-44221 Dortmund, Germany
morik@ls8.cs.uni-dortmund.de
http://www-ai.cs.uni-dortmund.de

**Abstract.** Designing the representation languages for the input and output of a learning algorithm is the hardest task within machine learning applications. Transforming the given representation of observations into a well-suited language $L_E$ may ease learning such that a simple and efficient learning algorithm can solve the learning problem. Learnability is defined with respect to the representation of the output of learning, $L_H$. If the predictive accuracy is the only criterion for the success of learning, the choice of $L_H$ means to find the hypothesis space with most easily learnable concepts, which contains the solution. Additional criteria for the success of learning such as comprehensibility and embeddedness may ask for transformations of $L_H$ such that users can easily interpret and other systems can easily exploit the learning results. Designing a language $L_H$ that is optimal with respect to all the criteria is too difficult a task. Instead, we design families of representations, where each family member is well suited for a particular set of requirements, and implement transformations between the representations. In this paper, we discuss a representation family of Horn logic. Work on tailoring representations is illustrated by a robot application.

## 1 Introduction

Machine learning has focused on the particular learning task of concept learning. Investigating this task has led to sound theoretical results as well as to efficient learning systems. However, some aspects of learning have not yet received the attention they deserve. Theoretical results are missing where they are urgently needed for successful applications of machine learning. If we contrast the theoretically analyzed setting of concept learning with the one found in real-world applications, we encounter quite a number of open research questions. Let me draw your attention to those questions that are related with tailoring representations.

The setting of concept learning that has been well investigated can be summarized as follows.

**Concept learning:** Given a set of examples in a representation language $L_E$, drawn according to some distribution, and background knowledge in a representation language $L_B$,

O. Watanabe, T. Yokomori (Eds.): ALT'99, LNAI 1720, pp. 1–12, 1999.

learn a hypothesis in a representation language $L_H$ that classifies further examples properly according to a given criterion.

Different paradigms vary assumptions about the distribution and about the existence of background knowledge. In the paradigm of probably approximately correct (PAC) learning, for instance, an unknown but fixed distribution is assumed and background knowledge is ignored. In the paradigm of inductive logic programming (ILP), the distribution is ignored, but background knowledge is taken into account. Different approaches vary the particular success criterion. For instance, information gain, minimal description length, or Bayes-oriented criteria are discussed. Structural risk minimization balances the error rate and the complexity of hypotheses. The variety of criteria can be subsumed under that of accuracy of predictions (i.e. correctness of classifications of new observations). In contrast, applications of machine learning are evaluated with respect to additional criteria:

**comprehensibility:** How easily can the learning results be interpreted by human decision makers?

**embeddedness:** Most learning results are produced in order to enhance the capabilities of another system (e.g., problem solving system, natural language system, robot), the so-called performance system. The criterion is here: How easily can learning results be used by the performance system?

These criteria are most often ignored in theoretical studies. Comprehensibility and embeddedness further constrain the choice of an appropriate hypothesis language $L_H$. The problem is that they frequently do so in a contradictory manner. A representation that is well-suited for a human user may be hard to handle by a performance system. A representation that is well-suited for a system to perform a certain task may be hard to be understood by a human user. To make things even worse, we also consider the input of the learning algorithm. A learning algorithm $A_i$ can be characterized by its input (i.e. $L_{Ei}$, $L_{Bi}$) and output (i.e. $L_{Hi}$) formats. Those pairs of input and output languages, for which an efficient and effective learning algorithm exists, are called *admissible* languages. In this way, $L_H$ is further constrained by the given data in $L_E$. It is hard or even impossible to design a representation $L_H$ which is

- efficiently learnable
- from data in a given format,
- easily understood by users,
- and can be put to direct use by a performance system.

Instead of searching for one representation that fulfills at the same time the requirements of the learning algorithm, the given data, the users, and the performance system, we may want to follow a more stepwise procedure. We divide the overall representation problem into several subproblems. Each subproblem consists of two parts, namely determining an appropriate representation and developing a transformation from a given representation into it. In order to not trade in a simple representation language for a complex transformation process, we design families of representations, where each family member is well suited for a particular set of requirements, and efficient transformations between the family members are possible. The subproblems are:

**Learnability:** The majority of theoretical analyses shows the learnability of concept classes under certain restrictions of the learning task, the representation languages, and the criterion for accuracy. Hence, this subject does not require justification. However, the transformation from a given representation into the desired one raises questions that have not yet been addressed frequently. The transformation here converts $L_{Hi}$ into $L_{Hj}$, where $L_{Hj}$ is better suited for learning.

**Optimizing input data:** The hardest task of machine learning applications is the design of a well-suited representation $L_{Ej}$. On one hand, the given representation *formalism* $L_{Ei}$ must be converted into the one accepted by the learning algorithm as input. On the other hand, the representation *language* (signature) can be optimized. The formalism remaining the same, the set of features (predicates) is changed. The standard procedure is to run the algorithm on diverse feature sets until one is found that leads to an acceptable accuracy of learning. Most feature construction or selection methods aim at overcoming this trial-and-error approach.

**Comprehensibility:** Although stated as a primary goal of machine learning from the very beginning on, the criterion of comprehensibility never became a hot topic of learning theory.

**Embeddedness or program optimization:** Learning results are supposed to enhance a procedure. Most often, the procedure is already implemented as a particular performance system. The learning result in $L_{Hi}$ must be transformed into the representation $L_{Hj}$ of the performance system. Quite often, the performance system offers restrictions that are not presupposed by the learning algorithm. In this case, the transformation may be turned into an optimization, exploiting the application's restrictions.

In this paper, a family of subsets of Horn logic is discussed and illustrated by a robot application.

## 2 Learnability of Restricted Horn Logic

The learnability subject does not need any justification here. However, the transformation of one representation $L_{Hi}$ into another one $L_{Hj}$ which is better suited for learning, does. An important question is, how to recognize those parts in a given representation (or concept class) automatically, that cause negative learnability results. The user may then be asked, whether the learning task could be weakened, or at least be warned that it may take exponential time to compute a result. For instance, detecting variables that occur in the head of a clause but not in its body prohibit the clause being generative. This can easily be checked automatically. Even suggestions for fixing the clause can be computed on the basis of the predicates defined so far [27] Alternatively, the learning algorithm may start with a simple representation and increase the complexity of the hypothesis space. Of course, this alternative is easier than the recognition of the complexity class.

Desired are learnability proofs that can be made operational in the sense that indicators for (non-)learnability are defined that can be recognized automatically. One example for an operational complexity criterion is the one used by the support vector machine [31]. The width of the margin separating positive and negative examples corresponds to the VC dimension of the hypothesis space, but can be calculated much easier.[1] According to this operational criterion hypothesis spaces of increasing complexity are tried by the learning algorithm. A rough indication of the complexity of hypotheses from the ILP paradigm is the number of literals in a clause. According to this criterion, the RDT algorithm searches fo increasingly complex hypotheses [8] and a similar procedure is followed in [5]. However, the number of literals is merely a heuristic measure of complexity.

Let me now illustrate operational proofs by [9]. The difficulty of first-order logic induction originates in first-order logic deduction. Hypothesis testing, saturation of examples with background knowledge, the comparison of competing hypotheses, and the reduction of hypotheses under equivalence all use the deductive inference. Since $\theta$–subsumption [25] is a correct and for not self-resolving, non tautological clauses a complete inference, most ILP systems use it.

$\theta$**–subsumption:** A clause $D$ $\theta$–subsumes a clause $C$ iff there exists a substitution $\theta$ such that $D\theta \subseteq C$.

$\theta$–subsumption is NP-complete because of the indeterminism of choosing $\theta$ in the general case. Hence, the clauses need to be restricted. Restricting Horn clauses to k-llocal clauses allows for polynomial learning [3]. William Cohen's proof maps k-llocal clauses on monomials for which learnability proofs exist. However, the proof is not operational. It just shows where it is worth to look for theoretically well-based algorithms. What we need is an operational proof of polynomial complexity of $\theta$–subsumption of k-llocal clauses in order to solve the deductive problem within induction. We then need a learning algorithm exploiting the restriction so that learning k-llocal clauses is polynomial. Desired is an automatic check, whether a clause is k-llocal, or not.

**k-llocal Horn clause:** Let $D = D_0 \leftarrow D_{DET}, D_{NONDET}$ be a Horn clause, where $D_{DET}$ is the deterministic and $D_{NONDET}$ is the indeterministic part of its body. Let $vars$ be a function computing the set of variables of a clause. $LOC_i \subseteq D_{NONDET}$ is a local part of $D$, iff
$(vars(LOC_i) \setminus vars(\{D_0, D_{DET}\})) \cap vars(D_{NONDET} \setminus LOC_i) = \emptyset$ and there does not exist $LOC_j \subset LOC_i$ which is also a local part of $D$.
A local part $LOC_i$ is k-llocal, iff
there exists a constant $k$ such that $k \geq | LOC_i |$.
A Horn clause is k-llocal, iff each local part of it is k-llocal.

---

[1] Determining the VC dimension is a problem in $O(n^{O(\log n)})$ where $n$ is the size of a matrix representing the concept class [26].

Jörg-Uwe Kietz presents a fast subsumption algorithm for $D = D_0 \leftarrow D_{DET}, LOC_1, ..., LOC_n$ and any Horn clause $C$ [9]. For the deterministic part of $D$, there exists exactly one substitution $\theta$. An efficient subsumption algorithm for deterministic Horn clauses is presented in [11]. In the indeterministic part of $D$, it is looked for local parts, i.e. for sets of literals which do not share an indeterministic variable. This is done by merging sets of literals which have a variable in common. In this way, the algorithm checks a given clause $D$, whether it is k-local, or not. This can be done polynomially. If the local part is bounded by some $k$, its subsumption is in $O(n \cdot (k^k \cdot \mid C \mid))$. If, however, $D_{Body}$ consists of one large local part, the subsumption is exponential. The proof of polynomial complexity in the number of literals of the clauses $D$ and $C$ corresponds directly to the fast subsumption algorithm. The algorithm guarantees efficient subsumption for k-local $D$, but can be applied to any Horn clause.

The least general generalization, LGG, of Gordon Plotkin [21] is then adjusted to k-llocal clauses and it is shown that the size of the LGG of k-llocal clauses does not increase exponentially (as does the LGG of unrestricted Horn clauses) and reduction of k-llocal clauses is polynomial, too [9]. Together with the negtive learnability results in [10], k-llocal clauses can be considered the borderline between learnable and not learnable indeterministic clauses. This concludes the illustration of what I mean by operational proofs.

# 3   Optimizing Input Data

The transformation of the given data within the same representation formalism is called feature construction/extraction, if new features are built on the basis of the given ones, and feature selection, if the most relevant subset of features is selected. An explicit construction is the invention and definition of new predicates as presented by [20], [29], and [32]. Including the transformation into the learning algorithm is called constructive induction [17], [2]. An implicit adding of new features is performed by the support vector machine [31]. Using a kernel function, the feature space is transformed such that the observations become linearly separable. A more complex input representation allows the algorithm to remain simple. Only because the enriched feature space need not be used for computation– the kernel functions are used instead –, transformation plus learning algorithm remain efficient. It is an open question how to make explicit, which of the added features contributed most to a good learning result.

Let me now turn to the transformation from one representation formalism to another one. A learning algorithm is selected because of both, its input and output formalisms (plus other properties). It may turn out, however, that there does not exist an algorithm with the desired input–output pair of languages. In this case, one of the options is to transform the data from the formalism in which they are available into the input format of the selected algorithm. The current interest in feature construction may stem from knowledge discovery in databases (KDD) [15]. The given database representation has to be transformed into one which is accepted by the learning algorithm. Of course, for an ILP learning algorithm there exists a 1:1 mapping from a database table to a predicate[7]. However, this simple transformation most often is not one that eases learning. Since the arity of predicates cannot be changed through learning, a huge number of irrelevant database attributes is carried along. Therefore, the transformation from database tables into predicates should map parts of the tables to predicates, where the database key is one of the arguments of the predicate. A tool that gives an ILP learner direct access to a relational database, provides different types of mappings from tables to predicates, and constructs SQL queries for hypothesis testing automatically has been developed [18]. However, the open question remains whether there are theoretically well-based indicators of the optimal mapping for a particular learning task. This is an essential question, since the number of possible mappings is only bounded by the size of the universal database relation. Therefore, it does not help that we may well compute the size of the hypothesis space for each mapping. What is required is a structure in the space of mappings that allows for efficient search.

A frequent task when applying an ILP algorithm is to transform numerical measurements into qualitative Horn logic clauses (facts). A mobile robot, for instance, reports its action and perception by multivariate time series. Each sensor and the moving engine deliver a measurement per moment. The ILP learner requires a description of a path and what has been sensed in terms of time intervals during which some assertions are true. Hence, the signal-to-symbol transformation needs to find adequate time intervals and assertions that summarize the measurements within the time interval. This task is different from time series analysis, where the curves of measurement are approximated. It corresponds to the analysis of event sequences, where events have to be automatically recognized. As opposed to current approaches which learn about event sequences (e.g., [33],[16]), the robot application asks for a representation that can be produced incrementally on-line [14]. For our robot application we have implemented a simple algorithm which constructs predicates of the form

increasing(MissionID, Angle, Sensor, FromTime, ToTime, RelToMove)

from measurements [19]. During the time interval FromTime, ToTime, the sensor preceives increasing distance while being oriented in a particular angle with respect to the global coordinates. The relation between measured distance and moved distance is expressed by the last argument. The algorithm reads in a measurement and compares it with the current summarizing assertion (i.e., a predicate with all arguments bound except for ToTime). Either ToTime is bound, the event has ended and a new one starts, or the next measurement is read in. This procedure has some parameters (e.g., tolerated variance). These are adjusted on the data so that the transformation itself is adaptive.

The language $L_E$ constructed has the nice property of fitting to general chain rules. Given an appropriate substitution $\sigma$, a literal $B_i$ of a chain rule can be unified with a ground fact $f \in L_E$, i.e. $B_i\sigma = f$.

**General chain rule:** Let $S$ be a literal or a set of literals. Let $args(S)$ be a function that returns the Datalog arguments of $S$. A normal clause is a general chain rule, iff its body literals can be arranged in a sequence

$$B_0 \leftarrow B_1, B_2, ..., B_k, B_{k+1}$$

such that there exist Datalog terms $X, Z \in args(B_0)$, $X, Y_1 \in args(B_1)$, $Y_1, Y_2 \in args(B_2)$, ..., $Y_{k-1}, Y_k \in args(B_k)$, and $Y_k, Z \in args(B_{k+1})$.

Obviously, chain rules are well-suited for the representation of event sequences, using the time points as chaining arguments. $L_E$ is constructed such that chain rules can be learned from them. In other words, having chain rules in mind for $L_H$ we transform the given data into facts that correspond to literals of $L_H$. Note, that this transformation is not motivated by the learning algorithm in order to make learning simpler. The aim is to design $L_E$ such that a $L_H$ can be learned which can easily embedded in the robot application.

## 4   Comprehensibility

It is often claimed that learning results are easier to understand than statistical results which demand a human interpreter who translates the results into conclusions for the customer of the statistical study. In particular, decision trees and rules were found to be easily undertandable. However, these statements lack justification.

In a user-independent way, proposed criteria for comprehensibility most often refer to the length of a description (the minimal description length (MDL) principle [24]). For decision trees, the number of nodes was used as a guideline for comprehensibility. For logic programs, the number of literals of a clause or the number of variables was used as an operational criterion for the ease of understanding [1] [2], [4]. Irene Stahl corrected the MDL for ILP by restricting the description length of examples to that of positive examples only [28]. Although presented as operationalisation of comprehensibility, compression may lead to almost incomprehensible descriptions[3]. Its value for hypothesis testing and structuring the hypothesis space not neglected, as a means to achieve comprehensible learning results it is questionable.

Ryszard Michalski has proposed to use natural language for communicating learning results. The ease of transforming $L_H$ into natural language can then be used as a criterion for the naturalness of the representation.

Edgar Sommer introduced the notion of extensional redundancy. Removing extensional redundancy compresses a theory, but compressions are not restricted to that. It is known from psychology that some redundancy eases understanding. Extensional redundancy aims at characterizing superfluous parts of a theory [27].

**Extensional redundancy:** Let $G$ be the set of goal concepts in a theory $T$. Let $Q$ be the set of instances of goal concepts that are derivable from $T$. Let $C$ be a clause in $T$ and $L$ be a literal in $C$.

---

[2] The reconstruction of the examples and background knowldge from the logic theory and the example encoding by a reference Turing machine leads to a measure of compression: the length of the output tape minus the length of the input tape.

[3] Think of compressed text files!

A literal $L$ is extensionally redundant in $C$ with respect to $g \in G$, iff $C$ is in the derivation of $g$ and $C \setminus \{L\}$.

A clause $C$ is extensionally redundant in $T$ with respect to $Q$, iff $T \vdash Q$ and $T \setminus \{C\} \vdash Q$.

Structure is a key to comprehensibility. Structure is achieved by the folding operations which leaves the minimal Herbrand model of a theory unchanged [30].

**fold:** Let $C, D \in T_i$ be ordered clauses of the form
$C = C_0 \leftarrow C_1, \cdots, C_m, C_{m+1}, \cdots, C_{m+n}$ and
$D = D_0 \leftarrow D_1, \cdots, D_m$.
Let $\sigma$ be a substitution satisfying the following conditions
1. $C_i = D_i\sigma, i = 1, ..., m$
2. let $X_1, ..., X_l$ be variables that occur in $D_{Body}$ but not in $D_{Head}$; each $X_j\sigma, j = 1, ..., l$ does not occur in $C_{Head}$ nor in $C_{m+1}, \cdots, C_{m+n}$; if $i \neq i$, then $X_i\sigma \neq X_j\sigma$.
3. $D$ is the only clause in $T_i$ whose head is unifiable with $D_0\sigma$.
If such a substitution exists, then
$C' = C_0 \leftarrow D_0\sigma, C_{m+1}, \cdots, C_{m+n}$ and
$T_{i+1} = fold(T_i, C, D) = T_i \setminus \{C\} \cup \{C'\}$.
Otherwise, $T_i$ remains unchanged.

Several stratification operators have been developed that structure a theory. The FENDER program folds clauses that define a target concept with an intermediate concept [27]. The intermediate concept is made of common partial premises. A common partial premise is a set of literals which most frequently occur together in the given theory. The literals must share a variable. This will be omitted in the folded clause. However, not all logically unnecessary variables are omitted. This is meant to not hide relevant information from the user, but only encapsulate internal details.

An alternative stratification method named prefix elimination has been developed particularly for chain programs [23], i.e. for better communicating event sequences. As opposed to FENDER which gathers common partial premises regardless of an ordering of literals, the prefix elimination method only replaces common prefixes of chained literals in a clause's body. Hence, applying prefix elimination to a chain program outputs a chain program. The prefix elimination method looks for common literal sequences in all clauses, not only ones that are used to define the same concept. It suppresses all unnecessary variables. This is meant to exhibit the time relations more clearly. An abstracted example from our robot application may illustrate the method.

**Example:** Let the theory $T_i$ be
$C_1 = alongWall(S, X, Z)$
$\leftarrow stand(V, O, X, Y_1), stable(V, O, Y_1, Y_2), decrPeak(S, O, Y_2, Z)$
$C_2 = alongDoor(S, X, Z)$
$\leftarrow stand(V, O, X, Y_1), stable(V, O, Y_1, Y_2), incrPeak(S, V, Y_2, Z)$
Prefix elimination returns $T_{i+1}$:

$$C_1' = alongWall(S, X, Z) \leftarrow standstable(V, O, X, Y_2), decrPeak(S, O, Y_2, Z)$$
$$C_2' = alongDoor(S, X, Z) \leftarrow standstable(V, O, X, Y_2), incrPeak(S, V, Y_2, Z)$$
$$D = standstable(V, O, X, Y_2) \leftarrow stand(V, O, X, Y_1), stable(V, O, Y_1, Y_2)$$

Two time intervals are summarized, but no information is abstracted away.

Compression and stratification are two operational criteria for the comprehensibility of logical theories. Whether they correspond to true needs of users should be studied empirically. Since the representation is to be understood by human users, the answer depends on general cognitive capabilities as well as on user-specific preferences which, in turn, depend on prior knowledge and training. Adjusting a representation to particular preferences is a learning task in its own right. A number of answer set equivalent representations could be presented to the user who selects his favorite one. The selections serve as positive examples and a profile of the user is learned which guides further presentations. Theoretical analysis of the user profiles could well lead to a refinement of compression which excludes incompehensibly compact theories.

## 5 Embeddedness or Program Optimization

Optimizing learning results for their use by a performance system is easier than optimizing them for human understanding, since the requirements of the system are known. In many cases the requirements by users and performance system are conflicting. However, they can both start from the same learning result, if $L_H$ has been chosen carefully. In our robotics application, we used the fact that chain programs correspond to definite finite automata (DFA). Since general chain programs – as opposed to elementary chain rules – are not equivalent to context free grammars, we cannot apply the transformation presented by [6]. The general chain rules can be translated into a context-free grammar, but a transformed grammar cannot be uniquely translated back into general chain rules. Hence, we may theoretically describe the learning results with reference to context-free grammars, but this analysis cannot be put to use. It is possible, however, to transform general chain rules into a DFA. Starting from a theory which has been stratified by prefix elimination, the mapping is as follows [23]:

- A clause head becomes a state of the DFA.
- A clause defining a prefix becomes a transition of the DFA.
- The clause head of an overall goal with its substitutions becomes an output.

The DFA is restricted to successful derivations. Compilation of learned theories consisting of 250 to 470 clauses took between 1 and 5 minutes CPU time [23]. A system using the learned and optimized knowledge was developed by Volker Klingspor [13], [22]. His system SHARC performs object-recognition, planning, and plan execution. The low-level steps of object recognition are performed in parallel, each sensor having its own process. Object recognition is performed by forward inference on optimized clauses using a marker passing strategy. Planning and plan execution is performed by backward inference on optimized clauses. The general chain rules are learned by GRDT, an ILP learner with declarative bias [12]. GRDT is not restricted to $L_H$ being general chain rules. The top goals to be learned were moving along a door and moving through a door. Guiding the mobile robot by a joy stick through and along doors in one environment resulted in the training data. The test was that the robot actually moved along or through other doors in a different but similar environment (i.e. the university building). No map was used. Many more experiments have been made using the simulation component of the PIONEER mobile robot. We were told before the project, that real-time behavior is impossible on the basis of logic programs, neuro-computing or other numerical processing would be mandatory. However, the real time from sending sensor measurements to SHARC until robot's reaction in almost all cases was below 0.005 seconds and at most 0.006 seconds [13]. This shows that learned clauses can navigate a robot in real time, if they are parallelized and optimized with respect to their use. In contrast, applying the learned clauses in their most comprehensible from is not fast enough for a robot application.

## 6   Conclusion

This paper tries to show that theory need not be restricted to the central learning step, leaving practicians alone with the design and optimization of $L_E$ and $L_H$. In contrast, developing operational indicators for the quality of a representation asks for theoretical analysis. Concerning the criteria of learnability, comprehensibility, and embeddedness, a brief overview of approaches towards well-based guidelines for the development and transformation of $L_E$ and $L_H$ is given. The question of how to design an appropriate $L_{Ej}$ from given data in $L_{Ei}$ is particularly stressed. On one hand, the design of $L_{Ej}$ is oriented towards making learning easier. On the other hand, the design of $L_{Ej}$ is oriented towards an admissible $L_H$ which can be optimized with respect to embeddedness.

The tailoring of representations is illustrated by a robot application.

- A general ILP learner with declarative bias, GRDT, outputs general chain clauses, because $L_E$ was made of ground chain facts.
- The original numerical data from the robot were transformed into ground chain facts by a simple procedure which uses parameter adjustment as its learning method.
- A theory can be optimized concerning comprehensibility by introducing intermediate predicates, which are then used for folding.
- A theory made of general chain rules can be optimized for real-time deductive inference using the prefix elimination method and the transformation into DFAs.

## References

[1] A.Srinivasan, S. Muggleton, and M. Bain. The justification of logical theories based on data compression. *Machine Intelligence*, 13, 1993.

[2] Eric Bloedorn and Ryszard Michalski. Data-driven constructive induction: Metodology and applications. In Huan Liu and Hiroshi Motoda, editors, *Feature Extraction, Construction, and Selection - A Data Mining Perpective*, chapter 4, pages 51 – 68. Kluwer, 1998.

[3] William W. Cohen. Learnability of restricted logic programs. In *ILP'93 Workshop*, Bled, 1993.

[4] D. Conklin and I. Witten. Complexity-based induction. *Machine Learning*, 16:203 – 225, 1994.

[5] Luc DeRaedt. *Interactive Theory Revision: an Inductive Logic Programming Approach*. Acad. Press, London [u.a.], 1992.

[6] G. Dong and S. Ginsburg. On the decomposition of chain datalog programs into p (left-)linear l-rule components. *Logic Programming*, 23:203 – 236, 1995.

[7] Saso Dzeroski. Inductive logic programming and knowledge discovery in databases. In Usama M. Fayyad, Gregory Piatetsky-Shapiro, Padhraic Smyth, and Ramasamy Uthurusamy, editors, *Advances in Knowledge Discovery and Data Mining*, chapter 1, pages 117–152. AAAI Press/The MIT Press, Menlo Park, California, 1996.

[8] J.-U. Kietz and S. Wrobel. Controlling the complexity of learning in logic through syntactic and task–oriented models. In Stephen Muggleton, editor, *Inductive Logic Programming.*, number 38 in The A.P.I.C. Series, chapter 16, pages 335–360. Academic Press, London [u.a.], 1992.

[9] Jörg Uwe Kietz. *Induktive Analyse relationaler Daten*. PhD thesis, Technische Universität Berlin, Berlin, oct 1996.

[10] Jörg-Uwe Kietz and Saso Dzeroski. Inductive logic programming and learnability. *SIGART–Bulletin*, 5(1):22–32, 1994.

[11] Jörg-Uwe Kietz and Marcus Lübbe. An effecient subsumption algorithm for inductive logic programming. In W. Cohen and H. Hirsh, editors, *Proceedings of the 11th International Conference on Machine Learning IML-94*, San Francisco, CA, 1994. Morgan Kaufmann.

[12] Volker Klingspor. GRDT: Enhancing model-based learning for its application in robot navigation. In S. Wrobel, editor, *Proc. of the Fourth Intern. Workshop on Inductive Logic Programming*, GMD-Studien Nr. 237, pages 107–122, St. Augustin, Germany, 1994. GMD.

[13] Volker Klingspor. *Reaktives Planen mit gelernten Begriffen*. PhD thesis, Univ. Dortmund, 1998.

[14] P. Laird. Identifying and using patterns in sequential data. In K.Jantke, S. Kobayashi, E. Tomita, and T. Yokomori, editors, *Procs. of 4th Workshop on Algorithmic Learning Theory*, pages 1 – 18. Springer, 1993.

[15] H. Liu and H. Motoda. *Feature Extraction, Construction, and Selection: A Data Mining Perspective*. Kluwer, 1998.

[16] H. Mannila, H. Toivonen, and A. Verkamo. Discovering frequent episode in sequences. In *Procs. of the 1st Int. Conf. on Knowledge Discovery in Databases and Data Mining*. AAAI Press, 1995.

[17] Ryszard S. Michalski and Yves Kodratoff. Research in machine learning and recent progress, classification of methods, and future directions. In Yves Kodratoff and Ryszard Michalski, editors, *Machine Learning - an Artificial Intelligence Approach*, volume III, chapter I, pages 3–30. Morgan Kaufmann, Los Altos, CA, 1990.

[18] Katharina Morik and Peter Brockhausen. A multistrategy approach to relational knowledge discovery in databases. *Machine Learning Journal*, 27(3):287–312, jun 1997.

[19] Katharina Morik and Stephanie Wessel. Incremental signal to symbol processing. In K.Morik, M. Kaiser, and V. Klingspor, editors, *Making Robots Smarter – Combining Sensing and Action through Robot Learning*, chapter 11, pages 185 –198. Kluwer Academic Publ., 1999.

[20] Stephen Muggleton and Wray Buntine. Machine invention of first-order predicates by inverting resolution. In *Proc. Fifth Intern. Conf. on Machine Learning*, Los Altos, CA, 1988. Morgan Kaufman.

[21] Gordon D. Plotkin. A note on inductive generalization. In B. Meltzer and D. Michie, editors, *Machine Intelligence*, chapter 8, pages 153–163. American Elsevier, 1970.

[22] Anke Rieger and Volker Klingspor. Program optimization for real-time performance. In K. Morik, V. Klingspor, and M. Kaiser, editors, *Making Robots Smarter – Combining Sensing and Action through Robot Learning*. Kluwer Academic Press, 1999.

[23] Anke D. Rieger. *Program Optimization for Temporal Reasoning within a Logic Programming Framework*. PhD thesis, Universit"at Dortmund, Germany, Dortmund, FRG, 1998.

[24] J. Rissanen. Modeling by shortest data description. *Automatica*, 14:465 – 471, 1978.

[25] J. Robinson. A machine-oriented logic based on the resolution principle. *Journal of the ACM*, 12(1):23–41, 1965.

[26] A. Shinohara. Complexity of computing vapnik-chervonenski dimension. In K.Jantke, S. Kobayashi, E. Tomita, and T. Yokomori, editors, *Procs. of 4th Workshop on Algorithmic Learning Theory*, pages 279 – 287. Springer, 1993.

[27] Edgar Sommer. *Theory Restructering: A Perspective on Design & Maintenance of Knowledge Based Systems*. PhD thesis, University of Dortmund, 1996.

[28] Irene Stahl. Compression measures in ILP. In Luc De Raedt, editor, *Advances in Inductive Logic Programming*, pages 295–307. IOS Press, 1996.

[29] Irene Stahl. Predicate invention in inductive logic programming. In Luc DeRaedt, editor, *Advances in Inductive Logic Programming*, pages 34 – 47. IOS Press, 1996.

[30] H. Tamaki and T. Sato. Unfold and fold transformation of logic programs. In *Procs. of 2nd Int. Conf. Logic Programming*, pages 127 – 138, 1984.

[31] Vladimir N. Vapnik. *The Nature of Statistical Learning Theory*. Springer, New York, 1995.

[32] Stefan Wrobel. *Concept Formation and Knowledge Revision*. Kluwer Academic Publishers, Dordrecht, 1994.

[33] Wei Zhang. A region-based approah to discovering temporal structures in data. In Ivan Bratko and Saso Dzeroski, editors, *Proc. of 16th Int. Conf. on Machine Learning*, pages 484 – 492. Morgan Kaufmann, 1999.

# Theoretical Views of Boosting and Applications

Robert E. Schapire

AT&T Labs – Research, Shannon Laboratory
180 Park Avenue, Room A279, Florham Park, NJ 07932, USA
www.research.att.com/~schapire

**Abstract.** Boosting is a general method for improving the accuracy of any given learning algorithm. Focusing primarily on the AdaBoost algorithm, we briefly survey theoretical work on boosting including analyses of AdaBoost's training error and generalization error, connections between boosting and game theory, methods of estimating probabilities using boosting, and extensions of AdaBoost for multiclass classification problems. Some empirical work and applications are also described.

## Background

Boosting is a general method which attempts to "boost" the accuracy of any given learning algorithm. Kearns and Valiant [29, 30] were the first to pose the question of whether a "weak" learning algorithm which performs just slightly better than random guessing in Valiant's PAC model [44] can be "boosted" into an arbitrarily accurate "strong" learning algorithm. Schapire [36] came up with the first provable polynomial-time boosting algorithm in 1989. A year later, Freund [16] developed a much more efficient boosting algorithm which, although optimal in a certain sense, nevertheless suffered from certain practical drawbacks. The first experiments with these early boosting algorithms were carried out by Drucker, Schapire and Simard [15] on an OCR task.

## AdaBoost

The AdaBoost algorithm, introduced in 1995 by Freund and Schapire [22], solved many of the practical difficulties of the earlier boosting algorithms, and is the focus of this paper. Pseudocode for AdaBoost is given in Fig. 1 in the slightly generalized form given by Schapire and Singer [40]. The algorithm takes as input a training set $(x_1, y_1), \ldots, (x_m, y_m)$ where each $x_i$ belongs to some *domain* or *instance space* $X$, and each *label* $y_i$ is in some label set $Y$. For most of this paper, we assume $Y = \{-1, +1\}$; later, we discuss extensions to the multiclass case. AdaBoost calls a given *weak* or *base learning algorithm* repeatedly in a series of rounds $t = 1, \ldots, T$. One of the main ideas of the algorithm is to maintain a distribution or set of weights over the training set. The weight of this distribution on training example $i$ on round $t$ is denoted $D_t(i)$. Initially, all weights are set equally, but on each round, the weights of incorrectly classified

O. Watanabe, T. Yokomori (Eds.): ALT'99, LNAI 1720, pp. 13–25, 1999.

Given: $(x_1, y_1), \ldots, (x_m, y_m)$ where $x_i \in X$, $y_i \in Y = \{-1, +1\}$
Initialize $D_1(i) = 1/m$.
For $t = 1, \ldots, T$:

- Train weak learner using distribution $D_t$.
- Get weak hypothesis $h_t : X \to \mathbb{R}$.
- Choose $\alpha_t \in \mathbb{R}$.
- Update:

$$D_{t+1}(i) = \frac{D_t(i) \exp(-\alpha_t y_i h_t(x_i))}{Z_t}$$

where $Z_t$ is a normalization factor (chosen so that $D_{t+1}$ will be a distribution).

Output the final hypothesis:

$$H(x) = \text{sign}\left(\sum_{t=1}^{T} \alpha_t h_t(x)\right).$$

**Fig. 1.** The boosting algorithm AdaBoost.

examples are increased so that the weak learner is forced to focus on the hard examples in the training set.

The weak learner's job is to find a *weak hypothesis* $h_t : X \to \mathbb{R}$ appropriate for the distribution $D_t$. In the simplest case, the range of each $h_t$ is binary, i.e., restricted to $\{-1, +1\}$; the weak learner's job then is to minimize the *error*

$$\epsilon_t = \Pr_{i \sim D_t}[h_t(x_i) \neq y_i].$$

Once the weak hypothesis $h_t$ has been received, AdaBoost chooses a parameter $\alpha_t \in \mathbb{R}$ which intuitively measures the importance that it assigns to $h_t$. In the figure, we have deliberately left the choice of $\alpha_t$ unspecified. For binary $h_t$, we typically set

$$\alpha_t = \tfrac{1}{2} \ln\left(\frac{1 - \epsilon_t}{\epsilon_t}\right). \tag{1}$$

More on choosing $\alpha_t$ follows below. The distribution $D_t$ is then updated using the rule shown in the figure. The *final hypothesis* $H$ is a weighted majority vote of the $T$ weak hypotheses where $\alpha_t$ is the weight assigned to $h_t$.

## Analyzing the Training Error

The most basic theoretical property of AdaBoost concerns its ability to reduce the training error. Specifically, Schapire and Singer [40], in generalizing a theorem of Freund and Schapire [22], show that the training error of the final hypothesis is bounded as follows:

$$\frac{1}{m} |\{i : H(x_i) \neq y_i\}| \leq \frac{1}{m} \sum_i \exp(-y_i f(x_i)) = \prod_t Z_t \qquad (2)$$

where $f(x) = \sum_t \alpha_t h_t(x)$ so that $H(x) = \text{sign}(f(x))$. The inequality follows from the fact that $e^{-y_i f(x_i)} \geq 1$ if $y_i \neq H(x_i)$. The equality can be proved straightforwardly by unraveling the recursive definition of $D_t$.

Eq. (2) suggests that the training error can be reduced most rapidly (in a greedy way) by choosing $\alpha_t$ and $h_t$ on each round to minimize

$$Z_t = \sum_i D_t(i) \exp(-\alpha_t y_i h_t(x_i)).$$

In the case of binary hypotheses, this leads to the choice of $\alpha_t$ given in Eq. (1) and gives a bound on the training error of

$$\prod_t \left[ 2\sqrt{\epsilon_t(1 - \epsilon_t)} \right] = \prod_t \sqrt{1 - 4\gamma_t^2} \leq \exp\left(-2\sum_t \gamma_t^2\right)$$

where $\epsilon_t = 1/2 - \gamma_t$. This bound was first proved by Freund and Schapire [22]. Thus, if each weak hypothesis is slightly better than random so that $\gamma_t$ is bounded away from zero, then the training error drops exponentially fast. This bound, combined with the bounds on generalization error given below prove that Ada-Boost is indeed a boosting algorithm in the sense that it can efficiently convert a weak learning algorithm (which can always generate a hypothesis with a weak edge for any distribution) into a strong learning algorithm (which can generate a hypothesis with an arbitrarily low error rate, given sufficient data).

Eq. (2) points to the fact that, at heart, AdaBoost is a procedure for finding a linear combination $f$ of weak hypotheses which attempts to minimize

$$\sum_i \exp(-y_i f(x_i)) = \sum_i \exp\left(-y_i \sum_t \alpha_t h_t(x_i)\right). \qquad (3)$$

Essentially, on each round, AdaBoost chooses $h_t$ (by calling the weak learner) and then sets $\alpha_t$ to add one more term to the accumulating weighted sum of weak hypotheses in such a way that the sum of exponentials above will be maximally reduced. In other words, AdaBoost is doing a kind of steepest descent search to minimize Eq. (3) where the search is constrained at each step to follow coordinate directions (where we identify coordinates with the weights assigned to weak hypotheses).

Schapire and Singer [40] discuss the choice of $\alpha_t$ and $h_t$ in the case that $h_t$ is real-valued (rather than binary). In this case, $h_t(x)$ can be interpreted as a "confidence-rated prediction" in which the sign of $h_t(x)$ is the predicted label, while the magnitude $|h_t(x)|$ gives a measure of confidence.

## Generalization Error

Freund and Schapire [22] showed how to bound the generalization error of the final hypothesis in terms of its training error, the size $m$ of the sample, the VC-dimension $d$ of the weak hypothesis space and the number of rounds $T$ of boosting. Specifically, they used techniques from Baum and Haussler [4] to show that the generalization error, with high probability, is at most

$$\hat{\Pr}\left[H(x) \neq y\right] + \tilde{O}\left(\sqrt{\frac{Td}{m}}\right)$$

where $\hat{\Pr}\left[\cdot\right]$ denotes empirical probability on the training sample. This bound suggests that boosting will overfit if run for too many rounds, i.e., as $T$ becomes large. In fact, this sometimes does happen. However, in early experiments, several authors [8, 14, 34] observed empirically that boosting often does *not* overfit, even when run for thousands of rounds. Moreover, it was observed that AdaBoost would sometimes continue to drive down the generalization error long after the training error had reached zero, clearly contradicting the spirit of the bound above. For instance, the left side of Fig. 2 shows the training and test curves of running boosting on top of Quinlan's C4.5 decision-tree learning algorithm [35] on the "letter" dataset.

In response to these empirical findings, Schapire et al. [39], following the work of Bartlett [2], gave an alternative analysis in terms of the *margins* of the training examples. The margin of example $(x, y)$ is defined to be

$$\frac{y \sum_t \alpha_t h_t(x)}{\sum_t |\alpha_t|}.$$

It is a number in $[-1, +1]$ which is positive if and only if $H$ correctly classifies the example. Moreover, as before, the magnitude of the margin can be interpreted as a measure of confidence in the prediction. Schapire et al. proved that larger margins on the training set translate into a superior upper bound on the generalization error. Specifically, the generalization error is at most

$$\hat{\Pr}\left[\text{margin}_f(x, y) \leq \theta\right] + \tilde{O}\left(\sqrt{\frac{d}{m\theta^2}}\right)$$

for any $\theta > 0$ with high probability. Note that this bound is entirely independent of $T$, the number of rounds of boosting. In addition, Schapire et al. proved that boosting is particularly aggressive at reducing the margin (in a quantifiable sense) since it concentrates on the examples with the smallest margins (whether positive or negative). Boosting's effect on the margins can be seen empirically, for instance, on the right side of Fig. 2 which shows the cumulative distribution of margins of the training examples on the "letter" dataset. In this case, even

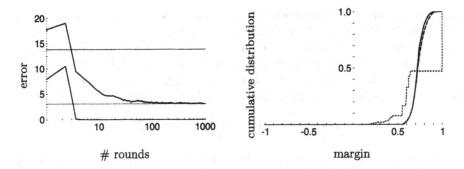

**Fig. 2.** Error curves and the margin distribution graph for boosting C4.5 on the letter dataset as reported by Schapire et al. [39]. *Left:* the training and test error curves (lower and upper curves, respectively) of the combined classifier as a function of the number of rounds of boosting. The horizontal lines indicate the test error rate of the base classifier as well as the test error of the final combined classifier. *Right:* The cumulative distribution of margins of the training examples after 5, 100 and 1000 iterations, indicated by short-dashed, long-dashed (mostly hidden) and solid curves, respectively.

after the training error reaches zero, boosting continues to increase the margins of the training examples effecting a corresponding drop in the test error.

Attempts (not always successful) to use the insights gleaned from the theory of margins have been made by several authors [6, 26, 32]. In addition, the margin theory points to a strong connection between boosting and the support-vector machines of Vapnik and others [5, 11, 45] which explicitly attempt to maximize the minimum margin.

## A Connection to Game Theory

The behavior of AdaBoost can also be understood in a game-theoretic setting as explored by Freund and Schapire [21, 23] (see also Grove and Schuurmans [26] and Breiman [7]). In classical game theory, it is possible to put any two-person, zero-sum game in the form of a matrix $\mathbf{M}$. To play the game, one player chooses a row $i$ and the other player chooses a column $j$. The loss to the row player (which is the same as the payoff to the column player) is $\mathbf{M}_{ij}$. More generally, the two sides may play randomly, choosing distributions $\mathbf{P}$ and $\mathbf{Q}$ over rows or columns, respectively. The expected loss then is $\mathbf{P}^{\mathrm{T}}\mathbf{M}\mathbf{Q}$.

Boosting can be viewed as repeated play of a particular game matrix. Assume that the weak hypotheses are binary, and let $\mathcal{H} = \{h_1, ...h_n\}$ be the entire weak hypothesis space (which we assume for now to be finite). For a fixed training set $(x_1, y_1), \ldots, (x_m, y_m)$, the game matrix $\mathbf{M}$ has $m$ rows and $n$ columns where

$$\mathbf{M}_{ij} = \begin{cases} 1 \text{ if } h_j(x_i) = y_i \\ 0 \text{ otherwise.} \end{cases}$$

The row player now is the boosting algorithm, and the column player is the weak learner. The boosting algorithm's choice of a distribution $D_t$ over training examples becomes a distribution $\mathbf{P}$ over rows of $\mathbf{M}$, while the weak learner's choice of a weak hypothesis $h_t$ becomes the choice of a column $j$ of $\mathbf{M}$.

As an example of the connection between boosting and game theory, consider von Neumann's famous minmax theorem which states that

$$\max_{\mathbf{Q}} \min_{\mathbf{P}} \mathbf{P}^{\mathrm{T}} \mathbf{M} \mathbf{Q} = \min_{\mathbf{P}} \max_{\mathbf{Q}} \mathbf{P}^{\mathrm{T}} \mathbf{M} \mathbf{Q}$$

for any matrix $\mathbf{M}$. When applied to the matrix just defined and reinterpreted in the boosting setting, this can be shown to have the following meaning: If, for any distribution over examples, there exists a weak hypothesis with error at most $1/2 - \gamma$, then there exists a convex combination of weak hypotheses with a margin of at least $2\gamma$ on all training examples. AdaBoost seeks to find such a final hypothesis with high margin on all examples by combining many weak hypotheses; so in a sense, the minmax theorem tells us that AdaBoost at least has the potential for success since, given a "good" weak learner, there must exist a good combination of weak hypotheses. Going much further, Ada-Boost can be shown to be a special case of a more general algorithm for playing repeated games, or for approximately solving matrix games. This shows that, asymptotically, the distribution over training examples as well as the weights over weak hypotheses in the final hypothesis have game-theoretic intepretations as approximate minmax or maxmin strategies.

## Estimating Probabilities

Classification generally is the problem of predicting the label $y$ of an example $x$ with the intention of minimizing the probability of an incorrect prediction. However, it is often useful to estimate the *probability* of a particular label. Recently, Friedman, Hastie and Tibshirani [24] suggested a method for using the output of AdaBoost to make reasonable estimates of such probabilities. Specifically, they suggest using a logistic function, and estimating

$$\Pr_f [y = +1 \mid x] = \frac{e^{f(x)}}{e^{f(x)} + e^{-f(x)}} \tag{4}$$

where, as usual, $f(x)$ is the weighted average of weak hypotheses produced by AdaBoost. The rationale for this choice is the close connection between the log loss (negative log likelihood) of such a model, namely,

$$\sum_i \ln \left( 1 + e^{-2y_i f(x_i)} \right) \tag{5}$$

and the function which, we have already noted, AdaBoost attempts to minimize:

$$\sum_i e^{-y_i f(x_i)}. \tag{6}$$

Specifically, it can be verified that Eq. (5) is upper bounded by Eq. (6). In addition, if we add the constant $1 - \ln 2$ to Eq. (5) (which does not affect its minimization), then it can be verified that the resulting function and the one in Eq. (6) have identical Taylor expansions around zero up to second order; thus, their behavior near zero is very similar. Finally, it can be shown that, for any distribution over pairs $(x, y)$, the expectations

$$E\left[\ln\left(1 + e^{-2yf(x)}\right)\right]$$

and

$$E\left[e^{-yf(x)}\right]$$

are minimized by the same function $f$, namely,

$$f(x) = \tfrac{1}{2}\ln\left(\frac{\Pr\left[y = +1 \mid x\right]}{\Pr\left[y = -1 \mid x\right]}\right).$$

Thus, for all these reasons, minimizing Eq. (6), as is done by AdaBoost, can be viewed as a method of approximately minimizing the negative log likelihood given in Eq. (5). Therefore, we may expect Eq. (4) to give a reasonable probability estimate.

Friedman, Hastie and Tibshirani also make other connnections between Ada-Boost, logistic regression and additive models.

## Multiclass Classification

There are several methods of extending AdaBoost to the multiclass case. The most straightforward generalization [22], called AdaBoost.M1, is adequate when the weak learner is strong enough to achieve reasonably high accuracy, even on the hard distributions created by AdaBoost. However, this method fails if the weak learner cannot achieve at least 50% accuracy when run on these hard distributions.

For the latter case, several more sophisticated methods have been developed. These generally work by reducing the multiclass problem to a larger binary problem. Schapire and Singer's [40] algorithm AdaBoost.MH works by creating a set of binary problems, for each example $x$ and each possible label $y$, of the form: "For example $x$, is the correct label $y$ or is it one of the other labels?" Freund and Schapire's [22] algorithm AdaBoost.M2 (which is a special case of Schapire and Singer's [40] AdaBoost.MR algorithm) instead creates binary problems, for each example $x$ with correct label $y$ and each *incorrect* label $y'$ of the form: "For example $x$, is the correct label $y$ or $y'$?"

These methods require additional effort in the design of the weak learning algorithm. A different technique [37], which incorporates Dietterich and Bakiri's [13] method of error-correcting output codes, achieves similar provable bounds to those of AdaBoost.MH and AdaBoost.M2, but can be used with any weak learner which can handle simple, binary labeled data. Schapire and Singer [40] give yet another method of combining boosting with error-correcting output codes.

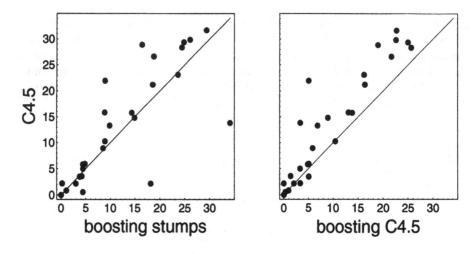

**Fig. 3.** Comparison of C4.5 versus boosting stumps and boosting C4.5 on a set of 27 benchmark problems as reported by Freund and Schapire [20]. Each point in each scatterplot shows the test error rate of the two competing algorithms on a single benchmark. The $y$-coordinate of each point gives the test error rate (in percent) of C4.5 on the given benchmark, and the $x$-coordinate gives the error rate of boosting stumps (left plot) or boosting C4.5 (right plot). All error rates have been averaged over multiple runs.

## Experiments and Applications

Practically, AdaBoost has many advantages. It is fast, simple and easy to program. It has no parameters to tune (except for the number of round $T$). It requires no prior knowledge about the weak learner and so can be flexibly combined with *any* method for finding weak hypotheses. Finally, it comes with a set of theoretical guarantees given sufficient data and a weak learner that can reliably provide only moderately accurate weak hypotheses. This is a shift in mind set for the learning-system designer: instead of trying to design a learning algorithm that is accurate over the entire space, we can instead focus on finding weak learning algorithms that only need to be better than random.

On the other hand, some caveats are certainly in order. The actual performance of boosting on a particular problem is clearly dependent on the data and the weak learner. Consistent with theory, boosting can fail to perform well given insufficient data, overly complex weak hypotheses or weak hypotheses which are too weak. Boosting seems to be especially susceptible to noise [12] (more on this later).

AdaBoost has been tested empirically by many researchers, including [3, 12, 14, 28, 31, 34, 43]. For instance, Freund and Schapire [20] tested AdaBoost on a set of UCI benchmark datasets [33] using C4.5 [35] as a weak learning algorithm, as well as an algorithm which finds the best "decision stump" or

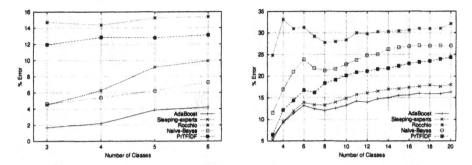

**Fig. 4.** Comparison of error rates for AdaBoost and four other text categorization methods (naive Bayes, probabilistic TF-IDF, Rocchio and sleeping experts) as reported by Schapire and Singer [41]. The algorithms were tested on two text corpora — Reuters newswire articles (left) and AP newswire headlines (right) — and with varying numbers of class labels as indicated on the $x$-axis of each figure.

single-test decision tree. Some of the results of these experiments are shown in Fig. 3. As can be seen from this figure, even boosting the weak decision stumps can usually give as good results as C4.5, while boosting C4.5 generally gives the decision-tree algorithm a significant improvement in performance.

In another set of experiments, Schapire and Singer [41] used boosting for text categorization tasks. For this work, weak hypotheses were used which test on the presence or absence of a word or phrase. Some results of these experiments comparing AdaBoost to four other methods are shown in Fig. 4. In nearly all of these experiments and for all of the performance measures tested, boosting performed as well or significantly better than the other methods tested. Boosting has also been applied to text filtering [42], "ranking" problems [18] and classification problems arising in natural language processing [1, 27].

The final hypothesis produced by AdaBoost when used, for instance, with a decision-tree weak learning algorithm, can be extremely complex and difficult to comprehend. With greater care, a more human-understandable final hypothesis can be obtained using boosting. Cohen and Singer [10] showed how to design a weak learning algorithm which, when combined with AdaBoost, results in a final hypothesis consisting of a relatively small set of rules similar to those generated by systems like RIPPER [9], IREP [25] and C4.5rules [35]. Cohen and Singer's system, called SLIPPER, is fast, accurate and produces quite compact rule sets. In other work, Freund and Mason [19] showed how to apply boosting to learn a generalization of decision trees called "alternating trees." Their algorithm produces a single alternating tree rather than an ensemble of trees as would be obtained by running AdaBoost on top of a decision-tree learning algorithm. On the other hand, their learning algorithm achieves error rates comparable to those of a whole ensemble of trees.

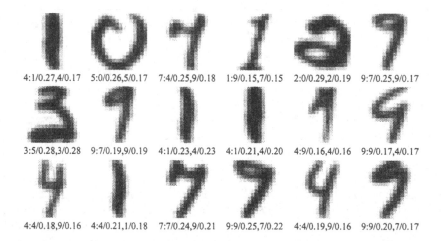

4:1/0.27,4/0.17  5:0/0.26,5/0.17  7:4/0.25,9/0.18  1:9/0.15,7/0.15  2:0/0.29,2/0.19  9:7/0.25,9/0.17

3:5/0.28,3/0.28  9:7/0.19,9/0.19  4:1/0.23,4/0.23  4:1/0.21,4/0.20  4:9/0.16,4/0.16  9:9/0.17,4/0.17

4:4/0.18,9/0.16  4:4/0.21,1/0.18  7:7/0.24,9/0.21  9:9/0.25,7/0.22  4:4/0.19,9/0.16  9:9/0.20,7/0.17

**Fig. 5.** A sample of the examples that have the largest weight on an OCR task as reported by Freund and Schapire [20]. These examples were chosen after 4 rounds of boosting (top line), 12 rounds (middle) and 25 rounds (bottom). Underneath each image is a line of the form $d{:}\ell_1/w_1,\ell_2/w_2$, where $d$ is the label of the example, $\ell_1$ and $\ell_2$ are the labels that get the highest and second highest vote from the combined hypothesis at that point in the run of the algorithm, and $w_1$, $w_2$ are the corresponding normalized scores.

A nice property of AdaBoost is its ability to identify *outliers*, i.e., examples that are either mislabeled in the training data, or which are inherently ambiguous and hard to categorize. Because AdaBoost focuses its weight on the hardest examples, the examples with the highest weight often turn out to be outliers. An example of this phenomenon can be seen in Fig. 5 taken from an OCR experiment conducted by Freund and Schapire [20].

When the number of outliers is very large, the emphasis placed on the hard examples can become detrimental to the performance of AdaBoost. This was demonstrated very convincingly by Dietterich [12]. Friedman et al. [24] suggested a variant of AdaBoost, called "Gentle AdaBoost" which puts less emphasis on outliers. In recent work, Freund [17] suggested another algorithm, called "Brown-Boost," which takes a more radical approach that de-emphasizes outliers when it seems clear that they are "too hard" to classify correctly. This algorithm is an adaptive version of Freund's [16] "boost-by-majority" algorithm. This work, together with Schapire's [38] work on "drifting games," reveal some interesting new relationships between boosting, Brownian motion, and repeated games while raising many new open problems and directions for future research.

# References

[1] Steven Abney, Robert E. Schapire, and Yoram Singer. Boosting applied to tagging and PP attachment. In *Proceedings of the Joint SIGDAT Conference on Empirical Methods in Natural Language Processing and Very Large Corpora*, 1999.

[2] Peter L. Bartlett. The sample complexity of pattern classification with neural networks: the size of the weights is more important than the size of the network. *IEEE Transactions on Information Theory*, 44(2):525–536, March 1998.

[3] Eric Bauer and Ron Kohavi. An empirical comparison of voting classification algorithms: Bagging, boosting, and variants. *Machine Learning*, to appear.

[4] Eric B. Baum and David Haussler. What size net gives valid generalization? *Neural Computation*, 1(1):151–160, 1989.

[5] Bernhard E. Boser, Isabelle M. Guyon, and Vladimir N. Vapnik. A training algorithm for optimal margin classifiers. In *Proceedings of the Fifth Annual ACM Workshop on Computational Learning Theory*, pages 144–152, 1992.

[6] Leo Breiman. Arcing the edge. Technical Report 486, Statistics Department, University of California at Berkeley, 1997.

[7] Leo Breiman. Prediction games and arcing classifiers. Technical Report 504, Statistics Department, University of California at Berkeley, 1997.

[8] Leo Breiman. Arcing classifiers. *The Annals of Statistics*, 26(3):801–849, 1998.

[9] William Cohen. Fast effective rule induction. In *Proceedings of the Twelfth International Conference on Machine Learning*, pages 115–123, 1995.

[10] William W. Cohen and Yoram Singer. A simple, fast, and effective rule learner. In *Proceedings of the Sixteenth National Conference on Artificial Intelligence*, 1999.

[11] Corinna Cortes and Vladimir Vapnik. Support-vector networks. *Machine Learning*, 20(3):273–297, September 1995.

[12] Thomas G. Dietterich. An experimental comparison of three methods for constructing ensembles of decision trees: Bagging, boosting, and randomization. *Machine Learning*, to appear.

[13] Thomas G. Dietterich and Ghulum Bakiri. Solving multiclass learning problems via error-correcting output codes. *Journal of Artificial Intelligence Research*, 2:263–286, January 1995.

[14] Harris Drucker and Corinna Cortes. Boosting decision trees. In *Advances in Neural Information Processing Systems 8*, pages 479–485, 1996.

[15] Harris Drucker, Robert Schapire, and Patrice Simard. Boosting performance in neural networks. *International Journal of Pattern Recognition and Artificial Intelligence*, 7(4):705–719, 1993.

[16] Yoav Freund. Boosting a weak learning algorithm by majority. *Information and Computation*, 121(2):256–285, 1995.

[17] Yoav Freund. An adaptive version of the boost by majority algorithm. In *Proceedings of the Twelfth Annual Conference on Computational Learning Theory*, 1999.

[18] Yoav Freund, Raj Iyer, Robert E. Schapire, and Yoram Singer. An efficient boosting algorithm for combining preferences. In *Machine Learning: Proceedings of the Fifteenth International Conference*, 1998.

[19] Yoav Freund and Llew Mason. The alternating decision tree learning algorithm. In *Machine Learning: Proceedings of the Sixteenth International Conference*, 1999. to appear.

[20] Yoav Freund and Robert E. Schapire. Experiments with a new boosting algorithm. In *Machine Learning: Proceedings of the Thirteenth International Conference*, pages 148–156, 1996.

[21] Yoav Freund and Robert E. Schapire. Game theory, on-line prediction and boosting. In *Proceedings of the Ninth Annual Conference on Computational Learning Theory*, pages 325–332, 1996.

[22] Yoav Freund and Robert E. Schapire. A decision-theoretic generalization of on-line learning and an application to boosting. *Journal of Computer and System Sciences*, 55(1):119–139, August 1997.

[23] Yoav Freund and Robert E. Schapire. Adaptive game playing using multiplicative weights. *Games and Economic Behavior*, to appear.

[24] Jerome Friedman, Trevor Hastie, and Robert Tibshirani. Additive logistic regression: a statistical view of boosting. Technical Report, 1998.

[25] Johannes Fürnkranz and Gerhard Widmer. Incremental reduced error pruning. In *Machine Learning: Proceedings of the Eleventh International Conference*, pages 70–77, 1994.

[26] Adam J. Grove and Dale Schuurmans. Boosting in the limit: Maximizing the margin of learned ensembles. In *Proceedings of the Fifteenth National Conference on Artificial Intelligence*, 1998.

[27] Masahiko Haruno, Satoshi Shirai, and Yoshifumi Ooyama. Using decision trees to construct a practical parser. *Machine Learning*, 34:131–149, 1999.

[28] Jeffrey C. Jackson and Mark W. Craven. Learning sparse perceptrons. In *Advances in Neural Information Processing Systems 8*, pages 654–660, 1996.

[29] Michael Kearns and Leslie G. Valiant. Learning Boolean formulae or finite automata is as hard as factoring. Technical Report TR-14-88, Harvard University Aiken Computation Laboratory, August 1988.

[30] Michael Kearns and Leslie G. Valiant. Cryptographic limitations on learning Boolean formulae and finite automata. *Journal of the Association for Computing Machinery*, 41(1):67–95, January 1994.

[31] Richard Maclin and David Opitz. An empirical evaluation of bagging and boosting. In *Proceedings of the Fourteenth National Conference on Artificial Intelligence*, pages 546–551, 1997.

[32] Llew Mason, Peter Bartlett, and Jonathan Baxter. Direct optimization of margins improves generalization in combined classifiers. Technical report, Deparment of Systems Engineering, Australian National University, 1998.

[33] C. J. Merz and P. M. Murphy. UCI repository of machine learning databases, 1999. www.ics.uci.edu/~mlearn/MLRepository.html.

[34] J. R. Quinlan. Bagging, boosting, and C4.5. In *Proceedings of the Thirteenth National Conference on Artificial Intelligence*, pages 725–730, 1996.

[35] J. Ross Quinlan. *C4.5: Programs for Machine Learning*. Morgan Kaufmann, 1993.

[36] Robert E. Schapire. The strength of weak learnability. *Machine Learning*, 5(2):197–227, 1990.

[37] Robert E. Schapire. Using output codes to boost multiclass learning problems. In *Machine Learning: Proceedings of the Fourteenth International Conference*, pages 313–321, 1997.

[38] Robert E. Schapire. Drifting games. In *Proceedings of the Twelfth Annual Conference on Computational Learning Theory*, 1999.

[39] Robert E. Schapire, Yoav Freund, Peter Bartlett, and Wee Sun Lee. Boosting the margin: A new explanation for the effectiveness of voting methods. *The Annals of Statistics*, 26(5):1651–1686, October 1998.

[40] Robert E. Schapire and Yoram Singer. Improved boosting algorithms using confidence-rated predictions. In *Proceedings of the Eleventh Annual Conference on Computational Learning Theory*, pages 80–91, 1998. To appear, *Machine Learning*.

[41] Robert E. Schapire and Yoram Singer. BoosTexter: A boosting-based system for text categorization. *Machine Learning*, to appear.

[42] Robert E. Schapire, Yoram Singer, and Amit Singhal. Boosting and Rocchio applied to text filtering. In *SIGIR '98: Proceedings of the 21st Annual International Conference on Research and Development in Information Retrieval*, 1998.

[43] Holger Schwenk and Yoshua Bengio. Training methods for adaptive boosting of neural networks. In *Advances in Neural Information Processing Systems 10*, pages 647–653, 1998.

[44] L. G. Valiant. A theory of the learnable. *Communications of the ACM*, 27(11):1134–1142, November 1984.

[45] Vladimir N. Vapnik. *The Nature of Statistical Learning Theory*. Springer, 1995.

# Extended Stochastic Complexity and Minimax Relative Loss Analysis

Kenji Yamanishi

Theory NEC Laboratory, Real World Computing Partnership,
C&C Media Research Laboratories, NEC Corporation,
4-1-1 Miyazaki, Miyamae-ku, Kawasaki, Kanagawa 216-8555, Japan,
`yamanisi@ccm.cl.nec.co.jp`

**Abstract.** We are concerned with the problem of sequential prediction using a given hypothesis class of continuously-many prediction strategies. An effective performance measure is the minimax relative cumulative loss (RCL), which is the minimum of the worst-case difference between the cumulative loss for any prediction algorithm and that for the best assignment in a given hypothesis class. The purpose of this paper is to evaluate the minimax RCL for general continuous hypothesis classes under general losses. We first derive asymptotical upper and lower bounds on the minimax RCL to show that they match $(k/2c) \ln m$ within error of $o(\ln m)$ where $k$ is the dimension of parameters for the hypothesis class, $m$ is the sample size, and $c$ is the constant depending on the loss function. We thereby show that the cumulative loss attaining the minimax RCL asymptotically coincides with the extended stochastic complexity (ESC), which is an extension of Rissanen's stochastic complexity (SC) into the decision-theoretic scenario. We further derive non-asymptotical upper bounds on the minimax RCL both for parametric and nonparametric hypothesis classes. We apply the analysis into the regression problem to derive the least worst-case cumulative loss bounds to date.

## 1 Introduction

### 1.1 Minimax Regret

We start with the minimax regret analysis for the sequential stochastic prediction problem. Let $\mathcal{Y}$ be an alphabet, which can be either discrete or continuous. We first consider the simplest case where $\mathcal{Y}$ is finite. Observe a sequence $y_1, y_2, \cdots$ where each $y_t (t = 1, 2, \cdots)$ takes a value in $\mathcal{Y}$. A *stochastic prediction algorithm* $\mathcal{A}$ performs as follows: At each round $t = 1, 2, ..., n$, $\mathcal{A}$ assigns a probability mass function over $\mathcal{Y}$ based on the past sequence $y^{t-1} = y_1 \cdots y_{t-1}$. The probability mass function can be written as a conditional probability $P(\cdot | y^{t-1})$. After the assignment, $\mathcal{A}$ receives an outcome $y_t$ and suffers a *logarithmic loss* defined by $-\ln P(y_t | y^{t-1})$. This process goes on sequentially. Note that $\mathcal{A}$ is specified by a sequence of conditional probabilities: $\{P(\cdot | y^{t-1}) : t = 1, 2, ..\}$. After observing a sequence $y^m = y_1 \cdots y_m$ of length $m$, $\mathcal{A}$ suffers a *cumulative logarithmic loss* $\sum_{t=1}^{m} \left( -\ln P(y_t | y^{t-1}) \right)$ where $P(\cdot | y_0) = P_0(\cdot)$ is given.

O. Watanabe, T. Yokomori (Eds.): ALT'99, LNAI 1720, pp. 26–38, 1999.

The goal of stochastic prediction is to make the cumulative loss as small as possible. We introduce a reference set of prediction algorithms, which we call a *hypothesis class*, then evaluate the cumulative loss for any algorithm relative to it. For sample size $m$, we define the *worst-case regret* for $\mathcal{A}$ relative to a hypothesis class $\mathcal{H}$ by

$$R_m(\mathcal{A} : \mathcal{H}) \stackrel{\text{def}}{=} \sup_{y^m} \left( \sum_{t=1}^m (-\ln P(y_t|y^{t-1})) - \inf_{f \in \mathcal{H}} \sum_{t=1}^m (-\ln f(y_t|y^{t-1})) \right),$$

which means that the worst-case difference between the cumulative logarithmic loss for $\mathcal{A}$ and that for the best assignment of a single hypothesis in $\mathcal{H}$. Further we define the *minimax regret* for sample size $m$ by

$$R_m(\mathcal{H}) = \inf_{\mathcal{A}} R_m(\mathcal{A} : \mathcal{H}),$$

where the infimum is taken over all stochastic prediction algorithms. Note that in the minimax regret analysis we require no statistical assumption for data-generation mechanism, but consider the worst-case with respect to sequences.

Notice here that for any $m$, a stochastic prediction algorithm specifies a joint probability mass function by

$$P(y^m) = \prod_{t=1}^m P(y_t|y^{t-1}). \tag{1}$$

Thus the minimax regret is rewritten as

$$R_m(\mathcal{H}) = \inf_P \sup_{y^m} \ln \frac{\sup_{f \in \mathcal{H}} f(y^m)}{P(y^m)}.$$

Shtarkov [9] showed that the minimax regret is attained by the joint probability mass function under the *normalized maximum likelihood*, defined as follows:

$$P(y^m) = \frac{\sup_{f \in \mathcal{H}} f(y^m)}{\sum_{y^m} \sup_{f \in \mathcal{H}} f(y^m)}$$

and then the minimax regret amounts to be

$$R_m(\mathcal{H}) = \sum_{y^m} \sup_{f \in \mathcal{H}} f(y^m). \tag{2}$$

Specifically consider the case where the joint distribution is given by a product of probability mass function belonging to a parametric hypothesis class given by $\mathcal{H}_k = \{P_\theta(\cdot) : \theta \in \Theta\}$ where $\Theta$ is a $k$-dimensional compact set in $\mathbb{R}^k$. Let $\hat{\theta}$ be the maximum likelihood estimator (m.l.e.) of $\theta$ from $y^m$ (i.e., $\hat{\theta} = \arg\max_{\theta \in \Theta} P_\theta(y^m)$ where $P_\theta(y^m) = \prod_{t=1}^m P_\theta(y_t)$). Rissanen [8] proved that under the condition that the central limit theorem holds for m.l.e. uniformly over $\Theta$, $R_m(\mathcal{H}_k)$ is asymptotically expanded as follows:

$$R_m(\mathcal{H}_k) = \frac{k}{2} \ln \frac{m}{2\pi} + \ln \int \sqrt{|I(\theta)|} d\theta + o(1), \tag{3}$$

where $I(\theta) \overset{\text{def}}{=} (E_\theta[-\partial^2 \ln P_\theta(y)/\partial\theta_i\partial\theta_j])_{i,j}$ denotes the Fisher information matrix and $o(1)$ goes to zero uniformly with respect to $y^m$ as $m$ goes to infinity.

For a given sequence $y^m$ and $\mathcal{H}_k$, the negative log-likelihood for $y^m$ under the joint probability mass function that attains the minimax regret is called the *stochastic complexity* (SC) of $y^m$ (relative to $\mathcal{H}_k$) [6],[7],[8], which we denote as $SC(y^m)$. That is,

$$SC(y^m) = -\ln P_{\hat{\theta}}(y^m) + \frac{k}{2}\ln\frac{m}{2\pi} + \ln\int\sqrt{|I(\theta)|}d\theta + o(1). \qquad (4)$$

The SC of $y^m$ can be thought of as an extension of Shannon's information in the sense that the latter measures the information of a data sequence relative to a single hypothesis while the former does so relative to a *class* of hypotheses.

## 1.2   Purpose of This Paper and Overview of Results

We extend the minimax regret analysis in two ways. One is to extend it into a general decision-theoretic scenario in which the hypothesis class is a class of real-valued functions rather than a class of probability mass functions, and the prediction loss is measured in terms of general loss functions (e.g., square loss,Hellinger loss) rather than the logarithmic loss. It is motivated by the fact that in real problems such as on-line regression and pattern-recognition, prediction should be made deterministically and a variety of loss functions should be used as a distortion measure for prediction.

We analyze the *minimax relative cumulative loss* (RCL), which is an extension of the minimax regret, under general losses. The minimax RCL has been investigated in the community of computational learning theory, but most of work are restricted to specific cases: 1) the case where general loss functions are used but a hypothesis class is finite (e.g., [10], [3]) and 2) the case where a hypothesis class is continuous but only specific loss functions such as the square loss and the logarithmic loss are used (e.g., [1], [4],[5],[2],[11]), or only specific hypothesis classes such as the Bernoulli model and the linear regression model (e.g., [2],[11]) are used. This paper offers a universal method of minimax RCL analysis relative to general continuous hypothesis classes under general loss functions.

We first derive asymptotical upper and lower bounds on the minimax RCL to show that they match $(k/2c)\ln m$ within error of $o(\ln m)$ where $k$ is the dimension of parameters for the hypothesis class, $m$ is the sample size, and $c$ is the constant depending on the loss function. According to [12], we introduce the *extended stochastic complexity* (ESC) to show that the ESC is an approximation to the minimax solution to RCL. The relation between ESC and the minimax RCL is an analogue of that between SC and the minimax regret. This gives a unifying view of the minimax RCL/the minimax regret analysis.

The other way of extension is to introduce a method of non-asymptotical analysis, while (3) is an asymptotical result, that is, it is effective only when the sample size is sufficiently large. Since sample size is not necessarily large enough in real situations, theoretical bounds that hold for any sample size would be practically useful.

Non-asymptotical bounds on the minimax regret and RCL were derived in [1],[5],[2],[11] for continuous hypothesis classes under specific losses. We take a new approach to derive non-asymptotical bounds on the minimax RCL both for parametric and non-parametric hypothesis classes under general losses.

The rest of this paper is organized as follows: Section 2 gives a formal definition of the minimax RCL. Section 3 overviews results on asymptotical analysis of the minimax RCL. Section 4 gives non-asymptotical analysis of the minimax RCL. Section 5 shows an application of our analysis to the regression problem.

## 2   Minimax RCL

For a positive integer $n$, let $\mathcal{X}$ be a subset of $\mathbb{R}^n$, which we call the *domain*. Let $\mathcal{Y} = \{0,1\}$ or $\mathcal{Y} = [0,1]$, which we call the *range*. Let $\mathcal{Z} = [0,1]$ or $\mathcal{Z}$ be a set of probability mass functions over $\mathcal{Y}$. We call $\mathcal{Z}$ the *decision space*. We set $\mathcal{D} = \mathcal{X} \times \mathcal{Y}$. We write an element in $\mathcal{D}$ as $D = (x,y)$. Let $L : \mathcal{Y} \times \mathcal{Z} \to \mathbb{R}^+ \cup \{0\}$ be a loss function.

A *sequential prediction algorithm* $\mathcal{A}$ performs as follows: At each round $t = 1, 2, \cdots$, $\mathcal{A}$ receives $x_t \in \mathcal{X}$ then outputs a predicted result $z_t \in \mathcal{Z}$ on the basis of $D^{t-1} = D_1 \cdots D_{t-1}$ where $D_i = (x_i, y_i)$ $(i = 1, \cdots, t-1)$. Then $\mathcal{A}$ receives the correct outcome $y_t \in \mathcal{Y}$ and suffers a loss $L(y_t, z_t)$. Hence $\mathcal{A}$ defines a sequence of maps: $\{f_t : t = 1, 2, \cdots\}$ where $f_t(x_t) = z_t$. A *hypothesis class* $\mathcal{H}$ is a set of sequential prediction algorithms.

**Definition 1.** *For sample size $m$, for a hypothesis class $\mathcal{H}$, let $\mathcal{D}^m(\mathcal{H})$ be a subset of $\mathcal{D}^m$ depending on $\mathcal{H}$. For any sequential prediction algorithm $\mathcal{A}$, we define the* worst-case relative cumulative loss (RCL) *by*

$$\mathcal{R}_m(\mathcal{A} : \mathcal{H}) \overset{\text{def}}{=} \sup_{D^m \in \mathcal{D}^m(\mathcal{H})} \left( \sum_{t=1}^{m} L(y_t, z_t) - \min_{f \in \mathcal{H}} \sum_{t=1}^{m} L(y_t, f_t(x_t)) \right),$$

*where $z_t$ is the output of $\mathcal{A}$ at the $t$th round. We define the* minimax RCL *by*

$$\mathcal{R}_m(\mathcal{H}) = \inf_{\mathcal{A}} \mathcal{R}_m(\mathcal{A} : \mathcal{H}), \tag{5}$$

*where the infimum is taken over all sequential prediction algorithms. We assume here that any prediction algorithm knows the sample size $m$ in advance.*

Consider the special case where $\mathcal{X} = \emptyset$, $\mathcal{Y} = \{0,1\}$, $\mathcal{Z} =$ the set of probability mass functions over $\mathcal{Y}$, and the loss function is the logarithmic loss: $L(y, P) = -\ln P(y)$. (Throughout this paper we call this case the *probabilistic case*.) We can easily check that in the probabilistic case the minimax RCL (5) is equivalent with the minimax regret (3).

Hereafter, we consider only the case where $\mathcal{Z} = [0,1]$, that is, the prediction is made deterministically. Below we give examples of loss functions for this case.

$L(y, z) = (y - z)^2$ (square loss),

$L(y, z) = y \ln \dfrac{y}{z} + (1 - y) \ln \dfrac{1 - y}{1 - z}$ (entropic loss),

$L(y, z) = \dfrac{1}{2} \left( (\sqrt{y} - \sqrt{z})^2 + (\sqrt{1 - y} - \sqrt{1 - z})^2 \right)$ (Hellinger loss),

$L(y, z) = \dfrac{1}{2} (-(2y - 1)(2z - 1) + \ln(e^{2z-1} + e^{-2z+1}) + B)$ (logistic loss),

where $B = \ln(1 + e^{-2})$.

For a loss function $L$, we define $L_0(z)$ and $L_1(z)$ by $L_0(z) \stackrel{\text{def}}{=} L(0, z)$ and $L_1(z) \stackrel{\text{def}}{=} L(1, z)$, respectively. We make the following assumption for $L$.

**Assumption 1** *The loss function $L$ satisfies:*
*1) $L_0(z)$ and $L_1(z)$ are twice continuously differentiable with respect to $z$. $L_0(0) = L_1(1) = 0$. For any $0 < z < 1$, $L_0'(z) > 0$ and $L_1'(z) < 0$.*
*2) Define $\lambda^*$ by*

$$\lambda^* \stackrel{\text{def}}{=} \left( \sup_{0 < z < 1} \frac{L_0'(z)L_1'(z)^2 - L_1'(z)L_0'(z)^2}{L_0'(z)L_1''(z) - L_1'(z)L_0''(z)} \right)^{-1}. \tag{6}$$

*Then $0 < \lambda^* < \infty$.*
*3) Let $G(y, z, w) = \lambda^*(L(y, z) - L(y, w))$. For any $y$, $z, w \in [0, 1]$, $\partial^2 G(y, z, w)/\partial y^2 + (\partial G(y, z, w)/\partial y)^2 \geq 0$.*

For example, $\lambda^* = 1$ for the entropic loss, $\lambda^* = 2$ for the square loss, and $\lambda^* = \sqrt{2}$ for the Hellinger loss. In the case of $\mathcal{Y} = \{0, 1\}$ instead of $\mathcal{Y} = [0, 1]$, Condition 3) is not necessarily required.

## 3   Asymptotical Results

According to [12], we introduce the notion of ESC in order to derive upper bounds on the minimax RCL.

**Definition 2.** *Let $\mu$ be a probability measure on a hypothesis class $\mathcal{H}$. For a given loss function $L$, for a sequence $D^m \in \mathcal{D}^m$, we define the* extended stochastic complexity *(ESC) of $D^m$ relative to $\mathcal{H}$ by*

$$I(D^m : \mathcal{H}) \stackrel{\text{def}}{=} -\frac{1}{\lambda^*} \ln \int e^{-\lambda^* \sum_{t=1}^{m} L(y_y, f_t(x_t))} \mu(df). \tag{7}$$

While SC was defined as the cumulative logarithmic loss that attains the minimax regret, ESC is not defined as the cumulative loss that attains the minimax RCL. This is because it is not possible to get an explicit form of the minimax solution to RCL for general losses. It will turn out in this section, however, that the ESC is a tight upper bound on the cumulative loss that attains the minimax RCL within error of $o(\ln m)$.

**Lemma 1.** *Under Assumption 1, there exists a sequential prediction algorithm such that for any $D^m$, its cumulative loss is upper-bounded by $I(D^m : \mathcal{H})$.*

Lemma 1 can be proven using Vovk's aggregating algorithm [10] with its analysis in [3].

In order to make a connection between ESC and the minimax RCL, we focus on the specific case where $\mathcal{H}$ is a parametric class such that any prediction algorithm in $\mathcal{H}$ is written as a sequence of functions each of which belongs to a parametric class $\mathcal{H}_k = \{f_\theta(\cdot) : \theta \in \Theta\}$ where $\Theta$ is a $k$-dimensional compact set in $\mathbb{R}^k$. In this case the ESC of $D^m$ relative to $\mathcal{H}_k$ is written as

$$I(D^m : \mathcal{H}_k) = -\frac{1}{\lambda^*} \ln \int d\theta \pi(\theta) e^{-\lambda^* \sum_{t=1}^m L(y_y, f_\theta(x_t))}, \qquad (8)$$

where $\pi(\theta)$ is a prior probability density over $\Theta$.

We make the following assumption for $L, \mathcal{H}_k$, and $\pi$.

**Assumption 2** *The following conditions hold for $L, \mathcal{H}_k$, and $\pi$:*
*1) Define a matrix $\hat{J}(\theta)$ by*

$$\hat{J}(\theta) \stackrel{\text{def}}{=} \frac{1}{m} \left( \frac{\partial^2 \sum_{t=1}^m L(y_t, f_\theta(x_t))}{\partial \theta_i \partial \theta_j} \Big|_\theta \right)_{i,j=1,\cdots k}$$

*and let $\mu(D^m : \theta)$ be the largest eigenvalue of $\hat{J}(\theta)$. Let $d = d_m$ be a sequence such that $d_m > k$, $\lim_{m \to \infty} d_m = \infty$, and $\lim_{m \to \infty} (d_m/m) = 0$. Let $\hat{\theta}$ be the minimum loss estimator of $\theta$ defined by $\hat{\theta} = \arg\min_{\theta \in \Theta} \sum_{t=1}^m L(y_t, f_\theta(x_t))$ Then for some $0 < \mu < \infty$,*

$$\sup_{D^m} \sup_{\theta:|\theta-\hat{\theta}|<(d_m/m)^{1/2}} \mu(D^m : \theta) \leq \mu.$$

*2) Let $N_m \stackrel{\text{def}}{=} \{\theta \in \Theta : |\theta - \hat{\theta}| \leq \sqrt{d_m/m}\}$ and $N'_m \stackrel{\text{def}}{=} \{\theta \in \mathbb{R}^k : |\theta - \hat{\theta}| \leq \sqrt{d_m/m}\}$. Then for some $0 < r < 1$, for all sufficiently large $m$, $\mathrm{vol}(N_m) \geq r \times \mathrm{vol}(N'_m)$ where $\mathrm{vol}(S)$ is Lebesgue volume of $S$.*
*3) For some $\underline{c} > 0$, for any $\theta \in \Theta$, $\pi(\theta) \geq \underline{c}$.*

The following lemma gives an asymptotical upper bound on the worst-case ESC.

**Lemma 2.** [12] *Let $\mathcal{D}^m(\Theta)$ be a subset of $\mathcal{D}^m$ such that $\partial \sum_{t=1}^m L(y_t, f_\theta(x_t))/\partial\theta|_{\theta=\hat{\theta}} = 0$. Under Assumption 2, for all $D^m \in \mathcal{D}^m(\Theta)$, we have*

$$I(D^m : \mathcal{H}_k) \leq \min_{\theta \in \Theta} \sum_{t=1}^m L(y_t, f_\theta(x_t)) + \frac{k}{2\lambda^*} \ln \frac{m\lambda^* \mu}{2\pi} + \frac{1}{\lambda^*} \ln \frac{1}{r\underline{c}} + o(1), \qquad (9)$$

*where $\lim_{m \to \infty} o(1) = 0$ uniformly over $\mathcal{D}^m(\Theta)$.*

Note that in the probabilistic case, $\lambda^* = 1$ hence the righthand side of (9) coincides the SC of (4) within error of $O(1)$.

The main technique to prove (9) is *Laplace's method*, which approximates an integral using a Gaussian integral in the neighborhood of the minimum loss estimator. The proof is sketched as follows:

*Proof.* For sample size $m$, let $\delta_m = \sqrt{d_m/m}$ for $d_m$ as in Assumption 2. For a minimum loss estimator $\hat{\theta}$ of $\theta$ from $D^m$, let $N_{\delta_m} = \{\theta \in \Theta : |\theta - \hat{\theta}| \leq \delta_m\}$ be a neighborhood of $\hat{\theta}$. We denote $\sum_{t=1}^{m} L(y_t, f_\theta(x_t))$ as $L(D^m : f_\theta)$. Then for all $D^m \in \mathcal{D}^m(\Theta)$, letting $\eta \in N_{\delta_m}$, we have

$$I(D^m : \mathcal{H}_k)$$
$$\leq -\frac{1}{\lambda^*} \ln \int_{N_{\delta_m}} d\theta \pi(\theta) \exp\left(-\lambda^* L(D^m : f_\theta)\right)$$
$$\leq -\frac{1}{\lambda^*} \ln \int_{N_{\delta_m}} d\theta \pi(\theta) \exp\left(-\lambda^* L(D^m : f_{\hat{\theta}}) - \frac{\lambda^* m}{2}(\theta - \hat{\theta})^T \hat{J}(\eta)(\theta - \hat{\theta})\right)$$
$$\leq -\frac{1}{\lambda^*} \ln \int_{N_{\delta_m}} d\theta \pi(\theta) \exp\left(-\lambda^* L(D^m : f_{\hat{\theta}}) - \frac{\lambda^* \mu m}{2} \sum_{i=1}^{k}(\theta_i - \hat{\theta}_i)^2\right)$$
$$\leq L(D^m : f_{\hat{\theta}}) - \frac{1}{\lambda^*} \ln \pi(\theta^*) + \ln \int_{N_{\delta_m}} d\theta \exp\left(-\frac{\lambda^* \mu m}{2} \sum_{i=1}^{k}(\theta_i - \hat{\theta}_i)^2\right), \quad (10)$$

where $\theta^*$ is the point in $N_{\delta_m}$ that attains the minimum of $\pi(\theta)$. The notations of $\hat{J}(\eta)$ and $\mu$ follow Assumption 2.

Let $N'_{\delta_m} = \{\theta \in \mathbb{R}^k : |\theta - \hat{\theta}| \leq \delta_m\}$. Then

$$\int_{N_{\delta_m}} \exp\left(-\frac{\lambda^* \mu m}{2} \sum_{i=1}^{k}(\theta_i - \hat{\theta}_i)^2\right) d\theta \geq r \int_{N'_{\delta_m}} \exp\left(-\frac{\lambda^* \mu m}{2} \sum_{i=1}^{k}(\theta_i - \hat{\theta}_i)^2\right) d\theta$$
$$\geq r\left(1 - \frac{k}{d_m}\right) \left(\frac{2\pi}{m}\right)^{k/2} \left(\sqrt{(\lambda^* \mu)^k}\right)^{-1}. \quad (11)$$

See [12] for the last inequality. Plugging (11) into (10) and letting $d_m$ go to infinity yield (9). □

Combining Lemmas 1 with 2 leads the following asymptotical upper bound on the minimax RCL.

**Theorem 1.** *Under Assumptions 1 and 2,*

$$\mathcal{R}_m(\mathcal{H}_k) \leq \frac{k}{2\lambda^*} \ln \frac{m\lambda^* \mu}{2\pi} + \frac{1}{\lambda^*} \ln \frac{1}{r\underline{c}} + o(1), \quad (12)$$

*where $\mathcal{D}^m(\mathcal{H})$ as in Definition 1 is set to $\mathcal{D}^m(\Theta)$.*

In order to investigate how tight (12) is, we derive an asymptotical lower bound on the minimax RCL.

**Theorem 2.** [13]. *When $L$ is the entropic loss or the square loss, for some regularity condition for $\mathcal{H}$,*

$$\mathcal{R}_m(\mathcal{H}_k) \geq \left( \frac{k}{2\lambda^*} - o(1) \right) \ln m. \tag{13}$$

*Furthermore, under some regularity conditions for $\mathcal{H}_k$ and a general $L$ in addition to Assumptions 1 and 2, (13) holds.*

(Note: The current forms of the regularity conditions required for general losses are very complicated [13] and remain to be simplified. )

By Theorems 1 and 2, we have the following corollary relating the ESC to the minimax regret. It is formally summarized as follows:

**Corollary 1.** *Let*

$$\mathcal{I}_m(\mathcal{H}_k) \overset{\text{def}}{=} \sup_{D^m \in \mathcal{D}^m(\Theta)} \left( I(D^m : \mathcal{H}_k) - \min_\theta \sum_{t=1}^m L(y_t, f_\theta(x_t)) \right).$$

*Then under the conditions as in Theorems 1 and 2,*

$$\lim_{m \to \infty} \frac{|\mathcal{I}_m(\mathcal{H}) - \mathcal{R}_m(\mathcal{H}_k)|}{\ln m} = 0.$$

Corollary 1 shows that the ESC can be thought of as the cumulative loss that attains the minimax RCL within error of $o(\ln m)$. It corresponds to the fact that SC is the cumulative logarithmic loss that attains the minimax regret. This gives a rationale that ESC is a natural extension of SC.

## 4    Non-asymptotical Results

### 4.1    Log-Loss Case

Bounds (4), (12) and (13) is *asymptotical* in the sense that they are effective only when the sample size $m$ is sufficiently large. This section derives non-asymptotical upper bounds on the minimax RCL, which might not be tight, but hold for any sample size. First, we overview the results by Cesa-Bianchi and Lugosi [1] for the probabilistic case under the logarithmic loss.

Let $(S, d)$ be a metric space where $S$ is a class of joint probability mass functions each of which is decomposed as in (1) and $d$ is the metric such that

$$d(f, g) = \left( \sum_{t=1}^m d_t^2(f, g) \right)^{1/2},$$

where $d_t(f, g) = \sup_{y^t} \left| \ln f(y_t | y^{t-1}) - \ln g(y_t | y^{t-1}) \right|$.

For $T \subset S$, for $\varepsilon > 0$, let $N(T, \varepsilon)$ be the cardinality of the smallest subset $T' \subset S$ such that for all $f \in T$, for some $g \in T'$, $d(f, g) \geq \varepsilon$.

The following theorem shows a non-asymptotical upper bound on the minimax regret.

**Theorem 3.** [1] *For any class* $\mathcal{H}$,

$$\mathcal{R}_m(\mathcal{H}) \leq \inf_{\varepsilon > 0} \left( \ln N(\mathcal{H}, \varepsilon) + 12 \int_0^\varepsilon \sqrt{\ln N(\mathcal{H}, \delta)} d\delta \right).$$

In deriving the above bound we don't require regularity condition for $\mathcal{H}$ such as the central limit theorem condition required for (3) to be satisfied. It actually holds regardless $\mathcal{H}$ is parametric or no-parametric.

Theorem 3 leads as a special case the following non-asymptotical upper bound on the minimax regret for parametric hypothesis classes.

**Corollary 2.** [1] *Consider a class* $\mathcal{H}$ *such that for some positive constants* $k$ *and* $c$, *for all* $\varepsilon > 0$,

$$\ln N(\mathcal{H}, \varepsilon) \leq k \ln \left( c\sqrt{m}/\varepsilon \right). \tag{14}$$

*Then for* $m \geq (288 \ln(c\sqrt{m}))/kc^2$, *we have*

$$\mathcal{R}_m(\mathcal{H}) \leq \frac{k}{2} \ln m + \frac{k}{2} \ln \frac{c^2 \ln(c\sqrt{m})}{k} + 5k. \tag{15}$$

Note that Condition (14) holds for most classes parametrized smoothly by a bounded subset of $\mathbb{R}^k$.

## 4.2   General-Loss Cases

Next for a decision-theoretic case under general losses other than the logarithmic loss, we derive non-asymptotical upper bounds on the minimax RCL in a different manner from Cesa-Bianchi and Lugosi's. First we investigate the case where the hypothesis class is parametric.

**Theorem 4.** [13] *Under Assumptions 1 and 2,*

$$\mathcal{R}_m(\mathcal{H}_k) \leq \frac{k}{2\lambda^*} \ln m + \frac{k}{2\lambda^*} \ln \left( \lambda^* \mu e F^2 V^{2/k} \right), \tag{16}$$

*where* $\mathcal{D}^m(\mathcal{H})$ *as in Definition 1 is set to* $\mathcal{D}^m(\Theta)$.

*Proof.* The main technique to prove (16) is to discretize the hypothesis class with an appropriate size and then to apply the aggregating algorithm over the discretized hypothesis class. The most important issue is how to choose the number of discrete points.

For $F \geq 1$, let $\Delta$ be a subset of $\Theta$ whose size is $N$ and for which the discretization scale is at most $F\sqrt{k}(V/N)^{1/k}$. That is, $\sup_{\theta \in \Theta} \min_{\theta' \in \Delta} |\theta - \theta'| \leq$

$F\sqrt{k}(V/N)^{1/k}$. This means that the discretization scale for each component in $\Delta$ is roughly uniform within a constant factor. It is a quite natural requirement for the discretization.

Let $\hat{\theta} = \arg\min_{\theta \in \Theta} \sum_{t=1}^{m} L(y_t, f_\theta(x_t))$ and $\bar{\theta} = \arg\min_{\theta \in \Delta} \sum_{t=1}^{m} L(y_t, f_\theta(x_t))$. We write the relative cumulative loss for any algorithm $\mathcal{A}$ as $R(\mathcal{A} : D^m)$. Letting $\hat{y}_t$ be the output of $\mathcal{A}$ at the $t$th round, we see

$$R(\mathcal{A} : D^m) = \left( \sum_{t=1}^{m} L(y_t, \hat{y}_t) - \sum_{t=1}^{m} L(y_t, f_{\bar{\theta}}(x_t)) \right) \tag{17}$$
$$+ \left( \sum_{t=1}^{m} L(y_t, f_{\bar{\theta}}(x_t)) - \sum_{t=1}^{m} L(y_t, f_{\hat{\theta}}(x_t)) \right).$$

Letting $\tilde{\mathcal{H}}_k = \{f_\theta(\cdot) : \theta \in \Delta\}$ and $\mathcal{A}$ be the aggregating algorithm AG using $\tilde{\mathcal{H}}_k$, by Lemma 1, we see

$$\sum_{t=1}^{m} L(y_t, \hat{y}_t) \leq I(D^m : \tilde{\mathcal{H}}_k)$$
$$= -\frac{1}{\lambda^*} \ln \frac{1}{N} \sum_{\theta \in \Delta} e^{-\lambda^* \sum_{t=1}^{m} L(y_t, f_\theta(x_t))}$$
$$\leq \sum_{t=1}^{m} L(y_t, f_{\bar{\theta}}(x_t)) + \frac{1}{\lambda^*} \ln N.$$

This leads:

$$\sup_{D^m \in \mathcal{D}^m(\Theta)} \left( \sum_{t=1}^{m} L(y_t, \hat{y}_t) - \sum_{t=1}^{m} L(y_t, f_{\bar{\theta}}(x_t)) \right) \leq \frac{1}{\lambda^*} \ln N. \tag{18}$$

By Taylor expansion argument, for all $D^m \in \mathcal{D}^m(\Theta)$,

$$\sum_{t=1}^{m} L(y_t, f_{\bar{\theta}}(x_t)) - \sum_{t=1}^{m} L(y_t, f_{\hat{\theta}}(x_t)) \leq \frac{\mu m}{2} |\hat{\theta} - \bar{\theta}|^2 \leq \frac{\mu m F^2 k}{2} \left( \frac{V}{N} \right)^{2/k}. \tag{19}$$

Plugging (18) and (19) into (17) yields

$$\sup_{D^m \in \mathcal{D}^m(\Theta)} R(\text{AG} : D^m) \leq \frac{1}{\lambda^*} \ln N + \frac{\mu m F^2 k}{2} \left( \frac{V}{N} \right)^{2/k}. \tag{20}$$

The minimum of (20) w.r.t. $N$ is attained by $N = \lceil (\lambda^* \mu m F^2)^{k/2} V \rceil$. Plugging this optimal size into (20) and choosing $\Delta$ so that $F$ is smallest yield (16).  $\square$

Next we investigate the case where the hypothesis class is nonparametric, but can be approximated by a sequence of parametric hypothesis classes.

**Theorem 5.** *Let* $\{\mathcal{H}_k : k = 1, 2, ..\}$ *be a sequence of classes such that* $\mathcal{H}_1 \subset \mathcal{H}_2 \subset \cdots$ *where* $\mathcal{H}_k$ *is a k-dimensional parametric hypothesis class. Let* $\mathcal{F}$ *be a hypothesis class such that for some* $C, \alpha > 0,$

$$\sup_{f \in \mathcal{F}} \inf_{h \in \mathcal{H}_k} \sup_{D^m} |L(D^m : f) - L(D^m : h)|/m \leq C/k^\alpha, \tag{21}$$

*where* $L(D^m : f) = \sum_{t=1}^{m} L(y_t, f(x_t))$. *Then under Assumption 1 and 2, for some* $A, B > 0$ *depending on* $\lambda^*, C,$ *and* $\alpha,$

$$\mathcal{R}_m(\mathcal{F}) \leq Am^{\frac{1}{\alpha+1}} \ln^{\frac{\alpha}{\alpha+1}} m + B\left(\frac{m}{\ln m}\right)^{\frac{1}{\alpha+1}} \ln\left(\lambda^* \mu e F^2 V^{2/k}\right).$$

*Proof.* Fix $k$. By (16) and (21), we have

$$\mathcal{R}_m(\mathcal{F}) \leq \mathcal{R}_m(\mathcal{H}_k) + \sup_{f \in \mathcal{F}} \inf_{h \in \mathcal{H}_k} \sup_{D^m} |L(D^m : f) - L(D^m : h)|$$

$$\leq \frac{k}{2\lambda^*} \ln m + \frac{k}{2\lambda^*} \ln\left(\lambda^* \mu e F^2 V^{2/k}\right) + \frac{mC}{k^\alpha}.$$

Setting $k = (2\lambda^* \alpha Cm/\ln m)^{\frac{1}{\alpha+1}}$ in the last inequality yields (22). $\qquad\square$

Condition (21) means that the worst-case approximation error for $\mathcal{H}_k$ to $\mathcal{F}$ is $O(1/k^\alpha)$. Eq. (16) is regarded as a special case of (22) where $\alpha$ is infinite.

## 5   Minimax RCL for Regression

We apply the results in Sections 3 and 4 into the regression problem. We consider the case where the hypothesis class is a class of linear functions of a feature vector and the distortion measure is the square loss. Such a case has entensively been investigated in the linear regression (LR) scenario in statistics. Our analysis is different from conventional ones in the following regards:

1) Although it is assumed in the classical LR that a noise is additive and is generated according to a Gaussian distribution, we don't make any probabilistic assumption either for a target distribution or a hypothesis class, but instead perform worst-case analysis in terms of the worst-case RCL. Additionally, we emphasize that we consider the regression problem in the on-line prediction scenario rather than in the batch-learning scenario as in the classical LR.

2) While most algorithms investigated in the classical LR take linear forms of a feature vector, we don't restrict ourselves into them, but rather consider non-linear prediction algorithms using a hypothesis class of linear functions.

Let $\mathcal{X} = \{x = (x^{(1)}, \cdots, x^{(k)}) \in [0,1]^k : (x^{(1)})^2 + \cdots + (x^{(k)})^2 \leq 1\}$ and $\mathcal{Y} = \mathcal{Z} = [0,1]$. Let $\Theta = \{\theta = (\theta_1, \cdots, \theta_k) \in [0,1]^k : \theta_1^2 + \cdots + \theta_k^2 \leq 1\}$. Let a hypothesis class be

$$\mathcal{H}_k = \{f_\theta(X) = \theta^T x : x \in \mathcal{X}, \theta \in \Theta\}.$$

This is known as a class of *linear predictors*. Let $L$ be the square loss function. Then $\lambda^* = 2$. For $\alpha > 0$, let $\pi(\theta) = e^{-\alpha\theta^T\theta}/V(\Theta)$ where $V(\Theta) = \int_\Theta e^{-\alpha\theta^T\theta} d\theta$.

Below we describe the aggregating algorithm [10],[12] using $\mathcal{H}_k$, denoted as AG. At the $t$th round, AG takes as input $D^{t-1}$ and $x_t$, then outputs $\hat{y}_t$ s.t.

$$\hat{y}_t = \frac{1}{2}\left(\left(-\frac{1}{2}\ln\int p(\theta|D^{t-1})e^{-2(\theta x)^2}d\theta\right)^{\frac{1}{2}} + 1 - \left(-\frac{1}{2}\ln\int p(\theta|D^{t-1})e^{-2(1-\theta x)^2}d\theta\right)^{\frac{1}{2}}\right),$$

where

$$p(\theta|D^{t-1}) = \frac{e^{-2(\theta-\mu_t)^T \Sigma_t(\theta-\mu_t)}}{\int e^{-2(\theta-\mu_t)^T \Sigma_t(\theta-\mu_t)}d\theta},$$

$$\Sigma_t^{(p,q)} = \alpha\delta_{p,q} + \sum_{j=1}^{t-1} x_j^{(p)} x_j^{(q)}, \quad \mu_t = \Sigma_t^{-1} A_t, \quad A_t^{(p)} = \sum_{j=1}^{t-1} y_j x_j^{(p)},$$

where $\Sigma^{(p,q)}$, $x_j^{(p)}$ and $A_t^{(p)}$ denote the $(p,q)$th component of $\Sigma$, the $p$th component of $x_j$, and the $p$th component of $A_t$, respectively ($p, q = 1, \cdots, k$), $\delta_{p,q} = 1$ if $p = q$ and $\delta_{p,q} = 0$ if $p \neq q$.

We can set $\mu = 2k, r = 1/2^k, \underline{c} = e^{-\alpha}/V(\Theta)$. By (1) we have the following upper bound on the worst-case RCL for AG:

$$\mathcal{R}_m(\text{AG} : \mathcal{H}_k) \leq \frac{k}{4}\ln\frac{2mk}{\pi} + \frac{1}{2}\ln 2^k e^\alpha V(\Theta) + o(1). \tag{22}$$

Note that the parameters in Theorem 4 are: $V = \pi^{k/2}/2^k\Gamma(1 + k/2)$ and $F = 1$. By (16), we have

$$\mathcal{R}_m(\mathcal{H}_k) \leq \frac{k}{4}\ln m + \frac{k}{4}\ln\left(\frac{ke\pi}{\Gamma(1 + k/2)^{2/k}}\right). \tag{23}$$

Vovk [11] derived a similar non-asymptotic upper bound on the worst-case RCL for the aggregating algorithm using linear predictors. His bound matches (23) up to the $\frac{k}{4}\ln m$ term.

Kivinen and Warmuth [4] proposed the gradient descent algorithm (GD) and the exponentiated gradient algorithm (EG) as sequential prediction algorithms using the linear predictors. Notice here that the outputs of both EG and GD are linear in $x$, whereas that of AG is not linear in $x$. They showed

$$\sup_{D^m} R(\text{GD} : D^m) = O(\sqrt{m}),$$

$$\sup_{D^m} R(\text{EG} : D^m) = O\left(k\sqrt{m\ln k}\right).$$

Eq.(22) shows that the upper bound on the worst-case RCL for AG is $O(k\ln m)$, which is smaller than those for GD and EG when $m$ is sufficiently large and the parameter size $k$ is fixed.

# References

1. Cesa-Bianchi,N., and Lugosi, G., Minimax regret under log loss for general classes of experts, in *Proc. of COLT'99,* (1999).
2. Freund,Y., Predicting a binary sequence almost as well as the optimal biased coin," in *Proc. of COLT'96,* 89-98 (1996).
3. Haussler, D., Kivinen, J., and Warmuth, M., Tight worst-case loss bounds for predicting with expert advice, *Computational Learning Theory: EuroCOLT'95,* Springer, 69-83 (1995).
4. Kivinen,J., and Warmuth,M., "Exponentiated gradient versus gradient descent for linear predictors," UCSC-CRL-94-16, 1994.
5. Opper,M., and Haussler,D., Worst case prediction over sequence under log loss, in *Proc. of IMA Workshop in Information, Coding, and Distribution,* Springer, 1997.
6. Rissanen, J., Stochastic complexity, *J. R. Statist. Soc. B,* vol.49, 3, 223-239(1987).
7. Rissanen, J., Stochastic Complexity in Statistical Inquiry, *World Scientific, Singapore,* 1989.
8. Rissanen, J., Fisher information and stochastic complexity, *IEEE Trans. on Inf. Theory,* vol.IT-42, 1, 40-47 (1996).
9. Shtarkov, Y.M., Universal sequential coding of single messages, *Probl. Inf. Transmission.,* 23(3):3-17 (1987).
10. Vovk, V.G., Aggregating strategies, in *Proc. of COLT'90,* Morgan Kaufmann, 371-386(1990).
11. Vovk, V.G., Competitive on-line linear regression, in *Proc. of Advances in NIPS'98,* MIT Press, 364-370(1998).
12. Yamanishi, K., A decision-theoretic extension of stochastic complexity and its applications to learning, *IEEE Tran. on Inf. Theory,* IT-44, 1424-1439(1998).
13. Yamanishi, K., Minimax relative loss analysis for sequential prediction algorithms using parametric hypotheses, in *Proc. of COLT'98,* ACM Press, pp:32-43(1998).

# Algebraic Analysis for Singular Statistical Estimation

Sumio Watanabe

P&I Lab., Tokyo Institute of Technology,
4259 Nagatsuta, Midori-ku, Yokohama, 226-8503 Japan
swatanab@pi.titech.ac.jp
http://watanabe-www.pi.titech.ac.jp/index.html

**Abstract.** This paper clarifies learning efficiency of a non-regular para-metric model such as a neural network whose true parameter set is an analytic variety with singular points. By using Sato's b-function we rig-orously prove that the free energy or the Bayesian stochastic complexity is asymptotically equal to $\lambda_1 \log n - (m_1 - 1) \log \log n +$ constant, where $\lambda_1$ is a rational number, $m_1$ is a natural number, and $n$ is the number of training samples. Also we show an algorithm to calculate $\lambda_1$ and $m_1$ based on the resolution of singularity. In regular models, $2\lambda_1$ is equal to the number of parameters and $m_1 = 1$, whereas in non-regular models such as neural networks, $2\lambda_1$ is smaller than the number of parameters and $m_1 \geq 1$.

## 1 Introduction

From the statistical point of view, layered learning machines such as neural networks are not regular models. In a regular statistical model, the set of true parameters consists of only one point and identifiable even if the learning model is larger than necessary to attain the true distribution (*over-realizable case*). On the other hand, if a neural network is in the over-realizable case, the set of true parameters is not one point or not a manifold, but an analytic variety with sin-gular points. For such non-regular and non-identifiable learning machines, the maximum likelihood estimator does not exist or is not subject to the asymp-totically normal distribution, resulting that their learning efficiency is not yet clarified [1] [2] [3][4][5]. However, analysis for the over-realizable case is necessary for selecting the optimal model which balances the function approximation error with the statistical estimation error [3].

In this paper, by employing algebraic analysis, we prove that the free energy $F(n)$ ( or called the Bayesian stochastic complexity or the average Bayesian factor) has the asymptotic form

$$F(n) = \lambda_1 \log n - (m_1 - 1) \log \log n + O(1),$$

where $n$ is the number of empirical samples. We also show that an algorithm to calculate the positive rational number $\lambda_1$ and the natural number $m_1$ using

O. Watanabe, T. Yokomori (Eds.): ALT'99, LNAI 1720, pp. 39–50, 1999.

Hironaka's resolution of singularities, and that $2\lambda_1$ is smaller than the number of parameters. Since the increase of the free energy $F(n+1) - F(n)$ is equal to the *generalization error* defined by the average Kullback distance of the estimated probability density from the true one, our result claims that non-regular statistical models such as neural networks are the better learning machines than the regular models if the Bayesian estimation is applied in learning.

## 2   Main Results

Let $p(y|x, w)$ be a conditional probability density from an input vector $x \in R^M$ to an output vector $y \in R^N$ with a parameter $w \in R^d$, which represents probabilistic inference of a learning machine. Let $\varphi(w)$ be a probability density function on the parameter space $R^d$, whose support is denoted by $W = \text{supp } \varphi \subset R^d$. We assume that training or empirical sample pairs $\{(x_i, y_i); i = 1, 2, ..., n\}$ are independently taken from $q(y|x)q(x)$, where $q(x)$ and $q(y|x)$ represent the true input probability and the true inference probability, respectively. In the Bayesian estimation, the estimated inference $p_n(y|x)$ is the average of the *a posteriori* ensemble,

$$p_n(y|x) = \int p(y|x, w)\rho_n(w)dw,$$

$$\rho_n(w) = \frac{1}{Z_n}\varphi(w)\prod_{i=1}^{n}p(y_i|x_i, w),$$

where $Z_n$ is a constant which ensures $\int \rho_n(w)dw = 1$. The learning efficiency or the generalization error is defined by the average Kullback distance of the estimated probability density $p_n(y|x)$ from the true one $q(y|x)$,

$$K(n) = E_n\{\int \log \frac{q(y|x)}{p_n(y|x)} q(x, y)dxdy\}$$

where $E_n\{\cdot\}$ shows the expectation value over all sets of training sample pairs.

In this paper we mainly consider the statistical estimation error and assume that the model can attain the true inference, in other words, there exists a parameter $w_0 \in W$ such that $p(y|x, w_0) = q(y|x)$. Let us define the average and empirical loss functions.

$$f(w) = \int \log \frac{p(y|x, w_0)}{p(y|x, w)} q(y|x)q(x)dxdy,$$

$$f_n(w) = \frac{1}{n}\sum_{i=1}^{n} \log \frac{p(y_i|x_i, w_0)}{p(y_i|x_i, w)}.$$

Note that $f(w) \geq 0$. By the assumption, the set of the true parameters $W_0 = \{w \in W ; f(w) = 0\}$ is not an empty set. $W_0$ is called an *analytic set* or *analytic variety* of the analytic function $f(w)$. Note that $W_0$ is not a manifold in general, since it has singular points.

From these definitions, it is immediately proven [4] that the average Kullback distance $K(n)$ is equal to the increase of the *free energy* $F(n)$.

$$K(n) = F(n+1) - F(n),$$

$$F(n) = -E_n\{\log \int \exp(-nf_n(w))\varphi(w)dw\},$$

where $F(n)$ is sometimes called *Bayesian stochastic complexity* or *Bayesian factor*. Theorem 1 and 2 are the main results of this paper. Let $C_0^\infty$ be a set of all compact support and $C^\infty$-class functions on $R^d$.

**Theorem 1** *Assume that $f(w)$ is an analytic function and $\varphi(w)$ is a probability density function on $R^d$. Then, there exists a real constant $C_1$ such that for any natural number $n$*

$$F(n) \leq \lambda_1 \ \log n - (m_1 - 1)\log\log n + C_1, \tag{1}$$

*where the rational number $-\lambda_1$ ($\lambda_1 > 0$) and a natural number $m_1$ is the largest pole and its multiplicity of the meromorphic function that is analytically continued from*

$$J(\lambda) = \int_{f(w)<\epsilon} f(w)^\lambda \overline{\varphi}(w)dw \quad (Re(\lambda) > 0).$$

*where $\epsilon > 0$ is a sufficiently small constant, and $\overline{\varphi}(w)$ is an arbitrary nonzero $C_0^\infty$-class function that satisfies $0 \leq \overline{\varphi}(w) \leq \varphi(w)$.*

**Theorem 2** *Let $\sigma > 0$ be a constant value. Assume that*

$$p(y|x, w) = \frac{1}{2\sigma^2}\exp(-\frac{\|y - \psi(x, w)\|^2}{2\sigma^2}),$$

*where $\psi(x, w)$ is an analytic function for $w \in R^d$ and a continuous function for $x \in R^M$. Also assume that $\varphi(w)$ is a $C_0^\infty$-class probability density function. Then, there exists a constant $C_2 > 0$ such that for any natural number $n$*

$$|F(n) - \lambda_1 \ \log n + (m_1 - 1)\log\log n| \leq C_2,$$

*where the rational number $-\lambda_1$ ($\lambda_1 > 0$) and a natural number $m_1$ is the largest pole and its multiplicity of the meromorphic function that is analytically continued from*

$$J(\lambda) = \int_{f(w)<\epsilon} f(w)^\lambda \varphi(w)dw \quad (Re(\lambda) > 0).$$

*where $\epsilon > 0$ is a sufficiently small constant.*

From Theorem 2, if the average Kullback distance $K(n)$ has an asymptotic expansion, then

$$K(n) = \frac{\lambda_1}{n} - \frac{m_1 - 1}{n\log n} + o(\frac{1}{n\log n}).$$

As is well known, regular statistical models have $\lambda_1 = d/2$ and $m_1 = 1$. However, non-regular models such as neural networks have smaller $\lambda_1$ and larger $m_1$ in general [3].

# 3 Proof of Theorem 1

**Lemma 1** *The upper bounds of the free energy is given by*

$$F(n) \leq -\log \int \exp(-nf(w))\varphi(w)dw.$$

[Proof of Lemma 1] From Jensen's inequality and $E_n(f_n - f) = 0$, lemma 1 is obtained. (Q.E.D.)

For a given $\epsilon > 0$, a set of parameters is defined by

$$W_\epsilon = \{w \in W \equiv \text{supp } \varphi; f(w) < \epsilon\}.$$

**Theorem 3** *(Sato, Bernstein, Björk, Kashiwara) Assume that there exists $\epsilon_0 > 0$ such that $f(w)$ is an analytic function in $W_{\epsilon_0}$. Then there exists a set $(\epsilon, P, b)$, where*
*(1) $\epsilon < \epsilon_0$ is a positive constant,*
*(2) $P = P(\lambda, w, \partial w)$ is a differential operator which is a polynomial for $\lambda$, and*
*(3) $b(\lambda)$ is a polynomial, such that*

$$P(\lambda, w, \partial w)f(w)^{\lambda+1} = b(\lambda)f(w)^\lambda \quad (^\forall w \in W_\epsilon, ^\forall \lambda \in C).$$

*The zeros of the equation $b(\lambda) = 0$ are real, rational, and negative numbers.*

[Explanation of Theorem] This theorem is proven based on the algebraic property of the ring of partial differential operators. See references [6][7][8]. The rationality of the zeros of $b(\lambda) = 0$ is shown based on the resolution of singularity [9][13]. The smallest order polynomial $b(\lambda)$ that satisfies the above relation is called a Sato-Bernstein polynomial or a b-function.

Hereafter $\epsilon > 0$ is taken smaller than that in this theorem. We can assume that $\epsilon < 1$ without loss of generality. For a given analytic function $f(w)$, let us define a complex function $J(\lambda)$ of $\lambda \in C$ by

$$J(\lambda) = \int_{W_\epsilon} f(w)^\lambda \varphi(w)dw.$$

**Lemma 2** *Assume that $\varphi(w)$ is a $C_0^\infty$-class function. Then, $J(\lambda)$ can be analytically continued to the meromorphic function on the entire complex plane, in other words, $J(\lambda)$ has only poles in $|\lambda| < \infty$. Moreover $J(\lambda)$ satisfies the following conditions.*
*(1) The poles of $J(\lambda)$ are rational, real, and negative numbers.*
*(2) For an arbitrary $a \in R$, $J(\infty + a\sqrt{-1}) = 0$, and $J(a \pm \infty \cdot \sqrt{-1}) = 0$.*

[Proof of Lemma 2] $J(\lambda)$ is an analytic function in the region $\mathrm{Re}(\lambda) > 0$. $J(\infty + a\sqrt{-1}) = 0$ is shown by the Lebesgue's convergence theorem. For $a > 0$, $J(a + \infty\sqrt{-1}) = 0$ is shown by the the Riemann-Lebesgue theorem. Let $P^*$ be the adjoint operator of $P = P(\lambda, w, \partial_w)$. Then, by Theorem 3,

$$J(\lambda) = \frac{1}{b(\lambda)} \int_{W_\epsilon} Pf(w)^{\lambda+1}\varphi(w)dw = \frac{1}{b(\lambda)} \int_{W_\epsilon} f(w)^{\lambda+1}P^*\varphi(w)dw$$

Because $P^*\varphi \in C^\infty$, $J(\lambda)$ can be analytically continued to $J(\lambda - 1)$ if $b(\lambda) \neq 0$. By analytic continuation, then even for $a < 0$, $J(a + \infty\sqrt{-1}) = 0$. For $b(\lambda) = 0$, then such $\lambda$ is a pole which is on the negative part of real axis. (Q.E.D.)

**Definition** Poles of the function $J(\lambda)$ are on the negative part of the real axis and contained in the set $\{m + \nu; m = 0, -1, -2, ..., b(\nu) = 0\}$. They are ordered from the bigger to the smaller by $-\lambda_1, -\lambda_2, -\lambda_3, \cdots$, ($\lambda_k > 0$ is a rational number.) and the multiplicity of $-\lambda_k$ is defined by $m_k$.

We define a function $I(t)$ from $R$ to $R$ by

$$I(t) = \int_{W_\epsilon} \delta(t - f(w))\varphi(w)dw, \tag{2}$$

where $\epsilon > 0$ is taken as above. By definition, if $t > \epsilon$ or $t < 0$ then $I(t) = 0$.

**Lemma 3** *Assume that $\varphi(w)$ is a $C_0^\infty$-class function. Then $I(t)$ has an asymptotic expansion for $t \to 0$. (The notation $\cong$ shows that the term can be asymptotically expanded.j*

$$I(t) \cong \sum_{k=1}^{\infty} \sum_{m=0}^{m_k-1} c_{k,m+1}\, t^{\lambda_k-1}(-\log t)^m \tag{3}$$

*where $m! \cdot c_{k,m+1}$ is the coefficient of the $(m + 1)$-th order in the Laurent expansion of $J(\lambda)$ at $\lambda = -\lambda_k$.*

[Proof of Lemma 3] The special case of this lemma is shown in [10]. Let $I_K(t)$ be the restricted sum in $I(t)$ from $k = 1$ to $k = K$. It is sufficient to show that, for an arbitrary fixed $K$,

$$\lim_{t \to 0}(I(t) - I_K(t))t^\lambda = 0 \quad (^\forall\lambda > -\lambda_{K+1} + 1). \tag{4}$$

From the definition of $J(\lambda)$, $J(\lambda) = \int_0^1 I(t)t^\lambda dt$. The simple calculation shows

$$\int_0^1 t^{\lambda+\lambda_k-1}(-\log t)^m dt = \frac{m!}{(\lambda + \lambda_k)^{m+1}}.$$ Therefore,

$$\int_0^1 (I(t) - I_K(t))t^\lambda dt = J(\lambda) - \sum_{k=1}^{K} \sum_{m=0}^{m_k-1} \frac{c_{k,m+1}}{(\lambda + \lambda_k)^{m+1}}.$$

By putting $t = e^{-x}$ and by using the inverse Laplace transform and the previous Lemma 2, the complex integral path can be moved by regularity, which leads eq.(4). (Q.E.D.)

[Proof of Theorem 1] By combining the above results, we have

$$F(n) \leq -\log \int_W \exp(-nf(w))\varphi(w)dw \leq -\log \int_{W_\epsilon} \exp(-nf(w))\overline{\varphi}(w)dw$$

$$= -\log \int_0^1 e^{-nt} I(t)dt = -\log \int_0^n e^{-t} I(\frac{t}{n})\frac{dt}{n}$$

$$\cong -\log\{\sum_{k=1}^{\infty} \sum_{m=0}^{m_k-1} \sum_{j=0}^{m} \frac{c_{k,m+1}(\log n)^j (m C_j)}{n^{\lambda_k}} \int_0^n e^{-t} t^{\lambda_k-1}(-\log t)^{m-j} dt\}$$

$$= \lambda_1 \log n - (m_1 - 1) \log\log n + O(1)$$

where $I(t)$ is defined by eq.(2) with $\overline{\varphi}(w)$ instead of $\varphi(w)$. (Q.E.D.)

## 4   Proof of Theorem 2

Hereafter, we assume that the model is given by

$$p(y|x, w) = \frac{1}{\sqrt{2\pi}} \exp(-\frac{1}{2}(y - \psi(x, w))^2)).$$

It is easy to generalize the result to a general standard deviation ($\sigma > 0$) case and a general output dimension ($N > 1$) case. For this model,

$$f(w) = \frac{1}{2}\int(\psi(x, w) - \psi(x, w_0))^2 q(x)dx$$

$$f_n(w) = \frac{1}{2n}\sum_{i=1}^n (\psi(x_i, w) - \psi(x_i, w_0))^2 - \frac{1}{n}\sum_{i=1}^n \eta_i(\psi(x_i, w) - \psi(x_i, w_0))$$

where $\{\eta_i \equiv y_i - \psi(x_i, w_0)\}$ are independent samples from the standard normal distribution.

**Lemma 4** *Let $\{x_i, \eta_i\}_{i=1}^n$ be a set of independent samples taken from $q(x)q_0(y)$, where $q(x)$ is a compact support and continuous probability density and $q_0(y)$ is the standard normal distribution. Assume that the function $\xi(x, w)$ is analytic for $w$ and continuous for $x$, and that the Taylor expansion of $\xi(x, w)$ among $\overline{w}$ absolutely converges in the region $T = \{w; |w_j - \overline{w}_j| < r_j\}$. For a given constant $0 < a < 1$, we define the region $T_a \equiv \{w; |w_j - \overline{w}_j| < ar_j\}$. Then, the followings hold.*
*(1) If $\int \xi(x, w)q(x)dx = 0$, there exists a constant $c'$ such that for an arbitrary $n$,*

$$A_n \equiv E_n\{\sup_{w \in T_a} |\frac{1}{\sqrt{n}}\sum_{i=1}^n \xi(x_i, w)|^2\} < c' < \infty$$

*(2) There exists a constant $c''$ such that for an arbitrary $n$,*

$$B_n \equiv E_n\Big\{ \sup_{w \in T_a} |\frac{1}{\sqrt{n}} \sum_{i=1}^{n} \eta_i \xi(x_i, w)|^2 \Big\} < c'' < \infty$$

[Proof of Lemma 4] We show (1). The statement (2) can be proven by the same method. This lemma needs proof because $\sup_{w \in T_a}$ is in the expectation. We denote $k = (k_1, k_2, ..., k_d)$ and

$$\xi(x, w) = \sum_{k=0}^{\infty} a_k(x)(w - \overline{w})^k = \sum_{k_1, ..., k_d = 0}^{\infty} a_{k_1 \cdots k_d}(x)(w_1 - \overline{w_1})^{k_1} \cdots (w_d - \overline{w_d})^{k_d}.$$

Let $K = \operatorname{supp} q(x)$ be a compact set. Since $\xi(x, w)$ is analytic for $w$, by Cauchy's integral formula for several complex functions, there exists $\delta > 0$ such that

$$|a_k(x)| \le M / \prod_{j=1}^{d} |r_j - \delta|^{k_j}, \quad M \equiv \max_{x \in K, w \in T_a} |\xi(x, w)|,$$

and that $\int a_k(x) q(x) dx = 0$. Thus

$$E_n\Big\{ |\frac{1}{\sqrt{n}} \sum_{i=1}^{n} a_k(x_i)|^2 \Big\}^{\frac{1}{2}} = \Big\{ \int |a_k(x)|^2 q(x) dx \Big\}^{\frac{1}{2}} \le \frac{M}{\prod_j |r_j - \delta|^{k_j}}.$$

Therefore,

$$A_n^{\frac{1}{2}} = E_n\Big\{ \sup_{w \in T_a} |\frac{1}{\sqrt{n}} \sum_{i=1}^{n} \xi(x_i, w)|^2 \Big\}^{\frac{1}{2}} = E_n\Big\{ \sup_{w \in T_a} |\frac{1}{\sqrt{n}} \sum_{i=1}^{n} \sum_{k=0}^{\infty} a_k(x_i)(w - \overline{w})^k|^2 \Big\}^{\frac{1}{2}}$$

$$\le \sum_{k=0}^{\infty} E_n\Big\{ \sup_{w \in T_a} |\frac{1}{\sqrt{n}} \sum_{i=1}^{n} a_k(x_i)(w - \overline{w})^k|^2 \Big\}^{\frac{1}{2}} < \infty$$

where $\delta$ is taken so that $a r_j < r_j - \delta$ $(j = 1, 2, ..., d)$. (Q.E.D.)

The function $\zeta_n(w)$ is defined as follows.

$$\zeta_n(w) = \frac{\sqrt{n}(f(w) - f_n(w))}{\sqrt{f(w)}}$$

Note that $\zeta_n(w)$ is holomorphic function of $w$ except $W_0$.

**Theorem 4** *Assume that $\psi(x, w)$ is analytic for $w \in R^d$ and continuous for $x \in R^M$. Also assume that $q(x)$ is a compact support and continuous function. Then, there exists a constant $C_3$ such that for arbitrary $n$*

$$E_n\Big\{ \sup_{w \in W \backslash W_0} |\zeta_n(w)|^2 \Big\} < C_3.$$

*where $W \subset R^d$ is a compact set.*

[Proof of Theorem 4] Outside of the neighborhood of $W_0$, this theorem can be proven by the previous lemma. We assume that $W = W_\epsilon$. By compactness of $W$, $W$ is covered by a union of finite small open sets. Thus we can assume $w \in W$ is in the neighborhood of $w_0 \in W$. By inductively applying the Weierstrass' preparation theorem [14] to the holomorphic function $\psi(x, w) - \psi(x, w_0)$, there exists a finite set of functions $\{g_j, h_j\}_{j=1}^J$, where $g_j(w)$ is a holomorphic function and $h_j(x, w)$ is a continuous function for $x$ and a holomorphic function for $w$, such that

$$\psi(x, w) - \psi(x, w_0) = \sum_{j=1}^{J} g_j(w) h_j(x, w). \tag{5}$$

where the matrix

$$M_{jk} \equiv \int h_j(x, w_0) \overline{h_k(x, w_0)} q(x) dx$$

is positive definite. Let $\alpha > 0$ be taken smaller than the minimum eigen value of the matrix $M_{jk}$. By the definition,

$$f(w) = \frac{1}{2} \sum_{j,k=1}^{J} g_j(w) \overline{g_k(w)} \int h_j(x, w) \overline{h_k(x, w)} q(x) dx,$$

is bounded by $f(w) \geq \frac{\alpha}{2} \sum_{j=1}^{J} |g_j(w)|^2$. by taking small $\epsilon > 0$. We define

$$A(w) = \frac{1}{2} \sum_{j,k=1}^{J} g_j(w) g_k(w) \frac{1}{n} \sum_{i=1}^{n} a_{jk}(x_i, w)$$

$$a_{jk}(x_i, w) = \int h_j(x, w) h_k(x, w) q(x) dx - h_j(x_i, w) h_k(x_i, w),$$

$$B(w) = \sum_{j=1}^{J} g_j(w) \{ \frac{1}{n} \sum_{i=1}^{n} \eta_i h_j(x_i, w) \}.$$

Then $A(w) + B(w) = f(w) - f_n(w)$. By the Cauchy-Schwarz inequality,

$$E_n\{|\zeta_n(w)|^2\} = E_n\{ \frac{n|f(w) - f_n(w)|^2}{f(w)} \}$$

$$\leq E_n\{ \frac{2n}{f(w)} (|A(w)|^2 + |B(w)|^2) \} \leq Const.$$

For the last inequalities, we applied the previous lemma 4. (Q.E.D.)

[Proof of Theorem 2] We define

$$\alpha_n = \sup_{w \in W \setminus W_0} |\zeta_n(w)|.$$

Then, by Theorem 4, $E_n\{\alpha_n^2\} < \infty$. The free energy or the Bayesian stochastic complexity satisfies

$$
\begin{aligned}
F(n) &= -E_n\{\log \int_W \exp(-nf_n(w))\varphi(w)dw\} \\
&= -E_n\{\log \int_W \exp(-nf(w) - \sqrt{nf(w)}\zeta_n(w))\varphi(w)dw\} \\
&\geq -E_n\{\log \int_W \exp(-nf(w) + \alpha_n\sqrt{nf(w)})\varphi(w)dw\}.
\end{aligned}
$$

Let us define $Z_i(n)$ $(i = 1, 2)$ by

$$
Z_i(n) = \int_{W(i)} \exp(-nf(w) + \alpha_n\sqrt{nf(w)})\varphi(w)dw
$$

where $W(1) = W_\epsilon$ and $W(2) = W \setminus W_\epsilon$. Then

$$
\begin{aligned}
F(n) &\geq -E_n\{\log(Z_1(n) + Z_2(n))\} \\
&= -E_n\{\log Z_1(n)\} - E_n\{\log(1 + \frac{Z_2(n)}{Z_1(n)})\}. \quad (6)
\end{aligned}
$$

Let $F_1(n)$ and $F_2(n)$ be the first and the second terms of eq.(6), respectively. For $F_1(n)$, the same procedure as the upper bound can be applied,

$$
\begin{aligned}
F_1(n) &\cong -E_n\Big[\log\{\sum_{k,m,j} \frac{c_{k,m+1} \cdot m\, C_j(\log n)^j}{n^{\lambda_k}} \int_0^n e^{-t+\alpha_n\sqrt{t}}t^{\lambda_k-1}(-\log t)^{m-j}dt\}\Big] \\
&= \lambda_1\log n - (m_1-1)\log\log n - E_n\{\log\int_0^n e^{-t+\alpha_n\sqrt{t}}\, t^{\lambda_1-1}dt\} + O(1) \\
&= \lambda_1\log n - (m_1-1)\log\log n + O(1)
\end{aligned}
$$

where we used $\alpha_n\sqrt{t} \leq (1/2)(t + \alpha_n^2)$. The term $F_2(n)$ is evaluated by using

$$
Z_1 \geq \int_{W_\epsilon} \exp(-nf(w))\varphi(w)dw \geq c_{1,m_1} \frac{(\log n)^{m_1-1}}{n^{\lambda_1}},
$$

and

$$
Z_2 \leq \int_{W\setminus W_\epsilon} \exp(-\frac{nf(w) - \alpha_n^2}{2})\varphi(w)dw \leq (1 - \varphi(W_\epsilon))\exp(-\frac{n\epsilon - \alpha_n^2}{2}),
$$

we obtain $Z_2/Z_1 \leq \exp(\alpha_n^2/2)$ for sufficiently large $n$. Hence

$$
F_2(n) \geq -E_n\{\log(1 + \exp(\frac{\alpha_n^2}{2}))\} \geq -E_n\{\frac{\alpha_n^2}{2}\} - E_n\{\log\frac{1 + \exp(\frac{\alpha_n^2}{2})}{\exp(\frac{\alpha_n^2}{2})}\} > -\infty.
$$

In the last inequality, we used Theorem 4. (Q.E.D.)

## 5  Algorithm to Calculate the Learning Efficiency

The important values $\lambda_1$ and $m_1$ can be calculated by resolution of singularities. Atiyah showed [13] that the following theorem is directly proven from Hironaka's theorem.

**Theorem 5** *(Hironaka) Let $f(w)$ be a real analytic function defined in a neighborhood of $0 \in R^d$. Then there exist an open set $U \supset 0$, a real analytic manifold $U'$ and a proper analytic map $g : U' \to U$ such that*
*(1) $g : U' \setminus A' \to U \setminus A$ is an isomorphism, where $A = f^{-1}(0)$ and $A' = g^{-1}(A)$,*
*(2) for each $P \in U'$ there are local analytic coordinates $(u_1, ..., u_d)$ centered at $P$ so that, locally near $P$, we have*

$$f(g(u_1, ..., u_d)) = h(u_1, .., u_d)u_1^{k_1}u_2^{k_2} \cdots u_d^{k_d}$$

*where $h$ is an invertive analytic function and $k_i \geq 0$.*

This theorem shows that the singularity of $f$ can be locally resolved. The following is an algorithm to calculate $\lambda_1$ and $m_1$.

**Algorithm to calculate the singular learning efficiency**
(1) Cover the analytic variety $W_0 = \{w \in \text{supp}\varphi; f(w) = 0\}$ by the finite union of open neighborhoods $U_\alpha$.
(2) For each neighborhood $U_\alpha$, find the analytic map $g$ by using blowing up.
(3) For each neighborhood, the function $J_\alpha(\lambda)$ is calculated.

$$J_\alpha(\lambda) \equiv \int_{U_\alpha} f(w)^\lambda \varphi(w)dw$$

$$= \int_{g^{-1}(U_\alpha)} f(g(w))^\lambda \varphi(g(u))|g'|du$$

$$= \int_{g^{-1}(U_\alpha)} h(u)^\lambda \prod_{i=1}^{d} u_i^{\lambda k_i} \varphi(g(u))|g'|du,$$

where $|g'|$ is Jacobian. The last integration can be done for each variable $u_i$, and poles and their multiplicities. of $J_\alpha(z)$ are obtained.
(4) By $J(\lambda) = \sum_\alpha J_\alpha(\lambda)$, poles and their multiplicities can be calculated.

**Example.1** (Regular Models) For the regular statistical models, by using the appropriate coordinate $(w_1, ..., w_d)$ the average loss function $f(w)$ can be locally written by

$$f(w) = \sum_{i=1}^{d} w_i^2.$$

The blowing up of the singularity, we find a map $g : (u_1, ..., u_d) \mapsto (w_1, ..., w_d)$,

$$w_1 = u_1, \qquad w_i = u_1 u_i \quad (2 \leq i \leq d)$$

Then the function $J(\lambda)$ is

$$J(\lambda) = \int u_1^{2\lambda}(1 + \sum_{i=2}^{d} u_i^2)^\lambda |u_1|^{d-1}\varphi(u_1, u_1u_2, u_1u_3, ..., u_1u_d)du_1 du_2 \cdots du_d$$

This function has the pole at $\lambda = -d/2$ with the multiplicity $m_1 = 1$. Therefore, the free energy is

$$F(n) \cong \frac{d}{2}\log n + O(1).$$

In this case, we also calculate the Sato's b-function [11].

**Example.2** If the model

$$p(y|x, a, b) = \frac{1}{\sqrt{2\pi}}\exp(-\frac{1}{2}(y - a\tanh(bx))^2)$$

is trained using samples from $p(y|x, 0, 0)$, then

$$f(a, b) = a^2 \int \tanh(bx)^2 q(x)dx.$$

In this case, the deepest singularity is the origin, and in the neighborhood of the origin, $f(a, b) = a^2b^2$. From this fact, it immediately follows that $\lambda_1 = 1/2$, $m_1 = 2$, resulting that

$$F(n) \cong \frac{1}{2}\log n - \log\log n + O(1).$$

**Example.3** Let us consider a neural network

$$p(y|x, a, b, c, d) = \frac{1}{\sqrt{2\pi}}\exp(-\frac{1}{2}(y - \psi(x, a, b, c, d))^2),$$
$$\psi(x, a, b, c, d) = a\tanh(bx) + c\tanh(dx).$$

Assume that the true regression function be $\psi(x, 0, 0, 0, 0)$. Then, the deepest singularity of $f(a, b, c, d)$ is $(0, 0, 0, 0)$ and in the neighborhood of the origin,

$$f(a, b, c, d) = (ab + cd)^2 + (ab^3 + cd^3)^2$$

since the higher order term can be bounded by the above two terms (see [12]). By using blowing-up twice, we can find a map $g : (x, y, z, w) \mapsto (a, b, c, d)$

$$a = x, \quad b = y^3w - yz, \quad c = zx, \quad d = y.$$

By using this transform, we obtain

$$f(g(x, y, z, w)) = x^2y^6[w^2 + \{(y^2w - z)^3 + z\}^2],$$
$$|g'(x, y, z, w)| = |xy^3|,$$

resulting that $\lambda_1 = 2/3$, and $m_1 = 1$, and $F(n) \cong (2/3)\log n + O(1)$.

For the more general cases, some inequalities were obtained [3][12]. It is shown in [11] that, for all cases, $2\lambda_1 \le d$.

# 6  Conclusion

Mathematical foundation for singular learning machines such as neural networks is established based on the algebraic analysis. The free energy or the stochastic complexity is asymptotically given by $\lambda_1 \log n - (m_1 - 1) \log \log n + const.$, where $\lambda_1$ and $m_1$ are calculated by resolution of singularities.

Analysis for the maximum likelihood case or the zero temperature limit is an important problem for the future. We expect that algebraic analysis also plays an important role for such analysis.

# References

1. Hagiwara, K., Toda, N., Usui, S.,: On the problem of applying AIC to determine the structure of a layered feed-forward neural network. Proc. of IJCNN Nagoya Japan. **3** (1993) 2263–2266
2. Fukumizu,K.:Generalization error of linear neural networks in unidentifiable cases. In this issue.
3. Watanabe,S.: Inequalities of generalization errors for layered neural networks in Bayesian learning. Proc. of ICONIP 98 (1998) 59–62
4. Levin, E., Tishby, N., Solla, S.A.: A statistical approaches to learning and generalization in layered neural networks. Proc. of IEEE **78(10)** (1990) 1568–1674
5. Amari,S., Fujita,N., Shinomoto,S.: Four Types of Learning Curves. Neural Computation **4 (4)** (1992) 608–618
6. Sato, M.,Shintani,T.: On zeta functions associated with prehomogeneous vector space. Anals. of Math., **100** (1974) 131–170
7. Bernstein, I.N.: The analytic continuation of generalized functions with respect to a parameter. Functional Anal. Appl.**6** (1972) 26–40.
8. Björk, J.E.: Rings of differential operators. Northholland (1979)
9. Kashiwara, M.: B-functions and holonomic systems. Inventions Math. **38** (1976) 33–53.
10. Gel'fand, I.M., Shilov, G.E.: Generalized functions. Academic Press, (1964).
11. Watanabe, S.:Algebraic analysis for neural network learning. Proc. of IEEE SMC Symp., 1999, to appear.
12. Watanabe,S.:On the generalization error by a layered statistical model with Bayesian estimation. IEICE Trans. **J81-A** (1998) 1442-1452. (The English version is to appear in Elect. and Comm. in Japan. John Wiley and Sons)
13. Atiyah, M.F.: Resolution of Singularities and Division of Distributions. Comm. Pure and Appl. Math. **13** (1970) 145–150
14. Hörmander,L.:An introduction to complex analysis in several variables. Van Nostrand. (1966)

# Generalization Error of Linear Neural Networks in Unidentifiable Cases

Kenji Fukumizu

RIKEN Brain Science Institute, Wako, Saitama 351-0198, Japan
fuku@brain.riken.go.jp
http://www.islab.brain.riken.go.jp/~fuku

**Abstract.** The statistical asymptotic theory is often used in theoretical results in computational and statistical learning theory. It describes the limiting distribution of the maximum likelihood estimator (MLE) as an normal distribution. However, in layered models such as neural networks, the regularity condition of the asymptotic theory is not necessarily satisfied. The true parameter is not identifiable, if the target function can be realized by a network of smaller size than the size of the model. There has been little known on the behavior of the MLE in these cases of neural networks. In this paper, we analyze the expectation of the generalization error of three-layer linear neural networks, and elucidate a strange behavior in unidentifiable cases. We show that the expectation of the generalization error in the unidentifiable cases is larger than what is given by the usual asymptotic theory, and dependent on the rank of the target function.

## 1 Introduction

This paper discusses a non-regular property of multilayer network models, caused by its structural characteristics. It is well-known that learning in neural networks can be described as the parametric estimation from the viewpoint of statistics. Under the assumption of Gaussian noise in the output, the least square error estimator is equal to the maximal likelihood estimator (MLE), whose statistical behavior is known in detail. Therefore, many researchers have believed that the behavior of neural networks is perfectly described within the framework of the well-known statistical theory, and have applied theoretical methodologies to neural networks.

It has been clarified recently that the usual statistical asymptotic theory on the MLE does not necessarily hold in neural networks ([1],[2]). This always happens if we consider the model selection problem in neural networks. Assume that we have a neural network model with $H$ hidden units as a hypothesis space, and that the target function can be realized by a network with a smaller number of hidden units than $H$. In this case, as we explain in Section 2, the true parameter in the hypothesis class, which realizes the target function, is high-dimensional and not identifiable. The distribution of the MLE is not subject to

O. Watanabe, T. Yokomori (Eds.): ALT'99, LNAI 1720, pp. 51–62, 1999.

the ordinary asymptotic theory in this case. We cannot apply any methods such as AIC and MDL, which are based on the asymptotic theory.

In this paper, we discuss the MLE of linear neural networks, as the simplest multilayer model. Also in this simple model, the true parameter loses identifiability if and only if the target is realized by a network with a smaller number of hidden units. As the first step to investigate the behavior of a learning machine in unidentifiable cases, we calculate the expectation of the generalization error of linear neural networks in asymptotic situations, and derive an approximate formula for large-scale networks. From these results, we see that the generalization error in unidentifiable cases is larger than what is derived from the usual asymptotic theory. While the ordinary asymptotic theory asserts that the expectation of the generalization error depends only on the number of parameters, the generalization error in linear neural networks depends on the rank of target function.

## 2 Neural Networks and Identifiability

### 2.1 Neural Networks and Identifiability of Parameter

A neural network model can be described as a parametric family of functions $\{f(\cdot; \theta) : \mathbb{R}^L \to \mathbb{R}^M\}$, where $\theta$ is a parameter vector. A three-layer neural network with $H$ hidden units is defined by

$$f^i(x; \theta) = \sum_{j=1}^{H} w_{ij} \, \varphi \left( \sum_{k=1}^{L} u_{jk} x_k + \zeta_j \right) + \eta_i, \quad (1 \leq i \leq M) \tag{1}$$

where $\theta = (w_{ij}, \eta_i, , u_{jk}, \zeta_j)$ summarizes all the parameters. The function $\varphi(t)$ is called an activation function. In the case of a multilayer perceptron, a bounded and non-decreasing function like $\tanh(t)$ is often used.

We consider regression problems, assuming that an output of the target system is observed with a noise. An observed sample $(x, y) \in \mathbb{R}^L \times \mathbb{R}^M$ satisfies

$$y = f(x) + z, \tag{2}$$

where $f(x)$ is the *target function*, which is unknown to a learner, and $z \sim N(0, \sigma^2 I_M)$ is a random vector representing noise, where $N(\mu, \Sigma)$ is a normal distribution with mean $\mu$ and variance-covariance matrix $\Sigma$. We use $I_M$ for the $M \times M$ unit matrix. An input vector $x$ is generated randomly with its probability $q(x)dx$. A set of $N$ training data, $\{(x^{(\nu)}, y^{(\nu)})\}_{\nu=1}^{N}$, is an independent sample from the joint probability $p(y|x)q(x)dxdy$, where $p(y|x)$ is defined by eq.(2).

We discuss the maximum likelihood estimator (MLE), denoted by $\hat{\theta}$, assuming the statistical model

$$p(y|x; \theta) = \frac{1}{(2\pi\sigma^2)^{M/2}} \exp\left(-\frac{1}{2\sigma^2} \|y - f(x; \theta)\|^2\right), \tag{3}$$

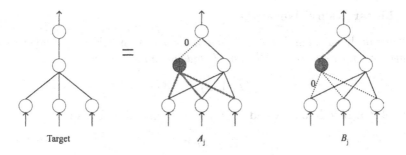

**Fig. 1.** Unidentifiable cases in neural networks

which has the same noise model as the target. Under these assumptions, it is easy to see that the MLE is equivalent to the least square error estimator, which minimizes the following *empirical error*:

$$E_{emp} = \sum_{\nu=1}^{N} \|y^{(\nu)} - f(x^{(\nu)}; \theta)\|^2. \tag{4}$$

We evaluate the accuracy of the estimation using the *expectation of generalization error*:

$$E_{gen} \equiv E_{\{(x^{(\nu)}, y^{(\nu)})\}} \left[ \int \|f(x; \hat{\theta}) - f(x)\|^2 q(x) dx \right]. \tag{5}$$

We sometimes call it simply *generalization error* if not confusing. It is easy to see that the expected log likelihood is directly related to $E_{gen}$ as

$$E_{\{(x^{(\nu)}, y^{(\nu)})\}} \left[ \int \int p(y|x) q(x)(-\log p(y|x; \theta)) dy dx \right] = \frac{1}{2\sigma^2} E_{gen} + const. \tag{6}$$

Throughout this paper, we assume that the target function is realized by the model; that is, there exists a true parameter $\theta_0$ such that $f(x; \theta_0) = f(x)$. One of the special properties of neural networks is that, if the target can be realized by a network with a smaller number of hidden units than the model, the set of true parameters that realize the target function is not a point but a union of high-dimensional manifolds (Fig.1). Indeed, the target can be realized in the parameter set where $w_{i1} = 0$ ($^\forall i$) holds and $u_{1k}$ takes an arbitrary value, and also in the set where $u_{1k} = 0$ ($^\forall i$) and $w_{i1}$ takes an arbitrary value, assuming $\varphi(0) = 0$. We say that the true parameter is *unidentifiable* if the set of true parameters is a union of manifolds whose dimensionality is more than one. The usual asymptotic theory cannot be applied if the true parameter is unidentifiable. The Fisher information matrix is singular in such a case ([3]). In the presence of noise in the output data, the MLE is located a little apart from the high-dimensional set.

## 2.2  Linear Neural Networks

We focus on linear neural networks hereafter, as the simplest multilayer model.
A *linear neural network (LNN) with $H$ hidden units* is defined by

$$f(x; A, B) = BAx, \qquad (7)$$

where $A$ is a $H \times L$ matrix and $B$ is a $M \times H$ matrix. We assume that

$$H \leq M \leq L$$

throughout this paper. Although $f(x; A, B)$ is just a linear map, the model is
not equal to the set of all linear maps from $\mathbb{R}^L$ to $\mathbb{R}^M$, but is the set of linear
maps of rank not greater than $H$. Then, the model is not equivalent to the linear
regression model $\{Cx \mid C : M \times L \text{ matrix}\}$. This model is known as reduced
rank regression in statistics ([4]).

The parameterization in eq.(7) has trivial redundancy. The transform
$(A, B) \mapsto (GA, BG^{-1})$ does not change the map for any non-singular matrix
$G$. Given a linear map of rank $H$, the set of parameters that realize the map
consists of an $H \times H$-dimensional manifold. However, we can easily eliminate this
redundancy if we restrict the parameterization so that the first $H$ rows of $A$ make
the unit matrix. Therefore, the essential number of parameters is $H(L+M-H)$.
In other words, we can regard $BA$ as a point in an $H(L + M - H)$-dimensional
space.

More essential redundancy arises when the rank of a map is less than $H$.
Even if we use the above restriction, the set of parameters that realize such a
map is still high-dimensional. Then, in LNN, the parameter $BA$ is identifiable if
and only if the rank of the target is equal to $H$. In this sense, we can regard linear
neural networks as a multilayer model, because it preserves the unidentifiability
explained in Section 2.1.

If the rank of the target is $H$, the usual asymptotic theory holds. It is well
known that $E_{gen}$ is given by

$$E_{gen} = \frac{\sigma^2}{N} \times H(L + M - H) + O(N^{-3/2}), \qquad (8)$$

using the number of parameters.

## 3  Generalization Error of Linear Neural Networks

### 3.1  Exact Results

It is known that the MLE of a LNN is exactly solved. We introduce the following
notations;

$$X = (x^{(1)}, \dots x^{(N)})^T, \quad Y = (y^{(1)}, \dots y^{(N)})^T, \quad \text{and} \quad Z = (z^{(1)}, \dots z^{(N)})^T. \qquad (9)$$

**Proposition 1** ([5]). *Let $V_H$ be an $M \times H$ matrix whose $i$-th column is the eigenvector corresponding to the $i$-th largest eigenvalue of $Y^T X (X^T X)^{-1} X^T Y$. Then, the MLE of a linear neural network is given by*

$$\hat{B}\hat{A} = V_H V_H^T Y^T X \left(X^T X\right)^{-1}. \tag{10}$$

Note that the MLE is unique even when the target is not identifiable, because the statistical data include noise. It distributes along the set of true parameters.

The expectation of the generalization error is given by the following

**Theorem 1.** *Assume that the rank of the target is $r$ ($\leq H$), and the variance-covariance matrix of the input $x$ is positive definite. Then, the expectation of the generalization error of a linear neural network is*

$$E_{gen} = \frac{\sigma^2}{N} \{r(L + M - r) + \phi(M - r, L - r, H - r)\} + O(N^{-3/2}), \tag{11}$$

*where $\phi(p, n, q)$ is the expectation of the sum of the $q$ largest eigenvalues of a random matrix following the Wishart distribution $W_p(n; I_p)$.*

(The proof is given in Appendix.)

The density function of the eigenvalues $\mu_1 \geq \ldots \geq \mu_p \geq 0$ of $W_p(n; I_p)$ is known as

$$\frac{1}{Z_n} \exp\left(-\frac{1}{2}\sum_{1=1}^{p}\mu_i\right) \prod_{i=1}^{p} \mu_i^{\frac{n-p-1}{2}} \prod_{1 \leq i \leq j \leq p} (\mu_i - \mu_j), \tag{12}$$

where $Z_n$ is a normalizing constant. However, the explicit formula of $\phi(p, n, q)$ is not known in general. In the following, we derive an exact formula in a simple case and an approximation for large-scale networks.

We can exactly calculate $\phi(2, n, 1)$ as follows. Since the expectation of the trace of a matrix from the distribution $W_2(n; I_2)$ is equal to 2, we have only to calculate $E[\mu_1 - \mu_2]$. By transforming the variable as $r = \frac{\mu_1 + \mu_2}{2}$ and $\omega = \cos^{-1} \sqrt{\mu_1 \mu_2}$), we can derive

$$E[\mu_1 - \mu_2] = \frac{1}{4\Gamma(n-1)} \int_0^{\infty} \int_0^{\frac{\pi}{2}} e^{-r} r^{n-3} \sin^{n-3}\omega (2r \cos \omega)^2 2r \sin \omega d\omega dr$$

$$= 2\sqrt{\pi} \frac{\Gamma(\frac{n+1}{2})}{\Gamma(\frac{n}{2})}. \tag{13}$$

Then, we obtain

$$E[\mu_1] = n + \sqrt{\pi} \frac{\Gamma(\frac{n+1}{2})}{\Gamma(\frac{n}{2})}. \tag{14}$$

From this fact, we can calculate the expectation of the generalization error in the case $H = M - 1$ and $r = H - 1$.

**Theorem 2.** *Assume $H = M - 1$, Then, the expectation of the generalization error in the case $r = H - 1$ and $r = H$ is give by*

$$
E_{gen} = \begin{cases} \frac{\sigma^2}{N}\left((M-1)(L+1) - 1 + \frac{\sqrt{\pi}\Gamma(\frac{L-M+3}{2})}{\Gamma(\frac{L-M+2}{2})}\right) & \text{if } r = H-1 \text{ (unidentifiable)}, \\ \frac{\sigma^2}{N}(M-1)(L+1) & \text{if } r = H \text{ (identifiable)}. \end{cases}
$$

$$(15)$$

The interesting point is that the generalization error changes depending on the identifiability of the true parameter. Since $\sqrt{\pi}\Gamma(\frac{n+1}{2})/\Gamma(\frac{n}{2}) > 1$ for $n \geq 2$, $E_{gen}$ in the unidentifiable case is larger than $E_{gen}$ in the identifiable case. If the number of input units is very large, from the Stirling's formula, the difference between these errors is approximated by $\frac{\sigma^2}{N}\sqrt{\pi L/2}$, which reveals much worse generalization in unidentifiable cases.

### 3.2   Generalization Error of Large Scale Networks

We analyze the generalization error of a large scale network in the limit when $L$, $M$, and $H$ go to infinity in the same order. Let $S \sim W_p(n; I_p)$ be a random matrix, and $\nu_1 \geq \nu_2 \geq \cdots \geq \nu_p \geq 0$ be the the eigenvalues of $n^{-1}S$. The empirical eigenvalue distribution of $n^{-1}S$ is defined by

$$
P_n := \frac{1}{p}(\delta(\nu_1) + \delta(\nu_2) + \cdots + \delta(\nu_p)),
$$

$$(16)$$

where $\delta(\nu)$ is the Dirac measure at $\nu$. The strong limit of $P_n$ is given by

**Proposition 2 ([6]).** *Let $0 < \alpha \leq 1$. If $n \to \infty$, $p \to \infty$ and $p/n \to \alpha$, then $P_n$ converges almost everywhere to*

$$
\rho_\alpha(u) = \frac{1}{2\pi\alpha}\frac{\sqrt{(u - u_m)(u_M - u)}}{u}\chi(u)du,
$$

$$(17)$$

*where $u_m = (\sqrt{\alpha} - 1)^2$, $u_M = (\sqrt{\alpha} + 1)^2$, and $\chi(u)$ denotes the characteristic function of $[u_m, u_M]$.*

Figure 2 shows the graph of $\rho_\alpha(u)$ for $\alpha = 0.5$.

We define $u_\beta$ as the $\beta$-percentile point of $\rho_\alpha(u)$; that is $\int_{u_\beta}^{u_M} \rho_\alpha(u)du = \beta$. If we transform the variable as $t = \left(u - \frac{u_m + u_M}{2}\right)/(2\sqrt{\alpha})$, the density of $t$ is

$$
\nu_\alpha(t) = \frac{2}{\pi}\frac{\sqrt{1 - t^2}}{2\sqrt{\alpha}t + 1 + \alpha},
$$

$$(18)$$

and the $\beta$-percentile point $t_\beta$ is given by $\int_{t_\beta}^{1} \nu_\alpha(t)dt = \beta$. Then, we can calculate

$$
\lim_{\substack{n,p \to \infty \\ p/n \to \alpha}} \frac{1}{np}\phi(p, n, \beta p) = \int_{u_\beta}^{u_M} u\rho(u)du = \frac{1}{\pi}\left\{\cos^{-1}(t_\beta) - t_\beta\sqrt{1 - t_\beta^2}\right\}.
$$

$$(19)$$

Combining this result with Theorem 1, we obtain

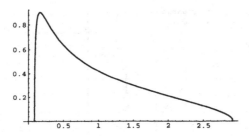

**Fig. 2.** Density of eigenvalues $\rho_{0.5}(u)$

**Theorem 3.** *Let $r$ ($r \leq H$) be the rank of the target. Then, we have*

$$E_{gen} \sim \frac{\sigma^2}{N} \left\{ r(L + M - r) + (L - r)(M - r)\frac{1}{\pi} \left( \cos^{-1}(t_\beta) - t_\beta \sqrt{1 - t_\beta^2} \right) \right\}$$
$$+ O(N^{-3/2}), \quad (20)$$

*when $L, M, H, r \to \infty$ with $\frac{M-r}{L-r} \to \alpha$ and $\frac{H-r}{M-r} \to \beta$.*

From elementary calculus, we can prove $\frac{1}{\pi}\{\cos^{-1}(t_\beta) - t_\beta\sqrt{1 - t_\beta^2}\} \geq \beta(1 + \alpha(1 - \beta))$ for $0 \leq \alpha \leq 1$ and $0 \leq \beta \leq 1$. Therefore, we see that in unidentifiable cases (*i.e.* $r < H$), $E_{gen}$ is greater than $\frac{\sigma^2}{N}H(L + M - H)$. Also in these results, $E_{gen}$ depends on the rank of the target. This shows clear difference from usual discussion on identifiable cases, in which $E_{gen}$ does not depend even on the model but only depends on the number of parameters (eq.(8)).

### 3.3   Numerical Simulations

First, we make experiments using LNN with 50 input, 20 hidden, and 30 output units. We prepare target functions of rank from 0 to 20. The generalization error of the MLE with respect to 10000 training data is calculated. The left graph of Fig.3 shows the average of the generalization errors over 100 data sets and the theoretical results given in Theorem 3. We see that the experimental and theoretical results coincide very much.

Next, we investigate the generalization error in an almost unidentifiable case, where the true parameter is identifiable but has very small singular values. We prepare a LNN with 2 input, 1 hidden, and 2 output units. The target function is $f(x; \theta_0) = \begin{pmatrix} \varepsilon \\ 0 \end{pmatrix}(\varepsilon \ 0)x$, where $\varepsilon$ is a small positive number. The target is identifiable for a non-zero $\varepsilon$. The right graph of Fig.3 shows the average of the generalization errors for 1000 training data. Surprisingly, while using 1000 training data for only 3 parameters, the result shows that the generalization errors for small $\varepsilon$ are much larger than what is given by the usual asymptotic theory. They are rather close to $E_{gen}$ of the unidentifiable case marked by $\times$.

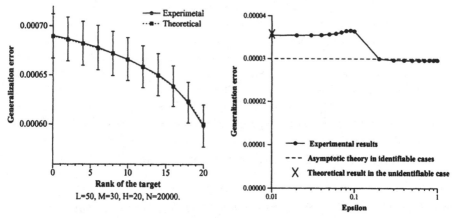

**Fig. 3.** Experimental results

## 4   Conclusion

This paper discussed the behavior of the MLE in unidentifiable cases of multi-layer neural networks. The ordinary methods based on the asymptotic theory cannot be applied to neural networks, if the target is realized by a smaller number of hidden units than the model. As the first step to clarifying the correct behavior of multilayer models, we elucidated the theoretical expression of the expectation of the generalization error for linear neural networks, and derived an approximate formula for large scale networks. From these results, we see that the generalization error in unidentifiable cases is larger than the generalization error in identifiable cases, and dependent on the rank of the target. This shows clear difference from ordinary models which always give a unique true parameter.

## Appendix

## A   Proof of Theorem 1

Let $C_0 = B_0 A_0$ be the coefficient of the target function, and $\Sigma$ be the variance-covariance matrix of the input vector $x$. From the assumption of the theorem, $\Sigma$ is positive definite. The expectation of the generalization error is given by

$$E_{gen} = E_{X,Y}[\text{Tr}[(\hat{B}\hat{A} - C_0)\Sigma(\hat{B}\hat{A} - C_0)^T]]. \tag{21}$$

We define an $M \times L$ random matrix $W$ by

$$W = Z^T X (X^T X)^{-1/2}. \tag{22}$$

Note that all the elements of $W$ are subject to the normal distribution $N(0, \sigma^2)$, mutually independent, and independent of $X$. From Proposition 1, we have

$$\hat{B}\hat{A} - C_0 = (V_H V_H^T - I_M)C_0 + V_H V_H^T W (X^T X)^{-1/2}. \tag{23}$$

This leads the following decomposition;

$$E_{gen} = E_{X,W}[\text{Tr}[C_0 \Sigma C_0^T (I_M - V_H V_H^T)]]$$
$$+ E_{X,W}[\text{Tr}[V_H V_H^T W (X^T X)^{-\frac{1}{2}} \Sigma (X^T X)^{-\frac{1}{2}} W^T]]. \quad (24)$$

We expand $(X^T X)^{1/2}$ and $X^T X$ as

$$(X^T X)^{1/2} = \sqrt{N} \Sigma^{1/2} + F,$$
$$X^T X = N\Sigma + \sqrt{N} K. \quad (25)$$

Then, the matrices $F$ and $K$ are of the order $O(1)$ as $N$ goes to infinity. We write $\varepsilon = \frac{1}{\sqrt{N}}$ hereafter for notational simplicity, and obtain the expansion of $\frac{1}{N} Y^T X (X^T X)^{-1} X^T Y$ as

$$T(\varepsilon) \equiv \frac{1}{N} Y^T X (X^T X)^{-1} X^T Y = T^{(0)} + \varepsilon T^{(1)} + \varepsilon^2 T^{(2)}, \quad (26)$$

where

$$T^{(0)} = C_0 \Sigma C_0^T,$$
$$T^{(1)} = C_0 K C_0^T + C_0 \Sigma^{1/2} W^T + W \Sigma^{1/2} C_0^T,$$
$$T^{(2)} = W W^T + W F C_0^T + C_0 F W^T. \quad (27)$$

Since the column vectors of $V_H$ are the eigenvectors of $T(\varepsilon)$, they are obtained by the perturbation of the eigenvectors of $T^{(0)}$. Following the method of Kato ([7], Section II), we will calculate the projection $P_j(\varepsilon)$ onto the eigenspace corresponding to the eigenvalue $\lambda_j(\varepsilon)$ of $T(\varepsilon)$, We call $P_j(\varepsilon)$ an eigenprojection.

Let $\lambda_1 \geq \ldots \geq \lambda_r > 0$ be the positive eigenvalues of $T^{(0)} = C_0 \Sigma C_0^T$, $P_i$ ($1 \leq i \leq r$) be the corresponding eigenprojections, and $P_0$ be the eigenprojections corresponding to the eigenvalue 0 of $T^{(0)}$. Then, from the singular value decomposition of $C_0 \Sigma^{1/2}$, we see that there exist projections $Q_i$ ($1 \leq i \leq r$) of $\mathbb{R}^L$ such that their images are mutually orthogonal 1-dimensional subspaces and the equalities

$$\Sigma^{1/2} C_0^T P_i C_0 \Sigma^{1/2} = \lambda_i Q_i \quad (28)$$

hold for all $i$. We define the total projection $\tilde{Q}$ by

$$\tilde{Q} = \sum_{i=1}^r Q_i. \quad (29)$$

First, let $\lambda_i(\varepsilon)$ ($1 \leq i \leq r$) be the eigenvalue obtained by the perturbation of $\lambda_i$, and $P_i(\varepsilon)$ be the eigenprojection corresponding to $\lambda_i(\varepsilon)$. Clearly, the equality

$$P_i(\varepsilon) = P_i + O(\varepsilon) \quad (30)$$

holds.

Next, we consider the perturbation of $P_0$. Generally, by the perturbation of eq.(26), the eigenvalue 0 of $T^{(0)}$ splits into several eigenvalues. Since the perturbation is caused by a positive definite random matrix, these eigenvalues are positive and different from each other almost surely. Let $\lambda_{r+1}(\varepsilon) > \cdots > \lambda_M(\varepsilon) > 0$ be the eigenvalues, and $P_{r+j}(\varepsilon)$ be the corresponding eigenprojections. We define the total projection of the eigenvalues $\lambda_{r+j}$ by

$$P_0(\varepsilon) = \sum_{j=1}^{M-r} P_{r+j}(\varepsilon). \tag{31}$$

The non-zero eigenvalues of $T(\varepsilon)P_0(\varepsilon)$ are $\lambda_{r+j}(\varepsilon)$ ($1 \leq j \leq M - r$). To obtain the expansion of $P_{r+j}(\varepsilon)$, we expand $T(\varepsilon)P_0(\varepsilon)$ as

$$T(\varepsilon)P_0(\varepsilon) = \sum_{n=1}^{\infty} \varepsilon^n \tilde{T}^{(n)} \tag{32}$$

Then, from Kato ([7],(2.20)), we see that the coefficient matrices of eq.(32) are in general given by

$$\tilde{T}^{(1)} = P_0 T^{(1)} P_0,$$
$$\tilde{T}^{(2)} = P_0 T^{(2)} P_0 - P_0 T^{(1)} P_0 T^{(1)} S - P_0 T^{(1)} S T^{(1)} P_0 - S T^{(1)} P_0 T^{(1)} P_0,$$
$$\begin{aligned}\tilde{T}^{(3)} = &-P_0 T^{(1)} P_0 T^{(2)} S - P_0 T^{(2)} P_0 T^{(1)} S - P_0 T^{(1)} S T^{(2)} P_0 - P_0 T^{(2)} S T^{(1)} P_0 \\ &- S T^{(1)} P_0 T^{(2)} P_0 - S T^{(2)} P_0 T^{(1)} P_0 + P_0 T^{(1)} P_0 T^{(1)} S T^{(1)} S \\ &+ P_0 T^{(1)} S T^{(1)} P_0 T^{(1)} S + P_0 T^{(1)} S T^{(1)} S T^{(1)} P_0 + S T^{(1)} P_0 T^{(1)} P_0 T^{(1)} S \\ &+ S T^{(1)} P_0 T^{(1)} S T^{(1)} P_0 + S T^{(1)} S T^{(1)} P_0 T^{(1)} P_0 - P_0 T^{(1)} P_0 T^{(1)} P_0 T^{(1)} S^2 \\ &- P_0 T^{(1)} P_0 S^2 T^{(1)} P_0 - P_0 T^{(1)} S^2 T^{(1)} P_0 T^{(1)} P_0 - S^2 T^{(1)} P_0 T^{(1)} P_0 T^{(1)} P_0, \end{aligned} \tag{33}$$

where $S$ is defined by

$$S = \sum_{i=1}^{r} \frac{1}{\lambda_i} P_i, \tag{34}$$

which is the inverse of $T^{(0)}$ in the image of $I - P_0$. Note that from eqs (28), (29), and (34), the equality

$$\Sigma^{1/2} C_0^T S C_0 \Sigma^{1/2} = \tilde{Q} \tag{35}$$

holds.

From the fact $T^{(0)} P_0 = 0$, we have

$$C_0 P_0 = 0. \tag{36}$$

Using eq.(35) and eq.(36), we can derive

$$\tilde{T}^{(1)} = 0, \qquad \tilde{T}^{(2)} = P_0 (WW^T - W\tilde{Q}W^T) P_0. \tag{37}$$

In particular, $P_{r+j}(\varepsilon)$ is the eigenprojection of

$$\frac{1}{\varepsilon^2} T(\varepsilon) P_0(\varepsilon) = \tilde{T}^{(2)} + \varepsilon \tilde{T}^{(3)} + \varepsilon^2 \tilde{T}^{(4)} + \cdots. \tag{38}$$

In the leading term $\tilde{T}^{(2)}$, $P_0 W(I_L - \tilde{Q})$ is the orthogonal projection of $W$ onto an $M - r$ dimensional subspace in the range and onto an $L - r$ dimensional subspace in the domain respectively. Thus, the distribution of the random matrix $\tilde{T}^{(2)}$ is equal to the Wishart distribution $W_{M-r}(L - r; \sigma^2 I_{M-r})$.

We expand $P_{r+j}(\varepsilon)$ as

$$P_{r+j}(\varepsilon) = P_{r+j} + \varepsilon P_{r+j}^{(1)} + \varepsilon^2 P_{r+j}^{(2)} + O(\varepsilon^3). \tag{39}$$

From Kato ([7], (2.14)), the coefficients are in general given by

$$P_{r+j}^{(1)} = - P_{r+j}\tilde{T}^{(3)}S_j - S_j\tilde{T}^{(3)}P_{r+j},$$
$$P_{r+j}^{(2)} = - P_{r+j}\tilde{T}^{(4)}S_j - S_j\tilde{T}^{(4)}P_{r+j} + P_{r+j}\tilde{T}^{(3)}S_j\tilde{T}^{(3)}S_j + S_j\tilde{T}^{(3)}P_{r+j}\tilde{T}^{(3)}S_j$$
$$+ S_j\tilde{T}^{(3)}S_j\tilde{T}^{(3)}P_{r+j} - P_{r+j}\tilde{T}^{(3)}P_{r+j}\tilde{T}^{(3)}S_j^2 - P_{r+j}\tilde{T}^{(3)}S_j^2 P_{r+j}$$
$$- S_j^2\tilde{T}^{(3)}P_{r+j}\tilde{T}^{(3)}P_{r+j}, \tag{40}$$

where $S_j$ is defined by

$$S_j = - \sum_{\substack{1 \leq k \leq M-r \\ k \neq j}} \frac{1}{\eta_j - \eta_k}P_{r+j} - \frac{1}{\eta_j}(I - P_0). \tag{41}$$

Here $\eta_1 \geq \ldots \geq \eta_{M-r}$ are the non-zero eigenvalues of $\tilde{T}^{(2)}$. The matrix $S_j$ is equal to the inverse of $\tilde{T}^{(2)} - \eta_j I_M$ in the image of $I - P_{r+j}$.

Using the expansions obtained above, we will calculate the generalization error. The first term of eq.(24) can be rewritten as

$$\sum_{j=H+1-r}^{M} E_{X,W}[\mathrm{Tr}[C_0 \Sigma C_0^T P_{r+j}(\varepsilon)]]. \tag{42}$$

Having $P_{r+j}C_0 = 0$ in mind, we obtain

$$\mathrm{Tr}[C_0 \Sigma C_0^T P_{r+j}^{(1)}] = 0,$$
$$\mathrm{Tr}[C_0 \Sigma C_0^T P_{r+j}^{(2)}] = \frac{1}{\eta_j^2}\mathrm{Tr}[C_0 \Sigma C_0^T(I - P_0)\tilde{T}^{(3)}P_{r+j}\tilde{T}^{(3)}(I - P_0)]. \tag{43}$$

Using eq.(36), eq.(37), and the fact that $C_0 \Sigma C_0^T(I - P_0)S = I - P_0$, we can derive from eq.(33)

$$\mathrm{Tr}[C_0 \Sigma C_0^T P_{r+j}^{(2)}] = \mathrm{Tr}[(T^{(1)} P_0 T^{(2)} - T^{(1)} P_0 T^{(1)} S T^{(1)})$$
$$P_{r+j}(T^{(2)} P_0 T^{(1)} - T^{(1)} S T^{(1)} P_0 T^{(1)})S]. \tag{44}$$

Furthermore, eq.(27) leads

$$T^{(1)} P_0 T^{(2)} P_{r+j} - T^{(1)} P_0 T^{(1)} S T^{(1)} P_{r+j} = C_0 \Sigma^{\frac{1}{2}} W^T P_0(WW^T - W\tilde{Q}W^T)P_{r+j}$$
$$= \eta_j C_0 \Sigma^{\frac{1}{2}} W^T P_{r+j}. \tag{45}$$

Finally, we obtain

$$\text{Tr}[C_0 \Sigma C_0^T P_{r+j}^{(2)}] = \text{Tr}[C_0 \Sigma^{1/2} W^T P_{r+j} W \Sigma^{1/2} C_0^T S] = \text{Tr}[P_{r+j} W \tilde{Q} W^T]. \quad (46)$$

The random matrices $P_{r+j}$ and $W\tilde{Q}W^T$ are independent, because $W\tilde{Q}$ and $W(I_L - \tilde{Q})$ are independent. Therefore,

$$\begin{aligned}
\text{E}_{X,w}[\text{Tr}[C_0 \Sigma C_0^T (I_M - V_H V_H^T)]] &= \varepsilon^2 \sum_{j=H-r+1}^{M-r} \text{E}_{X,w}[\text{Tr}[P_{r+j} W \tilde{Q} W^T]] \\
&= \sigma^2 \varepsilon^2 r(M - H) + O(\varepsilon^3) \quad (47)
\end{aligned}$$

is obtained.

Using eqs.(25) and (30), the second term of eq.(24) is rewritten as

$$\begin{aligned}
\text{E}_{X,w}[\text{Tr}[V_H V_H^T W (X^T X)^{-\frac{1}{2}} \Sigma (X^T X)^{-\frac{1}{2}} W^T]] \\
= \varepsilon^2 \text{E}_{X,w}\left[ \sum_{i=1}^{r} \text{Tr}[P_i W W^T] + \sum_{j=1}^{H-r} \text{Tr}[P_{r+j} W W^T] \right]. \quad (48)
\end{aligned}$$

Because $\sum_{i=1}^{r} P_i$ is a non-random orthogonal projection onto an $r$-dimensional subspace and the distribution of each element of $W$ is $N(0, \sigma^2)$, we have

$$\text{E}_{X,w}\left[ \text{Tr}\left[ \sum_{i=1}^{r} P_i W W^T \right] \right] = \sigma^2 r L. \quad (49)$$

We can calculate the second part of the right hand side of eq.(48) as

$$\begin{aligned}
\text{Tr}[P_{r+j} W W^T] &= \text{Tr}[P_{r+j} W \tilde{Q} W^T] + \text{Tr}[P_{r+j}(W W^T - W \tilde{Q} W^T)] \\
&= \text{Tr}[P_{r+j} W \tilde{Q} W^T] + \eta_j. \quad (50)
\end{aligned}$$

Because $\eta_j$ is the $j$-th largest eigenvalues of a random matrix from the Wishart distribution $W_{M-r}(L - r, \sigma^2 I_{M-r})$, we obtain

$$\text{E}_{X,w}[\sum_{j=1}^{H-r} \text{Tr}[P_{r+j} W W^T]] = \sigma^2 \{ r(H - r) + \phi(M - r, L - r, H - r) \}. \quad (51)$$

From eqs.(47), (49), and (51), we prove the the theorem.    □

## References

1. Hagiwara, K., Toda, N., Usui, S.: On the problem of applying AIC to determine the structure of a layered feed-forward neural network. Proc. 1993 Intern. Joint Conf. Neural Networks (1993) 2263–2266
2. Fukumizu, K.: Special statistical properties of neural network learning. Proc. 1997 Intern. Symp. Nonlinear Theory and its Applications (NOLTA'97) (1997) 747–750
3. Fukumizu, K.: A Regularity condition of the information matrix of a multilayer perceptron network. Neural Networks 9 (1996) 871–879
4. Reinsel, G.C., Velu, R.P.: Multivariate Reduced Rank Regression. Springer-Verlag, Berlin Heidelberg New York (1998)
5. Baldi, P. F., Hornik, K.: Learning in linear neural networks: a survey. IEEE Trans. Neural Networks 6 (1995) 837–858
6. Watcher, K.W.: The strong limits of random matrix spectra for sample matrices of independent elements. Ann. Prob. 6 (1978) 1–18
7. Kato, T.: Perturbation Theory for Linear Operators (2nd ed). Springer-Verlag, Berlin Heidelberg New York (1976)

# The Computational Limits to the Cognitive Power of the Neuroidal Tabula Rasa

Jiří Wiedermann*

Institute of Computer Science
Academy of Sciences of the Czech Republic
Pod vodárenskou věží 2
182 07 Prague 8
Czech Republic
wieder@uivt.cas.cz

**Abstract.** The neuroidal tabula rasa (NTR) as a hypothetical device which is capable of performing tasks related to cognitive processes in the brain was introduced by L.G. Valiant in 1994. Neuroidal nets represent a computational model of the NTR. Their basic computational element is a kind of a programmable neuron called neuroid. Essentially it is a combination of a standard threshold element with a mechanism that allows modification of the neuroid's computational behaviour. This is done by changing its state and the settings of its weights and of threshold in the course of computation. The computational power of an NTR crucially depends both on the functional properties of the underlying update mechanism that allows changing of neuroidal parameters and on the universe of allowable weights. We will define instances of neuroids for which the computational power of the respective finite-size NTR ranges from that of finite automata, through Turing machines, upto that of a certain restricted type of BSS machines that possess super–Turing computational power. The latter two results are surprising since similar results were known to hold only for certain kinds of analog neural networks.

## 1 Introduction

Nowadays, we are witnessing a steadily increasing interest towards understanding the algorithmic principles of cognition. The respective branch of computer science has been recently appropriately named as cognitive computing. This notion, coined by L.G. Valiant [8], denotes any computation whose computational mechanism is based on our ideas about brain computational mechanisms and whose goal is to model cognitive abilities of living organisms. There is no surprise that most of the corresponding computational models are based on formal models of neural nets.

Numerous variants of neural nets have been proposed and studied. They differ in the computational properties of their basic building elements, viz. neurons. Usually, two basic kinds of neurons are distinguished: discrete ones that compute

* This research was supported by GA ČR Grant No. 201/98/0717

O. Watanabe, T. Yokomori (Eds.): ALT'99, LNAI 1720, pp. 63–76, 1999.

with Boolean values, and analog (or continuous) ones that compute with any real or rational number between 0 and 1.

As far as the computational power of the respective neural nets is concerned, it is known that the finite nets consisting of discrete neurons are computationally equivalent to finite automata (cf. [5]). On the other hand, finite nets of analog neurons with rational weights, computing in discrete steps with rational values, are computationally equivalent to Turing machines (cf. [3]). If weights and computations with real values are allowed then the respective analog nets possess even super–Turing computational abilities [4]. No types of finite discrete neural nets are known that would be more powerful than the finite automata.

An important aspect of all interesting cognitive computations is learning. Neural nets learn by adjusting the weights on neural interconnections according to a certain learning algorithm. This algorithm and the corresponding mechanism of weight adjustment are not considered as part of the network.

Inspired by real biological neurons, Valiant suggested in 1988 [6] a special kind of programmable discrete neurons, called neuroids, in order to make the learning mechanism a part of neural nets. Based on its current state and current excitation from firings of the neighboring neuroids, a neuroid can change in the next step all its computational parameters (i.e., can change its state, threshold, and weights). In his monograph [7] Valiant introduced the notion of a neuroidal tabula rasa (NTR). It is a hypothetical device which is capable of performing tasks related to cognitive processes. Neuroidal nets serve as a computational model of the NTR. Valiant described a number of neuroidal learning algorithms demonstrating a viability of neuroidal nets to model the NTR. Nevertheless, insufficient attention has been paid to the computational power of the respective nets. Without pursuing this idea any further Valiant merely mentioned that the computational power of neuroids depends on the restriction put upon their possibilities to self–modify their computational parameters.

It is clear that by identifying a computational power of any learning device we get an upper qualitative limit on its learning or cognitive abilities. Depending on this limit, we can make conclusions concerning the efficiency of the device at hand and those related to its appropriateness to serve as a realistic model of its real, biological counterpart.

In this paper we will study the computational power of the neuroidal tabula rasa which is represented by neuroidal nets. The computational limits will be studied w.r.t the various restrictions on the update abilities of neuroidal computational parameters.

In Section 2 we will describe a broad class of neuroidal networks as introduced by Valiant in [7].

Next, in Section 3, three restricted classes of neuroidal nets will be introduced. They will include nets with a finite, infinite countable (i.e, integer), and uncountable (i.e., real) universe of weights, respectively.

Section 4 will briefly sketch the equivalence of the most restricted version of finite neuroidal nets — namely those with a finite set of parameters, with the finite automata.

In Section 5 we further show the computational equivalence of the latter neuroidal nets with the standard neural nets.

The next variant of neuroidal nets, viz. those with integer weights, will be considered in Section 6. We will prove that finite neuroidal nets with weights of size $S(n)$, which allow a simple arithmetic over their weights (i.e., adding or subtracting of the weights), are computationally equivalent to computations of any $S(n)$–space bounded Turing machine.

In Section 7 we will increase the computational power of the previously considered model of neuroidal nets by allowing their weights to be real numbers. The resulting model will turn to be computationally equivalent to the so–called additive BSS machine ([1]). This machine model is known for its ability to solve some undecidable problems.

Finally, in the conclusions we will discuss the merits of the results presented.

## 2   Neuroidal Nets

In what follows we will define neuroidal nets making use of the original Valiant's proposal [7], essentially including his notation.

**Definition 2.1** A neuroidal net $\mathcal{N}$ is a quintuple $\mathcal{N} = (G, W, X, \delta, \lambda)$, where

- $G = (V, E)$ is the directed graph describing the topology of the network; $V$ is a finite set of $N$ nodes called neuroids labeled by distinct integers $1, 2, \ldots, N$, and $E$ is a set of $M$ directed edges between the nodes. The edge $(i, j)$ for $i, j \in \{1, \ldots, N\}$ is an edge directed from node $i$ to node $j$.

- $W$ is the set of numbers called weights. To each edge $(i, j) \in E$ there is a value $w_{i,j} \in W$ assigned at each instant of time.

- $X$ is the finite set of the modes of neuroids which a neuroid can be in each instant. Each mode is specified as a pair $(q, p)$ of values where $q$ is the member of a finite set $Q$ of states, and $p$ is an integer from a finite set $T$ called the set of thresholds of the neuroid.

  $Q$ consists of two kinds of states called firing and quiescent states.

  To each node $i$ there is also a Boolean variable $f_i$ having value one or zero depending on whether the node $i$ is in a firing state or not.

- $\delta$ is the recursive mode update function of form $\delta : X \times W \to X$.

  Let $w_i \in W$ be the sum of those weights $w_{ki}$ of neuroid $i$ that are on edges $(k, i)$ coming from neuroids which are currently firing, i.e., formally $w_i = \sum_{\substack{k \text{ firing} \\ (k,i) \in E}} w_{ki} = \sum_{\substack{j \\ (j,i) \in E}} f_j w_{ji}$. The value of $w_i$ is called the excitation of $i$ at that time.

  The mode update function $\delta$ defines for each combination $(s_i, w_i)$ holding at time $t$ the mode $s' \in X$ that neuroid $i$ will transit to at time $t+1$: $\delta(s_i, w_i) = s'$.

- $\lambda$ is the recursive weight update function of form $\lambda : X \times W \times W \times \{0, 1\} \to W$. It defines for each weight $w_{ji}$ at time $t$ the weight $w'_{ji}$ to which it will transit at time $t+1$, where the new weight can depend on the values of each $s_i$, $w_i$, $w_{ji}$, and $f_j$ at time $t$: $\lambda(s_i, w_i, w_{ji}, f_j) = w'_{ji}$

The elements of sets $Q$, $T$, $W$, and $f_i$'s are called *parameters* of net $\mathcal{N}$.

A *configuration* of $\mathcal{N}$ at time $t$ is a list of modes of all neurons followed by a list of weights of all edges in $\mathcal{N}$ at that time. The respective lists of parameters are pertinent to neuroids ordered by their labels and to edges ordered lexicographically w.r.t. the pair of labels (of neuroids) that identify the edge at hand. Thus at any time a configuration is an element from $X^N \times W^M$.

The *computation of a neuroidal network* is determined by the *initial conditions* and the *input sequence*. The initial conditions specify the initial values of weights and modes of the neuroids. These are represented by the initial configuration. The input sequence is an infinite sequence of inputs or *stimuli* which specifies for each $t = 0, 1, 2, \ldots$ a set of neuroids along with the states into which these neuroids are forced to enter (and hence forced to fire or prevented from firing) at that time by mechanisms outside the net (by peripherals).

Formally, each stimulus is an $N$–tuple from the set $\{Q \cup *\}^N$. If there is a symbol $q$ at $i$–th position in the $t$–th $N$–tuple $s_t$, then this denotes the fact that the neuroid $i$ is forced to enter state $q$ at time $t$. The special symbol $*$ is used as don't–care symbol at positions which are not influenced by peripherals at that time.

A *computational step* of neuroidal net $\mathcal{N}$, which finds itself in a configuration $c_t$ and receives its input $s_t$ at time $t$, is performed as follows. First, neuroids are forced to enter into states as dictated by the current stimuli. Neurons not influenced by peripherals at that time retain their original state as in configuration $c_t$. In this way a new configuration $c'_t$ is obtained. Excitation $w_i$ is computed for this configuration now and the mode and weight updates are realized for each neuroid $i$ in parallel, in accordance with the respective function $\delta$ and $\lambda$. In this way a new configuration $c_{t+1}$ is entered.

The result of the computation after the $t$–th step is the $N$–tuple of states of all neuroids in $c_{t+1}$. This $N$–tuple is called the *action* at time $t$. Obviously, any action is an element in $Q^N$. Then the next computational step can begin.

The output of the whole computation can be seen as an infinite sequence of actions.

From the computational point of view any neuroidal net can be seen as a transducer which reads an infinite sequence of inputs (stimuli) and produces an infinite sequence of outputs (actions).

For more details about the model see [7].

## 3    Variants of Neuroidal Nets

In the previous definition of neuroidal nets we allowed set W to be any set of numbers and the weight and mode update functions to be arbitrary recursive functions. Intuitively it is clear that by restricting these conditions we will get variants of neural nets differing in their expressiveness as well as in their computing power. In his monograph Valiant [7] discusses this problem and suggests two extreme possibilities.

The first one considers such neuroidal nets where the set of weights of individual neuroids is finite. This is called a "simple complexity-theoretic model" in Valiant's terminology. We will also call the respective model of a neuroid as a "finite weight" neuroid. Note that in this case functions $\delta$ and $\lambda$ can both be described by finite tables.

The next possibility we will study are neuroidal nets where the universe of allowable weights and thresholds is represented by the infinite set of all integers. In this case it is no longer possible to describe the weight update function by a finite table. What we rather need is a simple recursive function that will allow efficient weight modifications. Therefore we will consider a weight update function which allows setting a weight to some constant value, adding or subtracting the weights, and assigning existing weights to other inputs edges. Such a weight update function will be called a *simple–arithmetic update function*. The respective neuroid will be called an "integer weight" neuroid. The *size* of each weight will be given by the number of bits needed to specify the respective weight value. This is essentially a model that is considered in [7] as the counterpart of the previous model.

The final variant of neuroidal nets which we will investigate is the variant of the previously mentioned model with real weights. The resulting model will be called *an additive real neuroidal net*.

## 4    Finite Weight Neuroidal Nets and Finite Automata

It is obvious that in the case of neuroidal nets with finite weights there is but a final number of different configurations a single neuroid can enter. Hence its computational activities like those of any finite neuroidal net, can be described by a single finite automaton (or more precisely: by a finite transducer). In order to get some insight into the relation between the sizes of the respective devices we will describe the construction of the respective transducer in more detail in the next theorem. In fact this transducer will be a Moore machine (i.e., the type of a finite automaton producing an output after each transition) since there is an output (action) produced by $\mathcal{N}$ after each computational move.

**Theorem 4.1** *Let $\mathcal{N}$ be a finite neuroidal net consisting of $N$ neuroids with a finite set of weights. Then there is a constant $c > 0$ and a finite Moore automaton $\mathcal{A}$ of size $\Theta(c^N)$ that simulates $\mathcal{N}$.*

**Sketch of the proof:** We will describe the construction of the Moore automaton $\mathcal{A} = (I, S, q_0, O, \Delta)$. Here $I$ denotes the input alphabet whose elements are $N$-tuples of the stimuli: $I = \{Q \cup *\}^N$. Set S is a set of states consisting of all configurations of $\mathcal{N}$, i.e., $S = X^N \times W^M$. State $q_0$ is the initial state and it is equal to the initial configuration of $\mathcal{N}$. Set $O$ denotes a set of outputs of $\mathcal{A}$. It will consist of all possible actions of $\mathcal{N} : O = Q^N$.

The transition function $\Delta : I \times S \to S \times O$ is defined as follows: $\Delta(i, s_1) = (s_2, o)$ if and only if the neuroid $\mathcal{N}$ in configuration $s_1$ and with input $i$ will enter configuration $s_2$ and produce output $o$ in one computational move. It is clear that the input–output behaviour of both $\mathcal{N}$ and $\mathcal{A}$ is equivalent.    □

Note that the size of the automaton is exponential w.r.t the size of the neuroidal net. In some cases such a size explosion seems to be unavoidable. For instance, a neuroidal net consisting of $N$ neuroids can implement a binary counter that can count up to $c^N$, where $c \geq 2$ is a constant which depends on the number of states of the respective neuroids. The equivalent finite automaton would then require at least $\Omega(c^N)$ states. Thus the advantage of using neuroidal nets instead of finite automata seems to lie in the description economy of the former devices.

The reverse simulation of a finite automaton by a finite neuroidal net is trivial. In fact, a single neuroid, with a single input, is enough. During the simulation, this neuroid transits to the same states as the simulated automaton would. There is no need for a neuroid to make use of its threshold mechanism.

# 5   Simulating Neuroidal Nets by Neural Nets

Neural nets are a restricted kind of neuroidal networks in which the neuroids can modify neither their weights nor their thresholds. The respective set of neuroidal states consists of only two states — of a firing and quiescent state. Moreover, the neurons are forced to fire if and only if the excitation reaches the threshold value. The computational behaviour of neural networks is defined similarly as that of the neuroidal ones.

It has been observed by several authors that neural nets are also computationally equivalent to the finite automata (cf. [5]). Thus, we get the following consequence of the previous theorem:

**Corollary 5.1** *The computational power of neuroidal nets with a finite set of weights is equivalent to that of standard non-programmable neural nets.*

In order to better appreciate the relationship between the sizes of the respective neuroidal and neural nets, we will investigate the direct simulation of finite neuroidal nets with finite weights by finite neural nets.

**Theorem 5.1** *Let $\mathcal{N} = (G, W, X, \delta, \lambda)$ be a finite neuroidal net consisting of $N$ neuroids and $M$ edges. Let the set of weights of $\mathcal{N}$ be finite. Let $|L|$, and $|D|$, respectively, be the number of all different sets of arguments of the corresponding weight and mode update function. Let $|S|$ be the set of all possible excitation values, $|S| \leq 2^{|W|}$.*
    *Then $\mathcal{N}$ can be simulated by a neural network $\mathcal{N}'$ consisting of $O((|X| + |S| + |L| + |D|)N + |W|M)$ neurons.*

**Proof:** It is enough to show that to any neuroid $i$ of $\mathcal{N}$ an equivalent neural network $C_i$ can be constructed. At any time the neuroid $i$ is described by its "instantaneous description", viz. its mode and the corresponding set of weights. The idea of simulation is to construct a neural net for all combinations of parameters that represent a possible instantaneous description of $i$. The instantaneous value of each parameter will be represented by a special module. There will also be two extra modules to realize the mode and weight update functions. Instead of changing the parameters the simulating neural

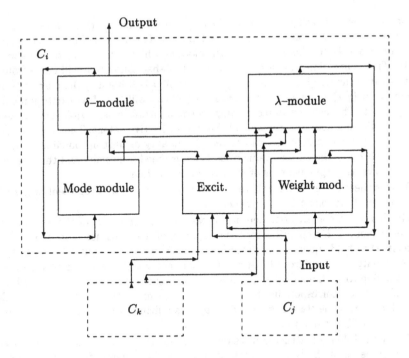

**Fig. 1.** Data flow in module $C_i$ simulating a single neuroid

net will merely "switch" among the appropriate values representing the parameters of the instantaneous description of the simulated neuroid. The details are as follows.

$C_i$ will consist of five different modules.

First, there are three modules called *mode module, excitation module, and weight module.* The purpose of each of these modules is to represent a set of possible values of the respective quantity that represents, in order of their above enumeration, a possible mode of a neuroid, a possible value of the total excitation coming from the firings of adjacent neurons, and possible weights for all incoming edges.

Thus the mode module $M_i$ consists of $|X|$ neurons. For each pair of form $(q,p) \in X$, with $q \in Q$ and $p \in T$, there is a corresponding neuron in $M_i$. Moreover, the neuron corresponding to the current mode of neuroid $i$ is firing, while all the remaining neurons in $M_i$ are in a quiescent state.

The weight module $W_i$ consists of a two–dimensional array of neurons. To each incoming edge to $i$ there is a row of $|W|$ neurons. Each row contains neurons corresponding to each possible value from the set $W$. If $(i,j) \in E$ is an incoming edge to $i$ carrying the weight $w_{ij} \in W$, then the corresponding neuron in the corresponding row of $W_i$ is firing.

The excitation module $E_i$ consists of $O(|S|)$ neurons. Among them, at each time only one neuron is firing, namely the one that corresponds to the current excitation $w_i$ of $i$. Let $w_i = \sum_{\substack{k \text{ firing} \\ (k,i) \in E}} w_{k,i} = \sum_{\substack{j \\ (j,i) \in E}} f_j w_{ji}$ at that time. In order to compute $w_i$, we have to add only those weights that occur at the connections from currently firing neuroids. Therefore we shall first check all pairs of form $\{f_j; w_{ji}\}$ to see which weight value $w_{ji}$ should participate in the computation of the total excitation. This will be done by dedicating special neurons $t_{ijk}$ to this task, with $k$ ranging over all weights in $W$. Each neuron $t_{ijk}$ will receive 2 inputs. The first one from a neuron from the $j$-th row and $k$-th column in the weight module, which corresponds to some weight $w \in W$. This connection will carry weight $w$. The other connection will come from $C_j$ and will carry the weight 1. Neuron $t_{ijk}$ will fire iff $j$ is firing and the current weight of connection $\{j, i\}$ is equal to $w$. In other words, $t_{ijk}$ will fire iff its excitation equals exactly $w + 1$. This calls for implementing an equality test which requires the presence of some additional neurons, but we will skip the respective details. The outcomes from all $t_{ijk}$ are then again summed and tested for equality against all possible excitation values. In this way the current value of $w_i$ is determined eventually and the respective neurons serve as output neurons of the excitation module.

Besides these three modules there are two more modules that represent, and realize the transition functions $\delta$ and $\lambda$, respectively.

The $\delta$-module contains one neuron for each set of arguments of the mode update function $\delta$. Neuron $d$, responsible for the realization of the transition of form $\delta(s_i, w_i) = s'_i$, has its threshold equal to 2. Its incoming edges from each output neuron in $M_i$ and from each output neuron from $E_i$ carry the weight equal to 1. Clearly, $d$ fires iff neurons corresponding to both quantities $s_i$ and $w_i$ fire. Firing of $e$ will subsequently inhibit the firing of a neuron corresponding to $s_i$ and excite the firing of a neuron corresponding to $s'_i$. Moreover, if the state corresponding to $s'_i$ is a firing state of $i$ then also a special neuron $out$ in $C_i$ is made to fire.

The $\lambda$-module is constructed n a similar way. It also contains one neuron per each set of arguments of the weight update function $\lambda$. The neuron $\ell$ responsible for the realization of the transition of form $\lambda(s_i, w_i, w_{ji}, f_j) = w'_{ji}$ has the threshold 4. Its incoming edges of weight 1 connect to it each output neuron in $M_i$, to each output neuron in $W_i$, to each neuron from the row corresponding to the $j$-th incoming edge of $i$, in $E_i$, and to the output from $C_j$. Clearly, $\ell$ fires iff neurons corresponding to all four quantities $s_i$, $w_i$, $w_{ji}$, and $f_j$ fire. Firing of $\ell$ will subsequently inhibit the firing of a neuron corresponding to $w_{ji}$ in $W_i$ and excite the firing of a neuron corresponding to $w'_{ji}$, also in $W_i$.

Schematically, the topology of network $C_i$ is sketched in Fig.1. For simplicity reasons only the flow of data is depicted by arrows.

The size of $C_i$ is given by the sum of all sizes of all its modules. The whole net $\mathcal{N}'$ thus contains $N$ mode–, excitation–, $\delta$– and $\lambda$–modules, of size $|X|$, $|S|$, $|D|$, and $|L|$, respectively. Moreover, for each of $M$ edges of $\mathcal{N}$ there is a complete row of $|W|$ neurons. This altogether leads to the size estimation as stated in the statement of the theorem.                                                                    □

From the previous theorem we can see that the size of a simulating neural network is larger than that of the original neuroidal network. It is linear in both the number of neuroids and edges of the neuroidal network. The constant of proportionality depends linearly on the size of "program" of individual neuroids, and exponentially on the size of the universe of weights. However, note that the neural net constructed in the latter theorem is much smaller than that obtained via the direct simulation of the finite automaton corresponding to the simulated neuroidal net. A neural net, simulating the automaton from the proof of theorem 4.1, would be of size $\Theta(c^N)$ for some constant $c > 0$.

To summarize the respective results, we see that when comparing finite neuroidal nets to standard, non-programmable neural nets, the programmability of the former does not increase their computational power; it merely contributes to their greater descriptive expressiveness.

# 6    Integer Weight Neuroidal Nets and Turing Machines

Now we will show that in the case of integer weights there exist neuroidal nets of the finite size that can simulate any Turing machine.

Since we will be interested in space–bounded machines w.l.o.g. we will first consider a single–tape Turing machine in place of a simulated machine. In order to extend our results also for sublinear space complexities we will later also consider single–tape machines with separate input tapes.

First we show that even a single neuroid is enough for simulation of a single tape Turing machine.

**Theorem 6.1** *Any single tape Turing machine[1] of time complexity $T(n)$ and of space complexity $S(n)$ can be simulated in time $O(T(n)S^2(n))$ by a single neuroid making use of integer weights of size $O(S(n))$ and of a simple arithmetic weight update function.*

**Sketch of the proof:** Since we are dealing with space–bounded Turing machines (TMs), w.l.o.g. we can consider only single–tape machines. Thus in what follows we will describe simulation of one computational step of a single–tape Turing machine $\mathcal{M}$ of space complexity $S(n)$ with tape alphabet $\{0, 1\}$. It is known (cf. [2]) that the tape of such a machine can be replaced by two stacks, $S_L$ and $S_R$, respectively. The first stack holds the contents of $\mathcal{M}$'s tape to the left from the current head position while the second stack represents the rest of the tape. The left or the right end of the tape, respectively, find themselves at the bottoms of the respective stacks. Thus we assume that $\mathcal{M}$'s head always scans the top of the right stack. For technical reasons we will add an extra symbol 1 to the bottom of each stack. During its computation $\mathcal{M}$ updates merely the top, or pushes the symbols to, or pops the symbols from the top of these stacks.

With the help of a neuroid $n$ we will represent machine $\mathcal{M}$ in a configuration described by the contents of its two stacks and by the state of the machine's finite state control in the following way. The contents of both stacks will be represented by two integers $v_L$ and $v_R$, respectively. Note that both $v_L, v_R \geq 1$ thanks to 1's at the bottoms of the respective stacks. The instantaneous state of $\mathcal{M}$ is stored in the states of $n$.

To simulate $\mathcal{M}$ we merely have to manipulate the above mentioned two stacks in a way that corresponds to the actions of the simulated machine. Thus, the net has to be able to read the top element of a stack, to delete it (to pop the stack), and to add (to push) a new element onto the top of the stack. W.r.t. our representation of a stack by an integer $v$, say, reading the top of a stack asks for determining the parity of $v$. Popping an element from or pushing it to a stack means computing of $\lfloor v/2 \rfloor$ and $2v$, respectively. All this must be done with the help of additions and subtractions.

The idea of the respective algorithm that computes the parity of any $v > 0$ is as follows. From $v$ we will successively subtract the largest possible power of 2, not

---

[1] Note that in the case of single tape machines the input size is counted into the space complexity and therefore we have $S(n)) \geq n$.

greater than $v$, until the value of $v$ drops to either 0 or 1. Clearly, in the former case, the original value of $v$ was even while in the latter case, it was odd.

More formally, the resulting algorithm looks as follows:

**while** $v > 1$ **do** $p1 := 1; p2 := 2$;
           **while** $p2 \leq v$ **do** $p1 := p1 + p1; p2 := p2 + p2$ **od**;
           $v := v - p1$
**od**;
**if** $v = 1$ **then** return(odd) **else** return(even) **fi**;

By a similar algorithm we can also compute the value of $\lfloor v/2 \rfloor$ (i.e., the value of $v$ shifted by one position to the right, losing thus its rightmost digit). This value is equal to the sum of the halves of the respective powers (as long as they are greater than 1) computed in the course of previous algorithm.

The time complexity of both algorithms is $O(S^2(n))$.

The "neuroidal" implementation of previous algorithms looks as follows. The algorithms will have to make use of the values representing both stacks, $v_L$ and $v_R$, respectively. Furthermore, they will need access to the auxiliary values $p1$, $p2$, $v$, and to the constant 1. All the previously mentioned values will be "stored" as weights of $n$. For technical reasons imposed by functionality restrictions of neuroids, which will become clearer later, we will need to store also the inverse values of all previously mentioned variables. These will be also stored in the weights of $n$.

Hencefore, the neuroid $n$ will have 12 inputs. These inputs are connected to $n$ via 12 connections. Making use of the previously introduced notation, the first six will hold the weights $w_1 = v_L$, $w_2 = v_R$, $w_3 = v$, $w_4 = p1$, $w_5 = p2$, and $w_6 = 1$. The remaining six will carry the same but inverse values.

The output of $n$ is connected to all 12 inputs.

The neuroid simulates each move of $\mathcal{M}$ in a series of steps. Each series perform one run of the previously mentioned (or of a similar) algorithm and therefore consists of $O(S^2(n))$ steps.

At the beginning of the series that will simulate the $(t+1)$-st move of $\mathcal{M}$, the following invariant is preserved by $n$ for any $t > 0$. Weights $w_1$ and $w_2$ represent the contents of the stacks after the $t$-th move and $w_7 = -w_1$ and $w_8 = -w_2$. The remaining weights are set to zero.

At the beginning of computation, the left stack is empty and the right stack contains the input word of $\mathcal{M}$. We will assume that $n$ will accept its input by entering a designated state. Also, the threshold of $n$ will be set to 0 all the time.

Assume that at time $t$ the finite control of $\mathcal{M}$ is in state $q$. Until its change, this state is stored in all forthcoming neuroidal states that $n$ will enter.

In order to read the symbol from the top of the right stack the neuroid has to determine the last binary digit of $w_2$ or, in other words, it has to determine the parity of $w_2$. To do so, we first perform all the necessary initialization assignments to auxiliary variables, and to their "counterparts" holding the negative values. In order to perform the necessary tests (comparisons), the neuroid must enter a firing state. Due to the neuroidal computational mechanism and thanks to the connection among the output of $n$ and all its inputs, all its non-zero weights will participate in the subsequent comparison of the total excitation against $n$'s threshold. It is here that we will make a proper use of weights with the opposite sign: the weights (i.e., variables) that should not be compared, and should not be forgotten, will participate in a comparison with opposite signs.

For instance, to perform the comparison $p2 \leq v$, we merely "switch off" the positive value of $p2$ and the negative value of $v$ from the comparison by temporarily setting the respective weights $w_5$ and $w_9$ to zero. All the other weight values remain as they were. As a result, after the firing step, $n$ will compare $v - p2$ against its threshold value (which is permanently set to 0) and will enter a state corresponding to the result of this comparison. After the comparison, the weights set temporarily to zero can be restored to their previous values (by assignments $w_5 := -w_{11}$ and $w_9 := -w_3$).

The transition of $\mathcal{M}$ into a state as dictated by its transition function is realized by $\mathcal{N}$ after updating the stacks appropriately, by storing the respective machine state into the state of $n$. The simulation ends by entering into the final state.

It is clear that the simulation runs in time as stated in the theorem. The size of any stack, and hence of any variable, never exceeds the value $S(n) + 1$. Hence the size of the weights of $n$ will be bounded by the same value.                                    □

Note that a similar construction, still using only one neuroid, would also work in case a multiple tape Turing machine should be simulated. In order to simulate a $k$–tape machine, the resulting neuroid will represent each tape by 12 weights as it did before. This will lead to a neuroid with $12k$ incoming edges.

Next we will also show that a simulation of an off–line Turing machine by a finite neuroidal network with unbounded weights is possible. This will enable us to prove a similar theorem as before which holds for arbitrary space complexities:

**Theorem 6.2** *Let $\mathcal{M}$ be an off–line multiple tape Turing machine of space complexity $S(n) \geq 0$. Then $\mathcal{M}$ can be simulated in a cubic time by a finite neuroidal net that makes use of integer weights of size $O(S(n))$ and of a simple arithmetic weight update function.*

**Sketch of the proof:** In order to read the respective inputs the neuroidal net will be equipped with the same input tape as the simulated Turing machine. Except the neuroid $n$ that takes care of a proper update of stacks that represent the respective machine tapes, the simulating net will contain also two extra neuroids that implement the control mechanism of the input head movement. For each move direction (left or right) there will be a special — so–called *move neuroid* — which will fire if and only if the input head has to move in a respective direction. The symbol read by the input head will represent an additional input to neuroid $n$ simulating the moves of $\mathcal{M}$.

The information about the move direction will be inferred by neuroid $n$. As can be seen from the description of the simulation in the previous theorem, $n$ keeps track on that particular transition of $\mathcal{M}$ that should be realized during each series of its steps simulating one move of $\mathcal{M}$.

Since $s$ can transmit this information to the respective move neuroids only via firing and cannot distinguish between the two target neuroids, we will have to implement a (finite) counter in each move neuroid. The counter will count the number of firings of $s$ occurring in an uninterrupted sequence. Thus at the end of the last step of $\mathcal{M}$'s move simulation (see the proof of the previous theorem) $s$ will send two successive firings to denote the left move and three firings for the right move. The respective signals will reach both move neuroids, but with the help of counting they will find which of them is in charge for moving the head. Some care over synchronization of all three neuroids must be taken.                                    □

It is clear that the computations of finite neuroidal nets with integer weights can be simulated by Turing machines. Therefore the computational power of both devices is the same.

In 1995, Siegelmann and Sonntag [4] proved that the computational power of certain analog neural nets is equivalent to that of Turing machines. They considered finite neural nets with fixed rational weights. At time $t$, the output of their analog neuron $i$ is a value between 0 and 1 which is determined by applying a so-called *piecewise linear activation* function $\phi$ to the excitation $w_i$ of $i$ at that time (see definition 2.1): $\phi : w_i \rightarrow \langle 0, 1 \rangle$. For negative excitation, $\phi$ takes the value 0, for excitation greater than 1 value 1, and for excitations between 0 and 1, $\phi(w_i) = w_i$. The respective net computes synchronously, in discrete time steps.

We will call the respective nets as *synchronous analog neural nets*.

Siegelmann and Sonntag's analog neural networks simulating a universal Turing machine consisted of 883 neurons. This can be compared with the simple construction from Theorem 5.1 requiring but a single neuroid. Nevertheless, the equivalency of both types of networks with Turing machines proves the following corollary:

**Corollary 6.1** *Finite synchronous analog neural nets are computationally equivalent to finite neuroidal nets with integer weights.*

## 7    Real Weight Neuroidal Nets and the Additive BSS Model

Now we will characterize the computational power of neuroidal nets with real parameters. We will compare their efficiency towards a restricted variant of the BSS model. The BSS model (cf. [1]) is a model that is similar to RAM which computes with real numbers under the unit cost model. In doing so, all four basic arithmetic operations of additions, subtractions, multiplication and division are allowed. The additive BSS model allows only for the former two arithmetic operations.

**Theorem 7.1** *The additive real model of neuroidal nets is computationally equivalent to the additive BSS model working over binary inputs.*

**Sketch of the proof:** The simulation of a finite additive real model of neuroidal net $\mathcal{N}$ on the additive BSS model $\mathcal{B}$ is a straightforward matter.

For the reverse simulation, assume that the binary input to $\mathcal{N}$ is provided to $\mathcal{B}$ by a mechanism similar to that from Theorem 6.2. One must first refer to the theorem (Theorem 1 in Chapter 21 in [1]) that shows that by a suitable encoding a computation of any additive machine can be done using a fixed finite amount of memory (in a finite number of "registers", each holding a real number) without exponential increase in the running time. The resulting machine $\mathcal{F}$ is then simulated by $\mathcal{N}$ in the following way: The contents of finitely many registers of $\mathcal{F}$ are represented as (real) weights of a single neuroid $r$. Addition or subtraction of weights, as necessary, is done directly by weight update function. A comparison of weights is done with the help of $r$'s threshold mechanism in a similar way to that in the proof of Theorem 6.1. To single out from the comparison the weights that should not be compared one can use a similar trick as in Theorem 6.1: to each such a weight a weight with the opposite sign is maintained.

The power of finite additive neuroidal nets with real weights comes from their ability to simulate oracular or nonuniform computations. For instance, in [1] it is shown that the additive real BSS machines decide all binary sets in exponential time. Their polynomial time coincides with the nonuniform complexity class P/*poly*.

## 8   Conclusions

The paper brings a relatively surprising result showing computational equivalence between certain kinds of discrete programmable and analog finite neural nets. This result offers new insights into the nature of computations of neural nets.

First, it points to the fact that the ability of changing weights is not a condition *sine qua non* for learning. A similar effect can be achieved by making use of reasonably restricted kinds of analog neural nets.

Second, the result showing computational equivalency of the respective nets supports the idea that all reasonable computational models of the brain are equivalent (cf. [9]).

Third, for modeling of cognitive or learning phenomena, the neuroidal nets seem to be preferred over the analog ones, due to the transparency of their computational or learning mechanism. As far as their appropriateness for the task at hand is concerned, neuroidal nets with a finite set of weights seem to present the maximal functionality that can be achieved by living organisms. As mathematical models also more powerful variants are of interest.

## References

1. Blum, M. — Cucker, F. — Shub, M. — Smale, M.: Complexity and Real Computation. Springer, New York, 1997, 453 p.
2. Hopcroft, J.E. — Ullman, J. D.: Formal Languages and their Relation to Automata. Addison–Wesley, Reading, Mass., 1969
3. Indyk, P.: Optimal Simulation of Automata by Neural Nets. Proc. of the 12th Annual Symp. on Theoretical Aspects of Computer Science STACS'95, LNCS Vol. 900, pp. 337–348, 1995
4. Siegelmann, H. T. — Sonntag, E.D.: On Computational Power of Neural Networks. *J. Comput. Syst. Sci.*, Vol. 50, No. 1, 1995, pp. 132–150
5. Šíma, J. — Wiedermann, J.: Theory of Neuromata. Journal of the ACM, Vol. 45, No. 1, 1998, pp. 155–178
6. Valiant, L.: Functionality in Neural Nets. Proc. of the 7th Nat. Conf. on Art. Intelligence, AAAI, Morgan Kaufmann, San Mateo, CA, 1988, pp. 629–634
7. Valiant, L.G.: Circuits of the Mind. Oxford University Press, New York, Oxford, 1994, 237 p., ISBN 0–19–508936–X

# The Consistency Dimension and Distribution-Dependent Learning from Queries
## (Extended Abstract)[*]

José L. Balcázar[1], Jorge Castro[1], David Guijarro[1], and Hans-Ulrich Simon[2]

[1] Dept. LSI, Universitat Politècnica de Catalunya, Campus Nord,
08034 Barcelona, Spain,
{balqui,castro,david}@lsi.upc.es
[2] Fakultät für Informatik, Lehrstuhl Mathematik und Informatik,
Ruhr-Universitaet Bochum, D-44780 Bochum,
simon@lmi.ruhr-uni-bochum.de

**Abstract.** We prove a new combinatorial characterization of polynomial learnability from equivalence queries, and state some of its consequences relating the learnability of a class with the learnability via equivalence and membership queries of its subclasses obtained by restricting the instance space. Then we propose and study two models of query learning in which there is a probability distribution on the instance space, both as an application of the tools developed from the combinatorial characterization and as models of independent interest.

## 1 Introduction

The main models of learning via queries were introduced by Angluin [2, 3]. In these models, the learning algorithm obtains information about the target concept asking queries to a teacher or expert. The algorithm has to output an exact representation of the target concept in polynomial time. Target concepts are formalized as languages over an alphabet. Frequently, it is assumed that the teacher can answer correctly two kinds of questions from the learner: membership queries and equivalence queries[1]. Unless otherwise specified, all our discussions are in the "proper learning" framework where the hypotheses come from the same class as the target concept. A combinatorial notion, called approximate fingerprints, turned out to characterize precisely those concept classes that can be learned from polynomially many equivalence queries of polynomial size [4, 6].

The essential intuition behind that fact is that the existence of queries that shrink the number of possibilities for the target concept by a polynomial factor is not only clearly sufficient, but also necessary to learn: if no such queries are available then adversaries can be designed that force any learner to spend too

---

[*] Work supported in part by the EC through the Esprit Program EU BRA program under project 20244 (ALCOM-IT) and the EC Working Group EP27150 (NeuroColt II) and by the spanish DGES PB95-0787 (Koala).
[1] Such a teacher is called sometimes "minimally adequate".

O. Watanabe, T. Yokomori (Eds.): ALT'99, LNAI 1720, pp. 77–92, 1999.
© Springer-Verlag Berlin Heidelberg 1999

many queries in order to identify the target. This intuition can be fully formalized along the lines of the cited works; the formalization can be found in [7].

Hellerstein et al. gave a beautiful characterization of polynomially (EQ,MQ)-learnable representation classes [8]. They introduced the notion of polynomial certificates for a representation class $\mathcal{R}$ and proved that $\mathcal{R}$ is polynomially learnable from equivalence and membership queries iff it has polynomial certificates.

The first main contribution of this paper is to propose a new combinatorial characterization of learnability from equivalence queries, surprisingly close to certificates, and quite different (and also simpler to handle) than the approximate fingerprints: the strong consistency dimension, that one can see as the analog of the VC dimension for query models.

Angluin [2, 3] showed that, when only approximate identification is required, equivalence queries can be substituted by a random sample. Thus, a PAC learning algorithm can be obtained from an exact learning algorithm that makes equivalence queries. In PAC learning, introduced by Valiant [11], one has to learn a target concept with high probability, in polynomial time (and, a fortiori, from a polynomial number of examples), within a certain error, under all probability distributions on the examples. Because of this last requirement, to learn under all distributions, PAC learning is also called distribution-free, or distribution-independent, learning. Distribution-independent learning is a strong requirement, but it can be relaxed to define PAC learning under specific distributions, or families of distributions. Indeed, several concept classes that are not known to be polynomially learnable, or known not to be polynomially learnable if RP $\neq$ NP, turn out to be polynomially learnable under some fixed distribution or families of distributions.

In comparison to PAC learning, one drawback of the query models is that they do not have this added flexibility of relaxing the "distribution-free" condition. The standard transformation sets them automatically at the "distribution-free" level. The second main contribution of this paper is the proposal of two learning models in which counterexamples are not adaptatively provided by a (helpful or treacherous) teacher, but instead are nonadaptatively sampled according to a probability distribution.

We prove that the distribution-free form of one of these models exactly coincides with standard learning from equivalence queries, while the other model is captured by the randomized version of the standard model. This allows us to extend, in a natural way, the query learning model to an explicit "distribution-free" setting where this restrictive condition can be naturally relaxed. Some of the facts that we prove of these new models make use of the consistency dimension characterization proved earlier as the first contribution of the paper.

Our notation and terminology is standard. We assume familiarity with the query-learning model. Most definitions will be given in the same section where they are needed. Generally, let $X$ be a set, called *instance space* or *domain* in the sequel. A *concept* is a subset of $X$, where we prefer sometimes to regard $C$ as a function from $X$ to $\{0,1\}$. A *concept class* is a set $\mathcal{C} \subseteq 2^X$ of concepts. An element of $X$ is called an *instance*. A pair $(x, b)$, where $b \in \{0,1\}$ is a binary label, is called *example for concept C* if $C(x) = b$. A *sample* is a collection of labeled instances. Concept $C$ is said to be *consistent with sample S* if $C(x) = b$ for all $(x, b) \in S$.

A *representation class* is a four-tuple $\mathcal{R} = (R, \Delta, \Phi, \Sigma)$. $\Sigma$ and $\Delta$ are finite alphabets. Strings of characters in $\Sigma$ are used to describe elements of the domain $X$, and strings of characters in $\Delta$ are used to encode concepts. $R \subseteq \Delta^*$ is the set of strings that are concept encodings or *representations*. Let $\Phi : R \longrightarrow 2^{\Sigma^*}$ be a function that maps these representations into concepts over $\Sigma$. For ease of technical exposition, we assume that, for each $r \in R$ there exists some $n \geq 1$ such that $\Phi(r) \subseteq \Sigma^n$. Thus each concept with a representation in $R$ has a domain of the form $\Sigma^n$ (as opposed to domain $\Sigma^*$).[2] The set $\mathcal{C} = \{\Phi(r) : r \in R\}$ is the concept class associated with $\mathcal{R}$.

We define the define the *size of concept* $C : \Sigma^n \to \{0, 1\}$ *w.r.t. representation class* $\mathcal{R}$ as the length of the shortest string $r \in R$ such that $C = \Phi(r)$, or as $\infty$ if $C$ is not representable within $\mathcal{R}$. This quantity is denoted by $|C|_{\mathcal{R}}$. With these definitions, $\mathcal{C}$ is a "doubly parameterized class", that is, it is partitioned into sets $\mathcal{C}_{n,m}$ containing all concepts from $\mathcal{C}$ with domain $\Sigma^n$ and size at most $m$. The kind of query-learning considered in this paper is proper in the sense that concepts and hypotheses are picked from the same class $\mathcal{C}$. We will however allow that the size of an hypothesis exceeds the size of the target concept. The number of queries needed in the worst case to obtain an affirmative answer from the teacher, or "learning complexity", given that the target concept belongs to $\mathcal{C}_{n,m}$ and that the hypotheses of the learner may be picked from $\mathcal{C}_{n,M}$, is denoted by $\mathrm{LC}_{\mathcal{R}}^{\mathcal{O}}(n, m, M)$, where $\mathcal{O}$ specifies the allowed query types. In this paper, either $\mathcal{O} = EQ$ or $\mathcal{O} = (EQ, MQ)$. We speak of polynomial $\mathcal{O}$-learnability if $\mathrm{LC}_{\mathcal{R}}^{\mathcal{O}}(n, m, M)$ is polynomially bounded in $n, m, M$.

We close this section with the definition of a version space. At any intermediate stage of a query-learning process, the learner knows (from the teacher's answers received so far) a sample $S$ for the target concept. The *current version space* $\mathcal{V}$ is the set of all concepts from $\mathcal{C}_{n,m}$ which are consistent with $S$. These are all concepts being still conceivable as target concepts.

## 2 The Strong Consistency Dimension and Its Applications

The proof, as it was given in [8], of the characterization of (EQ,MQ)-learning in terms of polynomial certificates implicitly contains concrete lower and upper bounds on the number of queries needed to learn $\mathcal{R}$. In Subsection 2.1, we make these bounds more explicit by introducing the so-called consistency dimension of $\mathcal{R}$ and writing the bounds in terms of this dimension (and some other parameters associated with $\mathcal{R}$). In Subsection 2.2, we define the notions of a "strong

---

[2] This is a purely technical restriction that allows us to present the main ideas in the most convincing way. It is easy to generalize the results in this paper to the case of domains with strings of varying length.

certificate" and of the "strong consistency dimension" and show that they fit the same purpose for EQ-learning as the former notions did for (EQ,MQ)-learning: we derive lower and upper bounds on the number of EQs needed to learn $\mathcal{R}$ in terms of the strong consistency dimension and conclude that $\mathcal{R}$ is polynomially EQ-learnable iff it has a polynomial strong certificate. In Subsection 2.3, we prove that the strong consistency dimension of a class equals the maximum of the consistency dimensions taken over all subclasses (induced by a restriction of the domain). This implies that the number of EQs needed to learn a concept class roughly equals the total number of EQs and MQs needed to learn the hardest subclass.

For ease of technical exposition, we need the following definitions. A *partially defined concept* $C$ on domain $\Sigma^n$ is a function from $\Sigma^n$ to $\{0, 1, *\}$, where "$*$" stands for "undefined". Since partially defined concepts and samples can be identified in the obvious manner, we use the terms "partially defined concept" and "sample" interchangeably in the sequel. The *support* of $C$ is defined as $\text{supp}(C) = \{x \in \Sigma^n : C(x) \in \{0, 1\}\}$. The *breadth* of $C$ is defined as the cardinality of its support and denoted as $|C|$. The *size* of $C$ is defined as the smallest size of a concept that is consistent with $C$. It is denoted as $|C|_{\mathcal{R}}$. Note that this definition coincides with the previous definition of size when $C$ has full support $\Sigma^n$. Sample $Q$ is called *subsample* of sample $C$ (denoted as $Q \sqsubseteq C$) if $\text{supp}(Q) \subseteq \text{supp}(C)$ and $Q, C$ coincide on $\text{supp}(Q)$. Throughout this section, $\mathcal{R} = (\Sigma, \Delta, R, \mu)$ denotes a representation class defining a doubly parameterized concept class $\mathcal{C}$.

## 2.1   Certificates and Consistency Dimension

$\mathcal{R}$ has *polynomial certificates* if there exist two-variable polynomials $p$ and $q$, such that for all $m, n > 0$, and for all $C : \Sigma^n \to \{0, 1\}$ the following condition is valid:

$$|C|_{\mathcal{R}} > p(n, m) \Rightarrow (\exists Q \sqsubseteq C : |Q| \le q(m, n) \wedge |Q|_{\mathcal{R}} > m) \tag{1}$$

The *consistency dimension* of $\mathcal{R}$ is the following three-variable function: $cdim_{\mathcal{R}}(n, m, M)$, where $M \ge m > 0$ and $n > 0$, is the smallest number $d$ such that for all $C : \Sigma^n \to \{0, 1\}$ the following condition is valid:

$$|C|_{\mathcal{R}} > M \Rightarrow (\exists Q \sqsubseteq C : |Q| \le d \wedge |Q|_{\mathcal{R}} > m) \tag{2}$$

An obviously equivalent but quite useful reformulation of Condition (2) is

$$(\forall Q \sqsubseteq C : |Q| \le d \Rightarrow |Q|_{\mathcal{R}} \le m) \Rightarrow |C|_{\mathcal{R}} \le M. \tag{3}$$

In words: if each subsample of $C : \Sigma^n \to \{0, 1\}$ of breadth at most $d$ has a consistent representation of size at most $m$, then $C$ has a consistent representation of size at most $M$.

The following result is (more or less) implicit in [8].

**Theorem 1**
$cdim_{\mathcal{R}}(n, m, M) \le LC_{\mathcal{R}}^{EQ, MQ}(n, m, M) \le \lceil cdim_{\mathcal{R}}(n, m, M) \cdot \log |\mathcal{C}_{n,m}| \rceil$

Note that the lower and the upper bound are polynomially related because

$$\log |C_{n,m}| \le m \cdot \log(1 + |\Delta|). \tag{4}$$

Clearly, Theorem 1 implies that $\mathcal{R}$ is polynomially (EQ,MQ)-learnable iff it has polynomial certificates. We omit the proof of Theorem 1.

## 2.2   Strong Certificates and Strong Consistency Dimension

We want to adapt the notions "certificate" and "consistency dimension" to the framework of EQ-learning. Surprisingly, we can use syntactically almost the same notions, except for a subtle but striking difference: the universe of $C$ will be extended from the set of all concepts over domain $\Sigma^n$ to the corresponding set of partially defined concepts. This leads to the following definitions.

   $\mathcal{R}$ has *polynomial strong certificates* if there exist two-variable polynomials $p$ and $q$, such that for all $m, n > 0$, and for all $C : \Sigma^n \to \{0, 1, *\}$ Condition (1) is valid.

   The *strong consistency dimension* of $\mathcal{R}$ is the following three-variable function: $scdim_{\mathcal{R}}(n, m, M)$, where $M \ge m > 0$ and $n > 0$, is the smallest number $d$ such that for all $C : \Sigma^n \to \{0, 1, *\}$ Condition (2) is valid. Again, instead of Condition (2), we can use the equivalent Condition (3). In words: if each subsample of $C : \Sigma^n \to \{0, 1, *\}$ of breadth at most $d$ has a consistent representation of size at most $m$, then $C$ has a consistent representation of size at most $M$.

**Theorem 2** $scdim_{\mathcal{R}}(n, m, M) \le LC_{\mathcal{R}}^{EQ}(n, m, M) \le \lceil scdim_{\mathcal{R}}(n, m, M) \cdot \ln |C_{n,m}| \rceil$

**Proof.**   For brevity reasons, let $q = LC_{\mathcal{R}}^{EQ}(n, m, M)$ and $d = scdim_{\mathcal{R}}(n, m, M)$.

   We prove the first inequality by exhibiting an adversary that forces any learner to spend as many queries as given by the strong consistency dimension. The minimality of $d$ implies that there is a sample $C$ such that still $|C|_{\mathcal{R}} > M$ but $(\forall Q \sqsubseteq C : |Q| \le d - 1 \Rightarrow |Q|_{\mathcal{R}} \le m)$. Thus, any learner, issuing up to $d - 1$ equivalence queries with hypotheses of size at most $M$, fails to be consistent with $C$, and a counterexample from $C$ can be provided such that there is still at least one consistent concept of size at most $m$ (a potential target concept). Hence, at least $d$ queries go by until an affirmative answer is obtained.

   In order to prove $q \le \lceil d \ln |C_{n,m}| \rceil$, we describe an appropriate EQ-learner $A$. $A$ keeps track of the current version space $\mathcal{V}$ (which is $C_{n,m}$ initially). For $i = 0, 1$, let $S_{\mathcal{V}}^i$ be the set

$$\{x \in \Sigma^n : \text{the fraction of concepts } C \in \mathcal{V} \text{ with } C(x) = 1 - i \text{ is less than } 1/d\}.$$

In other words, a very large fraction (at least $1 - 1/d$) of the concepts in $\mathcal{V}$ votes for output label $i$ on instances from $S_{\mathcal{V}}^i$. Let $C_{\mathcal{V}}$ be the sample assigning label $i \in \{0, 1\}$ to all instances from $S_{\mathcal{V}}^i$ and label "$*$" to all remaining instances (those without a so clear majority). Let $Q$ be an arbitrary but fixed subsample of $C_{\mathcal{V}}$ such that $|Q| \le d$. The definition of $S_{\mathcal{V}}^i$ implies (through some easy-to-check counting) that there exists a concept $C \in \mathcal{V} \subseteq C_{n,m}$ that is consistent with

$Q$. Applying Condition (3), we conclude that $|C_{\mathcal{V}}|_{\mathcal{R}} \leq M$, i.e., there exists an $H \in \mathcal{C}_{n,M}$ that is consistent with $C_{\mathcal{V}}$. The punchline of this discussion is: if $A$ issues the EQ with hypothesis $H$, then the next counterexample will shrink the current version space by a factor $1 - 1/d$ (or by a smaller factor). Since the initial version space contains $|\mathcal{C}_{n,m}|$ concepts and since $A$ is done as soon as $|\mathcal{V}| \leq 1$, a sufficiently large number of EQs is obtained by solving

$$(1 - 1/d)^q |\mathcal{C}_{n,m}| < e^{-q/d} |\mathcal{C}_{n,m}| \leq 1$$

for $q$. Clearly, $q = \lceil d \ln |\mathcal{C}_{n,m}| \rceil$ is sufficiently large.     ●

Since the lower and the upper bound in Theorem 2 are polynomially related according to Inequality (4), we obtain

**Corollary 3** $\mathcal{R}$ *is polynomially EQ-learnable iff it has a polynomial strong certificate.*

## 2.3   EQs Alone versus EQs and MQs

The goal of this subsection is to show that the number of EQs needed to learn a concept class is closely related to the total number of EQs and MQs needed to learn the hardest subclass. The formal statement of the main results requires the following definitions.

Let $S = (S_n)_{n \geq 1}$ with $S_n \subseteq \Sigma^n$ be a family of subdomains. The *restriction of a concept* $C : \Sigma^n \to \{0,1\}$ *to* $S_n$ is the partially defined concept (sample) with support $S_n$ which coincides with $C$ on its support. The class containing all restrictions of concepts from $\mathcal{C}$ to the corresponding subdomain from $S$ is called the *subclass of* $\mathcal{C}$ *induced by* $S$ and denoted as $\mathcal{C}|S$.

The notions polynomial certificate, consistency dimension, and learning complexity are adapted to the subclass of $\mathcal{C}$ induced by $S$ in the obvious way. $\mathcal{R}|S$ (in words: $\mathcal{R}$ restricted to $S$) *has polynomial certificates* if there exist two-variable polynomials $p$ and $q$, such that for all $m, n > 0$, and for all $C : \Sigma^n \to \{0,1,*\}$ such that $\mathrm{supp}(C) = S_n$, Condition (1) is valid. The *consistency dimension* of $\mathcal{R}|S$ is the following three-variable function: $\mathrm{cdim}_{\mathcal{R}}(S_n, m, M)$ is the smallest number $d$ such that for all $M \geq m > 0, n > 0$, and for all $C : \Sigma^n \to \{0,1,*\}$ such that $\mathrm{supp}(C) = S_n$, Condition (2) is valid. Again, instead of Condition (2), we can use the equivalent Condition (3).

Quantity $\mathrm{LC}_{\mathcal{R}}^{EQ,MQ}(S_n, m, M)$ is defined as the smallest total number of EQs and MQs needed to learn the class of concepts from $\mathcal{C}_{n,m}$ restricted to $S_n$ with hypotheses from $\mathcal{C}_{n,M}$ restricted to $S_n$. Quantity $\mathrm{LC}_{\mathcal{R}}^{EQ}(S_n, m, M)$ is understood analogously. Note that

$$\mathrm{LC}_{\mathcal{R}}^{EQ}(S_n, m, M) \leq \mathrm{LC}_{\mathcal{R}}^{EQ}(n, m, M) \tag{5}$$

is valid in general, because EQs become more powerful (as opposed to MQs which become less powerful) when we pass from the full domain to a subdomain (for the obvious reasons). We have the analogous inequality for the strong consistency dimension, but no such statement can be made for $LC_{\mathcal{R}}^{EQ,MQ}$ or the consistency dimension.

The following result is a straightforward generalization of Theorem 1.

**Theorem 4** $cdim_{\mathcal{R}}(S_n, m, M) \leq LC_{\mathcal{R}}^{EQ,MQ}(S_n, m, M) \leq \lceil cdim_{\mathcal{R}}(S_n, m, M) \cdot \log |(\mathcal{C}|\mathcal{S})_{n,m}| \rceil$.

We now turn to the main results of this section. The first one states that the strong consistency dimension of a class is the maximum of the consistency dimensions taken over all induced subclasses:

**Theorem 5** $scdim_{\mathcal{R}}(n, m, M) = \max_{S \subseteq \Sigma^n} cdim_{\mathcal{R}}(S, m, M)$.

**Proof.**     Let $d_*$ be the smallest $d$ which makes Condition (2) valid for all $C : \Sigma^n \to \{0, 1, *\}$. Let $d_*(S)$ be the corresponding quantity when $C$ ranges only over all samples with support $S$. It is evident that $d_* = \max_{S \subseteq \Sigma^n} d_*(S)$. The theorem now follows, because by definition $d_* = scdim_{\mathcal{R}}(n, m, M)$ and $d_*(S) = cdim_{\mathcal{R}}(S, m, M)$.     ●

**Corollary 6**     1. A representation class $\mathcal{R}$ has a polynomial strong certificate iff all its induced subclasses have a polynomial certificate.
2. A representation class is polynomially EQ-learnable iff all its induced subclasses are polynomially (EQ,MQ)-learnable.

The third result states that the number of EQs needed to learn a class equals roughly the total number of EQs and MQs needed to learn the hardest induced subclass.

**Corollary 7** $\max_{S \subseteq \Sigma^n} LC_{\mathcal{R}}^{EQ,MQ}(S, m, M) \leq LC_{\mathcal{R}}^{EQ}(n, m, M)$     and
$LC_{\mathcal{R}}^{EQ}(n, m, M) \leq \lceil \ln |\mathcal{C}_{n,m}| \cdot \max_{S \subseteq \Sigma^n} LC_{\mathcal{R}}^{EQ,MQ}(S, m, M) \rceil$.

Remember that the gap $\ln |\mathcal{C}_{n,m}|$ is bounded above by $m \cdot \ln(1 + |\Delta|)$.

## 3   Equivalence Queries with a Probability Distribution

Let now $\mathcal{D}$ denote a class of probability distributions on $X$, the instance space for a computational learning framework. The two subsections of this section introduce respective variants of equivalence query learning that somehow take such distributions into account.

We briefly describe now the first one. In the ordinary model of EQ-learning $\mathcal{C}$, with hypotheses from $\mathcal{H}$, the counterexamples for incorrect hypotheses are arbitrarily chosen, and we can think of an intelligent adversary making these choices. *EQ-learning $\mathcal{C}$ from $\mathcal{D}$-teachers* (still with hypotheses from $\mathcal{H}$) proceeds as ordinary EQ-learning, except for the following important differences:

1. Each run of the learning algorithm refers to an arbitrary but fixed pair $(C, D)$ such that $C \in \mathcal{C}$ and $D \in \mathcal{D}$, and to a given confidence parameter $0 < \delta < 1$.

2. The goal is *to learn C from the D-teacher*, i.e., $C$ is considered as target concept (as usual), and the counterexample to an incorrect hypothesis $H$ is randomly chosen according to the conditional distribution $D(\cdot/C \oplus H)$, where $\oplus$ denotes the symmetric difference of sets. Success is defined when this symmetric difference has zero probability. The learner must achieve a success probability of at least $1 - \delta$.

Clearly, the more restricted the class $\mathcal{D}$ of probability distributions, the easier the task for the learner. In this extended abstract, we focus on the following three choices of $\mathcal{D}$.

- $\mathcal{D}_{all}$ denotes the class of all probability distributions on $X$. This is the most general case.
- $\mathcal{D}_{unif}$ denotes the class of distributions that are uniform on a subdomain $S \subseteq X$ and assign zero probability to instances from $X \setminus S$. This case will be relevant in a later section.
- $\mathcal{D} = \{D\}$ is the most specific case, where $\mathcal{D}$ constains only a single probability distribution $D$. We use it only briefly in the last section.

Loosely speaking, the main results of this section are as follows:

- The next subsection proves that, for $\mathcal{D} = \mathcal{D}_{all}$, EQ-learning from $\mathcal{D}$-teachers is exactly as hard (same number of queries) as the standard model. (This result is only established for deterministic learners.) Thus, we are not actually introducing yet one more learning model, but characterizing an existing, widely accepted, one in a manner that provides the additional flexibility of the probability distribution parameter. Thus we obtain a sensible definition of distribution-dependent equivalence-query learning.
- In the next section, we introduce a combinatorial quantity, called the sphere number, and show that it represents an information-theoretic barrier in the model of EQ-learning from $\mathcal{D}_{unif}$-teachers (even for randomized learning algorithms). However, this barrier is overcome for each fixed distribution $D$ in the model of EQ-learning from the $D$-teacher.

### 3.1 Random versus Arbitrary Counterexamples

We use upper index $EQ[\mathcal{D}]$ to indicate that the $D$-teacher for some $D \in \mathcal{D}$ plays the role of the EQ-oracle.

**Theorem 8** $LC^{EQ[\mathcal{D}_{all}]}(\mathcal{C}, \mathcal{H}) = LC^{EQ}(\mathcal{C}, \mathcal{H})$.

**Proof.**     Let $A$ be an algorithm which EQ-learns $\mathcal{C}$ from $\mathcal{D}$-teachers with hypotheses from $\mathcal{H}$. Let $l \geq LC^{EQ}(\mathcal{C}, \mathcal{H})$ be the largest number of EQs needed by $A$ when we allow an adversary to return arbitrary counterexamples to hypotheses.[3]

---

[3] For the time being, there is no guarantee that $A$ succeeds at all, because it expects the counterexamples to be given from a $\mathcal{D}$-teacher. We will however see subsequently that there exists a distribution which sort of simulates the adversary.

Since $LC^{EQ}(C)$ is defined taking all algorithms into account, we lose no generality in assuming that $A$ always queries hypotheses that are consistent with previous counterexamples, so that all the counterexamples received along any run are different. There must exist a concept $C \in \mathcal{C}$, hypotheses $H_0, \ldots, H_{l-2} \in \mathcal{C}$ and instances $x_0, \ldots, x_{l-2} \in X$, such that the learner issues the $l-1$ incorrect hypotheses $H_i$ when learning target concept $C$, and the $x_i$ are the counterexamples returned to these hypotheses by the adversary, respectively. We claim that there exists a distribution $D$ such that, with probability $1-\delta$, the $D$-teacher returns the same counterexamples. This is technically achieved by setting $D(x_i) = (1-\alpha)\alpha^i$, for $i = 0, \ldots, l-3$, and $D(x_{l-2}) = \alpha^{l-2}$. An easy computation shows that the probability that the $D$-teacher presents another sequence of counterexamples as the adversary is at most $(l-2)\alpha$. Setting $\alpha = \delta/(l-2)$, the proof is complete. $\bullet$

Therefore, the distribution-free case of our model coincides with standard EQ-learning.

**Corollary 9** *Let $\mathcal{R} = (\Sigma, \Delta, R, \mu)$ be a representation class defining a doubly parameterized concept class $\mathcal{C}$. Then $LC_{\mathcal{R}}^{EQ[\mathcal{D}_{all}]}(n, m, M) = LC_{\mathcal{R}}^{EQ}(n, m, M)$ for all $M \geq m > 0, n > 0$.*

This obviously implies that learners for the distribution-free equivalence model can be transformed, through the standard EQ model, into distribution-free PAC learners. We note in passing that, applying the standard techniques directly on our model, we can prove the somewhat stronger fact that, for each individual distribution $\mathcal{D}$, a learner from $\mathcal{D}$-teachers can be transformed into an algorithm that PAC-learns over $\mathcal{D}$. We also can assume knowledge of a bound on the size of the target concept, by applying the usual trick of guessing it and increasing the guess whenever necessary.

## 3.2 EQ-Learning from Random Samples

In this subsection, we discuss another variant of the ordinary EQ-learning model. Given a representation class $\mathcal{C}$, *EQ-learning from $\mathcal{D}$-samples of size $p$ and with hypotheses from $\mathcal{H}$* proceeds as ordinary EQ-learning, except for the following differences:

1. Each run of the learning algorithm refers to an arbitrary but fixed pair $(C, D)$ such that $C \in \mathcal{C}$ and $D \in \mathcal{D}$, and to a given confidence parameter $0 < \delta < 1$.
2. The goal of the learner is to learn $C$ from (ordinary) EQs and a sample $P$ consisting of $p$ examples drawn independently at random according to $D$ and labeled correctly according to $C$. In other words, instead of EQ-learning $C$ from scratch, the learner gets $P$ as additional input. The learner must obtain an affirmative answer with a probability at least $1 - \delta$ of success.

Again the goal is to output a hypothesis for which the probability of disagreement with the target concept is zero; this time, the information about the distribution does not come from the counterexamples, but rather from the initial additional sample. We will show in this section that, for certain distributions, this model is strictly weaker than the model of EQ-learning from $\mathcal{D}$-teachers. However, in the distribution-free sense, it corresponds to the randomized version of the model described previously.

We first state (without proof) that each algorithm for EQ-learning from $\mathcal{D}$-samples can be converted into a randomized algorithm for EQ-learning from $\mathcal{D}$-teachers, such as those of the previous section, at the cost of a moderate overhead in the number of queries.

**Theorem 10** *Let $q$ be the number of EQs needed to learn $C$ from $\mathcal{D}$-samples of size $p$ and with hypothesis from $\mathcal{H}$. It holds, $LC^{EQ[\mathcal{D}]}(C, \mathcal{H}) \leq (p+1)(p+q)$.*

We show next an example that has an identification learning algorithm in the EQ from $\mathcal{D}$-teachers learning model, but does not have such algorithm in the EQ learning from $D$-samples model.

A $DNF_n$ formula is any sum $t_1 + t_2 + \cdots + t_k$ of monomials, where each monomial $t_i$ is the product of some literals chosen from $\{x_1, \ldots, x_n, \overline{x}_1, \ldots, \overline{x}_n\}$. Let $DNF = \cup_n DNF_n$ be the representation class of disjunctive normal form formulas.

Let us consider the class $\mathcal{D}$ of distributions $D$ defined in the following way. Assume that two different words $x_n$ and $y_n$ have been chosen for each $n \geq 1$. Consider the associated distribution $D$ defined by:

$$D(x_n) = 6/\pi^2(1/n^2 - 1/2^n)$$
$$D(y_n) = 6/(\pi^2 2^n)$$
$$D(z_n) = 0 \quad \text{for any word } z_n \text{ of length } n \text{ different from } x_n \text{ and } y_n.$$

$\mathcal{D}$ is obtained by letting $x_n$ and $y_n$ run over all pairs of different words of length $n$.

Let C be now any class able to represent concepts consisting of pairs $\{x_n, y_n\}$ within a reasonable size; for concreteness, pick DNF formulas consisting of complete minterms. A very easy algorithm learns them in our model of EQ from $\mathcal{D}$-teachers. The algorithm has to do at most two equivalence queries to know the value of the target formula $f$ on $x_n$ and $y_n$. First, it asks whether $f$ is identically zero. If a counterexample $e$ is given —$e$ must be $x_n$ or $y_n$— it will make a second query $f = t_e$?, where $t_e$ is the monomial that only evaluates to one on $e$ (the minterm). Thus we find whether either or both of $f(x_n)$ and $f(y_n)$ are 1, and if so we also know $x_n$ and/or $y_n$ themselves. Now the target formula is identified: the value of the formula on other points does not matter because they have zero probability.

However, it is not difficult to see that there is a distribution $D \in \mathcal{D}$ such that DNF formulas are not identifiable in the model of learning from EQ and $D$-samples. Here we refer to learning DNF's of size polynomial in $n$ from polynomially many equivalence queries of polynomial size, and with an extra initial sample of polynomial breadth. First we note that sampling according to $D \in \mathcal{D}$

there is a non-negligible probability of obtaining a sample that only contains copies of $x_n$.

**Lemma 11** *For any polynomial $q$ and $0 < \delta < 1$, there exists an integer $k_0$ such that for all $n \geq k_0$ the probability that a $D$-sample $S$ of size $q(n, 1/\delta)$ does not contain $y_n$ is greater than $\delta$.*

Then, the following negative result follows:

**Theorem 12** *There exist a distribution $D$ in $\mathcal{D}$ such that DNF is not EQ learnable from $D$-samples.*

The essential idea of the proof is that, after an initial sample revealing a single word, the algorithm is left with a task close enough to that of learning DNFs in the standard model with equivalence queries, which is impossible [4].

# 4  The Sphere Number and Its Applications

The remainder of the paper uses the machinery developed in Section 2 to obtain stronger results relating the models of the previous section, under one more technical condition: that the learning algorithm knows the size of the target concept, and never queries hypotheses longer than that. Some important learning algorithms do not have this property, but there are still quite a few (among the exact learners from equivalence queries only) that work in sort of an incremental fashion that leads to this property. The results become interesting because they lead to a precise characterization of randomized learners from $\mathcal{D}$-teachers.

We first rewrite our combinatorial material of the previous section in an extremely useful, geometrically intuitive form (1-spheres), and prove that for $m = M$ these structures capture clearly the strong consistency dimension. Applications follow in the next subsection.

## 4.1  Strong Consistency Dimension and 1-Spheres

A popular method for getting lower bounds on the number of queries is to show that the class of target concepts contains a basic "hard-to-learn" combinatorial structure. For instance, if the empty set is not representable but $N$ singletons are, then the number of EQs, needed to identify a particular singleton, is at least $N$. In this Subsection, we consider a conceptually similarly simple structure: the so-called 1-spheres. They are actually a disguised (read isomorphic) version of sets of singletons, with the empty set simultaneously forbidden. Then we show that the strong consistency dimension is lower bounded by the size of the largest 1-sphere that can be represented by $\mathcal{C}$. Moreover, for $M = m$ both quantities coincide.

To make the last statements precise, we need several definitions. Let $S$ be a finite set, and $S_0 \subseteq S$. The *1-sphere with support $S$ around center $S_0$*, denoted as $H^1_S(S_0)$ in the sequel, is the collection of sets $S_1 \subseteq S$ such that $|S_0 \oplus S_1| = 1$, where $\oplus$ denotes the symmetric difference of sets. In other words, $S_1 \subseteq S$ belongs to $H_S^1(S_0)$ if the Hamming distance between $S_0$ and $S_1$ is 1. Thus, it is formed by all the points at distance (radius) 1 from the center in Hamming space.

Let us now assume that $S \subseteq \Sigma^n$. Let $S'$ be an arbitrary subset of $S$. The sample $C' : \Sigma^n \to \{0, 1, *\}$ which represents $S'$ (as a subset of $S$) is the sample with support $S$ that assigns label 1 to all instances from $S'$, and label 0 to all instances from $S \setminus S'$. We say that $H_S^1(S_0)$ is representable by $C_{n,[m:M]}$ if the following two conditions are valid:

**(A)** Let $C_0$ be the sample with support $S$ which represents $S_0$. Then, $|C_0|_{\mathcal{R}} > M$.

**(B)** Each sample $C_1$ with support $S$, which represents a set $S_1 \in H_S^1(S_0)$, satisfies $|C_1|_{\mathcal{R}} \leq m$.

Thus, for the particular case of $M = m$, all points in Hamming space on the surface of the sphere are representable within size $m$ but the center is not; just as the above-mentioned use of singletons, which form the 1-sphere centered on the empty set. The *size* of $H_S^1(S_0)$ is defined as $|S|$. We define the three-variable function $\mathrm{sph}_{\mathcal{R}}(n, m, M)$, called *sphere number of $\mathcal{R}$* in the sequel, as the size of the largest 1-sphere which is representable by $C_{n,[m:M]}$.

We now turn to the main result of this subsection, which implies that the sphere number is another lower bound on $LC_{\mathcal{R}}^{EQ}(n, m, M)$.

**Theorem 13** $\mathrm{sph}_{\mathcal{R}}(n, m, M) \leq \mathrm{scdim}_{\mathcal{R}}(n, m, M)$ *with equality for* $M = m$.

**Proof.** For the sake of brevity, let $d = \mathrm{scdim}_{\mathcal{R}}(n, m, M)$ and $s = \mathrm{sph}_{\mathcal{R}}(n, m, M)$.

Let $H_S^1(S_0)$ be a largest 1-sphere that is representable by $C_{n,[m:M]}$. Thus, $|S| = s$. In order to prove $d \geq s$, we assume for sake of contradiction $d < s$. Consider the sample $C_0$ with support $S$ that represents $S_0$. By Condition (A), $|C_0|_{\mathcal{R}} > M$. According to Condition (2) applied to $C_0$, there exists a subsample $Q \sqsubseteq C_0$ such that $|Q| \leq d < s$ and $|Q|_{\mathcal{R}} > m$. Let $S_Q = \mathrm{supp}(Q) \subset S$. Let $Q_1$ be a sample with support $S$ that totally coincides with $Q$ (and thus with $C_0$) on $S_Q$, and coincides with $C_0$ on $S \setminus S_Q$ except for one instance. Clearly, $Q_1$ represents a set $S_1 \in H_S^1(S_0)$. By Condition (B), $|Q_1|_{\mathcal{R}} \leq m$. Since $|Q|_{\mathcal{R}} \leq |Q_1|_{\mathcal{R}}$, we arrived at a contradiction.

Finally, we prove $s \geq d$ for the special case that $M = m$. It follows from the minimality of $d$ and Condition (2) that there exists a sample $C : \Sigma^n \to \{0, 1, *\}$ such that the following holds:

1. $|C|_{\mathcal{R}} > m$.
2. $\exists Q_0 \sqsubseteq C : |Q_0| \leq d \wedge |Q_0|_{\mathcal{R}} > m$
3. $\forall Q \sqsubseteq C : (|Q| \leq d - 1 \Rightarrow |Q|_{\mathcal{R}} \leq m)$.

Let $S$ denote the support of $Q_0$. Note that $|S| = d$ (because otherwise the last two conditions become contradictory). Let $S_0 \subseteq S$ be the set represented by $Q_0$. We claim that $H_S^1(S_0)$ is representable by $C_{n,[m:m]}$ (which would conclude the proof). Condition (A) is obvious because $|Q_0|_{\mathcal{R}} > m$. Condition (B) can be seen as follows. For each $x \in S$, define $Q_x$ as the subsample of $C$ with support $S \setminus \{x\}$, and $Q'_x$ as the sample with support $S$ that coincides with $C$ on $S \setminus \{x\}$, but disagrees on $x$. Because each $Q_x$ is a subsample of $C$ of breadth $d-1$, it follows that $|Q_x|_{\mathcal{R}} \leq m$ for all $x \in S$. We conclude that the same remark applies to samples $Q'_x$, since a concept that is consistent with $Q_x$, but inconsistent with $Q_0$, must be consistent with $Q'_x$. Finally note that the samples $Q'_x$, $x \in S$, are exactly the representations of the sets in $H^1_S(S_0)$, respectively.                   •

## 4.2   Applications of the Sphere Number

In this subsection, $C$ denotes a concept class. The main results of this section are derived without referring to a representation class $\mathcal{R}$. We will however sometimes apply a general theorem to the special case where the concept class consists of concepts with a representation of size at most $m$.

It will be convenient to adapt some of our notations accordingly. For instance, we say that *1-sphere $H^1_S(S_0)$ is representable by $C$* if $S \subseteq X$ and the following two conditions are valid:

**(A)** $C$ does not contain a hypothesis $H$ that assigns label 1 to all instances in $S_0$ and label 0 to all instances in $S \setminus S_0$.

**(B)** For each $S' \in H^1_S(S_0)$, there exists a concept $C' \in C$ that assigns label 1 to all instances in $S'$ and label 0 to all instances in $S \setminus S'$.

The following notation will be used in the sequel. If $S = \{x_1, \ldots, x_s\}$, then $S_i = S_0 \oplus \{x_i\}$ for $i = 1, \ldots, s$. Thus, $S_1, \ldots, S_s$ are the sets belonging to $H^1_S(S_0)$. The concept from $C$ which represents $S_i$ in the sense of Condition (B) is denoted as $C_i$.

The *sphere number associated with $C$*, denoted as $\mathrm{sph}(C)$, is the size of the largest 1-sphere that is representable by $C$. Similar conventions are made for the learning complexity measure LC.

**Theorem 14** *Let $C = H^1_S(S_0)$ be a 1-sphere and $D$ an arbitrary but fixed distribution on $S$. Then, $LC^{EQ[D]}(C) \leq 1 + \lceil \log(1/\delta) \rceil$.*

**Proof.**   Let $S = \{x_1, \ldots, x_s\}$, and let $C_1, \ldots, C_s$ be the concepts from $C$ used to represent $S_1, \ldots, S_s \in H^1_S(S_0)$, respectively. Let $H_1, \ldots, H_s$ be a permutation of $C_1, \ldots, C_s$ sorted according to increasing values of $D(x_i)$. Consider the EQ-learner which issues its hypotheses in this order. It follows that as long as there exist counterexamples of a strictly positive probability, the probability that the teacher returns the counterexample $x_j$ associated with the target concept $C_j$ is at least $1/2$ per query. Thus, the probability that the target is not known after $\lceil \log(1/\delta) \rceil$ EQs is at most $\delta$. Thus, with probability at least $1 - \delta$, one more query suffices to receive answer YES.                   •

As the number of EQs needed to learn 1-spheres from arbitrary counterexamples equals the size $s$ of the 1-sphere, and the upper bound in Theorem 14 does not depend on $s$ at all, the model of EQ-learning from the $D$-teacher for a fixed distribution $D$ is, in general, more powerful than the ordinary model. The gap between the number of EQs needed in both models can be made arbitrarily large.

Recall that $\mathcal{D}_{unif}$ denotes the class of distributions that are uniform on a subdomain $S \subseteq X$ and assign zero probability to instances from $X \setminus S$.

**Theorem 15** *The following lower bound even holds for randomized learners:*

$$LC^{EQ}(\mathcal{C}) \geq LC^{EQ[\mathcal{D}_{unif}]}(\mathcal{C}) \geq (1 - \delta)sph(\mathcal{C}).$$

**Proof.** The first inequality is trivial. We prove the second one.

Let $S = \{x_1, \ldots, x_s\}$, and let $C_1, \ldots, C_s$ be the concepts from $\mathcal{C}$ used to represent $S_1, \ldots, S_s \in H_S^1(S_0)$, respectively. For $j = 1, \ldots, s$, let $D_j$ be the probability distribution that assigns zero probability to $x_j$ and is uniform on the remaining instances from $S$. Clearly, $D_j \in \mathcal{D}_{unif}$.

A learner must receive answer YES with probability at least $1 - \delta$ of success for each pair $(C, D)$, where $C \in \mathcal{C}$ is the target concept, and counterexamples are returned randomly according to $D \in \mathcal{D}$. It follows that, if target concept $C_j$ is drawn uniformly at random from $\{C_1, \ldots, C_s\}$, and counterexamples are subsequently returned according to $D_j$, answer YES is still obtained with probability at least $1 - \delta$ of success. Note that we randomize over the uniform distribution on the 1-sphere (random selection of the target concept), over the drawings of distribution $D_j$ conditioned to the current sets of counterexamples, respectively, and over the internal coin tosses of the learner.

Assume w.l.o.g. that all hypotheses are consistent with the counterexamples received so far. Let $C'$ be the next hypothesis, and $S' \subseteq S$ the subset of instances from $S$ being labeled 1 by $C'$. Because $H_S^1(S_0)$ is representable by $\mathcal{C}$, $S'$ must differ from $S_0$ on at least one element of $S$. If $S' = S_j$, then the learner receives answer YES. Otherwise, the set $U = (S' \oplus S_j) \setminus \{x_j\}$ is not empty. Note that the counterexample $x_i$ to $C'$ is picked from $U$ uniformly at random. This leads to the removal of only $C_i$ from the current version space $\mathcal{V}$.

The punchline of this discussion is that the following holds after the returnal of $q$ counterexamples:

1. The current version space $\mathcal{V}$ contains $s-q$ candidate concepts from $C_1, \ldots, C_s$. They are (by symmetry) statistically indistinguishable to the learner.
2. The next hypothesis is essentially a random guess in $\mathcal{V}$, that is, the chance to receive answer YES is exactly $1/|\mathcal{V}|$. The reason is that, from the perspective of the learner, all candidate target concepts in $\mathcal{V}$ are equally likely.[4]

---

[4] This might look unintuitive at first glance, because the learner does not necessarily draw the next hypothesis at random from $\mathcal{V}$ according to the uniform distribution. But notice that a random bit cannot be guessed with a probability of success larger than $1/2$ no matter which procedure for "guessing" is applied. This is the kind of argument that we used.

If answer YES is received before $s$ EQs were issued, then only because it was guessed within $\mathcal{V}$ by chance. We can illustrate this by thinking of two players. Player 1 determines at random a number between 1 and $s$ (the hidden target concept). Player 2 starts random guesses. The probability that the target number was determined after $q$ guesses is exactly $q/s$. Thus, at least $(1 - \delta)s$ guesses are required to achieve probability $1 - \delta$ of success.                                          •

**Corollary 16** *Let* $\mathcal{R} = (\Sigma, \Delta, R, \mu)$ *be a representation class defining a doubly parameterized concept class* $\mathcal{C}$. *The following lower bound holds for all* $m$ *and* $n$, *even for randomized learners:*

$$LC_{\mathcal{R}}^{EQ}(n, m, m) \geq LC_{\mathcal{R}}^{EQ[\mathcal{D}_{unif}]}(n, m, m) \geq (1 - \delta)sph_{\mathcal{R}}(n, m, m)$$

This means that, considering learning algorithms that do not make queries longer than the size of the target concept, the information-theoretic barrier for EQ-learning from arbitrary counterexamples is still a barrier for EQ-learning from $\mathcal{D}_{unif}$-teachers. This negative result even holds when the learner is randomized, so that this implies that it applies as well to the model of EQ-learning from $\mathcal{D}$-samples, which has been proved earlier to be subsumed by randomized learners from $\mathcal{D}$-teachers.

On the other hand, note that the results of this section generalize readily to the case in which the hypotheses queried come from a different class $\mathcal{H}$ larger than $\mathcal{C}$, or in particular to learners which query hypothesis of size up to $M > m$ when the target is known to have size at most $m$. The point is that, for this case, the last corollary does not have anymore the interpretation that we have described, since the sphere number no longer is guaranteed to coincide with the strong consistency dimension, so the lower bound for the learning complexity that we would obtain is no longer, in principle, the same information-theoretic barrier as for EQ-learning.

# References

[1] D. Angluin. Inference of reversible languages. *J. Assoc. Comput. Mach.*, 29:741–765, 1982.

[2] D. Angluin. Learning regular sets from queries and counterexamples. *Information and Computation*, 75:87–106, 1987.

[3] D. Angluin. Queries and concept learning. *Machine Learning*, 2:319–342, 1988.

[4] D. Angluin. Negative results for equivalence queries. *Machine Learning*, 5:121–150, 1990.

[5] J. Castro and J. L. Balcázar. Simple pac learning of simple decision lists. In *Sixth Internatinal Workshop, ALT'95*, pages 239–248, Fukuoka, Japan, 1995. LNAI. Springer.

[6] R. Gavaldà. On the power of equivalence queries. In *EUROCOLT'93*, pages 193–203. LNAI. Springer, 1993.

[7] Y. Hayashi, S. Matsumoto, A. Shinoara, and M. Takeda. Uniform characterization of polynomial-query learnabilities. In *First International Conference, DS'98*, pages 84–92, Fukuoka, Japan, 1998. LNAI. Springer.

[8] L. Hellerstein, K. Pillaipakkamnatt, V. Raghavan, and D. Wilkins. How many queries are needed to learn? *Journal of the ACM*, 43(5):840–862, 1996.

[9] M. Li and P. Vitányi. Learning simple concepts under simple distributions. *SIAM Journal on Computing*, 20(5):911–935, 1991.

[10] H. Simon. Learning decision lists an trees with equivalence queries. In *Second European Conference, EuroCOLT'95*, pages 322–336, Barcelona, Spain, 1995. Lecture Notes in Artificial Intelligence.

[11] L. Valiant. A theory of the learnable. *Comm. ACM*, 27:1134–1142, 1984.

# The VC-Dimension of Subclasses of Pattern Languages

Andrew Mitchell[1], Tobias Scheffer[2], Arun Sharma[1], and Frank Stephan[3]

[1] University of New South Wales, School of Computer Science and Engineering,
Sydney, 2052 NSW, Australia,
andrewm,arun@cse.unsw.edu.au
[2] Otto-von-Guericke-Universität Magdeburg, FIN/IWS, Universitätsplatz 2,
39106 Magdeburg, Germany,
scheffer@iws.cs.uni-magdeburg.de
[3] Mathematisches Institut, Universität Heidelberg, Im Neuenheimer Feld 294,
69120 Heidelberg, Germany,
fstephan@math.uni-heidelberg.de

**Abstract.** This paper derives the Vapnik Chervonenkis dimension of several natural subclasses of pattern languages. For classes with unbounded VC-dimension, an attempt is made to quantify the "rate of growth" of VC-dimension for these classes. This is achieved by computing, for each $n$, size of the "smallest" witness set of $n$ elements that is shattered by the class. The paper considers both erasing (empty substitutions allowed) and nonerasing (empty substitutions not allowed) pattern languages. For erasing pattern languages, optimal bounds for this size — within polynomial order — are derived for the case of 1 variable occurrence and unary alphabet, for the case where the number of variable occurrences is bounded by a constant, and the general case of all pattern languages. The extent to which these results hold for nonerasing pattern languages is also investigated. Some results that shed light on efficient learning of subclasses of pattern languages are also given.

## 1 Introduction

The simple and intuitive notion of pattern languages was formally introduced by Angluin [1] and has been studied extensively, both in the context of formal language theory and computational learning theory. We give a brief overview of the work on learnability of pattern languages to provide a context for the results in this paper. We refer the reader to Salomaa [20, 21] for a review of the work on pattern languages in formal language theory.

In the present paper, we consider both kinds of pattern languages: *erasing* (when empty substitutions are allowed) and *nonerasing* (when empty substitutions are *not* allowed). Angluin [2] showed that the class of nonerasing pattern languages is identifiable in the limit from only positive data in Gold's model [8]. Since its introduction, pattern languages and their variants have been a subject of intense study in identification in the limit framework (for a review, see Shinohara and Arikawa [24]). Learnability of the class of erasing pattern languages was

O. Watanabe, T. Yokomori (Eds.): ALT'99, LNAI 1720, pp. 93–105, 1999.
© Springer-Verlag Berlin Heidelberg 1999

first considered by Shinohara [23] in the identification in the limit framework. This class turns out to be very complex and it is still open whether for finite alphabet of size $> 1$, the class of erasing pattern languages can be identified in the limit from only positive data[1].

Since the class of nonerasing pattern languages is identifiable in the limit from only positive data, a natural question is if there is any gain to be had if negative data is also present. Lange and Zeugmann [14] observed that in the presence of both positive and negative data, the class of nonerasing pattern languages is identifiable with 0 mind changes; that is, there is a learner that after looking at a sufficient number of positive and negative examples comes up with the correct pattern for the language. This restricted "one-shot" version of identification in the limit is referred to as *finite identification*.

Since finite identification is a batch model, finite learning from both positive and negative data may be viewed as an idealized version of Valiant's [25] PAC model. In this paper, we show that even the VC-dimension of patterns with one single variable and an alphabet size of 1 is unbounded. This implies that even this restricted class of pattern languages is not learnable in Valiant's sense, even if we omit all polynomial time constraints from Valiant's definition of learning. This result (which holds for both the nonerasing and erasing cases) may appear to be at odds with the observation of Lange and Zeugmann [14] that the class of nonerasing pattern languages can be finitely learned from both positive and negative data. The apparent discrepancy between the two results is due to a subtle difference on the manner in which the two models treat data. In finite identification, the learner has the luxury of waiting for a finite, but unbounded, sample of positive and negative examples before making its conjecture. On the other hand, the learner in the PAC model is required to perform on any fixed sample of an "adequate" size. So, clearly the conditions in the PAC setting with respect to data presentation are more strict.

Since this restricted class and several other subclasses of pattern languages considered in this paper have unbounded VC-dimension, we make an attempt to quantify the rate of growth of VC-dimension for these classes. This is achieved by computing, for each $n$, size of the "smallest" witness set of $n$ elements that is shattered by the class. The motivation for computing such a *Vapnik Chervonenkis Witness Size* is as follows. Although classes with unbounded VC-dimension are not PAC-learnable in general, they may become learnable under certain constraints on the distribution. An often used constraint is that the distribution favors short strings. Therefore, an interesting question is: How large is the VC-dimension if only strings of a certain length are considered? Mathematically, it is perhaps more elegant to pose the question: What is the least length $m$ such that $n$ strings of size up to $m$ are shattered? We refer to this value of $m$ as the *Vapnik Chervonenkis Dimension Witness Size* for $n$ and express it as a function of $n$, $vcdws(n)$. Hence, higher the growth rate of the function $vcdws$,

---

[1] See Mitchell [17] where a subclass of erasing pattern languages is shown to be iden-
    tifiable in the limit from only positive data. This paper also shows that the class of
    erasing pattern languages is learnable if the alphabet size is 1 or $\infty$.

smaller is the "local" VC-dimension for strings up to a fixed length and "easier" it may be to learn the class under a suitably constrained variant of the PAC model.

Although the VC-dimension of 1-variable pattern languages is unbounded, we note that if at least one positive example is present, the VC-dimension of nonerasing pattern languages becomes bounded (this can be formally expressed in the terminology of version-spaces). Unfortunately, this does not help in the case of erasing pattern languages, as we are able to show that the VC-dimension of 1-variable erasing pattern languages is unbounded even in the presence of a positive example.

In $k$-variable patterns, the bound $k$ is on the number of distinct variables in the pattern and not on the total number of occurrences of all variables. We also consider the case where the number of occurrences of all the variables in a pattern is bounded. We show that the VC-dimension of the class of languages generated by patterns with at most 1 variable occurrence is 2. For variable occurrence count $\geq 2$, the VC dimension turns out to be unbounded provided the alphabet size is at least 2 and the pattern has at least two distinct variables. We also consider the case where the only requirement is that each variable occur exactly $n$ times in the pattern (so, there is neither any bound on the number of distinct variables nor any bound on the total number of variable occurrences). We show that the VC dimension of languages generated by patterns in which each variable occurs exactly once is unbounded. We note that this result also holds for any general $n$.

Having established several VC-dimension results, we turn our attention to issues involved in *efficient* learning of pattern language subclasses. One problem with efficient learning of pattern languages is the *NP*-completeness of the membership decision [1].[2] This NP-completeness result already implies that pattern languages cannot be learned polynomially in Valiant's sense when the hypotheses are patterns (because Valiant requires that, for a given instance, the output of the hypothesis must be computable in polynomial time). Schapire [22] strengthened this result by showing that pattern languages cannot be polynomially PAC-learned independent of the representation chosen for the hypotheses. Computing the output of a hypothesis cannot be done in polynomial time using *any* coding scheme which is powerful enough for learning pattern languages. Also, Ko, Marron and Tzeng [13] have shown that the problem of finding any pattern consistent with a set of positive and negative examples is *NP*-hard. Marron and Ko [16] considered necessary and sufficient conditions on a finite positive initial sample that allows exact identification of a target $k$-variable pattern from the initial sample and from polynomially many membership queries. Later, Marron [15] considered the exact learnability of $k$-variable patterns with polynomially

---

[2] Angluin [1] showed that the class of nonerasing pattern languages is not learnable with polynomially many queries if only equivalence, membership, and subset queries are allowed and as long as any hypothesis space with the same expressive power as the class being learned is considered. However, she gave an algorithm for exactly learning the class with a polynomial number of superset queries.

many membership queries, but where the initial sample consists of only a single positive example.

In the PAC setting, Kearns and Pitt [11] showed that $k$-variable pattern languages can be PAC-learned under product distributions[3] from polynomially many strings. At first blush, their result appears to contradict our claim that $k$-variable patterns have an unbounded VC-dimension. A closer look at their result reveals that they assume an upper bound on the length of substitution strings — which essentially bounds the VC-dimension of the class. When the substitutions of all variables are governed by independent and identical distributions, then $k$-variable pattern languages can (under a mild additional distributional assumption) even be learned linearly in the length of the target pattern and singly exponentially in $k$ [19].

In this paper we show that in the case of nonerasing pattern languages, the first positive example string contains enough information to bound the necessary sample size without any assumptions on the underlying distribution. (This result holds even for infinite alphabets.) Unfortunately, as already noted this result does not translate to the case of $k$-variable erasing pattern languages, as even in the presence of a positive example, the VC-dimension of single-variable erasing pattern languages is unbounded.

We finally consider some results in the framework of agnostic learning [9, 12]. Here no prior knowledge about the actual concept class being learned is assumed. The learner is required to approximate the observed distribution on classified instances almost as well as possible in the given hypothesis language (with high probability) in polynomial time. Agnostic learning may be viewed as the branch of learning theory closest to practical applications. Unfortunately, not even conjunctive concepts [12] and half-spaces [10] are agnostically learnable. Shallow decision trees, however, have been shown to be agnostically learnable [3, 6].

## 2   Preliminaries

The symbol $\epsilon$ denotes the empty string. Let $s$ be a string, word, or pattern. Then the *length* of $s$, denoted $|s|$, is the number of symbols in $s$. A pattern $\sigma$ is a string over elements from the basic language $\Sigma$ and variables from a variable alphabet; we use lower case Latin letters for elements of $\Sigma$ and upper case Latin letters for variables. The number of variables is the number of distinct variable symbols occurring in a pattern, the number of occurrences of variables is the total number of occurrences of variable symbols in a pattern. An erasing pattern language contains all words $x$ generated by the pattern in the sense that every variable occurrence $A$ is substituted within the whole word by the same string $\alpha_A \in \Sigma^*$, a non-erasing pattern language contains the words where

---

[3] More precisely, they require the positive examples in the sample to be generated according to a product distribution, but allow any arbitrary distribution for the negative examples.

the variables are substituted by non-empty strings only. Thus, in non-erasing pattern languages every word is at least as large as the pattern generating it.

For example, if $\sigma = aAbbBabAba$, then the length is 10, the number of variables 2 and the number of variable occurrences is 3. In an erasing pattern language, $\sigma$ generates the words $abbabba$ (by $A = \epsilon$ and $B = \epsilon$) and $abbaabba$ (by $A = \epsilon$ and $B = a$) which it does not generate in the nonerasing case. In both cases, erasing and nonerasing, $\sigma$ generates the word $aabbabaabbaba$ (by $A = a$ and $B = aba$). This allows us to define subclasses of pattern languages generated by a pattern with up to $k$ variables or up to $l$ variable occurrences.

**Quantifying Unbounded VC-Dimension.** The VC-dimension of a class $\mathcal{L}$ of languages is the size of the largest set of words $S$ such that $\mathcal{L}$ shatters $S$. The VC-dimension of a class $\mathcal{L}$ is unbounded iff, for every $n$, there are $n$ words $x_1, x_2, \ldots, x_n$ such that $\mathcal{L}$ shatters them. As motivated in the introduction, we introduce the function

$$vcdws(n) = \min\{\max\{|x_1|, |x_2|, \ldots, |x_n|\} : \mathcal{L} \text{ shatters } \{x_1, x_2, \ldots, x_n\}\}$$

where $vcdws$ stands for *Vapnik Chervonenkis Dimension Witness Size* and returns the size of the smallest witness for the fact that the VC-dimension is at least $n$. Determining $vcdws$ for several natural classes is one of the main results of the present work.

**Version Spaces.** Given a set of languages $\mathcal{L}$ and a set of positive and negative example strings $S$, the version space $VS(\mathcal{L}, S)$ consists of all languages in $\mathcal{L}$ that generate all the positive but none of the negative strings in $S$. It follows from Theorem 2.1 of Blumer *et al.* [5] that $\mathcal{L}$ can be PAC-learned with the sample $S$ and a finite number of additional examples if $VS(\mathcal{L}, S)$ has a finite VC-dimension. In Section 3 we will show that, for certain classes, the VC dimension of the version space remains infinite after a sample $S$ has been read while in Section 5 we show that, for other classes, the VC-dimension of the version space can turn from infinite to finite when the first positive example arrives.

# 3   VC-Dimension of Erasing Pattern Languages

Our first result shows that even the very restrictive class of 1-variable erasing pattern languages over the unary alphabet has an unbounded VC-dimension. This special case is the only one for which the exact value of $vcdws$ is known.

**Theorem 1.** *The VC-dimension of the class of erasing 1-variable pattern languages is unbounded. If the size of the alphabet is 1, then one can determine the exact size of the smallest witness by the formula $vcdws(n) = p_2 \cdot p_3 \cdot \ldots \cdot p_{n-1}$ where $p_m$ is the $m$-th prime number ($p_1 = 2, p_2 = 3, p_3 = 5, p_4 = 7, \ldots$).*

**Proof:** Let $\Sigma = \{a\}$. For the direction $vcdws(n) \leq p_2 \cdot p_3 \cdot \ldots \cdot p_{n-1}$, let $x_k = a^{m_k}$ where $m_k = p_1 \cdot p_2 \cdot \ldots \cdot p_{n-1}/p_k$, that is, $m_k$ is the product of the first $n-1$ primes except the $k$-th one. Let $x_n = \epsilon$. For every subset $E \subseteq \{x_1, x_2, \ldots, x_n\}$, let $p_E$ be the product of those $p_k$ where $k < n$ and $x_k \notin E$ and where $p_E = 1$ if $E \subseteq \{x_n\}$. Now the patterns $A^{p_E}$ and $a^{p_E} A^{p_E}$ generate a word $a^m$ with $m > 0$ iff $p_E$ divides $m$. Furthermore, the word $\epsilon$ is generated by $A^{p_E}$ but not by $a^{p_E} A^{p_E}$. So the language generated by $A^{p_E}$ contains exactly the $x_k \in E$ in the case $x_n \in E$; the language generated by $a^{p_E} A^{p_E}$ contains exactly the $x_k \in E$ in the case $x_n \notin E$. Since the longest $x_k$ is $x_1$ whose length is $p_2 \cdot p_3 \cdot \ldots \cdot p_{n-1}$ one has that $vcdws(n) \leq p_2 \cdot p_3 \cdot \ldots \cdot p_{n-1}$.

For the converse direction assume that the erasing 1-variable pattern languages shatter $E = \{a^{m_1}, a^{m_2}, \ldots, a^{m_n}\}$ where $m_1 < m_2 < \ldots < m_n$. Let $a^{d_k} A^{e_k}$ generate all elements in $E$ except $a^{m_k}$. Now one has, for $k' \in \{2, 3, \ldots, n\} - \{k\}$, that $a^{m_1} = a^{d_k + c_1 \cdot e_k}$ and $a^{m_{k'}} = a^{d_k + c_{k'} \cdot e_k}$, so $m_{k'} - m_1 = (c_{k'} - c_1) e_k$. On the other hand, $m_k - m_1$ is not a multiple of $e_k$ and $m_k - m_1$ has a prime factor $q_k$ which does not divide any difference $m_{k'} - m_1$. It follows that for every difference $m_k - m_1$ there is one prime number $q_k$ dividing all other differences $m_{k'} - m_1$ and therefore, any product of $n - 2$ of such different prime numbers must divide some difference $m_k - m_1$. The product $q_2 \cdot q_3 \cdot \ldots \cdot q_n / q_k$ is a lower bound for $m_k$ and, for the $k$ with the smallest number $q_k$, $m_k$ is at least the product of the primes $p_2 \cdot p_3 \cdot \ldots \cdot p_{n-1}$. So $vcdws(n) \geq p_2 \cdot p_3 \cdot \ldots \cdot p_{n-1}$. ∎

As noted, this is the only case where $vcdws$ has been determined exactly. It will be shown that more variables enable smaller values for $vcdws(n)$ while it is unknown whether larger alphabets give smaller values for $vcdws(n)$ in the case of erasing 1-variable pattern languages. The above proof even shows the following: Given any positive example $w$, there is still no bound on the VC-dimension of the version space of the class with respect to the example set $\{w\}$. Since the given $w$ takes the place of $x_n$ in the proof above, one now gets the upper bound $|w| + p_2 \cdot p_3 \cdot \ldots \cdot p_{n-1}$ instead of $p_2 \cdot p_3 \cdot \ldots \cdot p_{n-1}$ and uses for $x_k$ the words $wa^{m_k}$ with $m_k = p_1 \cdot p_2 \cdot \ldots \cdot p_{n-1} / p_k$ in the case $k < n$ and $x_k = w$ in the case $k = n$.

**Theorem 2.** *For any positive example $w$, the VC-dimension of the version space of the class of all erasing 1-variable pattern languages is unbounded and $vcdws(n) \leq |w| + p_2 \cdot p_3 \cdot \ldots \cdot p_n$.*

However, if two positive examples are present, then in some rare cases it may be possible to bound the number of patterns. For example, let the alphabet be $\Sigma = \{a, b\}$. Then if both strings $a$ and $b$ are in the language and are presented as positive examples, it is immediate that the only pattern language that satisfies this case is $\Sigma^*$.

An alternative to limiting the number of variables is limiting the number of variable occurrences. If the bound is 1, then the class is quite restrictive and has VC-dimension 2. However, as soon as the bound becomes 2, one has unbounded VC-dimension.

**Theorem 3.** *The VC-dimension of the class of erasing pattern languages generated by patterns with at most 1 variable occurrence is 2.*

One can generalize the result and show that every 1-variable erasing pattern language with up to $k$ occurrences of this variable has bounded Vapnik Chervonenkis dimension. This is no longer true for 2-variable erasing pattern languages with up to 2 occurrences.

**Theorem 4.** *The VC-dimension of the class of all erasing pattern languages generated by patterns with at most 2 variable occurrences is unbounded. Furthermore,* $vcdws(n) \leq (3n + 2) \cdot 2^n$.

**Proof:** For each $k$, let $x_k$ be the concatenation of all strings $a^n b \sigma b a^n$ where $\sigma \in \{a, b\}^n$ and the $k$-th character of $\sigma$ is a $b$. Now, for every subset $E$ of $\{x_1, x_2, \ldots, x_n\}$ let $\sigma_E$ be a strings of length $n$ such that $\sigma_E(k) = a$ if $x_k \notin E$ and $\sigma_E(k) = b$ if $x_k \in E$. Now the language generated by $Ab\sigma_E bB$ contains $x_k$ iff $b\sigma_E b$ is a substring of $x_k$ iff the $k$-th character in $\sigma_E$ is a $b$ which by definition is equivalent to $x_k \in E$. So, the set $\{x_1, x_2, \ldots, x_n\}$ is shattered. ∎

The corresponding theorem holds also for nonerasing pattern languages since $A$ and $B$ take at least the string $a^n$ or even something longer. A natural question is whether the lower bound is also exponential in $n$. The next theorem answers this question affirmatively.

**Theorem 5.** *For given $k$, the class of all pattern languages with up to $k$ variable occurrences satisfies* $vcdws(n) \geq 2^{(n-1)/(2k+1)}$.

**Proof:** Given $x_1, x_2, \ldots, x_n$, one needs $2^{n-1}$ patterns which contain $x_1$ and shatter $x_2, x_3, \ldots, x_n$. Let $m = |x_1|$ which is a lower bound for the size if $x_1, x_2, \ldots, x_n$ are the shortest words shattered by the considered class. A pattern generating $x_1$ has $h \leq k$ variable occurrences and, for the $l$-th variable occurrence in this word, one has a beginning entry $a_l \leq |x_1| \leq m$, and the length $b_l$ of the variable in $x_1$. Knowing $x_1$, each pattern generating $x_1$ has a unique description with the given parameters. So one gets the upper bound $1 + m^2 + m^4 + \ldots + m^{2k} \leq m^{2k+1}$ for the number of patterns generating $x_1$ and has $m^{2k+1} \geq 2^{n-1}$, that is, $m \geq 2^{(n-1)/(2k+1)}$. ∎

The next theorem is about the general case of the class of all erasing pattern languages. Strict lower bounds are $vcdws(n) \geq \log(n)/\log(|\Sigma|)$ for the case of alphabet size 2 or more and $vcdws(n) \geq n - 1$ for the case of alphabet size 1. These lower bounds are given by the size of the largest string within a set of $n$ strings. These straightforward bounds are modulo a linear factor optimal for the unary and binary alphabets.

**Theorem 6.** *For arbitrary erasing pattern languages:*
(a) *If* $\Sigma = \{a\}$ *then* $vcdws(n) \leq 2n$.
(b) *If* $\Sigma = \{a, b\}$ *then* $vcdws(n) \leq 4 + 2 \cdot \log(n)$.

**Proof (a)** In this case $\Sigma = \{a\}$. Let $x_1 = a^{n+1}, x_2 = a^{n+2}, \ldots, x_n = a^{n+n}$ and $E$ be a subset of $x_1, x_2, \ldots, x_n$. Now let $\sigma_E$ be the concatenation of those $A_k^{n+k}$ with $x_k \in E$: Taking $A_k = \{a\}$ and all other variables to $\epsilon$, the word generated by $\sigma_E$ is $x_k$. If at least two variables are not empty or one takes a string strictly longer than 1 then the overall length is at least $2n + 2$ and the word generated outside $\{x_1, x_2, \ldots, x_n\}$. So, $\sigma_E$ generates exactly those words $x_k$ which are in $E$ and the erasing pattern languages shatter $\{x_1, x_2, \ldots, x_n\}$.

**Proof (b)** In this case $\Sigma = \{a, b\}$. Let $m$ be the first integer such that the set $U_m$ contains at least $n$ strings where $U_m$ consists of all words $w \in \{a, b\}^m$ such that $a, b$ occur similar often in $w$, the first character of $w$ is $a$ and $aa, bb, ab$ and $ba$ are subwords of $w$. One can show that $m \leq 4 + 2 \cdot \log(n)$. Let $x_1, x_2, \ldots, x_n$ be different words in $U_m$. Now, for every $k$, let $\sigma_k$ be the pattern obtained from $x_k$ by replacing $a$ by $A_k$ and $b$ by $B_k$, and let $\sigma_E$ be the concatenation of those $\sigma_k$ where $x_k \in E$. Since every variable occurs in $\sigma_E$ $m/2$ times, one has that either one variable is assigned to some fixed $u \in \{a, b\}^2$ and the generated word is $u^{m/2}$ or there are two variables such that one of them is assigned to $a$ and the other one to $b$. Since $x_k \neq u^{m/2}$ — the word $u^{m/2}$ does not contain all subwords $aa, ab, ba, bb$ — and since $x_k \notin \{a^{m/2}b^{m/2}, b^{m/2}a^{m/2}\}$ and since the first character of $x_k$ is $a$ one can conclude that $A_l = a$ and $B_l = b$ for some $l$. Now the word generated by $\sigma_E$ is $x_l$ and $x_l = x_k$ only for $l = k$. Thus $\sigma_E$ generates exactly those $x_k$ with $x_k \in E$. ∎

The trivial lower bound is constant 1 for infinite alphabet $\Sigma$. But it is impossible to have constant upper bound for the size of the smallest witness, indeed there is, for every $k$, an $n$ with $vcwds(n) > k$.

# 4    VC-Dimension of Nonerasing Pattern Languages

Many of the theorems for erasing pattern languages can be adapted to the case of nonerasing pattern languages. In many theorems the upper bound increases by a sublinear factor (measured in the size of the previous value of the function $vcdws$). Furthermore one gets the following lower bound:

**Theorem 7.** *For any class of nonerasing pattern languages,* $vcdws(n) \geq \frac{n-1}{2 \cdot \log(n+2)}.$

**Proof:** Given $x_1, x_2, \ldots, x_n$, one needs $2^{n-1}$ patterns which contain $x_1$ and shatter $x_2, x_3, \ldots, x_n$. Let $m = |x_1|$ which is a lower bound for the size if $x_1, x_2, \ldots, x_n$ are the shortest words shattered by the considered class. A pattern generating $x_1$ can be described as follows: To each position one assigns either the value 0 if this position is covered by a constant from the pattern generating it, the value $h$ if it is the first character of some occurrence of the $h$-th variable ($h \leq m$) and $m + 1$ if it is some subsequent character of the occurrence of some variable. Together with $x_1$ itself, this string either describes uniquely the pattern generating $x_1$ or is invalid if, for example, some variable occurring twice has at each occurrence a different length. So one gets at most $(m+2)^m$ patterns which generate $x_1$. It follows that $(m+2)^m \geq 2^{n-1}$. This condition only holds if $m \geq \frac{n-1}{2 \cdot \log(n+2)}$. ∎

Furthermore, all lower bounds on $vcdws$ carry over from erasing pattern languages to nonerasing pattern languages. For upper bounds, the following bounds can be obtained by adapting the corresponding results for erasing pattern languages. In these three cases, the upper bounds are only slightly larger than those for the erasing pattern languages, but in the general case with an alphabet of size 2 or more, the above lower bound is $\frac{n-1}{2\cdot\log(n+2)}$ for nonerasing pattern languages while $4 + 2 \cdot \log(n)$ is an upper bound for the erasing pattern languages.

**Theorem 8.** *For 1-variable pattern languages, $vcdws(n) \leq p_1 \cdot p_2 \cdot \ldots \cdot p_n$, where $p_1, p_2, \ldots, p_n$ are the first $n$ prime numbers.*
*For patterns with exactly two variable occurrences, $vcdws(n) \leq (3n + 2) \cdot 2^n$.*
*If the alphabet size is 1, then $vcdws(n) \leq \frac{1}{2} \cdot (3n^2 + 5n)$ for the class of all nonerasing pattern languages.*

Note that in the case the alphabet size is two, one can — using the well-known fact that nonerasing pattern languages shatter the set of the $x_k = a^{k-1}ba^{n-k}$ — obtain that $vcdws(n) \leq n$.

# 5  Learning $k$-Variable Nonerasing Patterns

Having established several VC-dimension results in the previous section, we now present some PAC-learnability results. The fact that the VC dimension of $k$-variable pattern languages is infinite suggests that this class is not learnable. However, we will show that the version space becomes finite after the first positive example has been seen.

**Theorem 9.** *Let $\varepsilon$ and $\delta$ be given. Let $L$ be a $k$-variable pattern language and $D$ be an arbitrary distribution on $\Sigma^*$. Let $S$ be an initial set of positive sentences of size at least one and let $l_{min} = \min\{|w| \mid w \in S\}$. Regarding the version space, we can claim that $|VS(k\text{-variable pattern languages}, S)| \leq (l_{min} + k)^{l_{min}}$. Let $h$ be any pattern consistent with a sample of size at most $m \geq \frac{l_{min}}{\varepsilon} \log \frac{1}{\delta \cdot \log(l_{min}+k)}$. Then $P(Err_{L,D}[h] > \varepsilon) \leq \delta$.*

An exhaustive learner can find a consistent hypothesis (if one exists) after enumerating all possible $(l_{min}+k)^{l_{min}}$ patterns. In order to decide whether a pattern is consistent with a sample the learner has to check if $x \in L(h)$ for each example $x$ and pattern $h$. While this problem is NP-complete for general patterns, it can be solved polynomially for any fixed number of variables $k$.

**Theorem 10.** *Given a sample $S$ of positive and negative strings, a consistent nonerasing $k$-variable pattern $h$ can be found in $O((l_{min} + k)^{l_{min}} \cdot \max\{|x| \mid x \in S\}^k)$ – that is, learning is – as in the case of PAC – polynomial in parameters $\frac{1}{\delta}$ and $\frac{1}{\varepsilon}$ but depends exponentially on the parameters $l_{min}$ and $k$.*

An algorithm that learns a $k$-variable pattern still has a run time which grows exponentially in $l_{min}$. Under an additional assumption on $D$ and on the length of substitution strings, they become efficiently learnable for fixed $k$ [11].

**Patterns with $k$ variable occurrences.** If we restrict the patterns to have at most $k$ occurrences of any variables, they become even more easily learnable. The number of $k$-occurrence patterns which are consistent with an initial example $x$ is at most as large as the number of $k$-variable patterns – that is, the logarithm of the hypothesis space size is polynomial which makes the required sample size polynomial, too. However, the learner can find a consistent hypothesis much more quickly.

**Theorem 11.** *Pattern languages with up to $k$ occurrences of variables can be learned from a sample in $O(l_{min}^{2k-2} \cdot k^k)$ – that is, polynomially for fixed $k$.*

The idea of the proof is that up to $k$ substrings in the shortest example can be substituted by variables. Hence, we only need to try all "start and end positions" of the variables and to enumerate all possible identifications of some variables.

# 6   Length-Bounded Pattern Languages

In this section we show that length-bounded pattern languages are efficiently learnable – even in the agnostic framework. Due to lack of space our treatment here is informal.

We assume the alphabet size to be *finite*. There are $(|\Sigma| + k + 1)^k$ patterns of length at most $k$ ($|\Sigma|$ constants, up to $k$ variables, and an empty symbol). It follows immediately from Theorem 1 of [9] that $P(Err_{L,D}[h^*] < Err_{L,D}[h]-\varepsilon) \le \delta$ when $h$ minimizes the empirical error, $h^* = \inf_{h \in H}\{Err_{L,D}[h]\}$ is the truly best approximation of $L$ in $H$, and the sample size is at least $m \ge \frac{1}{\varepsilon^2} \log \frac{(|\Sigma|+k)^k}{\delta}$. In other words, by returning the hypothesis with the least empirical error a learner returns (with high probability) a hypothesis which is almost as good as the best possible hypothesis in the language. Hence, length bounded pattern languages are agnostically learnable. In order to find $h^*$, a learner can enumerate the hypothesis space in $O((|\Sigma| + k + 1)^k)$.

The union of length bounded patterns is the power set of the set of length bounded patterns – hence, this hypothesis space can be bounded to at most $2^{(|\Sigma|+k+1)^k}$. This implies that the sample complexity is $m \ge \frac{(|\Sigma|+k+1)^k}{\delta} \log \frac{1}{\delta \log(|\Sigma|+k+1)}$ (that is polynomial in $|\Sigma|, \frac{1}{\varepsilon}$, and $\frac{1}{\delta}$) but we still need to find an algorithm which finds a consistent hypothesis in polynomial time – together this proves that this class is polynomially learnable [4]. A greedy coverage algorithm which subsequently generates patterns which cover at least one positive and no negative example can be guaranteed to find a consistent hypothesis (if one exists) in $O((|\Sigma| + k)^k \cdot m^+)$ where $m^+$ is the number of positive examples (that is, polynomially for a fixed $k$).

In order to learn unions of length bounded pattern languages agnostically we would have to construct a polynomial algorithm which finds an empirical error minimizing hypothesis. Note that this is much more difficult: The greedy algorithm will find *a* consistent hypothesis – if one exists. It may occur that every positive instance is covered by a distinct pattern. In the agnostic framework, we would have to find *the* hypothesis which minimizes the observed error. An enumerative algorithm, however, would have a time complexity of $O(2^{(|\Sigma|+k)^k})$.

# 7  Conclusion

We studied the VC-dimension of several subclasses of pattern languages. We showed that even single variable pattern languages have an unbounded VC-dimension. For this and several other classes with unbounded VC-dimension we furthermore quantified the VC-dimension witness size, thus characterizing just how quickly the VC-dimension grows. We showed that the VC-dimension of the class of single variable pattern languages which are consistent with a positive example is unbounded; by contrast, the class of pattern languages with $k$ variable occurrences which are consistent with a positive example is finite. Hence, after the first positive example has been read, the sample size which is necessary or good generalization can be quantified. This result does seem to vindicate recent attempts by Reischuk and Zeugmann [18] (see also [7]) to study feasible average case learnability of single variable pattern languages by placing reasonable restrictions on the class of distributions.

## Acknowledgment

We would like to express our gratitude to the reviewers for several helpful comments that have improved the exposition of the paper. Andrew Mitchell is supported by an Australian Postgraduate Award. Tobias Scheffer is supported by grants WY20/1-1 and WY20/1-2 of the German Research Council (DFG), and an Ernst-von-Siemens fellowship. Arun Sharma is supported by the Australian Research Council Grants A49600456 and A49803051. Frank Stephan is supported by the German Research Council (DFG) grant Am 60/9-2.

# References

[1] D. Angluin. Finding patterns common to a set of strings. *Journal of Computer and System Sciences*, 21:46–62, 1980.

[2] D. Angluin. Inductive inference of formal languages from positive data. *Information and Control*, 45:117–135, 1980.

[3] P. Auer, R. C. Holte, and W. Maass. Theory and applications of agnostic PAC-learning with small decision trees. In *Proceedings of the 12th International Conference on Machine Learning*, pages 21–29. Morgan Kaufmann, 1995.

[4] A. Blumer, A. Ehrenfeucht, D. Haussler, and M. Warmuth. Occam's razor. *Information Processing Letters*, 24:377–380, 1987.

[5] A. Blumer, A. Ehrenfeucht, D. Haussler, and M. Warmuth. Learnability and the Vapnik-Chervonenkis dimension. *Journal of the ACM*, 36(4):929–965, 1989.

[6] D. Dobkin, D. Gunopoulos, and S. Kasif. Computing optimal shallow decision trees. In *Proceedings of the International Workshop on Mathematics in Artificial Intelligence*, 1996.

[7] T. Erlebach, P. Rossmanith, H. Stadtherr, A. Steger, and T. Zeugmann. Learning one-variable pattern languages very efficiently on average, in parallel, and by asking queries. In Ming Li and Akira Maruoka, editors, *Algorithmic Learning Theory: Eighth International Workshop (ALT '97)*, volume 1316 of *Lecture Notes in Artificial Intelligence*, pages 260–276, 1997.

[8] E. M. Gold. Language identification in the limit. *Information and Control*, 10:447–474, 1967.

[9] D. Haussler. Decision theoretic generalizations of the PAC model for neural net and other learning applications. *Information and Computation*, 100(1):78–150, 1992.

[10] K. Hoeffgen, H. Simon, and K. van Horn. Robust trainability of single neurons. Preprint, 1993.

[11] M. Kearns and L. Pitt. A polynomial-time algorithm for learning $k$-variable pattern languages. In R. Rivest, D. Haussler, and M. Warmuth, editors, *Proceedings of the Second Annual Workshop on Computational Learning Theory*. Morgan Kaufmann, 1989.

[12] M. Kearns, R. Schapire, and L. Sellie. Towards efficient agnostic learning. In *Proceedings of the Fifth Annual Workshop on Computational Learning Theory*, pages 341–352. ACM Press, 1992.

[13] K.-I Ko, A. Marron, and W.-G. Tseng. Learning string patterns and tree patterns from examples. In *Machine Learning: Proceedings of the Seventh International Conference*, pages 384–391, 1990.

[14] S. Lange and T. Zeugmann. Monotonic versus non-monotonic language learning. In G. Brewka, K. Jantke, and P. H. Schmitt, editors, *Proceedings of the Second International Workshop on Nonmonotonic and Inductive Logic*, volume 659 of *Lecture Notes in Artificial Intelligence*, pages 254–269. Springer-Verlag, 1993.

[15] A. Marron. Learning pattern languages from a single initial example and from queries. In D Haussler and L. Pitt, editors, *Proceedings of the First Annual Workshop on Computational Learning Theory*, pages 345–358. Morgan Kaufmann, 1988.

[16] A. Marron and K. Ko. Identification of pattern languages from examples and queries. *Information and Computation*, 74(2), 1987.

[17] A. Mitchell. Learnability of a subclass of extended pattern languages. In *Proceedings of the Eleventh Annual Conference on Computational Learning Theory*. ACM Press, 1998.

[18] R. Reischuk and T. Zeugmann. Learning one-variable pattern languages in linear average time. In *Proceedings of the Eleventh Annual Conference on Computational Learning Theory*, pages 198–208. ACM Press, 1998.

[19] P. Rossmanith and T. Zeugmann. Learning $k$-variable pattern languages efficiently stochastically finite on average from positive data. In *Proc. 4th International Colloquium on Grammatical Inference (ICGI-98)*, LNAI 1433, pages 13–24. Springer, 1998.

[20] A. Salomaa. Patterns (The Formal Language Theory Column). *EATCS Bulletin*, 54:46–62, 1994.

[21] A. Salomaa. Return to patterns (The Formal Language Theory Column). *EATCS Bulletin*, 55:144–157, 1994.

[22] R.E. Schapire. Pattern languages are not learnable. In M. Fulk and J. Case, editors, *Proceedings of the Third Annual Workshop on Computational Learning Theory*, pages 122–129. Morgan Kaufmann, 1990.

[23] T. Shinohara. Polynomial time inference of extended regular pattern languages. In *RIMS Symposia on Software Science and Engineering, Kyoto, Japan*, volume 147 of *Lecture Notes in Computer Science*, pages 115–127. Springer-Verlag, 1982.

[24] T. Shinohara and A. Arikawa. Pattern inference. In Klaus P. Jantke and Steffen Lange, editors, *Algorithmic Learning for Knowledge-Based Systems*, volume 961 of *Lecture Notes in Artificial Intelligence*, pages 259–291. Springer-Verlag, 1995.

[25] L. Valiant. A theory of the learnable. *Communications of the ACM*, 27:1134–1142, 1984.

# On the $V_\gamma$ Dimension for Regression in Reproducing Kernel Hilbert Spaces

Theodoros Evgeniou and Massimiliano Pontil

Center for Biological and Computational Learning, MIT
45 Carleton Street E25-201, Cambridge, MA 02142, USA
{theos,pontil}@ai.mit.edu

**Abstract.** This paper presents a computation of the $V_\gamma$ dimension for regression in bounded subspaces of Reproducing Kernel Hilbert Spaces (RKHS) for the Support Vector Machine (SVM) regression $\epsilon$-insensitive loss function $L_\epsilon$, and general $L_p$ loss functions. Finiteness of the $V_\gamma$ dimension is shown, which also proves uniform convergence in probability for regression machines in RKHS subspaces that use the $L_\epsilon$ or general $L_p$ loss functions. This paper presents a novel proof of this result. It also presents a computation of an upper bound of the $V_\gamma$ dimension under some conditions, that leads to an approach for the estimation of the empirical $V_\gamma$ dimension given a set of training data.

## 1 Introduction

The $V_\gamma$ dimension, a variation of the VC-dimension [11], is important for the study of learning machines [1,5]. In this paper we present a computation of the $V_\gamma$ dimension of real-valued functions $L(y, f(\mathbf{x})) = |y - f(\mathbf{x})|^p$ and (Vapnik's $\epsilon$-insensitive loss function $L_\epsilon$ [11]) $L(y, f(\mathbf{x})) = |y - f(\mathbf{x})|_\epsilon$ with $f$ in a bounded sphere in a Reproducing Kernel Hilbert Space (RKHS). We show that the $V_\gamma$ dimension is finite for these loss functions, and compute an upper bound on it. We also present a second computation of the $V_\gamma$ dimension in a special case of infinite dimensional RKHS, which is often the type of hypothesis spaces considered in the literature (i.e. Radial Basis Functions [9,6]). It also holds for the case when a bias is added to the functions, that is with $f$ being of the form $f = f_0 + b$, where $b \in R$ and $f_0$ is in a sphere in an infinite dimensional RKHS. This computation leads to an approach for computing the empirical $V_\gamma$ dimension (or random entropy of a hypothesis space [11]) given a set of training data, an issue that we discuss at the end of the paper. Our result applies to standard regression learning machines such as Regularization Networks (RN) and Support Vector Machines (SVM).

For a regression learning problem using $L$ as a loss function it is known [1] that finiteness of the $V_\gamma$ dimension for all $\gamma > 0$ is a necessary and sufficient condition for uniform convergence in probability [11]. So the results of this paper have implications for uniform convergence both for RN and for SVM regression [5].

O. Watanabe, T. Yokomori (Eds.): ALT'99, LNAI 1720, pp. 106–117, 1999.
© Springer-Verlag Berlin Heidelberg 1999

Previous related work addressed the problem of pattern recognition where $L$ is an indicator function [3,7]. The fat-shattering dimension [1] was considered instead of the $V_\gamma$ one. A different approach to proving uniform convergence for RN and SVM is given in [13] where covering number arguments using entropy numbers of operators are presented. In both cases, regression as well as the case of non-zero bias $b$ were marginally considered.

The paper is organized as follows. Section 2 outlines the background and motivation of this work. The reader familiar with statistical learning theory and RKHS can skip this section. Section 3 presents a proof of the results as well as an upper bound to the $V_\gamma$ dimension. Section 4 presents a second computation of the $V_\gamma$ dimension in a special case of infinite dimensional RKHS, also when the hypothesis space consists of functions of the form $f = f_0 + b$ where $b \in R$ and $f_0$ in a sphere in a RKHS. Finally, section 5 discusses possible extensions of this work.

## 2   Background and Motivation

We consider the problem of learning from examples as it is viewed in the framework of statistical learning theory [11]. We are given a set of $l$ examples $\{(\mathbf{x}_1, y_1), .., (\mathbf{x}_l, y_l)\}$ generated by randomly sampling from a space $X \times Y$ with $X \subset R^d$, $Y \subset R$ according to an unknown probability distribution $P(\mathbf{x}, y)$. Throughout the paper we assume that $X$ and $Y$ are bounded. Using this set of examples the problem of learning consists of finding a function $f : X \to Y$ that can be used given any new point $\mathbf{x} \in X$ to predict the corresponding value $y$.

The problem of learning from examples is known to be ill-posed [11,10]. A classical way to solve it is to perform Empirical Risk Minimization (ERM) with respect to a certain loss function, while restricting the solution to the problem to be in a "small" hypothesis space [11]. Formally this means minimizing the empirical risk $I_{\mathrm{emp}}[f] = \frac{1}{l} \sum_{i=1}^{l} L(y_i, f(\mathbf{x}_i))$ with $f \in \mathcal{H}$, where $L$ is the loss function measuring the error when we predict $f(\mathbf{x})$ while the actual value is $y$, and $\mathcal{H}$ is a given hypothesis space.

In this paper, we consider hypothesis spaces of functions which are hyperplanes in some feature space:

$$f(\mathbf{x}) = \sum_{n=1}^{\infty} w_n \phi_n(\mathbf{x}) \tag{1}$$

with:

$$\sum_{n=1}^{\infty} \frac{w_n^2}{\lambda_n} < \infty \tag{2}$$

where $\phi_n(\mathbf{x})$ is a set of given, linearly independent basis functions, $\lambda_n$ are given non-negative constants such that $\sum_{n=1}^{\infty} \lambda_n < \infty$. Spaces of functions of the form (1) can also be seen as Reproducing Kernel Hilbert Spaces (RKHS) [2,12] with kernel $K$ given by:

$$K(\mathbf{x}, \mathbf{y}) \equiv \sum_{n=1}^{\infty} \lambda_n \phi_n(\mathbf{x}) \phi_n(\mathbf{y}). \qquad (3)$$

For any function $f$ as in (1), quantity (2) is called the RKHS norm of $f$, $\|f\|_K^2$, while the number $D$ of features $\phi_n$ (which can be finite, in which case all sums above are finite) is the dimensionality of the RKHS.

If we restrict the hypothesis space to consist of functions in a RKHS with norm less than a constant $A$, the general setting of learning discussed above becomes:

$$\text{Minimize}: \quad \frac{1}{l} \sum_{i=1}^{l} L(y_i, f(\mathbf{x}_i))$$
$$\text{subject to}: \quad \|f\|_K^2 \le A^2. \qquad (4)$$

An important question for any learning machine of the type (4) is whether it is consistent: as the number of examples $(\mathbf{x}_i, y_i)$ goes to infinity the expected error of the solution of the machine should converge in probability to the minimum expected error in the hypothesis space [11,4]. In the case of learning machines performing ERM in a hypothesis space (4), consistency is shown to be related with uniform convergence in probability [11], and necessary and sufficient conditions for uniform convergence are given in terms of the $V_\gamma$ dimension (also known as level fat shattering dimension) of the hypothesis space considered [1,8], which is a measure of complexity of the space.

In statistical learning theory typically the measure of complexity used is the VC-dimension. However, as we show below, the VC-dimension in the above learning setting in the case of infinite dimensional RKHS is infinite both for $L_p$ and $L_\epsilon$, so it cannot be used to study learning machines of the form (4). Instead one needs to consider other measures of complexity, such as the $V_\gamma$ dimension, in order to prove uniform convergence in infinite dimensional RKHS. We now present some background on the $V_\gamma$ dimension [1].

The $V_\gamma$ dimension of a set of real-valued functions is defined as follows:

**Definition 1.** *Let $C \le L(y, f(\mathbf{x})) \le B$, $f \in \mathcal{H}$, with $C$ and $B < \infty$. The $V_\gamma$-dimension of $L$ in $\mathcal{H}$ (of the set $\{L(y, f(\mathbf{x})), \ f \in \mathcal{H}\}$) is defined as the maximum number $h$ of vectors $(\mathbf{x}_1, y_1) \dots, (\mathbf{x}_h, y_h)$ that can be separated into two classes in all $2^h$ possible ways using rules:*

$$\text{class 1 if: } L(y_i, f(x_i)) \ge s + \gamma$$
$$\text{class -1 if: } L(y_i, f(x_i)) \le s - \gamma$$

*for $f \in \mathcal{H}$ and some $C + \gamma \le s \le B - \gamma$. If, for any number $N$, it is possible to find $N$ points $(\mathbf{x}_1, y_1) \dots, (\mathbf{x}_N, y_N)$ that can be separated in all the $2^N$ possible ways, we will say that the $V_\gamma$-dimension of $L$ in $\mathcal{H}$ is infinite.*

For $\gamma = 0$ and for $s$ being free to change values for each separation of the data, this becomes the VC dimension of the set of functions [11]. In the case of hyperplanes (1), the $V_\gamma$ dimension has also been referred to in the literature [11] as the *VC dimension of hyperplanes with margin*. In order to avoid confusion with names, we call the *VC dimension of hyperplanes with margin* as the

$V_\gamma$ dimension of hyperplanes (for appropriate $\gamma$ depending on the margin, as discussed below).

The $V_\gamma$ dimension can be used to bound the covering numbers of a set of functions [1], which are in turn related to the generalization performance of learning machines. Typically the fat-shattering dimension [1] is used for this purpose, but a close relation between that and the $V_\gamma$ dimension [1] makes the two equivalent for the purpose of bounding covering numbers and hence studying the statistical properties of a machine. The $VC$ dimension has been used to bound the growth function $\mathcal{G}^\mathcal{H}(l)$. This function measures the maximum number of ways we can separate $l$ points using functions from hypothesis space $\mathcal{H}$. If $h$ is the $VC$ dimension, then $\mathcal{G}^\mathcal{H}(l)$ is $2^l$ if $l \leq h$, and $\leq (\frac{el}{h})^h$ otherwise [11] (where $e$ is the standard natural logarithm constant). In section 3 we will use the growth function of hyperplanes with margin to bound their VC dimension, which, as discussed above, is their $V_\gamma$ dimension that we are interested in.

Using the $V_\gamma$ dimension Alon et al. [1] gave necessary and sufficient conditions for uniform convergence in probability to take place in a hypothesis space $\mathcal{H}$. In particular they proved the following important theorem:

**Theorem 1.** *(Alon et al. , 1997 ) Let $C \leq L(y, f(\mathbf{x}))) \leq B$, $f \in \mathcal{H}$, $\mathcal{H}$ be a set of bounded functions. The ERM method uniformly converges (in probability) if and only if the $V_\gamma$ dimension of $L$ in $\mathcal{H}$ is finite for every $\gamma > 0$.*

It is clear that if for learning machines of the form (4) the $V_\gamma$ dimension of the loss function $L$ in the hypothesis space defined is finite for $\forall \gamma > 0$, then uniform convergence takes place. In the next section we present a proof of the finiteness of the $V_\gamma$ dimension, as well as an upper bound on it.

## 2.1   Why Not Use the VC-Dimension

Consider first the case of $L_p$ loss functions. Consider an infinite dimensional RKHS, and the set of functions with norm $\|f\|_K^2 \leq A^2$. If for any $N$ we can find $N$ points that we can shatter using functions of our set according to the rule:

$$\text{class } 1 \text{ if} : \ |y - f(\mathbf{x})|^p \geq s$$
$$\text{class } -1 \text{ if} : \ |y - f(\mathbf{x})|^p \leq s$$

then clearly the $VC$ dimension is infinite. Consider $N$ distinct points $(\mathbf{x}_i, y_i)$ with $y_i = 0$ for all $i$, and let the smallest eigenvalue of matrix $G$ with $G_{ij} = K(\mathbf{x}_i, \mathbf{x}_j)$ be $\lambda$. Since we are in infinite dimensional RKHS, matrix $G$ is always invertible [12], so $\lambda > 0$ since $G$ is positive definite and finite dimensional ($\lambda$ may decrease as $N$ increases, but for any finite $N$ it is well defined and $\neq 0$).

For any separation of the points, we consider a function $f$ of the form $f(\mathbf{x}) = \sum_{i=1}^N \alpha_i K(\mathbf{x}_i, \mathbf{x})$, which is a function of the form (1). We need to show that we can find coefficients $\alpha_i$ such that the RKHS norm of the function is $\leq A^2$. Notice that the norm of a function of this form is $\boldsymbol{\alpha}^T G \boldsymbol{\alpha}$ where $(\boldsymbol{\alpha})_i = \alpha_i$ (throughout the paper bold letters are used for noting vectors). Consider the set of linear equations

$$\mathbf{x}_j \in \text{class } 1: \quad \sum_{i=1}^{N} \alpha_i G_{ij} = s^{\frac{1}{p}} + \eta \quad \eta > 0$$
$$\mathbf{x}_j \in \text{class } -1: \quad \sum_{i=1}^{N} \alpha_i G_{ij} = s^{\frac{1}{p}} - \eta \quad \eta > 0$$

Let $s = 0$. If we can find a solution $\boldsymbol{\alpha}$ to this system of equations such that $\boldsymbol{\alpha}^T G \boldsymbol{\alpha} \leq A^2$ we can perform this separation, and since this is any separation we can shatter the $N$ points. Notice that the solution to the system of equations is $G^{-1}\boldsymbol{\eta}$ where $\boldsymbol{\eta}$ is the vector whose components are $(\boldsymbol{\eta})_i = \eta$ when $\mathbf{x}_i$ is in class 1, and $-\eta$ otherwise. So we need $(G^{-1}\boldsymbol{\eta})^T G (G^{-1}\boldsymbol{\eta}) \leq A^2 \Rightarrow \boldsymbol{\eta}^T G^{-1}\boldsymbol{\eta} \leq A^2$. Since the smallest eigenvalue of $G$ is $\lambda > 0$, we have that $\boldsymbol{\eta}^T G^{-1}\boldsymbol{\eta} \leq \frac{\boldsymbol{\eta}^T\boldsymbol{\eta}}{\lambda}$. Moreover $\boldsymbol{\eta}^T\boldsymbol{\eta} = N\eta^2$. So if we choose $\eta$ small enough such that $\frac{N\eta^2}{\lambda} \leq A^2 \Rightarrow \eta^2 \leq \frac{A^2\lambda}{N}$, the norm of the solution is less than $A^2$, which completes the proof.

For the case of the $L_\epsilon$ loss function the argument above can be repeated with $y_i = \epsilon$ to prove again that the VC dimension is infinite in an infinite dimensional RKHS.

Finally, notice that the same proof can be repeated for finite dimensional RKHS to show that the $VC$ dimension is never less than the dimensionality $D$ of the RKHS, since it is possible to find $D$ points for which matrix $G$ is invertible and repeat the proof above. As a consequence the VC dimension cannot be controlled by $A^2$. This is also discussed in [13].

## 3    An Upper Bound on the $V_\gamma$ Dimension

Below we always assume that data $X$ are within a sphere of radius $R$ in the feature space defined by the kernel $K$ of the RKHS. Without loss of generality, we also assume that $y$ is bounded between $-1$ and $1$. Under these assumptions the following theorem holds:

**Theorem 2.** *The $V_\gamma$ dimension $h$ for regression using $L_p$ ($1 \leq p < \infty$) or $L_\epsilon$ loss functions for hypothesis spaces $\mathcal{H}_A = \{f(\mathbf{x}) = \sum_{n=1}^{\infty} w_n \phi_n(\mathbf{x}) \mid \sum_{n=1}^{\infty} \frac{w_n^2}{\lambda_n} \leq A^2\}$ and $y$ bounded, is finite for $\forall \gamma > 0$. If $D$ is the dimensionality of the RKHS, then $h \leq O(min(D, \frac{(R^2+1)(A^2+1)}{\gamma^2}))$.*

**Proof.** Let's consider first the case of the $L_1$ loss function. Let $B$ be the upper bound on the loss function. From definition 1 we can decompose the rules for separating points as follows:

$$\begin{aligned} \text{class } 1 \text{ if } & y_i - f(\mathbf{x}_i) \geq s + \gamma \\ \text{or } & y_i - f(\mathbf{x}_i) \leq -(s + \gamma) \\ \text{class } -1 \text{ if } & y_i - f(\mathbf{x}_i) \leq s - \gamma \\ \text{and } & y_i - f(\mathbf{x}_i) \geq -(s - \gamma) \end{aligned} \quad (5)$$

for some $\gamma \leq s \leq B - \gamma$. For any $N$ points, the number of separations of the points we can get using rules (5) is not more than the number of separations we can get using the product of two indicator functions with margin (of hyperplanes with margin):

$$
\begin{aligned}
\text{function (a)}: \quad &\text{class } 1 \text{ if } y_i - f_1(\mathbf{x}_i) \geq s_1 + \gamma \\
&\text{class } -1 \text{ if } y_i - f_1(\mathbf{x}_i) \leq s_1 - \gamma \\
\text{function (b)}: \quad &\text{class } 1 \text{ if } y_i - f_2(\mathbf{x}_i) \geq -(s_2 - \gamma) \\
&\text{class } -1 \text{ if } y_i - f_2(\mathbf{x}_i) \leq -(s_2 + \gamma)
\end{aligned}
\tag{6}
$$

where $f_1$ and $f_2$ are in $\mathcal{H}_A$, $\gamma \leq s_1, s_2 \leq B - \gamma$. This is shown as follows.

Clearly the product of the two indicator functions (6) has less "separating power" when we add the constraints $s_1 = s_2 = s$ and $f_1 = f_2 = f$. Furthermore, even with these constraints we still have more "separating power" than we have using rules (5): any separation realized using (5) can also be realized using the product of the two indicator functions (6) under the constraints $s_1 = s_2 = s$ and $f_1 = f_2 = f$. For example, if $y - f(\mathbf{x}) \geq s + \gamma$ then indicator function (a) will give $+1$, indicator function (b) will give also $+1$, so their product will give $+1$ which is what we get if we follow (5). Similarly for all other cases.

As mentioned in the previous section, for any $N$ points the number of ways we can separate them is bounded by the growth function. Moreover, for products of indicator functions it is known [11] that the growth function is bounded by the product of the growth functions of the indicator functions. Furthermore, the indicator functions in (6) are hyperplanes with margin in the $D + 1$ dimensional space of vectors $\{\phi_n(\mathbf{x}), y\}$ where the radius of the data is $R^2 + 1$, the norm of the hyperplane is bounded by $A^2 + 1$, (where in both cases we add 1 because of $y$), and the margin is at least $\frac{\gamma^2}{A^2+1}$. The $V_\gamma$ dimension $h_\gamma$ of these hyperplanes is known [11,3] to be bounded by $h_\gamma \leq \min((D+1)+1, \frac{(R^2+1)(A^2+1)}{\gamma^2})$. So the growth function of the separating rules (5) is bounded by the product of the growth functions $(\frac{el}{h_\gamma})^{h_\gamma}$, that is $\mathcal{G}(l) \leq \left((\frac{el}{h_\gamma})^{h_\gamma}\right)^2$ whenever $l \geq h_\gamma$. If $h_\gamma^{reg}$ is the $V_\gamma$ dimension, then $h_\gamma^{reg}$ cannot be larger than the larger number $l$ for which inequality $2^l \leq (\frac{el}{h_\gamma})^{2h_\gamma}$ holds. From this, after some algebraic manipulations (take the log of both sides) we get that $l \leq 5h_\gamma$, therefore $h_\gamma^{reg} \leq 5 \min (D + 2, \frac{(R^2+1)(A^2+1)}{\gamma^2})$ which proves the theorem for the case of $L_1$ loss functions.

For general $L_p$ loss functions we can follow the same proof where (5) now needs to be rewritten as:

$$
\begin{aligned}
&\text{class } 1 \text{ if } y_i - f(\mathbf{x}_i) \geq (s + \gamma)^{\frac{1}{p}} \\
&\quad\quad \text{or } f(\mathbf{x}_i) - y_i \geq (s + \gamma)^{\frac{1}{p}} \\
&\text{class } -1 \text{ if } y_i - f(\mathbf{x}_i) \leq (s - \gamma)^{\frac{1}{p}} \\
&\quad\quad \text{and } f(\mathbf{x}_i) - y_i \leq (s - \gamma)^{\frac{1}{p}}
\end{aligned}
\tag{7}
$$

Moreover, for $1 < p < \infty$, $(s+\gamma)^{\frac{1}{p}} \geq s^{\frac{1}{p}} + \frac{\gamma}{pB}$ (since $\gamma = \left((s+\gamma)^{\frac{1}{p}}\right)^p - \left(s^{\frac{1}{p}}\right)^p = ((s+\gamma)^{\frac{1}{p}} - s^{\frac{1}{p}})(((s+\gamma)^{\frac{1}{p}})^{p-1} + \ldots + (s^{\frac{1}{p}})^{p-1}) \leq ((s+\gamma)^{\frac{1}{p}} - s^{\frac{1}{p}})(B + \ldots B) = ((s+\gamma)^{\frac{1}{p}} - s^{\frac{1}{p}})(pB)$ ) and $(s-\gamma)^{\frac{1}{p}} \leq s^{\frac{1}{p}} - \frac{\gamma}{pB}$ (similarly). Repeating the same argument as above, we get that the $V_\gamma$ dimension is bounded by $5 \min (D + 2, \frac{(pB)^2(R^2+1)(A^2+1)}{\gamma^2})$. Finally, for the $L_\epsilon$ loss function (5) can be rewritten as:

$$
\begin{aligned}
&\text{class } 1 \text{ if } y_i - f(\mathbf{x}_i) \geq s + \gamma + \epsilon \\
&\quad\text{or } f(\mathbf{x}_i) - y_i \geq s + \gamma + \epsilon \\
&\text{class } -1 \text{ if } y_i - f(\mathbf{x}_i) \leq s - \gamma + \epsilon \\
&\quad\text{and } f(\mathbf{x}_i) - y_i \leq s - \gamma + \epsilon
\end{aligned}
\tag{8}
$$

where calling $s' = s + \epsilon$ we can simply repeat the proof above and get the same upper bound on the $V_\gamma$ dimension as in the case of the $L_1$ loss function. (Notice that the constraint $\gamma \leq s \leq B - \gamma$ is not taken into account. Taking this into account may slightly change the $V_\gamma$ dimension for $L_\epsilon$. Since it is a constraint, it can only decrease - or not change - the $V_\gamma$ dimension).

These results imply that in the case of infinite dimensional RKHS the $V_\gamma$ dimension is still finite and is influenced only by $5 \frac{(R^2+1)(A^2+1)}{\gamma^2}$. In the next section we present a different upper bound on the $V_\gamma$ dimension in a special case of infinite dimensional RKHS.

## 4    The $V_\gamma$ Dimension in a Special Case

Below we assume that the data $\mathbf{x}$ are restricted so that for any finite dimensional matrix $G$ with entries $G_{ij} = K(\mathbf{x}_i, \mathbf{x}_j)$ (where $K$ is, as mentioned in the previous section, the kernel of the RKHS considered, and $\mathbf{x}_i \neq \mathbf{x}_j$ for $i \neq j$) the largest eigenvalue of $G$ is always $\leq M^2$ for a given constant $M$. We consider only the case that the RKHS is infinite dimensional. We note with $B$ the upper bound of $L(y, f(\mathbf{x}))$. Under these assumptions we can show that:

**Theorem 3.** *The $V_\gamma$ dimension for regression using $L_1$ loss function and for hypothesis space $\mathcal{H}_A = \{f(\mathbf{x}) = \sum_{n=1}^\infty w_n \phi_n(\mathbf{x}) + b \mid \sum_{n=1}^\infty \frac{w_n^2}{\lambda_n} \leq A^2\}$ is finite for $\forall \gamma > 0$. In particular:*

1. *If $b$ is constrained to be zero, then $V_\gamma \leq \left\lceil \frac{M^2 A^2}{\gamma^2} \right\rceil$*

2. *If $b$ is a free parameter, $V_\gamma \leq 4 \left\lceil \frac{M^2 A^2}{\gamma^2} \right\rceil$*

**Proof of part 1.**

Suppose we can find $N > \left\lceil \frac{M^2 A^2}{\gamma^2} \right\rceil$ points $\{(x_1, y_1), ..., (x_N, y_N)\}$ that we can shatter. Let $s \in [\gamma, B - \gamma]$ be the value of the parameter used to shatter the points.

Consider the following "separation"[1]: if $|y_i| < s$, then $(x_i, y_i)$ belongs in class 1. All other points belong in class -1. For this separation we need:

$$
\begin{aligned}
|y_i - f(x_i)| \geq s + \gamma, \text{ if } |y_i| < s \\
|y_i - f(x_i)| \leq s - \gamma, \text{ if } |y_i| \geq s
\end{aligned}
\tag{9}
$$

---

[1] Notice that this separation might be a "trivial" one in the sense that we may want all the points to be +1 or all to be -1 i.e. when all $|y_i| < s$ or when all $|y_i| \geq s$ respectively.

This means that: for points in class 1 $f$ takes values either $y_i + s + \gamma + \delta_i$ or $y_i - s - \gamma - \delta_i$, for $\delta_i \geq 0$. For points in the second class $f$ takes values either $y_i + s - \gamma - \delta_i$ or $y_i - s + \gamma + \delta_i$, for $\delta_i \in [0, (s - \gamma)]$. So (9) can be seen as a system of linear equations:

$$\sum_{n=1}^{\infty} w_n \phi_n(\mathbf{x}_i) = t_i. \tag{10}$$

with $t_i$ being $y_i + s + \gamma + \delta_i$, or $y_i - s - \gamma - \delta_i$, or $y_i + s - \gamma - \delta_i$, or $y_i - s + \gamma + \delta_i$, depending on $i$. We first use lemma 1 to show that for any solution (so $t_i$ are fixed now) there is another solution with not larger norm that is of the form $\sum_{i=1}^{N} \alpha_i K(\mathbf{x}_i, \mathbf{x})$.

**Lemma 1.** *Among all the solutions of a system of equations (10) the solution with the minimum RKHS norm is of the form:* $\sum_{i=1}^{N} \alpha_i K(\mathbf{x}_i, \mathbf{x})$ *with* $\boldsymbol{\alpha} = G^{-1}t$.

For a proof see the Appendix. Given this lemma, we consider only functions of the form $\sum_{i=1}^{N} \alpha_i K(\mathbf{x}_i, \mathbf{x})$. We show that the function of this form that solves the system of equations (10) has norm larger than $A^2$. Therefore any other solution has norm larger than $A^2$ which implies we cannot shatter $N$ points using functions of our hypothesis space.

The solution $\boldsymbol{\alpha} = G^{-1}t$ needs to satisfy the constraint:

$$\boldsymbol{\alpha}^T G \boldsymbol{\alpha} = t^T G^{-1} t \leq A^2$$

Let $\lambda_{max}$ be the largest eigenvalue of matrix $G$. Then $t^T G^{-1} t \geq \frac{t^T t}{\lambda_{max}}$. Since $\lambda_{max} \leq M^2$, $t^T G^{-1} t \geq \frac{t^T t}{M^2}$. Moreover, because of the choice of the separation, $t^T t \geq N\gamma^2$ (for example, for the points in class 1 which contribute to $t^T t$ an amount equal to $(y_i + s + \gamma + \delta_i)^2$: $|y_i| < s \Rightarrow y_i + s > 0$, and since $\gamma + \delta_i \geq \gamma > 0$, then $(y_i + s + \gamma + \delta_i)^2 \geq \gamma^2$. Similarly each of the other points "contribute" to $t^T t$ at least $\gamma^2$, so $t^T t \geq N\gamma^2$). So:

$$t^T G^{-1} t \geq \frac{N\gamma^2}{M^2} > A^2$$

since we assumed that $N > \frac{M^2 A^2}{\gamma^2}$. This is a contradiction, so we conclude that we cannot get this particular separation.

**Proof of part 2.**
Consider N points that can be shattered. This means that for any separation, for points in the first class there are $\delta_i \geq 0$ such that $|f(x_i) + b - y_i| = s + \gamma + \delta_i$. For points in the second class there are $\delta_i \in [0, s - \gamma]$ such that $|f(x_i) + b - y_i| = s - \gamma - \delta_i$. As in the case $b = 0$ we can remove the absolute values by considering for each class two types of points (we call them type 1 and type 2). For class 1, type 1 are points for which $f(x_i) = y_i + s + \gamma + \delta_i - b = t_i - b$. Type 2 are points for which $f(x_i) = y_i - s - \gamma - \delta_i - b = t_i - b$. For class 2, type 1

are points for which $f(x_i) = y_i + s - \gamma - \delta_i - b = t_i - b$. Type 2 are points for which $f(x_i) = y_i - s + \gamma + \delta_i - b = t_i - b$. Variables $t_i$ are as in the case $b = 0$. Let $S_{11}, S_{12}, S_{-11}, S_{-12}$ denote the four sets of points ($S_{ij}$ are points of class $i$ type $j$). Using lemma 1, we only need to consider functions of the form $f(x) = \sum_{i=1}^{N} \alpha_i K(x_i, x)$. The coefficients $\alpha_i$ are given by $\alpha = G^{-1}(t - b)$ there $b$ is a vector of $b$'s. As in the case $b = 0$, the RKHS norm of this function is at least

$$\frac{1}{M^2}(t - b)^T(t - b). \tag{11}$$

The $b$ that minimizes (11) is $\frac{1}{N}(\sum_{i=1}^{N} t_i)$. So (11) is at least as large as (after replacing $b$ and doing some simple calculations) $\frac{1}{2NM^2}\sum_{i,j=1}^{N}(t_i - t_j)^2$.

We now consider a particular separation. Without loss of generality assume that $y_1 \leq y_2 \leq \ldots \leq y_N$ and that $N$ is even (if odd, consider $N - 1$ points). Consider the separation where class 1 consists only of the "even" points $\{N, N - 2, \ldots, 2\}$. The following lemma is shown in the appendix:

**Lemma 2.** *For the separation considered, $\sum_{i,j=1}^{N}(t_i - t_j)^2$ is at least as large as* $\frac{\gamma^2(N^2-4)}{2}$.

Using Lemma 2 we get that the norm of the solution for the considered separation is at least as large as $\frac{\gamma^2(N^2-4)}{4NM^2}$. Since this has to be $\leq A^2$ we get that $N - \frac{4}{N} \leq 4\left[\frac{M^2A^2}{\gamma^2}\right]$, which completes the proof (assume $N > 4$ and ignore additive constants less than 1 for simplicity of notation).

In the case of $L_p$ loss functions, using the same argument as in the previous section we get that the $V_\gamma$ dimension in infinite dimensional RKHS is bounded by $\frac{(pB)^2M^2A^2}{\gamma^2}$ in the first case of theorem 3, and by $4\frac{(pB)^2M^2A^2}{\gamma^2}$ in the second case of theorem 3. Finally for $L_\epsilon$ loss functions the bound on the $V_\gamma$ dimension is the same as that for $L_1$ loss function, again using the argument of the previous section.

## 4.1   Empirical $V_\gamma$ Dimension

Above we assumed a bound on the eigenvalues of *any* finite dimensional matrix $G$. However such a bound may not be known a priori, or it may not even exist, in which case the computation is not valid. In practice we can still use the method presented above to measure the empirical $V_\gamma$ dimension given a set of $l$ training points. This can provide an upper bound on the random entropy of our hypothesis space [11].

More precisely, given a set of $l$ training points we build the $l \times l$ matrix $G$ as before, and compute it's largest eigenvalue $\lambda_{\max}$. We can then substitute $M^2$ with $\lambda_{\max}$ in the computation above to get an upper bound of what we call the empirical $V_\gamma$ dimension. This can be used directly to get bounds on the random entropy (or number of ways that the $l$ training points can be separated using rules (5)) of our hypothesis space. Finally the statistical properties of our learning machine can be studied using the estimated empirical $V_\gamma$ dimension (or the random entropy), in a way similar in spirit as in [13].

## 5   Conclusion

We presented a novel approach for computing the $V_\gamma$ dimension of RKHS for $L_p$ and $L_\epsilon$ loss functions. We conclude with a few remarks. First notice that in the computations we did not take into account $\epsilon$ in the case of $L_\epsilon$ loss function. Taking $\epsilon$ into account may lead to better bounds. For example, considering $|f(x) - y|_\epsilon^p, p > 1$ as the loss function, it is clear from the proofs presented that the $V_\gamma$ dimension is bounded by $\frac{p^2(B-\epsilon)^2 M^2 A^2}{\gamma^2}$. However the influence of $\epsilon$ seems to be minor (given that $\epsilon << B$).

An interesting observation is that the eigenvalues of the matrix $G$ appear in the computation of the $V_\gamma$ dimension. In the second computation we took into account only the largest and smallest eigenvalues. If the computation is made to upper bound the number of separations for a given set of points (random entropy or empirical $V_\gamma$ dimension) as discussed in section 4.1, then it may be possible that all the eigenvalues of $G$ are taken into account. This can lead to interesting relations with the work in [13].

### Acknowledgments
We would like to thank S. Mukherjee, T. Poggio, R. Rifkin, and A. Verri for useful discussions and comments.

## References

1. N. Alon, S. Ben-David, N. Cesa-Bianchi, and D. Haussler. Scale-sensitive dimensions, uniform convergence, and learnability. *J. of the ACM*, 44(4):615–631, 1997.
2. N. Aronszajn. Theory of reproducing kernels. *Trans. Amer. Math. Soc.*, 686:337–404, 1950.
3. P. Bartlett and J. Shawe-Taylor. Generalization performance of support vector machine and other pattern classifiers. In C. Burges B. Scholkopf, editor, *Advances in Kernel Methods-Support Vector Learning*. MIT press, 1998.
4. L. Devroye, L. Györfi, and G. Lugosi. *A Probabilistic Theory of Pattern Recognition*. Number 31 in Applications of mathematics. Springer, New York, 1996.
5. T. Evgeniou, M. Pontil, and T. Poggio. A unified framework for regularization networks and support vector machines. A.I. Memo No. 1654, Artificial Intelligence Laboratory, Massachusetts Institute of Technology, 1999.
6. F. Girosi, M. Jones, and T. Poggio. Regularization theory and neural networks architectures. *Neural Computation*, 7:219–269, 1995.
7. L. Gurvits. A note on scale-sensitive dimension of linear bounded functionals in Banach spaces. In *Proceedings of Algorithm Learning Theory*, 1997.
8. M. Kearns and R.E. Shapire. Efficient distribution-free learning of probabilistic concepts. *Journal of Computer and Systems Sciences*, 48(3):464–497, 1994.

9. M.J.D. Powell. The theory of radial basis functions approximation in 1990. In W.A. Light, editor, *Advances in Numerical Analysis Volume II: Wavelets, Subdivision Algorithms and Radial Basis Functions*, pages 105–210. Oxford University Press, 1992.
10. A. N. Tikhonov and V. Y. Arsenin. *Solutions of Ill-posed Problems*. W. H. Winston, Washington, D.C., 1977.
11. V. N. Vapnik. *Statistical Learning Theory*. Wiley, New York, 1998.
12. G. Wahba. *Splines Models for Observational Data*. Series in Applied Mathematics, Vol. 59, SIAM, Philadelphia, 1990.
13. R. Williamson, A. Smola, and B. Scholkopf. Generalization performance of regularization networks and support vector machines via entropy numbers. Technical Report NC-TR-98-019, Royal Holloway College University of London, 1998.

# Appendix

### Proof of Lemma 1

We introduce the $N \times \infty$ matrix $A_{in} = \sqrt{\lambda_n}\phi_n(\mathbf{x}_i)$ and the new variable $z_n = \frac{w_n}{\sqrt{\lambda_n}}$. We can write system (10) as follows:

$$A\mathbf{z} = \mathbf{t}. \tag{12}$$

Notice that the solution of the system of equation 10 with minimum RKHS norm, is equivalent to the Least Square (LS) solution of equation 12. Let us denote with $\mathbf{z}^0$ the LS solution of system 12. We have:

$$\mathbf{z}^0 = (A^\top A)^+ A^\top \mathbf{t} \tag{13}$$

where + denotes pseudoinverse. To see how this solution looks like we use Singular Value Decomposition techniques:

$$A = U\Sigma V^\top,$$
$$A^\top = V\Sigma U^\top,$$

from which $A^\top A = V\Sigma^2 V^\top$ and $(A^\top A)^+ = V_N \Sigma_N^{-2} V_N^\top$, where $\Sigma_N^{-1}$ denotes the $N \times N$ matrix whose elements are the inverse of the nonzero eigenvalues. After some computations equation (13) can be written as:

$$\mathbf{z}^0 = V\Sigma_N^{-1} U_N^\top \mathbf{t} = (V\Sigma_N U_N^\top)(U_N\Sigma_N^{-2}U_N^\top)\mathbf{t} = AG^{-1}\mathbf{t}. \tag{14}$$

Using the definition of $\mathbf{z}^0$ we have that

$$\sum_{n=1}^{\infty} w_n^0 \phi_n(\mathbf{x}) = \sum_{n=1}^{\infty}\sum_{i=1}^{N} \sqrt{\lambda_n}\phi_n(\mathbf{x})A_{ni}\alpha_i. \tag{15}$$

Finally, using the definition of $A_{in}$ we get:

$$\sum_{n=1}^{\infty} w_n^0 \phi_n(\mathbf{x}) = \sum_{i=1}^{N} K(\mathbf{x}, \mathbf{x}_i)\alpha_i$$

which completes the proof.

**Proof of Lemma 2**

Consider a point $(x_i, y_i)$ in $S_{11}$ and a point $(x_j, y_j)$ in $S_{-11}$ such that $y_i \geq y_j$ (if such a pair does not exist we can consider another pair from the cases listed below). For these points $(t_i - t_j)^2 = (y_i + s + \gamma + \delta_i - y_j - s + \gamma + \delta_j)^2 = ((y_i - y_j) + 2\gamma + \delta_i + \delta_j)^2 \geq 4\gamma^2$. In a similar way (taking into account the constraints on the $\delta_i$'s and on $s$) the inequality $(t_i - t_j)^2 \geq 4\gamma^2$ can be shown to hold in the following two cases:

$$
\begin{aligned}
(x_i, y_i) \in S_{11}, \; (x_j, y_j) \in S_{-11} \bigcup S_{-12}, \; y_i \geq y_j \\
(x_i, y_i) \in S_{12}, \; (x_j, y_j) \in S_{-11} \bigcup S_{-12}, \; y_i \leq y_j
\end{aligned}
\tag{16}
$$

Moreover

$$
\sum_{i,j=1}^{N}(t_i - t_j)^2 \geq 2 \left[ \sum_{i \in S_{11}} \left( \sum_{j \in S_{-11} \bigcup S_{-12}, y_i \geq y_j} (t_i - t_j)^2 \right) \right] + \\
2 \left[ \sum_{i \in S_{12}} \left( \sum_{j \in S_{-11} \bigcup S_{-12}, y_i \leq y_j} (t_i - t_j)^2 \right) \right].
\tag{17}
$$

since in the right hand side we excluded some of the terms of the left hand side. Using the fact that for the cases considered $(t_i - t_j)^2 \geq 4\gamma^2$, the right hand side is at least

$$
8\gamma^2 \sum_{i \in S_{11}} (\text{number of points } j \text{ in class } -1 \text{ with } y_i \geq y_j) + \\
+ 8\gamma^2 \sum_{i \in S_{12}} (\text{number of points } j \text{ in class } -1 \text{ with } y_i \leq y_j)
\tag{18}
$$

Let $I_1$ and $I_2$ be the cardinalities of $S_{11}$ and $S_{12}$ respectively. Because of the choice of the separation it is clear that (18) is at least

$$
8\gamma^2 \left( (1 + 2 + \ldots + I_1)) + (1 + 2 + \ldots + (I_2 - 1)) \right)
$$

(for example if $I_1 = 2$ in the worst case points 2 and 4 are in $S_{11}$ in which case the first part of (18) is exactly 1+2). Finally, since $I_1 + I_2 = \frac{N}{2}$, (18) is at least $8\gamma^2 \frac{N^2-4}{16} = \frac{\gamma^2(N^2-4)}{2}$, which proves the lemma.

# On the Strength of Incremental Learning

Steffen Lange[1] and Gunter Grieser[2]

[1] Universität Leipzig, Institut für Informatik
Augustusplatz 10–11, 04109 Leipzig, Germany
slange@informatik.uni-leipzig.de
[2] Technische Universität Darmstadt, Fachbereich Informatik
Alexanderstraße 10, 64283 Darmstadt, Germany
grieser@informatik.tu-darmstadt.de

**Abstract.** This paper provides a systematic study of incremental learning from noise-free and from noisy data, thereby distinguishing between
learning from only positive data and from both positive and negative
data. Our study relies on the notion of noisy data introduced in [22].

The basic scenario, named *iterative* learning, is as follows. In every learning stage, an algorithmic learner takes as input one element of an information sequence for a target concept and its previously made hypothesis
and outputs a new hypothesis. The sequence of hypotheses has to converge to a hypothesis describing the target concept correctly.

We study the following refinements of this scenario. *Bounded example-
memory* inference generalizes iterative inference by allowing an iterative
learner to additionally store an *a priori* bounded number of carefully
chosen data elements, while *feedback* learning generalizes it by allowing
the iterative learner to additionally ask whether or not a particular data
element did already appear in the data seen so far.

For the case of learning from noise-free data, we show that, where both
positive and negative data are available, restrictions on the accessibility
of the input data do not limit the learning capabilities if and only if
the relevant iterative learners are allowed to query the history of the
learning process or to store at least one carefully selected data element.
This insight nicely contrasts the fact that, in case only positive data
are available, restrictions on the accessibility of the input data seriously
affect the capabilities of all types of incremental learning (cf. [18]).

For the case of learning from noisy data, we present characterizations
of all kinds of incremental learning in terms being independent from
learning theory. The relevant conditions are purely structural ones. Surprisingly, where learning from only noisy positive data and from both
noisy positive and negative data, iterative learners are already exactly
as powerful as unconstrained learning devices.

## 1  Introduction

The theoretical investigations in the present paper derive their motivation to
a certain extent from the rapidly developing field of knowledge discovery in

O. Watanabe, T. Yokomori (Eds.): ALT'99, LNAI 1720, pp. 118–131, 1999.
© Springer-Verlag Berlin Heidelberg 1999

databases (abbr. KDD). KDD mainly combines techniques originating from machine learning, knowledge acquisition and knowledge representation, artificial intelligence, pattern recognition, statistics, data visualization, and databases to automatically extract new interrelations, knowledge, patterns and the like from huge collections of data (cf. [7], for a recent overview).

Among the different parts of the KDD process, like data presentation, data selection, incorporating prior knowledge, and defining the semantics of the results obtained, we are mainly interested in the particular subprocess of applying specific algorithms for learning something useful from the data. This subprocess is usually named data mining. There is one problem when invoking machine learning techniques to do data mining. Almost all machine learning algorithms are "in-memory" algorithms, i.e., they require the whole data set to be present in the main memory when extracting the concepts hidden in the data. However, if huge data sets are around, no learning algorithm can use all the data or even large portions of it simultaneously for computing hypotheses. Different methods have been proposed for overcoming the difficulties caused by huge data sets. For example, instead of doing the discovery process on all the data, one starts with significantly smaller samples, finds the regularities in it, and uses different portions of the overall data to verify what one has found.

Looking at data mining from this perspective, it becomes a true limiting process. That means, the actual hypothesis generated by the data mining algorithm is tested versus parts of the remaining data. Then, if the current hypothesis is not acceptable, the sample may be enlarged or replaced and the data mining algorithm will be restarted. Thus, from a theoretical point of view, it is appropriate to look at the data mining process as an ongoing, incremental one.

For the purpose of motivation and discussion of our research, we next introduce some basic notions. By $\mathcal{X}$ we denote any learning domain. Any collection $\mathcal{C}$ of sets $c \subseteq \mathcal{X}$ is called a concept class. Moreover, $c$ is referred to as concept. An algorithmic learner, henceforth called *inductive inference machine* (abbr. IIM), takes as input initial segments of an information sequence and outputs, once in a while, a hypothesis about the target concept. The set $\mathcal{H}$ of all admissible hypotheses is called *hypothesis space*. The sequence of hypotheses has to converge to a hypothesis describing the target concept correctly. If there is an IIM that learns a concept $c$ from all admissible information sequences for it, then $c$ is said to be *learnable in the limit* with respect to $\mathcal{H}$ (cf. [10]).

Gold's [10] model of learning in the limit relies on the unrealistic assumption that the learner has access to samples of growing size. Therefore, we investigate variations of the general approach that restrict the accessibility of the input data considerably. We deal with *iterative* learning, *k-bounded example-memory* inference, and *feedback* identification of indexable concept classes. All these models formalize *incremental learning*, a topic attracting more and more attention in the machine learning community (cf., e.g., [6,9,20,24]).

An iterative learner is required to produce its actual guess exclusively from its previous one and the next element in the information sequence presented. Iterative learning has been introduced in [26] and has further been studied by various authors (cf., e.g., [3,8,13,14,15,18,19]). Alternatively, we consider learners that are allowed to store up to $k$ carefully chosen data elements seen so far, where $k$ is *a priori* fixed ($k$-bounded example-memory inference). Bounded example-memory learning has its origins in [18]. Furthermore, we study feedback identification. The idea of feedback learning goes back to [26], too. In this setting, the iterative learner is additionally allowed to ask whether or not a particular data element did already appear in the data seen so far.

In the first part of the present paper, we investigate incremental learning from noise-free data. As usual, we distinguish the case of learning from only positive data and learning from both positive and negative data, synonymously learning from text and informant, respectively. A *text* for a concept $c$ is an infinite sequence that eventually contains all and only the elements of $c$. Alternatively, an *informant* for $c$ is an infinite sequence of all elements of $\mathcal{X}$ that are classified according to their membership in $c$.

Former theoretical studies mostly dealt with incremental concept learning from only positive data (cf. [3,8,18]). It has been proved that (i) all defined models of incremental learning are strictly less powerful than conservative inference (which itself is strictly less powerful than learning in the limit), (ii) feedback learning and bounded example-memory inference outperform iterative learning, and (iii) feedback learning and bounded example-memory inference extend the learning capabilities of iterative learners in different directions. In particular, it has been shown that any additional data element an iterative learner may store buys more learning power.

As we shall show, the situation changes considerably in case positive and negative data are available. Now, it is sufficient to store one carefully selected data element in the example-memory in order to achieve the whole learning power of unconstrained learning machines. As a kind of side-effect, the infinite hierarchy of more and more powerful bounded example-memory learners which has been observed in the text case collapses. Furthermore, also feedback learners are exactly as powerful as unconstrained learning devices. In contrast, similarly to the case of learning from positive data, the learning capabilities of iterative learners are again seriously affected.

In the second part of the present paper, we study incremental learning from noisy data. This topic is of interest, since, in real world-applications, one rarely receives perfect data. There are a lot of attempts to give a precise notion of what the term noisy data means (cf., e.g., [2,12,19]). In our study, we adopt the notion from [22] (see also [23]) which seems to have become standard when studying Gold-style learning (cf. [2,4,5]). This notion has the advantage that noisy data about a target concept nonetheless uniquely specify that concept. Roughly speaking, correct data elements occur infinitely often whereas incorrect data elements occur only finitely often. Generally, the model of noisy environments introduced in [22] aims to grasp situations in which, due to better simulation techniques or better technical equipment, the experimental data which a learner receives about an unknown phenomenon become better and better over time until they reflect the reality sufficiently well.

Surprisingly, where learning from noisy data is considered, iterative learners are exactly as powerful as unconstrained learning machines, and thus iterative learners are able to fully compensate the limitations in the accessibility of the input data. This nicely contrasts the fact that, where learning from noise-free text and noise-free informant, iterative learning is strictly less powerful than learning in the limit. Moreover, it immediately implies that all different models of incremental learning introduced above coincide. Furthermore, we characterize iterative learning from noisy data in terms being independent from learning theory. We show that an indexable class can be iteratively learned from noisy text if and only if it is inclusion-free. Alternatively, it is iteratively learnable from noisy informant if and only if it is discrete.

## 2   Preliminaries

Let $\mathbb{N} = \{0, 1, 2, \ldots\}$ be the set of all natural numbers. By $\langle .,. \rangle : \mathbb{N} \times \mathbb{N} \to \mathbb{N}$ we denote Cantor's pairing function. We write $A \# B$ to indicate that two sets $A$ and $B$ are incomparable, i.e., $A \setminus B \neq \emptyset$ and $B \setminus A \neq \emptyset$.

Any recursively enumerable set $\mathcal{X}$ is called a *learning domain*. By $\wp(\mathcal{X})$ we denote the power set of $\mathcal{X}$. Let $\mathcal{C} \subseteq \wp(\mathcal{X})$ and let $c \in \mathcal{C}$. We refer to $\mathcal{C}$ and $c$ as to a *concept class* and a *concept*. Sometimes, we will identify a concept $c$ with its characteristic function, i.e., we let $c(x) = +$, if $x \in c$, and $c(x) = -$, otherwise.

We deal with the learnability of indexable concept classes with uniformly decidable membership defined as follows (cf. [1]). A class of non-empty concepts $\mathcal{C}$ is said to be an *indexable concept class with uniformly decidable membership* if there are an effective enumeration $(c_j)_{j \in \mathbb{N}}$ of all and only the concepts in $\mathcal{C}$ and a recursive function $f$ such that, for all $j \in \mathbb{N}$ and all $x \in \mathcal{X}$, it holds $f(j, x) = +$, if $x \in c_j$, and $f(j, x) = -$, otherwise. We refer to indexable concept classes with uniformly decidable membership as to *indexable classes*, for short.

Next, we describe some well-known examples of indexable classes. First, let $\Sigma$ denote any fixed finite alphabet of symbols and let $\Sigma^*$ be the free monoid over $\Sigma$. Moreover, let $\mathcal{X} = \Sigma^*$ be the learning domain. We refer to subsets $L \subseteq \Sigma^+$ as to languages (instead of concepts). Then, the set of all context-sensitive languages, context-free languages, regular languages, and of all pattern languages form indexable classes (cf. [1,11]). Second, let $X_n = \{0,1\}^n$ be the set of all $n$-bit Boolean vectors. We consider $\mathcal{X} = \bigcup_{n \geq 1} X_n$ as learning domain. Then, the set of all concepts expressible as a monomial, a $k$-CNF, a $k$-DNF, and a $k$-decision list constitute indexable classes (cf. [21,25]).

Finally, we define some useful properties of indexable classes. Let $\mathcal{X}$ be the underlying learning domain and let $\mathcal{C}$ be an indexable class. Then, $\mathcal{C}$ is said to be *inclusion-free* iff $c \# c'$ for all distinctive concepts $c, c' \in \mathcal{C}$. Let $(w_j)_{j \in \mathbb{N}}$ be the lexicographically ordered enumeration of all elements in $\mathcal{X}$. For all $c \subseteq \mathcal{X}$, by $i^c$ we denote the *lexicographically ordered informant* of $c$, i.e., the infinite sequence $((w_j, c(w_j)))_{j \in \mathbb{N}}$. Then, $\mathcal{C}$ is said to be *discrete* iff, for every $c \in \mathcal{C}$, there is an initial segment of $c$'s lexicographically ordered informant $i^c$, say $i_x^c$, that separates $c$ from all other concepts $c' \in C$. More precisely speaking, for all $c' \in C$, if $c \neq c'$ then $i_x^c \neq i_x^{c'}$.

# 3  Formalizing Incremental Learning

## 3.1  Learning from Noise-Free Data

Let $\mathcal{X}$ be the underlying learning domain, let $c \subseteq \mathcal{X}$ be a concept, and let $t = (x_n)_{n\in\mathbb{N}}$ be an infinite sequence of elements from $c$ such that $\{x_n \mid n \in \mathbb{N}\} = c$. Then, $t$ is said to be a *text* for $c$. By $Text(c)$ we denote the set of all texts for $c$. Alternatively, let $i = ((x_n, b_n))_{n\in\mathbb{N}}$ be an infinite sequence of elements from $\mathcal{X} \times \{+, -\}$ such that $\{x_n \mid n \in \mathbb{N}\} = \mathcal{X}$, $\{x_n \mid n \in \mathbb{N}, b_n = +\} = c$, and $\{x_n \mid n \in \mathbb{N}, b_n = -\} = co\text{-}c = \mathcal{X} \setminus c$. Then, we refer to $i$ as an *informant* for $c$. By $Info(c)$ we denote the set of all informants for $c$. Moreover, let $t$ be a text, let $i$ be an informant, and let $y$ be a number. Then, $t_y$ and $i_y$ denote the initial segment of $t$ and $i$ of length $y+1$. Furthermore, we set $t_y^+ = \{x_n \mid n \leq y\}$, $i_y^+ = \{x_n \mid n \leq y, b_n = +\}$, and $i_y^- = \{x_n \mid n \leq y, b_n = -\}$.

As in [10], we define an *inductive inference machine* (abbr. *IIM*) to be an algorithmic mapping from initial segments of texts (informants) to $\mathbb{N}\cup\{?\}$. Thus, an IIM either outputs a hypothesis, i.e., a number encoding a certain computer program, or it outputs "?," a special symbol representing the case the machine outputs "no conjecture." Note that an IIM, when learning some target class $C$, is required to produce an output when processing any initial segment of any *admissible* information sequence, i.e., any initial segment of any text (informant) for any $c \in C$.

The numbers output by an IIM are interpreted with respect to a suitably chosen *hypothesis space* $\mathcal{H} = (h_j)_{j\in\mathbb{N}}$. Since we exclusively deal with indexable classes $C$, we always assume that $\mathcal{H}$ is also an indexing of some possibly larger class of non-empty concepts. Hence, membership is uniformly decidable in $\mathcal{H}$, too. Formally speaking, we deal with class comprising learning (cf. [27]). When an IIM outputs some number $j$, we interpret it to mean that it hypothesizes $h_j$.

In all what follows, a data sequence $\sigma = (d_n)_{n\in\mathbb{N}}$ for a target concept $c$ is either a text $t = (x_n)_{n\in\mathbb{N}}$ or an informant $i = ((x_n, b_n))_{n\in\mathbb{N}}$ for $c$. By convention, for all $y \in \mathbb{N}$, $\sigma_y$ denotes the initial segment $t_y$ or $i_y$.

We define convergence of IIMs as usual. Let $\sigma$ be given and let $M$ be an IIM. The sequence $(M(\sigma_y))_{y\in\mathbb{N}}$ of $M$'s hypotheses *converges* to a number $j$ iff all but finitely many terms of it are equal to $j$.

Now, we are ready to define *learning in the limit*.

**Definition 1 ([10])** *Let $C$ be an indexable class, let $c$ be a concept, and let $\mathcal{H} = (h_j)_{j\in\mathbb{N}}$ be a hypothesis space. An IIM M $Lim\,Txt_{\mathcal{H}}$ [$Lim\,Inf_{\mathcal{H}}$]–identifies $c$ iff, for every data sequence $\sigma$ with $\sigma \in Text(c)$ [$\sigma \in Info(c)$], there is a $j \in \mathbb{N}$ with $h_j = c$ such that the sequence $(M(\sigma_y))_{y\in\mathbb{N}}$ converges to $j$.*

*Then, M $Lim\,Txt_{\mathcal{H}}$ [$Lim\,Inf_{\mathcal{H}}$]–identifies $C$ iff, for all $c' \in C$, M $Lim\,Txt_{\mathcal{H}}$ [$Lim\,Inf_{\mathcal{H}}$]–identifies $c'$.*

*Finally, $Lim\,Txt$ $[Lim\,Inf]$ denotes the collection of all indexable classes $C'$ for which there are a hypothesis space $\mathcal{H}' = (h'_j)_{j \in \mathbb{N}}$ and an IIM $M$ such that $M\,Lim\,Txt_{\mathcal{H}'}$ $[Lim\,Inf_{\mathcal{H}'}]$–identifies $C'$.*

In the above definition, *Lim* stands for "limit". Suppose an IIM identifies some concept $c$. That means, after having seen only finitely many data of $c$ the IIM reaches its (unknown) point of convergence and it computes a correct and finite description of the target concept. Hence, some form of learning must have taken place.

In general, it is not decidable whether or not an IIM has already converged on a text $t$ (an informant $i$) for the target concept $c$. Adding this requirement to the above definition results in *finite learning* (cf. [10]). The corresponding learning types are denoted by *Fin Txt* and *Fin Inf*.

Next, we define *conservative* IIMs. Intuitively speaking, conservative IIMs maintain their actual hypothesis at least as long as they have not seen data contradicting it.

**Definition 2 ([1])** *Let $C$ be an indexable class, let $c$ be a concept, and let $\mathcal{H} = (h_j)_{j \in \mathbb{N}}$ be a hypothesis space. An IIM $M$ Consv $Txt_{\mathcal{H}}$ $[Consv\,Inf_{\mathcal{H}}]$–identifies $c$ iff $M\,Lim\,Txt_{\mathcal{H}}$ $[Lim\,Inf_{\mathcal{H}}]$–identifies $c$ and, for every data sequence $\sigma$ with $\sigma \in Text(c)$ $[\sigma \in Info(c)]$ and for any two consecutive hypotheses $k = M(\sigma_y)$ and $j = M(\sigma_{y+1})$, if $k \in \mathbb{N}$ and $k \neq j$, then $h_k$ is not consistent with $\sigma_{y+1}$.*[1]

*$M$ Consv $Txt_{\mathcal{H}}$ $[Consv\,Inf_{\mathcal{H}}]$–identifies $C$ iff, for all $c' \in C$, $M$ Consv $Txt_{\mathcal{H}}$ $[Consv\,Inf_{\mathcal{H}}]$–identifies $c'$.*

The learning types *Consv Txt* and *Consv Inf* are defined analogously as above.

The next theorem summarizes the known results concerning the relations between the standard learning models defined so far.

**Theorem 1 ([10], [16])**
    (1) *For all indexable classes $C$, we have $C \in Lim\,Inf$.*
    (2) *Fin Txt $\subset$ Fin Inf $\subset$ Consv Txt $\subset$ Lim Txt $\subset$ Consv Inf $=$ Lim Inf.*

Now, we formally define the different models of incremental learning.

An ordinary IIM $M$ has always access to the whole history of the learning process, i.e., it computes its actual guess on the basis of all data seen so far. In contrast, an *iterative* IIM is only allowed to use its last guess and the next data element in $\sigma$. Conceptually, an iterative IIM $M$ defines a sequence $(M_n)_{n \in \mathbb{N}}$ of machines each of which takes as its input the output of its predecessor.

**Definition 3 ([26])** *Let $C$ be an indexable class, let $c$ be a concept, and let $\mathcal{H} = (h_j)_{j \in \mathbb{N}}$ be a hypothesis space. An IIM $M$ $It\,Txt_{\mathcal{H}}$ $[It\,Inf_{\mathcal{H}}]$–identifies $c$ iff, for every data sequence $\sigma = (d_n)_{n \in \mathbb{N}}$ with $\sigma \in Text(c)$ $[\sigma \in Info(c)]$, the following conditions are fulfilled:*

(1) *for all $n \in \mathbb{N}$, $M_n(\sigma)$ is defined, where $M_0(\sigma) = M(d_0)$ as well as $M_{n+1}(\sigma) = M(M_n(\sigma), d_{n+1})$.*
(2) *the sequence $(M_n(\sigma))_{n \in \mathbb{N}}$ converges to a number $j$ with $h_j = c$.*

---

[1] In the text case, $\sigma^+_{y+1} \not\subseteq c_k$, and, in the informant case, $\sigma^+_{y+1} \not\subseteq c_k$ or $\sigma^-_{y+1} \not\subseteq co\text{-}c_k$.

*Finally, M It Txt*$_{\mathcal{H}}$ *[It Inf*$_{\mathcal{H}}$*]–identifies C iff, for each c' $\in$ C, M It Txt*$_{\mathcal{H}}$ *[It Inf*$_{\mathcal{H}}$*]–identifies c'.*

The learning types *It Txt* and *It Inf* are defined analogously to Definition 1.

Next, we consider a natural relaxation of iterative learning, named *k-bounded example-memory* inference. Now, an IIM $M$ is allowed to memorize at most $k$ of the data elements which it has already seen in the learning process, where $k \in \mathbb{N}$ is *a priori* fixed. Again, $M$ defines a sequence $(M_n)_{n\in\mathbb{N}}$ of machines each of which takes as input the output of its predecessor. Clearly, a $k$-bounded example-memory IIM outputs a hypothesis along with the set of memorized data elements.

**Definition 4** ([18]) *Let C be an indexable class, let c be a concept, and let $\mathcal{H} = (h_j)_{j\in\mathbb{N}}$ be a hypothesis space. Moreover, let $k \in \mathbb{N}$. An IIM M Bem*$_k$ *Txt*$_{\mathcal{H}}$ *[Bem*$_k$*Inf*$_{\mathcal{H}}$*]–identifies c iff, for every data sequence $\sigma = (d_n)_{n\in\mathbb{N}}$ with $\sigma \in$ Text(c) [$\sigma \in$ Info(c)], the following conditions are satisfied:*

(1) *for all $n \in \mathbb{N}$, $M_n(\sigma)$ is defined, where $M_0(\sigma) = M(d_0) = \langle j_0, S_0\rangle$ such that $S_0 \subseteq \{d_0\}$ and $card(S_0) \leq k$ as well as $M_{n+1}(\sigma) = M(M_n(\sigma), d_n) = \langle j_{n+1}, S_{n+1}\rangle$ such that $S_{n+1} \subseteq S_n \cup \{d_{n+1}\}$ and $card(S_{n+1}) \leq k$.*
(2) *the $j_n$ in the sequence $(\langle j_n, S_n\rangle)_{n\in\mathbb{N}}$ of M's guesses converge to a number $j$ with $h_j = c$.*

*Finally, M Bem*$_k$ *Txt*$_{\mathcal{H}}$ *[Bem*$_k$*Inf*$_{\mathcal{H}}$*]–identifies C iff, for each c' $\in$ C, M Bem*$_k$ *Txt*$_{\mathcal{H}}$ *[Bem*$_k$*Inf*$_{\mathcal{H}}$*]–identifies c'.*

For every $k \in \mathbb{N}$, the learning types *Bem*$_k$ *Txt* and *Bem*$_k$*Inf* are defined analogously as above. By definition, *Bem*$_0$ *Txt = It Txt* and *Bem*$_0$*Inf = ItInf*.

Next, we define learning by *feedback* IIMs. Informally speaking, a feedback IIM $M$ is an iterative IIM that is additionally allowed to make a particular type of queries. In each learning stage $n+1$, $M$ has access to the actual input $d_{n+1}$ and its previous guess $j_n$. $M$ is additionally allowed to compute a query from $d_{n+1}$ and $j_n$ which concerns the history of the learning process. That is, the feedback learner computes a data element $d$ and gets a "YES/NO" answer $A(d)$ such that $A(d) = 1$, if $d$ appears in the initial segment $\sigma_n$, and $A(d) = 0$, otherwise. Hence, $M$ can just ask whether or not the particular data element $d$ has already been presented in previous learning stages.

**Definition 5** ([26]) *Let C be an indexable class, let c be a concept, and let $\mathcal{H} = (h_j)_{j\in\mathbb{N}}$ be a hypothesis space. Let $Q : \mathbb{N} \times \mathcal{X} \to \mathcal{X}$ [$Q : \mathbb{N} \times \mathcal{X}_i \to \mathcal{X}_i$, where $\mathcal{X}_i = \mathcal{X} \times \{+, -\}$] be a total computable function. An IIM M, with a query asking function Q, FbTxt*$_{\mathcal{H}}$ *[FbInf*$_{\mathcal{H}}$*]–identifies c iff, for every data sequence $\sigma = (d_n)_{n\in\mathbb{N}}$ with $\sigma \in$ Text(c) [$\sigma \in$ Info(c)], the following conditions are satisfied:*

(1) *for all $n \in \mathbb{N}$, $M_n(\sigma)$ is defined, where $M_0(\sigma) = M(d_0)$ as well as $M_{n+1}(\sigma) = M(M_n(\sigma), A(Q(M_n(\sigma), d_{n+1})), d_{n+1})$.*
(2) *the sequence $(M_n(\sigma))_{n\in\mathbb{N}}$ converges to a number $j$ with $h_j = c$ provided A truthfully answers the questions computed by Q.*

*Finally, M FbTxt*$_{\mathcal{H}}$ *[FbInf*$_{\mathcal{H}}$*]–identifies C iff, for each c' $\in$ C, M FbTxt*$_{\mathcal{H}}$ *[FbInf*$_{\mathcal{H}}$*]–identifies c'.*

The learning types *FbTxt* and *FbInf* are defined analogously as above.

## 3.2    Learning from Noisy Data

In order to study iterative learning from noisy data we have to provide some more notations and definitions.

Let $\mathcal{X}$ be the underlying learning domain, let $c \subseteq \mathcal{X}$ be a concept, and let $t = (x_n)_{n \in \mathbb{N}}$ be an infinite sequence of elements from $\mathcal{X}$. Following [22], $t$ is said to be a *noisy text* for $c$ provided that every element from $c$ appears infinitely often, i.e., for every $x \in c$ there are infinitely many $n$ such that $x_n = x$, whereas only finitely often some $x \notin c$ occurs, i.e., $x_n \in c$ for all but finitely many $n \in \mathbb{N}$. By $NText(c)$ we denote the collection of all noisy texts for $c$. For every $y \in \mathbb{N}$, $t_y$ denotes the initial segment of $t$ of length $y + 1$. We let $t_y^+ = \{x_n \mid n \le y\}$.

Next, let $i = ((x_n, b_n))_{n \in \mathbb{N}}$ be any sequence of elements from $\mathcal{X} \times \{+, -\}$. Following [22], $i$ is said to be a *noisy informant* for $c$ provided that every element $x$ of $\mathcal{X}$ occurs infinitely often, almost always accomplished by the right classification $c(x)$. More formally, for all $x \in \mathcal{X}$, there are infinitely many $n \in \mathbb{N}$ such that $x_n = x$ and, for all but finitely many of them, $b_n = c(x)$. By $NInfo(c)$ we denote the collection of all noisy informants for $c$. For every $y \in \mathbb{N}$, $i_y$ denotes the initial segment of $i$ of length $y + 1$, $i_y^+ = \{x_n \mid n \le y, b_n = +\}$, and $i_y^- = \{x_n \mid n \le y, b_n = -\}$.

In contrast to the noise-free case, now an IIM receives as input finite sequences of a noisy text (noisy informant). When an IIM is supposed to identify some target concept class $\mathcal{C}$, then it has to output a hypothesis on every admissible information sequence, i.e., any initial segment of any noisy text (noisy informant) for any $c \in \mathcal{C}$. Analogously to the case of learning from noise-free data, we deal with class comprising learning (cf. [27]).

The learning types $LimNTxt$, $FinNTxt$, $ConsvNTxt$, $ItNTxt$, $Bem_kNTxt$, and $FbNTxt$ as well as $LimNInf$, $FinNInf$, $ConsvNInf$, $ItNInf$, $Bem_kNInf$, and $FbNInf$ are defined analogously to their noise-free counterparts by replacing everywhere text and informant by noisy text and noisy informant, respectively.

The following theorem summarizes the known results concerning learning of indexable concept classes from noisy data.

**Theorem 2 ([22])**

(1) $FinTxt \subset LimNTxt \subset LimTxt$.
(2) $FinInf \subset LimNInf \subset LimInf$.
(3) $LimNTxt \mathbin{\#} LimNInf$.

# 4    Incremental Learning from Noise-Free Data

## 4.1    The Text Case

In this subsection, we briefly review the known relations between the different variants of incremental learning and the standard learning models defined above.

All the models of incremental learning introduced above pose serious restrictions on the accessibility of the data provided during the learning process. Therefore, one might expect a certain loss of learning power. And indeed, conservative inference already forms an upper bound for any kind of incremental learning.

**Theorem 3 ([18])**

(1)  *It Txt $\subset$ Consv Txt.*
(2)  *Fb Txt $\subset$ Consv Txt.*
(3)  $\bigcup_{k \in \mathbb{N}} Bem_k Txt \subset Consv\,Txt.$

Moreover, bounded example-memory inference and feedback learning enlarge the learning capabilities of iterative identification, but the surplus power gained is incomparable. Moreover, the existence of an infinite hierarchy of more and more powerful bounded example memory learners has been shown.

**Theorem 4 ([18])**

(1)  *It Txt $\subset$ Fb Txt.*
(2)  *It Txt $\subset$ $Bem_1$ Txt.*
(3)  *For all $k \in \mathbb{N}$, $Bem_k Txt \subset Bem_{k+1} Txt.$*
(4)  *$Bem_1 Txt \setminus Fb Txt \neq \emptyset.$*
(5)  *$Fb Txt \setminus \bigcup_{k \in \mathbb{N}} Bem_k Txt \neq \emptyset.$*

A comparison of feedback learning and bounded example-memory inference with finite inference from positive and negative data illustrates another difference between both generalizations of iterative learning.

**Theorem 5 ([18])**

(1)  $\bigcup_{k \in \mathbb{N}} Bem_k Txt \# FinInf.$
(2)  *FinInf $\subset$ Fb Txt.*

Finally, finite inference from text is strictly less powerful than any kind of incremental learning.

**Theorem 6 ([18])** *Fin Txt $\subset$ It Txt.*


## 4.2    The Informant Case

Next, we study the strengths and the limitations of incremental learning from informant. Our first result deals with the similarities to the text case.

**Theorem 7** *FinInf $\subset$ ItInf $\subset$ LimInf.*

Moreover, analogously to the case of learning from only positive data, feedback learners and bounded example-memory learners are more powerful than iterative IIMs. But surprisingly, the surplus learning power gained is remarkable. The ability to make queries concerning the history of the learning process fully compensates the limitations in the accessibility of the input data.

**Theorem 8** *FbInf = LimInf.*

Even more surprisingly, the infinite hierarchy of more and more powerful $k$-bounded example-memory learners, parameterized by the number of data elements the relevant iterative learners may store, collapses in the informant case. The ability to memorize one carefully selected data element is also sufficient to fully compensate the limitations in the accessibility of the input data.

**Theorem 9** *$Bem_1 Inf = LimInf.*

*Proof.* It suffices to show that $Lim\,Inf \subseteq Bem_1Inf$. Let $\mathcal{C}$ be any indexable class and $(c_j)_{j\in\mathbb{N}}$ be any indexing of $\mathcal{C}$. By Theorem 1, $\mathcal{C} \in Lim\,Inf$.

Let $(w_j)_{j\in\mathbb{N}}$ denote the lexicographically ordered enumeration of all elements in $\mathcal{X}$. For all $m \in \mathbb{N}$ and all $c \subseteq \mathcal{X}$, we set $c^m = \{w_z \mid z \leq m, w_z \in c\}$ and $c^{\bar{m}} = \{w_z \mid z > m, w_z \in c\}$.

We let the required 1-bounded example-memory learner $M$ output as hypothesis a triple $(F, m, j)$ along with a singleton set containing the one data element stored. The triple $(F, m, j)$ consists of a finite set $F$ and two numbers $m$ and $j$. It is used to describe a finite variant of the concept $c_j$, namely the concept $F \cup c_j^{\bar{m}}$. Intuitively speaking, $c_j^{\bar{m}}$ is the part of the concept $c_j$ that definitely does not contradict the data seen so far, while $F$ is used to handle exceptions. For the sake of readability, we abstain from explicitly defining a hypothesis space $\mathcal{H}$ that provides an appropriate coding of all finite variants $h_{(F,m,j)} = F \cup c_j^{\bar{m}}$ of concepts in $\mathcal{C}$.

Let $c \in \mathcal{C}$ and let $i = ((x_n, b_n))_{n\in\mathbb{N}} \in Info(c)$. $M$ is defined in stages.

Stage 0. On input $(x_0, b_0)$ do the following:

Fix $m \in \mathbb{N}$ with $w_m = x_0$. Determine the least $j$ such that $c_j$ is consistent with $(x_0, b_0)$. Set $S = \{(x_0, b_0)\}$. Output $\langle(c_j^m, m, j), S\rangle$ and goto Stage 1.

Stage $n$, $n \geq 1$. On input $\langle(F, m, j), S\rangle$ and $(x_n, b_n)$ proceed as follows:

Let $S = \{(x, b)\}$. Fix $z, z' \in \mathbb{N}$ such that $w_z = x$ and $w_{z'} = x_n$. If $z' > z$, set $S' = \{(x_n, b_n)\}$. Otherwise, set $S' = S$. Test whether $h_{(F,m,j)} = F \cup c_j^{\bar{m}}$ is consistent with $(x_n, b_n)$. In case it is, goto (A). Otherwise, goto (B).

(A) Output $\langle(F, m, j), S'\rangle$ and goto Stage $n+1$.

(B) If $z' \leq m$, goto $(\beta1)$. If $z' > m$, goto $(\beta2)$.

($\beta1$) If $b_n = +$, set $F' = F \cup \{x_n\}$. If $b_n = -$, set $F' = F \setminus \{x_n\}$. Output $\langle(F', m, j), S'\rangle$ and goto Stage $n+1$.

($\beta2$) Determine $\ell = max\,\{z, z'\}$ and $F' = \{w_r \mid r \leq \ell, w_r \in h_{(F,m,j)}\}$. If $b_n = +$, set $F'' = F' \cup \{x_n\}$. If $b_n = -$, set $F'' = F' \setminus \{x_n\}$. Search for the least index $k > j$ such that $c_k$ is consistent with $(x_n, b_n)$. Then, output $\langle(F'', \ell, k), S'\rangle$ and goto Stage $n+1$.

Due to space limitations, the verification of $M$'s correctness is skipped.   $\square$

On the other hand, it is well-known that, where learning from informant, iterative learning with finitely many anomalies[2] is exactly as powerful as learning in the limit. Hence, Theorems 8 and 9 demonstrate the error correcting power of feedback queries and bounded example-memories.

Next, we summarize the established relations between the different models of incremental learning from text and their corresponding informant counterparts.

## Corollary 10

(1) $It\,Txt \subset It\,Inf$.
(2) $\bigcup_{k\in\mathbb{N}} Bem_k Txt \subset Bem_1 Inf$.
(3) $Fb\,Txt \subset Fb\,Inf$.

---

[2] In this setting, it suffices that an iterative learner converges to a hypothesis which describes a finite variant of the target concept.

Finally, we want to point out further differences between incremental learning from text and informant.

**Theorem 11**

(1) $ItInf \setminus LimTxt \neq \emptyset$.
(2) $Bem_1 Txt \setminus ItInf \neq \emptyset$.
(3) $FbTxt \setminus ItInf \neq \emptyset$.

The figure aside summarizes the observed separations and coincidences. Each learning type is represented as a vertex in a directed graph. A directed edge (or path) from vertex $A$ to vertex $B$ indicates that $A$ is a proper subset of $B$. Moreover, no edge (or path) between these vertices imply that $A$ and $B$ are incomparable.

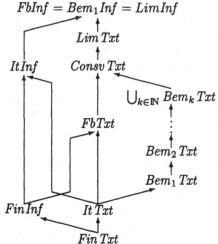

## 5  Incremental Learning from Noisy Data

### 5.1  Characterizations

In this section, we present characterizations of all models of learning from noisy text and noisy informant. First, we characterize iterative learning from noisy text in purely structural terms.

**Theorem 12** $C \in ItNTxt$ iff $C$ is inclusion-free.

Since $LimNTxt$ exclusively contains indexable classes that are inclusion-free (cf. [22]), by Theorem 1, and since, by definition, $ItNTxt \subseteq Bem_1 NTxt$ and $ItNTxt \subseteq FbNTxt$, we arrive at the following insight.

**Theorem 13**

(1) $ItNTxt = ConsvNTxt = LimNTxt$.
(2) $ItNTxt = FbNTxt = \bigcup_{k \in \mathbb{N}} Bem_k NTxt$.

Interestingly, another structural property allows us to characterize the collection of all indexable classes that can be iteratively learned from noisy informant.

**Theorem 14** $C \in ItNInf$ iff $C$ is discrete.

*Proof.* Necessity: Recently, it has been shown that every class of recursive enumerable languages that is learnable in the limit from noisy informant has to be discrete (cf. Stephan [22]; see also Case *et al.* [5], for the relevant details). Clearly, this result immediately translates in our setting. Now, since, by definition, $ItNInf \subseteq LimNInf$, we are done.

Sufficiency: Let $C$ be an indexable class that is discrete. Informally speaking, the required iterative learner $M$ behaves as follows. In every learning stage, $M$ outputs an index for some concept, say $c'$, along with a number $k$. The number $k$ is an lower bound for the length of the shortest initial segment of $c'$'s lexicographically ordered informant $i^{c'}$ that separates $c'$ from all other concepts in target class $C$. Since $M$ does not know whether a new data element is really correct, $M$ rejects its actual guess only in case the new data element contradicts the information represented in the initial segment $i_k^{c'}$. Moreover, since $M$ is supposed to learn in an iterative manner, $M$ has to use the input data to improve its actual lower bound $k$.

We proceed formally. Let $(c_j)_{j \in \mathbb{N}}$ be any indexing of $C$. For all $j \in \mathbb{N}$, $i^{c_j}$ denotes the lexicographically ordered informant of $c_j$. As before, let $(w_j)_{j \in \mathbb{N}}$ be the lexicographically ordered enumeration of all elements in $\mathcal{X}$. Moreover, let $f$ be any total recursive function such that, for all $z \in \mathbb{N}$, there are infinitely many $j \in \mathbb{N}$ with $f(j) = z$. We select a hypothesis space $\mathcal{H} = (h_{\langle j,k \rangle})_{j,k \in \mathbb{N}}$ that meets, for all $j, k \in \mathbb{N}$, $h_{\langle j,k \rangle} = c_{f(j)}$. The required iterative IIM $M$ is defined in stages. Let $c \in C$ and let $i = ((x_n, b_n))_{n \in \mathbb{N}}$ be any noisy informant for $c$.

Stage 0. On input $(x_0, b_0)$ do the following:
    Set $j_0 = 0$, set $k_0 = 0$, output $\langle j_0, k_0 \rangle$, and goto Stage 1.

Stage $n$, $n \geq 1$. On input $\langle j_{n-1}, k_{n-1} \rangle$ and $(x_n, b_n)$ do the following:
    Determine $p \in \mathbb{N}$ with $w_p = x_n$. If $p \leq k_{n-1}$, execute Instruction (A). Otherwise, execute Instruction (B).

(A) Test whether or not $b_n = c_{f(j_{n-1})}(x_n)$. In case it is, set $j_n = j_{n-1}$ and $k_n = k_{n-1}$. Otherwise, set $j_n = j_{n-1} + 1$ and $k_n = 0$. Output $\langle j_n, k_n \rangle$ and goto Stage $n + 1$.

(B) For all $z \leq p$, test whether $i_{k_{n-1}}^{c_{f(z)}} = i_{k_{n-1}}^{c_{f(j_{n-1})}}$ and $i_p^{c_{f(z)}} \neq i_p^{c_{f(j_{n-1})}}$. In case there is a $z$ successfully passing this test, set $j_n = j_{n-1}$ and $k_n = k_{n-1}+1$. Otherwise, set $j_n = j_{n-1}$ and $k_n = k_{n-1}$. Output $\langle j_n, k_n \rangle$ and goto Stage $n + 1$.

Due to space limitations, the verification of $M$'s correctness is skipped. $\square$

Analogously to the text case, all models of learning from noisy informant coincide, except $Fin\,NInf$.

**Theorem 15**

(1) $It\,NInf = Consv\,NInf = Lim\,NInf$.
(2) $It\,NInf = Fb\,NInf = \bigcup_{k \in \mathbb{N}} Bem_k\,NInf$.

Furthermore, the collection of all indexable classes that can be finitely learned from noisy text (noisy informant) is easily characterized as follows.

**Proposition 1** *Let $C$ be an indexable class. Then, the following statements are equivalent:*

(1) $C \in Fin\,NTxt$.
(2) $C \in Fin\,NInf$.
(3) $C$ contains at most one concept.

## 5.2 Comparisons with Other Learning Types

The characterizations presented in the last subsection form a firm basis for further investigations. They are useful to prove further results illustrating the relation of learning from noisy text and noisy informant to all the other types of learning indexable classes defined. Subsequently, $ItNTxt$ and $ItNInf$ are used as representatives for all models of learning from noisy data, except finite inference.

The next two theorems sharpen the upper bounds for learning from noisy data established in [22] (cf. Theorem 2 above).

**Theorem 16** $ItNTxt \subset Consv\,Txt$.

The next theorem puts the weakness of learning from noisy informant in the right perspective.

**Theorem 17** $ItNInf \subset Lim\,Txt$.

The reader should note that Theorem 17 cannot be sharpened to $ItNInf \subseteq Consv\,Txt$, since there are discrete indexable classes not belonging to $Consv\,Txt$ (cf. [16]). Since the class of all finite concepts is $Consv\,Txt$–identifiable and obviously not discrete, we may conclude:

**Theorem 18** $ItNInf \# Consv\,Txt$.

The next theorem provides us the missing piece in the overall picture.

**Theorem 19** $ItNTxt \# FinInf$.

The figure aside displays the established relations between the different models of learning from noisy data and the standard models of learning in the noise-free setting. The semantics of this figure is the same as that of the figure in the previous section. The displayed relations between the learning models $FinNTxt$, $FinNInf$, and $FinTxt$ are rather trivial. On the one hand, every singleton concept class is obviously $FinTxt$–identifiable. On the other hand, $FinTxt$ also contains richer indexable classes.

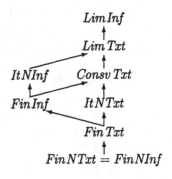

Recall that Assertion (3) of Theorem 2 rewrites into $ItNTxt \# ItNInf$. As we shall see, this result generalizes as follows: All models of iterative learning are pairwise incomparable, except $It\,Txt$ and $It\,Inf$.

**Theorem 20**

(1) $ItNTxt \# It\,Txt$.     (2) $ItNTxt \# It\,Inf$.

(3) $ItNInf \# It\,Txt$.     (4) $ItNInf \# It\,Inf$.

**Acknowledgment**

We thank the anonymous referees for their careful reading and comments which improved the paper considerably.

# References

1. D. Angluin. Inductive inference of formal languages from positive data. *Information and Control*, 45:117–135, 1980.
2. J. Case and S. Jain. Synthesizing learners tolerating computable noisy data. In *Proc. 9th ALT*, LNAI 1501, pp. 205–219. Springer-Verlag, 1998.

3. J. Case, S. Jain, S. Lange, and T. Zeugmann. Incremental concept learning for bounded data mining. *Information and Computation.* to appear.

4. J. Case, S. Jain, and A. Sharma. Synthesizing noise-tolerant language learners. In *Proc. 8th ALT*, LNAI 1316, pp. 228–243. Springer-Verlag, 1997.

5. J. Case, S. Jain, and F. Stephan. Vacillatory and BC learning on noisy data. In *Proc. 7th ALT*, LNAI 1160, pp. 285–289. Springer-Verlag, 1997.

6. A. Cornuéjols. Getting order independence in incremental learning. In *Proc. ECML*, LNAI 667, pp. 196–212. Springer-Verlag, 1993.

7. U.M. Fayyad, G. Piatetsky-Shapiro, P. Smyth, and R. Uthurusamy, editors. *Advances in Knowledge Discovery and Data Mining.* MIT Press, 1996.

8. M. Fulk, S. Jain, and D.N. Osherson. Open problems in systems that learn. *Journal of Computer and System Sciences*, 49:589–604, 1994.

9. R. Godin and R. Missaoui. An incremental concept formation approach for learning from databases. *Theoretical Computer Science*, 133:387–419, 1994.

10. M.E. Gold. Language identification in the limit. *Information and Control*, 10:447–474, 1967.

11. J.E. Hopcroft and J.D. Ullman. *Formal Languages and their Relation to Automata.* Addison-Wesley, 1969.

12. S. Jain. Program synthesis in the presence of infinite number of inaccuracies. In *Proc. 5th ALT*, LNAI 872, pp. 333–348. Springer-Verlag, 1994.

13. K.P. Jantke and H.R. Beick. Combining postulates of naturalness in inductive inference. *Journal of Information Processing and Cybernetics*, 17:465–484, 1981.

14. E. Kinber and F. Stephan. Mind changes, limited memory, and monotonicity. In *Proc. 8th COLT*, pp. 182–189. ACM Press, 1995.

15. S. Lange and R. Wiehagen. Polynomial-time inference of arbitrary pattern languages. *New Generation Computing*, 8:361–370, 1991.

16. S. Lange and T. Zeugmann. Language learning in dependence on the space of hypotheses. In *Proc. 6th COLT*, pp. 127–136. ACM Press, 1993.

17. S. Lange and T. Zeugmann. Learning recursive languages with bounded mind changes. *Int. Journal of Foundations of Computer Science*, 4:157–178, 1993.

18. S. Lange and T. Zeugmann. Incremental learning from positive data. *Journal of Computer and System Sciences*, 53:88–103, 1996.

19. D. Osherson, M. Stob, and S. Weinstein. *Systems that Learn, An Introduction to Learning Theory for Cognitive and Computer Scientists.* MIT Press, 1986.

20. S. Porat and J.A. Feldman. Learning automata from ordered examples. In *Proc. 1st COLT*, pp. 386–396. Morgan Kaufmann Publ., 1988.

21. R. Rivest. Learning decision lists. *Machine Learning*, 2:229–246, 1988.

22. F. Stephan. Noisy inference and oracles. In *Proc. 6th ALT*, LNAI 997, pp. 185–200. Springer-Verlag, 1995.

23. F. Stephan. Noisy inference and oracles. *Theoretical Computer Science*, 185:129–157, 1997.

24. L. Torgo. Controlled redundancy in incremental rule learning. In *Proc. ECML*, LNAI 667, pp. 185–195. Springer-Verlag, 1993.

25. L.G. Valiant. A theory of the learnable. *Communications of the ACM*, 27:1134–1142, 1984.

26. R. Wiehagen. Limes-Erkennung rekursiver Funktionen durch spezielle Strategien. *Journal of Information Processing and Cybernetics*, 12:93–99, 1976.

27. T. Zeugmann and S. Lange. A guided tour across the boundaries of learning recursive languages. In *Algorithmic Learning for Knowledge-Based Systems*, LNAI 961, pp. 193–262. Springer-Verlag, 1995.

# Learning from Random Text

Peter Rossmanith

Institut für Informatik
Technische Universität München
80333 München, Fed. Rep. of Germany
`rossmani@in.tum.de`

**Abstract.** Learning in the limit deals mainly with the question of *what* can be learned, but not very often with the question of *how fast*. The purpose of this paper is to develop a learning model that stays very close to Gold's model, but enables questions on the speed of convergence to be answered. In order to do this, we have to assume that positive examples are generated by some stochastic model. If the stochastic model is fixed (measure one learning), then all recursively enumerable sets are identifiable, while straying greatly from Gold's model. In contrast, we define *learning from random text* as identifying a class of languages for *every* stochastic model where examples are generated independently and identically distributed. As it turns out, this model stays close to learning in the limit. We compare both models keeping several aspects in mind, particularly when restricted to several strategies and to the existence of locking sequences. Lastly, we present some results on the speed of convergence: In general, convergence can be arbitrarily slow, but for recursive learners, it cannot be slower than some magic function. Every language can be learned with *exponentially small tail bounds*, which are also *the best possible*. All results apply fully to Gold-style learners, since his model is a proper subset of learning from random text.

## 1 Introduction

Learning in the limit as defined by Gold [5] has attracted much attention. It can be described as follows: The words of a language are presented to a learner in some order, where duplicates are allowed. At each point of time the learner has seen only a finite subset of the language and thus gets an increasingly improved idea of the language. The learner issues *hypotheses* that at some point have to converge to a correct one (and never to be changed afterwards).

The representation of a language as an infinite sequence, containing exactly the words of the language, is called a *text*. We will use the terms *learning in the limit*, *identification in the limit*, and *learning from text* synonymously.

Much work on learning from text has addressed the question concerning *what classes of languages are learnable* and of what restrictions and combinations of restrictions for learners do restrict the power of identification. A set of learners is called a *strategy*. The most important strategy is *recursive learners*. In this paper we will deal with recursive as well as non-recursive learners. Another type

O. Watanabe, T. Yokomori (Eds.): ALT'99, LNAI 1720, pp. 132–144, 1999.

of a strategy is *consistency* [1]. A learner is consistent if all hypotheses denote a language that at least *contains* all words thus far seen. It is well known that consistency does not generally restrict learning power, but it does restrict the power of recursive learners.

What has not been greatly adressed is *how fast* learning takes place. The reason for this is simple: With the exception of trivial cases there exists *no upper bound on the learning time* because texts can always be padded with useless information at the beginning. Therefore, this leaves *average case analysis* as a possible way to proceed. A prerequisite for this is a *stochastic model* for the texts. In general these models form a text by generating every word in the text independently from the others and with an equal probability distribution, which is well motivated by several scientific contexts. Results on learning pattern languages [3,13,10] and monomials [9] emerged as a consequence. These results are bounds on the average number of examples or on the time required to learn on average according to a commonly large class of probability distributions. Some of the papers also deal with aspects other than the average time or number of examples: They present tail bounds on the probability of convergence. More specifically, they show that some algorithm have *exponentially small tail bounds* [10]. There is also one general result: Every learner that is *conservative* and *set driven* automatically has small tail bounds as concerns every probability distribution [10]. Knowledge about tail bounds enables a learner to stop after a finite time and to announce his hypothesis as correct with high probability. There is a direct connection to *stochastically finite learning*, which was introduced in [10] (see also additional remarks in [9]).

In general, fixing probability distributions for each language in some class leads to a learning model that is much more powerful than that of identification in the limit: The whole class of recursively enumerable languages becomes learnable (see [8]). This model is called *measure one learning*. Kapur and Bilardi present an elegant way to construct simple learners for a collection of languages if there is some minimal knowledge about the underlying probability distributions [6]. They also show how knowledge about distributions provides indirect negative evidence.

In this paper we introduce the model *learning from random text*, which overcomes the difficulties above: It does not suffice to learn for fixed probability distributions, *every reasonable distribution* must be considered. In other words, a learner identifies a language from random text, if he converges to a correct hypothesis with probability one for every probability distribution for which the probability of a word is positive iff the word is a member of the language. This definition overcomes the difficulties mentioned above. Formal definitions are contained in the next section. (See also Kapur and Bilardi [7] for learning of indexed languages.)

In the first part of this paper we investigate some basic properties of this model. In particular, if a learner learns from text he also learns from random text, but not necessarily vice versa. With this in mind we generalize the classical model, due to the fact that a learner is now allowed to fail on certain texts.

These texts, which we call the *failure set* of the learner, must have measure zero for every admissible distribution. However, if a class is learnable from random text, it can also be learned from text. This is also valid if we restrict ourselves to recursive learners. This equivalence can be translated to all strategies holding no restriction on identification in the limit, for which are many.

To further compare the two models, we investigate some strategies that act as a restriction for recursive learning in the limit. *Set-driven learners* (whose hypotheses depend only on the *set* of examples seen, not on their multiplicity or order), *confident learners* (who converge on all texts for all languages), and *memory limited learners* (who can remember only a constant number of examples back in time). It will prove to be the case that the qualities of being set-driven or confident are restrictions for recursive learning from random text, too. The characteristic of limited memory, on the other hand, does not act as a restriction.

Every learner that learns in the limit has a *locking sequence* [2], whose existence plays a crucial part in many proofs. After reading a locking sequence as a prefix of a text, a learner never again changes his hypothesis. Blum and Blum showed that every learner has a locking sequence and that every initial prefix of a text is a prefix of a locking sequence [2]. When learning from random text, locking sequences do not necessarily exist. We offer a simple characterization in terms of topological properties of the failure set, showing whether or not locking sequences nevertheless exist. The topology concerned is the natural topology on the sequences of words from the languages to be learned: A locking sequence exists iff (1) the failure set is not comeager and iff (2) it is not dense. Similarly, every prefix of a text is aa prefix of a locking sequence iff (1) the failure set is meager and iff (2) it is nowhere dense.

In the second part of this paper we investigate the functions that map $n$ to the probability that the learner has not converged to the correct hypothesis after reading $n$ examples. This function will be called *convergence indicator*. The limit of a convergence indicator is zero for every admissible probability distribution, as to be expected. We show that, except for trivial cases, a convergence indicator cannot be smaller than *exponential*, i.e., it is always $\Omega(1)^n$. This is true regardless of the class of languages to be learned and the underlying probability distribution; hence we have a *lower bound*. Exists an upper bound as well? In other words, is it possible to learn arbitrarily slowly? The answer is generally 'yes', but for recursive learners 'no'. There exists some function $f$ such that *every* recursive learner's convergence indicator is $o(f(n))$. This forms a kind of magical barrier: Either you can learn faster or not at all.

After finding lower and upper bounds for the convergence behavior of individual learners, we have to consider the more general task of finding the best convergence behavior among all learners that learn a class of languages: We can always construct a learner that learns with exponentially small tail bounds, i.e, its convergence indicator is $O(1)^n$.

We also show that if a learner is *set-driven*, then his tail bounds are automatically exponentially small. This phenomenon has already been recognised for when a learner is simultaneously *set-driven* and *conservative* [10].

## 2    Preliminaries

This section contains fundamental definitions. The notation is almost identical to that in Osherson, Stob, and Weinstein's textbook [8]. The natural numbers are denoted by $N = \{1, 2, 3, \dots\}$. A *language* is a subset of natural numbers. Let $W_i$ be the language accepted by the $i$th Turing machine and $RE = \{W_1, W_2, \dots\}$ the *recursively enumerable languages*. A *text* is a sequence of natural number. If $t$ is a text, then $t_i$ denotes its $i$th component, i.e., $t = (t_1, t_2, \dots)$. The *range* $\mathrm{rng}(t)$ of a text $t$ is the set of all its components, i.e., $\mathrm{rng}(t) = \{t_1, t_2, \dots\}$. We say $t$ is a text for $L$ if $\mathrm{rng}(t) = L$. The set of all texts for $L$ is denoted by $\mathcal{T}_L$ and $\mathcal{T}$ is the set of all texts. The prefix of length $n$ of a text $t$ is denoted by $\bar{t}_n = (t_1, t_2, \dots, t_n)$. Let $\mathcal{F}$ be the set of all partial functions from $N$ to $N$. We will identify finite sequences with natural numbers. If $\phi \in \mathcal{F}$ and $\lim_{n \to \infty} \phi(\bar{t}_n) = i$, i.e., $\phi(\bar{t}_n) = i$ for all but finitely many $n$, we say that $\phi$ *converges on $t$ to $i$* and write $\phi(t) = i$. We say $\phi$ *converges on $t$* if it converges on $t$ to some $i$. If $W_{\phi(t)} = L$ for every text for $L$, then we say that $\phi$ *identifies $L$* (in the limit or from text). If $\mathcal{L} \subseteq RE$ and $\phi$ identifies every $L \in \mathcal{L}$ then we say that $\phi$ *identifies $\mathcal{L}$*.

Let $\mathcal{S} \subseteq \mathcal{F}$ be a *strategy*. Then $[\mathcal{S}]$ denotes the set of all classes $\mathcal{L} \subseteq RE$ that are learnable by some $\phi \in \mathcal{S}$. In particular, $[\mathcal{F}]$ are all learnable classes and $[\mathcal{F}^{rec}]$ all recursively learnable classes.

We define a topology $\mathcal{T}_L = (\mathcal{T}_{\mathbf{P}(L)}, O_L)$, where $\mathcal{T}_{\mathbf{P}(L)}$ is the set of all texts for all subsets of $L$. The open sets $O_L$ are defined by a base consisting of all sets $B^L_\sigma = \{t \in \mathcal{T}_{\mathbf{P}(L)} \mid \bar{t}_n = \sigma \text{ for } n = \mathrm{lh}(\sigma)\}$, i.e., all texts for all subsets of $L$ that have a prefix $\sigma$. ($\mathrm{lh}(\sigma)$ is the length of $\sigma$.) The induced topology is the sequence space over $L$. More details can be found in [8].

With the help of $\mathcal{T}_L$ we can define a probability space $(\mathcal{T}_{\mathbf{P}(L)}, \mathfrak{A}, M_L)$, where $\mathfrak{A}$, the measurable sets, is the smallest $\sigma$-Algebra that contains all basic open sets $B^L_\sigma$ and $M_L$ is an *admissible* probability measure defined via $M_L(B^L_\sigma) = \prod_{i=1}^{\mathrm{lh}(\sigma)} m_L(\sigma_i)$ where $m_L$ is a probability measure on $L$ and must fulfill $m_L(n) > 0$ iff $n \in L$ and $m_L(L) = 1$. The random variable $T$ denotes a *random text* for $L$; technically, $T$ is the identity function on $\mathcal{T}$. If $P$ is a predicate for texts, we use the usual abbreviation $M_L[P] = M_L(\{t \mid P(t)\})$. For example, $M_L[T \in B^L_\sigma] = M_L(\{t \in \mathcal{T} \mid T(t) \in B^L_\sigma\}) = M_L(\{t \in \mathcal{T} \mid t \in B^L_\sigma\}) = M_L(B^L_\sigma)$. We are now ready to define learning from random text formally.

**Definition 1** A learner $\phi \in \mathcal{F}$ *identifies* a language $L \subseteq RE$ *from random text* if $M_L[W_{\phi(T)} = L]$ for all admissible probability measures $M_L$. He *indentifies a class $\mathcal{L}$ from random text* if he identifies all $L \in \mathcal{L}$ from random text. The set of all classes identified by learners in $\mathcal{S}$ from random text is denoted by $[\![\mathcal{S}]\!]$.

## 3    Relations to Identification in the Limit

In this section we compare identification in the limit and identification from random text. The first result is that learning from random text is at least as powerful as learning from text for all strategies. Then we show that $[\mathcal{F}] = [\![\mathcal{F}]\!]$

and $[\mathcal{F}^{rec}] = [\![\mathcal{F}^{rec}]\!]$, i.e., that general learners, resp. recursive learners as a whole are equally powerful in both models. The next theorem is based on the simple fact that a random text is a *text* with probability one.

**Theorem 1** $[\mathcal{S}] \subseteq [\![\mathcal{S}]\!]$ *for every set of strategies* $\mathcal{S} \subseteq \mathcal{F}$.

*Proof.* If $\phi \in \mathcal{S}$ identifies a language $L$ from text then it identifies every text for $L$. We have to show that $\phi$ identifies $L$ on a random text with probability one.

Let us fix some measure $M_L$. We want to show that $M_L(\mathcal{T}_L) = 1$. We can write $\mathcal{T}_L = \mathcal{T}_{\mathbf{P}(L)} - \bigcup_{i \in L} \mathcal{T}_{L-\{i\}}$, i.e., the texts for $L$ are all texts whose range is a subset of $L$ minus all texts whose range is a proper subset of $L$. But $\mathcal{T}_{\mathbf{P}(L)}$ is the sure event and therefore $M_L(\mathcal{T}_{\mathbf{P}(L)}) = 1$. All that remains is to show that $M_L(\mathcal{T}_{L-\{i\}}) = 0$ for every $i \in L$. We can write

$$\mathcal{T}_{L-\{i\}} \subseteq X_n = \bigcup \{ B_\sigma^L \mid \mathrm{lh}(\sigma) = n \text{ and } \sigma \text{ contains no } i \}$$

and $M_L(X_n) = (1 - m_L(i))^n$ and consequently $\sum_{n=1}^{\infty} M_L(X_n) < \infty$. The Borel–Cantelli Lemma implies $M_L(\limsup X_n) = 0$ and $M_L(\mathcal{T}_{L-\{i\}}) = 0$, since $\mathcal{T}_{L-\{i\}} = \limsup X_n$. ($\limsup X_n$ is the set of all elements that appear in infinitely many $X_n$.) Consequently $M_L(\mathcal{T}_L) = 1$.

We have shown that $\phi$ identifies $L$ on all texts except on a measure zero set. Consequently it identifies $L$ from random text. $\qquad\square$

The difficulty in the next theorem is to find a learner that fails on no text, if we only know that a learner exists that fails only on a set of measure zero.

**Theorem 2** $[\mathcal{F}] = [\![\mathcal{F}]\!]$.

*Proof.* The $\subseteq$-part acts as a special case of Theorem 1.

To prove the opposite direction let $\phi \in \mathcal{F}$ identify a class of languages $\mathcal{L}$ from random text. We can assume w.l.o.g. that $\phi(\sigma) = \phi(\tau)$ whenever $W_{\phi(\sigma)} = W_{\phi(\tau)}$. We construct a $\psi \in \mathcal{F}$ that identifies $\mathcal{L}$.

The purpose of using $\psi$ is to simulate $\phi(t)$ on a random text constructed from $t$ with a particular probability distribution. The following is a detailed definition of $\psi$:

Let $\sigma = (n_1, n_2, \ldots, n_m)$ be some sequence. Here the measure $m_\sigma$ is defined as $m_\sigma(n_i) = \sum_{n_j = n_i} 2^{-j}$ for $i = 1, \ldots, m$ and $m_\sigma(n) = 0$ if $n \notin \mathrm{rng}(\sigma)$. In this way we obtain a sequence $m_{\bar{t}_n}$ of measures. There is a limit distribution $m_t(i) = \lim_{n \to \infty} m_{\bar{t}_n}(i)$ that is a probability measure. The corresponding probability measure on texts is $M_t$, which is defined as $M_t(B_\sigma^L) = \prod_{i=1}^{\mathrm{lh}(\sigma)} m_t(\sigma_i)$.

We know that $\lim_{n \to \infty} M_t[W_{\phi(\bar{T}_n)} = L] = 1$ if $t$ is a text for $L$ from Theorem 1 because $M_t$ is admissible for $L$. Let us fix the language $L$ and a text $t$ for $L$. We can then find for every $\frac{1}{3} > \epsilon > 0$ an $N \in \mathbf{N}$, so that $M_t[W_{\phi(\bar{T}_n)} = L] \geq 1 - \epsilon$ for all $n \geq N$. To compute $\psi(\bar{t}_n)$ it suffices to look at all $\phi(\sigma)$ where $\mathrm{lh}(\sigma) = n$ and $m_t(\sigma) > 0$. There must be an $i \in \{ \phi(\sigma) \mid M_t(B_\sigma^L) > 0 \text{ and } \mathrm{lh}(\sigma) = n \}$, so that

$$\sum_\sigma M_t(B_\sigma^L) \geq 1 - \epsilon$$

where the sum is taken over all $\sigma$ such that $M_t(B_\sigma^L) > 0$, $\mathrm{lh}(\sigma) = n$, and $\phi(\sigma) = i$. Moreover, $W_i = L$. We cannot define $\psi(\bar{t}_n)$ as that $i$ because $m_t$ is not known. However, $m_{\bar{t}_n}$ and $m_t$ are very similar. If $\sigma$ contains no $j \notin \mathrm{rng}(\bar{t}_n)$, then clearly $M_{\bar{t}_n}(B_\sigma^L) = M_t(B_\sigma^L)$. The $M_t$-measure of all $B_\sigma^L$ with $\mathrm{lh}(\sigma) = n$ and $\mathrm{rng}(\sigma) \not\subseteq \mathrm{rng}(\bar{t}_n)$ is at most $n2^{-n}$. Hence,

$$\sum_\sigma M_{\bar{t}_n}(B_\sigma^L) \geq 1 - \frac{\epsilon}{2} \;\Rightarrow\; \sum_\sigma M_t(B_\sigma^L) \geq 1 - \epsilon \;\Rightarrow\; \sum_\sigma M_{\bar{t}_n}(B_\sigma^L) \geq 1 - \frac{3}{2}\epsilon$$

for sufficiently large $n$ (such that $n2^{-n} < \epsilon/2$). Consequently, we can define $\psi(\bar{t}_n)$ as that $i$ for which the sum of all $M_{\bar{t}_n}(B_\sigma^L)$ over all $\sigma$ with $\mathrm{rng}(\sigma) = \mathrm{rng}(\bar{t}_n)$, $\mathrm{lh}(\sigma) = n$, and $\phi(\sigma) = i$ is bigger than $1/2$. If such an $i$ does not exist, then $\psi(\bar{t}_n)$ is undefined. It is not hard to see that $\psi$ identifies all $L \in \mathcal{L}$. $\square$

The same is valid for *recursive learners:*

**Theorem 3** $[\mathcal{F}^{rec}] = [\![\mathcal{F}^{rec}]\!]$.

*Proof.* The construction in Theorem 2 of $\psi(\bar{t}_n)$ is not effective (this refers to the "w.l.o.g."-section). Let $\phi \in \mathcal{F}^{rec}$ identify $\mathcal{L}$ from random text. We construct a different $\psi \in \mathcal{F}^{rec}$ that also identifies $\mathcal{L}$ from random text, but that has an additional property: If $\psi$ identifies a language $\mathcal{L}$ from random text then there is a single index $i$ for each admissible $M_L$ making $M_L[\phi(T) = i] = 1$ and $W_i = L$. In order to define $\psi$ we decompose $T$ into a countable number of disjoint texts $T^k$ for example by $T_n^k = T_{\langle k,n \rangle}$, where $\langle k, n \rangle = 2^k 3^n$. Then $\psi(\bar{T}_{\langle k,n \rangle}) = \min\{ \phi(\bar{T}_n^i) \mid 1 \leq i \leq k \}$. (If $m$ cannot be written as $\langle k, n \rangle$ then $\psi(\bar{T}_m) = \psi(\bar{T}_{\langle k,n \rangle})$ where $\langle k, n \rangle$ is the next smaller number of this form.) For each $i$ with $M_L[\phi(T) = i] > 0$ the probability that $\phi(T^k) = i$ for *some* $k$ is one. Therefore with probability one $\psi(T) = i$ where $i$ the minimal number with $M_L[\phi(T) = i] > 0$.

If we use $\psi$ instead of $\phi$ in the construction of Theorem 2, we can avoid deciding whether $W_i = W_j$. Then the construction becomes effective. $\square$

The remainder of this section deals with three strategies: set-driven, memory limited, and confident learners. If $[\mathcal{S}] = [\mathcal{F}]$, then $[\![\mathcal{S}]\!] = [\![\mathcal{F}]\!]$ (a simple corollary of the above theorem). If, however, $[\mathcal{S}] \subset [\mathcal{F}]$, then both $[\![\mathcal{S}]\!] = [\![\mathcal{F}]\!]$ and $[\![\mathcal{S}]\!] \subset [\![\mathcal{F}]\!]$ remain possible (the same applies for $\mathcal{F}^{rec}$ instead of $\mathcal{F}$). It is known that $[\mathcal{F}^{rec} \cap \mathcal{F}^{set-driven}] \subset [\mathcal{F}^{rec}]$ [11,4]. A learner is *set-driven* if each hypothesis depends only on the set of examples so far seen, but not on their order or multiplicity. The next theorem implies $[\mathcal{F}^{rec} \cap \mathcal{F}^{set-driven}] = [\![\mathcal{F}^{rec} \cap \mathcal{F}^{set-driven}]\!]$, since it states both models are equivalent for set-driven learners. If a learner is set-driven he cannot fail on a single text when learning from random text. Surprisingly, this is not true for rearrangement-independent learners, whose hypotheses depend only on the set of examples so far seen and on their number.

**Theorem 4** *Let $L \in \mathrm{RE}$ be a language where $\phi \in \mathcal{F}^{set\ driven}$ identifies $L$ from random text. Then $\phi$ identifies $L$.*

*Proof.* If $L$ is finite then $\phi$ locks as soon as it has seen all words form $L$. Otherwise it would converge on no text at all to the right hypothesis. Hence, it converges on all texts.

If $L$ is infinite, then take an arbitraty text $t = (n_1, n_2, n_3, \ldots)$ for $L$. We can assume that all $n_i$ are pairwise distinct, since $\phi$ is set-driven. Define $\mathcal{M} = \{\{n_1, n_2, \ldots, n_m\} \mid m \in \mathbf{N}\}$ and $S = \{t \in \mathcal{T} \mid \mathrm{rng}(\bar{t}_n) \in \mathcal{M} \text{ for all } n \in \mathbf{N}\}$. Then there is a measure $m_L$ such that $M_L(S) > 0$, e.g., $m_L(n_k) = ce^{-4^k}$ with $c = 1/\sum_{k=1}^{\infty} e^{-4^k}$ (a short computation shows $M_L(S) > 1/2$). Since $\phi$ is set-driven it converges on all texts from $S$ to the same hypothesis or it diverges on all of them. The latter cannot happen, since $S$ does not have a measure of zero. Therefore $\phi$ converges to the correct hypothesis on all of $S$. Since $t \in S$, $\phi$ identifies $t$. $\qquad\square$

**Corollary 1** $[\mathcal{S}] = [\![\mathcal{S}]\!]$ *for all* $\mathcal{S} \subseteq \mathcal{T}^{set\text{-}driven}$.

The same result does not hold for rearrangement-independent learners which shows that the *number* of examples plays a crucial role in this context.

**Theorem 5** *There is a* $\mathcal{S} \subseteq \mathcal{T}^{rearrangement\ independent}$ *such that* $[\mathcal{S}] \neq [\![\mathcal{S}]\!]$.

*Proof.* Let $\mathcal{L} = \{\{1\}, \mathbf{N}\}$ and $\phi$ defined via

$$\phi(\sigma) = \begin{cases} i \text{ if } \sigma = (1, 1, 1, \ldots, 1) \text{ or } \mathrm{rng}(\sigma) = \{1, 2, 3, \ldots, \mathrm{lh}(\sigma)\} \\ j \text{ otherwise.} \end{cases}$$

Obviously, $\phi$ is rearrangement independent (but not set-driven). While $\phi$ identifies $\mathcal{L}$ from random text, it does not identify $\mathcal{L}$. Now choose $\mathcal{S} = \{\phi\}$.

It is easy to see that $\phi$ identifies $\mathbf{N}$ from random text since $\phi$ identifies every text for $\mathbf{N}$ unless $t_1 \neq t_i$ for all $i > 1$. This happens with probability $\lim_{n \to \infty} (1 - m_L(1))^n = 0$. $\qquad\square$

Memory limited learners are an example of a natural strategy causing no restriction on learning from random text, but causing a restriction on learning in the limit. A learner $\phi$ is *memory limited* if there is a number $n$ such that $\phi(\sigma)$ depends only on $\phi(\sigma_1 \sigma_2 \ldots \sigma_{\mathrm{lh}(\sigma)-1})$ and $\sigma_{\mathrm{lh}(\sigma)}, \sigma_{\mathrm{lh}(\sigma)-1}, \ldots, \sigma_{\mathrm{lh}(\sigma)-n}$ for all sequences $\sigma$ [12]. A memory limited learner remembers only his last hypothesis and the last $n$ examples.

**Theorem 6** $[\mathcal{T}^{memory\ limited}] = [\mathcal{T}]$.

*Proof.* First we show that every random text is a fat text (a text that contains everything infinitely often) with probability one. Let $f : \mathbf{N} \to \mathbf{N} \times \mathbf{N}$ be an arbitrary bijective function. Then $T_{(i)} = (T_{f(i,1)}, T_{f(i,2)}, T_{f(i,3)}, \ldots)$ is a random text for every $i \in \mathbf{N}$. We have already shown that every random text is a text with probability one. Hence, $T$ contains an infinite number of texts $T_{(i)}$ with probability one.

Let $\mathcal{L} \subseteq RE$ and let $\phi$ identify $\mathcal{L}$ from random text. Then there is a $\psi$ that identifies $\mathcal{L}$ from text (Theorem 2) and we can assume that $\psi$ identifies $\mathcal{L}$ memory limited from fat text [8]. Since every random text is a fat text with probability one, $\psi$ identifies $\mathcal{L}$ from random text, too.                               □

Confidency is an example, where old proof techniques partially transfer to learning from random text. In most cases this is not possible, in particular if the proofs are based on locking sequence arguments. A learner is *confident* if he converges on all texts, even on texts for a language that he does not identify.

**Theorem 7** $[\mathcal{F}^{confident}] \subset [\mathcal{F}]$.

*Proof.* We can adapt the proof of $[\mathcal{F}^{confident}] \subset [\mathcal{F}]$ of Osherson, Stob, and Weinstein [8]. While the basic principle remains the same, the proof for learning from random text is much more involved as they use failure on single texts, while we have to provide sets with non-zero measure. Suppose $\phi \in \mathcal{F}$ identifies $RE_{fin}$ (the finite languages) from random text. Let $\sigma^0$ be the shortest sequence of zeros such that $W_{\phi(\sigma^0)} = \{0\}$. Such $\sigma^0$ exists, since $(0,0,\dots)$ is the only text for $\{0\}$ and therefore every random text coincides with it with probability 1. Let $\sigma^1$ be the shortest sequence of zeros and ones such that $W_{\phi(\sigma^0\sigma^1)} = \{0,1\}$. Let $L = \mathbf{N}$ and $M_L$ be admissible. Again, this $\sigma^1$ exists because $M_L(B_{\sigma^0}^{\{0,1\}} - B_{\sigma^0}^{\{0\}}) > 0$ and therefore are many sequences starting with $\sigma^0$ and on which $\phi$ even identifies $\{0,1\}$. Generally we define $\sigma^n$ to be the shortest sequence of $\{1,\dots,n\}$ such that $W_{\phi(\sigma^1\sigma^2\dots\sigma^n)} = \{1,2,\dots,n\}$. For analogous reasons as above $\sigma^n$ must exist.

However, $\phi$ obviously does not converge on $\sigma^1\sigma^2\sigma^3\dots$ and is therefore not confident. Since $RE_{fin} \in [\mathcal{F}]$ the claim follows.                               □

## 4   Locking Sequences

Locking sequences play a crucial role in many proofs. In general, no locking sequences may exist when learning from random text. The following theorems give simple characterizations, when locking sequences exist and when not.

**Lemma 1** $\mathcal{T}_L \cap B_\sigma^L$ and $B_\sigma^L$ are equivalent modula a meager set in $\mathcal{T}_L$.

*Proof.* $\mathcal{T}_L \cap B_\sigma^L = B_\sigma^L - \bigcup_{i \in L} B_\sigma^{L-\{i\}}$ and $B_\sigma^{L-\{i\}}$ is nowhere dense if $i \notin L$: Every non-void open set contains some basic open set $B_\tau^L$ that contains then itself $B_{\tau i}^L$, which is disjoint from $B_\sigma^{L-\{i\}}$.                               □

**Theorem 8** Let $\phi \in \mathcal{F}^{total}$ identify $L \in RE$ from random text. Let $M$ be the measure zero set of texts for $L$ on which $\phi$ does not identify $L$. Then the following three statements are equivalent: (1) Every $\sigma$ with $rng(\sigma) \subseteq L$ is prefix of a locking sequence for $L$. (2) $M$ is meager in $\mathcal{T}_L$. (3) $M$ is nowhere dense in $\mathcal{T}_L$.

*Proof.* We show $2 \Rightarrow 1 \Rightarrow 3 \Rightarrow 2$. Fix some admissible $M_L$ and let $\mathrm{rng}(\sigma) \subseteq L$. Since $\phi$ identifies $L$ on all texts in $\mathcal{T}_L - M$,

$$\mathcal{T}_L \cap B_\sigma^L \subseteq \bigcup \{ F_\phi^{-1}(\{t\}) \mid t \text{ is stabilized on } L \text{ and } \sigma \sqsubseteq t \} \cup M. \tag{1}$$

Since $B_\sigma^L$ and $\mathcal{T}_L \cap B_\sigma^L$ are equivalent modulo a meager set, $\mathcal{T}_L \cap B_\sigma^L$ is not contained in a meager set by the Baire category theorem. In particular, the right hand side of (1) is not meager and since $M$ is meager, some $F_\phi^{-1}(\{t\})$ cannot be nowhere dense if $t$ is stabilized on $L$ and $\sigma \sqsubseteq t$. Since $F_\phi^{-1}(\{t\})$ is closed this means that $\emptyset \neq \mathrm{Int}(F_\phi^{-1}(\{t\})) \subseteq F_\phi^{-1}(\{t\})$. As a non-void closed set $F_\phi^{-1}(\{t\})$ contains some basic open set $B_\tau^L$. The corresponding sequence $\tau \sqsupseteq \sigma$ is a locking sequence for $\phi$ on $L$.

$1 \Rightarrow 3$: Let us assume that $t$ is an accumulation point of $M$ and let $\sigma \sqsubset t$. Then every open subset of $B_\sigma^L$ is not disjoint from $M$. Hence $\sigma$ is not not a locking sequence. Since we can choose $\sigma$ arbitrarily, *no* prefix of $t$ is a locking sequence.

$3 \Rightarrow 2$: Every set that is nowhere dense is meager. □

**Theorem 9** *Let $\phi \in \mathcal{F}^{total}$ identify $L \in$ RE from random text. Let $M$ be the measure zero set of texts for $L$ on which $\phi$ does not identify $L$. Then the following conditions are equivalent: (1) $\phi$ has a locking sequence for $L$. (2) $M$ is not dense in $\mathcal{T}_L$. (3) $M$ is not comeager in $\mathcal{T}_L$.*

*Proof.* $1 \Rightarrow 2$: Assume $M$ is dense and $\sigma$ is a locking sequence. This is not possible since $B_\tau^L \cap M \neq \emptyset$ for every $\tau$ with $\mathrm{rng}(\tau) \subseteq L$ because $M$ is dense. Since $\sigma$ is a locking sequence, however, $B_\sigma^L \cap M = \emptyset$.

$2 \Rightarrow 3$: If a set is not dense, it is not comeager.

$3 \Rightarrow 1$: If $M$ is not comeager, then $\mathcal{T}_L - M$ is not meager because $\mathcal{T}_L$ is itself comeager. As before we can argue as follows:

$$\mathcal{T}_L - M \subseteq \{ F_\phi^{-1}(t) \mid t \text{ is stabilized on } L \}$$

Since $\mathcal{T}_L - M$ is not meager some $F_\phi^{-1}(t)$ is not nowhere dense and contains as a closed set some basic open set $B_\sigma^L$ and $\sigma$ is a locking sequence. □

The above two theorems are stated for total functions. The reason is that the proofs use $F_\phi$, which is a function that maps texts to texts — and not to "partial texts." It is possible, but very technical to modify the proofs for partial functions. A simpler way is the following, from which the same generalization immeadiately follows:

**Theorem 10** *Let $\phi \in \mathcal{F}$ identify $\mathcal{L} \subseteq$ RE from random text. Then there is a $\psi \in \mathcal{F}^{total}$ that identifies also $\mathcal{L}$ from random text and has the same failure sets as $\phi$ for every $L \in \mathcal{L}$. Moreover $\phi$ and $\psi$ have the same locking sequences for each $L \in \mathcal{L}$.*

*Proof.* Let $W_i \notin \mathcal{L}$. Define $\psi$ as

$$\psi(\sigma) = \begin{cases} \phi(\sigma) & \text{if } \phi(\sigma) \text{ is defined,} \\ i & \text{otherwise.} \end{cases}$$

Obviously, $\phi$ and $\sigma$ share the same locking sequences. If $\phi$ diverges on a text, $\psi$ diverges, too, or converges to $i$ thus failing to identify an $L \in \mathcal{L}$. If $\phi$ identifies some $L \in \mathcal{L}$ then $\psi$ converges to the same hypothesis. Hence, the failure sets are identical. □

Since $\phi \in \mathcal{F}$ and $\psi \in \mathcal{F}^{total}$ share conditions (1), (2), and (3) in Theorems 8 and 9, the three conditions are also equivalent for a partial function $\phi \in \mathcal{F}$.

Example how to use these characterizations: Can a learner fail on $t$ iff $t$ consists only of 1's with finitely many exceptions? The answer would be no, as there is obviously no locking sequence. Nevertheless the failure set is dense. Another application is the following theorem, which guarantees that confident learners have locking sequences. Nevertheless, confident learners *can* have non-void failure sets, but they cannot be dense.

**Theorem 11** *Every $\phi \in \mathcal{F}^{confident}$ that identifies a language $L$ from random text has a locking sequence for $L$.*

*Proof.* Since $\phi$ is confident it converges on every text. Therefore

$$\mathcal{T}_L \subseteq \bigcup \{ F_\phi^{-1}(t) \mid t \text{ is stabilized} \}$$

and again because of Baire's category theorem some $F_\phi^{-1}(t)$ is not nowhere dense and contains a basic open set $B_\sigma^L$. This $\sigma$ is a locking sequence. □

This theorem can also be easily generalized such that even every sequence is prefix of a locking sequence.

## 5   Tail Bounds

It can be shown that general learners can *learn arbitrarily slowly*, i.e., the probability that they still fail after $n$ rounds (the convergence indicator) converges arbitrarily slowly towards zero (the proof is based on ignoring larger and larger segments of the text, which slows down learning). However, the next theorem shows that recursive learners cannot learn arbitrarily slowly: Either they converge "fast" or they cannot learn at all.

**Theorem 12** *Let $L \in$ RE and let some $m_L$ be fixed. There is then a function $h: \mathbf{N} \to \mathbf{Q}$ such that $f(n) = o(h(n))$ for every $f$ that is a convergence indicator for a $\phi \in \mathcal{F}^{rec}$ that identifies $L$ with probability one.*

*Proof.* We define an oracle $O : \mathbf{N} \times \mathbf{Q}^+ \to \mathbf{Q}$ such that $|O(i, \epsilon) - m_L(i)| < \epsilon$, i.e., $O(i, \epsilon)$ is a rational number that is very near at $m_L(i)$, but still remains a rational number. Moreover, let $O(i, \epsilon) = 0$ iff $m_L(i) = 0$, i.e., iff $i \notin L$. The oracle $O$ is not uniquely determined; we just choose some $O$ with these properties.

An oracle Turing machine that has access to $O$ and additionally access to the *halting problem for Turing machines with oracle $O$* can compute a lower bound for $f(n)$ (the details are omitted).

Hence, whenever $\phi$ measure one identifies a language $L$ with convergence indicator $f$, then there is a function $g$ with $g(n) > f(n)$. Moreover, this $g$ is computable by some kind of oracle Turing machine whose oracle depends only on $m_L$, but not on $\phi$. Therefore, let $h$ be a function shrinking so slowly towards zero for $n \to \infty$ such that no oracle Turing machine as defined above can compute a function that shrinks slower (it can be easily constructed by diagonalization). This $h$ is the claimed function. □

The following theorem states that for each nontrivial learning problem *exponential tail bounds* can always be achieved and are also the best bounds possible.

**Theorem 13** *If $\mathcal{L} \in [\![\mathcal{F}]\!]$ (resp. $\mathcal{L} \in [\![\mathcal{F}^{rec}]\!]$) and $\mathcal{L}$ contains at least two languages that are not disjoint, then the convergence indicator for some $L \in \mathcal{L}$ is always $\Omega(1)^n$. On the other hand there is always a $\phi \in \mathcal{F}$ (resp. $\phi \in \mathcal{F}^{rec}$) that learns $\mathcal{L}$ from random text and whose convergence indicator for $L$ is $O(1)^n$.*

*Proof.* The lower bound follows from a text $(i, i, i, \dots)$ where $W_i$ is contained in two languages of $L$. Each learner fails on at least one of them. The upper bound follows from rearrangement-independent learners: If $\mathcal{L}$ is identified by a rearrangement-independent learner, its convergence indicator is $O(1)^n$, since he converges when the examples read contain a locking set. □

This proof also shows that every rearrangement-independent learner (and thus every conservative one) have automatically exponentially small tail bounds. It is already known that this is the case for learners that are simultaneously conservative (or rearrangement-independent) and conservative [10]. Then, however, there exists a tight relationsship between the tail bounds and the expected learning time, which is lacking if the learner is not conservative.

## 6   Conclusion

A stochastic model is a prerequisite to study the *speed of learning in inductive inference*, which was the main objective to start this line of research. There are several stochastic models available, where positive examples are generated independently and identically distributed according to a distribution. Kapur and Bilardi show how to construct learners in a uniform way [6].

If the same learner must identify a language for all reasonable probability distributions, then the only languages that are learnable are those that are also learnable in Gold's model of learning in the limit [5]. We call the latter stochastic model *learning from random text*. This model captures all classes of languages learnable in Gold's model and none else. However, learners restricted in some ways can learn more classes from random text than from text. An example are memory limited learners. On the other hand, for many strategies the two models coincide.

While there exist always locking sequences for Gold-style learners, this is not necessarily the case for learning from random text. The existence of locking sequences is closely related to the topological properties of the failure sets.

The general results on the *speed* of learning are as follows. One problem of inductive inference is a learner does never know whether he already converged or whether he will have to change his hypothesis somewhere in the future. Exponentially small tail bounds let the probability of the latter drop very fast, so exponentially small tail bounds are a useful property of a learner. We have seen that everything that can be learned at all can also be learned with exponentially small tail bounds, but not better. In particular, stochastically finite learning [10] is always possible in principle.

# References

1. D. Angluin. Finding patterns common to a set of strings. *Journal of Computer and System Sciences*, 21(1):46–62, 1980.

2. L. Blum and M. Blum. Toward a mathematical theory of inductive inference. *Information and Control*, 28:125–155, 1975.

3. T. Erlebach, P. Rossmanith, H. Stadtherr, A. Steger, and T. Zeugmann. Learning one-variable pattern languages very efficiently on average, in parallel, and by asking queries. In M. Li and A. Maruoka, editors, *Proceedings of the 8th International Workshop on Algorithmic Learning Theory*, number 1316 in Lecture Notes in Computer Science, pages 260–276. Springer-Verlag, October 1997.

4. M. A. Fulk. Prudence and other conditions on formal language learning. *Information and Computation*, 85:1–11, 1990.

5. E. M. Gold. Language identification in the limit. *Information and Control*, 10:447–474, 1967.

6. S. Kapur and G. Bilardi. Language learning from stochastic input. In *Proceedings of the 5th International Workshop on Computational Learning Theory*, pages 303–310. ACM, 1992.

7. S. Kapur and G. Bilardi. Learning of indexed families from stochastic input. In *The Australasian Theory Symposium (CATS'96)*, pages 162–167, Melbourne, Australia, January 1996.

8. D. Osherson, M. Stob, and S. Weinstein. *Systems That Learn: An Introduction for Cognitive and Computer Scientists*. MIT Press, Cambridge, Mass., 1986.

9. R. Reischuk and T. Zeugmann. A complete and tight average-case analysis of learning monomials. In C. Meinel and S. Tison, editors, *Proceedings of the 16th Symposium on Theoretical Aspects of Computer Science*, number 1563 in Lecture Notes in Computer Science, pages 414–423. Springer-Verlag, 1999.

10. P. Rossmanith and T. Zeugmann. Learning $k$-variable pattern languages efficiently stochastically finite on average from positive date. In V. Honavar and G. Slutzki, editors, *Proceedings of the 4th International Colloquium on Grammatical Inference*,

number 1433 in Lecture Notes in Artificial Intelligence, pages 13–24, Ames, Iowa, jul 1998. Springer-Verlag.

11. G. Schäfer. *Über Eingabeabhängigkeit und Komplexität von Inferenzstrategien.* PhD thesis, Rheinisch Westfälische Technische Hochschule Aachen, 1984. In German.

12. K. Wexler and P. Culicover. *Formal Principles of Language Acquisition.* MIT Press, Cambridge, Mass., 1980.

13. T. Zeugmann. Lange and Wiehagen's pattern learning algorithm: An average-case analysis with respect to its total learning time. *Annals of Mathematics and Artificial Intelligence,* 23(1–2):117–145, 1998.

# Inductive Learning with Corroboration

Phil Watson

Department of Computer Science,
University of Kent at Canterbury,
Canterbury, Kent CT2 7NZ, United Kingdom.
P.R.Watson@ukc.ac.uk

**Abstract.** The basis of inductive learning is the process of generating and refuting hypotheses. Natural approaches to this form of learning assume that a data item that causes refutation of one hypothesis opens the way for the introduction of a new (for now unrefuted) hypothesis, and so such data items have attracted the most attention. Data items that do not cause refutation of the current hypothesis have until now been largely ignored in these processes, but in practical learning situations they play the key role of *corroborating* those hypotheses that they do not refute.

We formalise a version of K.R. Popper's concept of *degree of corroboration* for inductive inference and utilise it in an inductive learning procedure which has the natural behaviour of outputting the most strongly corroborated (non-refuted) hypothesis at each stage. We demonstrate its utility by providing characterisations of several of the commonest identification types in the case of learning from text over class-preserving hypothesis spaces and proving the existence of canonical learning strategies for these types. In many cases we believe that these characterisations make the relationships between these types clearer than the standard characterisations. The idea of learning with corroboration therefore provides a unifying approach for the field.

*Keywords*: Degree of Corroboration; Inductive Inference; Philosophy of Science.

## 1 Introduction

The field of machine inductive inference has developed in an ad hoc manner, in particular in the characterisations of identification types which have been achieved. In this paper we wish to propose a new unifying framework for the field based on the philosophical work of K. R. Popper, and in particular his concept of *degree of corroboration*. We will demonstrate that many of the existing identification types in the case of learning from text allow an alternative characterisation using the concept of learning with corroboration; in particular this approach reveals the existence of canonical learning algorithms for the various types.

O. Watanabe, T. Yokomori (Eds.): ALT'99, LNAI 1720, pp. 145–156, 1999.
© Springer-Verlag Berlin Heidelberg 1999

We will be concerned with learning *indexable recursive families* of *recursive languages* from *text*. We restrict our attention to the standard case of *class-preserving* hypothesis spaces, i.e. those indexed recursive families $H_1, H_2, \ldots$ for $C$ such that for every $L \in C$ there exists at least one (and possibly many) $i$ such that $H_i$ describes $L$ and every $H_i$ describes some $L$ in $C$.

We assume the standard definitions in the field of machine inductive inference [Go67, An80, AS83]. Definitions of other concepts used in this paper may be found as follows: strong monotonic learning (*SMON-TXT*) [Ja91]; refuting inductive inference machines (RIIMs) [MA93, LW94]; justified refuting learning (*JREF-TXT*) [LW94]; set-driven learning (*s-\*-TXT*) [WC80, LZ94].

Our notation will mostly be standard. We mention the following points. $\mathbb{N}$ will be the natural numbers $0, 1, 2, \ldots$ while $\mathbb{N}^+$ will be the positive integers $1, 2, 3, \ldots$. Our languages $L$ will be non-empty sets of words over a fixed finite alphabet $\Sigma$; therefore $L \subseteq \Sigma^*$. We will write $(\Sigma^*)$ for the space of all finite and infinite sequences from $\Sigma^*$; therefore if $t$ is a text for language $L$, we have $t \in (\Sigma^*)$. We write $t_m$ for the finite initial subsequence of $t$ of length $m + 1$, and $t_m^+$ for the content of $t_m$, i.e. if $t = s_0, s_1, s_2, \ldots$ then $t_m^+ = \{s_i \mid i \leq m\}$. $Index(C)$ will be the set of all class-preserving recursive indexings $\mathcal{L}$ of class $C$ of recursive languages; such indexings will be our hypothesis spaces. If hypothesis $H \in \mathcal{L}$ describes language $L \in C$, where $\mathcal{L} \in Index(C)$, then we abuse notation slightly by writing $H = L$. Similarly if $H_1, H_2 \in \mathcal{L}$ describe the same $L \in C$ we write $H_1 = H_2$. We say that $t_m$ refutes $H$ iff $t_m^+ \not\subseteq H$. The set of all texts for $H$ will be written $Txt(H)$ while $Txts(\mathcal{L})$ will be the set of all texts $t$ such that $(\exists H \in \mathcal{L}) t \in Txt(H)$.

## 2    Degree of Corroboration

### 2.1    Popper's 'Logic of Scientific Discovery'

The philosopher K.R. Popper [Po34, Po54, Po57, Po63] defined a philosophical and logical system covering the epistemology and practice of science. A central plank of this system was the concept of *degree of corroboration*, $C(x, y)$, meaning the degree to which a theory $x$ receives support from the available evidence $y$. Evidence supporting $x$ causes $C(x, y)$ to increase in value, while evidence undermining $x$ causes $C(x, y)$ to decrease. A set of ten desiderata [Po34, Po57] defined $C(x, y)$. Space precludes a full discussion of these desiderata here; the reader is referred to [Wa99].

Popper's degree of corroboration is a practical measure enabling us to choose between unrefuted theories, given that a scientific theory is, by its very nature, incaple of proof (another major strand of Popper's work was concerned with settling this point). We should tentatively believe the best-corroborated hypothesis at any given time.

An interesting recent discussion of Popper's work is to be found in Gillies [Gi93, Gi96]. There a logical system is characterised as one with both inferential and control elements; in both Popper's work and the present paper corroboration plays the role of control. Indeed given the characterisations using canonical learners which we have obtained for standard learning types (Section 4) we may say that degree of corroboration is the *only* control element necessary in machine inductive inference. A more detailed discussion of Gillies's work may be found in [Wa99].

## 2.2   Our Differences from Popper's Approach - Discussion

**Restricted Domain** We wish to define a corroboration function analogous to Popper's but for use in the domain of inductive learning theory. This restricted domain enables us to make a number of simplifying assumptions compared to Popper's version.

First we note that we always wish to state how well a *hypothesis* is corroborated by *data*. This is already more specific than Popper's approach, in which he specifically allows the corroboration of, for example, one theory by another. Our hypotheses will be those of an *inductive inference machine* and will come from a particular *hypothesis space*, within which we aim to find a true description of the phenomenon producing the data, which will be a recursive language. The data will be a sequence of *examples* forming a *text* (or strictly speaking, forming at any particular time an initial segment of a text) for the phenomenon.

$c(H, t)$ will be the degree to which example text $t$ corroborates hypothesis $H$. Lower case is used to distinguish our versions of Popper's functions.

**Fixed Values** We assume that data is free of noise, and that we aim to find a hypothesis which *exactly* describes or explains the concept producing the data. Now the idea that data *undermines* (Popper's choice of word) a theory can be replaced by outright refutation in the case that data disagrees with the predictions of the theory. Thus all the possible negative values in Popper's scheme may be replaced in ours by $-1$, the corroboration value of refuted hypotheses.

Similarly the value 0, reserved by Popper for the degree of corroboration offered to $x$ by an independent theory $y$, subtly changes its meaning when we restrict ourselves to corroboration of hypotheses by data. The value 0 is now the corroboration given to any theory by the empty data set $\emptyset$, by vacuous data which gives us no help in choosing between competing hypotheses in our space, or in the case that the theory itself is tautological, metaphysical or otherwise not logically refutable.

**References to Probability** For historical reasons, Popper's desiderata are tied closely to definitions in probability; specifically, Popper sets out to demonstrate that degree of corroboration is in no sense a measure of probability. For our purposes, we have no need of any directly defined probabilistic measures. In a powerful argument, Popper identified the maximum degree of corroboration possible for a hypothesis with its logical *im*probability, and therefore with its scientific interest. Similarly, we use $c(H)$ to mean the highest degree of corroboration of which $H$ is capable; however we drop the reference to $P(\overline{x})$ in Popper's definition of $C(x)$ and instead add some natural restrictions on $c(H)$.

Popper's dependence on probabilistic definitions leads him to restrict the maximum degree of corroboration in any case to the value 1. Objections to this unnecessary restriction led him to drop it in [Po57], and we do likewise. Further, we may drop the restriction of degrees of corroboration to real number values altogether, and use any partially ordered set $S$ with a minimum element $-1$ such that $S-\{-1\}$ has a minimum element 0, and decidable (recursive) relations $\geq, \leq$ and $\bowtie$.

### 2.3   Our Definition of Degree of Corroboration

Let $H$ range over hypotheses from our space $\mathcal{L}$, and $t$ over texts and finite initial segments of texts. We assume that $c(H, t)$ ranges over some partially ordered set $S$ with minimum element $-1$ and an element 0 minimal in $S - \{-1\}$. We write $c(H)$ for the maximum degree of corroboration possible for $H$. Falsifiers$(H)$ is the set of potential data items in $\Sigma^*$ which refute $H$. If Falsifiers$(H_i) \subseteq$ Falsifiers$(H_j)$ then we will write $H_j \subseteq H_i$ to capture the natural Popperian sense that $H_j$ is more easily refuted (potentially more strongly corroborable) than $H_i$.

Our model of learning requires that $c(H, t)$ and comparison $(\leq)$ between degrees of corroboration are both recursive, but not necessarily that $c(H)$ is recursive or that $c(H_i) \leq c(H_j)$ is decidable.

First we formally define our corroboration functions.

**Definition 1.** *A corroboration function $c : \mathcal{L} \times (\Sigma^*) \to S$ over $\mathcal{L}$ maps hypotheses and texts to some set $S$ with minimum element $-1$ and an element 0 minimal in $S-\{-1\}$ such that $S$ has a decidable partial ordering $\leq$, and satisfies the following desiderata for all hypotheses $H, H' \in \mathcal{L}$ and all texts $t, t' \in (\Sigma^*)$:*

1. *$c(H, t) = -1$ iff there exists data in $t$ which refutes $H$.*
2. *$c(H, t) \geq 0$ iff $t$ does not refute $H$*
3. *$c(H, t) = 0$ if $t$ is empty or contains no data capable of refutation of any hypothesis in our space.*
4. *$c(H) = max\{Lim_{n\to\infty}c(H, t_n) \mid t$ is a text for $H\}$ is uniquely defined*
5. *$c(H) \geq c(H')$ if $H \subseteq H'$*
6. *If $t$ is a finite initial subsequence of $t'$ then either $c(H, t) \leq c(H, t')$ or $c(H, t') = -1$*

Note that item 5 in the definition implies that if $H = H'$ then $c(H) = c(H')$.

Our definition of degree of corroboration is simpler than Popper's because we have dropped all reference to probability and this gives us greater freedom when actually assigning values to our functions $c(H)$ and $c(H, t)$. We will see in the next section that certain inductive learning identification criteria will require corroboration functions with additional properties to those specified above.

## 3   Learning with Corroboration

In this section we cover the remaining assumptions and definitions necessary to define a theory of inductive learning with corroboration.

## 3.1   Hypotheses and Hypothesis Spaces

All forms of inductive inference suffer from the problem that the learner is required to choose one from among (typically) infinitely many hypotheses at each stage. Clearly no learner can consider all these hypotheses before it outputs a hypothesis or requests further data, so in effect there are only a limited number of hypotheses *in play* at any given time. Most authors gloss over this question as a matter of detail, or deal with it implicitly, but as we intend to propose a new unifying model for machine inductive inference, we feel constrained to deal with it explicitly.

We therefore assume that along with our hypothesis space $H_1, H_2, ...$ we have a recursive, monotonically increasing function $ip : \mathbb{N} \to \mathbb{N}$ with $Lim_{n \to \infty} ip(n) = \infty$ which gives the number of hypotheses in play at stage $n$ of any learning procedure with this hypothesis space. This leads to one slight concession with respect to our desiderata: hypotheses $H_j$ which are not yet in play at stage $n$ need not be considered to be either refuted or corroborated by $t_n$, the examples seen to that stage - we therefore arbitrarily assign $c(H_j, t_n) = 0$ for such $n, j$. This cannot cause confusion as these hypotheses are (by definition) not considered by any algorithm; it serves only to simplify some algorithms defined in the proofs.

## 3.2   Corroboration Functions and Canonical Learners with Corroboration

In the following section (Section 4) we examine the use of corroboration in inductive learning and prove that many of the most natural inductive learning identification types can be characterised by an existence condition for a suitable corroboration function over the hypothesis space. Our intention is that this corroboration function (which is invariably recursive so no undecidability results are implied, nor is any additional computing power gained illicitly) will be used as an oracle by a canonical learner for the appropriate type; this demonstrates that there is effectively a single best learning strategy for each identification type, and only the details of the corroboration function change depending on the hypothesis space.

The behaviour of a learner with corroboration is defined as follows.

**Definition 2.** *Turing machine $\mathcal{M}$, with oracle $c(H, t)$ is called a* learner with corroboration *if $c(H, t)$ is a recursive corroboration function and on input $t$ with hypotheses $H_1, .., H_p$ in play, $\mathcal{M}$ outputs some $i \leq p$ such that $c(H_i, t) > 0$ is maximal among the $c(H_j, t), j = 1, ..., p$, if defined, and requests more input otherwise.*

*If additionally $\mathcal{M}$ learns within identification type $*$, we call $\mathcal{M}$ a $*$-learner with corroboration.*

Clearly such a learner is consistent with Popper's dictum that we should prefer the most strongly corroborated hypothesis among competing hypotheses.

# 4   Characterising TXT-Identification Types in Learning with Corroboration

In this section we are concerned only with learning from *text*, and often abbreviate the names of identification types by dropping the *-TXT*. Our learners always work with respect to *class-preserving* hypothesis spaces.

Lack of space precludes the inclusion of most proofs. The proofs of the Theorems follow the form of the proof of Theorem 1 with additional details for the more complex learning types. The Corollaries concerning canonical learners rely on the observation that in each case the learner defined in the $\Leftarrow$ part of the proof of the preceding Theorem depends on $C$ only via $c$. All proofs may be found in [Wa99].

## 4.1   LIM- and s-LIM-Learning

**Definition 3.** *A corroboration function c over $\mathcal{L}$ is called* limiting *iff*

$$(\forall H \in \mathcal{L})(\forall t \in Txt(H))(\exists i)[H_i = H \wedge$$
$$(\exists n)(\forall m \geq n)(\forall j)[c(H_i, t_m) > c(H_j, t_m) \vee [c(H_i, t_m) \not< c(H_j, t_m) \wedge i \leq j]]]$$

**Theorem 1.** *$C \in LIM\text{-}TXT$ iff there exists $\mathcal{L} \in Index(C)$ such that there is a recursive limiting corroboration function c over $\mathcal{L}$.*

*Proof.* $(\Leftarrow)$

We define a learner $\mathcal{M}$ which uses such a recursive limiting $c$ to *LIM*-learn any $H \in \mathcal{L}$.

Let $t$ be a text. Let the hypotheses in play at stage $m$ be $H_1, ..., H_p$. At the $(m+1)$th stage (i.e. on input $t_m$) $\mathcal{M}$ behaves as follows.

$$\mathcal{M}(t_m) \begin{cases} = min(Best_m) & \text{if defined} \\ \text{requests more input} & \text{otherwise} \end{cases}$$

where

$$Best_m = \{i \mid i \leq p \wedge c(H_i, t_m) > 0 \wedge (\forall j \leq p)c(H_i, t_m) \not< c(H_j, t_m)\}$$

$\mathcal{M}$ *is recursive:* $\mathcal{M}$ recursively computes $c(H_i, t_m)$ for $i = 1, ..., p$ and forms the finite set of those $i$ for which $c(H_i, t_m)$ is maximal under the recursive relation $\leq$. $\mathcal{M}$ now outputs the minimum such $i$, unless the set is empty, in which case it requests more input.

*On presentation of a text t for $H$, $\mathcal{M}$ converges to some $j$ such that $H_j = H$:* fix $t$, an arbitrary text for $H$. Let $n$ be that stage defined in Definition 3. Now there is some $j$ with $H_j = H$ such that at stage $n$ and all subsequent stages $m$ $\mathcal{M}$ will output $j$ because $j = min(Best_m)$ by assumption that $c$ is a limiting corroboration function and the definition of $\mathcal{M}$.

$(\Rightarrow)$

Suppose $\mathcal{M}$ is an inductive learning machine which $LIM$-learns $C$ w.r.t. $\mathcal{L}$. We define a recursive $c$ which produces values (for degree of corroboration) ranging over $\mathbb{N} \cup \{-1\}$. Let

$$c(H_j, t_m) = \begin{cases} -1 & \text{if } t_m \text{ refutes } H_j \\ m+1 & \text{if } \mathcal{M}(t_m) = j \\ m & \text{otherwise} \end{cases}$$

$c$ *is recursive:* it is decidable for any $j$ whether $t_m$ refutes $H_j$, and by assumption $\mathcal{M}$ is an IIM.

$c$ *is a limiting corroboration function over* $\mathcal{L}$: it is easily checked that $c$ satisfies the conditions of Definition 1 and so $c$ is a corroboration function.

Let $t$ be any text for $H \in C$. By assumption there exists an index $j$ such that $H_j = H$ and a stage $n$ after which $\mathcal{M}$ always outputs $j$. Therefore at all stages $m \geq n$ we have $c(H_j, t_m) > c(H_k, t_m)$ for all $k \neq j$, which satisfies the requirements of Definition 3.

**Corollary 1.** *If $C \in LIM\text{-}TXT$ then there exists $\mathcal{L} \in Index(C)$ such that there is a recursive limiting corroboration function $c$ over $\mathcal{L}$ with the property that*

$$(\forall H \in \mathcal{L})(\forall t \in Txt(H))(\exists i)[H_i = H \wedge (\exists n)(\forall m \geq n)(\forall j \neq i)c(H_i, t_m) > c(H_j, t_m)]$$

**Corollary 2.** *There is a canonical $LIM$-learner with corroboration which will learn any $C \in LIM\text{-}TXT$ w.r.t. any $\mathcal{L} \in Index(C)$ using any recursive limiting corroboration function $c$ over $\mathcal{L}$ as an oracle.*

When considering the philosophical background for our model of learning, it seems clear that the order in which examples are presented to the learner, or the number of times the same example is repeated, has no significance. This leads us to the following definition.

**Definition 4.** *A corroboration function $c$ over $\mathcal{L} = H_1, H_2, \ldots$ is called* natural *if on all texts $t, u$, for all $m, n$ we have $t_m^+ = u_n^+ \Rightarrow (\forall i)c(H_i, t_m) = c(H_i, u_n)$.*

It might be objected that corroboration functions lacking the naturalness property should be disallowed. However, they are no more unnatural than non-set-driven learners (it is known [LZ94] that $s\text{-}LIM\text{-}TXT \subset LIM\text{-}TXT$).

**Theorem 2.** $C \in s\text{-}LIM\text{-}TXT$ *iff there exists $\mathcal{L} \in Index(C)$ such that there exists a recursive natural limiting corroboration function $c$ over $\mathcal{L}$.*

**Corollary 3.** *There is a canonical $s\text{-}LIM$-learner with corroboration which will learn any $C \in s\text{-}LIM\text{-}TXT$ w.r.t. any $\mathcal{L} \in Index(C)$ using any recursive natural limiting corroboration function $c$ over $\mathcal{L}$ as an oracle.*

## 4.2   Conservative and Strong Monotonic Learning

**Definition 5.** *A corroboration function* $c : \mathcal{L} \times (\Sigma^*) \to S$ *over* $\mathcal{L}$ *is called* attaining *if*

$$(\forall H \in \mathcal{L})(\forall t \in Txt(H))[(\exists j)(\exists n)[H_j = H \wedge c(H_j, t_n) = c(H_j)] \wedge$$
$$(\forall i)(\forall m)[c(H_i, t_m) = c(H_i) \Rightarrow$$
$$(\forall H' \in \mathcal{L})[[t_m \ refutes \ H' \vee H_i \not\supseteq H'] \wedge c(H', t_m) \not> c(H_i, t_m)]]$$

$c$ *is a* recursive attaining corroboration function *if both* $c$ *and* $c_f : \mathcal{L} \times S \to \{0, 1\}$ *are total and recursive, where:*

$$c_f(H_i, s) = \begin{cases} 1 \ if \ s = c(H_i) \\ 0 \ otherwise \end{cases}$$

Note that $c(H, \emptyset) = 0$ implies $(\forall i)c(H_i) \geq 0$.

**Theorem 3.** $\mathcal{C} \in CONSERV\text{-}TXT$ *iff there exists* $\mathcal{L} \in Index(\mathcal{C})$ *such that there exists a recursive attaining corroboration function* $c$ *over* $\mathcal{L}$.

**Corollary 4.** *There is a canonical CONSERV-learner with corroboration which will learn any* $\mathcal{C} \in CONSERV\text{-}TXT$ *w.r.t. any* $\mathcal{L} \in Index(\mathcal{C})$ *using as an oracle any recursive attaining corroboration function* $c$ *over* $\mathcal{L}$.

**Definition 6.** *A corroboration function* $c(H, t)$ *over* $\mathcal{L} = H_1, H_2, ...$ *is called* strict *if*

$$(\forall H_i \in \mathcal{L})(\forall t \in Txt(H_i))(\forall n)[c(H_i, t_n) = c(H_i) \Rightarrow (\forall H_j \supseteq t_n^+)H_j \supseteq H_i]$$

$c$ *is called a* recursive strict corroboration function *if both* $c$ *and* $c_f$ *are total and recursive, where* $c_f$ *is as defined in Definition 5.*

**Theorem 4.** $\mathcal{C} \in SMON\text{-}TXT$ *iff there exists* $\mathcal{L} \in Index(\mathcal{C})$ *such that there exists a recursive strict attaining corroboration function* $c$ *over* $\mathcal{L}$.

**Corollary 5.** *There exists a canonical SMON-learner with corroboration which SMON-learns any* $\mathcal{C} \in SMON\text{-}TXT$ *w.r.t. any* $\mathcal{L} \in Index(\mathcal{C})$ *using any recursive strict attaining corroboration function over* $\mathcal{L}$ *as an oracle.*

**Corollary 6.** *There is a canonical (CONSERV∪SMON)-learner with corroboration which will CONSERV-learn any* $\mathcal{C} \in CONSERV\text{-}TXT$ *w.r.t. any* $\mathcal{L} \in Index(\mathcal{C})$ *using any recursive attaining corroboration function* $c$ *over* $\mathcal{L}$ *as an oracle and will SMON-learn any* $\mathcal{C} \in SMON\text{-}TXT$ *w.r.t. any* $\mathcal{L} \in Index(\mathcal{C})$ *using any recursive strict attaining corroboration function* $c$ *for* $\mathcal{L}$ *as an oracle.*

### 4.3  FIN- and Refuting Learning

**Definition 7.** *Let* $\mathcal{L} = H_1, H_2, \ldots$ *be a hypothesis space. Then* $f : (\Sigma^*) \times \mathbb{N} \to \{0, 1\}$ *is called a* sufficiency function *over* $\mathcal{L}$ *if*

$$(\forall t)(\forall m)(\forall n)[f(t_m, n) = 1$$
$$\Rightarrow [(\forall j)t_m \text{ refutes } H_j \vee$$
$$(\exists i \le n)[t_m^+ \subseteq H_i \wedge (\forall k)[H_k = H_i \vee t_m \text{ refutes } H_k]]]]$$

*and* $(\forall t)(\forall j)(\forall k \ge j)(\forall n)(\forall m \ge n)[f(t_j, n) = 1 \Rightarrow f(t_k, m) = 1]$

**Definition 8.** *Let* $f$ *be a sufficiency function over* $\mathcal{L}$.

$f$ *is called an* inner sufficiency function *over* $\mathcal{L}$ *if it additionally holds that for every text* $t \in Txts(\mathcal{L})$, $(\exists m, n)f(t_m, n) = 1$.
*If instead it holds that for every text* $t \notin Txts(\mathcal{L})$, $(\exists m, n)f(t_m, n) = 1$, *then* $f$ *is called an* outer sufficiency function *over* $\mathcal{L}$.

Naturally the existence of a recursive (inner or outer) sufficiency function over $\mathcal{L}$ is a very strong condition and allows particularly strong forms of learning.

**Theorem 5.** $\mathcal{C} \in$ *FIN-TXT iff there exists* $\mathcal{L} \in Index(\mathcal{C})$ *such that there exists a recursive inner sufficiency function over* $\mathcal{L}$.

**Corollary 7.** *There exists a canonical FIN-learner which FIN-learns any* $\mathcal{C} \in$ *FIN-TXT w.r.t. any* $\mathcal{L} \in Index(\mathcal{C})$ *using any recursive inner sufficiency function over* $\mathcal{L}$ *as an oracle.*

We may use a sufficiency function to define a particularly strong form of corroboration function.

**Definition 9.** $c(H, t)$ *is called a* sufficient corroboration function *over* $\mathcal{L}$ *if there exists an inner sufficiency function* $f(t, n)$ *over* $\mathcal{L}$ *such that:*

$$(\forall t)(\forall i)(\forall m)[[c(H_i, t_m) > 0 \wedge c(H_i, t_m) = c(H_i)] \Rightarrow f(t_m, i) = 1]$$

*and*

$$(\forall t)(\forall m)(\forall n)[f(t_m, n) = 1 \Rightarrow (\exists i \le n)c(H_i, t_m) = c(H_i)]$$

$c$ *is called a* recursive sufficient corroboration function *if both* $c$ *and* $c_f$ *are total and recursive, where* $c_f$ *is as defined in Definition 5.*

**Theorem 6.** $\mathcal{C} \in$ *FIN-TXT iff there exists* $\mathcal{L} \in Index(\mathcal{C})$ *such that there exists a recursive sufficient corroboration function* $c$ *over* $\mathcal{L}$.

**Corollary 8.** *There exists a canonical FIN-learner with corroboration which FIN-learns any* $\mathcal{C} \in$ *FIN-TXT w.r.t. any* $\mathcal{L} \in Index(\mathcal{C})$ *using any recursive sufficient corroboration function over* $\mathcal{L}$ *as an oracle.*

**Theorem 7.** $C \in JREF\text{-}TXT$ iff there exists $\mathcal{L} \in Index(C)$ such that there exists a recursive outer sufficiency function $f$ over $\mathcal{L}$ and a recursive limiting corroboration function $c$ over $\mathcal{L}$.

**Corollary 9.** There exists a canonical JREF-learner with corroboration which JREF-learns any $C \in JREF\text{-}TXT$ w.r.t. any $\mathcal{L} \in Index(C)$ using any recursive outer sufficiency function and any recursive limiting corroboration function over $\mathcal{L}$ as oracles.

## 5    Example

The corroboration functions constructed in the $\Rightarrow$ proofs in Section 4 were simplistic. However in practical use, the existence or non-existence of appropriate corroboration functions may be suggested naturally by the space of hypotheses in use. We give an example of the use of corroboration functions to prove the learnability under certain identification criteria of a simple class.

Our example languages will be sets of points in the rational plane $Q^2$, so $\Sigma = \{(a, b) \mid a, b \in Q\}$.

*Example 1.* Let $C$ be the set of all closed circles of finite radius. Let $<, >$ be a fixed recursive bijection between $Q^2$ and $\mathbb{N}^+$ and $<<, >>$ a fixed recursive bijection between $Q^2$ and $Q$. A suitable hypothesis space $\mathcal{L} = H_1, H_2, \ldots$ is given by

$$H_{<a,b>} = \{(p, q) \mid a = << x, y >> \wedge (p - x)^2 + (q - y)^2 \le b^2\}$$

It is easily seen that $\mathcal{L}$ is a class-preserving recursive indexing of $C$.

Consider the following corroboration function $c : \mathcal{L} \times (\Sigma^*) \to Q \cup \{\infty\}$, which is based on the naturalistic idea that the further away a point is from $a$, the more severe a test it is of hypothesis $H_{<a,b>}$. For circles of non-zero radius $b$ we also include a scaling multiplier of $1/b^2$ into the corroboration function, so that smaller circles are potentially more highly corroborable than large ones.

$$c(H_{<a,b>}, t_m) = \begin{cases} 0 & \text{if } t_M^+ = \emptyset \\ -1 & \text{if } t_m \text{ refutes } H_{<a,b>}, \\ & \text{i.e. } [a = << x, y >> \\ & \wedge (\exists (c, d) \in t_m^+)[(c - x)^2 + (d - y)^2 > b^2]] \\ \infty & \text{if } b = 0 \wedge a = << x, y >> \wedge t_m^+ = \{(x, y)\} \\ 1/b^2 * max(a, b, t_m) & \text{otherwise} \end{cases}$$

where

$$max(a, b, t_m) = max\{((c - x)^2 + (d - y)^2)/b^2 \mid a = << x, y >> \wedge (c, d) \in t_m^+\}$$

With a little checking we see that $c$ is indeed a corroboration function under Definition 1, and is recursive and natural. $c$ is limiting because on any text $t$ for $H_i$ we have a stage $m$ at which $t_m$ contains two diametrically opposed points on the circumference of the circle defined by $H_i$. Then if we let $i = < a, b >$:

- $(\forall j)[[j =< c,d > \wedge d^2 < b^2] \rightarrow [t_m \text{ refutes } H_j \wedge c(H_j, t_m) = -1]]$
- $(\forall j)[[j =< c,d > \wedge d^2 > b^2] \rightarrow (\forall n \geq m)c(H_i, t_n) = 1/b^2 > 1/d^2 \geq c(H_j, t_n)$
- $(\forall j)[[j =< c,d > \wedge d^2 = b^2] \rightarrow [c = a \vee t_m \text{ refutes } H_j]]$

These are the only cases, so at all stages $n \geq m$ we have that $H_{<a,b>}$ is the most strongly corroborated hypothesis (except for $H_{<a,-b>}$, which is equally strongly corroborated and describes the same circle).

$c$ is also attaining because

- if $b = 0$ then $(\forall a)c(H_{<a,0>}) = \infty$
- if $b \neq 0$ then $(\forall a)c(H_{<a,b>}) = 1/b^2$

and for example $c(H_{<a,b>}, t_0) = c(H_{<a,b>})$ where $t = (x + b, y), \ldots$ is a text for $H_{<a,b>}$ and $a =<< x, y >>$.

The above suffices to prove that $C \in s\text{-}CONSERV\text{-}TXT$, by Theorem 3.

Finally we can see that $c$ is not strict because for example (let $b > 0$) $t = (x + b, y), \ldots$ results in $c(H_{<<<x,y>>,b>}, t_0) = 1/b^2 = c(H_{<<<x,y>>,b>})$ although many hypotheses $H_j$ with $H_{<<<x,y>>,b>} \not\subseteq H_j$ remain unrefuted. Nevertheless it is possible to find a recursive, strict, attaining, limiting, set-driven corroboration function over $\mathcal{L}$ by requiring that two diametrically opposed points on the circumference of $H_i$ must appear in the text before we set $c(H_i, t_m) = c(H_i)$. This proves that $C \in s\text{-}SMON\text{-}TXT$. The details are left as an exercise for the reader.

## 6 Conclusions and Future Work

We have proposed a unifying model for machine inductive inference based on the philosophical work of K.R. Popper, and obtained characterisations of many of the standard identification types in learning indexed families of recursive languages from text. In our model canonical learners use recursive oracles which compute a version of Popper's degree of corroboration. These learners then follow the natural strategy of preferring the most strongly (or at least a maximally strongly) corroborated hypothesis at any given time. Membership of a class of concepts within a particular identification criterion is then equivalent to the existence of a recursive corroboration function with certain properties depending on the identification type.

We intend to extend this unifying model of learning to include language learning from informant and related problems such as learning of partial recursive functions. An extension of our approach to learning from noisy data would be particularly interesting; in this case it is no longer certain that a single adverse data item refutes a hypothesis and we would be obliged to allow negative corroboration values other than $-1$, as in Popper's original model. Given the crucial role played by the hypothesis space in our model, it would also be interesting to extend this approach to cover exact and class comprising learning. Another interesting direction is to drop the requirement that our corroboration functions are recursive, thus obtaining a structure of 'degrees of unlearnability' analogous to the degrees of unsolvability of classical recursion theory.

## Acknowledgements

The author wishes to thank Prof. Dr. Steffen Lange of Universität Leipzig for his comments on an earlier draft, and also the anonymous referees.

# References

[An80] D. Angluin, Inductive inference of formal languages from positive data, *Information and Control* 45, 117-135, 1980.

[AS83] D. Angluin, C.H. Smith, Inductive inference: theory and methods, *Computing Surveys* 15, 237-269, 1983.

[Gi93] D. Gillies, *Philosophy of Science in the Twentieth Century*, Blackwell, 1993.

[Gi96] D. Gillies, *Artificial Intelligence and Scientific Method*, Oxford University Press, 1996.

[Go67] E.M. Gold, Language identification in the limit, *Information and Control* 10, 447-474, 1967.

[Ja91] K.P. Jantke, Monotonic and non-monotonic inductive inference, *New Generation Computing* 8, 349-460.

[LW94] S. Lange, P. Watson, Machine discovery in the presence of incomplete or ambiguous data, in S. Arikawa, K.P. Jantke (Eds.) Algorithmic Learning Theory, Proc. of the Fifth International Workshop on Algorithmic Learning Theory, Reinhardsbrunn, Germany, Springer LNAI 872, 438-452, 1994.

[LZ94] S. Lange, T. Zeugmann, Set-driven and rearrangement-independent learning of recursive languages, in S. Arikawa, K.P. Jantke (Eds.) Algorithmic Learning Theory, Proc. of the Fifth International Workshop on Algorithmic Learning Theory, Reinhardsbrunn, Germany, Springer LNAI 872, 453-468, 1994.

[MA93] Y. Mukouchi, S. Arikawa, Inductive inference machines that can refute hypothesis spaces, in K.P. Jantke, S. Kobayashi, E. Tomita, T. Yokomori (Eds.), Algorithmic Learning Theory, Proc. of the Fourth International Workshop on Algorithmic Learning Theory, Tokyo, Japan, Springer LNAI 744, 123-136, 1993.

[Po34] K.R. Popper, *The Logic of Scientific Discovery*, 1997 Routledge reprint of the 1959 Hutchinson translation of the German original.

[Po54] K.R. Popper, Degree of confirmation, *British Journal for the Philosophy of Science* 5, 143ff, 334, 359, 1954.

[Po57] K.R. Popper, A second note on degree of confirmation, *British Journal for the Philosophy of Science* 7, 350ff, 1957.

[Po63] K.R. Popper, *Conjectures and Refutations*, Routledge, 1963 (Fifth Edition, 1989).

[Wa99] P. Watson, Inductive Learning with Corroboration, Technical Report no. 6-99, Department of Computer Science, University of Kent at Canterbury, May 1999. Obtainable from http://www.cs.ukc.ac.uk/pubs/1999/782.

[WC80] K. Wexler, P. Culicover, *Formal Principles of Language Acquisition*, MIT Press, Cambridge, MA, 1980.

# Flattening and Implication

Kouichi Hirata[*]

Department of Artificial Intelligence,
Kyushu Institute of Technology,
Kawazu 680-4, Iizuka 820-8502, Japan
hirata@ai.kyutech.ac.jp

**Abstract.** *Flattening* is a method to make a definite clause function-free. For a definite clause $C$, flattening replaces every occurrence of a term $f(t_1, \cdots, t_n)$ in $C$ with a new variable $v$ and adds an atom $p_f(t_1, \cdots, t_n, v)$ with the associated predicate symbol $p_f$ with $f$ to the body of $C$. Here, we denote the resulting function-free definite clause from $C$ by $flat(C)$. In this paper, we discuss the relationship between flattening and implication. For a definite program $\Pi$ and a definite clause $D$, it is known that if $flat(\Pi) \models flat(D)$ then $\Pi \models D$, where $flat(\Pi)$ is the set of $flat(C)$ for each $C \in \Pi$. First, we show that the converse of this statement does not hold even if $\Pi = \{C\}$, that is, there exist definite clauses $C$ and $D$ such that $C \models D$ but $flat(C) \not\models flat(D)$. Furthermore, we investigate the conditions of $C$ and $D$ satisfying that $C \models D$ if and only if $flat(C) \models flat(D)$. Then, we show that, if (1) $C$ is not self-resolving and $D$ is not tautological, (2) $D$ is not ambivalent, or (3) $C$ is singly recursive, then the statement holds.

## 1 Introduction

The purpose of Inductive Logic Programming is to find a hypothesis that explains a given sample. It is a normal setting of Inductive Logic Programming that a hypothesis is a definite clause or a definite program and a sample is the set of (labeled) ground definite clauses. In this setting, the word "explain" is interpreted as either "subsume (denoted by $\succeq$)" or "imply (denoted by $\models$)". In the latter case, note that the problem of whether or not a definite clause $C$ implies another definite clause, called an *implication problem*, is undecidable in general [8]. On the other hand, if $C$ is function-free, then it is obvious that the implication problem is decidable.

*Flattening*, which has been first introduced in the context of Inductive Logic Programming by Rouveirol [14] (though similar ideas had already been used in other fields), is a method to make a definite clause function-free. For a definite clause $C$, flattening replaces every occurrence of a term $f(t_1, \cdots, t_n)$ in $C$ with a new variable $v$ and adds an atom $p_f(t_1, \cdots, t_n, v)$ with the associated predicate symbol $p_f$ with $f$ to the body of $C$. Additionally, the unit clause

---

[*] This work is partially supported by Japan Society for the Promotion of Science, Grants-in-Aid for Encouragement of Young Scientists 11780284.

$p_f(x_1, \cdots, x_n, f(x_1, \cdots, x_n)) \leftarrow$ is introduced to the background theory for each function symbol $f$ in $C$. We denote the resulting function-free definite clause by $flat(C)$ and the set of unit clauses by $defs(C)$.

Rouveirol [14] has investigated the several properties of flattening. Muggleton [9,11] has dealt with flattening in order to characterize his inverting implication. De Raedt and Džeroski [2] have analyzed their PAC-learnability of $jk$-clausal theories by transforming possibly infinite Herbrand models into approximately finite models according to flattening. Recently, Nienhuys-Cheng and de Wolf [13] have studied the properties of flattening with sophisticated discussion.

Rouveirol [14] (and Nienhuys-Cheng and de Wolf [13]) has shown that flattening "preserves" subsumption: Let $C$ and $D$ be definite clauses. Then, it holds that:

$$C \succeq D \text{ if and only if } flat(C) \succeq flat(D).$$

Also Rouveirol [14] (and Nienhuys-Cheng and de Wolf [13]) has claimed that flattening "preserves" implication: Let $\Pi$ be a definite program $\{C_1, \cdots, C_n\}$ and $D$ be a definite clause. We denote $\{flat(C_1), \cdots, flat(C_n)\}$ and $defs(C_1) \cup \cdots \cup defs(C_n)$ by $flat(\Pi)$ and $defs(\Pi)$, respectively. Then, Rouveirol's Theorem is described as follows:

$$\Pi \models D \text{ if and only if } flat(\Pi) \cup defs(\Pi) \models flat(D).$$

As the stronger relationship between flattening and implication than Rouveirol's Theorem, Nienhuys-Cheng and de Wolf [13] have shown the following theorem:

$$\text{If } flat(\Pi) \models flat(D), \text{ then } \Pi \models D.$$

If the converse of this theorem holds, then the several learning techniques for propositional logic such as [1,3] are directly applied to Inductive Logic Programming. On the other hand, if the converse holds, then the implication problem $\Pi \models D$ is decidable, because $flat(\Pi)$ and $flat(D)$ are function-free. However, it contradicts the undecidability of the implication problem [8,15] or the satisfiability problem [5]. In this paper, we show that the converse does not hold even if $\Pi = \{C\}$, that is, there exist definite clauses $C$ and $D$ such that:

$$C \models D \text{ but } flat(C) \not\models flat(D).$$

Furthermore, we investigate the conditions of $C$ and $D$ satisfying that $C \models D$ if and only if $flat(C) \models flat(D)$. Gottlob [4] has introduced the concepts of *self-resolving* and *ambivalent* clauses. A definite clause $C$ is *self-resolving* if $C$ resolves with a copy of $C$, and *ambivalent* if there exists an atom in the body of $C$ with the predicate symbol same as one of the head of $C$. As the corollary of Gottlob's results [4], we show that, if $C$ is not self-resolving and $D$ is not tautological, or $D$ is not ambivalent, then the statement holds. Furthermore, note that the $C$ in the counterexample stated above is given as a *doubly* recursive definite clause, that is, the body of $C$ contains two atoms that are unifiable with the head of a variant of $C$. Then, we show that, if $C$ is *singly* recursive, that is, the body of $C$ contains at most one atom that is unifiable with the head of a variant of $C$, then the statement also holds.

## 2    Preliminaries

A *literal* is an atom or the negation of an atom. A *positive literal* is an atom and a *negative literal* is the negation of an atom. A *clause* is a finite set of literals. A *unit clause* is a clause containing one positive literal. A *definite clause* is a clause containing one positive literal. A set of definite clauses are called a *definite program*. Conventionally, a definite clause is represented as $A \leftarrow A_1, \cdots, A_m$, where $A$ and $A_i$ $(1 \leq i \leq m)$ are atoms.

Let $C$ be a definite clause $A \leftarrow A_1, \cdots, A_m$. Then, the atom $A$ is called a *head* of $C$ and denoted by $head(C)$, and the sequence $A_1, \cdots, A_m$ of atoms is called a *body* of $C$ and denoted by $body(C)$.

Let $C$ and $D$ be definite clauses. We say that $C$ *subsumes* $D$, denoted by $C \succeq D$, if there exists a substitution $\theta$ such that $C\theta \subseteq D$, i.e., every literal in $C\theta$ also appears in $D$. Also we say that $C$ *implies* $D$ or $D$ is *a logical consequence of* $C$, denoted by $C \models D$, if every model of $C$ is also a model of $D$. $C$ is *logically equivalent to* $D$, denoted by $C \equiv D$, if $C \models D$ and $D \models C$. For definite programs $\Pi$ and $\Sigma$, $\Pi \succeq D$, $\Pi \succeq \Sigma$, $\Pi \models D$ and $\Pi \models \Sigma$ are defined similarly.

Let $C$ and $D$ be two clauses $\{L_1, \cdots, L_i, \cdots, L_l\}$ and $\{M_1, \cdots, M_j, \cdots, M_m\}$ which have no variables in common. If the substitution $\theta$ is an mgu for the set $\{L_i, \neg M_j\}$, then the clause $((C - \{L_i\}) \cup (D - \{\neg M_j\}))\theta$ is called a *(binary) resolvent* of $C$ and $D$. All of the resolvents of $C$ and $D$ are denoted by $Res(C, D)$.

Let $\Pi$ be a definite program and $C$ be a definite clause. An *SLD-derivation* of $C$ from $\Pi$ is a sequence $(R_1, C_0, \theta_1), \ldots, (R_k, C_{k-1}, \theta_k)$ such that $R_0 \in \Pi$, $R_k = C$, $C_{i-1}$ is a variant of an element of $\Pi$, $R_i \in Res(R_{i-1}, C_{i-1})$, and $\theta_i$ is an mgu of the selected literals of $R_{i-1}$ and $C_{i-1}$ for each $1 \leq i \leq k$. If an SLD-derivation of $C$ from $\Pi$ exists, we write $\Pi \vdash C$. In particular, $\{C\} \vdash D$ is denoted by $C \vdash D$.

**Theorem 1 ((Subsumption Theorem [13]))**. *Let $\Pi$ be a definite program and $D$ be a definite clause. Then, $\Pi \models D$ if and only if there exists a definite clause $E$ such that $\Pi \vdash E$ and $E \succeq D$.*

For a definite clause $C$, the *$l$th self-resolving closure* of $C$, denoted by $\mathcal{S}^l(C)$, is defined inductively as follows:

1. $\mathcal{S}^0(C) = \{C\}$,
2. $\mathcal{S}^l(C) = \mathcal{S}^{l-1}(C) \cup \{R \in Res(C, D) \mid D \in \mathcal{S}^{l-1}(C)\}$ $(l \geq 1)$.

Here, the logically equivalent clauses are regarded as identical. Note that $C \vdash D$ if and only if $D \in \mathcal{S}^l(C)$ for some $l \geq 0$. Then:

**Corollary 2 ((Implication between Definite Clauses [12]))**. *Let $C$ and $D$ be definite clauses. Then, $C \models D$ if and only if there exists a definite clause $E$ such that $E \in \mathcal{S}^l(C)$ and $E \succeq D$ for some $l \geq 0$.*

For each $n$-ary function symbol $f$, the associated $(n+1)$-ary predicate symbol $p_f$, called a *flattened predicate symbol* (on $f$), is introduced uniquely in the process of flattening. Also we call a definite clause $C$ or a definite program $\Pi$ *regular* if $C$ or $\Pi$ contains no flattened predicate symbols.

Let $C$ be a definite clause, $t$ be a term appearing in $C$ and $v$ be a variable not appearing in $C$. Then, $C|_t^v$ denotes the definite clause obtained from $C$ by replacing all occurrences of $t$ in $C$ with $v$.

There exist several variants (but equivalent) of the definition of flattening:

1. Do we introduce an equality theory [9,14] or not [2,13]?
2. Do we transform a constant symbol to an atom with an unary predicate symbol [2,14] or not [13]?

As the definition of flattening, we adopt the definition similar as De Raedt and Džeroski [2] that does not introduce an equality theory and does not transform a constant symbol.

Let $C$ be a definite clause. Then, the *flattened clause* $flat(C)$ of $C$ is defined as follows:

$$flat(C) = \begin{cases} C & \text{if } C \text{ is function-free,} \\ flat(C') & \text{if } t = f(t_1, \cdots, t_n)(n \geq 1) \text{ appears in } C, \end{cases}$$

where $C' = C|_t^v \cup \{\neg p_f(t_1, \cdots, t_n, v)\}$ and each $t_i$ $(1 \leq i \leq n)$ is a variable or a constant. Also $defs(C)$ is the set $\{p_f(x_1, \cdots, x_n, f(x_1, \cdots, x_n)) \leftarrow \quad | \quad f(t_1, \cdots, t_n) \text{ appears in } C\}$ of unit clauses. Furthermore, the number of calls of $flat$ that is necessary to obtain the function-free clause $flat(C)$ of $C$ is called a *rank* of $C$ and denoted by $rank(C)$.

For a definite program $\Pi = \{C_1, \cdots, C_n\}$, we define $flat(\Pi)$ and $defs(\Pi)$ as follows:

$$flat(\Pi) = \{flat(C_1), \cdots, flat(C_n)\},$$
$$defs(\Pi) = defs(C_1) \cup \cdots \cup defs(C_n).$$

## 3    Flattening and Implication

As the relationship between flattening and subsumption, Rouveirol [14] (and Nienhuys-Cheng and de Wolf [13]) has shown the following theorem:

**Theorem 3 ((Rouveirol [14], Nienhuys-Cheng & de Wolf [13]))**. *Let $C$ and $D$ be regular definite clauses. Then, $C \succeq D$ if and only if $flat(C) \succeq flat(D)$.*

Also Rouveirol [14] (and Nienhuys-Cheng and de Wolf [13]) has proposed the following relationship between flattening and implication. Let $\Pi$ be a regular definite program and $D$ be a regular definite clause. Then, Rouveirol's Theorem is described as follows:

**Theorem 4 ((Rouveirol [14], Nienhuys-Cheng & de Wolf [13]))**. *Let $\Pi$ be a regular definite program and $D$ be a regular definite clause. Then, $\Pi \models D$ if and only if $flat(\Pi) \cup defs(\Pi) \models flat(D)$.*

In Appendix, we discuss the proof of Rouveirol's Theorem.

Furthermore, Nienhuys-Cheng and de Wolf [13] have shown the following theorem, which is a stronger relationship between flattening and implication than Rouveirol's Theorem:

**Theorem 5 ((Nienhuys-Cheng & de Wolf [13]))**. *Let $\Pi$ be a regular definite program and $D$ be a regular definite clause. If $flat(\Pi) \models flat(D)$, then $\Pi \models D$.*

On the other hand, the converse of Theorem 5 does not hold even if $\Pi = \{C\}$:

**Theorem 6.** *There exist regular definite clauses $C$ and $D$ such that*

$$C \models D \text{ but } flat(C) \not\models flat(D).$$

*Proof.* Let $C$ and $D$ be the following regular definite clauses:

$$C = p(f(x_1), f(x_2)) \leftarrow p(x_1, x_3), p(x_3, x_2),$$
$$D = p(f(f(x_1)), f(f(x_2))) \leftarrow p(x_1, x_3), p(x_3, x_4), p(x_4, x_5), p(x_5, x_2).$$

By resolving $C$ to a copy of $C$ itself twice, it holds that $C \vdash D$ as Figure 1. Hence, it holds that $C \models D$.

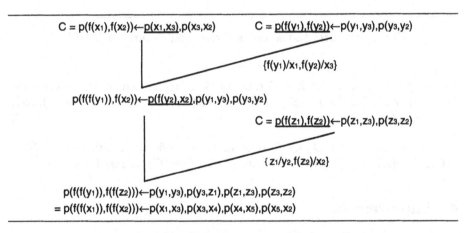

**Fig. 1.** The SLD-derivation of $D$ from $C$

On the other hand, $flat(C)$ and $flat(D)$ are constructed as follows:

$$flat(C) = p(x_1, x_2) \leftarrow p(x_3, x_4), p(x_4, x_5), p_f(x_3, x_1), p_f(x_5, x_2),$$
$$flat(D) = p(x_1, x_2) \leftarrow p(x_3, x_4), p(x_4, x_5), p(x_5, x_6), p(x_6, x_7),$$
$$p_f(x_3, x_8), p_f(x_8, x_1), p_f(x_7, x_9), p_f(x_9, x_2).$$

The first and second self-resolving closures of $flat(C)$ are constructed as Figure 2. Then, there exists no definite clause $E \in \mathcal{S}^2(flat(C))$ such that $E \succeq flat(D)$. By paying our attention to the number of atoms with the predicate $p_f$ and its relation, it holds that $flat(C) \models flat(D)$ if and only if there exists a definite clause

$$S^1(\mathit{flat}(C)) = \{\mathit{flat}(C)\}$$

$$\cup \left\{ \begin{array}{l} p(x_1,x_2){\leftarrow}p(x_3,x_4),p(x_5,x_6),p(x_6,x_7), \\ \qquad p_f(x_5,x_8),p_f(x_8,x_1),p_f(x_4,x_2),p_f(x_7,x_3) \\ p(x_1,x_2){\leftarrow}p(x_3,x_4),p(x_5,x_6),p(x_6,x_7), \\ \qquad p_f(x_3,x_1),p_f(x_7,x_8),p_f(x_8,x_2),p_f(x_5,x_4) \end{array} \right\},$$

$$S^2(\mathit{flat}(C)) = S^1(\mathit{flat}(C))$$

$$\cup \left\{ \begin{array}{l} p(x_1,x_2){\leftarrow}p(x_3,x_4),p(x_4,x_5),p(x_6,x_7),p(x_7,x_8), \\ \qquad p_f(x_3,x_9),p_f(x_9,x_1),p_f(x_8,x_{10}),p_f(x_{10},x_2), \\ \qquad p_f(x_5,x_{11}),p_f(x_6,x_{11}) \\ p(x_1,x_2){\leftarrow}p(x_3,x_4),p(x_5,x_6),p(x_7,x_8),p(x_8,x_9), \\ \qquad p_f(x_7,x_{10}),p_f(x_{10},x_{11}),p_f(x_{11},x_1),p_f(x_4,x_2), \\ \qquad p_f(x_6,x_3),p_f(x_9,x_5) \\ p(x_1,x_2){\leftarrow}p(x_3,x_4),p(x_5,x_6),p(x_7,x_8),p(x_8,x_9), \\ \qquad p_f(x_5,x_{10}),p_f(x_{10},x_1),p_f(x_4,x_2),p_f(x_7,x_6), \\ \qquad p_f(x_9,x_{11}),p_f(x_{11},x_3) \\ p(x_1,x_2){\leftarrow}p(x_3,x_4),p(x_5,x_6),p(x_7,x_8),p(x_8,x_9), \\ \qquad p_f(x_3,x_1),p_f(x_6,x_{10}),p_f(x_{10},x_2),p_f(x_7,x_{11}), \\ \qquad p_f(x_{11},x_4),p_f(x_9,x_5) \\ p(x_1,x_2){\leftarrow}p(x_3,x_4),p(x_5,x_6),p(x_7,x_8),p(x_8,x_9), \\ \qquad p_f(x_3,x_1),p_f(x_9,x_{10}),p_f(x_{10},x_{11}),p_f(x_{11},x_2), \\ \qquad p_f(x_5,x_4),p_f(x_7,x_6) \end{array} \right\}.$$

**Fig. 2.** The first and second self-resolving closures of $\mathit{flat}(C)$

$E \in S^2(\mathit{flat}(C))$ such that $E \succeq \mathit{flat}(D)$ by Corollary 2. Hence, we can conclude that there exists no definite clause $E \in S^2(\mathit{flat}(C))$ such that $E \succeq \mathit{flat}(D)$, so it holds that $\mathit{flat}(C) \not\models \mathit{flat}(D)$. □

For the definite clauses $C$ and $D$ given in Theorem 6, it holds that $\{\mathit{flat}(C)\} \cup \mathit{defs}(C) \vdash \mathit{flat}(D)$ as Figure 3, so it holds that $\{\mathit{flat}(C)\} \cup \mathit{defs}(C) \models \mathit{flat}(D)$.

## 4    Improvement

In this section, we investigate the conditions of definite clauses $C$ and $D$ satisfying that $C \models D$ if and only if $\mathit{flat}(C) \models \mathit{flat}(D)$.

First, we give the following lemma by Gottlob [4]. A definite clause $C$ is *self-resolving* if $C$ resolves with a copy of $C$. A definite clause $C$ is *ambivalent* if there exists an atom in $\mathit{body}(C)$ with the predicate symbol same as one of $\mathit{head}(C)$. Then:

**Lemma 7 ((Gottlob [4])).** *Let $C$ and $D$ be definite clauses.*

1. *Suppose that $C$ is not self-resolving and $D$ is not tautological. Then, $C \models D$ if and only if $C \succeq D$.*
2. *Suppose that $D$ is not ambivalent. Then, $C \models D$ if and only if $C \succeq D$.*

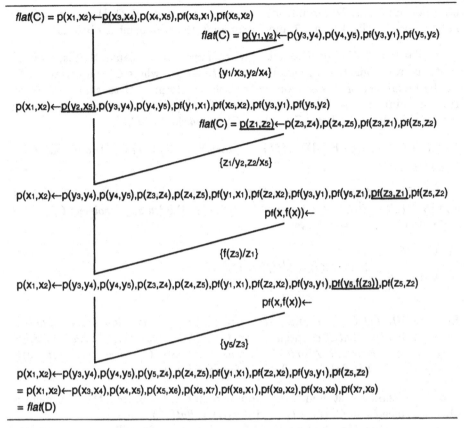

**Fig. 3.** The SLD-derivation of $flat(D)$ from $\{flat(C)\} \cup defs(C)$ in Theorem 6

By incorporating Lemma 7 with the previous theorems, we obtain the following corollary:

**Corollary 8.** *Let $C$ and $D$ be regular definite clauses.*

1. *Suppose that $C$ is not self-resolving and $D$ is not tautological. Then, $C \models D$ if and only if $flat(C) \models flat(D)$.*
2. *Suppose that $D$ is not ambivalent. Then, $C \models D$ if and only if $flat(C) \models flat(D)$.*

*Proof.* 1. By Lemma 7, $C \models D$ if and only if $C \succeq D$. By Theorem 3, $C \succeq D$ if and only if $flat(C) \succeq flat(D)$. By the definition of $\succeq$ and $\models$, if $flat(C) \succeq flat(D)$ then $flat(C) \models flat(D)$. So it holds that if $C \models D$ then $flat(C) \models flat(D)$. Hence, the statement holds by Theorem 5.

2. By the definition of ambivalence, the predicate symbol of the head of $D$ is different from all of the predicate symbols appearing in the body of $D$. This condition is preserved in $flat(D)$, because the flattened predicate symbols, which

does not appear in $D$, are introduced only in the body of $D$. Hence, $flat(D)$ is not ambivalent. By Lemma 7 and Theorem 3, the statement is obvious.     □

In Theorem 6, $C$ is given as a doubly recursive definite clause, that is, $body(C)$ contains two atoms that are unifiable with $head(C')$, where $C'$ is a variant of $C$. In the remainder of this section, we restrict the form of $C$ to *singly recursive*. Here, a definite clause $C$ is *singly recursive* if $body(C)$ contains at most one atom that is unifiable with $head(C')$, where $C'$ is a variant of $C$.

**Lemma 9 ((Gottlob [4]))**. *If $C \models D$, then $head(C) \succeq head(D)$ and $body(C) \succeq body(D)$.*

Let $C$ be a singly recursive definite clause. It is obvious that $|\mathcal{S}^l(C)| \leq l+1$ and $|\mathcal{S}^{l+1}(C) - \mathcal{S}^l(C)| \leq 1$ for each $l \geq 0$. Then, the $l$th self-resolvent $C_l$ of $C$ is defined inductively as follows:

1. $C_0 = C$,
2. $C_{l+1} = \begin{cases} D \text{ if } \mathcal{S}^{l+1}(C) - \mathcal{S}^l(C) = \{D\}, \\ C \text{ otherwise.} \end{cases}$

**Lemma 10.** *Let $C$ be a singly recursive regular definite clause with function symbols. Suppose that $C$ contains a term $t = f(t_1, \cdots, t_n)$, where each $t_i$ is either a variable or a constant. Also let $C'$ be a definite clause $C|_t^v \cup \{\neg p_f(t_1, \cdots, t_n, v)\}$. Then, it holds that $flat(C_l) \equiv flat(C'_l)$ for each $l \geq 0$.*

*Proof.* We show the statement by induction on $l$. If $l = 0$, then the statement is obvious, since $C_0 = C$, $C'_0 = C'$ and $flat(C) = flat(C')$.

Suppose that the statement holds for $l \leq k$. It is sufficient to show the case that $C$ is of the form $p(\bar{t}) \leftarrow p(\bar{s})$. Consider $C_{k+1}$ and $C'_{k+1}$. By the definition of the $(k+1)$th self-resolvent, $C_{k+1}$ is a resolvent of $C$ and $C_k$, and $C'_{k+1}$ is a resolvent of $C'$ and $C'_k$. Then, we can suppose that $C_{k+1}$ is of the form $(head(C) \leftarrow body(C_k)\mu)\theta$, where $\theta$ is an mgu of $head(C_k)\mu$ and $body(C)$ and $\mu$ is a renaming substitution. Hence, $C'_{k+1}$ is of the form $(head(C') \leftarrow body(C'_k)\mu', p_f(t_1, \cdots, t_n, v))\theta'$, where $\theta'$ is a substitution obtained from $\theta$ by replacing the binding $t\mu/x$ in $\theta$ with $v/x$, and $\mu'$ is a renaming substitution by adding the binding $u/v$ ($u$ is a new variable) to $\mu$. By induction hypothesis, it holds that $flat(C_k) \equiv flat(C'_k)$ and $flat(C) \equiv flat(C')$. By the forms of $C_{k+1}$ and $C'_{k+1}$, it holds that $flat(C_{k+1}) \equiv flat(C'_{k+1})$.     □

**Lemma 11.** *For a singly recursive definite clause $C$, it holds that $flat(C_l) \equiv (flat(C))_l$ for each $l \geq 0$.*

*Proof.* We show the statement by induction on $rank(C)$. If $rank(C) = 0$, then the statement is obvious, because $flat(C_l) = C_l$ and $flat(C) = C$ for each $l \geq 0$.

Suppose that the statement holds for $C$ such that $rank(C) \leq k$. Let $C$ be a singly recursive definite clause such that $rank(C) = k+1$. Since $C$ contains some function symbols, suppose that $C$ contains the term $t = f(t_1, \cdots, t_n)$, where each $t_i$ is either a variable or a constant. Let $C'$ be a definite clause $C|_t^v \cup \{\neg p_f(t_1, \cdots, t_n, v)\}$. Then, it holds that $flat(C') \equiv flat(C)$ and $rank(C') = k$. By Lemma 10, it holds that $flat(C_l') \equiv flat(C_l)$ for each $l \geq 0$. By induction hypothesis, it holds that $flat(C_l) \equiv flat(C_l') \equiv (flat(C'))_l \equiv (flat(C))_l$ for each $l \geq 0$. Hence, the statement holds for $rank(C) = k + 1$.     □

**Lemma 12.** *For a singly recursive definite clause $C$, it holds that $flat(C) \models flat(C_l)$ for each $l \geq 0$.*

*Proof.* We show the statement by induction on $l$. If $l = 0$, then $C_0 = C$, so the statement is obvious.

Suppose that the statement holds for $l \leq k$. Since $C_{k+1}$ is a resolvent of $C$ and $C_k$ and by Lemma 11, $flat(C_{k+1})$ is a resolvent of $flat(C)$ and $flat(C_k)$. By the soundness of SLD-resolution (*cf.* [7,13]), it holds that $\{flat(C), flat(C_k)\} \models flat(C_{k+1})$. By induction hypothesis, it holds that $flat(C) \models flat(C_k)$. Hence, it holds that $flat(C) \models flat(C_{k+1})$, so the statement holds for $l = k + 1$.     □

**Theorem 13.** *Let $C$ be a singly recursive regular definite clause and $D$ be a regular definite clause. Then, $C \models D$ if and only if $flat(C) \models flat(D)$.*

*Proof.* By Theorem 5, it is sufficient to show the only-if direction. We show it by induction of $rank(D)$. If $rank(D) = 0$, that is, $D$ is function-free, then so is $C$ by Lemma 9. Then, $flat(C) = C$ and $flat(D) = D$, so the statement is obvious.

Suppose that the statement holds for $D$ such that $rank(D) \leq k$. Let $D$ be a regular definite clause such that $rank(D) = k + 1$. Since $D$ contains some function symbols, suppose that $D$ contains a term $t = f(t_1, \cdots, t_n)$, where each $t_i$ $(1 \leq i \leq n)$ is a variable or a constant. Also let $D'$ be a definite clause $D|_t^v \cup \{\neg p_f(t_1, \cdots, t_n, v)\}$. Then, $rank(D) = k$ and $flat(D') \equiv flat(D)$. Suppose that $C \models D$. Then, by Corollary 2 and the definition of the $l$th self-resolvent, there exists an index $l \geq 0$ such that $C_l \succeq D$.

As similar as the proof of Lemma 19.6 in [13], we can construct the definite clause $C'$ from $C_l$ such that $C' \succeq D'$ and $flat(C_l) \equiv flat(C')$ as follows: Suppose that $C_l \theta \subseteq D'$. Let $\{s_1, \cdots, s_m\}$ be the set of distinct terms occurring in $C_l$ such that $s_i \theta = t$. If $s_i$ is a variable, then replace the binding $t/s_i$ with $v/s_i$. If $s_i$ is of the form $f(r_1, \cdots, r_n)$, in which case the $r_j$ are variables or constants, then replace all occurrences of $s_i$ in $C_l$ with a new variable $v_i$, add $\neg p_f(r_1, \cdots, r_n, v_i)$ in $C_l$, and add the binding $v/v_i$ to $\theta$. We call the definite clause resulting from these $m$ adjustments $C'$. Finally, replace all occurrences of $t$ in bindings in $\theta$ with $y$, and call the resulting substitution $\theta'$. Then, it holds that $C' \theta' \subseteq D'$, so $C' \succeq D'$. Hence, $C' \models D'$. Furthermore, by the construction of $C'$, it holds that $flat(C_l) \equiv flat(C')$.

By induction hypothesis, it holds that $flat(C') \models flat(D')$, so $flat(C_l) \models flat(D)$. By Lemma 12, it holds that $flat(C) \models flat(D)$. Hence, the statement holds for $rank(D) = k + 1$.     □

## 5    Conclusion

In this paper, we have investigated the relationship between flattening and implication [13,14]. Let $\Pi$ be a regular definite program and $C$ and $D$ be definite clauses. As the stronger relationship between flattening and implication than Rouveirol's Theorem [14], Nienhuys-Cheng and de Wolf [13] have shown the following theorem:

$$\text{If } flat(\Pi) \models flat(D), \text{ then } \Pi \models D.$$

In this paper, we have shown that there exist definite clauses $C$ and $D$ such that:

$$C \models D \text{ but } flat(C) \not\models flat(D).$$

Furthermore, we have shown that if $C$ and $D$ satisfy one of the following conditions, then it holds that $C \models D$ if and only if $flat(C) \models flat(D)$:

1. $C$ is not self-resolving and $D$ is not tautological,
2. $D$ is not ambivalent,
3. $C$ is singly recursive.

The class of definite clauses that flattening preserves implication is corresponding to the class that the implication problem is decidable [4,6,7], and the class of definite clauses that flattening does not preserve implication in the above sense is corresponding to the class that the implication problem is undecidable [8,15]. It is a future work to investigate the relationship between the classes of definite clauses that flattening preserves implication and that implication is decidable.

## Acknowledgment

The author would thank to anonymous referees for valuable comments.

## References

1. Angluin, D., Frazier, M. and Pitt, L.: *Learning conjunctions of Horn clauses*, Machine Learning **9**, 147–164, 1992.
2. De Raedt, L. and Džeroski, S.: *First-order jk-clausal theories are PAC-learnable*, Artificial Intelligence **90**, 375–392, 1994.
3. Frazier, M. and Pitt, L.: *Learning from entailment: An application to propositional Horn sentences*, Proc. 10th International Conference on Machine Learning, 120–127, 1993.
4. Gottlob, G.: *Subsumption and implication*, Information Processing Letters **24**, 109–111, 1987.
5. Hanschke, P. and Würtz, J.: *Satisfiability of the smallest binary program*, Information Processing Letters **45**, 237–241, 1993.
6. Leitsch, A.: *Implication algorithms for classes of Horn clauses*, Statistik, Informatik und Ökonomie, Springer, 172–189, 1988.

7. Leitsch, A.: *The resolution calculus*, Springer-Verlag, 1997.
8. Marcinkowski, J. and Pacholski, L.: *Undecidability of the Horn-clause implication problem*, Proc. 33rd Annual IEEE Symposium on Foundations of Computer Science, 354–362, 1992.
9. Muggleton, S.: *Inverting implication*, Proc. 2nd International Workshop on Inductive Logic Programming, ICOT Technical Memorandum TM-1182, 1992.
10. Muggleton, S. (ed.): *Inductive logic programming*, Academic Press, 1992.
11. Muggleton, S.: *Inverse entailment and Progol*, New Generation Computing **13**, 245–286, 1995.
12. Muggleton, S. and Page Jr., C., D.: *Self-saturation of definite clauses*, Proc. 4th International Workshop on Inductive Logic Programming, 162–174, 1994.
13. Nienhuys-Cheng, S.-H. and de Wolf, R.: *Foundations of inductive logic programming*, Lecture Notes in Artificial Intelligence **1228**, 1997.
14. Rouveirol, C.: *Extensions of inversion of resolution applied to theory completion*, in [10], 63–92.
15. Schmidt-Schauss, M.: *Implication of clauses is undecidable*, Theoretical Computer Science **59**, 287–296, 1988.

## Appendix: Rouveirol's Theorem

For Rouveirol's Theorem, it is clear that Rouveirol's original proof [14] is insufficient. On the other hand, Nienhuys-Cheng and de Wolf [13] have shown Rouveirol's Theorem as the consequence of Theorem 5 and the following lemma:

**Lemma 14.** *Let $\Pi$ be a regular definite program. Then, $flat(\Pi) \cup defs(\Pi) \models \Pi$.*

However, we obtain the following theorem:

**Theorem 15.** *There exist regular definite clauses $C$ and $D$ such that*

$$C \vdash D \text{ but } \{flat(C)\} \cup defs(C) \not\vdash flat(D).$$

*Proof.* Let $C$ and $D$ be the following regular definite clauses:

$$C = p(f(x_1, x_3), f(x_3, x_2)) \leftarrow p(x_1, x_3), p(x_3, x_2),$$
$$D = p(f(f(x_1, x_2), f(x_2, x_3)), f(f(x_2, x_3), f(x_3, x_4)))$$
$$\leftarrow p(x_1, x_2), p(x_2, x_3), p(x_2, x_3), p(x_3, x_4).$$

By resolving $C$ with $C$ itself twice, we can show that $C \vdash D$.

On the other hand, $flat(C)$ and $flat(D)$ are constructed as follows:

$$flat(C) = p(x_1, x_2) \leftarrow p(x_3, x_4), p(x_4, x_5), p_f(x_3, x_4, x_1), p_f(x_4, x_5, x_2),$$
$$flat(D) = p(x_1, x_2) \leftarrow p(x_3, x_4), p(x_4, x_5), p(x_4, x_5), p(x_5, x_6),$$
$$p_f(x_3, x_4, x_7), p_f(x_4, x_5, x_8), p_f(x_5, x_6, x_9),$$
$$p_f(x_7, x_8, x_1), p_f(x_8, x_9, x_2).$$

Also $defs(C) = \{p_f(x, y, f(x, y)) \leftarrow\}$.

The first and second self-resolving closures of $flat(C)$ are constructed as Figure 4. Note that $\{flat(C)\} \cup defs(C) \vdash flat(D)$ if and only if there exists a definite clause $E \in \mathcal{S}^2(flat(C))$ such that $flat(D)$ is obtained by resolving $E$

$$\mathcal{S}^1(flat(C)) = \{flat(C)\}$$

$$\cup \left\{ \begin{array}{l} p(x_1,x_2) \leftarrow p(x_3,x_4), p(x_5,x_6), p(x_6,x_7), \\ \qquad p_f(x_5,x_6,x_8), p_f(x_8,x_3,x_1), p_f(x_3,x_4,x_2), p_f(x_6,x_7,x_3) \\ p(x_1,x_2) \leftarrow p(x_3,x_4), p(x_5,x_6), p(x_6,x_7), \\ \qquad p_f(x_3,x_4,x_1), p_f(x_6,x_7,x_8), p_f(x_4,x_8,x_2), p_f(x_5,x_6,x_4) \end{array} \right\},$$

$$\mathcal{S}^2(flat(C)) = \mathcal{S}^1(flat(C))$$

$$\cup \left\{ \begin{array}{l} E_1 : p(x_1,x_2) \leftarrow p(x_3,x_4), p(x_4,x_5), p(x_6,x_7), p(x_7,x_8), \\ \qquad p_f(x_3,x_4,x_9), p_f(x_9,x_{10},x_1), p_f(x_7,x_8,x_{11}), p_f(x_{10},x_{11},x_2), \\ \qquad p_f(x_4,x_5,x_{10}), p_f(x_6,x_7,x_{10}) \\ E_2 : p(x_1,x_2) \leftarrow p(x_3,x_4), p(x_4,x_5), p(x_6,x_7), p(x_7,x_8), \\ \qquad p_f(x_3,x_4,x_{10}), p_f(x_9,x_{10},x_1), p_f(x_4,x_5,x_{11}), p_f(x_{10},x_{11},x_2), \\ \qquad p_f(x_7,x_8,x_{10}), p_f(x_6,x_7,x_9) \\ p(x_1,x_2) \leftarrow p(x_3,x_4), p(x_5,x_6), p(x_7,x_8), p(x_8,x_9), \\ \qquad p_f(x_8,x_3,x_1), p_f(x_3,x_4,x_2), p_f(x_{11},x_5,x_{10}), p_f(x_5,x_6,x_3), \\ \qquad p_f(x_7,x_8,x_{11}), p_f(x_8,x_9,x_5) \\ p(x_1,x_2) \leftarrow p(x_3,x_4), p(x_5,x_6), p(x_7,x_8), p(x_8,x_9), \\ \qquad p_f(x_{10},x_3,x_1), p_f(x_3,x_4,x_2), p_f(x_5,x_6,x_{10}), p_f(x_6,x_{11},x_3), \\ \qquad p_f(x_3,x_8,x_6), p_f(x_8,x_9,x_{11}) \\ p(x_1,x_2) \leftarrow p(x_3,x_4), p(x_5,x_6), p(x_7,x_8), p(x_8,x_9), \\ \qquad p_f(x_3,x_4,x_1), p_f(x_4,x_{10},x_2), p_f(x_{11},x_5,x_4), p_f(x_5,x_6,x_{10}), \\ \qquad p_f(x_7,x_8,x_{11}), p_f(x_8,x_9,x_5) \\ p(x_1,x_2) \leftarrow p(x_3,x_4), p(x_5,x_6), p(x_7,x_8), p(x_8,x_9), \\ \qquad p_f(x_3,x_4,x_1), p_f(x_4,x_{10},x_2), p_f(x_5,x_6,x_4), p_f(x_6,x_{11},x_{10}), \\ \qquad p_f(x_7,x_8,x_6), p_f(x_8,x_9,x_{11}) \end{array} \right\}.$$

**Fig. 4.** The first and second self-resolving closures of $flat(C)$

with $p_f(x, y, f(x, y)) \leftarrow$ some times. Then, we cannot obtain the above $E$ from each element in $\mathcal{S}^2(flat(C))$ except $E_1$ and $E_2$. Furthermore, the resolvent of $E_i$ $(i = 1, 2)$ with $p_f(x, y, f(x, y)) \leftarrow$ twice, where the selected atoms in $E_i$ are atoms of which the third argument's term is $x_{10}$, contains a term with $f$. Hence, it holds that $\{flat(C)\} \cup defs(C) \not\vdash flat(D)$. □

Hence, we cannot directly conclude Rouveirol's Theorem from Theorem 5 and Lemma 14.

Note that the definite clauses $C$ and $D$ in Theorem 15 are *not* a counterexample of the if-direction of Rouveirol's Theorem, because $E_1$ and $E_2$ subsume $flat(D)$ by the following substitutions $\sigma_1$ and $\sigma_2$:

$$\sigma_1 = \{x_4/x_6, x_5/x_7, x_6/x_8, x_7/x_9, x_8/x_{10}, x_9/x_{11}\},$$
$$\sigma_2 = \{x_4/x_3, x_5/x_4, x_6/x_5, x_4/x_7, x_5/x_8, x_7/x_9, x_8/x_{10}, x_9/x_{11}\}.$$

Rouveirol's Theorem seems to be correct, but it is necessary to improve the proof by [13,14] because of Theorem 6 and 15.

# Induction of Logic Programs Based on $\psi$-Terms

Yutaka Sasaki

NTT Communication Science Laboratories,
2-4 Hikaridai, Seika-cho, Soraku-gun, Kyoto 619-0237, Japan
sasaki@cslab.kecl.ntt.co.jp

**Abstract.** This paper extends the traditional *inductive logic programming* (ILP) framework to a $\psi$-term capable ILP framework. Aït-Kaci's $\psi$-terms have interesting and significant properties for markedly widening applicable areas of ILP. For example, $\psi$-terms allow partial descriptions of information, generalization and specialization of *sorts* (or *types*) placed instead of function symbols, and abstract descriptions of data using sorts; they have comparable representation power to *feature structures* used in natural language processing. We have developed an algorithm that learns logic programs based on $\psi$-terms, made possible by a bottom-up approach employing the *least general generalization (lgg)* extended for $\psi$-terms. As an area of application, we have selected information extraction (IE) tasks in which sort information is crucial in deciding the generality of IE rules. Experiments were conducted on a set of test examples and background knowledge consisting of *case frames* of newspaper articles. The results showed high precision and recall rates for learned rules for the IE tasks.

## 1 Introduction

In the traditional setting of *inductive logic programming* (ILP) [14], the input is a set of examples, which are usually ground instances, and background knowledge, which is a set of ground instances or logic programs. The output of ILP systems is a set of logic programs, such as pure Prolog programs. The form (*i.e.*, language) of the output is called a hypothesis language. The task of ILP systems is to find, based on the background knowledge, *good* hypotheses that cover most positive examples and least negative examples (if any).

Previously, as one direction of extending the scope of the representation power of examples and a hypothesis language of ILP, RHB$^+$ [19] was presented for learning logic programs based on $\tau$-terms which are logic terms whose variables have *sorts* (or *types*). $\tau$-terms, however, are a very restricted form of $\psi$-terms used in LOGIN [1] and LIFE [3].

For example, in the previously proposed framework, a positive example that expresses "Jack was injured" was represented as

$$injured(agent \Rightarrow Jack),$$

O. Watanabe, T. Yokomori (Eds.): ALT'99, LNAI 1720, pp. 169–181, 1999.
© Springer-Verlag Berlin Heidelberg 1999

using a *feature (or attribute) agent*. If *Jack* is defined as a sub-sort of *people*, this example could be generalized to

$$injured(agent \Rightarrow people)$$

However, the example

$$injured(agent \Rightarrow passenger(count \Rightarrow 10))$$

could not be generalized to

$$injured(agent \Rightarrow people(count \Rightarrow number)).$$

This is because RHB$^+$ would treat the *passenger* as a function symbol and would not be able to generalize the *passenger* to the sort *people*. This restricted the application range which had to learn from the data as to which of the original structures of natural language sentences to preserve.

This paper presents the design and algorithm of our new ILP system which is capable of handling $\psi$-terms. After explaining attractive points of $\psi$-terms, we formally define $\psi$-terms and explain their properties. Then previous type-oriented learner is briefly described and an algorithm for achieving an ILP system that learns logic programs based on $\psi$-terms is presented. As an application to test the feasibility of our system, *information extraction (IE)* is briefly introduced. After that, experimental results on IE tasks are shown. A discussion and conclusions conclude this paper.

## 2    Attractive Points of $\psi$-Terms

For the sake of introducing of features (or attributes) and sorts, $\psi$-terms enable the following advantages.

**partial descriptions** For example, term $name(first \Rightarrow peter)$ expresses the information of a person whose first name is known. This is equivalent to $name(first \Rightarrow peter, last \Rightarrow \top)$. In the process of unification[4], possibly other features can be added to the term.

**dynamic generalization and specialization** Sorts, placed at the positions of function symbols, can be dynamically generalized and specialized. For example, $person(id \Rightarrow name(first \Rightarrow person))$ is a generalized form of $man(id \Rightarrow name(first \Rightarrow Jack))$.

**abstract representation** Abstract representations of examples using sorts can reduce the amount of data. For example,

$$familiar(agent \Rightarrow person(residence \Rightarrow France), obj \Rightarrow French)$$

represents a number of ground instances, such as,

$$familiar(agent \Rightarrow Serge(residence \Rightarrow France), obj \Rightarrow French).$$

**coreference** Coreference enables the recursive representation of terms. For example, $X : person(spouse \Rightarrow person(spouse \Rightarrow X))$ refers to itself recursively [1].

**NLP applicability** $\psi$-terms have the same representation power as *feature structures* [8] which are used for formally representing the syntax and semantics of natural language sentences.

## 3  $\psi$-Terms

Given a set of sorts $\mathcal{S}$ containing the sorts $\top$ and $\bot$, the partial order $\leq$ on $\mathcal{S}$ such that $\bot$ is the least and $\top$ is the greatest element, and *features* (*i.e.*, labels or attributes) $\mathcal{F}$, $\psi$-terms are defined as follows [2].

### 3.1  Ordered Sorts

Sorts $\mathcal{S}$ have a partial order $\leq$. $\tau_1 \leq \tau_2$ means that $\tau_2$ is more general than $\tau_1$ [2]. A set of *sorts* $\mathcal{S}$ must include the *greatest element* $\top$ and the *least element* $\bot$. $s \vee t$ is defined as the *supremum* of sorts $s$ and $t$, and $s \wedge t$ is the *infimum* of sorts $s$ and $t$. Then, $\langle \mathcal{S}, \leq, \vee, \wedge \rangle$ forms a lattice [6].

If the given sort hierarchy is a tree without $\top$ and $\bot$, we add $r \leq \top$ for root sort $r$ and $\bot \leq l_i$ for leaf sort $l_i$. As a special treatment, we distinguish *constants* from sorts when we have to distinguish them for ILP purposes, while constants are usually regarded as sorts. Formally, constants $\mathcal{C}$ is $\mathcal{C} \subset \mathcal{S}$ and for $c \in \mathcal{C}$, $\forall t \; t < c \supset t = \bot$.

### 3.2  Definition of $\psi$-Terms

Informally, $\psi$-terms are Prolog terms whose variables are replaced with variable $Var$ of sort $s$, which is denoted as $Var{:}s$. Function symbols are also replaced with sorts. Terms have features (labels or attributes) for readability and for representing partial information.

For example,

$$injured(agent \Rightarrow X : people(of \Rightarrow number))$$

is an atomic formula based on $\psi$-terms whose features are *agent* and *of* and whose sorts are *people* and *number*.

The recursive definition of $\psi$-terms is as follows.

**Definition 1** (*$\psi$-terms*) A $\psi$-term *is either an* untagged *$\psi$-term or a* tagged $\psi$-term.

---

[1] Variables are also used as coreference tags. This is one of the most elegant ways to represent coreference.

[2] This is defined as $\tau_2 \sqsubseteq \tau_1$ in [8].

**Definition 2** (*tagged $\psi$-term*)

  − *A variable is a tagged $\psi$-term.*
  − *If $X$ is a variable and $t$ is an untagged $\psi$-term, $X : t$ is a tagged $\psi$-term.*

**Definition 3** (*untagged $\psi$-term*)

  − *A sort symbol is an untagged $\psi$-term.*
  − *If $s$ is a sort symbol, $l_1, ..., l_n$ are features and $t_1, ..., t_n$ are $\psi$-terms, $s(l_1 \Rightarrow t_1, ..., l_n \Rightarrow t_n)$ is an untagged $\psi$-term.*

**Definition 4** (*atomic formula*)

  − *If $p$ is a predicate, $l_1, ..., l_n$ are features and $t_1, ..., t_n$ are $\psi$-terms, $p(l_1 \Rightarrow t_1, ..., l_n \Rightarrow t_n)$ is an atomic formula.*

While terms have features, they are compatible with the usual atomic formulae of Prolog. The first-order term notation $p(t_1, ..., t_n)$ is syntactic sugar for the $\psi$-term notation $p(1 \Rightarrow t_1, ..., n \Rightarrow t_n)$ [2].

## 3.3   Least General Generalization

In the definition of the *least general generalization (lgg)* [17], the part that defines the term *lgg* should be extended to the *lgg* of $\psi$-terms [3].

Now, we operationally define the lgg of $\psi$-terms using the following notations. $a$ and $b$ represent untagged $\psi$-terms. $s$, $t$, and $u$ represent $\psi$-terms. $f$, $g$, and $h$ represent sorts. $X$, $Y$, and $Z$ represent variables. Given $t = f(l_1 \Rightarrow t_1, ..., l_n \Rightarrow t_n)$, the $l_i$ projection of $t$ is defined as $t.l_i = t_i$. For simplicity of the algorithm, we regard untagged $\psi$-term $a$ appearing without a variable to type $V : a$, where $V$ is a fresh variable. Note that a variable appearing nowhere typed is implicitly typed by $\top$.

**Definition 5** (*lgg of $\psi$-terms*)

  1. *$lgg(X : a, X : a) = X : a$.*
  2. *$lgg(s, t) = u$, where $s \neq t$ and the tuple $(s, t, u)$ is in the history Hist.*
  3. *If $s = X : f(l_1^s \Rightarrow s_1, .., l_n^s \Rightarrow s_n)$, $t = Y : g(l_1^t \Rightarrow t_1, .., l_m^t \Rightarrow t_m)$ and $s \neq t$, then $lgg(s, t) = u$, where $L = \{l_1^s, ..., l_n^s\} \cap \{l_1^t, ..., l_m^t\}$ and for features $l_i \in L$, $u = Z : h(l_1 \Rightarrow lgg(s.l_1, t.l_1), ..., l_{|L|} \Rightarrow lgg(s.l_{|L|}, t.l_{|L|}))$ with $h = f \vee g$ [4]. $(s, t, u)$ is added to Hist.*

---

[3]  The lgg of $\psi$-terms has already been described in [1]. We present an algorithm as an extension of Plotkin's lgg. The lgg of *feature terms*, which are equivalent to $\psi$-terms, can be found in [16].

[4]  Here, $\vee$ means the supremum of two sorts.

For example, the lgg of

$$injured(agent \Rightarrow passenger(of \Rightarrow 10))$$

and

$$injured(agent \Rightarrow men(of \Rightarrow 2))$$

is

$$injured(agent \Rightarrow people(of \Rightarrow number)).$$

**Definition 6** (*lgg of atoms based on $\psi$-terms*) *Let $P$ and $Q$ be atomic formulae (atoms). The lgg of atoms is defined as follows.*

1. *If $P = p(l_1^s \Rightarrow s_1, .., l_n^s \Rightarrow s_n)$ and $Q = p(l_1^t \Rightarrow t_1, .., l_m^t \Rightarrow t_m)$, then $lgg(P,Q) = p(l_1 \Rightarrow lgg(s.l_1, t.l_1), ..., l_{|L|} \Rightarrow lgg(s.l_{|L|}, t.l_{|L|}))$ where $L = \{l_1^s, ..., l_n^s\} \cap \{l_1^t, ..., l_m^t\}$.*
2. *If $P = p(l_1^s \Rightarrow s_1, .., l_n^s \Rightarrow s_n)$, $Q = q(l_1^t \Rightarrow t_1, .., l_m^t \Rightarrow t_m)$ and $p \neq q$, $lgg(P,Q)$ is undefined.*

Let $P$ and $Q$ be atoms and $L_1$ and $L_2$ be literals. The lgg of literals and clauses are defined as follows [12].

**Definition 7** (*lgg of literals based on $\psi$-terms*)

1. *If $L_1$ and $L_2$ are atomic, then $lgg(L_1, L_2)$ is the lgg of atoms.*
2. *If $L_1 = \neg P$ and $L_2 = \neg Q$, then $lgg(L_1, L_2) = lgg(\neg P, \neg Q) = \neg lgg(P, Q)$.*
3. *If $L_1 = \neg P$ and $L_2 = Q$ or $L_1 = P$ and $L_2 = \neg Q$, then $lgg(L_1, L_2)$ is undefined.*

**Definition 8** (*lgg of clauses*)
    Let clauses $c_1 = \{L_1, ..., L_n\}$ and $c_2 = \{K_1, ..., K_m\}$. Then $lgg(c_1, c_2) = \{L_{ij} = lgg(L_i, K_j) | L_i \in c_1, K_j \in c_2 \text{ and } lgg(L_i, K_j) \text{ is defined}\}$.

## 4    Previous Type-Oriented ILP System

This section briefly describes a summary of a previous ILP system. RHB$^+$ learns logic programs based on $\tau$-terms. $\tau$-terms are restricted forms of $\psi$-terms. Informally, $\tau$-terms are Prolog terms whose variables are replaced with *Var:type* and whose function symbols have features. It employs a combination of bottom-up and top-down approaches, following the result described in [23].

In the definition of *the least general generalization (lgg)* [17], the definition of the term *lgg* was extended to the $\tau$-term *lgg*. The other definitions of *lgg* were equivalent to the originals.

The special feature of RHB$^+$ is the *dynamic type restriction by positive examples* during clause construction. The restriction uses positive examples currently covered in order to determine appropriate types. For each variable $X_i$ appearing in the clause, RHB$^+$ computes the *supremum* of all types bound to $X_i$ when covered positive examples are unified with the current head in turn.

The search heuristic PWI is a weighted informativity employing a Laplace estimate [9]. Let $T = \{Head\!:\!-Body\,\} \cup BK$.

$$PWI(T) = -\frac{1}{|\hat{P}|} \times \log_2 \frac{|\hat{P}|+1}{|Q(T)|+2},$$

where $|\hat{P}|$ denotes the number of positive examples covered by $T$ and $Q(T)$ is the empirical content.

Type information was made use of for computing $|Q(T)|$. Let $Hs$ be a set of instances of *Head* generated by proving *Body* using backtracking. $|\tau|$ was defined as the number of constants under type $\tau$ in the type hierarchy. When $\tau$ is a constant, $|\tau|$ is defined as 1.

$$|Q(T)| = \sum_{h \in Hs} \prod_{\tau \in Types(h)} |\tau|,$$

where $Types(h)$ returns the set of types in $h$.

The stopping condition also utilized $|Q(T)|$ in the computation of the *Model Covering Ratio (MCR)*:

$$MCR(T) = \frac{|\hat{P}|}{|Q(T)|}.$$

RHB$^+$ was successfully applied to the IE task of extracting key information from 100 newspaper articles related to new product release [21]. This implies a potential of applying our $\psi$-term capable ILP system to the IE task.

## 5    New ILP Capable of $\psi$-Term

This section describes a novel relational learner $\psi$-RHB which learns logic programs based on $\psi$-terms.

Extending ILP to a $\psi$-term capable ILP is not straightforward. In top-down learning, the learner constructs all possible literals to be added to the current body. When considering only simple sorts which do not have any arguments, top-down approaches, like Foil, are efficient. However, when it comes to learning clauses with $\psi$-terms, it is not realistic to produce all kinds of literals that contain possible terms.

For example, if we have predicate $p$, sorts $t_1$ and $t_2$, features $l_1$ and $l_2$, and variable $X$, one of the possible literals is $p(l_1 \Rightarrow t_1(l_2 \Rightarrow X\!:\!t_1(l_1 \Rightarrow t_2)))$ because the predicate arity and term depth are unbound. The maximum depth of modification to the sort in a possible literal must be more than the maximum depth of modification to a sort seen in the given training examples. Moreover, at each level of a modification to a sort, the maximum number of features of the sort is the number of features $\mathcal{F}$. Therefore, generating all patterns of literals with $\psi$-terms is too time consuming and so not very practical. To cope with this problem, the learning strategy should be bottom-up.

## 5.1  Algorithms of $\psi$-Term Capable ILP

The positive examples are atomic formulae based on $\psi$-terms. The hypothesis language is a set of Horn clauses based on $\psi$-terms. The background knowledge also consists of atomic formulae. $\psi$-RHB, a $\psi$-term capable ILP system, employs a bottom-up approach, like Golem [15].

## Learning Algorithm

The learning algorithm of our ILP system is based on the Golem's algorithm [15] extended for $\psi$-terms.

The steps are as follows.

**Algorithm 1** *Learning algorithm*

1. *Given positive examples P, background knowledge BK.*
2. *Link sorts which have the same names in P and BK.*
3. *A set of hypotheses H* ={}.
4. *Select K pairs of examples $(A_i, B_i)$ as EP ($0 \leq i \leq K$).*
5. *Select sets of literals $AR_i$ and $BR_i$ as selected background knowledge according to the variable depth D.*
6. *Compute lggs of clauses $A_i{:}{-}AR_i$ and $B_i{:}{-}BR_i$.*
7. *Simplify the lggs by evaluating with weighted informativity PWI, which is the informativity defined in Section 4.*
8. *Select the best clause C, and add it to H if the score of C is better than the threshold $\delta$.*
9. *Remove covered examples from P.*
10. *If P is empty then return H; Otherwise, goto Step 4.*

In Step 2, we have to link sorts in the examples and the background knowledge because the OSF theory [4] which underlies the theory of $\psi$-terms is not formed under the *unique name assumption*. For example, if we have two terms $f(t)$ and $g(t)$, $t$ in $f(t)$ and $t$ in $g(t)$ are not identical. The OSF theory requires that they be represented as $f(X : t)$ and $f(X : t)$, if $t$ is identical in both of two terms. Therefore, the same sort symbols in the examples and in the background knowledge are linked and will be treated as identical symbols in the later steps.

In Step 5, to speed up the learning process, literals related to each pair of examples are selected. At first, $AR_i$ and $BR_i$ are empty. Then, (1) select the background knowledge literals $A_{sel}$ so that it has all literals whose sort symbols are identical to the sorts in $A_i$ or $AR_i$, and select $B_{sel}$ in the same manner using $B_i$ or $BR_i$. (2) Add literals $A_{sel}$ and $B_{sel}$ to sets $AR_i$ and $BR_i$, respectively. Repeat (1) and (2) $n$ times when the predefined variable depth is $n$. This iteration creates sets of literals.

We use $AR_i$ as the selected background knowledge for $A_i$, and $BR_i$ for $B_i$ in Step 6. What is computed in Step 6 is the following lgg of clauses.

$$lgg((A_i :- \bigwedge AR_i), (B_i :- \bigwedge BR_i)),$$

where $\bigwedge S$ is a conjunction of all of the elements in $S$. The *lggs* of clauses have the variable depth of at most $n$.

In Step 7, simplification of the lggs is achieved by checking all literals in the body as to whether removal of literals makes the score of the weighted informativity worse or not. For the purpose of informativity estimation, we use the concept of ground instances of atomic formulae based on $\psi$-terms. We call atomic formula $A$ ground instance if all of the sorts appearing in $A$ are constants. For example,

$$familiar(agent \Rightarrow Serge(residence \Rightarrow France), obj \Rightarrow French).$$

Moreover, literals in the body are checked as to whether they satisfy the input-output mode declarations of the predicates.

# 6    NLP Application

## 6.1    Information Extraction

This section presents a brief introduction of our target application: information extraction (IE). The task of information extraction involves extracting key information from a text corpus, such as newspaper articles or WWW pages, in order to fill empty slots of given *templates*. Information extraction techniques have been investigated by many researchers and institutions in a series of Message Understanding Conferences (MUC), which are not only technical meetings but also IE system contests on information extraction, conducted on common benchmarks.

The input for the information extraction task is a set of natural language texts (usually newspaper articles) with an empty *template*. In most cases, the articles describe a certain topic, such as corporate mergers or terrorist attacks in South America. The given templates have some slots which have field names, *e.g.*, "company name" and "merger date". The output of the IE task is a set of filled templates. IE tasks are highly domain dependent because the rules and dictionaries used to fill values in the template slots depend on the domain.

## 6.2    Problem in IE System Development

The domain dependence has been a serious problem for IE system developers. As an example, Umass/MUC-3 needed about 1500 person-hours of skilled labor to build the IE rules represented as a dictionary [13]. Worse, new rules have to be constructed from scratch when the target domain is changed.

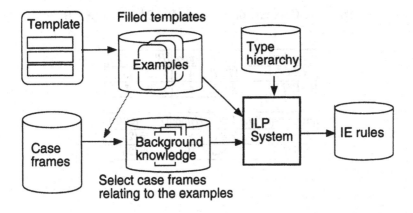

**Fig. 1.** Block diagram of the preparation of data for ILP

To cope with this problem, some researchers have studied methods to learn information extraction rules. On this background, we selected the IE task for an application of a $\psi$-term capable ILP. An IE task is appropriate for our application because natural languages contain a vast variety of nouns relating to a taxonomy (*i.e.*, sort hierarchy).

## 7  Experimental Results

For the purpose of estimating the performance of our system, we conducted experiments on the learning of IE rules. The IE tasks here involved the MUC-4 style IE and the template elements to be filled included two items [5]. We extracted articles related to accidents from a one-year newspaper corpus written in Japanese [6]. Forty two articles were related to accidents which resulted in some deaths and injuries. The template we used consisted of two slots: the number of deaths and injuries. We filled one template for each article. After parsing the sentences, tagged parse trees were converted into atomic formulae representing case frames.

Figure 1 shows the learning block diagram. Those case frames were given to our learner as background knowledge. *All of the 42 articles were able to be represented as case frames for the sake of the representation power of $\psi$-terms, while only 25 articles were able to be represented using $\tau$-terms.* Each slot of a filled template was given as a positive example. For the precision and recall, the standard evaluation metrics for IE tasks, we counted them by using four-fold cross validation on the 42 examples.

---

[5] This is a relatively simple setting compared to state-of-the-art IE tasks.

[6] We thank the Mainichi Newspaper Co. for permitting us to use the articles of 1992.

**Table 1.** Comparison between $RHB^+$ and $\psi\text{-}RHB$

| [deaths] | Time (sec) | $\|Hypo\|$ | $\|\hat{P}\|$ / $\|Q(T)\|$ |
|---|---|---|---|
| $RHB^+$ | 172.7 | 4 | 25/25 |
| $\psi\text{-}RHB$ | 954.2 | 4 | 25/25 |

| [injuries] | Time (sec) | $\|Hypo\|$ | $\|\hat{P}\|$ / $\|Q(T)\|$ |
|---|---|---|---|
| $RHB^+$ | 508.5 | 8 | 25/25 |
| $\psi\text{-}RHB$ | 3218.0 | 10 | 25/25 |

$$Precision = \frac{correct\ output\ answers}{output\ answers}$$

$$Recall = \frac{correct\ output\ answers}{all\ correct\ answers}$$

## 7.1 Natural Language Processing Tools

We used a sort hierarchy hand-crafted for the Japanese-English machine translation system ALT-J/E [11]. This hierarchy is a sort of concept thesaurus represented as a tree structure in which each node is called a category (i.e., a sort). An edge in the tree represents an is_a relation among the categories. The current version of the sort hierarchy is 12 levels deep and contains about 3000 category nodes. We also used the commercial-quality morphological analyzer, parser, and semantic analyzer of ALT-J/E.

Results after the semantic analysis were parse trees with case and semantic tags. We developed a logical form translator FEP2 which generates case frames expressed as atomic formulae from the parse trees.

## 7.2 Results

Table 1 and Table 2 show the results of our experiments. Table 1 shows the experimental results of RHB$^+$ and $\psi$-RHB using the same 25 examples as used in [19]. We used a SparcStation 20 for this experiment. $\psi$-RHB showed a high accuracy like RHB$^+$ but slowed down in exchange for its extended representation power in the hypothesis language.

Table 2 shows the experimental results on forty two examples. We used a AlphaStation 500/333MHz for this experiment. Overall, a very high precision, 90-97%, was achieved. 63-80% recall was achieved with all case frames including errors in the case selection and semantic tag selection. These selections had an error range of 2-7%. With only correct case frames, 67-88% recall was achieved.

It is important to note that the extraction of two different pieces of information showed good results. This indicates that our learner has high potential in IE tasks.

**Table 2.** Learning results of accidents

|                                | deaths | injuries |
|--------------------------------|--------|----------|
| Precision (all case frames)    | 96.7%  | 89.9%    |
| Recall (all case frames)       | 80.0%  | 63.2%    |
| Recall (correct case frames)   | 87.5%  | 66.7%    |
| Average time (sec.)            | 966.8  | 828.0    |

## 8  Discussion

The benefits of $\psi$-term capability, not just involving the $\tau$-term, in an application, depend on the writing style of the topic. In English, the expression "ABC Corp.'s printer" is commonly used and the logical term representation can be $printer(pos \Rightarrow$ "ABC Corp."). However, if the expression "ABC Corp. released a printer and ..." were very common, it could be $release($"ABC Corp.", $printer)$. In this case, since the required representation is within the $\tau$-term, extending the language from $\tau$-term based to $\psi$-term based does not pay for the higher computing cost.

In the IE community, some previous research has looked at generating IE rules from texts with filled templates, for example, AutoSlog-TS [18], CRYSTAL [22], LIEP [10], and RAPIER [7]. The main differences between our approach and the others are that

- we use semantic representations (*i.e.* case frames) created by a domain-independent parser and semantic analyzer.
- we use ILP techniques independent of both the parser and semantic analyzer.

Note that the second item means that learned logic programs may have several atomic formulae in the bodies. This point differentiates our approach from the simple generalization of a single case frame.

INDIE [5] learns a set of feature terms equivalent to $\psi$-terms. The learning is equivalent to the learning of a set of atomic formulae based on $\psi$-terms which cover all positive examples and no negative examples. Because its hypotheses are generated so as to exclude any negatives, it might be intolerant to noise.

Sasaki [20] reported a preliminary version ILP system which was capable of limited features of $\psi$-terms. Preliminary experiments are conducted on learning IE rules to extract information from only twenty articles.

## 9  Conclusions and Remarks

This paper has described an algorithm of a $\psi$-term capable ILP and its application to information extraction. The lgg of logic terms was extended to the lgg of $\psi$-terms. The learning algorithm is based on the lgg of clauses with $\psi$-terms.

Natural language processing relies on a vast variety of nouns relating to the sort hierarchy (or taxonomy) which plays a crucial role in generalizing data generated from the natural language. Therefore, the information extraction task matches the requirements of the $\psi$-term capable ILP.

Because of the modest robustness and performance of current natural language analysis techniques (for Japanese texts), errors were found in parsing, case selection, and semantic tag selection. The experimental results, however, show that learned rules achieve high precision and recall in IE tasks. Moreover, an important point is that all of the 42 articles related to the topic were able to be represented as case frames, which demonstrates the representation power of $\psi$-terms. This indicates that applying ILP to the learning from case frames will become more practical as NLP techniques progress in the near future.

# References

1. H. Aït-Kaci and R. Nasr, LOGIN: A logic programming language with built-in inheritance, *J. Logic Programming*, 3, pp.185-215, 1986.
2. H. Aït-Kaci and A. Podelski, *Toward a Meaning of LIFE*, PRL-RP-11, Digital Equipment Corporation, Paris Research Laboratory, 1991.
3. H. Aït-Kaci, B. Dumant, R. Meyer, A. Podelski, and P. Van Roy, *The Wild Life Handbook*, 1994.
4. H. Aït-Kaci, A. Podelski and S. C. Goldstein, Order-Sorted Feature Theory Unification, *J. Logic Programming*, Vol.30, No.2, pp.99-124, 1997.
5. E. Armengol and E. Plaza, Induction of Feature Terms with INDIE, *ECML-97*, pp.33-48, 1997.
6. Birkhoff, G., *Lattice Theory*, American Mathematical Society, 1979.
7. M. E. Califf and R. J. Mooney, Relational Learning of Pattern-Match Rules for Information Extraction, *ACL-97 Workshop in Natural Language Learning*, 1997.
8. B. Carpenter, *The Logic of Typed Feature Structures*, Cambridge University Press, 1992.
9. B. Cestnik, Estimating Probabilities: A Crucial Task in Machine Learning, *ECAI-90*, pp.147-149, 1990.
10. S. B. Huffman, Learning Information Extraction Patterns from Examples, *Statistical and Symbolic Approaches to Learning for Natural Language Processing*, pp. 246-260, 1996.
11. S. Ikehara, M. Miyazaki, and A. Yokoo, Classification of Language Knowledge for Meaning Analysis in Machine Translations, *Transactions of Information Processing Society of Japan*, Vol. 34, pp.1692-1704, 1993 (in Japanese).
12. N. Lavrač and S. Džeroski: *Inductive Logic Programming: Techniques and Applications*, Ellis Horwood, 1994.
13. W. Lehnert, C. Cardie, D. Fisher, J. McCarthy, E. Riloff and S. Soderland, University of Massachusetts: MUC-4 Test Results and Analysis, *Fourth Message Understanding Conference*, pp.151-158, 1992.
14. S. Muggleton, Inductive Logic Programming, *New Generation Computing*, 8(4), pp.295-318, 1991.
15. S. Muggleton and C. Feng, Efficient Induction of Logic Programs, in *Inductive Logic Programming*, Academic Press, 1992.
16. E. Plaza, Cases as terms: A feature term approach to the structured representation cases, *First Int. Conf. on Case-Based Reasoning*, pp. 263-276, 1995.

17. G. Plotkin, A Note on Inductive Generalization, in B. Jeltzer *et al.* eds., *Machine Intelligence 5*, pp.153-163, Edinburgh University Press, 1969.
18. E. Riloff, Automatically Generating Extraction Pattern from Untagged Text, *AAAI-96*, pp. 1044-1049, 1996.
19. Y. Sasaki and M. Haruno, RHB$^+$: A Type-Oriented ILP System Learning from Positive Data, *IJCAI-97*, pp.894-899, 1997.
20. Y. Sasaki, Learning of Information Extraction Rules using ILP — Preliminary Report, *The Second International Conference on The Practical Application of Knowledge Discovery and Data Mining*, pp.195-205, London, 1998.
21. Y. Sasaki, Applying Type-Oriented ILP to IE Rule Generation, *AAAI-99 Workshop on Machine Learning for Information Extraction*, pp.43-47,1999.
22. S. Soderland, D. Fisher, J. Aseltine, W. Lenert, CRYSTAL: Inducing a Conceptual Dictionary, *IJCAI-95*, pp.1314-1319, 1995.
23. J. M. Zelle and R. J. Mooney, J. B. Konvisser, Combining Top-down and Bottom-up Methods in Inductive Logic Programming, *ML-94*, pp.343-351, 1994.

# Complexity in the Case Against Accuracy: When Building One Function-Free Horn Clause Is as Hard as Any

Richard Nock

Department of Mathematics and Computer Science, Université des Antilles-Guyane, Campus de Fouillole, 97159 Pointe-à-Pitre, France
rnock@univ-ag.fr

**Abstract.** Some authors have repeatedly pointed out that the use of the accuracy, in particular for comparing classifiers, is not adequate. The main argument discusses the validity of some assumptions underlying the use of this criterion. In this paper, we study the hardness of the accuracy's replacement in various ways, using a framework very sensitive to these assumptions: Inductive Logic Programming. Replacement is investigated in three ways: completion of the accuracy with an additional requirement, replacement of the accuracy by the ROC analysis, recently introduced from signal detection theory, and replacement of the accuracy by a single criterion. We prove strong hardness results for most of the possible replacements. The major point is that allowing arbitrary multiplication of clauses appears to be totally useless. Another point is the equivalence in difficulty of various criteria. In contrast, the accuracy criterion appears to be tractable in this framework.

## 1 Introduction

As the number of classification learning algorithms is rapidly increasing, the question of finding efficient criteria to compare their results is of particular relevance. This is also of importance for the algorithms themselves, as they can naturally optimize directly such criteria to achieve good results. A criterion frequently encountered to address both problems is the accuracy, which received recently on these topics some criticisms about its adequacy [7].

The primary inadequacy of the accuracy stems from a tacit assumption that the overall accuracy controls by-class accuracies, or similarly that class distributions among examples are constant and relatively balanced [6]. This is obviously not true : skewed distributions are frequent in agronomy, or more generally in life sciences. As an example, consider the human DNA, in which no more than 6% are coding genes [7]. In that cases, the interesting, unusual class is often the rare one, and the well-balanced hypothesis may not lead to discover the unusual individuals. Moreover, in real-world problems, not only is this assumption false, but also of heavy consequences may be the misclassification of some examples, another cost which is not integrated in the accuracy. Fraud detection is a good

O. Watanabe, T. Yokomori (Eds.): ALT'99, LNAI 1720, pp. 182–193, 1999.

example of such situations [7], but medical domains are typical. As an example, consider the case where a mutagen molecule is predicted as non-mutagen, and the case where an harmless molecule is predicted as mutagen. In that cases, the interesting class has the heaviest misclassification costs, and the equal error costs assumption may produce bad results. Finally, the accuracy may be inadequate in some cases because other parameters are to be taken into account. Constraints on size parameters are sometimes to be used because we want to obtain small formulae, for interpretation purposes. As an example, consider again the problem of mutagenesis prediction, where two equally accurate formulae are obtained. If one is much smaller, it is more likely to provide useful descriptions for the mining expert.

We have chosen for our framework a field particularly sensitive to these problems, Inductive Logic Programming (ILP). ILP is a rapidly growing research field, concerned by the use of variously restricted subclasses of Horn clauses to build Machine Learning (ML) algorithms. According to [9], almost seventy applications use ILP formalism, twenty of which are science applications, which can be partitioned into biological (four) and drug design (sixteen) applications. ILP-ML algorithms have been applied with some success in areas of biochemistry and molecular biology [9]. Using ILP formalism, we argue that the replacement of the accuracy raises structural complexity issues. The argument is structured as follows.

First, to address the latter problems, we explain that the single accuracy requirement can be completed by an additional requirement to provide more adequate criteria. We integrate various constraints over two important kinds of parameters: by-class error functions, and representation parameters such as feature selection ratios, size constraints. We show that any of such integration leads to a very negative structural complexity result, similar to $NP$-Hardness, which is not faced by the accuracy optimization alone. The result has a side effect which can be presented as a "loss" in the formalism's expressiveness, a rare property in classical ML complexity issues. Indeed, it authorizes the construction of arbitrary large (even exponential sized) sets of Horn clauses, but which we prove having no more expressive power than a single Horn clause. We prove a threshold in intractability since it appears immediately with the additional requirement, and is not a function of the tightness of it. Furthermore, the effects of the constraints on optimal accuracies vanish as the number of predicates increases, as optimal accuracies with or without the additional constraints are asymptotically equal. Finally, for some criteria, their mixing with the accuracy brings the most negative result: not only does the intractability appears immediately with the criterion, but also the error cannot be dropped down under that of the unbiased coin. We then study the replacement of the accuracy criterion using a general method [6, 7], derived from statistical decision theory, based on a specific bi-criteria optimization. We show that this method leads to the same drawbacks. Finally, we investigate the replacement of the error by a single criterion, and show that it is also to be analyzed very carefully, as some of the "candidates" lead exactly to the same negative results presented before. The reductions are presented for a subclass of Horn formalism simple enough to be an element of the intersection of all classically encountered theoretical ILP studies.

## 2    Mono and Bi-criteria Solutions to Replace the Accuracy

Denote as $C$ and $\mathcal{H}$ two classes of concepts representations, respectively called *target's class* and *hypothesis class*. In real-world domains, we do not know the target concept's class, that is why we have to make ad hoc choices for $\mathcal{H}$ with a powerful enough formalism, yet ensuring tractability. Even if some benchmarks problems appear to be easily solvable [3], ML applications, and particularly ILP, face more difficult problems [9], for which the choice of $\mathcal{H}$ is crucial. Since most of the studies dealing with the accuracy replacement problem have been investigated with two classes [7], we also consider two-classes problems and not multi-class cases. It is not really important for us, as results already become hard in that setting. Let $c \in C$. Suppose that we have drawn examples following some unknown but fixed distribution $D$, labelled according to $c$. We can denote the accuracy of $h \in \mathcal{H}$ with respect to (w.r.t.) $c$ by $P_D(h = c) = \sum_{h(x)=c(x)} D(x)$.

### 2.1    Extending the Accuracy

The principal drawbacks of the accuracy are of two kinds: the equal costs assumption [6], and the well balanced assumption [7]. We propose a solution to the problem by the maximization of the accuracy subject to constraints. We also propose criteria on related problems, an example of such being the feature selection problem, in which we want to build formulae on restricted windows of the total features set. For any fixed positive rational $\nu$, we use the following adequate notion of distance between two reals $u, v : d_\nu(u, v) = \frac{|u-v|}{u+v+\nu}$. We also use eight rates on the examples (definitions differ slightly from [7]): $TP = \sum_{h(x)=1=c(x)} D(x)$ ; $TPR = TP/P$ ; $FP = \sum_{h(x)=1 \neq c(x)} D(x)$ ; $FPR = FP/N$; $TN = \sum_{h(x)=0=c(x)} D(x)$ ; $TNR = TN/N$ ; $FN = \sum_{h(x)=0 \neq c(x)} D(x)$ ; $FNR = FN/P$, with $N = \sum_{c(x)=0} D(x)$ and $P = \sum_{c(x)=1} D(x)$. In order to complete the accuracy requirements, we imagine seven types of additional constraints, each of them being parameterized by a number $\zeta$ (between 0 and 1). Each of them defines a subset of $\mathcal{H}$, which shall be parameterized by $D$ if the distribution controls the subset through the constraint. The first three subsets of $\mathcal{H}$ contain hypotheses for which the $FP$ and $FN$ are not far from each other, or a one-side error is upper bounded: $\mathcal{H}_{D,1}(\zeta) = \{h \in \mathcal{H}|d_\nu(FP, FN) \leq \zeta\}; \mathcal{H}_{D,2}(\zeta) = \{h \in \mathcal{H}|FN \leq \zeta\}; \mathcal{H}_{D,3}(\zeta) = \{h \in \mathcal{H}|FN \leq \frac{1}{\zeta}FP\}$. The two following subsets are parameterized by constraints equivalent to some frequently encountered in the information retrieval community [8], respectively (1 minus) the precision and (1 minus) the recall criteria: $\mathcal{H}_{D,4}(\zeta) = \{h \in \mathcal{H}|FP/(TP + FP) \leq \zeta\}$ ; $\mathcal{H}_{D,5}(\zeta) = \{h \in \mathcal{H}|FN/(TP + FN) \leq \zeta\}$. Define #P($h$) as the total number of different predicates of $h$, #W($h$) as the whole number of predicates of

$h$ (if one predicate is present $k$ times, it is counted $k$ times), and #T as the total number of different available predicates. The two last subsets of $\mathcal{H}$ are parameterized by formulae respectively having a sufficiently small fraction of the available predicates, or having a sufficiently small overall size: $\mathcal{H}_6(\zeta) = \{h \in \mathcal{H} | \#P(h)/\#T \leq \zeta\}$; $\mathcal{H}_7(\zeta) = \{h \in \mathcal{H} | \#W(h)/\#T \leq \zeta\}$. The division by the total number of different predicates in $\mathcal{H}_7(\zeta)$ is made only for technical reasons: to obtain hardness results for small values of $\zeta$ and thus, already for small sizes of formulae (in the last constraint). The first problem we address can be summarized as follows:

**Problem 1:** **Given $\zeta$ and $a \in \{1, 2, ..., 7\}$, can we find an algorithm returning a set of Horn clauses from $\mathcal{H}_{(D,)a}(\zeta)$ whose error is no more than a given $\gamma$, if such an hypothesis exists ?**

## 2.2   Replacing the Accuracy: The ROC Analysis

Receiver Operating Characteristic (ROC) analysis is a traditional methodology from signal detection theory [1]. It has been used in machine learning recently [6, 7] in order to correct the main drawbacks of the accuracy. In ROC space (this is the coordinate system), we visualize the performance of a classifier by plotting $TPR$ on the $Y$ axis, and $FPR$ on the $X$ axis. Figure 1 presents the ROC analysis, along with three possible outputs which we present and analyze. If a

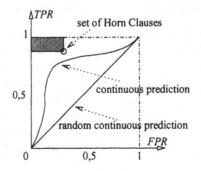

**Fig. 1.** The ROC analysis of a learning algorithm.

classifier produces a continuous output (such as an estimate of posterior probability of an instance's class membership [7]), for any possible value of $FPR$, we can get a value for $TPR$, by thresholding the output between its extreme bounds. If a classifier produces a discrete output (such as Horn clauses), then the classifier gives rise to a single point. If the classifier is the random choice of the class, either (if it is continuous) the curve is the line $y = x$, or (if it is discrete) there is a single dot, on the line $y = x$. One important thing to note is that the ROC representation gives the behavior of an algorithm without regarding the class distribution or the error cost [6]. And it allows to choose the best of some classifiers, by the following procedure. Fix as $K^+$ the cost of misclassifying a positive example, and $K^-$ the cost of misclassifying a negative example (these two costs depend on the problem). Then the *expected cost* of some classifier represented by point $(FPR, TPR)$ is given by the following formula: $\sum_{c(x)=1} D(x) \times (1 - TPR) \times K^+ + \sum_{c(x)=0} D(x) \times FPR \times K^-$. Two algorithms, whose corresponding point are respectively $(FPR_1, TPR_1)$ and $(FPR_2, TPR_2)$, have the same expected cost iff $(TPR_2 - TPR_1)/(FPR_2 - FPR_1) = (\sum_{c(x)=1} D(x)K^+)/(\sum_{c(x)=0} D(x)K^-)$. This gives the slope of an isoperformance line, which only depends on the relative weights of the examples, and the respective misclassification costs. Given one point on the ROC, the classifiers performing better are those on the "northwest" of the isoperformance line with the preceding slope, and to which the point belongs. If we want to find an algorithm $A$ performing *surely* better than an algorithm $B$, we therefore should strive to find $A$ such that its point lies into the rectangle whose opposite vertices are the $(0, 1)$ point (the perfect classification) and $B$'s point (a grey rectangle is shown on the top left of figure 1). From that, the second problem we address is the following (Note the constraint's weakness : the algorithm is required to work only on a *single* point):

**Problem 2: Given one point $(TPR_x, FPR_x)$ on the ROC, can we find an algorithm returning a set of Horn clauses whose point falls into the rectangle with opposite vertices $(0, 1)$ and $(TPR_x, FPR_x)$, if such an hypothesis exists ?**

### 2.3   Replacing the Accuracy by a Single Criterion

The question of whether the accuracy can be replaced by a single criterion instead of two (such as in ROC) has been raised in [6]. Some researchers [6] propose the use of the following criterion: $(1 - FPR) \times TPR$. A geometric interpretation of the criterion is the following [6]: it corresponds to the area of a rectangle whose opposite vertices are $(FPR, TPR)$ and $(1, 0)$. The typical isoperformance curve is now an hyperbola. The third problem we address is therefore:

**Problem 3: Given $\gamma$, can we find an algorithm returning a set of Horn clauses such that $(1 - FPR) \times TPR \geq \gamma$, if such an hypothesis exists ?**

## 3   Introduction to the Proof Technique

We present here the basic ILP notions which we use, with a basic introduction to our proofs. Technical parts are proposed in two appendices.

### 3.1   ILP Background Needed

The ILP background needed to understand this article can be summarized as follows. More formalization and details are given in [4], but they are not needed here. Given a Horn clause language $\mathcal{L}$ and a correct inference relation on $\mathcal{L}$, an ILP learning problem can be formalized as follows. Assume a background knowledge $\mathcal{BK}$ expressed in a language $\mathcal{LB} \subseteq \mathcal{L}$, and a set of examples $\mathcal{E}$ in a language $\mathcal{LE} \subseteq \mathcal{L}$. The goal is to produce an hypothesis $h$ in an hypothesis class $\mathcal{H} \subseteq \mathcal{L}$ consistent with $\mathcal{BK}$ and $\mathcal{E}$ such that $h$ and the background knowledge cover all positive examples and none of the negative ones. Sometimes the formalism cannot correctly classify all examples according to the preceding scenario, for the reason that the examples describe a complex concept. We may transform the ILP learning problem to a relaxed version, where we want the formulae to make sufficiently small errors over the examples. The choice of the representation languages for the background knowledge and the examples, and the inference relation greatly influence the complexity (or decidability) of the learning problem. A common restriction for both $\mathcal{BK}$ and $\mathcal{E}$ is to use ground facts. As in [5], we use $\theta$-subsumption as the inference relation (a clause $h_1$ $\theta$-subsumes a clause $h_2$ iff there exists a substitution $\theta$ such that $h_1\theta \subseteq h_2$ [5, 4]). In order to treat our problem as a classical ML problem, we use the following lemma, which authorizes us to create ordinary examples:

**Lemma 1.** *[5] Learning a Horn clause program from a set of ground background knowledge $\mathcal{BK}$ and ground examples $\mathcal{E}$ , the inference relation being generalized subsumption, is equivalent to learning the same program with $\theta$-subsumption, and empty background knowledge and examples defined as ground Horn clauses of the form $e \leftarrow b$, where $e \in \mathcal{E}$ and $b \in \mathcal{BK}$.*

In the following, we are interested in learning concepts in the form of (sets of) non recursive Horn clauses. It is important to note that all results are still valid when considering propositional, *determinate* or *local* Horn clauses, similarly to the study of [4], to which we refer for all necessary definitions. For the sake of simplicity in stating our results, we sometimes abbreviate "Function free Horn Clauses" by the acronym "*FfHC*".

## 3.2 Basic Tools for the Hardness Results

Concerning problem 1, fix $a \in \{1, 2, 3, 4, 5, 6, 7\}$. We want to approximate the best concept in $\mathcal{H}_{(D;)a}(\zeta)$ by one still in $\mathcal{H}_{(D;)a}(\zeta)$. However, the best concept in $\mathcal{H}_{(D;)a}(\zeta)$ generally does not have an error equal to the optimal one over $\mathcal{H}$ given $D$, $opt_{\mathcal{H}_D}(c)$. In fact, it has an error that we can denote $opt_{\mathcal{H}_{(D;)a}(\zeta)}(c) = \min_{h' \in \mathcal{H}_{(D;)a}(\zeta)} \sum_{h(x) \neq c(x)} D(x) \geq opt_{\mathcal{H}_D}(c)$. The goodness of the accuracy of a concept taken from $\mathcal{H}_{(D;)a}(\zeta)$ should be appreciated with respect to this latter quantity. Our results on problem 1 are all obtained by showing the hardness of solving the following decision problem:

**Definition 1.** *Approx-Constrained($\mathcal{H}, (a, \zeta)$):*
**Instance** : *A set of negative examples $S^-$, a set of positive examples $S^+$, a rational weight $0 < w(x_i) = \frac{n_i}{d_i} < 1$ for each example $x_i$, a rational $0 \leq \gamma < 1$. We assume that $\sum_{x \in S^+ \cup S^-} w(x_i) = 1$.*
**Question** : *$\exists ? h \in \mathcal{H}_{(D;)a}(\zeta)$ satisfying $\sum_{h(x) \neq c(x)} w(x) \leq \gamma$ ?*

Define as $n_e$ the size of the largest example we dispose of. Note that when the constraint is too tight, it can be the case that $\mathcal{H}_{(D;)a}(\zeta) = \emptyset$. Define as $|h|$ the size of some $h \in \mathcal{H}$ (in our case, it is the number of Horn clauses of $h$). In the non-empty subset of $\mathcal{H}$ where formulae are the most constrained (*i.e.* strengthening further the constraint gives an empty subset), define $n_{opt_{\mathcal{H}_{(D_i)a}(\varsigma)}}(c)$ as the size of the smallest hypothesis. Then, our reductions all satisfy $n_{opt_{\mathcal{H}_{(D_i)a}(\varsigma)}}(c) \leq (n_e)^3$. Note that the constraint makes generally $opt_{\mathcal{H}_{(D_i)a}(\varsigma)}(c) > opt_{\mathcal{H}_D}(c)$. However, the reductions all satisfy $d_\nu \left( opt_{\mathcal{H}_D}(c), opt_{\mathcal{H}_{(D_i)a}(\varsigma)}(c) \right) = o(1)$, *i.e.* asymptotic values coincide. In addition, the principal result we get (similar for all other problems) is that we can suppose that the whole time used to write the total set of Horn clauses is assimilated to $\mathcal{O}(n_e)$, for any set. By writing time, we mean time of any procedure consisting only in writing down clauses. Examples of such a procedure are "write down all clauses having $k$ literals", or even "write down *all* Horn clauses". Such procedures can be viewed as *for-to*, or *repeat* algorithms. This property authorizes the construction of Horn clause sets having arbitrary sizes, even exponential. Problem 2 is addressed by studying the complexity of the following decision problem.

**Definition 2.** *Approx-Constrained-ROC($\mathcal{H}, \gamma_{FPR}, \gamma_{TPR}$):*
**Instance** : *A set of negative examples $S^-$, a set of positive examples $S^+$, a rational weight $0 < w(x_i) = \frac{n_i}{d_i} < 1$ for each example $x_i$, a rational $0 \leq \gamma < 1$. We assume that $\sum_{x \in S^+ \cup S^-} w(x_i) = 1$.*
**Question** : *$\exists? h \in \mathcal{H}$ satisfying $1 - FPR \geq 1 - \gamma_{FPR}$ and $TPR \geq \gamma_{TPR}$?*

Concerning problem 3, the reductions study a single replacement criterion $\Gamma$, and the following decision problem.

**Definition 3.** *Approx-Constrained-Single($\mathcal{H}, \Gamma, \gamma$):*
**Instance** : *A set of negative examples $S^-$, a set of positive examples $S^+$, a rational weight $0 < w(x_i) = \frac{n_i}{d_i} < 1$ for each example $x_i$, a rational $0 \leq \gamma < 1$. We assume that $\sum_{x \in S^+ \cup S^-} w(x_i) = 1$.*
**Question** : *$\exists? h \in \mathcal{H}$ satisfying $\Gamma(h) \leq \gamma$?*

## 4    Hardness Results

**Theorem 1.** *We have:*
[1] *$\forall 0 < \varsigma < 1$, Approx-Constrained(FfHC, $(1, \varsigma)$) is Hard, when $\nu < (1 - \varsigma)/\varsigma$.*
[2] *$\forall 0 < \varsigma < \frac{1}{2}$, Approx-Constrained(FfHC, $(2, \varsigma)$) is Hard.*
[3] *$\forall a \in \{3, 4, 5, 6, 7\}, \forall 0 < \varsigma < 1$, Approx-Constrained(FfHC, $(a, \varsigma)$) is Hard.*

At that point, the notion of "hardness" needs to be clarified. By "Hard" we mean "cannot be solved in polynomial time under some particular complexity assumption". The notion of hardness used encompasses that of classical $NP$-completeness, since we use the results of [2] involving randomized complexity classes. All our hardness results are to be read with that precision in mind.
Due to space constraints, only proof of point [1] is presented in appendix 2; all other results strictly use the same type of reduction. Also, in appendix 1, we sketch the proof that all distributions under which our negative results are

proven lead to trivial positive results for the same problem when we remove the additional constraint, and optimize the accuracy alone. While negative results for optimizing the accuracy itself would naturally hold when considering the additional constraints, we therefore prove that optimizing the accuracy under constraint is a strictly more difficult problem, with non-trivial additional drawbacks. Furthermore, the upperbound error value ($\gamma$ in def. 1) in constraints 4, 5, 6, 7 can be fixed arbitrarily in $]0, 1/2[$, *i.e.* requiring the Horn clauses set to perform slightly better than the unbiased coin does not make the problem easier. We now show that the classical ROC components as described by [7] lead to the same results as those we claimed for the preceding bi-criteria optimizations. The problem is all the more difficult as the difficulty appears as soon as we choose to use ROC analysis, and is not a function of the ROC bounds.

**Theorem 2.** *Approx-Constrained-ROC(FfHC, $\gamma_{FPR}, \gamma_{TPR}$) is Hard; the result holds $\forall 0 < \gamma_{FPR}, \gamma_{TPR} < 1$.*

The distribution under which the negative result is proven is an easy distribution for the accuracy's optimization alone, similarly to those of the seven constraints. We now investigate the replacement of the accuracy by a single criterion. The negative result stated in the following theorem is to be read with all additional drawbacks mentioned for the previous theorems. Again, the distribution under which the theorem is proven is easy when optimizing the accuracy alone.

**Theorem 3.** $\exists \gamma_{max} > 0$ *such that* $\forall 0 < \gamma < \gamma_{max}$, *the problem Approx-Constrained-Single(FfHC,$(1 - FPR) \times TPR, \gamma$) is Hard.*

(Proof sketch included in appendix 2). As far as we know, $\gamma_{max} \geq \frac{175}{41616}$ (roughly $4.2 \times 10^{-3}$), but we think that this bound can be much improved.

# References

[1] J. P. Egan. *Signal detection theory and ROC analyses*. Academic Press, 1975.

[2] J. Hastad. Clique is hard to approximate within $n^{1-\epsilon}$. In *FOCS'96*, pages 627–636, 1996.

[3] R.C. Holte. Very simple classification rules perform well on most commonly used datasets. *Machine Learning*, pages 63–91, 1993.

[4] P. Jappy, R. Nock, and O. Gascuel. Negative robust learning results for horn clause programs. In *Proc. of the 13 th International Conference on ML*, 1996.

[5] J.-U. Kietz and S. Dzeroski. Inductive Logic Programming and learnability. *Sigart Bulletin*, pages 22–32, 1994.

[6] F. Provost and T. Fawcett. Analysis and visualization of classifier performance : comparison under imprecise class and cost distributions. In *Proc. of the $3^{rd}$ International Conference on KDD*, pages 43–48, 1997.

[7] F. Provost, T. Fawcett, and R. Kohavi. The Case Against Accuracy estimation for comparing induction algorithms. In *Proc. of the 15 th International Conference on ML*, pages 445–453, 1998.

[8] Sean Slattery and Mark Craven. Combining statistical and relational methods for learning in hypertext domains. In *Proc. of the Eighth International Conference on ILP*, pages 38–52, 1998.

[9] A. Srinivasan. Applications of ILP to problems in chemistry and biology. In *Proc. of the Eighth International Conference on ILP (Invited Talk)*, 1998.

# 5    Appendix 1: The Global Reduction

Reductions are achieved from the $NP$-Complete problem "Clique" [2], whose instance is a graph A graph $G = (X, E)$, and an integer $k$. The question is "Does there exist a clique of size $\geq k$ in $G$?". Of course, "Clique" is not hard to solve for any value of $k$. The following lemma establishes values of $k$ for which we can suppose that the problem is hard to solve ($\binom{n}{k} = n!/((n-k)!k!)$) is the binomial coefficient):

**Theorem 4.** *(i) We can suppose that $\binom{k}{2} \leq |E|$, and $k$ is not a constant, otherwise "Clique" is polynomial. (ii) For any $\alpha \in ]0,1[$, "Clique" is hard for the value $k = \alpha|X|$ or $k = |X|^\alpha$.*

*Proof.* (i) is immediate ; (ii) follows from [2]: it is proven that the largest clique size is not approximable to within $|X|^\beta$, for any constant $0 < \beta < 1$. Therefore, the graphs generated have a clique number which is either $l$, or greater than $l \times |X|^\beta$, with $l < |X|^{1-\beta}$. Therefore, the decision problem is intractable for values of $k > l$, which is the case if $k = \alpha|X|$ or $k = |X|^\alpha$, with $\alpha \in ]0,1[$.    □

The structure of the examples is the same for any of our reductions. Define a set of $|X|$ unary predicates $a_1(.), ..., a_{|X|}(.)$, in bijection with the vertices of $G$. To this set of unary predicates, we add two unary predicates, $s(.)$ and $t(.)$. The inferred predicate is denoted $q(.)$. The choice of unary predicates is made only for a simplicity purpose. We could have replaced each of them by $l$-ary predicates without changing our proof. Define a set of constant symbols useful for the description of the examples: $\{l_{i,j}, \forall (i,j) \in E\} \cup \{l_1, l_2, l_3, l_4\} \cup \{m_i, \forall i \in \{1, 2, ..., |X|\}\}$. Examples are described in the following way. Positive examples from $S^+$ are as follows:

$$\forall (i,j) \in E, p_{i,j} = q(l_{i,j}) \leftarrow \wedge_{k \in \{1,2,...,|X|\} \setminus \{i,j\}} a_k(l_{i,j}) \wedge t(l_{i,j}) \tag{1}$$
$$p_1 = q(l_1) \leftarrow \wedge_{k \in \{1,2,...,|X|\}} a_k(l_1) \wedge t(l_1) \tag{2}$$
$$p_2 = q(l_2) \leftarrow a_1(l_2) \tag{3}$$

Negative examples from $S^-$ are as follows:

$$\forall i \in \{1,2,...,|X|\}, n_i = q(m_i) \leftarrow \wedge_{k \in \{1,2,...,|X|\} \setminus \{i\}} a_k(m_i) \wedge t(m_i) \tag{4}$$
$$n'_1 = q(l_3) \leftarrow \wedge_{k \in \{1,2,...,|X|\}} a_k(l_3) \wedge s(l_3) \wedge t(l_3) \tag{5}$$
$$n'_2 = q(l_4) \leftarrow \wedge_{k \in \{1,2,...,|X|\}} a_k(l_4) \wedge s(l_4) \tag{6}$$

It comes that $n_{opt_{\mathcal{H}_{(D,)a^{(\zeta)}}}(c)} = \mathcal{O}(|X|^3)$ (coding size of positive examples) and $n_e = \mathcal{O}(|X|)$. Non-uniform weights are given to each example, depending on the constraint to be tackled with. The common-point to all reductions is that the weights of all examples $n_j$ (resp. all $p_{i,j}$) are equal (resp. to $w^-$ and $w^+$). In each reduction, examples and clauses satisfy:

**H$_1$** $p_2$ is forced to be badly classified.
**H$_2$** $n'_1$ is always badly classified.

**H₃** $w(n_2')$ ensures that $n_2'$ is always given the right class, forcing any clause to contain literal $t(.)$ (When we remove $n_2'$, we ensure that $p_2$ is removed too).

**Lemma 2.** *Any clause containing literal $s(.)$ can be removed.*

*Proof.* Suppose that one clause contains $s(.)$. Then it can be $\theta$-subsumed by $n_1'$ and by no other example (even if $n_2'$ exists, because of **H₃**); but $n_1'$ $\theta$-subsumes any clauses and also the empty clause. Therefore, removing the clause does not modify the value of any criteria based on the examples weights. Concerning the sixth constraint, the fraction of predicates used after removing the clause is at most the one before, thus, if the clause is an element of $\mathcal{H}_6(\zeta)$ before, it is still an element after. The same remark holds for the seventh constraint.          □

As a consequence, $p_1$ is always given the positive class (even by the empty clause!). We now give a general outline of the proof for Problem 1 ; reductions are similar for the other problems. Given $h = \{h_1, h_2, ..., h_l\}$ a set of Horn clauses, we define the set $\mathcal{I} = \{i \in \{1, 2, ..., |X|\} | \exists j \in \{1, 2, ..., l\}, a_i(.) \notin h_j\}$, and we fix $|\mathcal{I}| = k'$. In our proofs, we define two functions taking rational values, $E(k')$ and $F_a(k')$ $(k' \in \{1, 2, ..., |X|\}, a = 1, 2, 3, 4, 5, 6, 7)$. They are chosen such that:

- $E(k')$ is strictly increasing, $\sum_{x \in S^+ \cup S^- | h(x) \neq c(x)} w(x) \geq E(k')$ and $E(k) = \gamma$.
- $F_a(k')$ is strictly decreasing, is a lowerbound of the function inside $\mathcal{H}_{(D,)a}(\zeta)$, and $F_a(k) = \zeta$ (excepted for $a = 3, F_3(k) = 1/\zeta$).

$\forall a \in \{1, 2, 3, 4, 5, 6, 7\}$, if there exists an unbounded set of Horn clauses $h \in \mathcal{H}_{(D,)a}(\zeta)$ satisfying $\sum_{(x \in S^+ \wedge h(x)=0) \vee (x \in S^- \wedge h(x)=1)} w(x) \leq \gamma$, its error rate implies $k' \leq k$ and constraint implies $k' \geq k$. So $|\mathcal{I}| = k' = k$. The interest of the weights is then to force $\binom{k}{2}$ positive examples from the set $\{p_{i,j}\}_{(i,j) \in E}$ to be well classified, while we ensure the misclassification of at most $k$ negative examples of the set $\{n_i\}_{i \in \{1,2,...,|X|\}}$. It comes that these $\binom{k}{2}$ examples correspond to the $\binom{k}{2}$ edges linking the $|\mathcal{I}| = k$ vertices corresponding to negative examples badly classified. We therefore dispose of a clique of size $\geq k$.

Conversely, $\forall a \in \{1, 2, 3, 4, 5, 6, 7\}$, given some clique of size $k$ whose set of vertices is denoted $\mathcal{I}$, we show that singleton $h = q(X) \leftarrow \wedge_{i \in \{1,2,...,|X|\} \setminus \mathcal{I}} a_i(X) \wedge t(X)$ is $\in \mathcal{H}_{(D,)a}(\zeta)$, satisfying $\sum_{(x \in S^+ \wedge h(x)=0) \vee (x \in S^- \wedge h(x)=1)} w(x) \leq \gamma$. In this case, $n_{opt_{\mathcal{H}_{(D,)a}(\zeta)}(c)}$ drops down to $\mathcal{O}(n_e)$.

All distributions used in theorems 1 and 3 are such that $w^+ < w^-/|X|$, at least for graphs exceeding a fixed constant size. Also, due to the negative examples of weights $w^-$, if we remove the additional constraints and optimize the accuracy alone, we can suppose that the optimal Horn clause is a singleton: merging all clauses by keeping over predicates $a_j(.)$ only those present in all clauses does not decrease the accuracy. Under such a distribution, the optimal Horn clause necessarily contains all predicates $a_j(.)$, and the problem becomes trivial. The distribution in theorem 2 satisfies $w^+ = w^-$. This is also a simple distribution for the accuracy's optimization alone: indeed, the optimal Horn clause over predicates $a_j(.)$ is such that it contains no predicates $a_j(.)$ that does not appear at least in one positive example. If the graph instance of "Clique" is connex (and we can suppose so, otherwise the problem boils down to find the largest clique in one of the connected components), then the optimal Horn clause does not contain any of the $a_j(.)$.

# 6    Appendix 2: Proofs of Negative Results

## 6.1    Proof of Point [1], Theorem 1

Weights of positive examples: $w(p_2) = \frac{1}{2(1-\zeta)} \left( \zeta\nu + |X|^2 w^- (1+\zeta) \right)$; $\forall (i,j) \in E$,
$w(p_{i,j}) = w^+ = \frac{w^-}{(|X|+k)^2}$; $w(p_1) = \frac{1}{2} \left( 1 - \frac{\zeta\nu}{1-\zeta} \right) - \frac{1}{2} \left( w^- |X|^2 \left[ \frac{1+\zeta}{1-\zeta} + |X| - k \right] \right) - \frac{1}{2} \left( w^+ \left[ \frac{1-\zeta}{1+\zeta} \left( |E| - \binom{k}{2} \right) + |X| \right] \right)$. Weights of negative examples: $w(n'_2) = 1/2$; $\forall j \in \{1, 2, ..., |X|\}, w(n_j) = w^- = \frac{1}{|X|^2|E|^2}$; $w(n'_1) = \frac{1}{2} \left( \frac{1-\zeta}{1+\zeta} \left( |E| - \binom{k}{2} \right) w^+ \right) + \frac{1}{2} \left( (|X|^2 - k)w^- \right)$.

Fix $\gamma = \left( w(p_2) + w(n'_1) + kw^- + \left( |E| - \binom{k}{2} \right) \right) / 2$ (note that $w(n'_2)$ ensures that $n'_2$ is given the right class), and $k_{max} = 1 + \max_{2 \leq k'' \leq |X|:|E|-\binom{k''}{2}\geq 0} k''$. From the choice of weights, $\text{lcm}(\cup_{x_i \in S^+ \cup S^-} d_i) = \mathcal{O}(|X|^8)$ ("lcm" is the least common multiple), which is polynomial. Define the functions: $\forall k' \in \{0,1\}, E(k') = |E|w^+ + k'w^- + w(p_2) + w(n_1); \forall 2 \leq k' \leq k_{max}, E(k') = \left( |E| - \binom{k'}{2} \right) w^+ + k'w^- + w(p_2) + w(n_1); \forall k_{max} < k' \leq |X|, E(k') = k'w^- + w(p_2) + w(n_1)$. From the choice of weights, $E(k) = \gamma$. $\forall k' \in \{0,1\}, F_1(k') = \| |E|w^+ - k'w^- + w(p_2) - w(n_1)|/q$; $\forall 2 \leq k' \leq k_{max}, F_1(k') = | \left( |E| - \binom{k'}{2} \right) - k'w^- + w(p_2) - w(n_1)|/q$; $\forall k_{max} < k' \leq |X|, F_1(k') = | - k'w^- + w(p_2) - w(n_1)|/q$, with $q = \nu + |E|w^+ + k'w^- + w(p_2) + w(n_1)$. From the choice of weights, $F_1(k) = \zeta$.
The equation obtained when $k' < k_{max}$ takes its maximum for integer values when $k' = (|X| + k)^2 + 0,5 \pm 0,5 > |X|$. Furthermore, $\forall 1 \leq k_{max} \leq |X|, \left( |E| - \binom{k_{max}-1}{2} \right) w^+ < w^-$, which leads to $E(k_{max} - 1) < E(k_{max})$. In a more general way, $E(k')$ is strictly increasing over natural integers. Now remark that the numerator of $F_1(k')$ is strictly decreasing, and its denominator strictly increasing. Therefore, $F_1(k')$ is strictly decreasing. Furthermore $d_\nu \left( \sum_{h(x)\neq 1=c(x)} w(x), \sum_{h(x)\neq 0=c(x)} w(x) \right) \geq F_1(k')$. If $\exists h \in \mathcal{H}_{\{w_i\},1}(\zeta)$ satisfying $\sum_{h(x)\neq c(x)} w(x) \leq \gamma$, the error rate implies $k' \leq k$ and the constraint implies $k' \geq k$. Thus $|\mathcal{I}| = k' = k$. As pointed out in the preceding appendix, this leads to the existence of a clique of size $\geq k$.
Reciprocally, the Horn clause $h$ constructed in Appendix 1 satisfies both relations $h \in \mathcal{H}_{\{w_i\},1}(\zeta)$, and $\sum_{h(x)\neq c(x)} w(x) \leq \gamma$. Indeed, we have $\sum_{h(x)\neq 1=c(x)} w(x) = \left( |E| - \binom{k}{2} \right) w^+ + w(p_2)$, but also $\sum_{h(x)\neq 0=c(x)} w(x) = kw^- + w(n_1)$. Therefore, $d_\nu \left( \sum_{h(x)\neq 1=c(x)} w(x), \sum_{h(x)\neq 0=c(x)} w(x) \right) = F_1(k) = \zeta$ and $h \in \mathcal{H}_{\{w_i\},1}(\zeta)$. We have also $\sum_{h(x)\neq c(x)} w(x) = E(k) = \gamma$. The reduction is achieved. We end by re-

marking that $d_\nu\left(opt_{\mathcal{H}_{\{w_i\}}}(c), opt_{\mathcal{H}_{\{w_i\},1}(\varsigma)}(c)\right) \le (|E|w^+ + |X|w^-)/\left(\frac{\varsigma\nu}{1-\varsigma}+\nu\right)$, which is $o(1)$ (as $|X| \to \infty$ or $|E| \to \infty$), as claimed in subsection 3.2.

## 6.2    Proof Sketch of Theorem 3

Remark that $TPR(1-FPR) = TPR \times TNR$. Weights are as follows for positive examples (we do not use $p_2$):

$$\forall(i,j) \in E, w(p_{i,j}) = w^+ = \frac{\gamma}{(|X| - k)w^- \times \left[\binom{k}{2} + \frac{(|X|+1)^2 - \left(k - \frac{|X|+1}{3}\right)^2 - 3|X|}{6}\right]}$$

$w(p_1) = w^+ \times \left((|X| + 1)^2 - \left(k - \frac{|X|+1}{3}\right)^2 - 3|X|\right)/6$. Weights are as follows for negative examples (we do not use $n_2'$): $\forall j \in \{1, 2, ..., |X|\}, w(n_j) = w^- = 1/(|X| + k)$; $w(n_1') = 1 - |E|w^+ - |X|w^- - w(p_1)$. The choice of $\gamma_{max}$ comes from the necessity of keeping weights within correct limits. We explain how to the existence of a clique, by describing a polynomial of degree 3, $F(k')$ which upper-bounds $TPR \times TNR$, and of course has the desirable property of having its maximum for $k' = k$, with value $\gamma$, and with no other equal or greater values on the interval $[0, |X|]$. Similarly to the other proofs, the value $\gamma$ can only be reached when $k' = k$ represents $k$ "holes" among predicates $\{a_j(.)\}$, and this induces a size-$k$ clique in the graph. Define the function $F(k')$ as follows. $\forall k' \in \{0, 1\}, F(k') = w(p_1) \times (|X| - k')w^-; \forall 2 \le k' \le k_{max}, F(k') = \left(\binom{k'}{2}w^+ + w(p_1)\right)(|X| - k')w^-; \forall k_{max} < k' \le |X|, F(k') = (|E|w^+ + w(p_1))(|X| - k')w^-$. With our choice of weights, and inside the values of $k'$ for which we described $k$ (clearly, in the second $F(k')$), $F$ describes a polynomial of degree 3, shown in figure 2. $F$ upper-

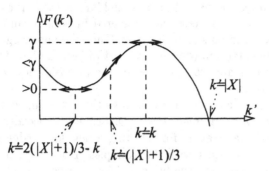

**Fig. 2.** Scheme of $F(k') = \left(\binom{k'}{2}w^+ + w(p_1)\right)(|X| - k')w^-$.

bounds $TPR \times TNR$ of any set of Horn clauses, and the demand on $TPR \times TNR$ leads to a single favorable case: the "holes" inside the set of Horn clauses describe a clique of size $k' = k$ in the graph.

# A Method of Similarity-Driven Knowledge Revision for Type Specializations

Nobuhiro Morita, Makoto Haraguchi, and Yoshiaki Okubo

Division of Electronics and Information Engineering, Hokkaido University
N-13 W-8, Sapporo 060-8628, JAPAN
{morita,makoto,yoshiaki}@db-ei.eng.hokudai.ac.jp

**Abstract.** This paper proposes a new framework of knowledge revision, called *Similarity-Driven Knowledge Revision*. Our revision is invoked based on a similarity observation by users and is intended to match with the observation. Particularly, we are concerned with a revision strategy according to which an inadequate variable typing in describing an object-oriented knowledge base is revised by specializing the typing to more specific one without loss of the original inference power. To realize it, we introduce a notion of *extended sorts* that can be viewed as a concept not appearing explicitly in the original knowledge base. If a variable typing with some sort is considered over-general, the typing is modified by replacing it with more specific extended sort. Such an extended sort can efficiently be identified by forward reasoning with *SOL-deduction* from the original knowledge base. Some experimental results show the use of SOL-deduction can drastically improve the computational efficiency.

## 1  Introduction

This paper proposes a novel method of knowledge revision (KR), called *Similarity-Driven Knowledge Revision*. In traditional KR methods previously proposed (e.g. [1]), their revision processes are triggered by some examples logically inconsistent with an original knowledge base. Then the knowledge base should be revised so that its extension (defined by a set of facts derived from it) becomes consistent with the examples. As a result, the inconsistency in the knowledge base will be removed.

Although we can have several revision methods to remove the conflict as a logical inconsistency, a *minimal revision principle* is especially preferred. Here the principle implies a strategy for selecting a new knowledge base that has a minimal extension consistent with the examples. Thus, both the notion of conflicts in knowledge bases and the basic revision strategy have been investigated in terms of extensions.

However, even if we find no extensional conflict in our knowledge base, we might need to revise it from an *non-extensional viewpoint*. We intend to utilize the revision from the non-extensional viewpoint to make our revision faster in the presence of extensional conflicts and to do revision even for cases not involving them.

O. Watanabe, T. Yokomori (Eds.): ALT'99, LNAI 1720, pp. 194–205, 1999.

**Fig. 1.** Extensional Relationship between *male* and *female*

As a first approach to such a non-extensional revision, this paper considers a conflict caused by an *over-general typing of variables* in an object-oriented knowledge base. When the knowledge base contains an over-general typing of some variable, then it deduces negative facts that will eventually be observed. However, it is not only way to find the over-general typing. This paper proposes to use a notion of *similarities between types* to find the inappropriateness, and tries to present a revision method based on it. As a type becomes more general, we have more chances to observe properties and rules shared by another type. Thus the possible class of similarities between types will contain a similarity that does not meet a user's intention.

Suppose we have a method for finding a similarity $\psi$ for a given knowledge base. There exist two cases where the similarity does not fit a user's intention: 1) $\psi$ shows the similarity between types $s_1$ and $s_2$, while the user considers they are not similar and 2) $\psi$ shows the dissimilarity between $s_1$ and $s_2$, while the user considers they are similar. This paper is especially concerned with a knowledge revision in the former case, assuming GDA, *Goal-Dependent Abstraction*, as an algorithm to find the similarities between types under an *order-sorted logic*, where the types are called *sorts* in the logic.

Given a knowledge base $\mathcal{KB}$ and a goal $G$ to be proved, GDA detects an appropriate similarity for $G$ between sorts $s_1$ and $s_2$ reflected in $\mathcal{KB}$ if the same property relevant to $G$ is shared for both $s_1$ and $s_2$. For example, suppose we have knowledge "if *female* has a property *has_long_hair*, then *female* has a property *takes_long_time_shower*" and "if *male* has the property *has_long_hair*, then *male* has the property *takes_long_time_shower*". It can be represented as the following order-sorted clauses:

"*takes_long_time_shower*$(X : female) \leftarrow$ *has_long_hair*$(X : female)$" and
"*takes_long_time_shower*$(X : male) \leftarrow$ *has_long_hair*$(X : male)$".

In these clauses, the description "$X : s$" is called a *variable typing* and means that the range of the value is restricted to an object (constant) belonging to the sort $s$. For the knowledge, GDA detects a similarity between *female* and *male* with respect to the property "*takes_long_time_shower*". However, this similarity seems not to fit our intuition very well. Such an unfitness would come from the fact that "*has_long_hair*" would be considered as a feasible feature for *female*, while not so for *male*, as illustrated in Fig. 1. This implies that the variable typing $X : male$ is inappropriate in the sense of *over-general*. We consider such a wrong typing as an intensional conflict in the original knowledge base and try to resolve it. The wrong typing $X : male$ is specialized (revised) by finding a new sort concept $s'$ that is a subconcept of *male* and has the concept "*male_with_long_hair*" as its subconcept, as shown in Fig. 1. In a word, such a new $s'$ is an imaginable subconcept of *male* that has the property "*has_long_hair*" as its feasible feature like *female* has. For the revised knowledge base, GDA detects a similarity between $s'$ and *female* that seems to fit our intuition.

Thus, our revision is triggered when we recognized an unfitness of detected similarity. Therefore, we call it *Similarity-Driven Knowledge Revision*.

A newly introduced imaginable concept is defined as an *extended sort*. An extended sort denotes a concept that does not appear explicitly in the original knowledge base. If a variable typing $X : s$ is considered over-general, the typing is modified by replacing the general sort $s$ with a more specific extended sort $s'$. In order for the extended sort to be meaningful, we present four conditions to be satisfied. It is theoretically showed that such an extended sort can be identified by a forward reasoning from the original knowledge base. Especially, a forward reasoning with *SOL-deduction* is adopted for an efficient computation. Some experimental results show that the use of SOL-deduction can drastically improve the computational efficiency.

## 2   Preliminaries

In this section, we introduce some fundamental terminologies and definitions [1].

Our knowledge base consists of the following three components.

**Sort Hierarchy:**   A *sort hierarchy* is given as a partially ordered set of sort symbols, $H = (S, \preceq)$. Each sort $s \in S$ denotes a sort concept and is interpreted as the set of possible instances of the concept. The relation $s \preceq s'$ means that $s$ is a subconcept of $s'$.

**Type Declaration:**   A *type declaration*, $TD$, is a finite set of typed constants that is of the form $\{c_1 : s_1, \ldots, c_n : s_n\}$, where $c_i$ is a constant symbol denoting an object and $s_i$ is a sort in $S$. A typed constant $c_i : s_i$ declares that the object denoted by $c_i$ *primarily* belongs to the sort concept $s_i$, where $s_i$ is called the *primary type* (or simply, *type*) of $c_i$ which is referred to as $[c_i]$. The extension of sort is defined as follows:

**Definition 1 (Extension of Sort).** Let $s$ be a sort. The extension of $s$, $A_s$, is defined as $A_s = \{c \mid [c] \preceq s\}$. We say that $c$ belongs to $s$, if $c \in A_s$. ∎

From the interpretation, it is obvious that if $s \preceq s'$ and $[c] = s$, then $c$ belongs to $s'$ as well as to $s$.

**Domain Theory:**   A *domain theory* (or simply, *theory*), $T$, is a set of function-free Horn clauses of the form $A \leftarrow B_1 \wedge \cdots \wedge B_k$, where $A$ and $B_i$ are positive literals of the form $p(t_1, \ldots, t_m)$ and each term $t_i$ is a typed variable $X_i : s_i$ or a typed constant. A typed variable $X_i : s_i$ means that the range of values is restricted to instances belonging to $s_i$. On the other hand, we assume that a predicate $p$ can take objects of any sort concept as its arguments.

---

[1] Throughout this paper, we assume that the notions with respect to First-Order Logic are familiar to the reader.

The inference under our knowledge base is the same as standard first-order deduction except the following point:

Every substitution $\theta = \{X_i : s_i/t_i\}$ should satisfy the type constraint that $[t_i] \preceq s_i$. That is, the variable must be instantiated to a variable or a constant of more specific sort concept [2].

# 3 Goal-Dependent Abstraction

In this section, we briefly present a framework of *Goal-Dependent Abstraction* that is used as the basis of our similarity finding algorithm GDA.

## 3.1 Abstraction Based on Sort Mapping

We first introduce a framework of *abstraction based on sort mapping*, an extended version of the framework of *abstraction based on predicate mapping* [3].

**Definition 2 (Sort Mapping).** Let $(S, \preceq)$ be a sort hierarchy. A *sort mapping* is a mapping $\psi : S \xrightarrow{\text{onto}} S'$, where $S'$ is an *abstract sort* set such that $S \cap S' = \phi$. ∎

A sort mapping can easily be extended to a mapping over a set of any expressions. For an expression $E$, $\psi(E)$ is defined as the expression obtained by mapping the sort symbols in $E$ under $\psi$.

For any expressions $E_1$ and $E_2$, if $\psi(E_1) = \psi(E_2) = E'$, then $E_1$ and $E_2$ are said to be *similar* and to be *instantiations* of $E'$ under $\psi$. Thus, a sort mapping can be viewed as a representation of *similarity between sorts*. Therefore, we often use the term "similarity" as a synonym for "sort mapping".

**Definition 3 (Theory Abstraction Based on Sort Mapping).** Let $\mathcal{KB} = < (S, \preceq), TD, T >$ be an order-sorted (concrete) knowledge base and $\psi : S \xrightarrow{\text{onto}} S'$ be a sort mapping. The *abstract domain theory* of $T$ based on $\psi$, $SortAbs_\psi(T)$, is defined as $SortAbs_\psi(T) = \{C' \mid \forall C \in \psi^{-1}(C') \ T \vdash C\}$, where for an expression $E'$, $\psi^{-1}(E')$ is defined as $\psi^{-1}(E') = \{E \mid \psi(E) = E'\}$. ∎

For example, assume we have a domain theory consisting of three clauses (facts) $p(X : s_1)$, $p(X : s_2)$ and $q(X : s_1)$. Based on a similarity $\psi$ such that $\psi(s_1) = \psi(s_2) = s'$, the first two clauses can be preserved as an abstract clause $p(X : s')$, while the last one cannot so. Thus, only such a property $p$ shared among *all* similar sorts are preserved by the abstraction process. Based on this interesting characteristic, a dynamic abstraction framework, called *Goal-Dependent Abstraction*, has been proposed [4,5].

---

[2] We consider in this paper only substitutions satisfying this constraint.

## 3.2  Appropriate Similarity for Goal

When we try to prove a goal from our knowledge base, the used (necessary) knowledge is completely dependent on the goal. Observing which properties (knowledge) can be preserved in the abstraction process based on a similarity, we define an appropriateness of similarity with respect to a given goal.

**Definition 4 (Appropriateness of Similarity for Goal).** Let $T$ be a theory, $\psi$ a similarity and $G$ a goal. Assume that $G$ can be proved from $T$ and $Proof(G)$ is the set of clauses in $T$ that are used in a proof of $G$. The similarity $\psi$ is said to be *appropriate for $G$* if $\psi(Proof(G)) \subseteq SortAbs_{\psi}(T)$. ∎

If a similarity $\psi$ is appropriate for a goal $G$, it is implied that the properties appearing in $Proof(G)$ (that is, the properties relevant to $G$) are shared among all similar sorts defined by $\psi$ [3]. Since such an appropriate similarity depends on a goal we try to prove, we can realize a goal-dependent aspect of abstraction based on an appropriate similarity for the given goal.

Given a knowledge base and a goal to be proved, an algorithm GDA detects an appropriate similarity for the goal. Discussing GDA in more detail is beyond the scope of this paper. Its precise description can be found in the literatures [4,5]. In our knowledge revision, GDA is used to detect a similarity reflected in our knowledge base. Our revision process is invoked when the detected similarity does not fit our intuition.

# 4    Similarity-Driven Knowledge Revision for Type Specialization

In this section, we propose a novel method of knowledge revision, called *Similarity-Driven Knowledge Revision*. Before giving a formal descriptions, we present some assumptions imposed in the following discussion.

Our knowledge revision is triggered by an observation of undesirable similarity that is reflected in a given original knowledge base. For a knowledge base and a goal $G$, assume GDA detects a similarity $\psi$ such that $s_1 \simeq_{\psi} s_2$. For the similarity, assume that a user considers they are not similar because the user recognizes some difference between $s_1$ and $s_2$ with respect to the plausibility of a property $p$ relevant to $G$, as illustrated in the first section. In this case, our knowledge base is tried to revise by specializing a variable typing with $s_1$ or $s_2$, which is considered too general with respect to the property $p$. However, since such a recognition of over-generality seems to highly depend on the user's subjectivity, our revision system would not be able to decide itself which variable typing to be specialized. Therefore, we assume that a variable typing to be specialized is given to the system by the user as an input.

In our knowledge base, the occurrence of a given variable typing to be specialized might not be identified *uniquely*. In that case, it would be desired to

---

[3] Briefly speaking, in terms of EBL method [6], this means that for any similar sort, the goal $G$ can be *explained* in the same way (that is, the same explanation structure).

adequately specialize all of the occurrences. Although one might consider that a naive way is to specialize them *individually*, the result of one specialization process deeply affects subsequent specializations. It is not so easy to obtain a good characterization of such a complicated revision at the present time. In this paper, therefore, we deal with only a case where a variable typing to be specialized can *uniquely* be identified.

## 4.1   Extended Sort

We first introduce a notion of *extended sort* that is a core concept in our revision.

In our method, a modification of the type $s$ of a variable is realized by finding a new sort $s'$ that is more specific than $s$. Such a newly introduced sort is precisely defined as an *extended sort*.

**Definition 5 (Extended Sort).** Let us consider a conjunction of atoms, $es$, and focus on a typed variable $X : s$ in $es$. Then, $es$ is called an *extended sort* with the *root variable* $X$. The root variable is referred to as $Root(es)$. ∎

An extended sort is interpreted as the set of possible instances of its root variable, as defined below. In the definition, a *Herbrand model* of a theory $T$ is a subset $\mathcal{M}$ of Herbrand base

$B = \{p(a_1, ..., a_n)|p$ is a predicate symbol and $a_j$ is a typed constant symbol$\}$

which satisfies a condition that for any clause $A \leftarrow Bs$ in $T$ and any ground substitution $\theta$, $A\theta \in \mathcal{M}$ whenever $Bs\theta \subseteq \mathcal{M}$.

**Definition 6 (Extension of Extended Sort).** Let $T$ be a theory and $\mathcal{M}$ be an Herbrand Model of $T$. Consider an extended sort $es$ such that $Root(es) = X$. The extension of $es$ with respect to $\mathcal{M}$, $E_{\mathcal{M}}(es)$, is defined as

$E_{\mathcal{M}}(es) = \{X\theta \mid \theta$ is a ground substitution to $es$ such that $es\theta \subseteq \mathcal{M}\}$.

For a constant $c$, if $c \in E_{\mathcal{M}}(es)$, then it is said that $c$ belongs to $es$. ∎

For example, $es = has\_a\_child(X : person, Y : person) \wedge likes(Y, Z : dog)$ with the root variable $X$ is interpreted as the set of persons each of which has a child who likes a dog. Thus the variables except the root variable are existentially quantified.

An ordering on extended sorts can be introduced based on their extensions.

**Definition 7 (Ordering on Extended Sorts).** Let $T$ be a theory and $\mathcal{ES}$ be the set of all extended sorts. For any extended sorts $es_1$ and $es_2$ in $\mathcal{ES}$, $es_1 \preceq_T es_2$ iff for any Herbrand Model $\mathcal{M}$ of $T$, $E_{\mathcal{M}}(es_1) \subseteq E_{\mathcal{M}}(es_2)$. ∎

Let us consider an extended sort, $es_1 = has\_son(X : father, Y : boy) \wedge dislikes(Y, X)$, whose root variable is $X$. $es_1$ means fathers each of which has a (young) son who dislikes his father. By the definition, $es_1$ is a subsort of *father* and *parent* under a sort hierarchy involving *father* $\prec$ *parent* and *boy* $\prec$ *young_person*. As a more general concept placed between $es_1$ and *parent*, we can suppose fathers each of which has a child who dislikes his/her parent, father or mother (possibly both of two). It will be expressed by an extended sort $es_2 = has\_child(X : father, W : young\_person), dislikes(W, Z : parent)$. It can be drawn from the following knowledge that $es_1$ is a special case of $es_2$:

- **Domain Theory:** We know $has\_child(X, Y) \leftarrow has\_son(X, Y)$. Therefore $es_1$ is a special case of $es_3 = has\_child(X : father, Y : boy), dislikes(Y, X)$.
- **Sort Hierarchy:** For the existentially quantified variables $Z : parent$ and $W : young\_person$ in $es_2$ to have their values, it suffices to have values in their subsort $father$ and $boy$, respectively. In addition, it is possible to identify $Z$ with $X$ (that is, $Z$ and $X$ are the same person). This is done by a substitution $\zeta = \{Z : parent/X : father, W : young\_person/Y : boy\}$. Thus any instance of $es_3$ turns out to be an instance of $es_2$.

As a result, it is found $es1$ is more specific than $es_2$ (via $es_3$). We can summarize this argument by the following proof-theoretic characterization of the ordering.

**Theorem 1.** Let $T$ be a theory and $es_1$ and $es_2$ be extended sorts such that $Root(es_1) = Root(es_2) = X$. Consider a ground substitution $\theta$ to $es_1$ that substitutes no constant appearing in $T$. Then for a ground substitution $\sigma$ to $es_2$ such that $X\theta = X\sigma$, $es_1 \preceq_T es_2$ iff $T \vdash es_2\sigma \leftarrow es_1\theta$. ∎

## 4.2   Revising Knowledge Base by Specializing Type of Variable

We describe here our specialization process for over-general variable typing.

For a knowledge base $\mathcal{KB} = <H, TD, T>$ and a goal $G$, let us assume that GDA detects a similarity $\psi$ such that $s_1 \simeq_\psi s_2$ and a user considers that $s_1$ and $s_2$ are not similar. In addition, assume the user considers a variable typing by $s_1$ to be over-general.

Let "$C = P \leftarrow ES$" be a clause in $Proof(G)$, where $ES$ is a conjunction of atoms and contains a typed variable $X : s_1$. Here we consider $ES$ as an extended sort whose root variable is $X$.

For an expression $E$, $E_{(t,t')}$ denotes the resultant expression obtained by replacing every occurrence of $t$ in $E$ with $t'$. Since GDA detects $s_1 \simeq_\psi s_2$, it is found from Definition 4 that the clause "$C_{(X:s_1, X:s_2)} = P_{(X:s_1, X:s_2)} \leftarrow ES_{(X:s_1, X:s_2)}$" is true (provable) under the original knowledge base. Nevertheless, this similarity does not fit the user's intuition.

This unfitness would be caused in a situation such as one illustrated in Fig. 1. In this example, the objects of $s_1$ satisfying $ES$ are a small part of $s_1$, while ones of $s_2$ satisfying $ES_{(X:s_1, X:s_2)}$ are most of $s_2$. In a word, the objects of $s_2$ satisfying $ES_{(X:s_1, X:s_2)}$ would be considered typical, while ones of $s_1$ satisfying $ES$ not so. In order for GDA not to detect a similarity between them, we introduce a new sort $s_1'$ which is a subsort of $s_1$ and subsumes $ES$ (refer to Fig. 1). Then, the original clause $C$ is modified into a new clause "$C_{(X:s_1, X:s_1')} = P_{(X:s_1, X:s_1')} \leftarrow ES_{(X:s_1, X:s_1')}$". Furthermore, the newly introduced sort $s_1'$ is adequately inserted into the original sort hierarchy and the original type declaration is modified. As a result, for the revised knowledge base, GDA detects a similarity between $s_1'$ and $s_2$ instead of one between $s_1$ and $s_2$. It should be emphasized here that since $s_1'$ subsumes the extended sort $ES$, the extension of the original knowledge base is not affected by this revision. That is, our revision can be considered *minimal*. Below we discuss our specialization process in more detail.

**Identifying Newly Introduced Sort:** The newly introduced sort $s_1'$ is precisely defined as an extended sort that is identified according to the following criterion.

**Definition 8 (Appropriateness of Introduced Extended Sort).** If an extended sort $es$ satisfies the following conditions, then it is considered as an *appropriate extended sort* to be introduced:

$C1 : ES \preceq_T es.$

$C2 :$ For any answer substitution $\theta$ to $es$ w.r.t. the knowledge
  base $\mathcal{KB}$, there exists a term $t$ such that $X : s_1/t \in \theta$.

$C3 : es \cap ES = \phi.$

$C4 :$ For any $es_0$ such that $es_0 \subseteq es$ and any selection of root variable in
  $P$ and $es_0$, $P \not\preceq_T es_0$. ∎

By the condition $C1$, it is guaranteed that the revision causes no influence on the extension of the original knowledge base. $C2$ is required in order for $s_1'$ to become a proper subsort of $s_1$. $C3$ and $C4$ are imposed to remove redundant descriptions.

An appropriate extended sort is basically computed in a generate-and-test manner. According to Theorem 1, a forward reasoning from $T \cup \{ES\theta\}$ is performed to obtain a candidate $es$ such that $T \cup \{ES\theta\} \vdash es\sigma$. Then the candidate is tested for its appropriateness based on the conditions $C2$, $C3$ and $C4$. If the candidate is verified to satisfy those conditions, the newly introduced sort $s_1'$ is defined by $es$. Based on the definition of $es$, the user might assign an adequate sort symbol to $s_1'$ if he/she prefers.

For an efficient computation of $es$, we present an useful theorem and propose to adopt a reasoning method, *SOL-deduction* [7].

**Theorem 2.** Let $C = P \leftarrow ES$ be the clause in $Proof(G)$ to be replaced in the revision, and $es$ be an extended sort such that $Root(es) = Root(ES) = X : s$. If $es$ satisfies $C1$, $C2$ and $C4$, then $(T - \{C\}) \cup \{ES\theta\} \vdash es\sigma$ and $T - \{C\} \not\vdash es\sigma$, where $\theta$ is a ground substitution to $ES$ that substitutes no constant appearing in $T$ and $\sigma$ is a ground substitution to $es$ such that $X\theta = X\sigma$. ∎

From the theorem, it is sufficient for our candidate generation to perform a forward reasoning from $(T - \{C\}) \cup \{ES\theta\}$, instead of from $T \cup \{ES\theta\}$. Since removing $C$ from $T$ will reduce the cost of the forward reasoning, we can expect an efficient candidate generation.

In addition, the theorem says that any candidate derived from $T - \{C\}$ is quite useless to obtain an appropriate extended sort. That is, it is sufficient to have candidates that can *newly* be derived by adding $ES\theta$ to $T - \{C\}$. If we have a method by which we can efficiently obtain such candidates, desired extended sorts can be obtained more efficiently. We can obtain such an efficient method with the help of *SOL-deduction* [7]. Briefly speaking, for a theory $T$ and a clause $C$, by performing SOL-deduction from $T \cup \{C\}$, we can *centrally* obtain all clause that can *newly* be derived by adding $C$ to $T$. This characteristic of SOL-deduction is quite helpful for our task of candidate generation. However, it should be noted that we still have to test for the appropriateness based on $C2$, $C3$ and $C4$.

**Inserting Extended Sort into Sort Hierarchy:** After the computation of the newly introduced sort $s_1'$ (defined as $es$), we have to modify the original sort hierarchy by inserting $s_1'$ into an adequate position. Such a position is identified according to the following theorems.

**Theorem 3.** Let $es$ be an extended sort such that $Root(es) = X : s$. For any Herbrand Model $\mathcal{M}$, $E_{\mathcal{M}}(es) \subseteq A_s$. ∎

The theorem says that the new sort $s_1'$ should be a subsort of $s_1$ in the resultant hierarchy.

**Theorem 4.** Let $es$ be an extended sort such that $Root(es) = X : s$. If there exists an answer substitution $\theta$ to $es$ with respect to $\mathcal{KB}$ such that $X\theta = Y : t$ (where $Y$ is a new variable), then for any Herbrand Model $\mathcal{M}$, $A_t \subseteq E_{\mathcal{M}}(es)$. ∎

Let $\Theta$ be the set of answer substitutions to $es$. Consider the set of sorts $Subs_{es}$ such that $Sub_{es} = \{s \mid \theta \in \Theta$ and $X : s_1/Y : s$ appears in $\theta\}$. Theorem 4 says that $s_1'$ should have every sort in $Sub_{es}$ as its subsort in the resultant hierarchy.

**Modifying Type Declaration:** As well as the modification of sort hierarchy, a modification of type declaration might be needed.

The modification have to be performed according to the condition that $\forall c \in E_{\mathcal{M}_T}(es)$, $c$ belongs to $s_1'$, where $\mathcal{M}_T$ is the Least Herbrand Model of $T$. The next theorem shows how to modify the original type declaration.

**Theorem 5.** Let $es$ be an extended sort such that $Root(es) = X : s$. The next two statements are equivalent:

- $c \in E_{\mathcal{M}_T}(es)$.
- There exists an answer substitution $\theta$ to $es$ with respect to $\mathcal{KB}$ such that $X\theta = c$, or $X\theta = Y : t$ (where $Y$ is a new variable) and $c \in A_t$. ∎

In the case where an answer substitution $\theta$ such that $X\theta = Y : t$ is obtained, no modification of type declaration is necessary. In this case, since the original sort hierarchy is modified and $t$ becomes a subsort of $s_1'$ as the result, $c \in A_t$ obviously belongs to $s_1'$.

In the case where an answer substitution $\theta$ such that $X\theta = c$ is obtained, let $\Theta$ be the set of answer substitutions to $es$. Consider the set of constants $Inst_{es}$ defined as $Inst_{es} = \{c \mid \theta \in \Theta$ and $X : s_1/c$ appears in $\theta\}$. From Theorem 5, for any $c \in Inst_{es}$, we have to modify the original type declaration $TD$ into $TD'$ based on which it is implied that $c$ belongs to $s_1'$. Let us assume that for a constant $c \in Inst_{es}$, $c : t \in TD$. We have to take two cases into account. In the first case where $t = s_1$, the original type $s_1$ of $c$ is simply replaced with $s_1'$. In the second case where $t \neq s_1$, the type $s_1$ of $c$ is replaced with a sort $s_c$ that corresponds to a common subsort of $t$ and $s_1'$, since the type of a constant should be unique. As such a $s_c$, it might be necessary to introduce a quite new sort and then the sort hierarchy might be modified following the introduction.

Our revision process is summarized as an algorithm in Fig. 2.

**Input:** A knowledge base $\mathcal{KB} = <H, TD, T>$.
$Proof(G)$: the set of clauses that is used to prove a goal $G$ from $\mathcal{KB}$.
A sort $s$ to be specialized.
**Output:** A revised knowledge base $\mathcal{KB}' = <H', TD', T'>$.

1. Extract a clause $C = P \leftarrow ES$ from $Proof(G)$ such that a variable typed with $s$ appears in its body, and the variable $X$ typed with $s$ to the root variable of $ES$.
2. Derive $es\sigma$ from $(T - \{C\}) \cup \{ES\theta\}$ by a forward reasoning with SOL-deduction, where $\theta$ is a ground substitution to $ES$ that substitutes no constant appearing in $\mathcal{KB}$.
   Then make sure that $es$ satisfies the appropriateness conditions $C2$, $C3$ and $C4$. If such a $es$ cannot be found, terminate with failure.
3. Inform that a new sort $s'$ to be introduced can be defined as $es$.
4. Revise $H$ to $H'$ by replacing the clause $C$ in $T$ with $C' = P_{(X:s, X:s')} \leftarrow ES_{(X:s, X:s')}$.
5. Modify $H$ into $H'$ by inserting the new sort $s'$ into an adequate position.
6. Modify $TD$ into $TD'$ by redeclaring with $s'$ or with a quite new sort $s''$ if necessary. In the latter case, modify $H'$ following the introduction of $s''$.
7. Output the new knowledge base $\mathcal{KB}' = <H', TD', T'>$ and terminate.

**Fig. 2.** Algorithm for Knowledge Revision by Type Specialization

## Sort Hierarchy $H$ and Type Declaration $TD$ :

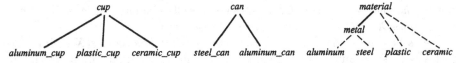

| cup | | | can | | material | | | |
| aluminum_cup | plastic_cup | ceramic_cup | steel_can | aluminum_can | aluminum | steel | plastic | ceramic |

metal

## Domain Theory $T$:

$throw\_away\_on\_friday(X) \leftarrow incombustible(X)$.
$throw\_away\_on\_tuesday(X) \leftarrow combustible(X)$.
$incombustible(X : cup) \leftarrow made\_of(X : cup, Y : metal)$.
$incombustible(X : can) \leftarrow made\_of(X : can, Y : metal)$.
$has\_handle(X : cup) \leftarrow made\_of(X : cup, Y : metal)$.

$made\_of(X : aluminum\_cup, aluminum : metal)$.
$made\_of(X : plastic\_cup, plastic : material)$.
$made\_of(X : ceramic\_cup, ceramic : material)$.
$made\_of(X : steel\_can, steel : metal)$.
$made\_of(X : aluminum\_can, aluminum : metal)$.

**Fig. 3.** Order-Sorted Knowledge Base

## 4.3  Example of Similarity-Driven Knowledge Revision

We illustrate here our revision processes for a knowledge base shown in Fig. 3 [4].
For the knowledge base and a goal $G = throw\_away\_on\_friday(X)$, we obtain
$$Proof(G) = \{ \ throw\_away\_on\_friday(X) \leftarrow incombustible(X),$$
$$incombustible(X : cup) \leftarrow made\_of(X : cup, Y : metal),$$
$$made\_of(X : cup, aluminum : metal) \ \}.$$
And GDA detects a similarity $\psi$ such that $cup \simeq_\psi can$. Let us assume that contrary to the similarity, a user considers that $cup$ and $can$ are not similar and considers a variable typing with $cup$ to be over-general.

A clause in $Proof(G)$ whose body contains a variable typed with $cup$ is $C = incombustible(X : cup) \leftarrow made\_of(X : cup, Y : metal)$, where $made\_of(X : cup, Y : metal)$ is considered as an extended sort $ES$ whose root variable is

---

[4] In the figure, the sort hierarchy and type declaration are given in a hierarchical form. A plain line denotes a "is a subsort of" relation and a dotted line corresponds to a declaration of constant type. For example, it is declared that the type of a constant $aluminum$ is a sort $metal$.

**Table 1.** Experimental Results

| KB Size | R. Type | Num. of Atoms | Exec. Time | KB Size | R. Type | Num. of Atoms | Exec. Time |
|---------|---------|---------------|------------|---------|---------|---------------|------------|
| 10 | FWR-$T$ | 4 | 80 | 40 | FWR-$T$ | 6 | 1130 |
| | FWR-$T_C$ | 2 | 50 | | FWR-$T_C$ | 2 | 1020 |
| | SOL-$T$ | 4 | 10 | | SOL-$T$ | 6 | 40 |
| | SOL-$T_C$ | 2 | 0 | | SOL-$T_C$ | 2 | 20 |

$X$. According to Theorem 2, consider a ground instance of $ES$ with a substitution $\theta = \{X : cup/a, Y : metal/b\}$, where $a$ and $b$ are constants not appearing in the original knowledge base. By a forward reasoning from $(T - \{C\}) \cup \{made\_of(a, b)\}$, an atom $has\_handle(a)$ can be derived.

As the next step, $has\_handle(X : cup)$ is tested for its appropriateness. The answer substitution to the goal $has\_handle(X : cup)$ is $\{X : cup/Y : aluminum\_cup\}$, where $Y$ is a new variable. Therefore, $has\_handle(X : cup)$ satisfies $C2$. It is obvious that it satisfies $C3$. Furthermore, since $incombustible(X : cup) \not\preceq_T has\_handle(X : cup)$, $C4$ is satisfied as well. Therefore, it is verified that $has\_handle(X : cup)$ is an appropriate extended sort.

Let $s$ be a new sort defined by the extended sort $has\_handle(X : cup)$. The sort $s$ is tried to put to an adequate position in the original sort hierarchy. It is easily found that $s$ becomes a subsort of $cup$. Moreover, since $s$ subsumes the extended sort $ES = made\_of(X : cup, Y : metal)$, only $aluminum\_cup$ can become a subsort of $s$.

The original type declaration does not need to be modified in this revision.

Finally, replace the original clause $C$ with $C_{(X:cup, X:s)} = incombustible(X : s) \leftarrow made\_of(X : s, Y : metal)$.

The extension of the newly introduced sort $s$ is defined as one of $has\_handle(X : cup)$. Some sort symbol meaning "cup with handle" might be assigned to $s$.

## 5   Experimental Results

We have implemented a knowledge revision system based on our algorithm and made an experimentation to verify its usefulness [5]. We show the results here.

As discussed previously, we have four ways to obtain an extended sort to be introduced: 1) by forward reasoning from $T \cup \{ES\theta\}$, 2) by forward reasoning from $(T - \{C\}) \cup \{ES\theta\}$. 3) by SOL-deduction from $T \cup \{ES\theta\}$. 4) by SOL-deduction from $(T - \{C\}) \cup \{ES\theta\}$. In our experimental results, they are referred to as reasoning types, "FWR-$T$", "FWR-$T_C$", "SOL-$T$" and "SOL-$T_C$", respectively. We provided two knowledge bases consisting of 10 clauses and 40 clauses. For each knowledge base and reasoning type, the number of atoms defining an extended sort and the execution time (msec.) were examined. Our experimental results are shown in Table 1.

The results show that the removal of $C$ affects the quality of computed extended sorts. For both knowledge bases, some unnecessary atoms were derived

---

[5] Our system has been written in SICStus Prolog and run on a SPARC-station 5.

by the reasonings from $T$. Moreover, such a meaningless derivation undesirably affects the execution times. It is, therefore, considered that the removal of $C$ is effective to improve both the efficiency and the quality of our knowledge revision.

The experimental results also show that the use of SOL-deduction can drastically reduce the execution time. The reduction ratios tend to be large as knowledge base grows. This implies that the use of SOL-deduction would be useful to improve the efficiency of our revision even in a real domain. We are currently considering a *legal domain* [4] as an attractive application field for our method.

## 6    Concluding Remarks

In this paper, we presented a novel framework of Similarity-Driven Knowledge Revision. Our revision process is invoked by an observation of undesirable similarity reflected in the original knowledge base. The knowledge base is revised by specializing an over-general variable typing $X : s$ into more specific $X : s'$. The central task is to find an extended sort $es$ by which $s'$ is precisely defined and is an imaginable subsort of $s$. For the efficient computation of the extended sort, we presented an effective proof-theoretic property and proposed the use of SOL-deduction. A drastic improvement of the efficiency was empirically verified.

An important future work is to investigate this kind of knowledge revision in a case where several over-general variable typings are found. Further investigation would be needed to obtain a good characterization of this complicated revision.

Contrary to the assumption on similarity observation in this paper, it would also be worth studying a revision method in a case where a dissimilarity between two sorts is detected by GDA, while the user considers they are similar. In this case, it might be needed to add some new clauses to the original knowledge base as well as modifying variable typings.

## References

1. S. Wrobel. Concept Formation and Knowledge Revision, Kluwer Academic Publishers, Netherlands, 1994.
2. C. Walter. Many-Sorted Unification, *Journal of the Association for Computing Machinery*, Vol. 35 No. 1, 1988, pp.1–17.
3. D. J. Tenenberg. Abstracting First-Order Theories, *Change of Representation and Inductive Bias* (P. D. Benjamin, ed. ), Kluwer Academic Publishers, USA, 1989, pp. 67–79.
4. T. Kakuta, M. Haraguchi and Y. Okubo. A Goal-Dependent Abstraction for Legal Reasoning by Analogy, *Artificial Intelligence & Law*, Vol.5, Kluwer Academic Publishers, Netherlands, 1997, pp. 97–118.
5. Y. Okubo and M. Haraguchi. Constructing Predicate Mappings for Goal-Dependent Abstraction, *Annals of Mathematics and Artificial Intelligence*, Vol.23, 1998, pp. 169–197.
6. T. Mitchell, R. Keller and S. Kedar-Cabelli. Explanation-Based Generalization: A Unifying View, *Machine Learning*, Vol.1, 1986, pp. 47–80.
7. K. Inoue. Liner Resolution for Consequence-Finding, *Artificial Intelligence*, Vol. 56 No. 2–3, 1992, pp 301–353.

# PAC Learning with Nasty Noise

Nader H. Bshouty*, Nadav Eiron, and Eyal Kushilevitz

Computer Science Department, Technion, Haifa 32000, Israel.
{bshouty,nadav,eyalk}@cs.technion.ac.il

**Abstract.** We introduce a new model for learning in the presence of noise, which we call the *Nasty Noise* model. This model generalizes previously considered models of learning with noise. The learning process in this model, which is a variant of the PAC model, proceeds as follows: Suppose that the learning algorithm during its execution asks for $m$ examples. The examples that the algorithm gets are generated by a nasty adversary that works according to the following steps. First, the adversary chooses $m$ examples (independently) according to the fixed (but unknown to the learning algorithm) distribution $D$ as in the PAC-model. Then the powerful adversary, upon seeing the specific $m$ examples that were chosen (and using his knowledge of the target function, the distribution $D$ and the learning algorithm), is allowed to remove a fraction of the examples at its choice, and replace these examples by the same number of arbitrary examples of its choice; the $m$ modified examples are then given to the learning algorithm. The only restriction on the adversary is that the number of examples that the adversary is allowed to modify should be distributed according to a binomial distribution with parameters $\eta$ (the noise rate) and $m$.

On the negative side, we prove that no algorithm can achieve accuracy of $\epsilon < 2\eta$ in learning any non-trivial class of functions. On the positive side, we show that a polynomial (in the usual parameters, and in $\epsilon - 2\eta$) number of examples suffice for learning any class of finite VC-dimension with accuracy $\epsilon > 2\eta$. This algorithm may not be efficient; however, we also show that a fairly wide family of concept classes can be *efficiently* learned in the presence of nasty noise.

## 1 Introduction

Valiant's *PAC model* of learning [23] is one of the most important models for learning from examples. Although being an extremely elegant model, the PAC model has some drawbacks. In particular, it assumes that the learning algorithm has access to a *perfect* source of random examples. Namely, upon request, the learning algorithm can ask for random examples and in return gets pairs $(x, c_t(x))$ where all the $x$'s are points in the input space distributed *identically and independently* according to some fixed probability distribution $D$, and $c_t(x)$ is the *correct* classification of $x$ according to the target function $c_t$ that the algorithm tries to learn.

Since Valiant's seminal work, there were several attempts to relax these assumptions, by introducing models of *noise*. The first such noise model, called the

---

* Some of this research was done while this author was at the Department of Computer Science, the University of Calgary, Canada.

O. Watanabe, T. Yokomori (Eds.): ALT'99, LNAI 1720, pp. 206–218, 1999.
© Springer-Verlag Berlin Heidelberg 1999

*Random Classification Noise* model, was introduced in [2] and was extensively studied, e.g., in [1,6,10,14,15,17]. In this model the adversary, before providing each example $(x, c_t(x))$ to the learning algorithm tosses a biased coin; whenever the coin shows "H", which happens with probability $\eta$, the classification of the example is flipped and so the algorithm is provided with the, wrongly classified, example $(x, 1 - c_t(x))$. Another (stronger) model, called the *Malicious Noise* model, was introduced in [24], revisited in [18], and was further studied in [8,11,12,13,21]. In this model the adversary, whenever the $\eta$-biased coin shows "H", can replace the example $(x, c_t(x))$ by some arbitrary pair $(x', b)$ where $x'$ is any point in the input space and $b$ is a boolean value. (Note that this in particular gives the adversary the power to "distort" the distribution $D$.)

In this work, we present a new model which we call the *Nasty (Sample) Noise* model. In this model, the adversary gets to see the whole sample of examples requested by the learning algorithm before giving it to the algorithm and then modify $E$ of the examples, *at its choice*, where $E$ is a random variable distributed by the binomial distribution with parameters $\eta$ and $m$, where $m$ is the size of the sample[1]. The modification applied by the adversary can be arbitrary (as in the Malicious Noise model).[2] Intuitively speaking, the new adversary is more powerful than the previous ones – it can examine the whole sample and then remove from it the most "informative" examples and replace them by less useful and even misleading examples (whereas in the Malicious Noise Model for instance, the adversary also may insert to the sample misleading examples but does not have the freedom to choose which examples to remove). The relationships between the various models are shown in Table 1.

| | Random Noise-Location | Adversarial Noise-Location |
|---|---|---|
| Label Noise Only | Random Classification Noise | Nasty Classification Noise |
| Point and Label Noise | Malicious Noise | Nasty Sample Noise |

**Table 1.** Summary of models for PAC-learning from noisy data

We argue that the newly introduced model, not only generalizes the previous noise models, including variants such as Decatur's CAM model [13] and CPCN model [14], but also, that in many real-world situations, the assumptions previous models made about the noise seem insufficient. For example, when training data is the result of some physical experiment, noise may tend to be stronger in boundary areas rather than being uniformly distributed over all inputs. While special models were devised to describe this situation in the exact-learning setting (for example, the incomplete boundary query model of Blum et al., [5]), it may be regarded as a special case of Nasty Noise, where the adversary chooses to provide unreliable answers on sample points that are near the boundary of the target concept (or to remove such points from the sample). Another situation to which our model is related is the setting of Agnostic Learning. In this model, a

---

[1] This distribution makes the number of examples modified be the same as if it were determined by $m$ independent tosses of an $\eta$-biased coin. However, we allow the adversary's choice be dependent on the sample drawn.

[2] We also consider a weaker variant of this model, called the *Nasty Classification Noise* model, where the adversary may modify only the classification of the chosen points (as in the Random Classification Noise model).

concept class is not given. Instead, the learning algorithm needs to minimize the empirical error while using a hypothesis from a predefined hypotheses class (see, for example, [19] for a definition of the model). Assuming the best hypothesis classifies the input up to an $\eta$ fraction, we may alternatively see the problem as that of learning the hypotheses class under nasty noise of rate $\eta$. However, we note that the success criterion in the agnostic learning literature is different from the one used in our PAC-based setting.

We show two types of results. Sections 3 and 4 show information theoretic results, and Sect. 5 shows algorithmic results. The first result, presented in Sect. 3, is a bound on the quality of learning possible with a nasty adversary. This result shows that any learning algorithm cannot learn any non-trivial concept class with accuracy less than $2\eta$ when the sample contains nasty noise of rate $\eta$. It is complemented by a matching positive result in Sect. 4 that shows that any class of finite VC-dimension can be learned by using a sample of polynomial size, with any accuracy $\epsilon > 2\eta$. The size of the sample required is polynomial in the usual PAC parameters and in $1/\Delta$ where $\Delta = \epsilon - 2\eta$ is the margin between the requested accuracy $\epsilon$ and the above mentioned lower bound.

The main, quite surprising, result (presented in Sect. 5) is another positive result showing that *efficient* learning algorithms are still possible in spite of the powerful adversary. More specifically, we present a composition theorem (analogous to [3,8] but for the nasty-noise learning model) that shows that any concept class that is constructed by composing concept classes that are PAC-learnable from a hypothesis class of fixed VC-dimension, is efficiently learnable when using a sample subject to nasty noise. This includes, for instance, the class of all concepts formed by any boolean combination of half-spaces in a constant dimension Euclidean space. The complexity here is, again, polynomial in the usual parameters and in $1/\Delta$. The algorithm used in the proof of this result is an adaptation to our model of the PAC algorithm presented in [8].

Our results may be compared to similar results available for the Malicious Noise model. For this model, Cesa-Bianchi et al. [11] show that the accuracy of learning with malicious noise is lower bounded by $\eta/(1 - \eta)$. A matching algorithm for learning classes similar to those presented here with malicious noise is presented in [8]. As for the Random Classification Noise model, learning with arbitrary small accuracy, even when the noise rate is close to a half, is possible. Again, the techniques presented in [8] may be used to learn the same type of classes we examine in this work with Random Classification Noise.

## 2   Preliminaries

In this section we provide basic definitions related to learning in the PAC model, with and without noise. A learning task is specified using a *concept class*, denoted $C$, of boolean concepts defined over an *instance space*, denoted $\mathcal{X}$. A boolean concept $c$ is a function $c : \mathcal{X} \mapsto \{0,1\}$. The concept class $C$ is a set of boolean concepts: $C \subseteq \{0,1\}^{\mathcal{X}}$.

Throughout this paper we sometimes treat a concept as a set of points instead of as a boolean function. The set that corresponds to a concept $c$ is simply $\{x|c(x) = 1\}$. We use $c$ to denote both the function and the corresponding set interchangeably. Specifically, when a probability distribution $D$ is defined over $\mathcal{X}$, we use the notation $D(c)$ to refer to the probability that a point $x$ drawn from $\mathcal{X}$ according to $D$ will have $c(x) = 1$.

## 2.1    The Classical PAC Model

The *Probably Approximately Correct (PAC)* model was originally presented by Valiant [23]. In this model, the learning algorithm has access to an oracle PAC that returns on each call a labeled example $(x, c_t(x))$ where $x \in \mathcal{X}$ is drawn (independently) according to a fixed distribution $D$ over $\mathcal{X}$, unknown to the learning algorithm, and $c_t \in C$ is the target function the learning algorithm should "learn".

**Definition 1.** *A class $C$ of boolean functions is* PAC-learnable *using hypothesis class $\mathcal{H}$ in polynomial time if there exists an algorithm that, for any $c_t \in C$, any $0 < \epsilon < 1/2$, $0 < \delta < 1$ and any distribution $D$ on $\mathcal{X}$, when given access to the PAC oracle, runs in time polynomial in $\log |\mathcal{X}|$, $1/\delta$, $1/\epsilon$ and with probability at least $1 - \delta$ outputs a function $h \in \mathcal{H}$ for which:* $\Pr_D[c_t(x) \neq h(x)] \leq \epsilon$.

## 2.2    Models for Learning in the Presence of Noise

Next, we define the model of PAC-learning in the presence of *Nasty Sample Noise* (NSN for short). In this model, a learning algorithm for the concept class $C$ is given access to an (adversarial) oracle $\mathrm{NSN}_{C,\eta}(m)$. The learning algorithm is allowed to call this oracle *once* during a single run. The learning algorithm passes a single natural number $m$ to the oracle, specifying the size of the sample it needs, and gets in return a labeled sample $S \in (\mathcal{X} \times \{0,1\})^m$. (It is assumed, for simplicity, that the algorithm knows in advance the number of examples it needs; It is possible to extend the model to circumvent this problem.)

The sample required by the learning algorithm is constructed as follows: As in the PAC model, a distribution $D$ over the instance space $\mathcal{X}$ is defined, and a target concept $c_t \in C$ is chosen. The adversary then draws a sample $S_g$ of $m$ points from $\mathcal{X}$ according to the distribution $D$. Having full knowledge of the learning algorithm, the target function $c_t$, the distribution $D$, and the sample drawn, the adversary chooses $E = E(S_g)$ points from the sample, where $E(S_g)$ is a random variable. The $E$ points chosen by the adversary are removed from the sample and replaced by any other $E$ point-and-label pairs by the adversary. The $m - E$ points not chosen by the adversary remain unchanged and are labeled by their correct labels according to $c_t$. The modified sample of $m$ points, denoted $S$, is then given to the learning algorithm. The only limitation that the adversary has on the number of examples that it may modify is that it should be distributed according to the binomial distribution with parameters $m$ and $\eta$, namely:

$$\Pr[E = n] = \binom{m}{n} \eta^n (1 - \eta)^{m-n},$$

where the probability is taken by first choosing $S_g \in D^m$ and then choosing $E$ according to the corresponding random variable $E(S_g)$.

**Definition 2.** *An algorithm $\mathcal{A}$ is said to learn a class $C$ with nasty sample noise of rate $\eta \geq 0$ with accuracy parameter $\epsilon > 0$ and confidence parameter $\delta < 1$ if, given access to any oracle $NSN_{C,\eta}(m)$, for any distribution $D$ and any target $c_t \in C$ it outputs a hypothesis $h : \mathcal{X} \mapsto \{0,1\}$ such that, with probability at least $1 - \delta$ the hypothesis satisfies* $\Pr_D[h \triangle c_t] \leq \epsilon$.

We are also interested in a restriction of this model, which we call the *Nasty Classification Noise* learning model (NCN for short). The only difference between the NCN and NSN models is that the NCN adversary is only allowed to modify the labels of the $E$ chosen sample-points, but it cannot modify the $E$ points themselves. Previous models of learning in the presence of noise can also be readily shown to be restrictions of the Nasty Sample Noise model: The Malicious Noise model corresponds to the Nasty Noise model with the adversary restricted to introducing noise into points that are chosen uniformly at random, with probability $\eta$, from the original sample. The Random Classification Noise model corresponds to the Nasty Classification Noise model with the adversary restricted so that noise is introduced into points chosen uniformly at random, with probability $\eta$, from the original sample, and each point that is chosen gets its label flipped.

## 2.3   VC Theory Basics

The VC-dimension [25], is widely used in learning theory to measure the complexity of concept classes. The VC-dimension of a class $\mathcal{C}$, denoted VCdim($\mathcal{C}$), is the maximal integer $d$ such that there exists a subset $Y \subseteq \mathcal{X}$ of size $d$ for which all $2^d$ possible behaviors are present in the class $\mathcal{C}$, and VCdim($\mathcal{C}$) = $\infty$ if such a subset exists for any natural $d$. It is well known (e.g., [4]) that, for any two classes $\mathcal{C}$ and $\mathcal{H}$ (over $\mathcal{X}$) of VC-dimension $d$, the class of negations $\{c | \mathcal{X} \setminus c \in \mathcal{C}\}$ has VC-dimension $d$, and the class of unions $\{c \cup h | c \in \mathcal{C}, \ h \in \mathcal{H}\}$ has VC-dimension at most $2\max\{\text{VCdim}(\mathcal{C}), \text{VCdim}(\mathcal{H})\} + 1 = O(d)$. Following [3] we define the dual of a concept class:

**Definition 3.** *The dual $\mathcal{H}^{\perp} \subseteq \{0,1\}^{\mathcal{H}}$ of a class $\mathcal{H} \subseteq \{0,1\}^{\mathcal{X}}$ is defined to be the set $\{x^{\perp} | x \in \mathcal{X}\}$ where $x^{\perp}$ is defined by $x^{\perp}(h) = h(x)$ for all $h \in \mathcal{H}$.*

If we view a concept class $\mathcal{H}$ as a boolean matrix $M_{\mathcal{H}}$ where each row represents a concept and each column a point from the instance space, $\mathcal{X}$, then the matrix corresponding to $\mathcal{H}^{\perp}$ is the transpose of the matrix $M_{\mathcal{H}}$. The following claim, from [3], gives a tight bound on the VC dimension of the dual class:

**Claim 1:** For every class $\mathcal{H}$,   VCdim($\mathcal{H}$) $\geq \lfloor \log \text{VCdim}(\mathcal{H}^{\perp}) \rfloor$.

In the following discussion we limit ourselves to instance spaces $\mathcal{X}$ of finite cardinality. The main use we make of the VC-dimension is in constructing $\alpha$-nets. The following definition and theorem are from [7]:

**Definition 4.** *A set of points $Y \subseteq \mathcal{X}$ is an $\alpha$-net for concept class $\mathcal{H} \subseteq \{0,1\}^{\mathcal{X}}$ under distribution $D$ over $\mathcal{X}$, if for every $h \in \mathcal{H}$ such that $D(h) \geq \alpha$, $Y \cap h \neq \emptyset$.*

**Theorem 1.** *For any class $\mathcal{H} \subseteq \{0,1\}^{\mathcal{X}}$ of VC-dimension $d$, any distribution $D$ over $\mathcal{X}$, and any $\alpha > 0$, $\delta > 0$, if $m \geq \max\{\frac{4}{\alpha} \log \frac{2}{\delta}, \frac{8d}{\alpha} \log \frac{13}{\alpha}\}$ examples are drawn i.i.d. from $\mathcal{X}$ according to the distribution $D$, they constitute an $\alpha$-net for $\mathcal{H}$ with probability at least $1 - \delta$.*

In [22], Talagrand proved a similar result:

**Definition 5.** *A set of points* $Y \subseteq \mathcal{X}$ *is an* $\alpha$*-sample for the concept class* $\mathcal{H} \subseteq \{0,1\}^{\mathcal{X}}$ *under the distribution* $D$ *over* $\mathcal{X}$*, if it holds that every* $h \in \mathcal{H}$ *satisfies* $\left| D(h) - \frac{|Y \cap h|}{|Y|} \right| \leq \alpha.$

**Theorem 2.** *There is a constant* $c_1$*, such that for any class* $\mathcal{H} \subseteq \{0,1\}^{\mathcal{X}}$ *of VC-dimension* $d$*, and distribution* $D$ *over* $\mathcal{X}$*, and any* $\alpha > 0$*,* $\delta > 0$*, if* $m \geq \frac{c_1}{\alpha^2} (d + \log \frac{1}{\delta})$ *examples are drawn i.i.d. from* $\mathcal{X}$ *according to the distribution* $D$*, they constitute an* $\alpha$*-sample for* $\mathcal{H}$ *with probability at least* $1 - \delta$*.*

### 2.4  Consistency Algorithms

Let $P$ and $N$ be subsets of points from $\mathcal{X}$. We say that a function $h : \mathcal{X} \mapsto \{0,1\}$ is consistent on $(P, N)$ if $h(x) = 1$ for every "positive point" $x \in P$ and $h(x) = 0$ for every "negative point" $x \in N$. A *consistency algorithm* (see [8]) for a pair of classes $(\mathcal{C}, \mathcal{H})$ (both over the same instance space $\mathcal{X}$), receives as input two subsets of the instance space, $(P, N)$, runs in time $t(|P \cup N|)$, and satisfies the following. If there is a function in $\mathcal{C}$ that is consistent with $(P, N)$, the algorithm outputs "YES" and some $h \in \mathcal{H}$ that is consistent with $(P, N)$, or "NO" if no consistent $h \in \mathcal{H}$ exist (there is no restriction on the output in the case that there is a consistent function in $\mathcal{H}$ but not in $\mathcal{C}$).

Given a subset of points of the instance space $Q \subseteq \mathcal{X}$, we will be interested in the set of all possible partitions of $Q$ into positive and negative examples, such that there is a function $h \in \mathcal{H}$ and a function $c \in \mathcal{C}$ that are both consistent with this partition. This may be formulated as: $S_{\mathrm{CON}}(Q) = \{P \mid \mathrm{CON}(P, Q \setminus P) = \text{"YES"}\}$ where CON is a consistency algorithm for $(\mathcal{C}, \mathcal{H})$. Bshouty [8] shows the following, based on the Sauer Lemma [20]:

**Lemma 1.** *For any set of points* $Q$*,* $|S_{CON}(Q)| \leq |Q|^{VC\text{-}dim(H)}$*.*

Furthermore, an efficient algorithm for generating this set of partitions (along with the corresponding functions $h \in \mathcal{H}$) is presented, assuming that $\mathcal{C}$ is PAC-learnable from $\mathcal{H}$ of constant VC dimension. The algorithm's output is denoted $\hat{S}_{\mathrm{CON}}(Q) \triangleq \{((P, Q \setminus P), h) \mid P \in S_{\mathrm{CON}}(Q) \text{ and } h \text{ is consistent with } (P, Q \setminus P)\}.$

## 3  Information Theoretic Lower Bound

In this section we show that no learning algorithm (not even inefficient ones) can learn a "non-trivial" concept class with accuracy $\epsilon$ better than $2\eta$ under the NSN model; in fact, we prove that this impossibility result holds even for the NCN model.

**Definition 6.** *A concept class* $\mathcal{C}$ *over an instance space* $\mathcal{X}$ *is called non-trivial if there exist two points* $x_1, x_2 \in \mathcal{X}$ *and two concepts* $c_1, c_2 \in \mathcal{C}$*, such that* $c_1(x_1) = c_2(x_1)$ *and* $c_1(x_2) \neq c_2(x_2)$*.*

**Theorem 3.** *Let* $\mathcal{C}$ *be a non-trivial concept class,* $\eta$ *be a noise rate and* $\epsilon < 2\eta$ *be an accuracy parameter. Then, there is no algorithm that learns the concept class* $\mathcal{C}$ *with accuracy* $\epsilon$ *under the NCN model (with rate* $\eta$*).*

**Proof sketch:**     We base our proof on the method of induced distributions introduced in [18, Theorem 1]. We show that there are two concepts $c_1, c_2 \in C$ and a probability distribution $D$ such that $\text{Pr}_D(c_1 \triangle c_2) = 2\eta$ and an adversary can force the labeled examples shown to the learning algorithm to be distributed identically both when $c_1$ is the target and when $c_2$ is the target.

Let $c_1$ and $c_2$ be the two concepts whose existence is guaranteed by the fact that $C$ is a non-trivial class, and let $x_1, x_2 \in X$ be the two points that satisfy $c_1(x_1) = c_2(x_1)$ and $c_1(x_2) \neq c_2(x_2)$. We define the probability distribution $D$ to be $D(x_1) = 1 - 2\eta$, $D(x_2) = 2\eta$, and $D(x) = 0$ for all $x \in X \setminus \{x_1, x_2\}$. Clearly, we indeed have $\text{Pr}_D(c_1 \triangle c_2) = \text{Pr}_D(x_2) = 2\eta$.

The adversary will modify exactly half of the sample points of the form $(x_2, \epsilon)$ to $(x_2, 1 - \epsilon)$. This would result with the learning algorithm being given a sample effectively drawn from the following induced distribution:

$$\text{Pr}(x_1, c_1(x_1)) = 1 - 2\eta \quad \text{and} \quad \text{Pr}(x_2, c_1(x_2)) = \text{Pr}(x_2, c_2(x_2)) = \eta.$$

This induced distribution would be the same no matter whether the true target is $c_1$ or $c_2$. Therefore, according to the sample that the learning algorithm sees, it is impossible to differentiate between the case where the target function is $c_1$ and the case where the target function is $c_2$.     □

Note that in the above proof we indeed take advantage of the "nastiness" of the adversary. Unlike the malicious adversary, our adversary can focus all its "power" on just the point $x_2$, causing it to suffer a relatively high error rate, while examples in which the point is $x_1$ do not suffer any noise. Finally, since any NCN adversary is also a NSN adversary, Theorem 3 implies the following:

**Corollary 1.** *Let $C$ be a non-trivial concept class, $\eta > 0$ be the noise rate, and $\epsilon < 2\eta$ be an accuracy parameter. There is no algorithm that learns the concept class $C$ with accuracy $\epsilon$ under the NSN model, with noise rate $\eta$.*

## 4     Information Theoretic Upper Bound

In this section we provide a positive result that complements the negative result of Sect. 3. This result shows that, given a sufficiently large sample, any hypothesis that performs sufficiently well on the sample (even when this sample is subject to nasty noise) satisfies the PAC learning condition. Formally, we analyze the following generic algorithm for learning any class $C$ of VC-dimension $d$, whose inputs are a certainty parameter $\delta > 0$, the nasty error rate parameter $\eta < \frac{1}{2}$ and the required accuracy $\epsilon = 2\eta + \Delta$:

**Algorithm NastyConsistent:**

1. Request a sample $S = \{(x, b_x)\}$ of size $m \geq \frac{c}{\Delta^2}\left(d + \log \frac{2}{\delta}\right)$
2. Output any $h \in C$ such that $|\{x \in S : h(x) \neq b_x\}| \leq m(\eta + \Delta/4)$ (if no such $h$ exists, choose any $h \in C$ arbitrarily).

**Theorem 4.** *Let $C$ be any class of VC-dimension $d$. Then, (for some constant $c$) algorithm NastyConsistent is a PAC learning algorithm under nasty sample noise of rate $\eta$.*

*Proof.* By Hoeffding's inequality [16], with probability $1 - \delta/2$ the number of sample points that are modified by the adversary $E$ is at most $m(\eta + \Delta/4)$.

Now, we note that the target function $c_t$, errs on at most $E$ points of the sample shown to the learning algorithm (as it is completely accurate on the non-modified sample $S_g$). Thus, with high probability Algorithm NastyConsistent will be able to choose a function $h \in C$ that errs on no more that $(\eta + \Delta/4)m$ points of the sample shown to it. However, in the worst case, these errors of the function $h$ occur in points that were not modified by the adversary. In addition, $h$ may be erroneous for all the points that the adversary did modify. Therefore, all we are guaranteed in this case, is that the hypothesis $h$ errs on no more that $2E$ points of the original sample $S_g$. By Theorem 2, there exists a constant $c$ such that, with probability $1 - \delta/2$, the sample $S_g$ is a $\frac{\Delta}{2}$-sample for the class of symmetric differences between functions from $C$. By the union bound we therefore have that, with probability at least $1 - \delta$, $E \leq (\eta + \Delta/4)m$, meaning that $|S_g \cap (c_t \Delta h)| \leq (2\eta + \Delta/2)m$, and that $S_g$ is a $\Delta/2$-sample for the class of symmetric differences, and so: $\Pr_D[(c_t \Delta h)] \leq 2\eta + \Delta = \epsilon$ as required.    □

## 5    Composition Theorem for Learning with Nasty Noise

Following [3] and [8], we define the notion of "composition class": Let $C$ be a class of boolean functions $g : \mathcal{X} \mapsto \{0,1\}^n$. Define the class $C^\star$ to be the set of all boolean functions $F(x)$ that can be represented as $f(g_1(x), \ldots, g_k(x))$ where $f$ is any boolean function, and $g_i \in C$ for $i = 1, \ldots, k$. We define the size of $f(g_1, \ldots, g_k)$ to be $k$. Given a vector of hypotheses $(h_1, \ldots, h_t) \in \mathcal{H}^t$ define the set $\mathcal{W}(h_1, \ldots, h_t)$ to be the set of sub-domains $W_a = \{x | (h_1(x), \ldots, h_t(x)) = a\}$ for all possible vectors $a \in \{0,1\}^t$.

We now show a variation of the algorithm presented in [8] that can learn the class $C^\star$ with a nasty sample adversary, assuming that the class $C$ is PAC-learnable from a class $\mathcal{H}$ of constant VC dimension $d$. The algorithm builds on the fact that a consistency algorithm CON for $(C, \mathcal{H})$ can be constructed, given an algorithm that PAC learns $C$ from $\mathcal{H}$ [8]. This algorithm can learn the concept class $C^\star$ with any confidence parameter $\delta$ and with accuracy $\epsilon$ that is arbitrarily close to the lower bound of $2\eta$, proved in the previous section. Its sample complexity and computational complexity are both polynomial in $k$, $1/\delta$ and $1/\Delta$, where $\Delta = \epsilon - 2\eta$.

The algorithm is based on the following idea: Request a large sample from the oracle and randomly pick a smaller sub-sample from the sample retrieved. The random choice of a sub-sample neutralizes some of the power the adversary has, since the adversary cannot know which examples are the ones that will be most "informative" for us. Then use the consistency algorithm for $(C, \mathcal{H})$ to find one representative from $\mathcal{H}$ for any possible behavior on the smaller sub-sample. These hypotheses from $\mathcal{H}$ now define a division of the instance space into "cells", where each cell is characterized by a specific behavior of all the hypotheses picked. The final hypotheses is simply based on taking a majority vote among the complete sample inside each such cell.

To demonstrate the algorithm, we consider (informally) the specific, relatively simple, case where the class to be learned is the class of $k$ intervals on the line (see Fig. 1). The algorithm, given a sample as input, proceeds as follows:

1. The algorithm uses a "small", random sub-sample to divide the line into sub-intervals. Each two adjacent points in the sub-sample define such a sub-interval.
2. For each such sub-interval the algorithm calculates a majority vote on the complete sample. The result is our hypothesis.

The number of points (which in this specific case is the number of sub-intervals) the algorithm chooses in the first step depends on $k$. Intuitively, we want the total weight of the sub-intervals containing the target's end-points to be relatively small (this is what is called the "bad part" in the formal analysis that follows). Naturally, there will be $2k$ such "bad" sub-intervals, so the larger $k$ is, the larger the sub-sample needed. Except for these "bad" sub-intervals, all other subintervals on which the algorithm errs have to have at least half of their points modified by the adversary. Thus the total error will be roughly $2\eta$, plus the weight of the "bad" sub-intervals.

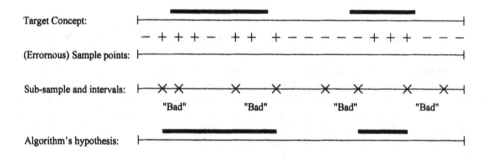

**Fig. 1.** Example of NastyLearn for intervals.

Now, we proceed to a formal description of the learning algorithm. Given the constant $d$, the size $k$ of the target function[3], the bound on the error rate $\eta$, the parameters $\delta$ and $\Delta$, and two additional parameters $M, N$ (to be specified below), the algorithm proceeds as follows:

**Algorithm NastyLearn:**

1. Request a sample $S$ of size $N$.
2. Choose uniformly at random a sub-sample $R \subseteq S$ of size $M$.
3. Use the consistency algorithm for $(\mathcal{C}, \mathcal{H})$ to compute
   $$\hat{S}_{CON}(R) = \{((P_1, R \setminus P_1), h_1), \ldots, ((P_t, R \setminus P_t), h_t)\}.$$
4. Output the hypotheses $H(h_1, \ldots, h_t)$, computed as follows: For any $W_a \in \mathcal{W}(h_1, \ldots, h_t)$ that is not empty, set $H$ to be the majority of labels in $S \cap W_a$. If $W_a$ is empty, set $H$ to be 0 on any $x \in W_a$.

---

[3] The algorithm can use the "doubling" technique in case that $k$ is not given to it. In this case however, the sample size is not known in advance and so we need to use the extended definition of the Nasty Noise model that allows repetitive queries to the oracle.

**Theorem 5.** *Let*

$$M = max\left(\frac{24k}{\Delta}\log\frac{8}{\delta}, \frac{c_2dk}{\Delta}\log\frac{78k}{\Delta}\right) \quad and \quad N = \frac{M^{c_1d2^d}k^2}{\Delta^2}\left(2^dd + \log\frac{4}{\delta}\right)$$

*where $c_1$ and $c_2$ are constants. Then, Algorithm NastyLearn learns the class $C^*$ with accuracy $\epsilon = 2\eta + \Delta$ and confidence $\delta$ in time polynomial in $k$, $\frac{1}{\delta}$, and $\frac{1}{\Delta}$.*

Before commencing with the actual proof, we present a technical lemma:

**Lemma 2.** *Assuming $N$ is set as in the statement of Theorem 5, with probability at least $1 - \frac{\delta}{4}$, $E$ (the number of points in which errors are introduced) is at most $(\eta + \Delta/12)N$.*

For lack of space, the proof is omitted (see [9] for details). We are now ready to present the proof of Theorem 5:

*Proof.* To analyze the error made by the hypothesis that the algorithm generates, let us denote the adversary's strategy as follows:

1. Generate a sample of the requested size $N$ according to the distribution $D$, and label it by the target concept $F$. Denote this sample by $S_g$.
2. Choose a subset $S_{out} \subseteq S_g$ of size $E = E(S_g)$, where $E(S_g)$ is a random variable (as defined in Sect. 2.2).
3. Choose (maliciously) some other set of points $S_{in} \subseteq \mathcal{X} \times \{0,1\}$ of size $E$.
4. Hand to the learning algorithm the sample $S = (S_g \setminus S_{out}) \cup S_{in}$.

Assume the target function $F$ is of the form $F = f(g_1, \ldots, g_k)$. For all $i \in \{1, \ldots, k\}$, denote by $h_{j_i}$, where $j_i \in \{1, \ldots, t\}$, the hypothesis the algorithm have chosen in step 3 that exhibits the same behavior $g_i$ has over the points of $R$ (from the definition of $\hat{S}_{CON}$ we are guaranteed that such a hypothesis exists). By definition, there are no points from $R$ in $h_{j_i}\triangle g_i$, so:

$$R \cap (h_{j_i}\triangle g_i) = \emptyset. \tag{1}$$

As the VC-dimension of both the class $\mathcal{C}$ of all $g_i$'s and the class $\mathcal{H}$ of all $h_i$'s is $d$, the class of all their possible symmetric differences also has VC-dimension $O(d)$ (see Sect. 2.3). By applying Theorem 1, when viewing $R$ as a sample taken from $S$ according to the uniform distribution, and by choosing $M$ to be as in the statement of the theorem, $R$ will be an $\alpha$-net (with respect to the uniform distribution over $S$) for the class of symmetric differences, with $\alpha = \Delta/6k$, with probability at least $1 - \delta/4$. Note that there may still be points in $S$ which are in $h_{j_i}\triangle g_i$. Hence, we let $S^{(i)} = S \cap (h_{j_i}\triangle g_i)$. Now, by using (1) we get that $\frac{|S^{(i)}|}{|S|} \leq \frac{\Delta}{6k}$ with probability at least $1 - \delta/4$, simultaneously for all $i$.

For every sub-domain $B \in \mathcal{W}(h_1, \ldots, h_t)$ we define:

$$N_B \triangleq |S_g \cap B| \qquad\qquad , N_B^{in} \triangleq |S_{in} \cap B|$$
$$N_B^{out,g} \triangleq \left|S_{out} \cap B \cap \overline{\bigcup_i(h_{j_i}\triangle g_i)}\right| \quad , N_B^{out,b} \triangleq |S_{out} \cap B \cap \bigcup_i(h_{j_i}\triangle g_i)|$$
$$N_B^\alpha \triangleq |S \cap B \cap \bigcup_i(h_{j_i}\triangle g_i)|$$

In words, $N_B$ and $N_B^{in}$ simply stand for the size of the restriction of the original (noise-free) sample $S_g$ and the noisy examples $S_{in}$ introduced by the adversary to the sub-domain $B$. The other definitions are based on the distinction between the "good" part of $B$, where the $g_i$s and the $h_{j_i}$s behave the same, and the "bad" part, which is present due to the fact that the $g_i$s and the $h_{j_i}$s exhibit the same behavior only on the sub-sample $R$, rather than on the complete sample $S$.

Since the hypothesis takes a majority vote in each sub-domain, then it will err on the domain $B \cap (\overline{\bigcup_i (h_{j_i} \triangle g_i)})$ if the number of examples left untouched in $B$ is less than the number of examples in $B$ that were modified by the adversary, plus those that were misclassified by the $h_{j_i}$s (with respect to the $g_i$s). This may be formulated as the following condition: $N_B^{in} + N_B^{\alpha} \geq N_B - N_B^{out,g} - N_B^{\alpha}$. Therefore, the total error the algorithm may experience is at most:

$$D\left[\bigcup_i h_{j_i} \triangle g_i\right] + \sum_{B:\ N_B \leq N_B^{in} + N_B^{out,g} + 2N_B^{\alpha}} D(B).$$

We now calculate a bound for each of the two terms above separately. To bound the second term, note that by Theorem 2 our choice of $N$ guarantees $S_g$ to be a $\frac{\Delta}{6|W(h_1,\ldots,h_t)|}$-sample for our domain with probability at least $1 - \delta/4$. Note that from the definition of $W(h_1,\ldots,h_t)$ and from the Sauer Lemma [20] we have that $|W(h_1,\ldots,h_t)| \leq t^{VCdim(\mathcal{H}^{\perp})}$, which, with Claim 1 and Lemma 1 yields:

$$|W(h_1,\ldots,h_t)| \leq M^{VCdim(\mathcal{H})VCdim(\mathcal{H}^{\perp})} \leq M^{d2^d}$$

Our choice of $N$ indeed guarantees, with probability at least $1 - \delta/4$ that:

$$\sum_{B:\ N_B \leq N_B^{in} + N_B^{out,g} + 2N_B^{\alpha}} D(B) \leq \sum_{B:\ N_B \leq N_B^{in} + N_B^{out,g} + 2N_B^{\alpha}} \left(\frac{N_B}{N} + \frac{\Delta}{6|W(h_1,\ldots,h_t)|}\right)$$

$$\leq \frac{\Delta}{6} + \sum_{B \in W(h_1,\ldots,h_t)} \frac{N_B^{in} + N_B^{out,g} + 2N_B^{\alpha}}{N}$$

From the above choice of $N$, it follows that $S_g$ is also a $\frac{\Delta}{6|W(h_1,\ldots,h_t)|}$-sample for the class of symmetric differences of the form $h_{j_i} \triangle g_i$. Thus, with probability at least $1 - \delta/4$, we have:

$$\sum_{i=1}^{k} D(h_{j_i} \triangle g_i) \leq \frac{2\Delta}{6} + \sum_{B \in W(h_1,\ldots,h_t)} \frac{N_B^{out,b}}{N}.$$

The total error made by the hypothesis (assuming that none of the four bad events happen) is therefore bounded by:

$$\Pr_D[H \triangle F] \leq \frac{3\Delta}{6} + \sum_{B \in W(h_1,\ldots,h_t)} \frac{N_B^{in} + N_B^{out,g} + N_B^{out,b} + 2N_B^{\alpha}}{N} \leq 2\eta + \Delta = \epsilon,$$

as required. This bound holds with certainty at least $1 - \delta$.   $\square$

# References

1. J. A. Aslam and S. E. Decatur, "General Bounds on Statistical Query Learning and PAC Learning with Noise via Hypothesis Boosting", *FOCS93*, pp. 282-291, 1993.
2. D. Angluin and P. Laird, "Learning from Noisy Examples", *Machine Learning*, Vol. 2, pp. 343-370, 1988.
3. S. Ben-David, N. H. Bshouty and E. Kushilevitz, "A Composition Theorem for Learning Algorithms with Applications to Geometric Concept Classes", *STOC97*, pp. 324-333, 1997.
4. S. Ben-David and A. Litman, "Combinatorial Variability of Vapnik–Chervonenkis Classes with Applications to Sample Compression Schemes", *Discrete Applied Math* 86, pp. 3-25, 1998.
5. A. Blum, P. Chalasani, S. A. Goldman, and D. K. Slonim, "Learning with Unreliable Boundary Queries", *COLT95*, pp. 98-107, 1995.
6. A. Blum, M. Furst, J. Jackson, M. J. Kearns, Y. Mansour, and S. Rudich, "Weakly Learning DNF and Characterizing Statistical Query Learning Using Fourier Analysis", *STOC94*, 1994.
7. A. Blumer, A. Ehrenfeucht, D. Haussler and M. K. Warmuth, "Learnability and the Vapnik-Chervonenkis dimension", *J. of the ACM*, 36(4), pp. 929-965, 1989.
8. N. H. Bshouty, "A New Composition Theorem for Learning Algorithms", *STOC98*, pp. 583-589, 1998.
9. N. H. Bshouty, N. Eiron and E. Kushilevitz, "PAC Learning with Nasty Noise", Technical Report CS0693, Department of Computer Science, The Technion — Israel Institute of Technology.
10. N. H. Bshouty, S. A. Goldman, H. D. Mathias, S. Suri, and H. Tamaki, "Noise-Tolerant Distribution-Free Learning of General Geometric Concepts", *STOC96*, pp. 151-160, 1996.
11. N. Cesa-Bianchi, E. Dichterman, P. Fischer, and H. U. Simon, "Noise-Tolerant Learning near the Information-Theoretic bound", *STOC96*, pp. 141-150, 1996.
12. N. Cesa-Bianchi, P. Fischer, E. Shamir and H. U. Simon, "Randomized hypotheses and Minimum Disagreement hypotheses for Learning with Noise", proceedings of *EuroCOLT 97*, pp. 119-133, 1997.
13. S. E. Decatur, "Learning in Hybrid Noise Environments Using Statistical Queries", in *Learning from Data: Artificial Intelligence and Statistics V*, D. Fisher and H. J. Lenz, (Eds.), 1996.
14. S. E. Decatur, "PAC Learning with Constant-Partition Classification Noise and Applications to Decision Tree Induction", *Proceedings of the Sixth International Workshop on Artificial Intelligence and Statistics*, pp. 147-156, 1997.
15. S. E. Decatur and R. Gennaro, "On Learning from Noisy and Incomplete Examples", *COLT95*, pp. 353-360, 1995.
16. W. Hoeffding, "Probability Inequalities for Sums of Bounded Random Variables", J. of the American Statistical Association, 58(301), pp. 13-30, 1963.
17. M. Kearns, "Efficient Noise-Tolerant Learning from Statistical Queries", Proc. 25th ACM Symposium on the Theory of Computing, pp. 392-401, 1993.
18. M. J. Kearns and M. Li, "Learning in the Presence of Malicious Errors", SIAM J. on Computing, 22:807-837, 1993.
19. M. J. Kearns, R. E. Schapire, and L. M. Sellie, "Toward Efficient Agnostic Learning", *Machine Learning*, vol. 17(2), pp. 115-142, 1994.
20. N. Sauer, "On the Density of Families of sets", *Journal of Combinatorial Theory*, 13:145-147, 1972.
21. R. E. Schapire, "The Design and Analysis of Efficient Learning Algorithms", MIT Press, 1991.
22. M. Talagrand, "Sharper Bounds for Gaussian and Empirical Processes", *Annals of Probability*, 22:28-76, 1994.

23. L. G. Valiant, "A Theory of the Learnable", Comm. ACM, 27(11):1134-1142, 1984.
24. L. G. Valiant, "Learning Disjunctions of Conjunctions", *IJCAI85*, pp. 560–566, 1985.
25. V. N. Vapnik and A. Y. Chervonenkis, "On the Uniform Convergence of Relative Frequencies of Events to Their Probabilities", Theory Probab. Appl. 16, no. 2 pp. 264–280, 1971.

# Positive and Unlabeled Examples Help Learning*

Francesco De Comité, François Denis, Rémi Gilleron, and Fabien Letouzey

LIFL, URA 369 CNRS, Université de Lille 1
59655 Villeneuve d'Ascq FRANCE
{decomite, denis, gilleron, letouzey}@lifl.fr

**Abstract.** In many learning problems, labeled examples are rare or expensive while numerous unlabeled and positive examples are available. However, most learning algorithms only use labeled examples. Thus we address the problem of learning with the help of positive and unlabeled data given a small number of labeled examples. We present both theoretical and empirical arguments showing that learning algorithms can be improved by the use of both unlabeled and positive data. As an illustrating problem, we consider the learning algorithm from statistics for monotone conjunctions in the presence of classification noise and give empirical evidence of our assumptions. We give theoretical results for the improvement of Statistical Query learning algorithms from positive and unlabeled data. Lastly, we apply these ideas to tree induction algorithms. We modify the code of C4.5 to get an algorithm which takes as input a set LAB of labeled examples, a set POS of positive examples and a set UNL of unlabeled data and which uses these three sets to construct the decision tree. We provide experimental results based on data taken from UCI repository which confirm the relevance of this approach.

**Key words:** PAC model, Statistical Queries, Unlabeled Examples, Positive Examples, Decision Trees, Data Mining

## 1 Introduction

Usual learning algorithms only use labeled examples. But, in many machine learning settings, gathering large sets of unlabeled examples is easy. This remark has been made about text classification tasks and learning algorithms able to classify text from labeled and unlabeled documents have recently been proposed ([BM98], [NMTM98]). We also argue that, for many machine learning problems, a "natural" source of positive examples (that belong to a single class) is available and positive data are abundant and cheap. For example consider a classical domain, such as the diagnosis of diseases: unlabeled data are abundant (all patients); positive data may be numerous (all the patients who have the disease); but, labeled data are rare if detection tests for this disease are expensive. As a

---

* This research was partially supported by "Motricité et Cognition" : Contrat par objectifs région Nord/Pas-de-Calais

O. Watanabe, T. Yokomori (Eds.): ALT'99, LNAI 1720, pp. 219–230, 1999.

second example, consider mailing for a specific marketing action: unlabeled data are all the clients in the database; positive data are all the clients who asked information about the product concerned by the marketing action before the mailing was done; but, labeled data are rare and expensive because a survey has to be done on a part of the database of all clients. We do not address text classification problems in the present paper, but they are concerned too: for a web-page classification problem, unlabeled web-pages can be inexpensively gathered, a set of web pages you are interested in is available in your bookmarks, labeled web-pages are fairly expensive but a small set of hand labeled web-pages can be designed.

It has been proved in [Den98] that many concepts classes, namely those which are learnable from statistical queries, can be efficiently learned in a PAC framework using positive and unlabeled data only. But the price to pay is an increase in the number of examples needed to achieve learning (although it remains of polynomial size). We consider the problem of learning with a small set of labeled examples, a set of positive examples and a large set of unlabeled examples. We assume that unlabeled examples are drawn according to some hidden distribution $D$, that labeled examples are drawn according to the standard example oracle $EX(f, D)$, and that positive examples are drawn according to the oracle $EX(f, D_f)$ where $D_f$ is the distribution $D$ restricted to positive examples. The reader should note that our problem is different from the problem of learning with imbalanced training sets (see [KM97]) because we use three sources of examples. In the method we discuss here, labeled examples are only used to estimate the target weight (the proportion of positive examples among all examples); therefore, if an estimate of the target weight is available for the problem, only positive and unlabeled data are needed. We present experimental results showing that unlabeled data and positive data can efficiently boost accuracy of the statistical query learning algorithm for monotone conjunctions in the presence of classification noise. Such boosting can be explained by the fact that SQ algorithms are based on the estimate of probabilities. We prove that these estimates could be replaced by: an estimate of the weight of the target concept with respect to (w.r.t.) the hidden distribution using the (small) set of labeled examples and estimates of probabilities which can be computed from positive and unlabeled data only. If the sets of unlabeled and positive data are large enough, all estimates can be calculated within the accuracy of the estimate of the weight of the target concept. We present theoretical arguments in the PAC framework showing that a gain in the size of the query space (or its VC dimension) can be obtained on the number of labeled examples. But as usual, the results could be better for real problems.

In the last section of the paper, we consider standard methods of decision tree induction and examine the commonly used C4.5 algorithm described in [Qui93]. In this algorithm, when refining a leaf into an internal node, the decision criterion is based on statistical values. Therefore, C4.5 can be seen as a statistical query algorithm and the above ideas can be applied. We adapt the code of C4.5. Our algorithm takes as inputs three sets: a set of labeled examples, a set of positive examples and a set of unlabeled examples. The information gain criterion used by C4.5 is modified such that the three sets are used. The reader should note that labeled examples are used only once for the computation of the weight of the target concept under the hidden distribution. We provide some promising experimental results, but further experiments are needed for an experimental validation of our approach.

## 2   Preliminaries

### 2.1   Basic Definitions and Notations

For each $n \geq 1$, $X_n$ denotes an instance space on $n$ attributes. A concept $f$ is a subset of some instance space $X_n$ or equivalently a $\{0,1\}$-valued function defined on $X_n$. For each $n \geq 1$, let $C_n \subset 2^{X_n}$ be a set of concepts. Then $C = \bigcup C_n$ denotes a concept class over $X = \bigcup X_n$. The *size* of a concept $f$ is the size of a smallest representation for a given representation scheme. An *example* of a concept $f$ is a pair $\langle x, f(x) \rangle$, which is *positive* if $f(x) = 1$ and *negative* otherwise. We denote by $Pos(f)$ the set of all $x$ such that $f(x) = 1$. If $D$ is a distribution defined over $X$ and if $A$ is a subset of the instance space $X$, we denote by $D(A)$ the probability of the event $[x \in A]$ and we denote by $D_A$ the induced distribution. For instance, if $f$ is a concept over $X$ such that $D(f) \neq 0$, $D_f(x) = D(x)/D(f)$ if $x \in Pos(f)$ and 0 otherwise. We denote by $\overline{f}$ the complement of the set $f$ in $X$ and $f \Delta g$ the symmetric difference between $f$ and $g$. A *monotone conjunction* is a conjunction of boolean variables . For each $x \in \{0,1\}^n$, we use the notation $x(i)$ to indicate the $i$th bit of $x$. If $V$ is a subset of $\{x_1, \dots, x_n\}$, the conjunction of variables in $V$ is denoted by $\Pi_{x_i \in V} x_i$. If $V = \emptyset$, $\Pi_{x_i \in V} x_i = 1$.

### 2.2   PAC and SQ Models

Let $f$ be a target concept in some concept class $C$. Let $D$ be the hidden distribution defined over $X$. In the PAC model [Val84], the learner is given access to an example oracle $EX(f, D)$ which returns at each call an example $\langle x, f(x) \rangle$ drawn randomly according to $D$. A concept class $C$ is *PAC learnable* if there exist a learning algorithm $L$ and a polynomial $p(., ., ., .)$ with the following property: for any $f \in C$, for any distribution $D$ on $X$, and for any $0 < \epsilon < 1$ and $0 < \delta < 1$, if $L$ is given access to $EX(f, D)$ and to inputs $\epsilon$ and $\delta$, then with probability at least $1 - \delta$, $L$ outputs a hypothesis concept $h$ satisfying $error(h) = D(f \Delta h) \leq \epsilon$ in time bounded by $p(1/\epsilon, 1/\delta, n, size(f))$.

The SQ-model [Kea93] is a specialization of the PAC model in which the learner forms its hypothesis solely on the basis of estimates of probabilities. A *statistical query* over $X_n$ is a mapping $\chi : X_n \times \{0,1\} \to \{0,1\}$ associated with a tolerance $0 < \tau \leq 1$. In the SQ-model the learner is given access to a statistics oracle $STAT(f, D)$ which, at each query $(\chi, \tau)$, returns an estimate of $D(\{x \mid \chi(\langle x, f(x) \rangle) = 1\})$ within accuracy $\tau$. Let $C$ be a concept class over $X$. We say that $C$ is *SQ-learnable* if there exist a learning algorithm $L$ and polynomials

$p(.,.,.), q(.,.,.)$ and $r(.,.,.)$ with the following property: for any $f \in C$, for any distribution $D$ over $X$, and for any $0 < \epsilon < 1$, if $L$ is given access to $STAT(f, D)$ and to an input $\epsilon$, then, for every query $(\chi, \tau)$ made by $L$, the predicate $\chi$ can be evaluated in time $q(1/\epsilon, n, size(f))$, and $1/\tau$ is bounded by $r(1/\epsilon, n, size(f))$, $L$ halts in time bounded by $p(1/\epsilon, n, size(f))$ and $L$ outputs a hypothesis $h \in C$ satisfying $D(f \Delta h) \leq \epsilon$.

It is clear that given access to the example oracle $EX(f, D)$, it is easy to simulate the statistics oracle $STAT(f, D)$ drawing a sufficiently large set of labeled examples. This is formalized by the following result:

**Theorem 1.** *[Kea93] Let $C$ be a class of concepts over $X$. Suppose that $C$ is SQ learnable by algorithm $L$. Then $C$ is PAC learnable, and furthermore:*

- *If $L$ uses a finite query space $Q$ and $\alpha$ is a lower bound on the allowed approximation error for every query made by $L$, the number of calls of $EX(f, D)$ is $O(1/\alpha^2 \log |Q|/\delta)$*
- *If $L$ uses a query space $Q$ of finite VC dimension $d$ and $\alpha$ is a lower bound on the allowed approximation error for every query made by $L$, the number of calls of $EX(f, D)$ is $O(d/\alpha^2 \log 1/\delta)$*

The reader should note that this result has been extended to white noise PAC models: the Classification Noise model of Angluin and Laird [AL88]; the Constant Partition Classification Noise Model [Dec97]. The proofs may be found in [Kea93] and [Dec97]. Also note that almost all the concept classes known to be PAC learnable are SQ learnable and are therefore PAC learnable with classification noise.

## 3 Learning Monotone Conjunctions in the Presence of Classification Noise

In this section, the target concept is a monotone conjunction over $\{x_1, \ldots, x_n\}$. In the noise free case, a learning algorithm for monotone conjunctions is:

---

**Learning Monotone Conjunctions - Noise Free Case**
**input:** $\epsilon, \delta$
   $V = \emptyset$
   Draw a sample $S$ of $m(\epsilon, \delta)$ examples
   **for** i=1 to n **do**
      **if** for every positive example $\langle x, 1 \rangle$, $x(i) = 1$ **then** $V \leftarrow V \cup \{x_i\}$
**output:** $h = \Pi_{x_i \in V} x_i$

---

It can be proved that $O(1/\epsilon \log 1/\delta + n/\epsilon)$ examples are enough to guarantee that the hypothesis $h$ output by the learning algorithm has error less than $\epsilon$ with confidence at least $1 - \delta$. The given algorithm is not noise-tolerant. In the presence of classification noise, it is necessary to compute an estimate $\widehat{p_1}(x_i = 0)$ of $p_1(x_i = 0)$ which is the probability that a random example according to the hidden distribution $D$ is positive and satisfies $x(i) = 0$. Then only variables such that this estimate is small enough are included in the output hypothesis. Let us suppose that examples are drawn according to a noisy oracle which, on each call, first draws an instance $x$ according to $D$ together with its correct label and then flips the label with probability $0 \leq \eta < 1/2$. Let us suppose that the noise rate $\eta$ is known, then we can consider the following learning algorithm of monotone conjunctions from statistics in the presence of classification noise:

---

**Learning Monotone Conjunctions - Noise Tolerant Case**
**input:** $\epsilon$, $\delta$ , $\eta$
  $V = \emptyset$
  Draw a sample $S$ of $m(\epsilon, \delta, \eta)$ examples
  *the size of $S$ is sufficient to ensure that the following estimates*
  *are accurate to within $\epsilon/(2n)$ with a confidence greater that $1 - \delta$*
  **for** i=1 to n **do**
    compute an estimate $\widehat{p_1}(x_i = 0)$ of $p_1(x_i = 0)$
    **if** $\widehat{p_1}(x_i = 0) \leq \epsilon/(2n)$ **then** $V \leftarrow V \cup \{x_i\}$
**output:** $h = \Pi_{x_i \in V} x_i$

---

If the noise rate is not known, we can estimate it with techniques described in [AL88]. We do not consider that case because we want to show the best expected gain.

Let $q_1(x_i = 0)$ (resp. $q_0(x_i = 0)$) be the probability that a random example according to the noisy oracle is positive (resp. negative) and satisfies $x(i) = 0$. We have:

$$p_1(x_i = 0) = \frac{(1 - \eta)q_1(x_i = 0) - \eta q_0(x_i = 0)}{1 - 2\eta} \tag{1}$$

Thus we can estimate $p_1(x_i = 0)$ using estimates of $q_1(x_i = 0)$ and $q_0(x_i = 0)$. Then simple algebra and standard Chernoff bound may be used to prove that $O\left[(n^2 \log n)/(\epsilon^2(1 - 2\eta)^2) \log 1/\delta\right]$ examples are sufficient to guarantee that the hypothesis $h$ output by the learning algorithm has error less than $\epsilon$ with confidence at least $1 - \delta$. The reader should note that this bound is quite larger than the noise free case one. We now make the assumption that labeled examples are rare, but that sources of unlabeled examples and positive examples are available to the learner. Unlabeled examples are drawn according to $D$. A noisy positive oracle, on each call, draws examples from the noisy oracle until it gets one with label 1.

We raise the following problems:

- How can we use positive and unlabeled examples in the previous learning algorithm?
- What could be the expected gain?

In the learning algorithm of conjunctions from statistics with noise, an estimate of $p_1(x_i = 0)$ is calculated using (1). From usual formulas for conditional probabilities, $q_1(x_i = 0)$ may be expressed as the probability $q(1)$ that a labeled example is positive according to the noisy oracle times the probability $q_f(x_i = 0)$ that a positive example (drawn according to the positive noisy oracle) satisfies $x(i) = 0$. Now, using the formula for probabilities of disjoint events, $q_0(x_i = 0)$ is equal to the probability $q(x_i = 0)$ that an unlabeled example (drawn according to D) satisfies $x(i) = 0$ minus $q_1(x_i = 0)$. Thus, to compute an estimate of $p_1(x_i = 0)$, we use the following equations: $q_1(x_i = 0) = q(1) \times q_f(x_i = 0)$, $q_0(x_i = 0) = q(x_i = 0) - q_1(x_i = 0)$ and $p_1(x_i = 0) = [(1 - \eta)q_1(x_i = 0) - \eta q_0(x_i = 0)]/(1 - 2\eta)$. Consequently, to compute estimates of $p_1(x_i = 0)$ for all $i$, we have to compute an estimate of $q(1)$ with labeled examples, estimates of $q_f(x_i = 0)$ for every $i$ using the source of positive examples, and compute estimates of $q_0(x_i = 0)$ for every $i$ using the source of unlabeled examples. The reader should note that labeled examples are used *only* once for the calculation of an estimate of the probability that a labeled example is positive. Thus, we have given a positive answer to our first question: unlabeled examples and positive examples can be used in the learning algorithm of conjunctions from statistics. We now raise the second question, that is: what could be the expected gain? We give below an experimental answer to these questions.

We compare three algorithms:

- The first one is the learning algorithm of conjunctions from statistics where only labeled examples are used
- The second one computes an estimate of $q(1)$ from labeled examples and uses exact values for $q_f(x_i = 0)$ and $q_0(x_i = 0)$. That amounts to say that an *infinite* pool of positive and unlabeled data is available
- The third one computes an estimate of $q(1)$ from labeled examples and estimates of $q_f(x_i = 0)$ and $q_0(x_i = 0)$ from a *finite* number of positive and unlabeled examples

Each of these three algorithms outputs an ordered list $V = (x_{\sigma(1)}, \ldots, x_{\sigma(n)})$ of variables such that, for each $i$, $\widehat{p_1}(x_{\sigma(i)} = 0) \leq \widehat{p_1}(x_{\sigma(i+1)} = 0)$. For a given ordered list $V$, and for each $i$, we define $g_i(V) = \Pi_{j \leq i} x_{\sigma(j)}$. The minimal error of an ordered list $V$ is defined as $error_{min}(V) = min\{error(g_i(V)) \mid 0 \leq i \leq n\}$ which is the least error rate we can hope. We compare the minimal errors for the three algorithms. First, let us make more precise these three algorithms. We recall that labeled examples are drawn from a noisy oracle, that positive examples are drawn from the noisy oracle restricted to positive examples, and that the noise rate $\eta$ is known.

---

**Algorithm $L(LAB_N)$**
**input:** a sample $LAB$ of $N$ labeled examples
   for i=1 to n **do**
      $\widehat{q_1}(x_i = 0) = |\{\langle x, c \rangle \in LAB \mid x(i) = 0 \wedge c = 1\}|/N$
      $\widehat{q_0}(x_i = 0) = |\{\langle x, c \rangle \in LAB \mid x(i) = 0 \wedge c = 0\}|/N$
      $\widehat{p_1}(x_i = 0) = \frac{(1-\eta)\widehat{q_1}(x_i=0)-\eta\widehat{q_0}(x_i=0)}{1-2\eta}$
   **output:** ordered list $V = (x_{\sigma(1)}, \ldots, x_{\sigma(n)})$

| Algorithm $L(LAB_N, POS_\infty, UNL_\infty)$ | Algorithm $L(LAB_N, POS_M, UNL_M)$ |
|---|---|
| **input:** a sample $LAB$ of $N$ labeled examples | **input:** a sample $LAB$ of $N$ labeled examples, |
| $\widehat{q}(1) = \|\{\langle x, c\rangle \in LAB \mid c = 1\}\|/N$ | a sample $POS$ of $M$ positive examples |
| **for** i=1 to n **do** | and a sample $UNL$ of $M$ unlabeled examples |
| compute exactly $q_f(x_i = 0)$ | $\widehat{q}(1) = \|\{\langle x, c\rangle \in LAB \mid c = 1\}\|/N$ |
| compute exactly $q(x_i = 0)$ | **for** i=1 to n **do** |
| $\widehat{q_1}(x_i = 0) = \widehat{q}(1) \times q_f(x_i = 0)$ | $\widehat{q_f}(x_i = 0) = \|\{\langle x, c\rangle \in POS \mid x(i) = 0\}\|/M$ |
| $\widehat{q_0}(x_i = 0) = q(x_i = 0) - \widehat{q_1}(x_i = 0)$ | $\widehat{q}(x_i = 0) = \|\{x \in UNL \mid x(i) = 0\}\|/M$ |
| $\widehat{p_1}(x_i = 0) = \frac{(1-\eta)\widehat{q_1}(x_i=0) - \eta\widehat{q_0}(x_i=0)}{1-2\eta}$ | $\widehat{q_1}(x_i = 0) = \widehat{q}(1) \times \widehat{q_f}(x_i = 0)$ |
| **output:** ordered list $V = (x_{\sigma(1)}, \dots, x_{\sigma(n)})$ | $\widehat{q_0}(x_i = 0) = \widehat{q}(x_i = 0) - \widehat{q_1}(x_i = 0)$ |
| | $\widehat{p_1}(x_i = 0) = \frac{(1-\eta)\widehat{q_1}(x_i=0) - \eta\widehat{q_0}(x_i=0)}{1-2\eta}$ |
| | **output:** ordered list $V = (x_{\sigma(1)}, \dots, x_{\sigma(n)})$ |

Now, we describe experiments and experimental results [1]. The concept class is the class of monotone conjunctions over $n$ variables $x_1, \dots, x_n$ for some $n$. The target concept is a conjunction containing five variables. The class $\mathcal{D}$ of distributions is defined as follows: $D \in \mathcal{D}$ is characterized by a tuple $(\rho_1, \dots, \rho_n) \in [0, \rho]^n$ where $\rho = 2(1 - 2^{-\frac{1}{5}}) \simeq 0.26$; for a given $D \in \mathcal{D}$, all values $x(i)$ are selected independently of each other, and $x(i)$ is set to 0 with probability $\rho_i$ and set to 1 with probability $1 - \rho_i$. Note that $\rho$ has been chosen such that, if each $\rho_i$ is drawn randomly and independently in $[0, \rho]$, the average weight of the target concept $f$ w.r.t. $D$ is 0.5. We suppose that examples are drawn accordingly to noisy oracles where the noise rate $\eta$ is set to 0.2.

**Experiment 1.** The number $n$ of variables is set to 100. We compare the averages of minimal errors for algorithms $L(LAB_N)$ and $L(LAB_N, POS_\infty, UNL_\infty)$ as functions of the number $N$ of labeled examples. For a given $N$, averages of minimal errors for an algorithm are obtained doing $k$ times the following:

- $f$ is a randomly chosen conjunction of five variables
- $D$ is chosen randomly in $\mathcal{D}$ by choosing randomly and independently each $\rho_i$
- $N$ examples are drawn randomly w.r.t. $D$, they are labeled according to the target concept $f$, then the correct label is flipped with probability $\eta$
- Minimal errors for $L(LAB_N)$ and $L(LAB_N, POS_\infty, UNL_\infty)$ are computed

and then compute the averages over the $k$ iterations. We set $k$ to 100. The results can be seen in Fig. 1. The top plot corresponds to $L(LAB_N)$ and the bottom plot to $L(LAB_N, POS_\infty, UNL_\infty)$.

**Experiment 2.** We now consider a more realistic case: there are $M$ positive examples and an equal number of unlabeled examples. We show that together with a small number $N$ of labeled examples, these positive and unlabeled examples give about as much information as do $M$ labeled examples alone. We compare the averages of minimal errors for algorithms $L(LAB_N, POS_M, UNL_M)$ and $L(LAB_M)$ as functions of $M$. The number $n$ of variables is set to 100. The number $N$ of labeled examples is set to 10. The results can be seen in Fig. 1.

---

[1] Sources and scripts can be found at
ftp://grappa.univ-lille3.fr/pub/Softs/posunlab.

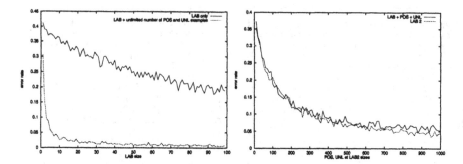

**Fig. 1.** results of experiments 1 and 2. For experiment 1: target size = 5; 100 variables; 100 iterations. This figure shows the gain we can expect using free positive and unlabeled data. For experiment 2: target size = 5; 100 variables; 100 iterations; $size(LAB) = 10$; $size(POS) = size(UNL) = size(LAB2) = M$; $M$ ranges from 10 to 1000 by step 10. These curves show that with only 10 labeled examples, the learning algorithm performs almost as well with $M$ positive and $M$ unlabeled examples as with $M$ labeled examples.

## 4   Theoretical Framework

Let $C$ be a class of concepts over $X$. Suppose that $C$ is SQ learnable by some algorithm $L$. Let $f$ be the target concept and let us consider a statistical query $\chi$ made by $L$. The statistics oracle $STAT(f, D)$ returns an estimate $\widehat{D}_\chi$ of $D_\chi = D(\{x \mid \chi(\langle x, f(x)\rangle) = 1\})$ within some given accuracy. We may write: $D_\chi = D(\{x \mid \chi(\langle x, 1\rangle) = 1 \land f(x) = 1\}) + D(\{x \mid \chi(\langle x, 0\rangle) = 1 \land f(x) = 0\}) = D(\{x \mid \chi(\langle x, 1\rangle) = 1\} \cap f) + D(\{x \mid \chi(\langle x, 0\rangle) = 1\} \cap \overline{f}) = D(A \cap f) + D(B \cap \overline{f})$ where the sets $A$ and $B$ are defined by: $A = \{x \mid \chi(\langle x, 1\rangle) = 1\}$, $B = \{x \mid \chi(\langle x, 0\rangle) = 1\}$. Furthermore, let $A$ be any subset of the instance space $X$ and $f$ be a concept over $X$, we have $D(A \cap f) = D_f(A) \times D(f)$ and $D(A \cap \overline{f}) = D(A) - D(A \cap f)$. From the preceding equations, we obtain that $D_\chi = D(f) \times (D_f(A) - D_f(B)) + D(B)$.

Now, in order to estimate $D_\chi$, it is sufficient to estimate $D(f)$, $D_f(A)$, $D_f(B)$ and $D(B)$. If we get an estimate of $D(f)$ within accuracy $\alpha$ and estimates of $D_f(A)$, $D_f(B)$ and $D(B)$ within accuracy $\beta$, it can be easily shown that $D(f) \times (D_f(A) - D_f(B)) + D(B)$ is an estimate of $D(f)$ within accuracy $\alpha + \beta(3 + 2\alpha)$.

As usual, $D(f)$ can be estimated using the oracle $EX(f, D)$. We can estimate $D_f(A)$ and $D_f(B)$ using the POS oracle $EX(f, D_f)$. We can estimate $D(B)$ with the UNL oracle $EX(1, D)$. So we can modify any statistical query based algorithm so that it uses the EX, POS and UNL oracles. Furthermore, if the standard algorithm makes $N$ queries, labeled, positive and unlabeled example sources will be used to estimate respectively 1, $2N$ and $N$ queries.

In this paper, we make the assumption that labeled examples are "expensive" and that unlabeled and positive examples are "cheap". If we make the stronger assumption that positive and unlabeled data are free, we can estimate $D_f(A)$,

$D_f(B)$ and $D(B)$ within arbitrary accuracy, i.e. $\beta = 0$. If $\tau_{min}$ is the smallest tolerance needed by the learning algorithm $L$ and whatever is the number of queries made by $L$, we see that we only need labeled examples to estimate **only one** probability, say $D(f)$, within accuracy $\tau_{min}$. Let $Q$ be the query space used by $L$. Theorem 1 gives an upper bound of the number of calls of $EX(f, D)$ necessary to simulate the statistical queries needed by $L$. We see that we can expect to divide this number of calls by $VCDIM(Q)$.

A more precise theoretical study remains to be done. For instance, it should be interesting to estimate the expected improvements of the accuracy when the number of labeled examples is fixed depending on the number of positive and unlabeled examples. This could be done for each usual statistical query learning algorithm.

# 5   Tree Induction from Labeled, Positive, and Unlabeled Data

C4.5, and more generally decision tree based learning algorithms are SQ-like algorithms because attribute test choices depend on statistical queries. After a brief presentation of C4.5 and as C4.5 is an SQ algorithm, we describe in Sect. 5.2 how to adapt it for the treatment of positive and unlabeled data. We finally discuss experimental results of a modified version of C4.5 which uses positive and unlabeled examples.

## 5.1   C4.5, a Top-Down Decision Tree Algorithm

Most algorithms for tree induction use a top-down, greedy search through the space of decision trees. The *splitting criterion* used by C4.5 [Qui93] is based on a statistical property, called *information gain*, itself based on a measure from information theory, called *entropy*. Given a sample $S$ of some target concept, the entropy of $S$ is $Entropy(S) = \sum_{i=1}^{c} -p_i \log_2 p_i$ where $p_i$ is the proportion of examples in $S$ belonging to the class $i$. The information gain is the expected reduction in entropy by partitioning the sample according to an attribute test $t$. It is defined as

$$Gain(S, t) = Entropy(S) - \sum_{v \in Values(t)} \frac{N_v}{N} Entropy(S_v) \qquad (2)$$

where $Values(t)$ is the set of every possible value for the attribute test $t$, $N_v$ is the cardinality of the set $S_v$ of examples in $S$ for which $t$ has value $v$ and $N$ is the cardinality of $S$.

## 5.2   C4.5 with Positive and Unlabeled Data

Let $X$ be the instance space, we only consider binary classification problems. The classes are denoted by 0 and 1, an example is said to be positive if its label is 1. Let $POS$ be a sample of positive examples of some target concept $f$, let $LAB$ be a sample of labeled examples and let $UNL$ be a set of unlabeled data. Let $D$ be the hidden distribution which is defined over $X$. $POS$ is a set of examples $\langle x, f(x) = 1 \rangle$ returned by an example oracle $EX(f, D_f)$, $LAB$ is a set of examples $\langle x, f(x) \rangle$ returned by an example oracle $EX(f, D)$ and $UNL$ is a set of instances $x$ drawn according to the distribution $D$. The entropy of a sample $S$ is defined by $Entropy(S) = -p_0 \log_2 p_0 - p_1 \log_2 p_1$. In this formula, $S$ is the set of training examples associated with the current node $n$ and $p_1$ is the proportion of positive examples in $S$. Let $D_n$ be the filtered distribution, that is the hidden distribution $D$ restricted to instances reaching the node $n$, let $X_n$ be the set of instances reaching the node $n$: $p_1$ is an estimation of $D_n(f)$. Now, in the light of the results of Sect. 4, we modify formulas for the calculation of the information gain. We have $D_n(f) = D(X_n \cap f)/D(X_n)$. Using the equation $D(X_n \cap f) = D_f(X_n) \times D(f)$, we obtain $D_n(f) = D_f(X_n) \times D(f) \times 1/D(X_n)$.

We can estimate $D_f(X_n)$ using the set of positive examples associated with the node $n$, we can estimate $D(f)$ with the complete set of labeled examples, and we can estimate $D(X_n)$ with unlabeled examples. More precisely, let $POS^n$ be the set of positive examples associated with the node $n$, let $UNL^n$ be the set of unlabeled examples associated with the node $n$, and let $LAB_1$ be the set of positive examples in the set of labeled examples $LAB$, the entropy of the node $n$ is calculated using the following:

$$p_1 = \inf \left( \frac{|POS^n|}{|POS|} \times \frac{|LAB_1|}{|LAB|} \times \frac{|UNL|}{|UNL^n|}, 1 \right); p_0 = 1 - p_1 \qquad (3)$$

The reader should note that $\frac{|LAB_1|}{|LAB|}$ is independent of the node $n$. We now define the information gain of the node $n$ by $Gain(n, t) = Entropy(n) - \sum_{v \in Values(t)} (N_v^n/N^n) Entropy(nv)$ where $Values(t)$ is the set of every possible value for the attribute test $t$, $N^n$ is the cardinality of $UNL^n$, $N_v^n$ is the cardinality of the set $UNL_v^n$ of examples in $UNL^n$ for which $t$ has value $v$, and $nv$ is the node below $n$ corresponding to the value $v$ for the attribute test $t$.

## 5.3   Experimental Results

We applied the results of the previous section to C4.5 and called the resulting algorithm C4.5PosUnl. The differences as compared with C4.5 are the following:

- C4.5PosUnl takes as input three sets: $LAB$, $POS$ and $UNL$
- $|LAB_1|/|LAB|$ which appears in (3) is calculated only once
- For the current node, entropy and gain are calculated using (3)
- When gain ratio is used, split information is calculated with unlabeled examples
- The majority class is chosen using (3)
- halting criteria during the top-down tree generation are evaluated on $UNL$
- When pruning the tree, classification errors are estimated with the help of proportions $p_0$ and $p_1$ from (3)

We consider two data sets from the *UCI Machine Learning Database* [MM98]: kr-vs-kp and adult. The majority class is chosen as positive. We fix the sizes of the test set, set of positive examples, and set of unlabeled examples. These values are set to:

- For kr-vs-kp: 1000 for the test set, 600 for the set of positive examples, and to 600 for the set of unlabeled examples
- For adult: 15000 for the test set, 10000 for the set of positive examples, and to 10000 for the set of unlabeled examples

We let the number of labeled examples vary, and compare the error rate of C4.5 and C4.5PosUnl. For a given size of *LAB*, we iterate 100 times the following: all sets are selected randomly (for *POS*, a larger set is drawn and only the selected number of positive examples are kept), we compute the error rate for C4.5 with input *LAB* and the error rate for C4.5PosUnl with input *LAB*, *POS* and *UNL*. Then, we average out the error rates over the 1000 experiments.

The results can be seen in Fig. 2. The error rates are promising when the number of labeled examples is small (e.g. less than 100). We think that the better results of C4.5 for higher number of examples is due to our pruning algorithm which does not use in the best way positive and unlabeled examples (C4.5PosUnl trees are consistently larger than C4.5 ones).

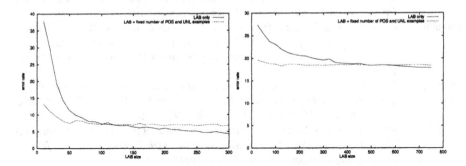

**Fig. 2.** error rate of C4.5 and C4.5PosUnl averaged over 100 trials. The left figure shows the results on the kr-vs-kp data set and the right one corresponds to the adult data set.

adult and kr-vs-kp were selected in this paper because they are well known and contain many examples. The experiments were run on all other two-class UCI problems (ftp://grappa.univ-lille3.fr/pub/Experiments/C45PosUnl).

## 6   Conclusion

In many practical learning situations, labeled data are rare or expensive to collect while a great number of positive and unlabeled data are available. In this paper, we have given experimental and theoretical evidence that these kind of examples can efficiently be used to boost statistical query learning algorithms. A lot of work remains to be done, in several directions:

- More precise theoretical results must be stated, at least for specific statistical query learning algorithms
- C4.5 should be modified further, especially the pruning algorithm which must be adapted to the data types presented in this paper
- We intend to collect real data of the kind studied here (labeled, positive and unlabeled) to test this new variant of C4.5
- Our method can be applied to any statistical query algorithm. It would be interesting to know if it can be appropriate elsewhere

# References

[AL88]       D. Angluin and P. Laird. Learning from noisy examples. *Machine Learning*, 2(4):343–370, 1988.

[BM98]       A. Blum and T. Mitchell. Combining labeled and unlabeled data with co-training. In *Proc. 11th Annu. Conf. on Comput. Learning Theory*, pages 92–100. ACM Press, New York, NY, 1998.

[Dec97]      S. E. Decatur. Pac learning with constant-partition classification noise and applications to decision tree induction. In *Proceedings of the Fourteenth International Conference on Machine Learning*, 1997.

[Den98]      F. Denis. Pac learning from positive statistical queries. In *ALT 98, 9th International Conference on Algorithmic Learning Theory*, volume 1501 of *Lecture Notes in Artificial Intelligence*, pages 112–126. Springer-Verlag, 1998.

[Kea93]      M. Kearns. Efficient noise-tolerant learning from statistical queries. In *Proceedings of the 25th ACM Symposium on the Theory of Computing*, pages 392–401. ACM Press, New York, NY, 1993.

[KM97]       M. Kubat and S. Matwin. Addressing the curse of imbalanced training sets : One-sided selection. In *Proceedings of the 14th International Conference on Machine Learning*, pages 179–186, 1997.

[MM98]       C.J. Merz and P.M. Murphy. UCI repository of machine learning databases, 1998.

[NMTM98]  K. Nigam, A. McCallum, S. Thrun, and T. Mitchell. Learning to classify text from labeled and unlabeled documents. In *Proceedings of the 15th National Conference on Artificial Intelligence, AAAI-98*, 1998.

[Qui93]      J. R. Quinlan. *C4.5: Programs for Machine Learning*. Morgan Kaufmann, San Mateo, CA, 1993.

[Val84]      L.G. Valiant. A theory of the learnable. *Commun. ACM*, 27(11):1134–1142, November 1984.

# Learning Real Polynomials with a Turing Machine

Dennis Cheung

Department of Mathematics, City University of Hong Kong
83 Tat Chee Avenue, Kowloon, HONG KONG
50000548@plink.cityu.edu.hk

**Abstract.** We provide an algorithm to PAC learn multivariate polynomials with real coefficients. The instance space from which labeled
samples are drawn is $\mathbb{R}^N$ but the coordinates of such samples are known
only approximately. The algorithm is iterative and the main ingredient
of its complexity, the number of iterations it performs, is estimated using the condition number of a linear programming problem associated
to the sample. To the best of our knowledge, this is the first study of
PAC learning concepts parameterized by real numbers from approximate
data.

## 1 Introduction

In the PAC model of learning one often finds concepts parameterized by real
numbers. Examples of such concepts appear in the first pages of well-known
textbooks such as [7]. The algorithmics for learning such concepts follows the
same pattern as that for learning concepts parameterized by Boolean values.
One randomly selects a number of elements $x_1, \ldots, x_m$ in the instance space $X$.
Then, with the help of an oracle, one decides which of them satisfy the target
concept $c^*$. Finally, one computes a hypothesis $c^h$ which is consistent with the
sample, i.e. a concept $c^h$ which is satisfied by exactly those $x_i$ which satisfy $c^*$.

A main result from Blumer et al. [3] provides a bound for the size $m$ of the
sample above in order to guarrantee that the error of $c^h$ is less than $\varepsilon$ with
probability at least $1 - \delta$, namely

$$m \geq C_0 \left( \frac{1}{\varepsilon} \log \left( \frac{1}{\delta} \right) + \frac{\text{VCdim}(\mathcal{C})}{\varepsilon} \log \left( \frac{\delta}{\varepsilon} \right) \right) \qquad (1)$$

where $C_0$ is a universal constant and $\text{VCdim}(\mathcal{C})$ is the Vapnick-Chervonenkis
dimension of the concept class at hand. This result is specially useful when
concepts are not discrete entities (i.e. not representable using words over a finite
alphabet) since in this case one can bound the size of the sample without using
the VC dimension.

A particularly important case of concepts parameterized by real numbers is
the one in which the membership test of an instance $x \in X$ to a concept $c$ in the
concept class $\mathcal{C}$ can be expressed by a quantifier-free first-order formula. In this

O. Watanabe, T. Yokomori (Eds.): ALT'99, LNAI 1720, pp. 231–240, 1999.
© Springer-Verlag Berlin Heidelberg 1999

case, concepts in $\mathcal{C}_{n,N}$ are parameterized by elements in $\mathbb{R}^n$, the instance space $X$ is the Euclidean space $\mathbb{R}^N$, and the membership of $x \in X$ to $c \in \mathcal{C}$ is given by the truth of $\Psi_{n,N}(x,c)$ where $\Psi_{n,N}$ is a quantifier-free first-order formula of the theory of the reals with $n + N$ free variables. In this case, a result of Goldberg and Jerrum [5] bounds the VC-dimension of $\mathcal{C}_{n,N}$ by

$$\mathrm{VCdim}(\mathcal{C}_{n,N}) \leq 2n\log(8eds). \tag{2}$$

Here $d$ is a bound for the degrees of the polynomials appearing in $\Psi_{n,N}$ and $s$ is a bound for the number of distinct atomic predicates in $\Psi_{n,N}$.

One may say that, at this stage, the problem of PAC learning a concept $c^* \in \mathcal{C}_{n,N}$ is solved. Given $\varepsilon, \delta > 0$ we simply compute $m$ satisfying (1) with the VC-dimension replaced by the bound in (2). Then we randomly draw $x_1, \ldots, x_m \in X$ and finally we compute a hypothesis $c^h \in \mathcal{C}_{n,N}$ consistent with the membership of $x_i$ to $c^*$, $i = 1, \ldots, m$ (which we obtain from some oracle). To obtain $c^h$ we may use any of the algorithms proposed recently to solve the first-order theory of the reals (cf. [6, 8, 1]).

It is however at this stage that our research has its starting point by remarking that, from a practical viewpoint, we can not exactly read the elements $x_i$. Instead, we obtain rational approximations $\tilde{x}_i$. As an example, imagine that we want to learn how to classify some kind of stones according as to whether a stone satisfies a certain concept $c^*$ or not. For each stone we measure $N$ parameters —e.g. radioactivity, weight, etc.— and we have access to a collection of such stones already classified. That is, for each stone in the collection, we know whether the stone satisfies $c^*$. When we measure one of the parameters $x_i$ of a stone, say the weight, we don't obtain the exact weight but an approximation $\tilde{x}_i$. The membership of this stone to $c^*$ depends nevertheless on $x = (x_1, \ldots, x_N)$ and not on $\tilde{x}$. Our problem thus, becomes that of learning $c^*$ from approximate data. A key feature is that we know the precision $\rho$ of these approximations and that we can actually modify $\rho$ in our algorithm to obtain better approximations. In our example this corresponds to fixing the number of digits appearing on the display of our measuring instrument.

In this paper we give an algorithm to learn from approximate data for a particular learning problem namely, PAC learning the coefficients of a multivariate polynomial from the signs ($\geq 0$ or $< 0$) the polynomial takes over a sample of points. While there are several papers dealing with this problem (e.g. [11, 2]) they either consider Boolean variables, i.e. $X = \{0,1\}^N$, or they work over finite fields. To the best of our knowledge, the consideration of rounded-off real data is new.

In studying the complexity of our algorithm we will naturally deal with a classical theme in numerical analysis, that of conditioning, and we will find the common dependence of running time on the condition number of the input (cf. [4]).

## 2    The Problem

Consider the class $\mathcal{P}_{d,N}^O$ of real polynomials of degree $d$ in $N$ variables which have a certain fixed monomial structure. That is, fix a subset $O \subset \mathbb{N}^N$ such that for all $\alpha = (\alpha_1, \ldots, \alpha_N) \in O$, $\alpha_1 + \cdots + \alpha_N \leq d$. Thus, the elements in $\mathcal{P}_{d,N}^O$ have the form

$$f = \sum_{\alpha \in O} c_\alpha y^\alpha$$

with $c_\alpha \in \mathbb{R}$, and $y^\alpha = y_1^{\alpha_1} \cdots y_N^{\alpha_N}$. Let $n$ be the cardinality of $O$. We will denote by $c$ the vector of coefficients of $f$ and assume an ordering of the elements in $O$ so that $c = (c_1, \ldots, c_n)$. Also, to emphasize the dependance of $f$ on its coefficient vector we will write the polynomial above as $f_c$.

Our goal is to PAC learn a target polynomial $f_{c^*}$ with coefficients $c^*$. The instance space is $\mathbb{R}^N$ and we assume a probability distribution $\mathcal{D}$ over it. For an instance $y \in \mathbb{R}^N$, we say that $y$ satisfies $c^*$ when $f_{c^*}(y) \geq 0$. This makes $\mathcal{P}_{d,N}^O$ into a concept class by associating to each $f \in \mathcal{P}_{d,N}^O$ the concept set $\{y \in \mathbb{R}^N \mid f(y) \geq 0\}$.

The error of a hypothesis $f_{c^h}$ is given by

$$\text{Error}\,(c^h) = \text{Prob}\,(\text{sign}\,(f_{c^*}(y)) \neq \text{sign}\,(f_{c^h}(y)))$$

where the probability is taken according to $\mathcal{D}$ and the sign function is defined by

$$\text{sign}\,(z) = \begin{cases} 1 \text{ if } z \geq 0 \\ 0 \text{ otherwise} \end{cases}$$

As usual, we will suppose that an oracle $\text{EX}_{c^*} : \mathbb{R}^N \to \{0, 1\}$ is available computing $\text{EX}_{c^*}(y) = \text{sign}\,(f_{c^*}(y))$. We finally recall that a randomized algorithm PAC learns $f_{c^*}$ with error $\varepsilon$ and confidence $\delta$ when it returns a concept $c^h$ satisfying $\text{Error}\,(c^h) \leq \varepsilon$ with probability at least $1 - \delta$.

Should we be able to deal with arbitrary real numbers, the following algorithm would PAC learn $f_{c^*}$.

**Algorithm 1**
Input: $N, d, \epsilon$ and $\delta$
1. Compute $m$ using (1) and (2)
2. Draw $m$ random points $y^{(i)} \in \mathbb{R}^N$
3. Use the function $\text{EX}_{c^*}$ to obtain $\text{sign}\,(f_{c^*}(y^{(i)}))$ for $i = 1, \ldots, m$
4. From step 3, we obtain a number of linear inequalities in $c$ and these inequalities can be writen in matrix form

$$\begin{cases} B_1 c < 0 \\ B_2 c \leq 0 \end{cases}$$

5. Find any vector $c^h$ satisfying the system in step 4
6. Output: $c^h$

Note that, to execute step 5, we don't need the general algorithms for solving the first-order theory over the reals mentioned in the preceding section but only an algorithm to find a feasible point of a linear programming instance whose feasible set is non-empty (since $c^*$ belongs to it).

If real data can not be dealt with exactly, we need to proceed differently. We begin to do so in the next section, by discussing our model of round-off.

## 3    Round-Off and Errors

Let $y \in \mathbb{R}^N$. We say that $\tilde{y} \in \mathbb{Q}^N$ approximates $y$ with precision $\rho$, $0 < \rho < 1$ (or that $\tilde{y}$ is a measure of $y$ with such precision) when

$$|y_j - \tilde{y}_j| \leq \rho |y_j| \qquad \text{for } j = 1, \ldots, N.$$

*Remark. The definition above is the usual definition of relative precision found in numerical analysis. Numbers here are represented in the form*

$$z = \pm a \times 10^e$$

*where $e \in \mathbb{Z}$, $a = 0$ or $a \in [1, 10)$, and $a$ is written with $|\log_{10} \rho|$ digits. The number $a$ is called the* mantissa *of $z$ and the number $e$ its* exponent. *For instance*

$$3.14159 \times 10^0$$

*approximates $\pi$ with precision $10^{-6}$.*

*There is a strong correlation between $\rho$ and the number of digits (or bits) necessary to write down $\tilde{y}_j$. However, this correlation does not translate into a definite relation since the magnitude of $y_j$ (among other things) also contribute to determining this number of digits. For instance the number $1.23456 \times 10^{12}$ will use 13 digits when written down. On the other hand, $4.00000 \times 10^0$ only needs one digit. And both have precision $10^{-6}$.*

In our learning problem, we fix a precision $\rho$ and we measure each instance $y^{(i)}$ in our sample to obtain $\tilde{y}^{(i)}$. Consequently, when we compute $B_1$ and $B_2$ we do not obtain those matrices but rather some approximations $\tilde{B}_1$ and $\tilde{B}_2$. Our first result bounds the relative error (the precision) for the entries of $\tilde{B}_1$ and $\tilde{B}_2$.

**Theorem 1.** *Let $b$ be any entry of $B_1$ or $B_2$. If $|y_j^{(i)} - \tilde{y}_j^{(i)}| \leq \rho |y_j^{(i)}|$ for $i = 1, \ldots, m$ and $j = 1, \ldots, N$ then*

$$\frac{|b - \tilde{b}|}{|b|} \leq \sigma = (1 + \rho)^d - 1.$$

$\square$

A crucial remark at this stage is that if the feasible set of the system

$$\begin{cases} B_1 c < 0 \\ B_2 c \le 0 \end{cases}$$

has empty interior, no matter how small is $\rho$, the system

$$\begin{cases} \tilde{B}_1 c < 0 \\ \tilde{B}_2 c \le 0 \end{cases}$$

may have not solutions at all. Therefore, in the sequel, we will search only for interior solutions of the system. That is, we will search for solutions of the system

$$(\text{LP1}) \qquad Bc < 0 \qquad \text{with} \qquad B = \begin{bmatrix} B_1 \\ B_2 \end{bmatrix}.$$

Our problem remains to find a solution of $Bc < 0$ knowing only $\tilde{B}$. In the next section we will give a first step in this direction.

## 4    Narrowing the Feasible Set

Consider the system

$$(\text{LP2}) \quad \tilde{B}c < 0.$$

Let $A = (B, -B)$ and

$$(\text{LP3}) \begin{cases} Ax < 0 \\ x \ge 0 \end{cases}$$

with $x \in \mathbb{R}^{2n}$. Similarly, let $\tilde{A} = (\tilde{B}, -\tilde{B})$ and

$$(\text{LP4}) \begin{cases} \tilde{A}x < 0 \\ x \ge 0 \end{cases}$$

The following lemma is immediate.

**Lemma 2.** *For $i = 1, \ldots, m$ and $j = 1, \ldots, 2n$,* $\dfrac{|a_{ij} - \tilde{a}_{ij}|}{|a_{ij}|} \le \sigma = (1 + \rho)^d - 1.$

$\square$

Define $\overline{A}$ as follows. For $i = 1, \ldots, m$ and $j = 1, \ldots, 2n$ let

$$\overline{a}_{ij} = \begin{cases} \dfrac{\tilde{a}_{ij}}{1 - \sigma} & \text{if } \tilde{a}_{ij} \ge 0 \\[2mm] \dfrac{\tilde{a}_{ij}}{1 + \sigma} & \text{if } \tilde{a}_{ij} < 0. \end{cases}$$

Now consider the system

$$(\text{LP5}) \begin{cases} \overline{A}x < 0 \\ x \ge 0. \end{cases}$$

**Theorem 3.** *If $x$ is a solution of (LP5) and $x = (u,v)$ with $u,v \in \mathbb{R}^n$ then $c = u - v$ is a solution of (LP1).*    □

Theorem 3 inspires the following algorithm.

> **Algorithm 2**
> Input: $N, d, \epsilon$ and $\delta$
> 1. Compute $m$ using (1) and (2)
> 2. Get $m$ random points $y^{(i)} \in \mathbb{R}^N$
> 3. Use the function $\text{EX}_{c^*}$ to obtain $\text{sign}\,(f_{c^*}(y^{(i)}))$ for $i = 1, \ldots, m$
> 4. $\rho := (3/2)^{1/d} - 1$
> 5. Measure $y^{(i)}$ with precision $\rho$ to obtain $\widetilde{y}^{(i)}$, $i = 1, \ldots, m$
> 6. Write down the system (LP2), i.e., $\tilde{B}c < 0$
> 7. Transform system (LP2) to (LP4) and then to (LP5), as described above
> 8. If there is any vector $x^h$ satisfying (LP5)
>      return $c^h := u^h - v^h$ and HALT
>    else
>      $\rho := \rho^2$
>      go to step 5

*Remark.* The initial value $\rho_0$ for the precision is set to $(3/2)^{1/d} - 1$ since this implies $\sigma = 1/2$. We actually can take for $\rho_0$ the largest power of 2 smaller than $(3/2)^{1/d} - 1$.

At each iteration of the algorithm $\rho$ is squared. This corresponds to doubling the number of bits of the mantissas in the measures $\widetilde{y}^{(i)}_j$.

Before stepping into the analysis of Algorithm 2, we derive an upper bound for the relative error of $\overline{A}$ as an approximation of $A$. In the next statement, and in the rest of this paper, $\|\ \|$ denotes the 2-norm in Euclidean space.

**Proposition 4.** *If $\rho \leq (3/2)^{1/d} - 1$ then for $i = 1, \ldots, m$*

$$\frac{\|a_i - \overline{a}_i\|}{\|a_i\|} \leq 4\sigma.$$

□

## 5    Complexity and Condition

Algorithm 2 can be implemented on a Turing machine (modulo the oracle $\text{EX}_{c^*}$). Its running time its determined by two quantities:

1) the number of iterations performed by the algorithm, and
2) the bit-size of the rational numbers involved in the intermediate computations.

Notice that the cost of each iteration is dominated by step 8 and, more precisely, by checking the existence of a solution of (LP5). This is a linear programming problem over the rationals and, as such, it can be solved in polynomial time by either the ellipsoid method or the interior point method (see, e.g., [10]).

These methods work in time bounded by a polynomial of low degree in the dimension of the input system and linear in the largest bit-size of its entries. In our problem, the dimension of the input system is fixed $(m \times 2n)$ through all the iterations and is itself polynomial in $n, d, \varepsilon$ and $|\log \delta|$.

The bit-size of the entries of (LP5) presents a more complicated issue. It depends, on the one hand, on the largest and smaller (in absolute value) quantities among the $y_j^{(i)}$ and, on the other hand, on the precision $\rho$ with which these quantities are measured. The first number,

$$L = \max \left\{ |y_j^{(i)}|, \frac{1}{|y_j^{(i)}|} \;\middle|\; i \le m, \, j \le 2n, \, y_j^{(i)} \ne 0 \right\}$$

is not controlled by Algorithm 2. It is actually a random variable dependent on the distribution $\mathcal{D}$. The second number, the precision $\rho$, affects the bit-size of $\tilde{y}_j^{(i)}$ as observed in Remark 1.

In the rest of this paper we will focus on estimating the number of iterations performed by Algorithm 2. In doing so, it will be necessary to traverse the territory of linear programming and numerical analysis.

Let $b_i \in \mathbb{R}^n$ be the $i$th row of $B$ and $b_i^\perp$ be the hyperplane perpendicular to $b_i$ and passing through the origin. Note that $b_i^\perp$ is the boundary of the half-space defined by the inequality $b_i c < 0$.

**Definition 5.** *For every $c \in \mathbb{R}^n$ let $\theta_i(B, c)$ be the acute angle, i.e. $0 \le \theta_i(B, c) \le \frac{\pi}{2}$, between $c$ and the hyperplane $b_i^\perp$. Also, let*

$$\theta(B, c) = \min_{i=1,\ldots,m} \theta_i(B, c).$$

*Finally, let the condition number of $B$ be*

$$\mathcal{C}(B) = \min_{c \in \mathrm{Sol}(B)} \frac{1}{\sin \theta(B, c)}.$$

*Here $\mathrm{Sol}(B)$ denotes the set of points $c \in \mathbb{R}^n$ such that $Bc < 0$. We will denote by $\bar{c}$ any point in $\mathrm{Sol}(B)$ for which this minimum is attained.*

*Remark.* Note that $\bar{c}$ actually maximizes $\theta(B, c)$. Also, for $c \in \mathrm{Sol}(B)$, let $d_i$ be the distance between $c$ and $b_i^\perp$. Then, $d_i = \|c\| \sin \theta_i(B, c)$. So, we can rewrite $\mathcal{C}(B)$ as

$$\mathcal{C}(B) = \min_{c \in \mathrm{Sol}(B)} \frac{\|c\|}{\min_{i \le m} d_i}.$$

The expression $\frac{\min d_i}{\|c\|}$ can be seen as the (normalized) distance from $c$ to the boundary of $\mathrm{Sol}(B)$. So, $\bar{c}$ is a solution of (LP1) having a maximal distance to this boundary and $\mathcal{C}(B)$ is the inverse of this distance.

*Intuitively, if $C(B)$ is small (i.e. if $\theta(B, \bar{c})$ is large) a greater error can be allowed in the coefficients of $B$ and we may need less iterations in Algorithm 2. The following theoren, our main result, quantifies this fact.*

**Theorem 6.** *If $C(B) < \infty$ then the algorithm will halt and return a solution $c^h$. Furthermore, the number of iterations is bounded by the smallest integer greater than*

$$\log_2 \left( \frac{\log_2\left[\left(1 + \frac{1}{4\sqrt{2}C(B)}\right)^{\left(\frac{1}{d}\right)} - 1\right]}{\log_2(\rho_0)} \right)$$

*where $\rho_0$ is the value of $\rho$ set in step 4.* □

*Remark. Theorem 6 bounds the number of iterations in Algorithm 2 as a function of $C(B)$. We end this section by noting that $C(B)$ is actually a random variable since $B$ depends on the random sample $y^{(1)}, \ldots, y^{(m)}$. The number of iterations in Algorithm 2 is a random variable as well. Its expected value can be bounded by replacing $C(B)$ by its expected value in the bound of Theorem 6.*

## 6    A Characterization of $C(B)$

Condition numbers are defined in numerical analysis mainly for continuous functions $\varphi : \mathbb{R}^n \to \mathbb{R}^m$. At a point $x \in \mathbb{R}^n$, the condition number $\mu(x)$ measures the largest possible value

$$\frac{\|\varphi(x + \Delta) - \varphi(x)\|}{\|\Delta\|}$$

over all infinitesimal perturbations $\Delta$ of the point $x$.

A recurrent theme is the relation between $\mu(x)$ and the distance from $x$ to the set $\Sigma$ of *ill-posed* inputs, i.e. to the set of points $x \in \mathbb{R}^n$ such that $\mu(x) = \infty$. For a number of problems, the condition number $\mu(x)$ is the inverse to the distance from $x$ to $\Sigma$ (often multiplied by $\|x\|$ to scale properly).

For computational problems which are not describable by a function $\varphi$ as above the definition of condition number is less clear (we have been very sketchy here, for a more detailed discusion on condition numbers see [4, 12]). For linear programming problems, several condition numbers were defined in the last few years (e.g. [9, 13]). The one introduced by Renegar is defined precisely in terms of distance to ill-posedness.

Let $Bc \leq 0$ be a feasible system, i.e. $\text{Sol}(B) \neq \emptyset$. Also, let

$$D(B) = \sup\{\Delta \mid \max |b_{ij} - b'_{ij}| < \Delta \Rightarrow \text{Sol}(B') \neq \emptyset\}.$$

Renegar defines the condition number of $B$ to be

$$C(B) = \frac{\max |b_{ij}|}{D(B)}.$$

A variation of Renegar's condition number, also in the spirit of the inverse to the distance to infeasibility (but normalized differently) is the following. Let

$$D^*(B) = \sup\left\{ \Delta \;\middle|\; \max \frac{\|b_i - b_i'\|}{\|b_i\|} < \Delta \Rightarrow \text{Sol}(B') \neq \emptyset \right\}$$

and

$$C^*(B) = \frac{1}{D^*(B)}.$$

In this section, we will state some relationships between $C(B)$, $C^*(B)$ and $C(B)$.

**Theorem 7.** $C(B) = C^*(B)$.    □

**Proposition 8.** $C^*(B) \leq \sqrt{n}C(B)$.    □

One can prove that an upper bound for $C(B)$ in terms of $C^*(B)$ with the format of Proposition 8 —i.e. with the form $C(B) \leq f(n,m)C^*(B)$ for some function $f$ of the dimensions $n$ and $m$— can not exist. A key difference between $C(B)$ and $C^*(B)$ is that while both condition numbers are homogeneous of degree zero in $B$ (i.e. $C(\lambda B) = C(B)$ for all $\lambda > 0$), $C^*(B)$ is actually multi-homogeneous in its rows and $C(B)$ is sensitive to differences in row scaling. The next two propositions make this more precise.

**Proposition 9.** Let $\lambda_1, \ldots, \lambda_m > 0$ and $b_i' = \lambda_i b_i$ for $i = 1, \ldots, m$. Denote by $B'$ the matrix whose $i$th row is $b_i'$. Then $C^*(B) = C^*(B')$.    □

**Proposition 10.**

$$C^*(B) \geq \frac{\min_i \|b_i\|}{\sqrt{n}\max_{i,j} |b_{ij}|} C(B).$$

□

**Acknowledgement.** The ideas of Renegar [9] have been a source of inspiration for our work. We are also indebted to Steve Smale who first suggested to us the subject of this paper.

# References

[1] BASU, S., R. POLLACK, and M.-F. ROY (1994). On the combinatorial and algebraic complexity of quantifier elimination. In *35th annual IEEE Symp. on Foundations of Computer Science*, pp. 632–641.

[2] BERGADANO, F., N. BSHOUTY, and S. VARRICHIO (1996). Learning multivariate polynomials from substitutions and equivalence queries. Preprint.

[3] BLUMER, A., A. EHRENFEUCHT, D. HAUSSLER, and M. WARMUTH (1989). Learnability and the vapnik-chervonenkis dimension. *J. of the ACM 36*, 929–965.

[4] CUCKER, F. (1999). Real computations with fake numbers. To appear in *Proceedings of ICALP'99*.

[5] GOLDBERG, P. and M. JERRUM (1995). Bounding the Vapnik-Chervonenkis dimension of concept classes parameterized by real numbers. *Machine Learning 18*, 131–148.

[6] HEINTZ, J., M.-F. ROY, and P. SOLERNO (1990). Sur la complexité du principe de Tarski-Seidenberg. *Bulletin de la Société Mathématique de France 118*, 101–126.

[7] KEARNS, M. and U. VAZIRANI (1994). *An Introduction to Computational Learning Theory*. The MIT Press.

[8] RENEGAR, J. (1992). On the computational complexity and geometry of the first-order theory of the reals. Part I. *Journal of Symbolic Computation 13*, 255–299.

[9] RENEGAR, J. (1995). Incorporating condition measures into the complexity theory of linear programming. *SIAM Journal of Optimization 5*, 506–524.

[10] SCHRIJVER, A. (1986). *Theory of Linear and Integer Programming*. John Wiley & Sons.

[11] SHAPIRE, R. and L. SELLIE (1993). Learning sparse multivariate polynomials over a field with queries and counterexamples. In *6th ACM Workshop on Computational Learning Theory*, pp. 17–26.

[12] SMALE, S. (1997). Complexity theory and numerical analysis. In A. Iserles (Ed.), *Acta Numerica*, pp. 523–551. Cambridge University Press.

[13] VAVASIS, S. and Y. YE (1995). Condition numbers for polyhedra with real number data. *Oper. Res. Lett. 17*, 209–214.

# Faster Near-Optimal Reinforcement Learning: Adding Adaptiveness to the $E^3$ Algorithm

Carlos Domingo*

Dept. of Math. and Comp. Science, Tokyo Institute of Technology
Meguro-ku, Ookayama, Tokyo, Japan
carlos@is.titech.ac.jp

**Abstract.** Recently, Kearns and Singh presented the first provably efficient and near-optimal algorithm for reinforcement learning in general Markov decision processes. One of the key contributions of the algorithm is its explicit treatment of the exploration-exploitation trade off. In this paper, we show how the algorithm can be improved by substituting the exploration phase, that builds a model of the underlying Markov decision process by estimating the transition probabilities, by an adaptive sampling method more suitable for the problem. Our improvement is two-folded. First, our theoretical bound on the worst case time needed to converge to an almost optimal policy is significatively smaller. Second, due to the adaptiveness of the sampling method we use, we discuss how our algorithm might perform better in practice than the previous one.

## 1 Introduction

In reinforcement learning, an agent faces the problem of learning how to behave in an unknown dynamic environment in order to achieve a goal. Instead of receiving examples as in the supervised learning model, the learning agent must discover by interaction with the environment how to behave to get the most reward [9].

Reinforcement learning has been receiving increasing attention in the last few years from both, machine learning practitioners and theoreticians. The formal modeling of the environment as a Markov decision process (see next section for a formal definition) makes it particularly suitable for obtaining theoretical results that might also be applicable to real-world problems. Recently, learning theoretical style results have been obtained, being the algorithm $E^3$ of Kearns and Singh [5] one of the most relevant. The $E^3$ algorithm is the first reinforcement learning algorithm that provably achieves near-optimal performance in polynomial time for general Markov decision processes, in contrast with previous asymptotic results. One of the key contributions of the algorithm is an explicit treatment of the exploration versus exploitation dilemma inherent to any reinforcement learning problem. In other words, any reinforcement learning

* Supported by the EU Science and Technology Fellowship Program (STF13) of the European Commission.

O. Watanabe, T. Yokomori (Eds.): ALT'99, LNAI 1720, pp. 241–251, 1999.

algorithm has to spend some time obtaining information about the environment, the exploration phase, and then, use that information to discover an almost optimal policy, the exploitation phase. Obviously, a too long exploration phase might lead to a poor bound while, a too short one, might not allow the algorithm to find an almost optimal policy. The $E^3$ algorithm provides an explicit method for deciding when to switch between the two phases.

A close look at the analysis of the $E^3$ algorithm reveals that the factor that strongly dominates the time bound (a polynomial of degree 4 in all the relevant problem parameters) comes from the sampling process used by the authors to estimate the transition probabilities during the exploration phase. Not only the bound is too large for any practical purposes, it also fails to satisfy the following intuitively desirable property. Given a certain state $i$ in a Markov decision process, suppose that one of the transition probabilities from state $i$ to state $j$ executing action $a$ has a very high probability, for instance 0.9. Intuitively, most of the time when we apply action $a$ from state $i$ we will land on state $j$ and then, we should be able to realize very quickly that the probability of that particular transition is large. On the other hand, suppose that another state $i'$ has transition probabilities uniformly distributed among all the reachable states. In this case, when applying action $a$ from $i'$ we will be landing all the time in different states. Intuitively, in this case, more experience will be required to obtain a good approximation of all these transition probabilities. However, the $E^3$ algorithm will execute action $a$ from both states, $i$ and $i'$ exactly the same number of times. In other words, the number of times that we need to execute an action from certain state in the exploration phase is fixed in advance to a worst case bound independent of the underlying Markov decision process.

The improvement proposed here solves the two problems just mentioned. We substitute the static batch sampling method used in the original $E^3$ algorithm by a *sequential sampling* method adapted to this problem from the one proposed in [8]. This algorithm does sampling sequentially and has a stopping condition that depends on the current estimated. Thus, the amount of sampling needed to estimate certain transition probability will depend *adaptively* on the unknown underlying value being estimated, satisfying the intuition outlined above. In other words, our version of $E^3$ will perform differently depending on how it is the underlying Markov decision process. That is it, it will adapt to the situation at hand instead of being always in the worst case.

Moreover, even in the worst case, we will still use less amount of examples than the fixed worst case bound provided in [5]. Due to the nature of our sampling method, we can obtain estimators that are multiplicatively close to the original probabilities instead of additively close as in the original $E^3$. This will allow us to modify the proof of correctness so that, the amount of sampling required will be smaller, even in the worst case. Since the time spend estimating the underlying model dominates the overall time bound, this will lead us to reduce it from a polynomial of degree 4 to a polynomial of degree 2 in worst case, a significant reduction.

Adaptive sampling has been studied since long time ago (see, for instance, the book by Walt [10]) and has also been recently used in the context of database query estimation [8] and knowledge discovery [1,2]. Furthermore, adaptivity is a very desirable property for an algorithm that is expected to be used in practical applications. See the discussion about the relevance of adaptivity in the context of learning and discovery science in [11].

As noted by the authors, a practical implementation based on the algorithmic ideas provided by them would enjoy performance on natural bounds that is considerably better than what their bounds indicate. In fact, our improvement corroborates that intuition since our modification uses all the ideas strongly related to the reinforcement learning problem proposed while substituting the method of sampling used by a more appropriate one for this problem in an ad-hoc manner. It is important to notice that our method while being more efficient also keeps the same theoretical guarantees of reliability as the one used by the original $E^3$ algorithm.

This paper is organized as follows. In Section 2 we provide the formal definitions related to reinforcement learning. Then, we move on Section 3 where we review in detail the $E^3$ algorithm and its proof. In Section 4 we show how to modify the $E^3$ algorithm by the adaptive sampling method and sketch a proof of its correctness. We will conclude in Section 5 discussing our result and future related work.

## 2   Preliminaries and Definitions

A *Markov decision process (MDP)* $M$ can be defined by a tuple $(S, A, T, R)$ where: S consists of a set of *states* $S = \{1, \ldots, N\}$; A is a set of *actions* $A = \{a_1, \ldots, a_k\}$; $T$ represents the set of *transition probabilities* for each state-action pair $(i, a)$ where $P_M^a(ij) \geq 0$ specifies the probability of landing in state $j$ when executing action $a$ from state $i$ in $M$ [1]; $R$ represents the rewards $R : S \rightarrow [0, R_{max}]$ where $R(i)$ is the reward obtained by the agent in state $i$.

A policy defines how the agent behaves on the Markov decision process. More formally, a policy $\pi$ in a Markov decision process $M$ over a set of states $\{1, \ldots, N\}$ with actions $\{a_1, \ldots, a_k\}$ is a mapping $\pi : \{1, \ldots, N\} \rightarrow \{a_1, \ldots, a_k\}$.

Once a Markov decision process and a policy have been defined, we will discuss about how good is that policy using the two standard asymptotic measures of return of a policy: the expected *average return* and the expected *discounted return*. Since the goal of the $E^3$ algorithm, as well as our improved version, is to obtain finite time convergence results, in this draft we will be talking only about $T$-step expected average return and this can be translated to expected discounted return through the *horizon time* $1/(1 - \gamma)$ or to the expect average return through the *mixing time* of the optimal policy as described in [5].

Let $M$ be a Markov decision process and a let $\pi$ be a policy in $M$. The $T$-*step (expected) average return* from state $i$ is defined as $U_M^\pi(i, T) = \sum_p \Pr_M^\pi[p] U_M(p)$

---

[1] Note that $\sum_j P_M^a(ij) = 1$ for any pair $(i, a)$.

where the sum is over all $T$-paths $p$ in $M$ that start at $i$, $\Pr_M^\pi[p]$ is the probability of crossing path $p$ in $M$ executing $\pi$ and $U_M(p)$ is the average return along path $p$ defined as $U_M(p) = \frac{1}{T}(R_{i_1} + \cdot + R_{i_T})$. Moreover, we define the optimal $T$-step average return from $i$ in $M$ by $U_M^{\pi^*}(i, T) = \max_\pi U_M^\pi(i, T)$.

Thus, the goal in reinforcement learning will be the following. Given parameters $\epsilon$ (the error), $\delta$ (the confidence) and $T$ (the time horizon in the case of discounted return and the mixing time of the optimal policy in the case of infinite horizon average return) we would like to have a reinforcement learning algorithm that with probability larger than $1 - \delta$ obtains a policy such that the expect return of the policy is $\epsilon$ close to the optimal one.

## 3    The $E^3$ Algorithm

Before going into the details of our improved version, we will need to review in certain detail algorithm $E^3$ and its proof of correctness and reliability.

The $E^3$ algorithm is what is usually called an *indirect* or *model-based* reinforcement learning algorithm. That it is, it builds a partial model of the underlying Markov decision process and then, it attempts to compute an optimal policy from it. Thus, there are two phases clearly distinct that we review in the following.

One phase consists in obtaining knowledge of the underlying Markov model from experience on it. The kind of experience that the algorithm has access to consist of, given that the agent is in a particular state at a a particular time step, choose the action to perform, execute it and land on a (possibly) different state from where a further experiment can be performed. Kearns and Singh coined this action as *balanced wandering* meaning that upon arrival in a state, the algorithm tries the action that has been tried the fewest number of times. Since we assume that the world where the agent moves is modeled with a MDP, the state reached when choosing an action from certain state is determined according to the transition probabilities distribution. This experience is gathered at each state the algorithm visits and used to build an approximate model of the transition probabilities distribution in the obvious way. This phase is what it is known as the *exploration phase*.

The other phase, known as the *exploitation phase*, consists on making use of the statistics gathered so far to compute a policy that, hopefully, at some point will be close to the optimal one in the sense made precise in Section 2.

These two phases are interleaved during the learning process. That is, the algorithm collects statistics by experimenting on the MDP (therefore, it is in the exploration phase) and at some point, it decides to switch to the exploitation phase and attempts to compute an optimal policy using the approximate model constructed so far. Whenever the policy is still not close enough to the optimal, it goes back to the exploration phase and tries to collect new statistics about the unknown part of the underlying MDP and so on. Thus, it is important to notice that the algorithm might choose in some cases not to build a complete model of the underlying MDP if doing so it is not necessary to achieve a close to optimal return.

One of the main contributions of the $E^3$ algorithm was to provide an explicit method for deciding when to switch between phases, hence, the name Explicit Explore or Exploit ($E^3$) for the algorithm. For this, a crucial definition was that of a *known* state, a state that has been visited enough number of times so that the estimates of the transition probabilities from that state are close enough to their true values. We will state here their definition for future comparison with the new one we will provide in Section 4. Recall that $\epsilon$, $\delta$ and $T$ are the input parameters of the algorithm as described in Section 2.

**Definition 1.** *[5] Let $M$ be a Markov decision process over $N$ states. We say that a state $i$ of $M$ is* **known** *if each action has been executed from $i$ at least $m_{kn} = \mathcal{O}((NTR_{max})/\epsilon)^4 \log(1/\delta))$ times.*

An important observation is that, given the definition above, we cannot do balanced wandering forever before at least one state becomes *known*. By the Pigeonhole Principle, at most after $N(m_{kn} - 1) + 1$ steps of balanced wandering, some state becomes known.

When the agent lands in a known state (either previously known or that just becomes known at this point for the first time), the algorithm does the following. The algorithm builds a new MDP with the set of currently known states. More precisely, if $S$ is the set of currently known states in $M$, it constructs a MDP $M_S$ induced on $S$ by $M$ where all transitions between states in $S$ are preserved and the rest are redirected to a new *absorbing* state that intuitively represents all the unknown and unvisited states.

Notice that even though the algorithm does not known $M_S$ it has a good approximation of it thanks to the definition of known state, we will refer to this approximation as $\hat{M}_S$. The notion of approximation used is the following.

**Definition 2.** *[5] Let $M$ and $\hat{M}$ be two Markov decision processes over the same set of states. Then, we will say that $\hat{M}$ is an $\alpha$-**approximation** of $M$ if for any pair of states $i$ and $j$ and any action $a$, the following inequalities are satisfied:*

$$P_M^a(ij) - \alpha \leq \hat{P}_M^a(ij) \leq P_M^a(ij) + \alpha$$

It can be shown by a straightforward application of the Hoeffding bound that if a state is known as defined in Definition 1 then $\hat{M}_S$ is a $\mathcal{O}((\epsilon/(NTR_{max}))^2)$-approximation of $M_S$. Moreover, Kearns and Singh proved a *Simulation Lemma* that stated that, in this case, the expected $T$-return of any policy in $\hat{M}_S$ is close to the expected return of the same policy in $M_S$.

The other key lemma in their analysis is the *Exploit or Explore Lemma* that states that, either the optimal policy achieves high return just by using the set of known states $S$ (which can be detected thanks to $M_S$ and the Simulation Lemma) or the optimal policy has high probability of leaving $S$ (which again the algorithm can detect by finding a *exploration* policy that quickly reaches the additional absorbing state in $\hat{M}_S$). Thus, performing two on-line computations on $\hat{M}_S$, the algorithm is provided with either a way to compute a policy with near-optimal return for the next $T$ steps or to obtain new statistics on an unknown or unvisited state. The computation time required for this off-line computations is shown to be bounded by $\mathcal{O}(N^2 T/\epsilon)$.

Putting all these pieces together Kearns and Singh showed that the $E^3$ algorithm achieves, with probability larger than $1 - \delta$, a return that is $\epsilon$ close to the return of the optimal policy in time polynomial in $N, T, 1/\epsilon$, and $\log(1/\delta)$. The main factor in the overall bound comes from the definition of known states, that is, the number of times that a state needs to be visited during the exploration phase before we can attempt to compute an optimal policy. We refer to their paper [5] for further details.

Our improvement affects only the part concerning the exploration phase. In the following section we will show how a more efficient sampling method will allow us to declare a state as *known* more quickly obtaining a significant reduction on the overall running time while keeping the same theoretical guarantees of reliability. Our improvement does not affect the rest of the algorithm and thus, the same lemmas can be used almost exactly the same way as in the original $E^3$ algorithm to proof the correctness of the overall algorithm.

## 4    Knowing the States Faster: Adding Adaptivity to the Exploration Phase

As we mentioned in the introduction, the key idea for improving $E^3$ relies on using a different sampling method for estimating the transition probabilities. This will result on a substantial reduction on the number of statistics need before a state is declared known. For this, we need first to modify the notion of approximation given in Definition 2.

**Definition 3.** *Let $M$ and $\hat{M}$ be two Markov decision processes over the same set of states. Then, we say that $\hat{M}$ is an $\alpha$-**strong** approximation of $M$ if for any pair of states $i$ and $j$, and any action $a$ such that $P_M^a(ij) \geq \alpha$, the following inequalities are satisfied:*

$$(1 - \alpha)P_M^a(ij) \leq P_{\hat{M}}^a(ij) \leq (1 + \alpha)P_M^a(ij)$$

The differences between this definition and the original one are the following. We require that only the transitions that are not "too small" are approximated in a multiplicative way while, previously, every transition was required to be approximated but just in an additive way. The following key lemma related to the one that was already proved in [5] holds under the definition of approximation given above.

**Lemma 1.** *(Modified Simulation Lemma) Let $M$ be any Markov decision process over $N$ states and let $\hat{M}$ be an $\mathcal{O}(\epsilon/(NTR_{max}))$-strong approximation of $M$. Then for any policy $\pi$, number of steps $T$ and for any state $i$, $U_M^\pi(i,T) - \epsilon \leq U_{\hat{M}}^\pi(i,T) \leq U_M^\pi(i,T) + \epsilon$.*

*Proof.* The proof follows the same lines of the proof of the related lemma provided in [5]. For simplicity of notation, let us denote by $\alpha = c\epsilon/(4NTR_{max})$ where $c$ is some constant smaller than 1 and let us fix throughout the proof a policy $\pi$ and a start state $i$.

We first consider the contribution to the return of the transitions that are not approximated in $\hat{M}$, that it is, the transitions whose transition probabilities are smaller than $\alpha$. Since we have $N$ states, the total probability of all these transitions is at most $\alpha N$. Moreover, the probability that in $T$ steps we cross any of these transitions can be bounded by $\alpha NT$. Thus, the total contribution to the expected return of any of these transitions is at most $\alpha NTR_{max}$. By our definition of $\alpha$ this quantity is smaller than $c\epsilon$.

Let us consider the paths that do not cross any transition whose transition probability is smaller than $\alpha$. By our definition of $\alpha$-strong approximation, for any path $p$ of length $T$ the following holds:

$$(1 - \alpha)^T \mathrm{Pr}_M^\pi[p] \leq \mathrm{Pr}_{\hat{M}}^\pi[p] \leq (1 + \alpha)^T \mathrm{Pr}_M^\pi[p]$$

Recall that $U_M^\pi(i, T) = \sum_p \mathrm{Pr}_M^\pi[p] U_M(p)$. Since the inequality above holds for any path $T$, it also holds when we take the expected value. In other words, the following inequality can be derived from the inequality above:

$$c\epsilon + (1 - \alpha)^T U_M^\pi(i, T) \leq U_{\hat{M}}^\pi(i, T) \leq (1 + \alpha)^T U_M^\pi(i, T) + c\epsilon$$

where the factor $c\epsilon$ comes from our previous calculation of the error introduced by the small transitions not required to be approximated in the definition of $\alpha$-strong approximation. Now we should show that our choice of $\alpha$ together with the inequality obtained above implies the lemma. We will show it only for the upper bound, the lower bound can be shown in a similar manner. For showing the upper bound, we need to show that the following two inequalities hold:

$$(1 + \alpha)^T U_M^\pi(i, T) \leq U_M^\pi(i, T) + \epsilon/2 \quad \text{and} \quad c\alpha \leq \epsilon/2$$

The second inequality easily follows by choosing an appropriate value for $c$ in the definition of $\alpha$. For the first one, showing that $(1+\alpha)^T \leq 1+\epsilon/(2R_{max})$ holds will suffice since the average reward is bounded by $R_{max}$. To see this, notice that from the Taylor expansion of $\log(1 + \alpha)$ one can show that $T \log(1 + \alpha)$ is less than $T\alpha/2$ and standard calculus shows that $2^x \leq 1 + 2x$. Thus, choosing $\alpha$ such that $T\alpha \leq \epsilon/(2R_{max})$ will suffice and this can be obviously satisfied by our choice of $\alpha$ and an appropriate choice of $c$. $\qquad\qquad\square$

As in [5], the appropriate definition of known state should be derived from the Simulation Lemma. We will use the following one.

**Definition 4.** *Let $\alpha = \mathcal{O}(\epsilon/(NTR_{max}))$. An state $i$ will be denoted as well-known when for any action $a$ such that $P_M^a(ij) \geq \alpha$,*

$$(1 - \alpha)P_M^a(ij) \leq P_{\hat{M}}^a(ij) \leq (1 + \alpha)P_M^a(ij)$$

Notice that a straightforward application of Chernoff bounds is not appropriate to determine how many times we need to visit a state before it can be declared as *well-known*. This is because the required approximation is multiplicative and, then the number of visits needed that we will obtain if we derive it from the Chernoff bound will depend on the true transition probabilities, a number that is unknown to the algorithm. In fact, it is precisely what it is being estimated. On the other hand, the Hoeffding bound cannot be used here to derive the number of necessary steps since it only provides an additive approximation while we want a multiplicative one. For the statements of the Chernoff and Hoeffding bounds we refer the reader to [6].

To get around this difficulty, we will use a sequential sampling algorithm based on the one proposed by Lipton et.al. [7,8] for database query estimation. This algorithm will substitute the following steps of the $E^3$ algorithm. Recall that when the algorithm is in the exploration phase, it does balanced wandering. That is, it just executes the least used action from the state where the agent is currently located, updates the estimates according to the landing state and, in case the number of times that the state has been visited becomes larger than the required by the definition of known state given in Section 3, then it is declared as *known*.

1  *AdaExploStep* /* for state $i$ */
2  **if** state $i$ is visited for the first time **then**
3      $\alpha = \mathcal{O}(\epsilon/NTR_{max})$; $\beta = 10\ln(2kN/\delta)/\alpha^2$
4      **for** all states $j \in S$ and actions $a \in A$ **do**
5          $m_a = 0$; $N_M^a(ij) = 0$;
6  apply action $a$ (least used breaking ties randomly);
7  let $j$ the landing state, $N_M^a(ij) = N_M^a(ij) + 1$;
8  $m_a = m_a + 1$;
9  **if** $(N_M^a(ij) \geq 3\ln(2kN/\delta)(1+\alpha)/\alpha^2)$ **then**
10      declare $P_M^a(ij)$ as estimated by $\hat{P}_M^a(ij) = N_M^a(ij)/m_a$;
11 **if** $(m_a \geq \beta)$ **then**
12      declare all remaining $P_M^a(ij')$ as estimated by $\hat{P}_M^a(ij') = N_M^a(ij)/m_a$
13 **if** all $P_M^a(ij)$ are estimated for all states $j$ and actions $a$ **then**
14      declare $i$ as *well-known*.

**Fig. 1.** Adaptive exploration step for state $i$.

Our approach is the following. Every time we land on an unknown or unvisited state $i$ in the exploration phase we will execute an *Adaptive Exploration Step* (AdaExploStep for short). A pseudo code for AdaExploStep is provided in Figure 1 and we discuss it now. First, if the state is unvisited, we will initialize variables $N_M^a(ij)$ that will be used for estimating the real transitions probabilities $P_M^a(ij)$, the number of times every action $a$ has been used from it $m_a$ and, the two parameters of the algorithm $\alpha$ and $\beta$. Then, we will choose the action to execute (the least used, breaking ties randomly), we will denote by $j$ the landing state and update $N_M^a(ij)$ accordingly. Then, we will check two conditions whose meaning is the following. The first condition (line 9 of Figure 1) controls whether the estimator $\hat{P}_M^a(ij) = N_M^a(ij)/m_a$ of $P_M^a(ij)$ is already $\alpha$ close to it in a multiplicative sense as desired. Notice that for doing this we are just using value $N_M^a(ij)$. The second condition (line 11 of Figure 1) checks whether we have done enough sampling so we can guarantee with high probability that all the transition probabilities that have not been declared estimated yet must be smaller than $\alpha$. Finally, when all the transition probabilities for all the actions are declared as estimated, the state is declared well-known. In the following theorem we discuss the reliability and complexity of the procedure just described.

**Theorem 1.** *Let $i$ be a state in a Markov decision process $M$ and let $\alpha = \mathcal{O}(\epsilon/NTR_{max})$. Then, if procedure AdaExploStep declares state $i$ as well-known, with probability more than $1-\delta$, it does it correctly in at most $m = \mathcal{O}(k\ln(2kN/\delta)/\alpha^2\sigma)$ steps where $\sigma$ is the maximum between the smallest transition probability and $\alpha$.*

*Proof.* Let us start proving the correctness, that is, that the estimates $\hat{P}_M^a(ij)$ output by procedure AdaExploStep satisfy Definition 4 with high probability. For this, let us fix first one particular transition probability $p = P_M^a(ij)$ and let us denote by $\alpha = \mathcal{O}(\epsilon/NTR_{max})$ the desired accuracy on the estimate. Furthermore, let us suppose that the algorithm declares $p$ as estimated in the first if-then condition, that is, $N(p) = N_M^a(ij)$ becomes larger than $c = 3\ln(2kN/\delta)(1+\alpha)/\alpha^2$. Notice that since $N(p)$ only increases at most by 1 at every step, at the stopping step $N(p)$ satisfies $c \leq N(p) \leq c+1$. Thus, since the estimator output by the algorithm is $\hat{p} = N(p)/m_a$, it can be easily verified that for any values of $m_a$ satisfying

$$\frac{c}{p(1+\alpha)} \leq m_a \leq \frac{c+1}{p(1-\alpha)}$$

estimate $\hat{p}$ is within the desired range, that is, $(1-\alpha)p \leq \hat{p} \leq (1+\alpha)p$. Therefore, the probability of error can be bounded by the probability of stopping before $l_1 = c/(p(1+\alpha))$ steps (and thus, $\hat{p} > p(1+\alpha)$) plus the probability of stopping after $l_2 = (c+1)/(p(1-\alpha))$ steps (and thus, $\hat{p} < p(1-\alpha)$). Moreover, notice that the stopping condition is monotone in the following sense. If it is satisfied at step $l$ then it will also be satisfied at any step $l' > l$ and if it has not been satisfied at step $l$, then it has also not been satisfied at any step $l' < l$, no matter what are the results of the random trials. Therefore, we need to consider only the two extreme points $l_1$ and $l_2$. Applying the Chernoff bound to bound those two probabilities and by our choice of $c$ we can conclude that the probability that $\hat{p}$ does not correctly estimate $p$ is less than $\delta/(2kN)$. Since there are at most $kN$ transition probabilities being estimated simultaneously, by the union bound, the probability that any of them fails is at most $\delta/2$.

We have just shown that, with high probability, any transition probability $p \geq \alpha$ that is declared as estimated by the first condition satisfies Definition 4. More over, it takes at most $(c + 1)/(p(1 + \alpha))$ steps. By our choice of $c$ and noticing that $(1 + \alpha)/(1 - \alpha)$ is smaller than $5/3$ for any $\alpha$ less than $0.25$, it follows that the algorithm will estimate $p$ in at most $5 \ln(2kN/\delta)/(\alpha^2 p)$ steps.

Now, let us discuss the second if-then condition. The meaning of this condition is the following. If we are doing too many steps in the same state and there are still transition probabilities that have not been yet declared as estimated, then, those transitions are "small" with high probability and we can declare the state as well-known satisfying Definition 4 without further steps. To show the correctness of this condition, suppose that the algorithm stops in the second condition and let $q = P_M^a(ij)$ a transition probability that was not yet declared as estimated. Thus, from the first if-then condition (not yet satisfied) we know that $N(q) = N_M^a(ij)$ should be smaller than $c$ and from the second if-then condition (just satisfied) we know that $m_a \geq d$, where $d = 10 \ln(2kN/\delta)/\alpha^2$. Thus, the probability that $q$ is larger than $\alpha$ can be bounded by the probability that $q - N(q)/d$ is larger than $\alpha - c/d$. Applying the Hoeffding bound and by our choice of $d$ and $c$ it can be derived that this probability is smaller than $\delta/(kN)$. Again, using the union bound we can bound by $\delta/2$ the probability that a transition probability larger than $\alpha$ is incorrectly declared classified by the second condition.

Finally, the probability that the algorithm makes a mistake in either bound is bound by $\delta/2 + \delta/2$ and the theorem follows.                    □

We have just seen that AdaExploStep correctly declares the states as well-known. Moreover, if $S$ is the set of well-known states, then $\hat{M}_S$ will be a strong approximation of $M_S$ in the sense of Definition 3 and thus, by Lemma 1 it will appropriately simulate $M_S$. Thus, it can be used to compute the off-line policies the same way as it was used in the original $E^3$ algorithm.

## 5   Conclusion

We have seen how we can modify the exploration phase of the $E^3$ algorithm by an adaptive sampling method so that is possible to improve its overall time bound. Moreover, we have argued that due to the adaptiveness of our method, it should be more suitable for practical purposes and part of our future work will be to implement our version of $E^3$ and test it experimentally.

Notice that algorithm $E^3$ as well as our improvement suffer the problem of being polynomial in the number of states $N$, something that might be impractical in certain problems. One possible way around this problem is to consider factored MDP, that it is, MDP whose transition model can be factored as a dynamic Bayesian network. A generalization of the $E^3$ algorithm to that case has been recently obtained in [4]. Our method seems to be applicable also to improve that generalization although some technical points need to be carefully checked and this will be part of our future job.

# 6    Acknowledgments

I would like to thanks Denis Therien for inviting me to the McGill Annual Workshop on Computational Complexity where I learned all the neat things about reinforcement learning from this year main speaker Michael Kearns. I also would like to thank Michael for kindly providing me all the details about the $E^3$ algorithm. Finally, thanks to the anonymous referees for several comments that help me to improve the presentation of the paper.

# References

1. Carlos Domingo, Ricard Gavaldà and Osamu Watanabe. Practical Algorithms for On-line Selection. In *Proceedings of the First International Conference on Discovery Science*, DS'98. Lecture Notes in Artificial Intelligence 1532:150–161, 1998.
2. Carlos Domingo, Ricard Gavaldà and Osamu Watanabe. Adaptive Sampling Methods for Scaling Up Knowledge Discovery Algorithms. To appear in *Proceedings of the Second International Conference on Discovery Science*, DS'99, December 1999.
3. Leslie Pack Kaebling, Michael L. Littman and Andrew W. Moore. Reinforcement Learning: A Survey. *Journal of Artificial Intelligence Research* 4 (1996) 237–285.
4. Michael Kearns and Daphne Koller. Efficient Reinforcement Learning in Factored MDPs. To appear in the *Proc. of the International Joint Conference on Artificial Intelligence*, IJCAI'99.
5. Michael Kearns and Satinder Singh. Near-Optimal Reinforcement Learning in Polynomial Time. In *Machine Learning: Proceedings of the 16th International Conference*, ICML'99, pages 260–268, 1998.
6. M.J. Kearns and U.V. Vazirani. *An Introduction to Computational Learning Theory*. Cambridge University Press, 1994.
7. Richard J. Lipton and Jeffrey F. Naughton. Query Size Estimation by Adaptive Sampling. *Journal of Computer and System Science*, 51:18–25, 1995.
8. Richard J. Lipton, Jeffrey F. Naughton, Donovan Schneider and S. Seshadri. Efficient sampling strategies for relational database operations. *Theoretical Computer Science*, 116:195–226, 1993.
9. R.S. Sutton and A. G. Barto. *Reinforcement Learning: An Introduction.* Cambridge, MA. MIT Press.
10. Abraham Wald. *Sequential Analysis*. Wiley Mathematical, Statistics Series, 1947.
11. Osamu Watanabe. From Computational Learning Theory to Discovery Science. In *Proc. of the 26th International Colloquium on Automata, Languages and Programming*, Invited talk of ICALP'99. Lecture Notes in Computer Science 1644:134–148, 1999.

# A Note on Support Vector Machine Degeneracy

Ryan Rifkin, Massimiliano Pontil, and Alessandro Verri*

Center for Biological and Computational Learning, MIT
45 Carleton Street E25-201, Cambridge, MA 02142, USA
{rif,pontil,verri}@ai.mit.edu

**Abstract.** When training Support Vector Machines (SVMs) over non-separable data sets, one sets the threshold $b$ using any dual cost coefficient that is strictly between the bounds of 0 and $C$. We show that there exist SVM training problems with dual optimal solutions with all coefficients at bounds, but that *all* such problems are degenerate in the sense that the "optimal separating hyperplane" is given by $\mathbf{w} = \mathbf{0}$, and the resulting (degenerate) SVM will classify all future points identically (to the class that supplies more training data). We also derive necessary and sufficient conditions on the input data for this to occur. Finally, we show that an SVM training problem can always be made degenerate by the addition of a *single* data point belonging to a certain unbounded polyhedron, which we characterize in terms of its extreme points and rays.

## 1 Introduction

We are given $l$ examples $(\mathbf{x}_1, y_1), \ldots, (\mathbf{x}_l, y_l)$, with $\mathbf{x}_i \in \mathrm{I\!R}^n$ and $y_i \in \{-1, 1\}$ for all $i$. The SVM training problem is to find a hyperplane and threshold $(\mathbf{w}, b)$ that separates the positive and negative examples with maximum margin, penalizing misclassifications linearly in a user-selected penalty parameter $C > 0$.[1] This formulation was introduced in [2]. For a good introduction to SVMs and the nonlinear programming problems involved in their training, see [3] or [1]. We train an SVM by solving either of the following pair of dual quadratic programs:

$$(P) \quad \min_{\mathbf{w}, b, \Xi} \tfrac{1}{2}\|\mathbf{w}\|^2 + C(\textstyle\sum_{i=1}^{\ell} \xi_i) \qquad\qquad (D) \quad \max_{\Lambda} \Lambda \cdot \mathbf{1} - \tfrac{1}{2}\Lambda \mathbf{D} \Lambda$$

$$y_i(\mathbf{w} \cdot \mathbf{x}_i + b) \geq 1 - \xi_i \qquad\qquad \Lambda \cdot \mathbf{y} = 0$$
$$\xi_i \geq 0 \qquad\qquad\qquad \lambda_i \leq C$$
$$\lambda_i \geq 0$$

where we used the vector notations $\Xi = (\xi_1, \ldots, \xi_l), \Lambda = (\alpha_1, \ldots, \alpha_l)$. $\mathbf{D}$ is the symmetric positive semidefinite matrix defined by $D_{ij} \equiv y_i y_j \mathbf{x}_i \cdot \mathbf{x}_j$. Throughout this note, we use the convention that if an equation contains $i$ as an unsummed subscript, the corresponding equation is replicated for all $i \in \{1, \ldots, l\}$.

---

* INFM-DISI, Università di Genova, Via Dodecaneso 35, 16146 Genova, Italy
[1] Actually, we penalize linearly points for which $y_i(\mathbf{w} \cdot \mathbf{x}_i + b) < 1$; such points are not actually "misclassifications" unless $y_i(\mathbf{w} \cdot \mathbf{x}_i + b) < 0$.

O. Watanabe, T. Yokomori (Eds.): ALT'99, LNAI 1720, pp. 252–263, 1999.
© Springer-Verlag Berlin Heidelberg 1999

In practice, the dual program is solved.[2] However, for this pair of primal-dual problems, the KKT conditions are necessary and sufficient to characterize optimal solutions. Therefore, $\mathbf{w}, b, \Xi$, and $\Lambda$ represent a pair of primal and dual optimal solutions if and only if they satisfy the KKT conditions. Additionally, any primal and dual feasible solutions with identical objective values are primal and dual optimal. The KKT conditions (for the primal problem) are as follows:

$$\mathbf{w} - \sum_{i=1}^{\ell} \lambda_i y_i \mathbf{x}_i = 0 \tag{1}$$

$$\sum_{i=1}^{\ell} \lambda_i y_i = 0 \tag{2}$$

$$C - \lambda_i - \mu_i = 0 \tag{3}$$

$$y_i(\mathbf{x}_i \cdot \mathbf{w} + b) - 1 + \xi_i \geq 0 \tag{4}$$

$$\lambda_i \{ y_i(\mathbf{x}_i \cdot \mathbf{w} + b) - 1 + \xi_i \} = 0 \tag{5}$$

$$\mu_i \xi_i = 0 \tag{6}$$

$$\xi_i, \lambda_i, \mu_i \geq 0 \tag{7}$$

The $\mu_i$ are Lagrange multipliers associated with the $\xi_i$; they do not appear explicitly in either (P) or (D). The KKT conditions will be our major tool for investigating the properties of solutions to (P) and (D).

Suppose that we have solved (D) and possess a dual optimal solution $\Lambda$. Equation (1) allows us to determine $\mathbf{w}$ for the associated primal optimal solution. Further suppose that there exists an $i$ such that $0 < \lambda_i < C$. Then, by equation (3), $\mu_i > 0$, and by equation (6), $\xi_i = 0$. Because $\lambda_i \neq 0$, equation (5) tells us that $y_i(\mathbf{x}_i \cdot \mathbf{w} + b) - 1 + \xi_i = 0$. Using $\xi_i = 0$, we see that we can determine the threshold $b$ using the equation $b = 1 - y_i(\mathbf{x}_i \cdot \mathbf{w})$.

Once $b$ is known, we can determine the $\xi_i$ by noting that $\xi_i = 0$ if $\lambda_i \neq C$ (by equations (3) and (6)), and that $\xi_i = 1 - y_i(\mathbf{x}_i \cdot \mathbf{w} + b)$ otherwise (by equation (5)). However, this is not strictly necessary, as it is $\mathbf{w}$ and $b$ that must be known in order to classify future instances.

We note that our ability to determine $b$ and $\Xi$ is crucially dependent on the existence of a $\lambda_i$ strictly between 0 and $C$. Additionally, the optimality conditions, and therefore the SVM training algorithm derived in Osuna's thesis [3], depend on the existence of such a $\lambda_i$ as well. On page 49 of his thesis Osuna states that "We have not found a proof yet of the existence of such $\lambda_i$, or conditions under which it does not exist." Other discussions of SVM's ( [1], [2]) also implicitly assume the existence of such a $\lambda_i$.

In this paper, we show that there need not exist a $\lambda_i$ strictly between bounds. Such cases are a subset of *degenerate* SVM training problems: those problems

---

[2] SVMs in general use a nonlinear kernel mapping. In this note, we explore the linear simplification in order to gain insight into SVM behavior. Our analysis holds identically in the nonlinear case.

where the optimal separating "hyperplane" is $\mathbf{w} = 0$, and the optimal solution is to assign all future points to the same class. We derive a strong characterization of SVM degeneracy in terms of conditions on the input data. We go on to show that any SVM training problems can be made degenerate via the addition of a *single* training point, and that, assuming the two classes are of different cardinalities, this new training point can fall anywhere in a certain unbounded polyhedron. We provide a strong characterization of this polyhedron, and give a mild condition which will insure non-degeneracy.

## 2    Support Vector Machine Degeneracy

In this section, we explore SVM training problems with a dual optimal solution satisfying $\lambda_i \in \{0, C\}$ for all $i$.

We begin by noting and dismissing the trivial example where all training points belong to the same class, say class 1. In this case, it is easily seen that $\Lambda = 0$, $\Xi = 0$, $\mathbf{w} = 0$, and $b = 1$ represent primal and dual optimal solutions, both with objective value 0.

**Definition 1.** *A vector $\Lambda$ is a $\{0, C\}$-solution for an SVM training problem $\mathcal{P}$ if $\Lambda$ solves (D), $\lambda_i \in \{0, C\}$ for all $i$ and $\Lambda \neq 0$ (note that this includes cases where $\lambda_i = C$ for all $i$).*

We demonstrate the existence of problems having $\{0, C\}$-solutions with an example where the data lie in $\mathbb{R}^2$:

| $\mathbf{x}$ | $y$ |
|---|---|
| $(2,3)$ | $1$ |
| $(2,2)$ | $-1$ |
| $(1,2)$ | $1$ |
| $(1,3)$ | $-1$ |

$$D = \begin{bmatrix} 13 & -10 & 8 & -11 \\ -10 & 8 & -6 & 8 \\ 8 & -6 & 5 & -7 \\ -11 & 8 & -7 & 10 \end{bmatrix}$$

Suppose $C = 10$. The reader may easily verify that $\Lambda = (10, 10, 10, 10)$, $\mathbf{w} = 0$, $b = -1$, $\Xi = (0, 2, 0, 2)$ are feasible primal and dual solutions, both with objective value 40, and are therefore optimal. Actually, given our choice of $\Lambda$ and $w$, we may set $b$ anywhere in the closed interval $[-1, 1]$, and set $\Xi = (1 + b, 1 - b, 1 + b, 1 - b)$.

We have demonstrated the possibility of $\{0, C\}$-solutions, but the above example seems highly abnormal. The data are distributed at the four corners of a unit square centered at $(1.5, 2.5)$, with opposite corners being of the same class. The "optimal separating hyperplane" is $\mathbf{w} = 0$, which is not a hyperplane at all. We now proceed to formally show that *all* SVM training problems which admit $\{0, C\}$-solutions are degenerate in this sense.

The following lemma is obvious from inspection of the KKT conditions:

**Lemma 1.** *Suppose that $\Lambda$ is a $\{0, C\}$-solution to an SVM training problem $\mathcal{P}_1$ with $C = C_1$. Given a new SVM training problem $\mathcal{P}_2$ with identical input data and $C = C_2$, $(C_2/C_1) \cdot \Lambda$ is dual optimal for $\mathcal{P}_2$. The corresponding primal optimal solution(s) is (are) unchanged.*

We see that $\{0, C\}$-solutions are not dependent on a particular choice of $C$. This in turn implies the following:

**Lemma 2.** *If $\Lambda$ is a $\{0, C\}$-solution to an SVM training problem $\mathcal{P}$, $\mathbf{D} \cdot \Lambda = 0$.*

PROOF: Since $\mathbf{D}$ is symmetric positive semidefinite, we can write $\mathbf{D} = \mathbf{R}\Sigma\mathbf{R}^T$, where $\Sigma$ is a diagonal matrix with the (nonnegative) eigenvalues of $\mathbf{D}$ in descending order on the diagonal, $\mathbf{R}$ is an orthogonal basis of corresponding eigenvectors of $\mathbf{D}$, and $\mathbf{R}\mathbf{R}^T = \mathbf{I}$. If $\mathbf{D} \cdot \Lambda \neq 0$, then for some index $k$, $\sigma_k \geq 0$ and $\mathbf{R}_k \cdot \Lambda \neq 0$.

For any value of $C$, let $\Lambda_C$ be the $\{0, C\}$-solution obtained by adjusting $\Lambda$ appropriately. This solution is dual optimal for a problem having input data identical to $\mathcal{P}$, with a new value of $C$, by Lemma 1.

$$\Lambda_C \mathbf{D} \Lambda_C = \sum_{j=1}^{l} \sigma_j \|\mathbf{R}_j \cdot \Lambda_C\|^2$$

$$\geq \sigma_k \|\mathbf{R}_k \cdot \Lambda_C\|^2$$

$$= \sigma_k C^2 \|\mathbf{R}_k \cdot \Lambda_1\|^2$$

Define $S$ to be the number of non-zero elements in $\Lambda$. As we vary $C$, the optimal dual objective value of our family of $\{0, C\}$-solutions is given by:

$$f_\Lambda(C) = \Lambda_C \cdot 1 - \frac{1}{2}\Lambda_C \mathbf{D} \Lambda_C$$

$$\leq SC - \frac{1}{2}\sigma_k C^2 \|\mathbf{R}_k \cdot \Lambda_1\|^2$$

However, if

$$C^* > \frac{2S}{\sigma_k \|\mathbf{R}_k \cdot \Lambda_1\|^2}$$

$f_\Lambda(C^*) < 0$. This is a contradiction, for $\Lambda = 0$ is feasible in $\mathcal{P}$ with objective value zero, and zero is therefore a *lower bound* on the value of any optimal solution to $\mathcal{P}$, regardless of the value of $C$.

**Theorem 1.** *If $\Lambda$ is a $\{0, C\}$-solution to an SVM training problem $\mathcal{P}$, $\mathbf{w} = 0$ in all primal optimal solutions.*

PROOF:

Any optimal solution must, along with $\Lambda$, satisfy the KKT conditions. Exploiting this, we see:

$$0 = \mathbf{D} \cdot \Lambda$$

$$\Longrightarrow 0 = \Lambda \mathbf{D} \Lambda$$

$$= \sum_{i=1}^{l} \sum_{j=1}^{l} \lambda_i D_{ij} \lambda_j$$

$$= \sum_{i=1}^{l} \sum_{j=1}^{l} \lambda_i y_i y_j \mathbf{x}_i \mathbf{x}_j \lambda_j$$

$$= \left( \sum_{i=1}^{l} \lambda_i y_i \mathbf{x}_i \right) \cdot \left( \sum_{j=1}^{l} \lambda_j y_j \mathbf{x}_j \right)$$

$$= \mathbf{w} \cdot \mathbf{w}$$

$$\Longrightarrow \mathbf{w} = \mathbf{0}$$

This is a key result. It states that if our dual problem admits a $\{0, C\}$-solution, the "optimal separating hyperplane" is $\mathbf{w} = \mathbf{0}$. In other words, it is of no value to construct a hyperplane at all, no matter how expensive misclassifications are, and the optimal classifier will classify all future data points using only the threshold $b$. Our data must be arranged in such a way that we may as well "de-metrize" our space by throwing away all information about where our data points are located, and classify all points identically.

The converse of this statement is false: given an SVM training problem $\mathcal{P}$ that admits a primal solution with $\mathbf{w} = \mathbf{0}$, it is *not* necessarily the case that all dual optimal solutions are $\{0, C\}$-solutions, nor even that a $\{0, C\}$-solution necessarily *exists*, as the following example, constructed from the first example by "splitting" a data point into two new points whose *average* is one of the original points, shows:

| $\mathbf{x}$ | $y$ |
|---|---|
| $(2, 3)$ | $1$ |
| $(2, 2)$ | $-1$ |
| $(1, 1.5)$ | $1$ |
| $(1, 2.5)$ | $1$ |
| $(1, 3)$ | $-1$ |

$$\mathbf{D} = \begin{bmatrix} 13 & -10 & 6.5 & 9.5 & -11 \\ -10 & 8 & -5 & -7 & 8 \\ 6.5 & -5 & 3.25 & 4.75 & -5.5 \\ 9.5 & -7 & 4.75 & 7.25 & -8.5 \\ -11 & 8 & -5.5 & -8.5 & 10 \end{bmatrix}$$

Again letting $C = 10$, the reader may verify that setting $\mathbf{\Lambda} = (10, 10, 5, 5, 10)$, $\mathbf{w} = \mathbf{0}, b = -1, \Xi = (0, 20, 0, 20, 0, 0)$ are feasible primal and dual solutions, both with objective value 40, and are therefore optimal. With more effort, the reader may verify that $\mathbf{\Lambda} = \{10, 10, 5, 5, 10\}$ is the unique optimal solution to the dual problem, and therefore no $\{0, C\}$-solution exists.

Although our initial motivation was to study problems with optimal solutions having every dual coefficient $\lambda_i$ at bounds, we gain additional insight by studying the following, broader class of problems.

**Definition 2.** *An SVM training problem $\mathcal{P}$ is **degenerate** if there exists an optimal primal solution to $\mathcal{P}$ in which $\mathbf{w} = \mathbf{0}$.*

By Theorem 1, any problem that admits a $\{0, C\}$-solution is degenerate. As in the $\{0, C\}$-solution case, one can use the KKT conditions to easily show that the degeneracy of an SVM training problem is independent of the particular choice of the parameter $C$, and that $\mathbf{w} = 0$ in *all* primal optimal solutions of a degenerate training problem.

For degenerate SVM training problems, even though there is no optimal separating hyperplane in the normal sense, we still call those data points that contribute to the "expansion" $\mathbf{w} = 0$ with $\lambda_i \neq 0$ support vectors. Given an SVM training problem $\mathcal{P}$, define $K_i$ to be the index set of points in class $i$, $i \in \{1, -1\}$.

**Lemma 3.** *Given a degenerate SVM training problem $\mathcal{P}$, assume without loss of generality that $|K_{-1}| \leq |K_1|$. Then all points in class $-1$ are support vectors; furthermore, $\lambda_i = C$ if $i \in K_{-1}$. Additionally, if $|K_{-1}| = |K_1|$, the (unique) dual optimal solution is $\Lambda = \mathbf{C}$.*

PROOF:Because $\mathbf{w} = 0$, the primal constraints reduce to:

$$y_i b \geq 1 - \xi_i$$

If $|K_{-1}| < |K_1|$, the optimal value of $b$ is 1, and $\xi_i$ is positive for $i \in |K_{-1}|$. Therefore, $\lambda_i = C$ for $i \in K_{-1}$ (by Equations 6 and 3).

Assume $|K_{-1}| = |K_1|$. We may (optimally) choose $b$ anywhere in the range $[-1, 1]$. If $b \leq 0$, all points in class 1 have $\lambda_i = C$, and if $b \geq 0$, all points in class $-1$ have $\lambda_i = C$. In either case, there are at least $|K_{-1}|$ points in a single class satisfying $\lambda_i = C$. But equation ( 2) says that the sum of the $\lambda_i$ for each class must be equal, and since no $\lambda_i$ may be greater then $C$, we conclude that every $\lambda_i$ is equal to $C$ in *both* classes.

Finally, we derive conditions on the input data for a degenerate SVM training problem $\mathcal{P}$.

**Theorem 2.** *Given an SVM training problem $\mathcal{P}$, assume without loss of generality that $|K_{-1}| \leq |K_1|$. Then:*
*a. $\mathcal{P}$ is degenerate if and only if there exists a set of multipliers $\Omega$ for the points in $K_1$ satisfying:*

$$0 \leq \omega_i \leq 1$$

$$\sum_{i \in K_{-1}} \mathbf{x}_i = \sum_{i \in K_1} \omega_i \mathbf{x}_i$$

$$\sum_{i \in K_1} \omega_i = |K_{-1}|$$

*b. $\mathcal{P}$ admits a $\{0, C\}$-solution if and only if $\mathcal{P}$ is degenerate and the $\omega_i$ in part (a) may all be chosen to be 0 or 1.*

PROOF:

(a, $\Rightarrow$) Suppose $\mathcal{P}$ is degenerate. Consider a modification of $\mathcal{P}$ with identical input data, but $C = 1$; this problem is also degenerate. All points in class $-1$ are support vectors, and their associated $\lambda_i$ are at 1, by Lemma 3. Letting $\Lambda$

be any dual optimal solution to $\mathcal{P}$, we see that letting $\omega_i = \lambda_i$ for $i \in K_1$ and applying Equation ( 2) demonstrates the existence of the $\omega_i$.

(a, $\Leftarrow$) Given $\omega_i$ satisfying the condition, we easily see that $\lambda_i = C$ for $i \in K_{-1}, \lambda_i = \omega_i C$ for $i \in K_1$ induces a pair of optimal primal and dual solutions to $\mathcal{P}$ with $\mathbf{w} = \mathbf{0}$ using the KKT conditions.

(b, $\Rightarrow$) Given a $\{0, C\}$-solution, $\mathbf{w} = \mathbf{0}$ in an associated primal solution by Theorem 1, and setting $\omega_i = \lambda_i / C$ for $i \in K_1$ satisfies the requirements on $\mathbf{\Omega}$.

(b, $\Leftarrow$) Let $\lambda_i = \omega_i C$ for $i \in K_1$, and apply the KKT conditions.

## 3   The Degenerating Polyhedron

Theorem 2 indicates that it is *always* possible to make an SVM training problem degenerate by adding a *single* new data point. We now proceed to characterize the set of individual points whose addition will make a given problem degenerate. For the remainder of this section, we assume that $|K_{-1}| \leq |K_1|$, and we denote $\sum_{i \in K_{-1}} \mathbf{x}_i$ by $\mathbf{V}$, and $|K_{-1}|$ by $n$.

Suppose we choose, for each $i \in K_1$, an $\omega_i \in [0, 1]$, satisfying $n - 1 \leq \sum_{i \in K_1} \omega_i < n$. It is clear from the conditions of Theorem 2 that if we add a *new* data point

$$\mathbf{x}_c = \frac{V - \sum_{i \in K_1} \omega_i \mathbf{x}_i}{n - \sum_{i \in K_1} \omega_i} \tag{8}$$

that the problem becomes degenerate, where the new point has a multiplier given by $\omega_c = n - \sum_{i \in K_1} \omega_i$, and that all single points whose additions would make the problem degenerate can be found in such a manner. We denote the set of points so obtained by $\mathbf{X_D}$.

We introduce the following notation. For $k \leq n$, we let $S_k$ denote the set containing all possible sums of $k$ points in $K_1$. Given a point $\mathbf{s} \in S_k$, we define an indicator function $\chi_{\mathbf{s}} : K_1 \to \{0, 1\}$ with the property $\chi_{\mathbf{s}}(\mathbf{x}_i) = 1$ if and only if $\mathbf{x}_i$ is one of the $k$ points of $K_1$ that were summed to make $\mathbf{x}$.

The region $\mathbf{X_D}$ is in fact a polyhedron whose extreme points and extreme rays are of the form $V - x$ for $x \in S_{n-1}$ and §$_n$, respectively. More specifically, we have the following theorem; the proof is not difficult, but it is rather technical, and we defer it to Appendix A:

**Theorem 3.** *Given a non-degenerate problem* $\mathcal{P}$, *consider the polyhedron*

$$\mathbf{P_D} \equiv \{ \sum_{\mathbf{s}^p \in S_{n-1}} \lambda_{\mathbf{s}^p}(\mathbf{V} - \mathbf{s}^p) + \sum_{\mathbf{s}^r \in S_n} \alpha_{\mathbf{s}^r}(\mathbf{V} - \mathbf{x}^r) \mid \lambda_{\mathbf{s}^p}, \alpha_{\mathbf{s}^r} \geq 0, \sum_{\mathbf{s}^p \in S_{n-1}} \lambda_{\mathbf{s}^p} = 1 \}$$

*Then* $\mathbf{P_D} = \mathbf{X_D}$.

An example is shown in Figure 1. The dark region represents the set of those points that, when added to the class 1, will make the problem degenerate. This set can be obtained following the construction in Appendix A.

On the one hand, the idea that the addition of a single data point can make an SVM training problem degenerate seems to bode ill for the usefulness of the method. Indeed, SVMs are in some sense not robust. This is a consequence of the fact that because errors are penalized in the $L_1$ norm, a *single* outlier can have *arbitrarily large* effects on the separating hyperplane. However, the fact that we are able to precisely characterize the "degenerating" polyhedron allows us to provide a positive result as well. We begin by noting that in the example of Figure 1, the entire polyhedron of points whose addition make the problem degenerate is located well away from the initial data. This is not a coincidence. Indeed, using Theorem 3, we may easily derive the following theorem:

**Theorem 4.** *Given a non-degenerate problem $P$ with $|K_{-1}| \le |K_1|$, suppose there exists a hyperplane $w$ through $V/n$, the center of mass of $K_{-1}$, such that all points in $K_1$ lie on one side of $w$, and the closest distance between a point in $K_1$ and $w$ is $d$. Then all points in the "degenerating" polyhedron $P_D$ lie at least $(|K_{-1}| - 1) * d$ from $w$ on the other side of $w$ from $K_1$.*

Using Theorem 2 we can easily show that if the center of mass of the points in the smaller class $(V/n)$ does not lie in the convex hull of the points in the larger class, our problem is not degenerate, and we may apply Theorem 4 to bound below the distance at which an outlier would have to lie from $V/n$ in order to make the problem degenerate. We conclude that if the class with larger cardinality lies well away from and entirely to one side of a hyperplane through the center of mass of the class of smaller cardinality, our problem is nondegenerate, and any single point we could add to make the problem degenerate would be an extreme outlier, lying on the opposite side of the smaller class from the larger class.

## 4   Nonlinear SVMs and Further Remarks

The conditions we have derived so far apply to the construction of a linear decision surface. It should be clear that similar arguments apply to nonlinear kernels. In particular, degenerate SVMs will occur if and only if the data satisfy the conditions of Theorem 2 *after* undergoing the nonlinear mapping to the high-dimensional space. It is not necessary that the data be degenerate in the original input space, although examples could be derived where they were degenerate in both spaces, for a particular kernel choice. *The important message of Theorem 2, however, is that while degenerate SVMs are possible, the requirements on the input data are so stringent that one should never expect to encounter them in practice.* On another note, if a degenerate SVM does occur, one simply sets the threshold $b$ to 1 or $-1$, depending on which class contributes more points to the training set. Thus in all cases, we are able to determine the threshold $b$. Of course, the wisdom of this approach depends on the data distribution. If our two classes lie largely on top of each other, than classifying according to the larger class may indeed be the best we can do (assuming our examples were drawn

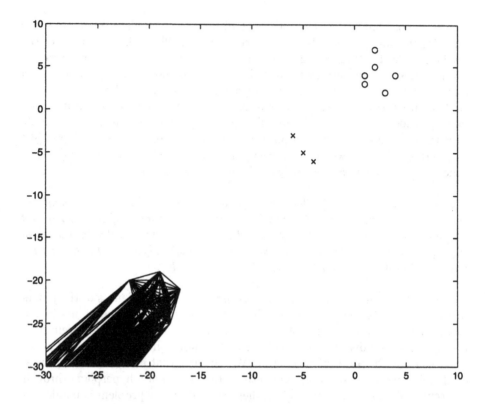

**Fig. 1.** A sample problem, and the "degenerating" polyhedron: whenever a point in the polyhedron is added to the class 1 (circle), the problem has the degenerate solution $\mathbf{w} = b = 0$

randomly from the input distribution). If, instead, our dataset looks more like that of Figure 1, we are better off removing outliers and resolving.

Finally, a brief remark on complexity is in order. The quadratic program (D) can be solved in polynomial time, and solving this program will allow us to determine whether a given SVM training problem $\mathcal{P}$ is degenerate. However, the problem of determining whether or not a $\{0, C\}$-solution exists is not so easy. Certainly, if $\mathcal{P}$ is *not* degenerate, no $\{0, C\}$-solution exists, but the converse is false. Determining the existence of a $\{0, C\}$-solution may be quite difficult: if we require the $\mathbf{x}_i$ to lie in $\mathbb{R}^1$, determining whether a $\{0, C\}$-solution exists is already equivalent to solving the weakly NP-complete problem SUBSET-SUM (see [4] for more information on NP-completeness).[3]

---

[3] Because the problem is only weakly NP-complete, given a bound on the size of the numbers involved, the problem is polynomially solvable.

# References

1. C. Burges. A tutorial on support vector machines for pattern recognition. In *Data Mining and Knowledge Discovery*. Kluwer Academic Publishers, Boston, 1998. (Volume 2).
2. C. Cortes and V. Vapnik. Support vector networks. *Machine Learning*, 20:1–25, 1995.
3. E. Osuna. *Support Vector Machines: Training and Applications*. PhD thesis, Massachusetts Institute of Technology, 1998.
4. M. Garey and D. Johnson. *Computers and Intractability: A Guide to the Theory of NP-Completeness* W. Freeman and Company, San Francisco, 1979.

# A    Proof of Theorem 3

**Theorem 5.** *Given a non-degenerate problem $\mathcal{P}$, consider the polyhedron*

$$\mathbf{P_D} \equiv \{ \sum_{\mathbf{s}^p \in S_{n-1}} \lambda_{\mathbf{s}^p}(\mathbf{V} - \mathbf{s}^p) + \sum_{\mathbf{s}^r \in S_n} \alpha_{\mathbf{s}^r}(\mathbf{V} - \mathbf{x}^r) \mid \lambda_{\mathbf{s}^p}, \alpha_{\mathbf{s}^r} \geq 0, \sum_{\mathbf{s}^p \in S_{n-1}} \lambda_{\mathbf{s}^p} = 1 \}$$

PROOF:

(a, $\mathbf{P_D} \subseteq \mathbf{X_D}$) Given a set of $\lambda_{\mathbf{x}^p}$ and $\alpha_{\mathbf{s}^r}$ satisfying $\lambda_{\mathbf{s}^p}, \alpha_{\mathbf{s}^r} \geq 0$, $\sum_{\mathbf{s}^p \in S_{n-1}} \lambda_{\mathbf{s}^p} = 1$, we define $A \equiv \sum_{\mathbf{s}^r \in S_n} \alpha_{\mathbf{s}^r}$, and set

$$\omega_c = \frac{1}{1+A},$$

and, for $i \in K_1$, we set

$$\omega_i = \omega_c \Big( \sum_{\mathbf{s}^p \in S_{n-1}} \lambda_{\mathbf{s}^p} \chi_{\mathbf{s}^p}(\mathbf{x}_i) + \sum_{\mathbf{s}^p \in S_{n-1}} \lambda_{\mathbf{s}^p} \chi_{\mathbf{s}^r}(\mathbf{x}_i) \Big)$$

Then $0 \leq \omega_i \leq 1$ for each $i \in K_1$, and

$$\sum_{i \in K_1} \omega_i = \frac{n-1+nA}{1+A} = n - \frac{1}{1+A},$$

which is in $[n-1, n)$, so we conclude that the assigned $\omega_i$ are valid. Finally, substituting into Equation ( 8), we find:

$$\frac{V - \sum_{i \in K_1} \omega_i \mathbf{x}_i}{n - \sum_{i \in K_1} \omega_i} = \frac{V - \frac{1}{1+A} \sum_{i \in K_1} \Big( \sum_{\mathbf{s}^p \in S_{n-1}} \lambda_{\mathbf{s}^p} \chi_{\mathbf{s}^p}(\mathbf{x}_i) + \sum_{\mathbf{s}^r \in S_n} \alpha_{\mathbf{s}^r} \chi_{\mathbf{s}^r}(\mathbf{x}_i) \Big) \mathbf{x}_i}{\frac{1}{1+A}}$$

$$= (1+A)V - \sum_{\mathbf{s}^p \in S_{n-1}} \lambda_{\mathbf{s}^p} \mathbf{s}^p - \sum_{\mathbf{s}^r \in S_n} \alpha_{\mathbf{s}^r} \mathbf{s}^r$$

$$= \sum_{\mathbf{s}^p \in S_{n-1}} \lambda_{\mathbf{s}^p}(V - \mathbf{s}^p) + \sum_{\mathbf{s}^r \in S_n} \alpha_{\mathbf{s}^r}(V - \mathbf{s}^r)$$

We conclude that $\mathbf{P_D} \subseteq \mathbf{X_D}$.

(b, $\mathbf{X_D} \subseteq \mathbf{P_D}$) Our proof is by construction: given a set of $\omega_i$, $i \in K_1$, we show how to choose $\lambda_{\mathbf{s}^p}$ and $\alpha_{\mathbf{s}^r}$ so that:

$$\lambda_{\mathbf{s}^p} \geq 0 \quad \forall \mathbf{s}^p \in S_{n-1}$$

$$\sum_{\mathbf{s}^p \in S_{n-1}} \lambda_{\mathbf{s}^p} = 1$$

$$\alpha_{\mathbf{s}^r} \geq 0 \quad \forall \mathbf{x}_r \in S_n$$

$$\frac{V - \sum_{i \in K_1} \omega_i \mathbf{x}_i}{n - \sum_{i \in K_1} \omega_i} = \sum_{\mathbf{s}^p \in S_{n-1}} \lambda_{\mathbf{s}^p}(V - \mathbf{s}^p) + \sum_{\mathbf{s}^r \in S_n} \alpha_{\mathbf{s}^r}(V - \mathbf{s}^r)$$

If we impose the reasonable "separability" conditions:

$$\frac{V}{n - \sum_{i \in K_1} \omega_i} = \sum_{\mathbf{s}^p \in S_{n-1}} \lambda_{\mathbf{s}^p} V + \sum_{\mathbf{s}^r \in S_n} \alpha_{\mathbf{s}^r} V$$

$$\frac{\sum_{i \in K_1} \omega_i \mathbf{x}_i}{n - \sum_{i \in K_1} \omega_i} = \sum_{\mathbf{s}^p \in S_{n-1}} \lambda_{\mathbf{s}^p} \mathbf{s}^p + \sum_{\mathbf{s}^r \in S_n} \alpha_{\mathbf{s}^r} \mathbf{s}^r$$

we can easily derive the following:

$$\sum_{\mathbf{s}^r \in S_n} \alpha_{\mathbf{s}^r} = \frac{(\sum_{i \in K_1} \omega_i + 1) - n}{n - \sum_{i \in K_1} \omega_i} \equiv A$$

We are now ready to describe the actual construction. We will first assign the $\alpha_{\mathbf{s}^r}$, then the $\lambda_{\mathbf{s}^p}$. We describe in detail the assignment of the $\alpha_{\mathbf{s}^r}$, the assignment of the $\lambda_{\mathbf{s}^p}$ is essentially similar. We begin by initializing each $\alpha_{\mathbf{s}^p}$ to 0. At each step of the algorithm, we consider the "residual":

$$\frac{V - \sum_{i \in K_1} \omega_i \mathbf{x}_i}{n - \sum_{i \in K_1} \omega_i} - \sum_{\mathbf{s}^r \in S_n} \alpha_{\mathbf{s}^r}(V - \mathbf{s}^r) \tag{9}$$

Note that by expanding each $\mathbf{s}^r$ in the $n$ points of $K_1$ which sum to it, we can represent (9) as a multiple of $V$ minus a linear combination of the points of $K_1$ — we will maintain the invariant that this linear combination is actually a nonnegative combination. During a step of the algorithm, we select the $n$ points of $K_1$ that have the largest coefficients in this expansion. If there is a tie, we expand the set to include all points with coefficients equal to the $n$th largest coefficient. Let $j$ be the number of points in the set that share the $n$th largest coefficient, and let $k\ (\geq n)$ be the total size of the selected set. We select the $\left(\frac{j}{n-k+j}\right)$ points $\mathbf{s}^r$ containing the remaining $\max(k-j,0)$ points with the largest coefficients, and $n-k+j$ of the $j$ points which contain the $n$th largest coefficient. We will then add equal amounts of each of these $\mathbf{s}^r$ to our representation until some pair of coefficients in the residual that were unequal become equal. This can happen in one of two ways: either the smallest of the coefficients in our set can become equal to a new, still smaller coefficient, or the second smallest coefficient in the set can become equal to the smallest (this can only happen in the case where $k > n$.) At each step of the algorithm, the total number of different coefficients in the residual is reduced by at least one, so, within $|K_1|$ steps, we will be able to assign all the $\alpha_{\mathbf{s}^r}$ (note that at each step of our algorithm, we increase $\left(\frac{j}{n-k+j}\right)$ of the $\alpha_{\mathbf{s}^r}$). The only way the algorithm could break down is if, at some step, there were fewer than $n$ points in $K_1$ with nonzero coefficients in the residual. Trivially, the algorithm does not break down at the first step — there must always be at least $n$ points with non-zero coefficients initially. To show that the algorithm does not break down at a later step, assume that after assigning coefficients to the $\mathbf{s}^r$ totaling $k(< A)$, we are left with $j(< n)$ non-zero coefficients. Noting that our algorithm requires that each of the $j$ remaining points with non-zero coefficients is part of each $\mathbf{s}^r$ with a non-zero coefficient, we can see that the the residual value of each of these $j$ points is no more then $\frac{1}{n-w} - k$. We derive the following bound on the *initial* sum of the coefficients, which we call $I_{sum}$:

$$I_{sum} \leq j\left(\frac{1}{n - \sum\limits_{i \in K_1} \omega_i} - k\right) + kn$$

$$= \frac{j}{n - \sum\limits_{i \in K_1} \omega_i} + k(n - j)$$

$$\leq \frac{n - 1}{n - \sum\limits_{i \in K_1} \omega_i} + k$$

$$< \frac{n - 1}{n - \sum\limits_{i \in K_1} \omega_i} + \frac{\sum\limits_{i \in K_1} \omega_i + 1 - n}{n - \sum\limits_{i \in K_1} \omega_i}$$

$$= \frac{\sum\limits_{i \in K_1} \omega_i}{n - \sum\limits_{i \in K_1} \omega_i}$$

But this is a contradiction, $I_{sum}$ must be equal to $\dfrac{\sum\limits_{i \in K_1} \omega_i}{n - \sum\limits_{i \in K_1} \omega_i}$ . We conclude that we are able to assign the $\alpha_{\mathbf{s}^r}$ successfully. Extremely similar arguments hold for the $\lambda_{\mathbf{s}^p}$.

# Learnability of Enumerable Classes of Recursive Functions from "Typical" Examples

Jochen Nessel

University of Kaiserslautern, Postfach 3049, D-67653 Kaiserslautern, Germany
nessel@informatik.uni-kl.de

**Abstract.** The paper investigates whether it is possible to learn every enumerable classes of recursive functions from "typical" examples. "Typical" means, there is a computable family of finite sets, such that for each function in the class there is *one* set of examples that can be used in *any* suitable hypothesis space for this class of functions. As it will turn out, there are enumerable classes of recursive functions that are not learnable from "typical" examples. The learnable classes are characterized.

The results are proved within an abstract model of learning from examples, introduced by Freivalds, Kinber and Wiehagen. Finally, the results are interpreted and possible connections of this theoretical work to the situation in real life classrooms are pointed out.

## 1 Introduction

This work started with the following question. Assume a teacher has to teach five pupils the concepts from a given concept class. Is it always possible to come up with one finite set of examples for each concept, such that all pupils will learn the intended concept when given the corresponding set of examples?

This seems to be a very natural question; in fact every teacher will ask herself the question, as to which examples she should present to her pupils to have all of them learn, for example, arithmetic.

In inductive inference, a pupil is mostly represented by a learning machine $M$ and a hypothesis space $\varphi$, which is usually some numbering. The machine is fed examples of some unknown concept – which has to be represented in $\varphi$ – and outputs one or more hypotheses, which are interpreted with respect to $\varphi$. The machine has learned the concept successfully, if its last hypothesis is a correct description for what it had to learn.

Some of the results in learning theory depend fundamentally on the choice of an appropriate hypothesis space; see for example [6], [7]. This problem of finding a suitable hypothesis space for a target class could be avoided, if there were examples so "typical" for the concepts in the target class, that they would suffice to learn in *any* hypothesis space.

In this paper, we will investigate this problem for the relatively manageable case of enumerable sets of recursive functions. The used learning model was introduced by Freivalds, Kinber and Wiehagen; cf. [2]. One of their intentions was to

O. Watanabe, T. Yokomori (Eds.): ALT'99, LNAI 1720, pp. 264–275, 1999.

model the teacher–pupil–scenario encountered real life classrooms; more on this in the next section. Even in this rather easy case, there are enumerable classes of recursive functions, that do not have "typical" examples. The paper gives a recursion theoretic characterization of the enumerable classes learnable from "typical" examples. It would be nice though, to have a deeper understanding of which classes fall within this characterization.

The next section gives formal definitions, some basic results and further motivation regarding the models used for this investigation. In section three we give the main results. Due to lack of space, only a few proofs could be included entirely in the main part of the paper, the rest is sketched. The last section is devoted to conclusions, open problems and an attempt to give connections of this theoretical work to real life teaching. It might be argued that this has no place in work on machine learning. But the author is convinced, that if machine learning might give insights into how humans learn or problems they might face while learning, the possibility to discuss this insights should not be passed by.

## 2  Definitions, Notations, and Basic Results

In the following, familiarity with standard mathematical and recursion theoretic notation and concepts, as given for example in [10], is assumed.

$\mathcal{P}^n$ will denote the set of *partial recursive functions* of $n$ arguments; by definition $\mathcal{P} = \mathcal{P}^1$. $\mathcal{R}$ will stand for the set of *recursive functions*. Sometimes, functions are identified with their graphs; for example "$020^\infty$" may stand for the function that is everywhere zero with exception of argument 1, where it assumes value 2. For a function $f$, $f(x)\downarrow$ means that $f$ is defined on argument $x$. A function $f$ is an *initial segment* of a function $g \in \mathcal{R}$, if $domain(f) = \{0, \ldots, n\}$ for some $n$ and furthermore $f \subseteq g$. For any recursive $f$, let $f^n$ stand for a standard encoding of the initial segment of $f$ with length $n$. This will later ease the definition of the learning machines, that can then be thought off as machines with a fixed number of input parameters.

All functions in $\mathcal{P}^2$ are called *numberings*. Let $\varphi$ and $\psi$ range over numberings and let $\eta$ be any fixed standard acceptable numbering; cf. [10]. A numbering $\varphi$ *has decidable equality*, if the set $\{(i,j) \mid \varphi_i = \varphi_j\}$ is recursive. A numbering is called *one-one*, if every function appears at most once in it. A numbering $\varphi$ is said to be *reducible* to a numbering $\psi$, written $\varphi \preceq \psi$, if there exists $r \in \mathcal{R}$ such that $\varphi_i = \psi_{r(i)}$ for all $i$. The function $r$ is then called a *reduction*. Two numberings $\varphi$ and $\psi$ are called *equivalent*, written $\varphi \equiv \psi$, if both $\varphi \preceq \psi$ and $\psi \preceq \varphi$ hold.

Define $\mathcal{P}_\varphi = \{f \mid$ there exists $i$ such that $\varphi_i = f\}$. If $\mathcal{P}_\varphi \subseteq \mathcal{P}_\psi$, then $\varphi$ is a *subnumbering* of $\psi$.

Let $U$ range over subsets of $\mathcal{R}$. $U$ is said to be *enumerable*, if there is a numbering $\varphi$ satisfying $\mathcal{P}_\varphi = U$.

Let $\varphi$ be any numbering. A numbering $ex$ *contains good examples for* $\varphi$ if the following conditions are fulfilled: (1) $ex_i \subseteq \varphi_i$ for all $i$, and (2) there is $e \in \mathcal{R}$ such that $e(i) = card(domain(ex_i))$ for all $i$.

In particular, part (2) implies that $domain(ex_i)$ is finite and recursive. Therefore, the *set of good examples* $\{(x, ex_i(x)) \mid x \in domain(ex_i)\}$ can easily be computed from $i$, i.e. there is an effective algorithm that computes on input $i$ the good examples given by $ex_i$, returns them and stops; cf. [2]. We will say "$ex$ are good examples for $\varphi$" synonymously for "there is a numbering $ex$ containing good examples for $\varphi$".

An *inference machine* is any computable device that takes given, finite sets of examples to natural numbers, which will be interpreted as programs with respect to some previously selected numbering.

**Definition 1.** *(See [2].) $U$ is called learnable from good examples with respect to $\varphi$ (written $U \in Gex\text{-}Fin_\varphi$) if there exist good examples $ex$ for $\varphi$ and an inference machine $M$, such that for all $i$ such that $\varphi_i \in U$ and all finite $A$ such that $ex_i \subseteq A \subseteq \varphi_i$ the following holds: $M(A){\downarrow}$ and $\varphi_{M(A)} = \varphi_i$.*
*Let $Gex\text{-}Fin = \{U \mid U \in Gex\text{-}Fin_\varphi \text{ for some } \varphi\}$.*

Note that we require only functions in the target class $U$ to be identified. Furthermore, we require $M$ to learn from any finite superset of the good examples, as long as this set is contained in the target function. This is done in order to avoid some coding tricks, like presenting the only example $(i, \varphi_i(i))$ in order to learn $\varphi_i$, which would have nothing in common with the learning problem we would like to model.

Other models consider learning to be a limiting process.

**Definition 2.** *(See [3].) An inference machine $M$ is said to identify a recursive function $f$ with respect to $\varphi$ in the limit if, for all $n$, $M(f^n){\downarrow} = i_n$ and there exists an $i_{n_0}$ such that $i_m = i_{n_0}$ for all $m \geq n_0$, and furthermore $\varphi_{i_{n_0}} = f$.*

In other words, an inference machine learning some $f$ can change its mind about a correct description for $f$ a finite number of times, but must eventually converge to an index for $f$ in $\varphi$.

**Definition 3.** *$U$ is learnable in the limit with respect to $\varphi$ (written $U \in EX_\varphi$) if there is an inference machine, that identifies every $f \in U$ with respect to $\varphi$.*
*Define $EX = \{U \mid U \in EX_\varphi \text{ for some } \varphi\}$.*

There are two major differences between these two definitions: (1) a "good-example-machine" receives *one finite* set of examples, whereas a "Gold-machine" over time will see every value of the target function; and (2): a good-example-machine is only allowed one guess, whereas a Gold-machine can change its guess finitely many times.

So it would be natural to expect the relation $Gex\text{-}Fin \subset EX$. But surprisingly, Freivalds, Kinber and Wiehagen in [2] proved

**Theorem 1.** *$EX \subset Gex\text{-}Fin$.*

Beside the formal proof, there is an intuitive argument supporting this result: when the good-example-machine gets its examples, which are computed from a program of the function to be learned, it *knows* that these examples are the *important* part of the target function and can concentrate its efforts on processing this important information. On the other hand, the Gold-machine might not be able to distinguish the important part of what it sees from unimportant information and therefore cannot learn a function it is presented, even though it may change its mind a finite number of times.

Furthermore, the result states, that for every function in every EX-learnable class, there *is* such an *important* part of that function which suffices to identify it with respect to the other functions in $U$.

Theorem 1 is one reason the Gex-model was used for this study, since it contains everything that can be learned in the limit if all examples are demonstrated. The other reason is, that the Gex–model seems to model the usual pupil–teacher–situation pretty well, which is interesting in its own right. To see this, imagine the good examples $ex_i = \{(x, ex_i(x)) \mid x \in domain(ex_i)\}$ to be computed by a teacher, who wants a pupil $(M, \varphi)$ – i.e., the "learning-algorithm" $M$ the pupil knows, together with the pupils "knowledge-base" $\varphi$ – to learn concept $\varphi_i$. The pupil is then given a superset of those examples by the teacher, processes them, and hopefully comes up with a representation of the intended concept. We will follow this thoughts in the conclusions some more.

Suppose we want to learn an enumerable class $U$. It is rather easy to see that there exist infinitely many enumerations for any such $U$. Furthermore, the following holds:

**Proposition 1.** *Let $U$ be any enumerable class and $\varphi$ any numbering satisfying $\mathcal{P}_\varphi = U$. Then $U \in Gex\text{-}Fin_\varphi$ iff $\{(i,j) \mid \varphi_i = \varphi_j\}$ is recursive.*

*Proof.* (Sketch) "$\Rightarrow$" Assume a) $U \in Gex\text{-}Fin_\varphi$, where b) $\varphi \in \mathcal{R}^2$. Then a) is easily seen to imply $\varphi_i = \varphi_j$ iff $ex_i \subseteq \varphi_j$ and $ex_j \subseteq \varphi_i$; while b) together with the properties of good examples implies that the latter test is recursive.

"$\Leftarrow$" If equality in $\varphi$ is decidable, it is very easy to compute good examples, since $\varphi_j \neq \varphi_j$ yields the existence of an $x$ such that $\varphi_i(x)\downarrow \neq \varphi_j(x)\downarrow$. □

Let us now consider an arbitrary enumerable class $U$ of recursive functions. The following is a well known result from recursion theory; see [5] for references.

**Proposition 2.** *For every enumerable class $U$ there exists a numbering $\varphi$ such that $\mathcal{P}_\varphi = U$ and $\{(i,j) \mid \varphi_i = \varphi_j\}$ is recursive.*

So, by Proposition 1 we get that for any enumerable class $U$ there are inference machines able to learn $U$ in the $Gex\text{-}Fin$–sense with respect to $\varphi$. Now it is easy to see that there are infinitely many numberings enumerating $U$ and all have recursive equality.

Let $f$ be any function from $U$. Is there a set of examples so *typical* for $f$, such that a teacher could present those examples to *any* machine able to learn $U$ – and hence $f$ – and it comes up with a correct description for $f$?

The results in the next section will show, that there exist classes of recursive functions that do not have "typical" examples.

# 3   Results

**Definition 4.** *Let $U$ be an enumerable class of recursive functions.*

$$Hyp(U) = \{\varphi \mid U \in \textit{Gex-Fin}_\varphi\}$$

The abbreviation *Hyp* should remind the fact, that this set contains all suitable hypothesis spaces for the class $U$. Now Propositions 2 and 1 imply that $Hyp(U) \neq \emptyset$ for all enumerable classes $U$.

Next we define what it means for an enumerable class of functions to be learnable with typical examples.

**Definition 5.** *Let $U$ be an enumerable class of recursive functions. We say $U \in \textit{Gex-Fin}$ with typical examples, if there exist $\varphi \in Hyp(U)$ and good examples ex for $U$ with respect to $\varphi$ such that $U \in \textit{Gex-Fin}_\varphi$ with the good examples given by ex, and for all $\psi \in Hyp(U)$ there exist good examples $ex'$ such that $U \in \textit{Gex-Fin}_\psi$ with examples $ex'$ and furthermore, for all $i, j$, we have that $\varphi_i = \psi_j$ implies $ex_i = ex'_j$.*

In other words, $U$ is learnable from typical examples, if there is a way to choose the examples for any $f \in U$ to be equal in all suitable hypothesis spaces. This seems to capture our intention pretty well, since a teacher can now present this set of examples to all inference machines and all of them will learn $f$. So, the examples are so "typical" for $f$ with respect to the other functions in $U$, that *every* machine able to learn $U$, can do so when given the "typical" examples.

Note that this definition implies the typical examples to be uniformaly computable for each admissible hypothesis space.

The first result in this section characterizes the enumerable sets of recursive functions that may be learned with typical examples.

**Theorem 2.** *Let $U$ be an enumerable class of recursive functions. $U \in \textit{Gex-Fin}$ with typical examples iff $\varphi \equiv \psi$ holds for all $\varphi, \psi \in Hyp(U)$.*

*Proof.* "$\Rightarrow$" The reduction $r$ to be defined takes $\varphi$-indices to $\psi$-indices by just searching for a function with the same set of good examples, which exists by assumption and definition of typical examples.

"$\Leftarrow$" From Proposition 1 we get that the set $Hyp(U)$ contains every one-one-numbering of $U$, since for those numberings equality is obviously decidable. Let $\varphi$ be any one-one-numbering of $U$. Proposition 1 implies $U \in \textit{Gex-Fin}_\varphi$; let $ex$ be the good examples witnessing this. Pick any $\psi \in Hyp(U)$. Then, by assumption, $\psi \preceq \varphi$ via some $r \in \mathcal{R}$. Define $ex'_i = ex_{r(i)}$ for all $i$. Since $ex$ are good examples for $\varphi$ and $\varphi_{r(i)} = \psi_i$ for all $i$, $ex'$ contains good examples for $\psi$. Furthermore, if $\psi_i = \psi_j$ then $r(i) = r(j)$, because $\varphi$ is one-one, and therefore $ex'_i = ex'_j$. This yields that equality in $\psi$ is decidable and, applying Proposition 1, we get $U \in \textit{Gex-Fin}$ with typical examples.    $\square$

Proofs for the following theorem are already known, see [5] and the references therein for a short survey; especially [9]. A new proof is given here that allows the observations we need in order to make our point concerning the existence of typical examples.

**Theorem 3.** *There exists an enumerable class of recursive functions that has one-one numberings $\varphi$ and $\psi$ such that $\varphi \not\equiv \psi$.*

The two constructed numberings being one-one implies $\{\varphi, \psi\} \subseteq Hyp(\mathcal{P}_\varphi)$. But now Theorem 2 implies that $\mathcal{P}_\varphi$ is not learnable with typical examples.

*Proof.* We will construct two numberings $\varphi$ and $\psi$ in parallel and diagonalize against all functions possibly witnessing $\varphi \preceq \psi$. Recall that $\eta$ is a numbering of all partial recursive functions.

Initialize: For all $i$, set $\varphi_i := \psi_i := \emptyset$ and $\ell_i := 0$. Set $D := \emptyset$ and $n := 0$.
Step $s$: Set $\varphi_n := 1^s 0^\infty$, $\ell_n := s$, $\psi_n := 1^s 0$, $D := D \cup \{n\}$, $n := n + 1$.
  For $i = 1$ to $n - 1$, $i \in D$ do:
      Compute $j = \eta_{\ell_i}(i)$ for at most $s$ steps.
      (1)   If $j$ is still undefined, then $\psi_i := \psi_i 0$, i.e. extend $\psi_i$ with another
            zero.
      (2)   If $j = i$, then
                  set $\psi_i := \psi_i 1^\infty$ and terminate $\psi_i$,
                  set $\varphi_n := \psi_i$, $\psi_n := \varphi_i$, $n := n + 1$.
      (3)   If $j \neq i$, then $\psi_i := \psi_i 0^\infty$ and terminate $\psi_i$.
  next $i$

(a) First note that $\varphi$ and $\psi$ are computable, everywhere defined and $\mathcal{P}_\varphi = \mathcal{P}_\psi$; this follows immediately from the construction.

(b) Furthermore, $\varphi$ and $\psi$ are one-one: the functions in both numberings take as values only 0 and 1. For every $s$, at most two functions start with $1^s 0$. Furthermore, every function begins with $1^s 0$ for some suitable $s$. If there are two such functions, one continues with $0^\infty$ and the one is terminated by ending it with $1^\infty$; cf. (2) in the construction above.

(c) Finitely, $\{j \mid$ there is $i$ such that $\ell_i = j\} = \mathbb{N}$: obviously, in every step $s$ some $\ell_n$ will assume the value $s$.

So we have – by (a) and (b) – that $\mathcal{P}_\varphi = \mathcal{P}_\psi$ is an enumerable set of functions and both $\varphi$ and $\psi$ are one-one. It remains to prove that $\varphi \not\preceq \psi$.

Assume by way of contradiction, there is a recursive function $\eta_c$ satisfying $\varphi_n = \psi_{\eta_c(n)}$ for all $n$. By (c) there exists $i$ such that $\ell_i = c$. Since $\eta_{\ell_i}$ is recursive, $\eta_{\ell_i}(i) \downarrow = j$. There are two possible cases:

$i = j$ : Then $\psi_i = 1^{\ell_i} 0^k 1^\infty$ for some suitable $k$, since the construction will be terminated in (2). But $\varphi_i = 1^{\ell_i} 0^\infty$ and therefore $\varphi_i \neq \psi_i$. Contradiction.

$i \neq j$ : In this case $\varphi_i = \psi_i = 1^{\ell_i} 0^\infty$ by (3) of the construction. Since $\psi$ is one-one, $\psi_j \neq \psi_i$ follows. Contradiction.

So, $\varphi \not\preceq \psi$ and hence the theorem follows. $\qquad\square$

**Corollary 1.** *Let $\varphi$ and $\psi$ be the numberings constructed in the proof of Theorem 3. Assume $\mathcal{P}_\varphi \in Gex\text{-}Fin_\varphi$ with good examples $ex$ and $\mathcal{P}_\varphi \in Gex\text{-}Fin_\psi$ with good examples $ex'$. Then there exist infinitely many $i$ such that*

(1) $ex_i \subseteq \psi_i$ and $ex'_i \subseteq \varphi_i$,
(2) $\varphi_i \neq \psi_i$.

*Proof.* Due to space restriction we only give an informal argument. If $\varphi_i \neq \psi_i$, then there exists $j$ such that $\varphi_i = \psi_j$ and $\varphi_j = \psi_i$. The set $\{i \mid \varphi_i = \psi_i\}$ is not recursive and therefore so is the question, whether there is a $j$ as mentioned above. The functions $\varphi_i$ and $\psi_i$ have the same beginning and since it is not known if they will differ later, the good examples – once for $\varphi$ and once for $\psi$ – have to be selected from this common part. If the two functions differ, i.e. if there exists $j$ as indicated above, then the good examples $ex_j$ ($ex'_j$, resp.) can be selected as to contain a difference between $\varphi_i$ and $\varphi_j$ ($\psi_i$ and $\psi_j$, resp.). So, $\varphi_i$ and $\psi_i$ are not equal, but the examples were picked from the common part. This yields the assertion. □

Let us interpret this result. Pick any $i$ satisfying conditions (1) and (2) of the corollary. Note that (1) implies $ex_i \cup ex'_i \subseteq \varphi_i$ and $ex_i \cup ex'_i \subseteq \psi_i$. Hence, $ex_i \cup ex'_i$ is an admissible input for any inference machine $M_1$ witnessing $\mathcal{P}_\varphi \in Gex\text{-}Fin_\varphi$ as well as for any inference machine $M_2$ witnessing $\mathcal{P}_\varphi \in Gex\text{-}Fin_\psi$. Since both numberings are one-one and by definition of the inference process, we get $\varphi_{M_1(ex_i \cup ex'_i)} = \varphi_i$ and $\psi_{M_2(ex_i \cup ex'_i)} = \psi_i$. So, both machines learn a function from the input $ex_i \cup ex'_i$, but since $\varphi_i \neq \psi_i$, they have learned different functions from the same set of examples. The corollary states that this will happen for infinitely many concepts in $\mathcal{P}_\varphi$, regardless of how the teacher selects the examples for the machines $M_1$ and $M_2$ and their respective hypothesis spaces $\varphi$ and $\psi$.

Now we will prove the theorems for the general case. Again we stress that the fact stated in Theorem 4 is already known. On the other hand, the proof given here had to be made from scratch in order to guarantee the properties we need to formulate and prove Corollary 2.

**Theorem 4.** *For each $2 \leq a \in \mathbb{N}$ there exist numberings $\varphi^1, \ldots, \varphi^a$ with the following properties for all $0 \leq i, j \leq a$:*

(1) $\varphi^i \in \mathcal{R}^2$ and is one-one,
(2) $\mathcal{P}_{\varphi^i} = \mathcal{P}_{\varphi^j}$ and
(3) $i \neq j$ implies $\varphi^i \not\equiv \varphi^j$.

*Proof.* Let $a \geq 2$ be given. We will construct the numberings $\varphi^1, \ldots, \varphi^a$ in parallel by diagonalizing against all possible $\binom{a}{2}$-tuples of reductions among the $\varphi^i$. There are easier ways to prove part (3) of the theorem, but this will enable us to prove an analogue to Corollary 1.

The construction below uses lists. Let [] denote the empty list. For some non-empty list $L = [a, b, c, d]$, as you would expect, $Head(L) = a$ and $Tail(L) = [b, c, d]$.

Now we will give a short explanation of the variables used in the construction and hope this will increase readability a little bit.

In $\ell_i$ we code the reductions we will diagonalize against with the set of functions beginning with $1^{\ell_i}0$. Of course we could get this information by scanning the beginning part of each function, but this keeps notation easier. In $L_i$ we keep a *list* of reductions, in the order we want to diagonalize against them. The variable $m_i$ will denote the biggest value, for which all the functions starting with $1^{\ell_i}0$ have been already defined. If we write $c_{ij}$, we will mean reduction $\eta_{c_{ij}}$ which is supposed to reduce $\varphi^i$ to $\varphi^j$. Finally, we use $b_x$ and $b_y$ to store the index of the "biggest" function beginning with $1^{\ell_i}0$ in $\varphi^x$ and $\varphi^y$. By "biggest" we mean the function $f$ with the largest $x \in domain(f)$ such that $f(x) = 1$ up to the arguments defined until now. Note that it will be possible to compute those, since we have knowledge of $m_i$.

Initialize: $\varphi_i^j := \emptyset$ for all $j \in \{1, \ldots, a\}, i \geq 0$.
$\quad \ell_i := m_i := n := 0$ and $L_i = []$ for all $i \geq 0$.
Step $s$: $\ell_n := s = \langle c_{12}, c_{13}, \ldots, c_{1a}, c_{23}, \ldots, c_{a-1\,a} \rangle$
$\quad L_n = [c_{12}, c_{23}, c_{34}, \ldots, c_{a-1\,a}, \text{"rest"}]$, where "rest" is the list resulting from
$\quad$ erasing $c_{12}, c_{23}, c_{34}, \ldots, c_{a-1\,a}$ from the list $[c_{12}, c_{13}, \ldots, c_{1a}, c_{23}, \ldots, c_{a-1\,a}]$
$\quad$ [* For example $L_n = [c_{12}, c_{23}, c_{34}, c_{45}, c_{13}, c_{14}, c_{15}, c_{24}, c_{25}, c_{35}]$ *]
$\quad$ for $j = 1$ to $a$ do: $\varphi_n^j := 1^{\ell_n}0$; $m_n = \ell_n$; end for;
$\quad$ $n := n + 1$;
$\quad$ for $i = 1$ to $n - 1$, $\ell_i \neq 0$ do:
$\quad\quad$ if $L_i = []$ then    [* all reductions have been taken care off *]
$\quad\quad\quad$ for all $\varphi_z^j$, $j \in \{1, \ldots, a\}$, $z \leq n$, that begin with $1^{\ell_i}0$, define $\varphi_z^j(m_i + 1) := 0$.
$\quad\quad\quad$ end for
$\quad\quad$ $m_i := m_i + 1$.
$\quad\quad$ else    [* there still are reductions we need to diagonalize against *]
$\quad\quad$ $c := Head(L_i) = c_{xy}$
$\quad\quad$ if $x + 1 = y$ then    [* still in the "first part" of the diagonalization *]
$\quad\quad\quad$ compute $r := \eta_c(i)$ for at most $s$ steps.
$\quad\quad\quad$ if $r = i$ then
$\quad\quad\quad\quad$ [* so we have $\varphi_i^x = \varphi_i^y = 1^{\ell_i}0X0$, where 'X' is some suitable
$\quad\quad\quad\quad$ sequence of zeros and ones of length $m_i - \ell_i - 2$ *]
$\quad\quad\quad\quad$ $\varphi_i^x := 1^{\ell_i}0X000$;
$\quad\quad\quad\quad$ $\varphi_n^j := 1^{\ell_i}0X010$ for all $1 \leq j \leq x$;
$\quad\quad\quad\quad$ $\varphi_i^j := 1^{\ell_i}0X010$ for all $y \leq j \leq a$;
$\quad\quad\quad\quad$ $\varphi_n^j := 1^{\ell_i}0X000$ for all $y \leq j \leq a$;
$\quad\quad\quad\quad$ for all $\varphi_z^j$, $j \in \{1, \ldots, a\}$, $z \leq n$, that start with $1^{\ell_i}0$ and have
$\quad\quad\quad\quad$ not yet been defined for arguments $m_i + 1$ and $m_i + 2$, let
$\quad\quad\quad\quad$ $\varphi_z^j(m_i + 1) := \varphi_z^j(m_i + 2) := 0$.
$\quad\quad\quad\quad$ end for
$\quad\quad\quad\quad$ $n := n + 1$, $m_i := m_i + 2$; $L_i := Tail(L_i)$.
$\quad\quad$ else    [* i.e., $x + 1 < y$, the "second part" of the diagonalization *]
$\quad\quad\quad$ $b_x :=$ index of "biggest function" beginning with $1^{\ell_i}0$ in $\varphi^x$.
$\quad\quad\quad$ $b_y :=$ index of $\varphi_{b_x}^x$ in $\varphi^y$.
$\quad\quad\quad$ compute $r := \eta_c(b_x)$ for at most $s$ steps.
$\quad\quad\quad$ if $r = b_y$ then
$\quad\quad\quad\quad$ [* again $\varphi_i^x = \varphi_i^y = 1^{\ell_i}0X0$; see above *]
$\quad\quad\quad\quad$ $\varphi_{b_x}^x := 1^{\ell_i}0X000$;
$\quad\quad\quad\quad$ $\varphi_{b_y}^y := 1^{\ell_i}0X010$;
$\quad\quad\quad\quad$ $\varphi_n^j := 1^{\ell_i}0X010$ for all $j \in \{1, \ldots, a\} \setminus \{y\}$;

$$\varphi_n^y := 1^{\ell_i}0X000;$$

for all $\varphi_z^j$, $j \in \{1,\ldots,a\}$, $z \leq n$, that start with $1^{\ell_i}0$, and
have not yet been defined for arguments $m_i + 1$ and $m_i + 2$,
let $\varphi_z^j(m_i + 1) := \varphi_z^j(m_i + 2) := 0$.
end for

$$n := n + 1, \ m_i := m_i + 2; \ L_i := Tail(L_i).$$

if the computation of $\eta_c(i)$, or resp. $\eta_c(b_x)$ does not terminate, then
for all $\varphi_z^j$, $j \in \{1,\ldots,a\}$, $z \leq n$, that egin with $1^{\ell_i}0$, define $\varphi_z^j(m_i + 1) := 0$.
end for

$$m_i := m_i + 1.$$

end for

(a) Note that $\varphi^i \in \mathcal{R}^2$ and $\mathcal{P}_{\varphi^i} = \mathcal{P}_{\varphi^j}$ for all $i, j \in \{1,\ldots,a\}$ follows immediately from construction.

(b) Every $\varphi^i$ is one-one. This can be argued in the same way as in the proof of Theorem 2.

(c) For any $\binom{a}{2}$-tuple $(c_{12}, c_{13}, \ldots, c_{1a}, c_{23}, \ldots, c_{a-1 \, a})$ of indices of recursive functions, $\eta_{c_{ij}}$ does not reduce $\varphi^i$ to $\varphi^j$. Again, this can easily be seen, since the construction takes care that every possible reduction is wrong.

It remains to prove that $i \neq j$ implies $\varphi^i \not\equiv \varphi^j$ for $i, j \in \{1,\ldots,a\}$. Assume $i < j$, otherwise just exchange $i$ and $j$. Suppose by way of contradiction, that $\eta_k$ reduces $\varphi^i$ to $\varphi^j$. Hence $k$ is an index of a recursive function. Let $(k,\ldots,k)$ be an $\binom{a}{2}$-tuple. Obviously, it only contains indices of recursive functions. By (c) we have that, for all indices $c_{ij}$ in this tuple, $\eta_{c_{ij}}$ does not reduce $\varphi^i$ to $\varphi^j$. This contradicts our choice of $k$. The theorem follows.    □

**Corollary 2.** *Let $a \geq 2$ and $\varphi^1,\ldots,\varphi^a$ be the numberings constructed in the proof of Theorem 4. Assume $\varphi^i \in Gex\text{-}Fin_{\varphi^i}$ with good examples $ex^i$ for all $i \in \{1,\ldots,a\}$. Then there exist infinitely many $n$ such that*

(1) $ex_n^i \subseteq \varphi_n^j$ *for all* $i, j \in \{1,\ldots,a\}$ *and*
(2) $\varphi_n^i \neq \varphi_n^j$ *for all* $i, j \in \{1,\ldots,a\}$.

*Proof.* (Sketch) A self referential argument shows, that the construction used in the proof of Theorem 4 would make a mistake, if conditions (1) and (2) of the formulation of the corollary were not fulfilled.    □

This corollary somewhat strengthens the remarks following Corollary 1. Here we have the situation that, for infinitely many $n$, $(\bigcup_{j=1}^a ex_n^j) \subseteq \varphi_n^i$ and $\varphi_n^i \neq \varphi_n^k$ for all $i, k \in \{1,\ldots,a\}$. Condition (2) now implies that every machine learns a different function when presented with the examples $\bigcup_{j=1}^a ex_n^j$. The other comments apply here as well.

Furthermore note, that there *exist* families $\{ex_j^i\}_{j \geq 0, i \in \{1,\ldots,a\}}$ of finite sets, which we also might call "good examples" for now, such that $ex_j^i \subseteq \varphi_{j'}^{i'}$ iff $\varphi_j^i = \varphi_{j'}^{i'}$, for all $i, i' \in \{1,\ldots,a\}$ and $j, j' \geq 0$.

To see this, one checks the proof of Theorem 4, which yields that for every function $f$ in the generated numberings only finitely many $x$ exist, such that $f(x) \neq 0$. So there exist families containing examples with all and only those $x$.

It is easy to see, that now these sets of good examples are equal if and only if so are the corresponding functions. This obviously yields the assertion stated above. But none of this families is computable, since this would clearly contradict the corollary.

On the other hand: it would be easy to compute these families "in the limit". And hence, a teacher with lots of experience might know a good part of this typical examples for his area of expertise.

One might ask if this phenomenon can also be achieved for infinitely many numberings. As the following theorem, cf. [9], shows, there is indeed an infinite sequence of pairwise non-equivalent numberings, all of them enumerating the same class of recursive functions. The proof used here is conceptionally much simpler than the original one in [9].

**Theorem 5.** *There exists a sequence $\varphi^i$, $i \geq 0$, of numberings such that for all $i, j$ the following properties are satisfied:*

(1) $\varphi^i \in \mathcal{R}^2$, $\varphi^j \in \mathcal{R}^2$ *and both numberings are one-one,*
(2) $\mathcal{P}_{\varphi^i} = \mathcal{P}_{\varphi^j}$,
(3) $i \neq j$ *implies $\varphi^i \not\equiv \varphi^j$.*

*Proof.* (Sketch) This is again a diagonalization, but this time it is made sure that, for $i < j$, $\varphi^i$ can not be reduced to $\varphi^j$. In essence, the argument used to prove Theorem 3 is repeated an infinite number of times. The only thing to take care of is the accounting of which functions were used in the construction, in order to fulfill condition (2). $\square$

But there is no analogue for Corollaries 1 and 2. An analogue to the corollaries in the finite case would require for any choice of the good examples a sequence of indices $n_k$, $k \geq 0$, such that $\varphi^i_{n_k} \neq \varphi^j_{n_k}$ and $\bigcup_{k \geq 0} ex^k_{n_k} \subseteq \varphi^i_{n_i}$ for all $i, j$. Note that in the corollaries above we have that one index $n$ fulfills this requirement and do not need a whole sequence. But requiring one index $n$ would complicate the previous proof and is not needed for the following argument.

For each $\varphi^i$ in the sequence constructed in Theorem 5, $\mathcal{P}_{\varphi^i} \in Gex\text{-}Fin_{\varphi^i}$ holds by Proposition 1. Furthermore, this can be achieved with good examples $gex^i$ that satisfy, for all $i, j$, the following conditions: $card(gex^i_j) > max(\{i, j\})$ and furthermore $gex^i_j$ is an initial segment of $\varphi^i_j$. To see this, assume $\mathcal{P}_{\varphi^i} \in Gex\text{-}Fin_{\varphi^i}$ with good examples $ex^i$ for some $i$. Define $gex^i_j$, for all $j$, by $gex^i_j = \{(x, \varphi^i_j(x)) \mid 0 \leq x \leq max(\{i, j, max(domain(ex^i_j))\})\}$. Since the inference machine witnessing $\mathcal{P}_{\varphi^i} \in Gex\text{-}Fin_{\varphi^i}$ has to learn from all finite supersets of the good examples $ex^i$ as well, obviously $gex^i$ also are good examples for $\mathcal{P}_{\varphi^i}$ with respect to $\varphi^i$.

This yields that for every sequence $n_k$, the set $E = \bigcup_{k \geq 0} gex^k_{n_k}$ will be infinite. For every $x$ there is at least one $y$ such that $(x, y) \in E$, since the good examples are initial segments. Therefore $E$ can be contained in at most one function. In fact, $E$ might not even be a function, but a relation. An analogue to the corollaries in the finite case therefore can not hold.

# 4    Conclusion, Open Problems, and Interpretation

Theorem 4 and Corollary 2 witness the following fact: for every $n \geq 2$, there is an enumerable class of recursive functions and $n$ hypothesis spaces, such that, no matter how the teacher chooses the examples for some concepts within the class, *each* machine witnessing the learnability for one of those hypothesis spaces will learn a *different* function when confronted with this set of examples. Even worse, they *all* produce seemingly identical hypotheses consistent with the given examples, so that it is impossible for the teacher to know, whether the machines have successfully learned the intended function or not.

Of course, there are unanswered questions.

What do concept classes look like that fulfill the corollaries? What are necessary or/and sufficient conditions for those? Or, rephrased in recursion theoretic terms: given two recursive numberings $\varphi$ an $\psi$, what is needed to be able to test "pointwise equality" between them? I.e., is there an $f \in \mathcal{R}$ such that $f(i) = 1$ iff $\varphi_i = \psi_i$?

Another interesting question is, which classes of recursive functions have the property, that all their numberings with decidable equality are reducible to one another, or, equivalently, that all their one-one numberings are equal with respect to $\preceq$. This would characterize the classes of functions that are learnable with typical good examples, by using Theorem 2, in a different way. For enumerable classes, necessary and sufficient conditions are known in order to assure that *all* of their numberings are equivalent with respect to $\preceq$; cf. [5] and the references therein. But it is easy to see that there is an enumerable class $U$ of functions, such that all one-one numberings of $U$ are equivalent, but not all enumerations of $U$ are. For example, let $U = \{f_i \mid i \in \mathbb{N}\} \cup \{$ constant zero function$\}$, where $f_i$ is always 0, with exception of $i$, where it takes value 1. Obviously, all one-one numberings of $U$ are equivalent, and it is easy to construct two numberings of $U$ that are not equivalent, by exploiting the fact that the constant zero function is an "accumulation point" for $U$. (The function $f$ is an accumulation point for $U$, if for all $n \in \mathbb{N}$ there exists $m_n$ such that $m_n < m_{n+1}$ and $f(x) = g_n(x)$ for all $x < m_n$ and $f(m_n) \neq g_n(m_n)$ for some $g_n$ in $U$.)

In the comments following Corollary 2 it is mentioned, that "typical" examples could be computed in the limit. It could be interesting to find an intuitive definition for "limit computable examples", without "shifting" most of the inference process into this limiting computation.

The reader only interested in mathematical results may now stop reading. The following tries to give some connections of the obtained results to real life teaching and interpret them in that context.

As mentioned before, the pair $(M, \varphi)$ might be thought of as a pupil: the pupils learning algorithm $M$ and its knowledge base $\varphi$. In a classroom the following might happen: a teacher gives two pupils $(M_1, \varphi)$ and $(M_2, \psi)$ the examples for some concepts he wants them to learn. The pupils process those examples and return an identical hypothesis $i$, as it happens even in the theoretical case, see the comments following Corollary 2 on page 270. Now, if the teacher does not know which knowledge base a pupil is using, he might not know, if both pupils have learned the intended concept. As a consequence, he will have to submit them both to a series of tests, in order to check what they learned. And eventually, he will have to correct mistakes the pupils made. Normally this is achieved by presenting new examples to the pupil in order to make it see its mistake and learn the correct concept.

The corollaries show that there are concept classes and sets of pupils, such that for some concepts the teacher has to compute a different set of examples for each pupil. But this is only feasible in small classrooms, since otherwise the teacher just will not have the time to dedicate enough time to each student and compute a different set example for each one. So the model reflects the well know fact, that smaller classrooms improve learning performance. In addition one might notice that all students have the same learning potential, since all knowledge bases contain the same set of functions. Hence no pupil could be considered "stupid", they just generate and test ideas in a different way. This might be a reason why some pupils like some teachers and learn better with them: teacher and pupil use a similar "knowledge base", the teacher for generating and the pupil for testing the examples. So it is to expect that they will achieve good learning performance. Of course, there might, and most likely will, be other reasons, but it would be interesting to test this hypothesis in a real classroom.

I am grateful to R. Wiehagen, C. Smith and the referees for many valuable suggestions and to W. and A. Nessel for carefully reading a draft of this work.

# References

1. Jain, S., Lange, S., Nessel, J. (1997), Learning of r.e. Languages from Good Examples, in Li, Maruoka, Eds., *Eighth International Workshop on Algorithmic Learning Theory*, 32 - 47, Lecture Notes in Artificial Intelligence 1316, Springer Verlag.
2. Freivalds, R., Kinber, E.B., Wiehagen, R. (1993), On the power of inductive inference from good examples. *Theoretical Computer Science* 110, 131 - 144.
3. Gold, E.M. (1967), Language identification in the limit. *Information and Control* 10, 447 - 474.
4. Goldman, S.A., Mathias, H.D. (1996), Teaching a smarter learner. *Journal of Computer and System Sciences* 52, 255 - 267.
5. Kummer, M. (1995), A Learning-Theoretic Characterization of Classes of Recursive Functions, *Information Processing Letters* 54, 205 - 211.
6. Lange, S., Nessel, J., Wiehagen, R. (1998), Learning recursive languages from good examples, *Annals of Mathematics and Artificial Intelligence* 23, 27 - 52.
7. Lange, S., Zeugmann, T. (1993), Language Learning in Dependence on the Space of Hypotheses, Proceedings of the Sixth Annual ACM Conference on Computational Learning Theory, 127 - 136, ACM Press.
8. Lange, S., Zeugmann, T. (1993), Learning recursive languages with bounded mind-changes, *International Journal of Foundations of Computer Science* 2, 157 - 178.
9. Marchenkov, S. S. (1972), The computable enumerations of families of recursive functions, *Algebra i Logika* 11, 588-607; English Translation *Algebra and Logic* 15, 128 - 141, 1972.
10. Rogers, H. Jr. (1987), *Theory of Recursive Functions and Effective Computability*, MIT Press, Cambridge, Massachusetts.

# On the Uniform Learnability of Approximations to Non-recursive Functions

Frank Stephan[1],[*] and Thomas Zeugmann[2],[**]

[1] Mathematisches Institut, Universität Heidelberg, Im Neuenheimer Feld 294,
69120 Heidelberg, Germany
fstephan@math.uni-heidelberg.de
[2] Department of Informatics, Kyushu University, Kasuga 816-8580, Japan
thomas@i.kyushu-u.ac.jp

**Abstract.** Blum and Blum (1975) showed that a class $B$ of suitable recursive approximations to the halting problem is reliably $EX$-learnable. These investigations are carried on by showing that $B$ is neither in $NUM$ nor robustly $EX$-learnable. Since the definition of the class $B$ is quite natural and does not contain any self-referential coding, $B$ serves as an example that the notion of robustness for learning is quite *more restrictive* than intended.

Moreover, variants of this problem obtained by approximating any given recursively enumerable set $A$ instead of the halting problem $K$ are studied. All corresponding function classes $\mathcal{U}(A)$ are still $EX$-inferable but may *fail* to be reliably $EX$-learnable, for example if $A$ is non-high and hypersimple. Additionally, it is proved that $\mathcal{U}(A)$ is neither in $NUM$ nor robustly $EX$-learnable provided $A$ is part of a recursively inseparable pair, $A$ is simple but not hypersimple or $A$ is neither recursive nor high. These results provide more evidence that there is still some need to find an adequate notion for "naturally learnable function classes."

## 1. Introduction

Though algorithmic learning of recursive functions has been intensively studied within the last three decades there is still some need to elaborate this theory further. For the purpose of motivation, let us shortly recall the basic scenario.

An algorithmic learner is fed growing initial segments of the graph of the target function $f$. Based on the information received, the learner computes a

* Supported by the Deutsche Forschungsgemeinschaft (DFG) under Research Grant no. Am 60/9-2.
** Supported by the Grant-in-Aid for Scientific Research in Fundamental Areas from the Japanese Ministry of Education, Science, Sports, and Culture under grant no. 10558047. Part of this work was done while visiting the Laboratoire d'Informatique Algorithmique: Fondements et Applications, Université Paris 7. This author is gratefully indebted to Maurice Nivat for providing financial support and inspiring working conditions.

O. Watanabe, T. Yokomori (Eds.): ALT'99, LNAI 1720, pp. 276–290, 1999.
© Springer-Verlag Berlin Heidelberg 1999

hypothesis on each input. The sequence of all computed hypotheses has to converge to a correct, finite and global description of the target $f$. We shall refer to this scenario by saying that $f$ is *EX-learnable* (cf. Definition 1).

Clearly, what one is really interested in are powerful learning algorithms that cannot only learn one function but all functions from a given class of functions. Gold [11] provided the first such powerful learner, i.e., the *identification by enumeration* algorithm and showed that it can learn every class contained in *NUM*. Here *NUM* denotes the family of all function classes that are subsets of some recursively enumerable class of recursive functions.

There are, however, learnable classes of recursive functions which are not contained in *NUM*. The perhaps most prominent example is the class *SD* of self-describing recursive functions, i.e., of all those functions that compute a program for themselves on input 0. Clearly, *SD* is *EX*-learnable.

Since Gold's [11] pioneering paper a huge variety of learning criteria have been proposed within the framework of inductive inference of recursive functions (cf., e.g., [3,6,8,9,15,19,21]). By comparing these inference criteria to one another, it became popular to show separation results by using function classes with self-referential properties. On the one hand, the proof techniques developed are mathematically quite elegant. On the other hand, these separating examples may be considered to be a bit artificial, because of the use of self-describing properties. Hence, Bārzdiņš suggested to look at versions of learning that are closed under computable transformations (cf. [20,28]). For example, a class $\mathcal{U}$ is *robustly EX-learnable*, iff, for every computable operator $\Theta$ such that $\Theta(\mathcal{U})$ is a class of recursive functions, the class $\Theta(\mathcal{U})$ is *EX*-learnable, too (cf. Definition 4). There have been many discussions which operators are admissible in this context (cf., e.g., [10,14,16,20,23,28]). At the end, it turned out to be most suitable to consider only general recursive operators, that is, operators which map every total function to a total one. The resulting notion of robust *EX*-learning is the most general one among all notions of robust *EX*-inference.

Next, we state the two main questions that are studied in the present paper.

(1) What is the overall theory developed so far telling us about the learnability of "naturally defined function classes?"
(2) What is known about the robust *EX*-learnability of such "naturally defined function classes?"

Clearly an answer to the first question should tell us something about the usefulness of the theory, and an answer to the second problem should, in particular, provide some insight into the "naturalness" of robust *EX*-learning. However, our knowledge concerning both questions has been severely limited. For function classes in *NUM* everything is clear, i.e., their learnability has been proved with respect to many learning criteria including robust *EX*-learning. Next, let us consider one of the few "natural" function classes outside *NUM* that have been considered in the literature, i.e., the class $\mathcal{C}$ of all recursive complexity functions. Then, using Theorem 2.4 and Corollary 2.6. in [23], one can conclude that $\mathcal{C}$ is not robustly *EX*-learnable for many complexity measures including space, since there is no recursive function that bounds every function in $\mathcal{C}$ for all but finitely many arguments. On the other hand, $\mathcal{C}$ itself is still learnable with respect to many inference criteria by using the identification by enumeration learner.

The latter result already provides some evidence that the notion of robust $EX$-learning may be too restrictive. Nevertheless, the situation may be completely different if one looks at classes of $\{0,1\}$-valued recursive functions, since their learnability differs sometimes considerably from the inferability of arbitrary function classes (cf., e.g., [17,26]). As far as these authors are aware of, one of the very few "natural classes" of $\{0,1\}$-valued recursive functions that may be a candidate to be not included in $NUM$ has been proposed by Blum and Blum [6]. They considered a class $\mathcal{B}$ of approximations to the halting problem $K$ and showed that $\mathcal{B}$ is reliably $EX$-learnable. This class $\mathcal{B}$ is quite natural and not self-describing. It remained, however, open whether or not $\mathcal{B}$ is in $NUM$.

Within the present work, it is shown that $\mathcal{B}$ is neither in $NUM$ nor robustly $EX$-learnable. Moreover, we study generalizations of Blum and Blum's [6] original class by considering classes $\mathcal{U}(A)$ of approximations for any recursively enumerable set $A$. In particular, it is shown that all these classes remain $EX$-learnable but not necessarily reliably $EX$-inferable (cf. Theorems 14 and 16). Furthermore, we show $\mathcal{U}(A)$ to be neither in $NUM$ nor robustly $EX$-learnable provided $A$ is part of a recursively inseparable pair, $A$ is simple but not hypersimple or $A$ is neither recursive nor high (cf. Theorems 13 and 17).

Thus the results obtained enlarge our knowledge concerning the learnability of "naturally defined" function classes. Additionally, all those classes $\mathcal{U}(A)$ which are not in $NUM$ as well as $\mathcal{B}$ are natural examples for a class which is on the one side not self-describing and on the other side not robustly learnable. So all these $\mathcal{U}(A)$ provide some incidence that the presently discussed notions of robust and hyperrobust learning [1,7,10,14,16,23,28] destroy not only coding tricks but also the learnability of quite natural classes.

Due to the lack of space, many proofs are only sketched or omitted. We refer the reader to [25] for a full version of this paper.

## 2. Preliminaries

Unspecified notations follow Rogers [24]. $\mathbb{N} = \{0, 1, 2, \ldots\}$ and $\mathbb{N}^*$ denote the set of all natural numbers and the set of all finite sequences of natural numbers, respectively. $\{0,1\}^*$ stands for the set of all finite $\{0,1\}$-valued sequences and for all $x \in \mathbb{N}$ we use $\{0,1\}^x$ for the set of all $\{0,1\}$-valued sequences of length $x$.

The classes of all partial recursive and recursive functions of one, and two arguments over $\mathbb{N}$ are denoted by $\mathcal{P}$, $\mathcal{P}^2$, $\mathcal{R}$, and $\mathcal{R}^2$, respectively. $f \in \mathcal{P}$ is said to be monotone provided for all $x, y \in \mathbb{N}$ we have, if both $f(x)$ and $f(y)$ are defined then $f(x) \le f(y)$. $\mathcal{R}_{0,1}$ and $\mathcal{R}_{mon}$ denotes the set of all $\{0,1\}$-valued recursive functions and of all monotone recursive functions, respectively.

Furthermore, we write $f^n$ instead of the string $(f(0), \ldots, f(n))$, for any $n \in \mathbb{N}$ and $f \in \mathcal{R}$. Sometimes it will be suitable to identify a recursive function with the sequence of its values, e.g., let $\alpha = (a_0, \ldots, a_k) \in \mathbb{N}^*$, $j \in \mathbb{N}$, and $p \in \mathcal{R}_{0,1}$; then we write $\alpha j p$ to denote the function $f$ for which $f(x) = a_x$, if $x \leq k$, $f(k+1) = j$, and $f(x) = p(x-k-2)$, if $x \geq k+2$. Furthermore, let $g \in \mathcal{P}$ and $\alpha \in \mathbb{N}^*$; we write $\alpha \preceq g$ iff $\alpha$ is a prefix of the sequence of values associated with $g$, i.e., for all $x \leq k$, $g(x)$ is defined and $g(x) = a_x$.

Any function $\psi \in \mathcal{P}^2$ is called a numbering. Moreover, let $\psi \in \mathcal{P}^2$, then we write $\psi_i$ for the function $x \to \psi(i, x)$ and set $\mathcal{P}_\psi = \{\psi_i \mid i \in \mathbb{N}\}$ as well as $\mathcal{R}_\psi = \mathcal{P}_\psi \cap \mathcal{R}$. Consequently, if $f \in \mathcal{P}_\psi$, then there is a number $i$ such that $f = \psi_i$. If $f \in \mathcal{P}$ and $i \in \mathbb{N}$ are such that $\psi_i = f$, then $i$ is called a $\psi$–program for $f$. Let $\psi$ be any numbering, and $i, x \in \mathbb{N}$; if $\psi_i(x)$ is defined (abbr. $\psi_i(x)\downarrow$) then we also say that $\psi_i(x)$ converges. Otherwise, $\psi_i(x)$ is said to diverge (abbr. $\psi_i(x)\uparrow$).

A numbering $\varphi \in \mathcal{P}^2$ is called a Gödel numbering or acceptable numbering (cf. [24]) iff $\mathcal{P}_\varphi = \mathcal{P}$, and for any numbering $\psi \in \mathcal{P}^2$, there is a $c \in \mathcal{R}$ such that $\psi_i = \varphi_{c(i)}$ for all $i \in \mathbb{N}$. In the following, let $\varphi$ be any fixed Gödel numbering. As usual, we define the halting problem to be the set $K = \{i \mid i \in \mathbb{N}, \varphi_i(i)\downarrow\}$. Any function $\Phi \in \mathcal{P}^2$ satisfying $dom(\varphi_i) = dom(\Phi_i)$ for all $i \in \mathbb{N}$ and $\{(i, x, y) \mid i, x, y \in \mathbb{N}, \Phi_i(x) \leq y\}$ is recursive is called a complexity measure (cf. [5]).

Furthermore, let $NUM = \{\mathcal{U} \mid (\exists \psi \in \mathcal{R}^2)[\mathcal{U} \subseteq \mathcal{P}_\psi]\}$ denote the family of all subsets of all recursively enumerable classes of recursive functions.

Next, we define the concepts of learning mentioned in the introduction.

**Definition 1.**   Let $\mathcal{U} \subseteq R$ and $M : \mathbb{N}^* \to \mathbb{N}$ be a recursive machine.

(a) (Gold [11]) $M$ is an EX-learner for $\mathcal{U}$ iff, for each function $f \in \mathcal{U}$, $M$ converges syntactically to $f$ in the sense that there is a $j \in \mathbb{N}$ with $\varphi_j = f$ and $j = M(f^n)$ for all but finitely many $n \in \mathbb{N}$.

(b) (Angluin [2]) $M$ is a conservative EX-learner for $\mathcal{U}$ iff $M$ EX-learns $\mathcal{U}$ and $M$ makes in addition only necessary hypothesis changes in the sense that, whenever $M(\sigma\eta) \neq M(\sigma)$ then the program $M(\sigma)$ is inconsistent with the data $\sigma\eta$ by either $\varphi_{M(\sigma)}(x)\uparrow$ or $\varphi_{M(\sigma\eta)}(x)\downarrow \neq \sigma\eta(x)$ for some $x \in dom(\sigma\eta)$.

(c) (Bārzdins [4], Case and Smith [8]) $M$ is a BC-learner for $\mathcal{U}$ iff, for each function $f \in \mathcal{U}$, $M$ converges semantically to $f$ in the sense that $\varphi_{M(f^n)} = f$ for all but finitely many $n \in \mathbb{N}$.

A class $\mathcal{U}$ is EX-learnable iff it has a recursive EX-learner and EX denotes the family of all EX-learnable function classes. Similar we define when a class is conservatively EX-learnable or BC-learnable. We write BC for the family of all BC-learnable function classes.

Note that $EX \subset BC$ (cf. [8]). As far as we are aware of, it has been open whether or not conservative learning constitutes a restriction for EX-learning of recursive functions. The negative answer is provided by the next proposition.

**Proposition 2.** $EX =$ conservative-EX.

Nevertheless, whenever suitable, we shall design a conservative learner instead of just an EX-learner, thus avoiding the additional general transformation given by the proof of Proposition 2.

Next, we define reliable inference. Intuitively, a learner $M$ is reliable provided it converges if and only if it learns. There are several variants of reliable learning, so we will give a justification of our choice below.

**Definition 3 (Blum and Blum [6], Minicozzi [21]).** Let $\mathcal{U} \subseteq R$; then $\mathcal{U}$ is said to be *reliably EX-learnable* if there is a machine $M \in \mathcal{R}$ such that

(1)  $M$ $EX$-learns $\mathcal{U}$ and
(2)  for all $f \in \mathcal{R}$, if the sequence $(M(f^n))_{n \in \mathbb{N}}$ converges, say to $j$, then $\varphi_j = f$.

By $\mathcal{REX}$ we denote the family of all reliably $EX$-learnable function classes.

Note that one can replace the condition "$f \in \mathcal{R}$" in (2) of Definition 3 by "$f \in \mathcal{P}$" or "all total $f$." This results in a different model of reliable learning, say $\mathcal{PEX}$ and $\mathcal{TEX}$, respectively. Then for every $\mathcal{U} \subseteq \mathcal{R}_{0,1}$ such that $\mathcal{U} \in \mathcal{PEX}$ or $\mathcal{U} \in \mathcal{TEX}$ one has $\mathcal{U} \in NUM$ (cf. [6,12,26]). On the other hand, there are classes $\mathcal{U} \subseteq \mathcal{R}_{0,1}$ such that $\mathcal{U} \in \mathcal{REX} \setminus NUM$ (cf. [12]). As a matter of fact, our Theorem 6 below together with Blum and Blum's [6] result $\mathcal{B} \in \mathcal{REX}$ provides a much easier proof of the same result than Grabowski [12].

Finally, we define robust $EX$-learning. This involves the notion of general recursive operators. A general recursive operator is a computable mapping that maps functions over $\mathbb{N}$ to functions over $\mathbb{N}$ and every total function has to be mapped to a total function. For a formal definition and more information about general recursive operators the reader is referred to [13,22,27].

**Definition 4 (Jain, Smith and Wiehagen [16]).** Let $\mathcal{U} \subseteq \mathcal{R}$; then $\mathcal{U}$ is said to be *robustly EX-learnable* if $\Theta(\mathcal{U})$ is $EX$-learnable for every general recursive operator $\Theta$. By robust-$EX$ we denote the family of all robustly $EX$-learnable function classes.

# 3.  Approximating the Halting Problem

Within this section, we deal with Blum and Blum's [6] class $\mathcal{B}$. First, we define the class of approximations to the halting problem considered in [6].

**Definition 5.** Let $\tau \in \mathcal{R}$ be such that for all $i \in \mathbb{N}$

$$\varphi_{\tau(i)}(x) = \begin{cases} 1, & \text{if } \Phi_i(x)\downarrow \text{ and } \Phi_x(x) \leq \Phi_i(x) \\ 0, & \text{if } \Phi_i(x)\downarrow \text{ and } \neg[\Phi_x(x) \leq \Phi_i(x)] \\ \uparrow, & \text{otherwise.} \end{cases}$$

Now, we set $\mathcal{B} = \{\varphi_{\tau(i)} \mid i \in \mathbb{N} \text{ and } \Phi_i \in \mathcal{R}_{mon}\}$.

Blum and Blum [6] have shown $\mathcal{B} \in \mathcal{REX}$ but left it open whether or not $\mathcal{B} \in NUM$. It is not, as our next theorem shows.

**Theorem 6.** $\mathcal{B} \notin NUM$.

**Proof.** First, recall that $K$ is part of a recursively inseparable pair (cf. [22, Exercise III.6.23.(a)]). That is, there is an r.e. set $H$ such that $K \cap H = \emptyset$ and for every recursive set $A \supseteq H$ we have $|A \cap K| = \infty$. Now, we fix any enumeration $k_0, k_1, k_2, \ldots$ and $h_0, h_1, h_2, \ldots$ of $K$ and $H$, respectively. Suppose to the contrary, that there exists a numbering $\psi \in \mathcal{R}^2$ such that $B \subseteq \mathcal{R}_\psi$. Next, we define for each $\psi_e$ a function $g_e \in \mathcal{P}$ as follows. For all $e, x \in \mathbb{N}$ let

$g_e(x) =$ "Search for the least $n$ such that for $n = s + y$ either (A), (B) or (C) happens:

(A) $y = h_s \wedge \psi_e(y) = 1$
(B) $y = k_s \wedge \psi_e(y) = 0 \wedge y > x$
(C) $\psi_e(y) > 1$

If (A) happens first, then set $g_e(x) = s + y$.
If (B) happens first, then let $g_e(x) = \Phi_y(y) + y$.
If (C) happens first, then let $g_e(x) = 0$."

**Claim 1.** $g_e \in \mathcal{R}$ *for all* $e \in \mathbb{N}$.

If there is at least one $y$ such that $\psi_e(y) > 1$, then $g_e \in \mathcal{R}$. Now let $\psi_e \in \mathcal{R}_{0,1}$ and suppose that there is an $x \in \mathbb{N}$ with $g_e(x)\!\uparrow$ . Then there are no $s, y$ such that $y = h_s$ and $\psi_e(y) = 1$. Hence, $M = \{y \mid y \in \mathbb{N} \wedge \psi_e(y) = 0\} \supseteq H$ and $M$ is recursive. Thus, $|M \cap K| = \infty$. So there must be a $y > x$ such that $\psi_e(y) = 0$ and an $s \in \mathbb{N}$ with $y = k_s$. Thus (B) must happen, and since $y = k_s$, we conclude $\Phi_y(y)\!\downarrow$ . Hence, $g_e(x)\!\downarrow$ , too, a contradiction. This proves Claim 1.

**Claim 2.** *Let $e$ be any number such that $\psi_e = \varphi_{\tau(i)}$ for some $\varphi_{\tau(i)} \in B$. Then $g_e(x) > \Phi_i(x)$ for all $x \in \mathbb{N}$.*

Assume any $i, e$ as above, and consider the definition of $g_e(x)$. Suppose $g_e(x) = s + y$ for some $s, y$ such that $y = h_s$ and $\psi_e(y) = 1$. Since $\psi_e(y) = \varphi_{\tau(i)}(y) = 1$ implies $\Phi_y(y) \leq \Phi_i(y)$, and hence $y \in K$, we get a contradiction to $K \cap H = \emptyset$. Thus, this case cannot happen.

Consequently, in the definition of $g_e(x)$ condition (B) must have happened. Thus, some $s, y$ such that $y > x$, $y = k_s$ and $\psi_e(y) = 0$ have been found. Since $y = k_s$, we conclude $\Phi_y(y)\!\downarrow$ and thus $g(x) > \Phi_y(y)$. Because of $\psi_e(y) = \varphi_{\tau(i)}(y) = 0$, we obtain $\Phi_i(y) < \Phi_y(y)$ by the definition of $\varphi_{\tau(i)}$. Now, putting it all together, we get $g(x) > \Phi_y(y) > \Phi_i(y) \geq \Phi_i(x)$, since $y > x$ and $\Phi_i \in \mathcal{R}_{mon}$. This proves Claim 2.

**Claim 3.** *For every $b \in \mathcal{R}$ there exists an $i \in \mathbb{N}$ such that $\Phi_i \in \mathcal{R}_{mon}$ and $b(x) < \Phi_i(x)$ for all $x \in \mathbb{N}$.*

Let $r \in \mathcal{R}$ be such that for all $j, x \in \mathbb{N}$ we have

$$\varphi_{r(j)}(0) = \begin{cases} 0, & \text{if } \neg[\Phi_j(0) \leq b(0)] \\ \varphi_j(0) + 1, & \text{otherwise} \end{cases}$$

and for $x > 0$

$$\varphi_{r(j)}(x) = \begin{cases} 0, & \text{if } \Phi_j(n) \text{ is defined for all } n < x \ \wedge \\ & \quad \neg[\Phi_j(x) \leq \Phi_j(x-1) \vee \Phi_j(x) \leq b(x)] \\ \varphi_j(x) + 1, & \text{if } \Phi_j(n) \text{ is defined for all } n < x \ \wedge \\ & \quad [\Phi_j(x) \leq \Phi_j(x-1) \vee \Phi_j(x) \leq b(x)] \\ \uparrow, & \text{otherwise.} \end{cases}$$

We prove that neither equivalence queries alone nor membership queries alone suffice to learn $MCFD$. For these negative results we use techniques similar to those in [3,6,8].

On the other hand, we show that $MCFD$ is learnable using both types of queries. Our algorithm is a modification of Angluin et al.'s algorithm [4] to learn conjunctions of Horn clauses. We also show that the size of equivalent minimal covers of functional dependencies is polynomially related.

Some related work can be found in [9,10] where the authors study how prior knowledge can speed up the task of learning. They propose functional dependencies ("determinations" in their terminology) as a form of prior knowledge. They pose the question of whether prior knowledge can be learned. This paper investigates that direction.

The paper is organized as follows. In Section 2 we introduce definitions related to functional dependencies, and some algorithms that are folk-knowledge. We need them to prove some properties that will be used throughout the paper. In Sections 3 and 4 we prove negative results for membership queries and equivalence queries respectively. Finally, Section 5 shows the learning algorithm using membership and equivalence queries.

## 2    Preliminaries

In what follows, we give some definitions, properties and algorithms related to functional dependencies, most of which can be found in any databases text book (see [11,5]). For definitions concerning the model of learning via queries we refer the reader to [2].

### 2.1    Functional Dependencies and Minimal Covers

A relation scheme $R = \{A_1, A_2, \ldots, A_n\}$ is a set of attributes. Each attribute $A_i$ takes values from domain $DOM(A_i)$. An instance $r$ of relation scheme $R$ is a subset of $DOM(A_1) \times DOM(A_2) \times \ldots \times DOM(A_n)$. The size of an instance $r$ is the number of $n$-tuples of $r$.

Given $R$ and $X, Y$ subsets of $R$, the functional dependency $X \longrightarrow Y$ is a constraint on the values that instances of $R$ can take. More precisely, we say $X \longrightarrow Y$, read "$X$ functionally determines $Y$", if for every instance $r$ of $R$, and for every pair $\langle t_1, t_2 \rangle$ of tuples of $r$, $t_1(X) = t_2(X) \Longrightarrow t_1(Y) = t_2(Y)$ (where $t_1(Z) = t_2(Z)$ means that tuples $t_1$ and $t_2$ coincide in the value of all attributes in $Z$). Given a functional dependency $X \longrightarrow Y$, we call $X$ the antecedent of the functional dependency and $Y$ the consequent.

We say that a functional dependency $X \longrightarrow Y$ is logically implied by a set of functional dependencies $F$ if every instance $r$ of $R$ that satisfies the dependencies in $F$ also satisfies $X \longrightarrow Y$. If $r$ does not satisfy $X \longrightarrow Y$, then we say that $r$ violates $X \longrightarrow Y$.

Now $\mathcal{U}(A)$ consists of all those $f_e$ where $\Phi_e \in \mathcal{R}_{mon}$.

Next, comparing $\mathcal{U}(K)$ to the original class $\mathcal{B}$ of Blum and Blum [6] one can easily prove the following. For every $f \in \mathcal{B}$ there is a function $g \in \mathcal{U}(K)$ such that for all $x \in \mathbb{N}$ we have $f(x) = 1$ implies $g(x) = 1$. Hence, the approximation $g$ is at least as good as $f$. The converse is also true, i.e., for each $g \in \mathcal{U}(K)$ there is an $f \in \mathcal{B}$ such that $g(x) = 1$ implies $f(x) = 1$ for all $x \in \mathbb{N}$. Therefore, we consider our new classes of approximations as natural generalizations of Blum and Blum's [6] original definition.

Moreover, note that there is a function $gen_A$ which computes for every $e$ of a monotone $\Phi_e$ a program $gen_A(e)$ for the function $f$ associated with $\Phi_e$:

$$\varphi_{gen_A(e)}(x) = \begin{cases} 1, & \text{if } \Phi_A(x) \leq \Phi_e(x)\!\downarrow \ \wedge \ (\forall y < x)[\Phi_e(y) \leq \Phi_e(y+1)] \\ 0, & \text{if } \neg[\Phi_A(x) \leq \Phi_e(x)\!\downarrow] \ \wedge \ (\forall y < x)[\Phi_e(y) \leq \Phi_e(y+1)] \\ \uparrow, & \text{otherwise.} \end{cases}$$

Now, if $A$ is recursive, everything is clear, since we have the following.

**Theorem 11.** *If $A$ is recursive then $\mathcal{U}(A) \in NUM$.*

The direct generalization of Theorem 6 would be that $\mathcal{U}(A)$ is not in $NUM$ for every non-recursive r.e. set $A$ and every measure $\Phi_A$. Unfortunately, there are some special cases where this is still unknown to us.

We obtained many intermediate results which give incidence that $\mathcal{U}(A)$ is not in $NUM$ for any non-recursive r.e. set $A$. First, every non-recursive set $A$ has a sufficiently "slow" enumeration such that $\mathcal{U}(A) \notin NUM$ for this underlying enumeration and the corresponding $\Phi_A$. Second, for many classes of sets we can directly show that $\mathcal{U}(A) \notin NUM$, whatever measure $\Phi_A$ we choose. Besides the cases where $A$ is part of a recursively inseparable pair or $A$ is simple but not hypersimple, the case of the non-recursive and non-high sets $A$ is interesting, in particular, since the proof differs from that for the two previous cases.

Recall that a set $A$ is *simple* iff $A$ is both r.e. and infinite, $\overline{A}$ is infinite but there is no infinite recursive set $R$ disjoint to $A$. A set $A$ is *hypersimple* iff $A$ is both r.e. and infinite, and there is no function $f \in \mathcal{R}$ such that $f(n) \geq \bar{a}_n$ for all $n \in \mathbb{N}$, where $\bar{a}_0, \bar{a}_1, \ldots$ is the enumeration of $\overline{A}$ in strictly increasing order (cf. Rogers [24]). Using this definition of hypersimple sets, one can easily show the following lemma.

**Lemma 12.** *A set $A \subseteq \mathbb{N}$ is hypersimple iff*
(a)  *$A$ is r.e. and both $A$ and $\overline{A}$ are infinite*
(b)  *for all functions $g \in \mathcal{R}$ with $g(x) \geq x$ for all $x \in \mathbb{N}$ there exist infinitely many $x \in \mathbb{N}$ such that $\{x, x+1, \ldots, g(x)\} \subseteq A$.*

Now, we are ready to state the announced theorem.

**Theorem 13.** *$\mathcal{U}(A)$ is not in $NUM$ for the following r.e. sets $A$.*
(a)  *$A$ is part of a recursively inseparable pair.*
(b)  *$A$ is simple but not hypersimple.*
(c)  *$A$ is neither recursive nor high.*

**Proof.** We sketch only the proof of Assertion (c) here. Assume by way of contradiction $\mathcal{U}(A) \in NUM$. Thus, there is a $\psi \in \mathcal{R}^2$ such that $\mathcal{U}(A) \subseteq \mathcal{R}_\psi$. Assume without loss of generality that $0 \in A$. The $A$-recursive function $d_A(x) = \max\{\Phi_A(y) \mid y \leq x$ and $y \in A\}$ is total and recursive relative to $A$. If now $m(x) \geq d_A(x)$, then the function generated by $m$ in accordance to Definition 10 is equal to the characteristic function of $A$.

$$A(x) = f_m(x) = \begin{cases} 1, & \text{if } \Phi_A(x) \leq m(x) \\ 0, & \text{if } \neg[\Phi_A(x) \leq m(x)]. \end{cases}$$

So one can define the following $A$-recursive function $h$:

$$h(x) = \min\{y \geq x \mid (\forall j \leq x)(\exists z)[(x \leq z \leq y) \wedge \psi_j(z) \neq A(z)]\}.$$

Since $A$ is not recursive, no function $\psi_j$ can be a finite variant of $A(x)$, and thus $h$ is total. Using $h$ we next the following total $A$-recursive function $g$ by $g(x) = \sum_{y=x}^{h(x)} d_A(y)$. Since $A$ is not high, there is a function $b \in \mathcal{R}$ such that $b(x) \geq g(x)$ for infinitely many $x$. By Claim 3 in the demonstration of Theorem 6, there exists an $e \in \mathbb{N}$ such $\Phi_e \in \mathcal{R}_{mon}$ and $\Phi_e(x) > b(x)$ for all $x \in \mathbb{N}$. Thus, $\Phi_e(x) \geq g(x)$ for infinitely many $x$.

Next, for every $\psi_k \in \mathcal{R}_\psi$ there exists an $x > k$ such that $\Phi_e(x) > g(x)$. Consider all $y = x, x+1, \ldots, h(x)$. By the definition of $g$ and by $\Phi_e \in \mathcal{R}_{mon}$, we have $\Phi_e(y) \geq d_A(y)$ for all these $y$. Thus, by the choice of $d_A$ and the definition of $\varphi_{gen_A(e)}$ we arrive at $\varphi_{gen_A(e)}(y) = A(y)$ for all $y = x, x+1, \ldots, h(x)$. But now the definition of the function $h$ guarantees that $\psi_k(z) \neq \varphi_{gen_A(e)}(z)$ for some $z$ with $x \leq z \leq h(x)$. Consequently, $\varphi_{gen_A(e)}$ differs from all $f_k$ in contradiction to the assumption $\mathcal{U}(A) \in NUM$. ∎

## 5.  Reliable and $EX$-Learnability of $\mathcal{U}(A)$

Blum and Blum [6] showed $\mathcal{B} \in \mathcal{REX}$. The $EX$-learnability of $\mathcal{U}(A)$ alone can be generalized to every r.e. set $A$, but this is not possible for reliability. But before dealing with $\mathcal{REX}$-inference, we show that every $\mathcal{U}(A)$ is $EX$-learnable.

**Theorem 14.** $\mathcal{U}(A)$ is $EX$-learnable for all r.e. sets $A$.

**Proof.** If $A$ is recursive, then $\mathcal{U}(A) \in NUM$ (cf. Theorem 11) and thus $EX$-learnable. So let $A$ be non-recursive and let $\Phi_A$ be a recursive enumeration of $A$. An $EX$-learner for the class $\mathcal{U}(A)$ is given as follows.

- On input $\sigma$, disqualify all $e$ such that there are $x \in dom(\sigma)$ and $y \leq |\sigma|$ satisfying one of the following three conditions:
  (a) $\Phi_{gen_A(e)}(x) \leq |\sigma|$ and $\varphi_{gen_A(e)}(x) \neq \sigma(x)$
  (b) $\sigma(x) = 0$, $\Phi_A(x) \leq y$ and $\neg[\Phi_e(x) \leq y]$
  (c) $\Phi_e(x+1) \leq y$ and $\neg[\Phi_e(x) \leq y]$.
- Output $gen_A(e)$ for the smallest $e$ not yet disqualified.

The algorithm disqualifies only such indices $e$ where $\varphi_{gen_A(e)}$ is either defined and false or undefined for some $x \in dom(\sigma)$. Thus the learner is conservative.

Since the correct indices are never disqualified, it remains to show that the incorrect ones are. This clearly happens if $\varphi_{gen_A(e)}(y) \downarrow \neq \sigma(y)$ for some $y$. Otherwise let $z$ be the first undefined place of $\varphi_{gen_A(e)}$. This undefined place is either due to the fact that $\Phi_e(x) > \Phi_e(x+1)$ for some $x < z$ or that $\Phi_e(z)\uparrow$. In the first case, $e$ is eventually disqualified by condition (c), in the second case, either $\Phi_e(x+1)\downarrow$ for some first $x \geq z$, then $e$ is again eventually disqualified by condition (c) or $\Phi_e(x)\uparrow$ for some $x \in A$ above $z$ and so $e$ is disqualified by condition (b). Hence, the learning algorithm is correct.    $\blacksquare$

The result that $\mathcal{B}$ is reliably $EX$-learnable can be generalized to halves of recursively inseparable pairs and to simple but not hypersimple sets.

**Theorem 15.** $\mathcal{U}(A)$ *is reliably EX-learnable if*
(a)    $A$ *is part of a recursively inseparable pair or*
(b)    $A$ *is simple but not hypersimple.*

**Proof.** The central idea of the proof is that conditions (a) and (b) allow to identify a class of functions which contains all recursive functions which are too difficult to learn and on which the learner then signals infinitely often divergence. The recursive functions outside this class turn out to be $EX$-learnable and contain the class $\mathcal{U}(A)$.

The learner $M$ does not need to succeed on functions $f \notin \mathcal{R}_{0,1}$ or if $f(x) = 1$ for almost all $x \in A$. Now, the second condition can be checked indirectly for $f \in \mathcal{R}_{0,1}$ and the $A$ in the precondition of the theorem.

In case (a), let $A$ and $B = \{b_0, b_1, \ldots\}$ form a recursively inseparable pair. If $f(x) = 1$ for almost all $x \in A$ then $f(b_s) = 1$ for some $b_s$. So one defines that $\sigma$ disqualifies if $\sigma(x) \geq 2$ for some $x$ or if $\sigma(b_s)\downarrow = 1$ for some $s \leq |\sigma|$.

In case (b), the set $A$ is simple but not hypersimple. By Lemma 12 there is a function $g \in \mathcal{R}$ with $g(x) \geq x$ for all $x \in \mathbb{N}$ such that $\overline{A}$ intersects every interval $\{x, x+1, \ldots, g(x)\}$. But if $f(x) = 1$ for almost all $x \in A$, then, by the simplicity of $A$, $f(x) = 1$ for almost all $x$ and there is an $x$ with $f(y) = 1$ for all $y \in \{x, x+1, \ldots, g(x)\}$. So one defines that $\sigma$ disqualifies if $\sigma(x) \geq 2$ for some $x$ or if there is an $x$ and $\sigma(y) = 1$ for all $y \in \{x, x+1, \ldots, g(x)\}$.

The reliable $EX$-learner $N$ is a modification of the learner $M$ from Theorem 14 which copies $M$ on all $\sigma$ except those which disqualify — on them, $N$ always outputs a guess for $\sigma 0^\infty$ and thus either converges to some $\sigma 0^\infty$ or diverges by infinitely many changes of the hypothesis. Let $e(\sigma)$ be a program for $\sigma 0^\infty$ and let

$$N(\sigma) = \begin{cases} e(\sigma), & \text{if } \sigma \text{ is disqualified} \\ M(\sigma), & \text{otherwise.} \end{cases}$$

For the verification, note that for every $f \in \mathcal{U}(A)$ we have $f(x) = 0$ for all $x \in \overline{A}$. Thus, if $f \in \mathcal{U}(A)$ then no $\sigma \preceq f$ is disqualified and therefore $N$ is an $EX$-learner for $\mathcal{U}(A)$.

Assume now that $N$ converges to an $e'$ on some recursive function $f$. If this happens for a function $f$ such that some $\sigma' \preceq f$ has been disqualified then $f = \sigma 0^\infty$ and so also $\varphi_{e'} = \sigma 0^\infty$ for some $\sigma \preceq f$. Thus, $N$ converges to a correct program for $f$ in this case.

Otherwise, no $\sigma' \preceq f$ is disqualified. Since $N$ copies the indices of $M$ and those are all of the form $gen_A(e)$, there is a least $e$ with $e' = gen_A(e)$. If $f(x) = 0$ for infinitely many $x \in A$, then $M$ converges only to $gen_A(e)$ if $\varphi_{gen_A(e)} = f$ and the algorithm is correct in that case.

Finally, consider the subcase that $f(x) = 0$ for only finitely many $x \in A$. Consequently, in case (a) $f(x) = 1$ for some $x \in B$ and in case (b) there must be an $x$ such that $f(y) = 1$ for all $y = x, x + 1, \ldots, g(x)$. In both cases, some $\sigma' \preceq f$ is disqualified, thus this case cannot occur. Hence, $N$ is reliable.     ∎

**Theorem 16.** *If $A$ is hypersimple and not high then $\mathcal{U}(A) \notin \mathcal{REX}$.*

**Proof.** Let $A$ be a hypersimple non-high set, let $\Phi_A$ be a corresponding measure, and assume to the contrary that $\mathcal{U}(A) \in \mathcal{REX}$. Then also the union

$$\mathcal{U}(A) \cup \{\alpha 1^\infty \mid \alpha \in \{0,1\}^*\}$$

is $EX$-learnable, since every class in $NUM$ is also in $\mathcal{REX}$ and $\mathcal{REX}$ is closed under union (cf. [6,21]). Given an $EX$-learner $M$ for the above union, one can define the following function $h_1$ by taking

$$h_1(x) = \min\{s \geq x \mid (\forall \sigma \in \{0,1\}^x)\,(\forall y \leq x)\,[M(\sigma 1^s) \neq M(\sigma) \vee$$
$$\Phi_{M(\sigma)}(y) \leq s \wedge \varphi_{M(\sigma)}(y) = \sigma(y)]\}.$$

The function $h_1$ is total since any guess $M(\sigma)$ either computes the function $\sigma 1^\infty$ or is eventually replaced by a new guess on $\sigma 1^\infty$. Note that $h_1 \in \mathcal{R}_{mon}$ and $h_1(x) \geq x$ for all $x$.

Since $A$ is not recursive, there is no total function dominating $\Phi_A$. Thus one can define a recursive function $h_2(x)$ by taking

$$h_2(x) = \text{ the smallest } s \text{ such that there is a } y \text{ with } x \leq y \leq s \wedge$$
$$h_1(y + h_1(y)) < s \wedge \Phi_A(y) + \Phi_A(y + 1) + \ldots + \Phi_A(y + h_1(y)) < s.$$

Since $A$ is hypersimple, we directly get from Lemma 12 that $h_2 \in \mathcal{R}$. Consider for every $f \in \mathcal{U}(A)$ the index $i$ to which $M$ converges and an index $j$ with $f = \varphi_{gen_A(j)}$.

Assume now that $M$ has converged to $i$ at $z \leq x$. Consider the $y, s$ from the definition of $h_2$ and let $\sigma = f(0), \ldots, f(y)$. If $M(\sigma 1^{h_1(y)}) \neq M(\sigma)$ then there is some $y' \in \{y, y+1, \ldots, y+h_1(y)\}$ with $f(y') = 0$. As a consequence, $\Phi_j(y') < \Phi_A(y') < h_2(y)$. Since $\Phi_j \in \mathcal{R}_{mon}$, we know $\Phi_j(y) < s$. Otherwise, $\Phi_i(x) \leq h_1(y)$ and $\varphi_i(x)$ has converged. Since $y \leq h_2(x)$, we conclude $\Phi_i(x) \leq h_1(h_2(x))$. So one can give the following definition for $f$ by case-distinction where the first case is taken which is applicable and where $\sigma = f(0), \ldots, f(z)$.

$$\varphi_{e(i,j,\sigma)}(x) = \begin{cases} \sigma(x), & \text{if } x \in dom(\sigma) \\ \varphi_i(x), & \text{if } \Phi_i(x) \le h_1(h_2(x)) \\ 1, & \text{if } \Phi_A(x) \le \Phi_j(x) \le h_2(x) \\ 0, & \text{otherwise.} \end{cases}$$

Since the search-conditions in the second and third case are bounded by a recursive function in $x$, the family of all $\varphi_{e(i,j,\sigma)}$ contains only total functions and its universal $i, j, \sigma, x \to \varphi_{e(i,j,\sigma)}(x)$ is computable in all parameters. Furthermore, for the correct $i, j, \sigma$ as chosen above, $\varphi_{e(i,j,\sigma)}$ equals the given $f$ since, for all $x > z$, either $\varphi_i(x)$ converges within $h_1(h_2(x))$ steps to $f(x)$ or $\Phi_A(x) \le \Phi_j(x) \le h_2(x)$. It follows that this family covers $\mathcal{U}(A)$ and that $\mathcal{U}(A)$ is in $NUM$ which, a contradiction to Theorem 13, since $A$ is neither recursive nor high. ∎

# 6. Robust Learning

A mathematical elegant proof method to separate learning criteria is the use of classes of self-describing functions. On the one hand, these examples are a bit artificial, since they use coding tricks. On the other hand, natural objects like cells contain a description of themselves. Nevertheless, from a learning theoretical point some criticism remains in order, since a learner needs only to fetch some code from the input.

Therefore, Bārzdiņš suggested to look at restricted versions of learning: For example, a class $S$ is robustly $EX$-learnable, iff, for every operator $\Theta$, the class $\Theta(S)$ is $EX$-learnable. There were many discussions, which operators $\Theta$ are admissible in this context and how to deal with those cases where $\Theta$ maps some functions in $S$ to partial functions. At the end, it turned out that it is most suitable to consider only general recursive operators $\Theta$ which map every total function to a total one [16]. This notion is among all notions of robust $EX$-learning the most general one in the sense that every class $S$ which is robustly $EX$-learnable with respect to any criterion considered in the literature is also robustly $EX$-learnable with respect to the model of Jain, Smith and Wiehagen [16].

Although the class $\mathcal{B}$ is quite natural and does not have any obvious self-referential coding, the class $\mathcal{B}$ is not robustly $EX$-learnable — so while on the one hand the notion of robust $EX$-learning still permits topological coding tricks [16,23], it does on the other hand already rule out the natural class $\mathcal{B}$. The provided example gives some incidence, that there is still some need to find a adequate notion for a "natural $EX$-learnable class."

Every class in $NUM$ is robustly $EX$-learnable, in particular the class $\mathcal{U}(A)$ for a recursive set $A$ (cf. Theorem 11). The next theorem shows that $\mathcal{U}(A)$ is not robustly $EX$-learnable for any nonrecursive sets $A$ which are part of a recursively inseparable pair, which are simple but not hypersimple or which are neither recursive nor high. Thus, here the situation is parallel to the one at Theorem 13.

**Theorem 17.** $\mathcal{U}(A)$ *is not robustly EX-learnable for the following r.e. sets* $A$.
(a)  $A$ *is part of a recursively inseparable pair.*
(b)  $A$ *is simple but not hypersimple.*
(c)  $A$ *is neither recursive nor high.*

# 7. Conclusions

The main topic of the present investigations have been the class $\mathcal{B}$ of Blum and Blum [6] and the natural generalizations $\mathcal{U}(A)$ of it obtained by using r.e. sets $A$ as a parameter. It is has been shown that for large families of r.e. sets $A$, these classes $\mathcal{U}(A)$ are not in *NUM*. Furthermore, they can be always *EX*-learned. Moreover, for some but not all sets $A$ there is also a $\mathcal{REX}$-learner. Robust *EX*-learning is impossible for all non-recursive sets $A$ that are part of recursively inseparable pair, for simple but not hypersimple sets $A$ and for all sets $A$ that are non-high and non-recursive. Since the classes $\mathcal{U}(A)$ are quite natural, this result adds some incidence that "natural learnability" does not coincide with robust learnability as defined in the current research.

Future work might address the remaining unsolved question whether $\mathcal{U}(A)$ is outside *NUM* for all non-recursive sets $A$. Additionally, one might investigate whether $\mathcal{U}(A)$ is robustly *BC*-learnable for some sets $A$ such that $\mathcal{U}(A)$ is not robustly *EX*-inferable. It would be also interesting to know whether or not $\mathcal{U}(A)$ can be reliably *BC*-learned for sets $A$ with $\mathcal{U}(A) \notin \mathcal{REX}$ (cf. [18] for more information concerning reliable *BC*-learning). Finally, there are some ways to generalize the notion of $\mathcal{U}(A)$ to every $K$-recursive set $A$ and one might investigate the learning theoretic properties of the so obtained classes.

# References

1. A. Ambainis and R. Freivalds. Transformations that preserve learnability. In *Proccedings of the 7th International Workshop on Algorithmic Learning Theory* (ALT'96) (S. Arikawa and A. Sharma, Eds.) Lecture Notes in Artificial Intelligence Vol. 1160, pages 299–311, Springer-Verlag, Berlin, 1996.
2. D. Angluin. Inductive inference of formal languages from positive data. *Information and Control*, 45:117–135, 1980.
3. D. Angluin and C.H. Smith. A survey of inductive inference: Theory and methods. *Computing Surveys*, 15:237–289, 1983.
4. J. Bārzdins. Prognostication of automata and functions. *Information Processing* '71, (1) 81–84. Edited by C. P. Freiman, North-Holland, Amsterdam, 1971.
5. M. Blum. A machine-independent theory of the complexity of recursive functions. *Journal of the Association for Computing Machinery*, 14:322–336.
6. L. Blum and M. Blum. Towards a mathematical theory of inductive inference. *Information and Control*, 28:125–155, 1975.
7. J. Case, S. Jain, M. Ott, A. Sharma and F. Stephan. Robust learning aided by context. In *Proceedings of 11th Annual Conference on Computational Learning Theory* (COLT'98), pages 44–55, ACM Press, New York, 1998.

8. J. Case and C.H. Smith. Comparison of identification criteria for machine inductive inference. *Theoretical Computer Science* 25:193–220, 1983.
9. R. Freivalds. Inductive inference of recursive functions: Qualitative theory. In *Baltic Computer Science* (J. Bārzdiņš and D. Bjørner, Eds.), Lecture Notes in Computer Science Vol. 502, pages 77–110. Springer-Verlag, Berlin, 1991.
10. M. Fulk. Robust separations in inductive inference. In *Proceedings of the 31st Annual Symposium on Foundations of Computer Science* (FOCS), pages 405–410, St. Louis, Missouri, 1990.
11. M.E. Gold. Language identification in the limit. *Information and Control*, 10:447–474, 1967.
12. J. Grabowski. Starke Erkennung. *In* Strukturerkennung diskreter kybernetischer Systeme, (R. Linder, H. Thiele, Eds.), Seminarberichte der Sektion Mathematik der Humboldt-Universität Berlin Vol. 82, pages 168–184, 1986.
13. J.P. Helm. On effectively computable operators. *Zeitschrift für mathematische Logik und Grundlagen der Mathematik (ZML)*, 17:231–244, 1971.
14. S. Jain. *Robust Behaviourally Correct Learning.* Technical Report TRA6/98 at the DISCS, National University of Singapore, 1998.
15. S. Jain, D. Osherson, J.S. Royer and A. Sharma. *Systems That Learn: An Introduction to Learning Theory.* MIT-Press, Boston, MA., 1999.
16. S. Jain, C. Smith and R. Wiehagen. On the power of learning robustly. In *Proceedings of Eleventh Annual Conference on Computational Learning Theory* (COLT), pages 187–197, ACM Press, New York, 1998.
17. E.B. Kinber and T. Zeugmann. Inductive inference of almost everywhere correct programs by reliably working strategies. *Journal of Information Processing and Cybernetics*, 21:91–100, 1985.
18. E.B. Kinber and T. Zeugmann. One-sided error probabilistic inductive inference and reliable frequency identification. *Information and Computation*, 92:253–284, 1991.
19. R. Klette and R. Wiehagen. Research in the theory of inductive inference by GDR mathematicians – A survey. *Information Sciences*, 22:149–169, 1980.
20. S. Kurtz and C.H. Smith. On the role of search for learning. In *Proceedings of the 2nd Annual Workshop on Computational Learning Theory* (R. Rivest, D. Haussler and M. Warmuth, Eds.) pages 303–311, Morgan Kaufman, 1989.
21. E. Minicozzi. Some natural properties of strong-identification in inductive inference. *Theoretical Computer Science*, 2:345–360, 1976.
22. P. Odifreddi. *Classical Recursion Theory.* North-Holland, Amsterdam, 1989.
23. M. Ott and F. Stephan. Avoiding coding tricks by hyperrobust learning. *Proceedings of the Fourth European Conference on Computational Learning Theory* (EuroCOLT) (P. Fischer and H.U. Simon, Eds.) Lecture Notes in Artificial Intelligence Vol. 1572, pages 183–197, Springer-Verlag, Berlin, 1999.
24. H.Jr. Rogers. *Theory of Recursive Functions and Effective Computability.* McGraw–Hill, New York, 1967.
25. F. Stephan and T. Zeugmann. On the Uniform Learnability of Approximations to Non-Recursive Functions. DOI Technical Report DOI-TR-166, Department of Informatics, Kyushu University, July 1999.
26. T. Zeugmann. A-posteriori characterizations in inductive inference of recursive functions. *Journal of Information Processing and Cybernetics (EIK)*, 19:559–594, 1983.

27. T. Zeugmann. On the nonboundability of total effective operators. *Zeitschrift für mathematische Logik und Grundlagen der Mathematik (ZML)*, 30:169–172, 1984.
28. T. Zeugmann. On Bārzdiņš' conjecture. In *Proceedings of the International Workshop on Analogical and Inductive Inference* (AII'86) (K.P. Jantke, Ed.), Lecture Notes in Computer Science Vol. 265, pages 220–227. Springer-Verlag, Berlin, 1986.

# Learning Minimal Covers of Functional Dependencies with Queries[*]

Montserrat Hermo[1] and Víctor Lavín[2]

[1] Dpto. Lenguajes y Sistemas Informáticos
UPV/EHU, P.O. Box 649, E-20080 San Sebastián, SPAIN
jiphehum@si.ehu.es
[2] Dpto. Sistemas Informáticos y Programación
Universidad Complutense E-28040 Madrid, SPAIN
vlavin@eucmos.sim.ucm.es

**Abstract.** Functional dependencies play an important role in the design of databases. We study the learnability of the class of minimal covers of functional dependencies ($MCFD$) within the exact learning model via queries. We prove that neither equivalence queries alone nor membership queries alone suffice to learn the class. In contrast, we show that learning becomes feasible if both types of queries are allowed. We also give some properties concerning minimal covers.

## 1 Introduction

Functional dependencies were introduced by Codd [7] as a tool for designing relational databases. Based on this concept, a well developed formalism has arisen, the theory of normalization. This formalism helps to build relational databases that lack undesirable features, such as redundancy in the data and update anomalies.

We study the learnability of the class $MCFD$ (minimal covers of functional dependencies) in the model of learning with queries due to Angluin [1,2]. In this model the learner's goal is to identify an unknown target concept $c$ in some class $C$. In order to obtain information about the target, the learner has available two types of queries: membership and equivalence queries. In a membership query the learner supplies an instance $x$ from the domain and gets answer *YES* if $x$ belongs to the target, and *NO* otherwise. The input to an equivalence query is some hypothesis $h$, and the answer is either *YES* if $h \equiv c$ or a counterexample in the symmetric difference of $c$ and $h$.

The class $C$ is learnable if the learner can identify any target concept $c$ in time polynomial in the size of $c$ and the length of the largest counterexample received.

[*] Partially supported by the Spanish DGICYT through project PB95-0787 (KOALA).

O. Watanabe, T. Yokomori (Eds.): ALT'99, LNAI 1720, pp. 291–300, 1999.
© Springer-Verlag Berlin Heidelberg 1999

By the fixed point theorem [24] there is an $i \in \mathbb{N}$ such that $\varphi_{r(i)} = \varphi_i$. Now, one inductively shows that $\varphi_i = 0^\infty$, $\Phi_i \in \mathcal{R}_{mon}$ and $b(x) < \Phi_i(x)$ for all $x \in \mathbb{N}$ and Claim 3 follows.

Finally, by Claim 1, all $g_e \in \mathcal{R}$, and thus there is a function $b \in \mathcal{R}$ such that $b(x) \geq g_e(x)$ for all $e \in \mathbb{N}$ and all but finitely many $x \in \mathbb{N}$ (cf. [6]). Together with Claim 2, this function $b$ contradicts Claim 3, and hence $B \notin NUM$.  ∎

The next result can be obtained by looking at $\mathcal{U}(K)$ in Theorems 15 and 17.

**Theorem 7.** $B$ *is* $\mathcal{REX}$-*inferable but not robustly* $EX$-*learnable.*

Theorems 6 and 7 immediately allow the following separation, thus reproving Grabowski's [12] Theorem 5.

**Corollary 8.** $NUM \cap \wp(\mathcal{R}_{0,1}) \subset \mathcal{REX} \cap \wp(\mathcal{R}_{0,1})$.

Finally, we ask whether or not the condition $\Phi_i \in \mathcal{R}_{mon}$ in the definition of the class $B$ is necessary. The affirmative answer is given by our next theorem. That is, instead of $B$, we now consider the class $\tilde{B} = \{\varphi_{\tau(i)} \mid i \in \mathbb{N} \text{ and } \Phi_i \in \mathcal{R}\}$.

**Theorem 9.** $\tilde{B}$ *is not* $BC$-*learnable.*

Next, we generalize the approach undertaken so far by considering classes $\mathcal{U}(A)$ of approximations to any recursively enumerable (abbr. r.e.) set $A$.

# 4.  Approximating Arbitrary r.e. Sets

The definition of Blum and Blum's [6] class uses implicitly the measure $\Phi_K$ defined as $\Phi_K(x) = \Phi_x(x)$ for measuring the speed by which $K$ is enumerated. Using this notion $\Phi_K$, the class $B$ of approximations of $K$ is defined as

$$B = \{f \in \mathcal{R}_{0,1} \mid (\exists \Phi_e \in \mathcal{R}_{mon})\,(\forall x)\,[f(x) = 1 \Leftrightarrow \Phi_K(x) \leq \Phi_e(x)]\}.$$

Our main idea is to replace $K$ by an arbitrary r.e. set $A$ and to replace $\Phi_K$ by a measure $\Phi_A$ of (the enumeration speed of) $A$. Such a measure satisfies the following two conditions:

- The set $\{(x, y) \mid \Phi_A(x)\!\downarrow \leq y\}$ is recursive.
- $x \in A \Leftrightarrow (\exists y)\,[\Phi_A(x) \leq y]$.

Here, $\Phi_A$ is intended to be taken as the function $\Phi_i$ of some index $i$ of $A$, but sometimes we might also take the freedom to look at some other functions $\Phi_A$ satisfying the two requirements above. The natural definition for a class $\mathcal{U}(A)$ corresponding to the class $B$ in the case $A = K$ based on an underlying function $\Phi_A$ is the following.

**Definition 10.** Given an r.e. set $A$, an enumeration $\Phi_A$ and a total function $\Phi_e$, let

$$f_e(x) = \begin{cases} 1, & \text{if } \Phi_A(x) \leq \Phi_e(x) \\ 0, & \text{if } \neg[\Phi_A(x) \leq \Phi_e(x)]. \end{cases}$$

**Definition 1.** *The closure of a set of dependencies $F$, denoted by $F^+$, is the set of functional dependencies that are logically implied by $F$.*

**Definition 2.** *Let $F$ and $G$ be sets of dependencies. $F$ is equivalent to $G$ ($F \equiv G$) if $F^+ = G^+$.*

**Definition 3.** *The closure of a set of attributes $X$, written $X^+$, with respect to a set of dependencies $F$, is the set of attributes $A$ such that $X \longrightarrow A$ is in $F^+$.*

Given a relation scheme $R$, $X \subseteq R$ and a set of functional dependencies $F$, the following algorithm (see [5]) computes $X^+$ with respect to $F$, in time polynomial in $|R|$ and $|F|$.

**Algorithm Closure**

> input $X$;
> $X^+ = X$;
> **repeat**
>> $OLDX^+ := X^+$;
>> **for** each dependency $V \longrightarrow W$ in $F$ **do**
>>> **if** $V \subseteq X^+$ **then** $X^+ := X^+ \cup W$;
>>> **end if**
>> **end for**
> **until** $OLDX^+ = X^+$;

It is easy to test whether two sets of dependencies $F$ and $F'$ are equivalent: for each dependency $X \longrightarrow Y$ in $F(F')$, test whether $X \longrightarrow Y$ is in $F'(F)$ using the above algorithm to compute $X^+$ with respect to $F'(F)$ and then checking whether $Y \subseteq X^+$. We will use this test in Subsection 2.2 to prove some properties concerning minimal covers.

**Definition 4.** *Let $F$ be a set of dependencies. A set of dependencies $G$ is a minimal cover for $F$ if:*

1. *$G \equiv F$.*
2. *The consequent of each dependency in $G$ is a single attribute.*
3. *For no dependency $X \longrightarrow A$ in $G$, $G - \{X \longrightarrow A\} \equiv F$.*
4. *For no dependency $X \longrightarrow A$ in $G$ and proper subset $Y$ of $X$,*
   *$(G - \{X \longrightarrow A\}) \cup \{Y \longrightarrow A\} \equiv F$.*

We outline a procedure to find a minimal cover –there can be several– for a given set of dependencies $F$ (see [11] for more details). First, using the property that a functional dependency $X \longrightarrow Y$ holds if and only if $X \longrightarrow A$ holds for all $A$ in $Y$, we decompose all dependencies in $F$ so that condition 2 of the definition is fulfilled. Then, for conditions 3 and 4, we check repeatedly whether dropping a dependency (or some attribute in the antecedent of a dependency) from $F$ yields a set $F'$ equivalent to $F$. If it is so we substitute $F'$ for $F$, and keep applying the procedure until neither dependencies nor attributes can be eliminated.

Note that it follows from the above that the size of a minimal cover for $F$ is never much bigger that the size of $F$ itself (at most a multiplicative factor in the number of attributes), what makes learning minimal covers as interesting as learning sets of general functional dependencies.

## 2.2 Some Properties of Minimal Covers

Now we prove that the size of equivalent minimal covers is polynomially related. First we need a lemma.

**Lemma 1.** *Let $R$ be a relation scheme, let $F$ and $F'$ be minimal covers of functional dependencies over $R$. If $F \equiv F'$ then any dependency $X \longrightarrow A$ in $F$ can be inferred from $F'$ using at most $|R|$ dependencies of $F'$.*

**Proof.** Let us assume, by way of contradiction, that more than $|R|$ dependencies of $F'$ are needed to infer $X \longrightarrow A$. Then, at least two of them, say $D_1$ and $D_2$, must have the same consequent. If we run Algorithm Closure to compute $X^+$, the last one of $D_1$ and $D_2$ examined by the algorithm does not force the inclusion of any new attribute into $X^+$, and thus is unnecessary. □

**Corollary 1.** *Let $R$ be a relation scheme, let $F$ and $F'$ be minimal covers of functional dependencies over $R$. If $F \equiv F'$ then $|F'| \le |R| * |F|$.*

**Proof.** Suppose, by contradiction, that $|F'| > |R| * |F|$. Then there is some dependency $D \in F'$ that, by Lemma 1, is not used to infer any of the dependencies in $F$. Let $G$ be $F' - \{D\}$. Clearly $F^+$ can be inferred from $G$, and since $F^+ = (F')^+$ then $D$ is redundant in $F'$, that is, $F'$ is not a minimal cover. □

In Sections 3 and 4 we define some target classes containing sets of dependencies, that must be inequivalent and minimal covers. The following lemmas will allow us to ensure such requirements.

**Lemma 2.** *Let $F$ be a set of functional dependencies over $R = \{A_1, \ldots A_n, B\}$ such that the consequent of each dependency in $F$ is the attribute $B$. If for all $X \longrightarrow B$ in $F$ it holds that $X$ does not contain the antecedent of any other dependency of $F$, then $F$ is a minimal cover for $F$.*

**Proof.** Obviously $F$ satisfies conditions *1* and *2* of Definition 4. To check that $F$ satisfies conditions *3* and *4* note that for every dependency $X \longrightarrow B$ in $F$, and for all proper subset $Y$ of $X$, $X^+$ with respect to $F - \{X \longrightarrow B\}$ and $Y^+$ with respect to $F$ do not contain $B$. □

**Lemma 3.** *Let $F_1$ and $F_2$ be sets of dependencies whose consequents are the single attribute $B$. If there exists a dependency $Y \longrightarrow B$ in $F_1$, such that $Y$ does not contain the antecedent of any dependency of $F_2$, then both sets are inequivalent.*

**Proof.** Let $Y \longrightarrow B$ be the dependency of the hypothesis. As $B \notin Y^+$ with respect to $F_2$, $F_1 \not\equiv F_2$. □

## 3  Membership Queries

To show that $MCFD$ is not learnable using membership queries alone, a standard adversary technique is used. We define a large target class, from which the target cover will be selected, in such a way that the answer to any membership query eliminates few elements from the target class. This will force the learner to make a superpolynomial number of queries to identify the target cover.

**Theorem 1.** *The class $MCFD$ cannot be learned using a polynomial number of polynomially-sized membership queries.*

**Proof.** Let $R = \{A_1, A_2, \ldots A_n, B\}$, for $n$ even, be a relation scheme and let $p$ be any polynomial. The target class $T_n$ will contain $2^{\frac{n}{2}}$ covers, all of them having dependencies

$$A_1 A_2 \longrightarrow B, A_3 A_4 \longrightarrow B, \ldots, A_{n-1} A_n \longrightarrow B.$$

Besides, each cover contains a distinguished dependency, whose antecedent has one attribute picked up from the antecedent of each dependency above, and $B$ as the consequent. By Lemma 2 all covers in the target class $T_n$ are minimal, and by Lemma 3 they are logically inequivalent.

Using $T_n$ as the target class, suppose the learner makes a membership query with instance $r$ of size at most $p(n)$. The adversary considers every pair of tuples $\langle t_1, t_2 \rangle$ in $r$, and answers according to the following rule:

- If $t_1(B) = t_2(B)$ for every pair $\langle t_1, t_2 \rangle$, then the answer is *YES*. No cover is eliminated from $T_n$.
- Otherwise, let $S$ be the set of all pairs $\langle t_1, t_2 \rangle$ such that $t_1(B) \neq t_2(B)$:
  - If for some $\langle t_1, t_2 \rangle \in S$ there exist attributes $A_{2i+1}, A_{2(i+1)}$ $(0 \leq i \leq \frac{n}{2} - 1)$ such that $t_1(A_{2i+1} A_{2(i+1)}) = t_2(A_{2i+1} A_{2(i+1)})$, then the answer is *NO*. Again no cover is eliminated from $T_n$.
  - If none of the conditions above hold then the answer is *YES*. Note that this answer removes $\frac{p(n)}{2}$ covers from $T_n$ in the worst case, the case being that $r$ can be partitioned into pairs $\langle t_1, t_2 \rangle$, where $t_1$ and $t_2$ coincide in the value of exactly $\frac{n}{2}$ attributes.

Therefore, to identify the target cover the learner must make at least $\frac{2^{\frac{n}{2}}}{p(n)} - 1$ membership queries.    $\square$

## 4  Equivalence Queries

As in the case of membership queries, to prove nonlearnability with equivalence queries alone we use an adversary argument. First, we need a lemma.

**Lemma 4.** *Let $F$ be a minimal cover defined over $R = \{A_1, A_2, \ldots, A_n, B\}$, containing $p$ dependencies, each of them having consequent $B$, and antecedent with at least $\sqrt{n}$ attributes from $\{A_1, A_2, \ldots, A_n\}$. There exists some instance $r$ of $R$ with the following properties:*

- $r$ has two tuples $\langle t_1, t_2 \rangle$.
- $r$ satisfies $F$.
- The number of attributes $A_i \in \{A_1, A_2, \ldots A_n\}$ for which $t_1(A_i) \neq t_2(A_i)$ is at most $1 + \sqrt{n}(\ln p)$.

**Proof.** Since all antecedents of dependencies in $F$ have at least $\sqrt{n}$ attributes from $\{A_1, A_2, \ldots, A_n\}$, there must be some attribute $A_i$ that occurs in at least $\frac{p}{\sqrt{n}}$ of them. We now can delete from $F$ the dependencies that have $A_i$ in their antecedent, and apply the same procedure to the remaining set of dependencies. After doing so $k$ times we are left with a set of at most $p(1 - \frac{1}{\sqrt{n}})^k$ dependencies. Taking $k = 1 + \sqrt{n}(\ln p)$, we obtain $p(1 - \frac{1}{\sqrt{n}})^k < 1$. Therefore, there is a set $X$ with at most $1 + \sqrt{n}(\ln p)$ attributes such that all the antecedents of dependencies in $F$ have some attribute in $X$.

The instance $r = \langle t_1, t_2 \rangle$ where $t_1(A) \neq t_2(A)$ for all $A \in X$ and $t_1(R - X) = t_2(R - X)$ surely satisfies $F$. □

**Theorem 2.** *The class MCDF cannot be learned using a polynomial number of polynomially-sized equivalence queries.*

**Proof.** Let $R = \{A_1, A_2, \ldots, A_n, B\}$ be a relation scheme. We define the target class, $T_n$, that contains every cover $G$ that satisfies the following:

- $G$ has $\sqrt{n}$ dependencies of the form $A_{i_1} A_{i_2} \ldots A_{i_{\sqrt{n}}} \longrightarrow B$.
- The antecedents of the dependencies in $G$ are pairwise disjoint.

By Lemma 2 and Lemma 3 all covers in $T_n$ are minimal and logically inequivalent. The cardinality of $T_n$ is

$$|T_n| = \frac{n!}{(\sqrt{n})! \sqrt{n} + 1}$$

Now, to an equivalence query on input $F$, of size at most $p = n^c$, where $c$ is a constant, the adversary answers as follows:

- If there is some dependency $X \longrightarrow A_i$ in $F$, where $A_i \in \{A_1, A_2, \ldots A_n\}$, then give as a counterexample the instance $r = \langle t_1, t_2 \rangle$ where $t_1(A_i) \neq t_2(A_i)$ and $t_1(R - \{A_i\}) = t_2(R - \{A_i\})$. Clearly this counterexample does not remove any cover from $T_n$.
- Otherwise, if there is some dependency $X \longrightarrow B$ in $F$ and $|X| < \sqrt{n}$, then return as a counterexample the instance $r = \langle t_1, t_2 \rangle$ where $t_1(X) = t_2(X)$ and $t_1(A) \neq t_2(A)$ for all $A \in R - X$. No cover in $T_n$ is violated by this instance, although it violates $F$.
- If none of the cases above hold then Lemma 4 guarantees the existence of an instance $r = \langle t_1, t_2 \rangle$ that satisfies $F$, and whose tuples disagree in the values of at most $1 + c\sqrt{n}(\ln n)$ attributes. In this case give that instance as counterexample. The covers that will be eliminated by the counterexample are those for which the antecedent of every dependency has at least one

attribute in which the tuples of $r$ disagree. Therefore, the number of covers that $r$ eliminates from $T_n$ is at most

$$E_n = \left(\frac{1 + c\sqrt{n}(\ln n)}{\sqrt{n}}\right) \frac{(n - \sqrt{n})!}{((\sqrt{n} - 1)!)^{\sqrt{n}}(\sqrt{n})!}$$

The fraction of covers removed from $T_n$, that is, $\frac{E_n}{|T_n|}$, is at most

$$\frac{(1 + c\sqrt{n}(\ln n))^{\sqrt{n}}}{(\sqrt{n})!} \frac{(\sqrt{n})^{\sqrt{n}}}{(n - \sqrt{n})^{\sqrt{n}}}$$

which is superpolynomially small in $n$.                                     □

## 5   The Learning Algorithm

In this section we show that a slight modification of Angluin *et al.*'s algorithm *HORN* for learning conjunctions of Horn clauses, using membership and equivalence queries, yields an algorithm that learns *MCFD*.

First, we discuss the meaning of positive and negative counterexamples in the setting of functional dependencies. Let us assume that the counterexamples are instances of two tuples (obviously, a one-tuple instance never can be a counterexample). In this case, a positive counterexample $\langle t_1, t_2\rangle$ tells that no dependency having its antecedent contained in the set of attributes where $t_1$ and $t_2$ agree, and its consequent outside, can be in the target cover. In contrast, a negative counterexample indicates that at least one dependency satisfying the conditions just mentioned must be in the target.

Note that the significance of these counterexamples is the same as the meaning of counterexamples in the case of Horn clauses, if we translate "set of attributes where $t_1$ and $t_2$ agree" into "set of variables assigned true". Also note that there is no syntactic difference between a conjunction of Horn clauses and a minimal cover for a set of functional dependencies[1], hence the input to equivalence queries has the same "shape", no matter what oracle $-EQ_{HORN}$ or $EQ_{MCFD}-$ we use.

---

[1] There is an exception to this statement. The counterpart to a Horn clause $c$ with no positive literal should be a functional dependency $f$ with the empty set as consequent. The difference is not merely syntactic but also semantic, since $f$ does not impose any constraint on the instance space, that is, $f$ is superfluous unlike $c$. This fact rules out the straightforward transformation of the target class used by Angluin [3] to prove approximate fingerprints for $CNF$ (and implicitly for conjunctions of Horn clauses) into a target class for proving non-learnability with equivalence queries alone for $MCFD$. The reason is that, once transformed, the class would contain just one minimal cover: the empty one. Also the counterpart to a Horn clause $c$ with no negative literals should be a functional dependency $f$ with the empty set in the antecedent. However, in this case the meaning of both $c$ and $f$ is alike

Therefore, were we to learn $MCFD$ over an instance space containing only two-tupled examples, the transformation of $HORN$ would be straightforward: substitute $EQ_{MCFD}$ and $MQ_{MCFD}$ for $EQ_{HORN}$ and $MQ_{HORN}$ respectively; whenever $EQ_{MCFD}$ provides a counterexample $\langle t_1, t_2 \rangle$, convert $\langle t_1, t_2 \rangle$ into a boolean vector by setting to *true* the attributes (variables) where $t_1$ and $t_2$ agree and *false* elsewhere; finally, perform the reverse mapping before asking any membership query. One last remark, if we wanted the learning algorithm to be *proper*, in the sense that inputs to equivalence queries be in the class $MCFD$, we should transform the hypotheses generated into minimal covers. This can be done in polynomial time.

Now, we wish to address the problem of learning in the general case, that is, when the instance space is not restricted to contain only two-tupled instances. The key observation is that, to detect the violation of some dependency or the need of its inclusion in the current hypothesis, it suffices to consider pairs of tuples. When a $k$-tupled positive counterexample is received, we consider all $\binom{k}{2}$ pairs of tuples, and for each of them proceed to remove from the current hypothesis the dependencies that are violated. If the counterexample is negative then we ask $\binom{k}{2}$ membership queries to detect a pair of tuples –there must be at least one– that violates some dependency in the target cover, and proceed accordingly, that is, trying to identify the dependency in order to include it in the current hypothesis. Thus, we have reduced the problem of learning $MCFD$ over an unrestricted instance space to that of learning when the instances have two tuples.

We present now the algorithm that learns $MCFD$. We follow the notation in [4] as much as possible. For $x$ and $y$ boolean vectors, $true(x)$ is the set of attributes assigned *true* by $x$; $x \cap y$ is the boolean vector such that $true(x \cap y) = true(x) \cap true(y)$. Given a two-tupled relation $r$, $sketch(r)$ is the boolean vector whose *true* values correspond to the attributes for which the tuples of $r$ agree. For boolean vector $x$, $rel(x)$ maps $x$ onto a relation $r$ (there are many) such that $sketch(r) = x$. Finally, if $x$ is a boolean vector such that $true(x) = \{A_1, A_2, \ldots A_k\}$, then $FD(x)$ denotes the set of functional dependencies

$$FD(x) = \{A_1, A_2, \ldots A_k \longrightarrow B : B \notin true(x)\}.$$

The algorithm maintains a sequence $S$ of boolean vectors that are *sketches* of negative counterexamples, each of them violating distinct dependencies of the target cover. This sequence is used to generate a new hypothesis $F$ by taking the union of $FD(x)$ for all $x$ in $S$. Since we want a *proper* learning algorithm, we must transform the hypothesis $F$ thus generated into a minimal cover $G$, prior to any equivalence query. Note that when a positive counterexample is received we eliminate dependencies from $F$ instead of $G$. In doing so we preserve the parallelism with algorithm $HORN$, where a hypothesis may contain clauses that are implied by other clauses in the same hypothesis. This is to prevent the algorithm from possibly entering an infinite loop. On the other hand, it is obvious that the counterexample provided by an equivalence query is independent of whether the input to that query is a minimal cover or not, as long as they are equivalent. (For more explanations and ideas behind the algorithm see [4]).

Set $S$ to be the empty sequence; /* $s_i$ denotes the i-th boolean vector of $S$ */
Set $F$ to be the empty hypothesis;
Set $G$ to be the empty hypothesis; /* $G$ is a minimal cover for $F$ */
**while** $EQ_{MCFD}(G) \neq YES$ **loop**
       Let $r$ be the counterexample relation returned by the equivalence query;
       **if** $r$ violates at least one functional dependency of $F$
           **then** /* $r$ is a positive example */
               remove from $F$ every dependency that $r$ violates;
           **else** /* $r$ is a negative example */
               ask (at most $\binom{|r|}{2}$) queries to $MQ_{MCFD}$ until a
               negative answer is got for some $\langle t_1, t_2 \rangle$ in $r$;
               x:= sketch $(\langle t_1, t_2 \rangle)$;
               **for each** $s_i$ in $S$ such that $true(s_i \cap x)$
                        is properly contained in $true(s_i)$ **loop**
                 $MQ_{MCFD}(rel(s_i \cap x))$;
               **end loop**;
               **if** any of these queries is answered $NO$
               **then**
                   let $i =\min \{j : MQ_{MCFD}(rel(s_j \cap x)) = NO\}$;
                   replace $s_i$ with $s_i \cap x$;
               **else**
                   add $x$ as the last element in the sequence $S$;
               **end if** ;
               $F = \bigcup_{s \in S} FD(s)$;
       **end if**;
       set $G$ to be a minimal cover for $F$;
**end loop**;
return $G$;
**end**;

The correctness of the algorithm follows from the correctness of $HORN$ and the comments above. About the query and time complexity, the algorithm makes as many equivalence queries as $HORN$ makes. However, both the number of membership queries and the time complexity are increased, since the counterexamples can have an arbitrary number of tuples, and for each counterexample received the algorithm has to compute a minimal cover. In any case, the complexity is polynomial in the size of the target cover, the number of attributes of the relation scheme and the number of tuples of the largest counterexample.

# References

1. D. Angluin. "Learning Regular Sets from Queries and Counterexamples". *Information and Computation*, 75, 87-106, 1987.

2. D. Angluin. "Queries and Concept Learning". *Machine Learning*, 2(4), 319-342, 1988.

3. D. Angluin. "Negative Results for Equivalence Queries". *Machine Learning*, 5, 121-150, 1990.

4. D. Angluin, M. Frazier and L. Pitt. "Learning Conjunctions of Horn Clauses". *Machine Learning*, 9, 147-164, 1992.

5. R. Elmasri and S. B. Navathe. *Fundamentals of Database Systems*. Benjamin-Cummings Pub. Redwood City, California, 1994.

6. J. Castro, D. Guijarro and V. Lavín. "Learning Nearly Monotone k-term DNF". *Information Processing Letters*, 67(2), 75-79, 1998.

7. E.F. Codd. "A Relational model for Large Shared Data Banks". *Comm. of the ACM*, 13(6), 377-387, 1970.

8. D. Guijarro, V. Lavín and V. Raghavan. "Learning Monotone Term Decision Lists". *To appear in Theoretical Computer Science. Proceedings of EUROCOLT'97*, 16-26, 1997.

9. S. Mahadevan and P. Tadepalli. "Quantifying Prior Determination Knowledge using PAC Learning Model". *Machine Learning*, 17(1), 69-105, 1994.

10. P. Tadepalli and S. Russell. "Learning from Examples and Membership Queries with Structured Determinations". *Machine Learning*, 32, 245-295, 1998.

11. J.D. Ullman. *Principles of Database and Knowledge-Base Systems*. Computer Science Press, Inc. 1988.

# Boolean Formulas Are Hard to Learn for Most Gate Bases

Víctor Dalmau

Departament LSI, Universitat Politècnica de Catalunya,
Mòdul C5. Jordi Girona Salgado 1-3. Barcelona 08034, Spain,
dalmau@lsi.upc.es

**Abstract.** Boolean formulas are known not to be PAC-predictable even with membership queries under some cryptographic assumptions. In this paper, we study the learning complexity of some subclasses of boolean formulas obtained by varying the basis of elementary operations allowed as connectives. This broad family of classes includes, as a particular case, general boolean formulas, by considering the basis given by {AND, OR, NOT}. We completely solve the problem. We prove the following *dichotomy theorem*: For any set of basic boolean functions, the resulting set of formulas is either polynomially learnable from equivalence queries or membership queries alone or else it is not PAC-predictable even with membership queries under cryptographic assumptions. We identify precisely which sets of basic functions are in which of the two cases. Furthermore, we prove than the learning complexity of formulas over a basis depends only on the absolute expressivity power of the class, ie., the set of functions that can be represented regardless of the size of the representation. In consequence, the same classification holds for the learnability of boolean circuits.

## 1 Introduction

The problem of learning an unknown boolean formula under some determined protocol has been widely studied. It is well known that, even restricted to propositional formulas, the problem is hard [4, 18] in the usual learning models. Therefore researchers have attempted to learn subclasses of propositional boolean formulas obtained by enforcing some restrictions on the structure of the formula, specially subclasses of boolean formulas in disjunctive normal form (DNF). For example, $k$-DNF formulas, $k$-term DNF formulas, monotone-DNF formulas, Horn formulas, and their dual counterparts [1, 5, 2] have all been shown exactly learnable using membership and equivalence queries in Angluin's model [1] while the question of whether DNF formulas are learnable is still open. Another important class of problems can be obtained by restricting the number of occurrences of a variable. For example, whereas there is a polynomial-time algorithm to learn read-once formulas with equivalence and membership queries [3], the problem of learning read-thrice boolean formulas is hard under cryptographic assumptions [4].

O. Watanabe, T. Yokomori (Eds.): ALT'99, LNAI 1720, pp. 301–312, 1999.
© Springer-Verlag Berlin Heidelberg 1999

In this paper we take a different approach. We study the complexity of learning subclasses of boolean formulas obtained placing some restrictions in the elementary boolean functions that can be used to build the formulas. In general, boolean formulas are constructed by using elementary functions from a complete basis, generally {AND, OR, NOT}. In this paper we will allow formulas to use as a basis any arbitrary set of boolean functions.

More precisely, let $F = \{f_1, \ldots, f_m\}$ be a finite set of boolean functions. A formula in FOR($F$) can be any of (a) a boolean variable, or (b) an expression of the form $f(g_1, \ldots, g_k)$ where $f$ is a $k$-ary function in $F$ and $g_1, \ldots, g_k$ are formulas in FOR($F$).

For example, consider the problem of learning a monotone boolean formula. Every such formula can be expressed as a formula in the class FOR({AND, OR}). The main result of this paper characterizes the complexity of learning FOR($F$) for every finite set $F$ of boolean functions. The most striking feature of this characterization is that for any $F$, FOR($F$) is either polynomially learnable with equivalence or membership queries alone or, under some cryptographic assumptions, not polynomially predictable even with membership queries.

This dichotomy is somewhat surprising since one might expect that any such large and diverse family of concept classes would include some representatives of the many intermediate learning models such as exact learning with equivalence and membership queries, PAC learning with and without membership queries and PAC-prediction without membership queries.

Furthermore, we give an interesting classification of the polynomially learnable classes. We show that, in a sense that will be made precise later, FOR($F$) is polynomially learnable if and only if at least one of the following conditions holds:

(a) Every function $f(x_1, x_2, \ldots, x_n)$ in $F$ is definable by an expression of the form $c_0 \vee (c_1 \wedge x_1) \vee (c_2 \wedge x_2) \vee \cdots \vee (c_n \wedge x_n)$ for some boolean coefficients $c_i$ $(1 \leq i \leq n)$.

(b) Every function $f(x_1, x_2, \ldots, x_n)$ in $F$ is definable by an expression of the form $c_0 \wedge (c_1 \vee x_1) \wedge (c_2 \vee x_2) \wedge \cdots \wedge (c_n \vee x_n)$ for some boolean coefficients $c_i$ $(1 \leq i \leq n)$.

(a) Every function $f(x_1, x_2, \ldots, x_n)$ in $F$ is definable by an expression of the form $c_0 \oplus (c_1 \wedge x_1) \oplus (c_2 \wedge x_2) \oplus \cdots \oplus (c_n \wedge x_n)$ for some boolean coefficients $c_i$ $(1 \leq i \leq n)$.

There is another rather special feature of this result. Learnability of boolean formulas over a basis $F$ depends only on the set of functions that can be expressed as a formula in FOR($F$) but it does not depend on the size of the representation. As a consequence of this fact, the same dichotomy holds for representation classes which, in terms of absolute expressivity power, are equivalent to formulas, such as boolean circuits.

As an intermediate tool for our study we introduce a link with some well known algebraic structure, called *clones* in Universal Algebra. In particular, we make use of very remarkable result on the structure of boolean functions proved by Post [21]. This approach has been successful in the study of other computational problems such as satisfiability, tautology and counting problems of boolean formulas [23], learnability of quantified formulas [9] and Constraint Satisfaction Problems [13, 14, 15, 16, 12].

Finally we mention some similar results: a dichotomy result for satisfiability, tautology and some counting problems over closed sets of boolean functions [23], the circuit value problem [11, 10], the satisfiability of generalized formulas [24], the inverse generalized satisfiability problem [17], the generalized satisfiability counting problem [7], the approximability of minimization and maximization problems [6, 19, 20], the optimal assignments of Generalized Propositional Formulas [22] and the learnability of quantified boolean formulas [8].

## 2  Learning Preliminaries

Most of the terminology about learning comes from [4]. Strings over $X = D^*$ will represent both examples and concept names. A *representation of concepts* $C$ is any subset of $X \times X$. We interpret an element $\langle u, x \rangle$ of $X \times X$ as consisting of a *concept name* $u$ and an *example* $x$. The example $x$ is a member of the concept $u$ if and only if $\langle u, x \rangle \in C$. Define the *concept represented by* $u$ as $K_C(u) = \{x : \langle u, x \rangle \in C\}$. The *set of concepts represented by* $C$ is $K_C = \{K_C(u) : u \in X\}$.

Along these pages we use two models of learning, all of them fairly standard: Angluin's model of exact learning with queries defined by Angluin [1], and the model of PAC-prediction with membership queries as defined by Angluin and Kharitonov [4].

To compare the difficulty of learning problems in the prediction model we use a slight generalization of the *prediction-preserving reducibility with membership queries* [4].

**Definition 1.** *Let $C$ and $C'$ be representations of concepts. Let $\perp$ and $\top$ be elements not in $X$. Then $C$ is* pwm-reducible *to $C'$, denoted $C \leq_{pwm} C'$, if and only if there exist four mappings $g, f, h$, and $j$ with the following properties:*

1. *There is a nondecreasing polynomial $q$ such that for all natural numbers $s$ and $n$ and for $u \in X$ with $|u| \leq s$, $g(s, n, u)$ is a string $u'$ of length at most $q(s, n, |u|)$.*
2. *For all natural numbers $s$ and $n$, for every string $u \in X$ with $|u| \leq s$, and for every $x \in X$ with $|x| \leq n$, $f(s, n, x)$ is a string $x'$ and $x \in K_C(u)$ if and only if $x' \in K_{C'}(g(s, n, u))$. Moreover, $f$ is computable in time bounded by a polynomial in $s$, $n$, and $|x|$, hence there exists a nondecreasing polynomial $t$ such that $|x'| \leq t(s, n, |x|)$.*
3. *For all natural numbers $s$ and $n$, for every string $u \in X$ with $|u| \leq s$, for every $x' \in X$, and for every $b \in \{\top, \perp\}$, $h(s, n, x')$ is a string $x \in X$, and $j(s, n, x', b)$ is either $\perp$ or $\top$. Furthermore $x' \in K_{C'}(g(s, n, u))$ if and only if $j(s, n, x', b) = \top$, where $b = \top$ if $x \in K_C(u)$ and $b = \perp$ otherwise. Moreover, $h$ and $j$ are computable in time bounded by a polynomial in $s$, $n$, and $|x'|$.*

*In (2), and independently in (3), the expression "$x \in K_C(u)$" can be replaced with "$x \notin K_C(u)$", as discussed in [4].*

The following results are obtained adapting slightly some proofs in [4].

**Lemma 1.** *The pwm-reduction is transitive, i.e., let $C, C'$ and $C''$ be representations of concepts, if $C \leq_{pwm} C' \leq_{pwm} C''$ then $C \leq_{pwm} C''$.*

**Lemma 2.** *Let $C$ and $C'$ be representations of concepts. If $C \leq_{pwm} C'$ and $C'$ is polynomially predictable with membership queries, then $C$ is also polynomially predictable with membership queries.*

## 3   Clones

Let $D$ be finite set called *domain*. An $n$-adic *function* over $D$ is a map $f : D^n \longrightarrow D$. Let $\mathcal{F}^D$ be the set of all the functions over the domain $D$. Let $\mathcal{P}$ be a class of functions over $D$. Let $\mathcal{P}_n$ be the $n$-adic functions in $\mathcal{P}$. We shall say that $\mathcal{P}$ is a clone if it satisfies the following conditions:

$C_1$ For each $n \geq m \geq 1$, $\mathcal{P}$ contains the *projection function* $\text{proj}_{n,m}$, defined by

$$\text{proj}_{n,m}(x_1, \ldots, x_n) = x_m$$

$C_2$ For each $n, m \geq 1$, each $f \in \mathcal{P}_n$ and each $g_1, \ldots, g_n \in \mathcal{P}_m$. $\mathcal{P}_m$ contains the composite function $h = f[g_1, \ldots, g_n]$ defined by

$$h(x_1, \ldots, x_m) = f(g_1(x_1, \ldots, x_m), \ldots, g_n(x_1, \ldots, x_m))$$

If $F \subseteq \mathcal{F}^D$ is any set of functions over $D$, there is a smallest clone containing all of the functions in $F$; this is the clone generated by $F$, and we denote it $\langle F \rangle$ If $F = \{f_1, \ldots, f_k\}$ is a finite set, we may write $\langle f_1, \ldots, f_k \rangle$ for $\langle F \rangle$, and refer to $f_1, \ldots, f_k$ as generators of $\langle F \rangle$. The set of clones over a finite domain $D$ is closed under intersection and therefore it constitutes a lattice, with meet ($\wedge$) and join ($\vee$) operations defined by:

$$\bigwedge_{i \in I} C_i = \bigcap_{i \in I} C_i \qquad \bigvee_{i \in I} C_i = \left\langle \bigcup_{i \in I} C_i \right\rangle$$

There is a smallest clone which is the intersection of all clones; we shall denote it $\mathcal{I}_D$. It is easy to see that $\mathcal{I}_D$ contains exactly the projections over $D$.

### 3.1   Boolean Case

Operations on a 2-element set, say $D = \{0, 1\}$ are boolean operations. The lattice of the clones over the boolean domain was studied by Post, leading to a full description [21]. The proof is too long to be included here. We will give only the description of the lattice.

A usual way to describe a poset $(P, \leq)$ (and a lattice in particular) is by depicting a *diagram* with the relation *coverage*, where for every $a, b \in P$ we say

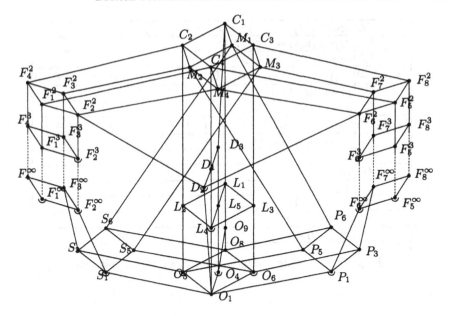

**Fig. 1.** Post Lattice

that $a$ covers $b$ if $b \leq a$ and if $c$ is an element in $P$ such that $b \leq c \leq a$, then either $c = a$ or $c = b$. The diagram of the lattice of clones on $D = \{0, 1\}$, often called *Post's lattice* is depicted in Figure 1. The clones are labeled according their standard names.

A clone $C$ is *join irreducible* iff $C = C_1 \vee C_2$ always implies $C = C_1$ or $C = C_2$. In Figure 1, the join irreducible clones of the diagram are denoted by $\smile$. Since $\langle \mathcal{P} \rangle = \bigvee_{f \in \mathcal{P}} \langle f \rangle$, it follows that the join irreducible clones are generated by a single operation, furthermore, it suffices to present a generating operation for each join irreducible clone of Post's lattice. Table 2 associates to every join irreducible clone $C$, its generating operation $\varphi_C$.

For a $n$-ary boolean function $f$ define its *dual* $\mathrm{dual}(f)$ by

$$\mathrm{dual}(f)(x_1, \ldots, x_n) = \neg f(\neg x_1, \ldots, \neg x_n).$$

Obviously, $\mathrm{dual}(\mathrm{dual}(f)) = f$. Furthermore, $f$ is self-dual iff $\mathrm{dual}(f) = f$. For a class $F$ of boolean functions define $\mathrm{dual}(F) = \{\mathrm{dual}(f) : f \in F\}$. The classes $F$ and $\mathrm{dual}(F)$ are called dual. Notice that $\langle \mathrm{dual}(F) \rangle = \mathrm{dual}(\langle F \rangle)$.

## 4   The Dichotomy Theorem

A *base* $F$ is a finite set of boolean functions $\{f_1, f_2, \ldots, f_n\}$ ($f_i$  $1 \leq i \leq n$, denotes both the function and its symbol). We follow the standard definitions of boolean circuits and boolean formulas. The class of boolean circuits over the basis $F$, denoted by $\mathrm{CIR}(F)$, is defined to be the set of all the boolean circuits

| | |
|---|---|
| $D_2$ | $\varphi_{D_2}(x,y,z) = (x \wedge y) \vee (x \wedge z) \vee (y \wedge z)$ |
| $F_1^\infty$ | $\varphi_{F_1^\infty}(x,y,z) = x \vee (y \wedge \bar{z})$ |
| $F_2^\infty$ | $\varphi_{F_2^\infty}(x,y,z) = x \vee (y \wedge z)$ |
| $F_2^i \ (i \geq 2)$ | $\varphi_{F_2^i}(x_1,\ldots,x_{i+1}) = \bigwedge_{j=1}^{i+1}(x_1 \vee \cdots \vee x_{j-1} \vee x_{j+1} \vee \cdots \vee x_{i+1})$ |
| $F_5^\infty$ | $\varphi_{F_5^\infty}(x,y,z) = x \wedge (y \vee \bar{z})$ |
| $F_6^\infty$ | $\varphi_{F_6^\infty}(x,y,z) = x \wedge (y \vee z)$ |
| $F_6^i \ (i \geq 2)$ | $\varphi_{F_6^i}(x_1,\ldots,x_{i+1}) = \bigvee_{j=1}^{i+1}(x_1 \wedge \cdots \wedge x_{j-1} \wedge x_{j+1} \wedge \cdots \wedge x_{i+1})$ |
| $L_4$ | $\varphi_{L_4}(x,y,z) = x \oplus y \oplus z$ |
| $O_1$ | $\emptyset$ |
| $O_4$ | $\varphi_{O_4}(x) = \bar{x}$ |
| $O_5$ | $\varphi_{O_5}(x) = 1$ |
| $O_6$ | $\varphi_{O_6}(x) = 0$ |
| $P_1$ | $\varphi_{P_1}(x,y) = x \wedge y$ |
| $S_1$ | $\varphi_{S_1}(x,y) = x \vee y$ |

**Fig. 2.** Generating operations for meet irreducible clones

where every gate is a function in $F$. The class of boolean formulas over the basis $F$, denoted by $\mathrm{FOR}(F)$ is the class of circuits in $\mathrm{CIR}(F)$ with fan-out $\leq 1$.

Given a boolean circuit $C$ over the input variables $x_1, x_2, \ldots, x_n$, we denote by $[C]$ the function computed by $C$ when the variables are taken as arguments in lexicographical order. In the same way, given a finite set of boolean functions $F$ we define $[\mathrm{CIR}(F)]$ as the class of functions computed by circuits in $\mathrm{CIR}(F)$. Similarly, given a boolean formula $\Phi$ over the variables $x_1, x_2, \ldots, x_n$, we denote by $[\Phi]$ the function computed by $\Phi$ when the variables are taken as arguments in lexicographical order. In the same way, given a finite set of boolean functions $F$ we define $[\mathrm{FOR}(F)]$ as the class of functions computed by formulas in $\mathrm{FOR}(F)$. Given a boolean circuit $C \in \mathrm{CIR}(F)$, it is possible to construct a formula $\Phi \in \mathrm{FOR}(F)$ computing the same function than $C$ (the size of $\Phi$ can be exponentially bigger than the size of $C$ but we are not concerned with the size of the representation). Thus $[\mathrm{FOR}(F)] = [\mathrm{CIR}(F)]$.

In fact, it is direct to verify that the class of functions $[\mathrm{CIR}(F)]$ contains the projections and it is closed under composition. Therefore, it constitutes a clone. More precisely, $[\mathrm{CIR}(F)]$ is exactly the clone generated by $F$, in our terminology

$$[\mathrm{CIR}(F)] = [\mathrm{FOR}(F)] = \langle F \rangle, \text{ for all bases } F.$$

The use of clone theory to study computational problems over boolean formulas was introduced in [23] studying the complexity of some computational problems over boolean formulas, such as satisfiability, tautology and some counting problems.

We say that an $n$-ary function $f$ is disjunctive if there exists some boolean coefficients $c_i \ (0 \leq i \leq n)$ such that

$$f(x_1, \ldots, x_n) = c_0 \vee (c_1 \wedge x_1) \vee (c_2 \wedge x_2) \vee \cdots \vee (c_n \wedge x_n).$$

Similarly, we say that an $n$-ary function $f$ is conjunctive if there exists some boolean coefficients $c_i$ $(0 \le i \le n)$ such that

$$f(x_1, \ldots, x_n) = c_0 \wedge (c_1 \vee x_1) \wedge (c_2 \vee x_2) \wedge \cdots \wedge (c_n \vee x_n).$$

Accordingly, we say that an $n$-ary function $f$ is linear if there exists some boolean coefficients $c_i$ $(0 \le i \le n)$ such that

$$f(x_1, \ldots, x_n) = c_0 \oplus (c_1 \wedge x_1) \oplus (c_2 \wedge x_2) \oplus \cdots \oplus (c_n \wedge x_n).$$

Let $F$ be a set of boolean functions. We will say that $F$ is disjunctive (resp. conjunctive, linear) iff every function in $F$ is disjunctive (resp. conjunctive, linear). We will say that $F$ is basic iff $F$ is disjunctive, conjunctive or linear.

For any set of boolean formulas (circuits) $\mathcal{B}$, we define $\mathcal{C}_\mathcal{B}$ as the representation of concepts formed from formulas (circuits) in $\mathcal{B}$. More precisely, $\mathcal{C}_\mathcal{B}$ contains all the tuples of the form $\langle C, x \rangle$ where $C$ represents a formula (circuit) in $\mathcal{B}$ and $x$ is a model satisfying $C$.

In this section we state and prove the main result of the paper.

**Theorem 1.** (*Dichotomy Theorem for the Learnability of Boolean Circuits and Boolean Formulas*) *Let $F$ be a finite set of boolean functions. If $F$ is basic, then $\mathcal{C}_{\mathrm{CIR}(F)}$ is both polynomially exactly learnable with $n+1$ equivalence queries, and polynomially exactly learnable with $n+1$ membership queries. Otherwise, $\mathcal{C}_{\mathrm{FOR}(F)}$ is not polynomially predictable with membership queries under the assumption that any of the following three problems are intractable: testing quadratic residues modulo a composite, inverting RSA encryption, or factoring Blum integers.*

We refer the reader to Angluin and Kharitonov [4] for definitions of the cryptographic concepts. We mention that the non-learnability results for boolean circuits hold also with the weaker assumption of the existence of public-key encryption systems secure against CC-attack, as discussed in [4].

## Proof of Theorem 1

Learnability of formulas over disjunctive, conjunctive and linear bases is rather straightforward. Notice that if a basis $F$ is disjunctive (resp. conjunctive, linear) then every function computed by a circuit in $\mathrm{CIR}(F)$ is also disjunctive (resp. conjunctive, linear). Thus, learning a boolean circuit over a basic basis is reduced to finding the boolean coefficients of the canonical expression. It is easy to verify that this task can be done in polynomial time with $n + 1$ equivalence queries or $n + 1$ membership queries, as stated in the theorem.

Now, we study which portion of Post's lattice is covered by these cases. Consider clone $L_1$ with generating set $L_1 = \langle \varphi_{O_4}, \varphi_{O_5}, \varphi_{O_6}, \varphi_{L_4} \rangle$. Since all the operations in the generating set of $L_1$ are linear, then the clone $L_1$ is linear. Similarly, clone $P_6$, generated by operations $\varphi_{O_5}$, $\varphi_{O_6}$ and $\varphi_{P_1}$ is conjunctive, since so is every operation in the generating set. Finally clone $S_6$, generated by operations $\varphi_{O_5}$, $\varphi_{O_6}$ and $\varphi_{S_1}$ is disjunctive, since so is every operation in the generating set. Thus, every clone contained in $L_1$, $P_6$, or $S_6$ is linear, conjunctive or disjunctive respectively. Actually, clone $L_1$ (resp. $P_6$, $S_6$) has been chosen carefully among the linear (resp. conjunctive, disjunctive) clones. It corresponds to the maximal linear (resp. conjunctive, disjunctive) clone in Post's lattice. It has been obtained as the join of all the linear (resp. conjunctive, disjunctive) clones and, in consequence, has the property that every linear (resp. conjunctive, disjunctive) clone is contained in $L_1$ (resp. $P_6$, $S_6$).

Let us study non-basic clones. With a simple inspection of Post's lattice we can infer that any clone not contained in $L_1$, $S_6$ or $P_6$ contains any of the following operations: $\varphi_{F_2^\infty}$, $\varphi_{F_6^\infty}$, $\varphi_{D_2}$. In Section 4.1 it is proved that if $\langle F \rangle$ contains any of the previous functions, then the class FOR($F$) is not PAC-predictable even with membership queries under the assumptions of the theorem.

∎

## 4.1   Three Fundamental Non-learnable Functions

Let $\mathcal{B} = \{\text{AND}, \text{OR}, \text{NOT}\}$ be the usual complete basis for boolean formulas. In [4], it is proved that $\mathcal{C}_{\text{FOR}(\mathcal{B})}$ is not polynomially predictable under the assumptions of Theorem 1. In this section we generalize the previous result to all bases $F$ able to "simulate" any of the following three basic non-learnable functions: $\varphi_{F_2^\infty}$, $\varphi_{F_6^\infty}$, and $\varphi_{D_2}$. This three functions can be regarded as the basic causes for non-learnability in formulas.

The technique used to prove non-learnability results is a two-stage pwm-reduction from FOR($\mathcal{B}$). First, we prove as an intermediate result that monotone boolean formulas are as hard to learn, as general boolean formulas.

**Lemma 3.** *The class $\mathcal{C}_{\text{FOR}(\mathcal{B})}$ is pwm-reducible to $\mathcal{C}_{\text{FOR}(\{\text{AND},\text{OR}\})}$.*

**Proof.** Let $\Phi$ be a boolean formula with $x_1, \ldots, x_n$ as input variables. We can assume that NOT operations are applied only to input variables. Otherwise by using repeatedly De Morgan's law we can move every NOT function towards the input variables.

Consider the formula $\Psi$ with $x_1, \ldots, x_n, y_1, \ldots, y_n$ as input variables, obtained modifying slightly formula $\Phi$ as follows: replace every NOT function applied to variable $x_i$, by the new input variable $y_i$. Finally, we define the formula $\Upsilon$ with $x_1, \ldots, x_n, y_1, \ldots, y_n$ as input variables to be:

$$\Upsilon(x_1, \ldots, x_n, y_1, \ldots, y_n) =$$

$$\left( \Psi(x_1, \ldots, x_n, y_1, \ldots, y_n) \vee \bigvee_{1 \le i \le n} (x_i \wedge y_i) \right) \wedge$$

$$\wedge \bigwedge_{1 \le i \le n} (x_i \vee y_i)$$

Formula $\Upsilon$ evaluates the following function:

$$\Upsilon(x_1, \ldots, x_n, y_1, \ldots, y_n) = \begin{cases} \Phi(x_1, \ldots, x_n) & \text{if } \forall i : 1 \le i \le n, \ x_i \ne y_i \\ 0 & \text{if } \exists i : 1 \le i \le n, \ x_i = y_i = 0 \\ 1 & \text{otherwise} \end{cases}$$

For every natural number $s$ and for every concept representation $u \in \mathcal{C}_{\mathrm{FOR}(B)}$ such that $|u| \leq s$, let $\Phi$ be the boolean formula with $n$ input variables represented by $u$, let $u'$ be the representation of the monotone boolean formula $\Upsilon$ obtained from $\Phi$ as described above. We define $g(s, n, u) = u'$. For every assignments $x$ and $y$ of length $n$ we define $f(s, n, x) = x\bar{x}$, $h(s, n, xy) = x$ and

$$j(s, n, xy, b) = \begin{cases} b & \text{if } x = \bar{y} \\ \bot & \text{if } \exists i : 1 \leq i \leq n, x_i = y_i = 0 \\ \top & \text{otherwise} \end{cases}$$

Clearly, $f$, $g$, $h$ and $j$ satisfy the conditions (1), (2) and (3) in Definition 1 and therefore define a pwm-reduction.

Technical note: In the proof of this prediction with membership reduction and in the next ones, functions $f, g, h, j$ have been defined only partially to keep the proof clear. It is trivial to extend them to obtain complete functions preserving conditions (1), (2) and (3). ∎

Now, we have to see that $\mathcal{C}_{\mathrm{FOR}(\{\mathrm{NOT},\mathrm{AND}\})}$ is pwm-reducible to $\mathcal{C}_{\mathrm{FOR}(F)}$ if $F$ is able to "generate" any of the following functions: $\varphi_{F_2^\infty}$, $\varphi_{F_6^\infty}$ or $\varphi_{D_2}$. Let us do a case analysis.

**Theorem 2.** *Let $F$ be a set of boolean functions. If $\varphi_{F_2^\infty} \in \langle F \rangle$ then $\mathcal{C}_{\mathrm{FOR}(\{\mathrm{AND},\mathrm{OR}\})}$ is pwm-reducible to $\mathcal{C}_{\mathrm{FOR}(F)}$.*

**Proof.** Clone $\langle F \rangle$ includes the operation $\varphi_{F_2^\infty}(x, y, z) = x \vee (y \wedge z)$. Thus, there exists some formula $\Phi_{F_2^\infty}$ in $\mathrm{FOR}(F)$ over three variables $x, y, z$ such that $[\Phi_{F_2^\infty}] = \varphi_{F_2^\infty}$.

Clearly, with the operation $\varphi_{F_2^\infty}$ and the additional help of constant 0 it is possible to simulate functions AND and OR,

$$\mathrm{AND}(x, y) = \varphi_{F_2^\infty}(0, x, y)$$

$$\mathrm{OR}(x, y) = \varphi_{F_2^\infty}(x, y, y)$$

Let $\Psi$ be an arbitrary monotone boolean formula in $\mathrm{FOR}(\{\mathrm{AND}, \mathrm{OR}\})$ over the input variables $x_1, x_2 \ldots, x_n$.

Let $\Upsilon_2$ be the boolean formula over the input variables $x_1, \ldots, x_n, c_0$ obtained from $\Psi$ by replacing every occurrence $\mathrm{AND}(x, y)$ by $\Phi_{F_2^\infty}(c_0, x, y)$ and, similarly, every occurrence of $\mathrm{OR}(x, y)$ by $\Phi_{F_2^\infty}(x, y, y)$.

Finally, let $\Upsilon_1$ be the boolean formula defined by:

$$\Upsilon_1(x_1, x_2, \ldots, x_n, c_0) = \Phi_{\Upsilon_2^\infty}(\Upsilon_2(x_1, x_2 \ldots, x_n, c_0), c_0, c_0),$$

By construction we have

$$\Upsilon_2(x_1, x_2, \ldots, x_n, 0) = \Psi(x_1, x_2, \ldots, x_n), \text{ and}$$

$$\Upsilon_1(x_1, x_2, \ldots, x_n, c_0) = \begin{cases} \Psi(x_1, x_2, \ldots, x_n) & \text{if } c_0 = 0 \\ 1 & \text{otherwise} \end{cases}$$

Now we are in position to define the pwm-reduction. Let $g$ be the function assigning to every monotone boolean formula $\Psi$, an associated formula $\Upsilon_1$ in FOR($F$) constructed as described above. Let $f$ be the function adding the value of the constant zero to the end of string, i.e.,

$$f(s, n, \langle x_1, x_2, \ldots, x_n \rangle) = \langle x_1, x_2, \ldots, x_n, 0 \rangle.$$

Mapping $h$ produces the inverse result. That is, given an string removes the last value (corresponding to the constant 0).

$$h(s, n, \langle x_1, \ldots, x_n, c_0 \rangle) = \langle x_1, \ldots, x_n \rangle$$

Finally, function $j$ is defined by

$$j(s, n, \langle x_1, \ldots, x_n, c_0 \rangle, b) = \begin{cases} b & \text{if } c_0 = 0 \\ \top & \text{otherwise} \end{cases}$$

Thus, it is immediate to verify that $f$, $g$, $h$, and $j$ define a pwm-reduction from $\mathcal{C}_{\{\text{AND,OR}\}}$ to $\mathcal{C}_{\text{FOR}(F)}$.    ∎

By duality we have,

**Theorem 3.**    *Let $F$ be a set of boolean functions. If $\varphi_{F_6}^\infty \in \langle F \rangle$ then $\mathcal{C}_{\text{FOR}(\{\text{AND,OR}\})}$ is pwm-reducible to $\mathcal{C}_{\text{FOR}(F)}$.*

Finally we study clones containing $\varphi_{D_2}$.

**Theorem 4.**    *Let $F$ be a set of boolean functions. If $\varphi_{D_2} \in \langle F \rangle$ then $\mathcal{C}_{\text{FOR}(\{\text{AND,OR}\})}$ is pwm-reducible to $\mathcal{C}_{\text{FOR}(F)}$.*

**Proof.** For this proof we will use the fact that operation $\varphi_{D_2}$ satisfies the self-duality property. Thus, every function in $\langle \varphi_{D_2} \rangle$ is self-dual. Clone $\langle F \rangle$ includes the majority operation $\varphi_{D_2}(x, y, z) = (x \wedge y) \vee (x \wedge z) \vee (y \wedge z)$. Thus, there exists some formula $\Phi_{D_2}$ in FOR($F$) over three variables $x, y, z$ such that the function computed by $F_{D_2}$ is $\varphi_{D_2}$.

Clearly, with the operation $\varphi_{D_2}$ and the additional help of constants it is possible to simulate functions AND and OR,

$$\text{AND}(x, y) = \varphi_{D_2}(0, x, y)$$

$$\text{OR}(x, y) = \varphi_{D_2}(1, x, y)$$

For every monotone boolean formula $\Psi$ in FOR($\{\text{AND, OR}\}$) over the input variables $x_1, x_2 \ldots, x_n$ we construct an associated formula $\Upsilon_1$ over the variables $x_1, x_2 \ldots, x_n, c_0, c_1$ defined by

$$\Upsilon_1(x_1, x_2, \ldots, x_n, c_0, c_1) = \Phi_{D_2}(\Upsilon_2(x_1, x_2 \ldots, x_n, c_0, c_1), c_0, c_1),$$

where $\Upsilon_2$ is the formula over the input variables $x_1, x_2, \ldots, x_n, c_0, c_1$ obtained from $\Psi$ in a similar way to the previous proof: we replace every occurrence of AND$(x, y)$ by $\Phi_{D_2}(c_0, x, y)$ and every occurrence of OR$(x, y)$ by $\Phi_{D_2}(c_1, x, y)$.

By construction we have (the case $c_0 = 1 \land c_1 = 0$ is a consequence of the self-duality of $D_2$),

$$\Upsilon_2(x_1, x_2, \ldots, x_n, c_0, c_1) = \begin{cases} \Psi(x_1, x_2, \ldots, x_n) & \text{if } c_0 = 0 \land c_1 = 1 \\ \neg\Psi(\neg x_1, \neg x_2, \ldots, \neg x_n) & \text{if } c_0 = 1 \land c_1 = 0 \\ \text{undetermined} & \text{otherwise} \end{cases}$$

$$\Upsilon_1(x_1, x_2, \ldots, x_n, c_0, c_1) = \begin{cases} \bot & \text{if } c_0 = c_1 = 0 \\ \top & \text{if } c_0 = c_1 = 1 \\ \Psi(x_1, x_2, \ldots, x_n) & \text{if } c_0 = 0 \land c_1 = 1 \\ \neg\Psi(\neg x_1, \neg x_2, \ldots, \neg x_n) & \text{if } c_0 = 1 \land c_1 = 0 \end{cases}$$

Now we are in position to define the pwm-reduction. Let $g$ be the function assigning to every monotone boolean formula $\Psi$ in $\text{FOR}(\{\text{AND}, \text{OR}\})$, an associated formula $\Upsilon_1$ in $\text{FOR}(F)$ constructed as described above. Let $f$ be the function adding the value of the constants to the end of string, i.e.,

$$f(s, n, \langle x_1, x_2, \ldots, x_n \rangle) = \langle x_1, x_2, \ldots, x_n, 0, 1 \rangle.$$

Mapping $h$ removes the last two values (corresponding to the constants) and, moreover, $h$ negates the values of the assignment if the values of the constants are flipped,

$$h(s, n, \langle x_1, \ldots, x_n, c_0, c_1 \rangle) = \begin{cases} \langle x_1, \ldots, x_n \rangle & \text{if } c_0 = 0 \lor c_1 = 1 \\ \langle \neg x_1, \ldots, \neg x_n \rangle & \text{otherwise} \end{cases}$$

Finally, function $j$ is defined by

$$j(s, n, \langle x_1, \ldots, x_n, c_0, c_1 \rangle, b) = \begin{cases} 0 & \text{if } c_0 = 0 \land c_1 = 0 \\ b & \text{if } c_0 = 0 \land c_1 = 1 \\ \neg b & \text{if } c_0 = 1 \land c_1 = 0 \\ 1 & \text{if } c_0 = 1 \land c_1 = 1 \end{cases}$$

Thus, it is immediate to verify that $f$, $g$, $h$, and $j$ define a pwm-reduction from $\mathcal{C}_{\{\text{AND},\text{OR}\}}$ to $\mathcal{C}_{\text{CIR}(F)}$. ∎

# References

[1] D. Angluin. Queries and Concept Learning. *Machine Learning*, 2:319–342, 1988.
[2] D. Angluin, M. Frazier, and L. Pitt. Learning Conjunctions of Horn Clauses. *Machine Learning*, 9:147–164, 1992.
[3] D. Angluin, L. Hellerstein, and M. Karpinski. Learning Read-Once Formulas with Queries. *Journal of the ACM*, 40:185–210, 1993.
[4] D. Angluin and M. Kharitonov. When won't Membership Queries help. *Journal of Computer and System Sciences*, 50:336–355, 1995.
[5] U. Berggren. Linear Time Deterministic Learning of $k$-term DNF. In *6th Annual ACM Conference on Computational Learning Theory, COLT'93*, pages 37–40, 1993.

[6] N. Creignou. A Dichotomy Theorem for Maximum Generalized Satisfiability Problems. *Journal of Computer and System Sciences*, 51(3):511–522, 1995.

[7] N. Creignou and M. Hermann. Complexity of Generalized Satisfiability Counting Problems. *Information and Computation*, 125:1–12, 1996.

[8] V. Dalmau. A Dichotomy Theorem for Learning Quantified Boolean Formulas. *Machine Learning*, 35(3):207–224, 1999.

[9] V. Dalmau and P. Jeavons. Learnability of Quantified Formulas. In *4th European Conference on Computational Learning Theory Eurocolt'99*, volume 1572 of *Lecture Notes in Artificial Intelligence*, pages 63–78, Berlin/New York, 1999. Springer-Verlag.

[10] L.M. Goldschlager. A Characterization of Sets of *n*-Input Gates in Terms of their Computational Power. Technical Report 216, Basser Department of Computer Science, The University of Sidney, 1983.

[11] L.M. Goldschlager and I. Parberry. On the Construction of Parallel Computers from various bases of Boolean Circuits. *Theoretical Computer Science*, 43:43–58, 1986.

[12] P. Jeavons, D. Cohen, and M.C. Cooper. Constraints, Consistency and Closure. *Artificial Intelligence*, 101:251–265, 1988.

[13] P. Jeavons, D. Cohen, and M. Gyssens. A Unifying Framework for Tractable Constraints. In *1st International Conference on Principles and Practice of Constraint Programming, CP'95, Cassis (France), September 1995*, volume 976 of *Lecture Notes in Computer Science*, pages 276–291. Springer-Verlag, 1995.

[14] P. Jeavons, D. Cohen, and M. Gyssens. A Test for Tractability. In *2nd International Conference on Principles and Practice of Constraint Programming CP'96*, volume 1118 of *Lecture Notes in Computer Science*, pages 267–281, Berlin/New York, August 1996. Springer-Verlag.

[15] P. Jeavons, D. Cohen, and M. Gyssens. Closure Properties of Constraints. *Journal of the ACM*, 44(4):527–548, July 1997.

[16] P. Jeavons and M. Cooper. Tractable Constraints on Ordered Domains. *Artificial Intelligence*, 79:327–339, 1996.

[17] D. Kavvadias and M. Sideri. The Inverse Satisfiability Problem. In *2nd Computing and Combinatorics COCOON'96*, volume 1090 of *Lecture Notes in Computer Science*, pages 250–259. Springer-Verlag, 1996.

[18] Michael Kearns and Leslie Valiant. Cryptographic limitations on learning Boolean formulae and finite automata. *Journal of the ACM*, 41(1):67–95, January 1994.

[19] S. Khanna, M. Sudan, and L. Trevisan. Constraint Satisfaction: The Approximability of Minimization Problems. In *12th IEEE Conference on Computational Complexity*, 1997.

[20] S. Khanna, M. Sudan, and P. Williamson. A Complete Classification fo the Approximability of Maximation Problems Derived from Boolean Constraint Satisfaction. In *29th Annual ACM Symposium on Theory of Computing*, 1997.

[21] E.L. Post. *The Two-Valued Iterative Systems of Mathematical Logic*, volume 5 of *Annals of Mathematics Studies*. Princeton, N.J, 1941.

[22] S. Reith and H. Vollmer. The Complexity of Computing Optimal Assignments of Generalized Propositional Formulae. Technical Report TR196, Department of Computer Science, Universität Würzburg, 1999.

[23] S. Reith and K.W. Wagner. The Complexity of Problems Defined by Subclasses of Boolean Functions. Technical Report TR218, Department of Computer Science, Universität Würzburg, 1999.

[24] T.J. Schaefer. The Complexity of Satisfiability Problems. In *10th Annual ACM Symposium on Theory of Computing*, pages 216–226, 1978.

# Finding Relevant Variables in PAC Model with Membership Queries

David Guijarro[1]*, Jun Tarui[2], and Tatsuie Tsukiji[3]

[1] Department LSI, Universitat Politècnica de Catalunya,
Jordi Girona Salgado, 1-3, Barcelona 08034, Spain
**david@lsi.upc.es**
[2] Department of Communications and Systems, University of
Electro-communications, Chogugaoka, Chofu-shi, Tokyo 182, Japan
**jun@sw.cas.uec.ac.jp**
[3] School of Informatics and Sciences, Nagoya University, Nagoya 464-8601, Japan
**tsukiji@info.human.nagoya-u.ac.jp**

**Abstract.** A new research frontier in AI and data mining seeks to develop methods to automatically discover relevant variables among many irrelevant ones. In this paper, we present four algorithms that output such crucial variables in PAC model with membership queries. The first algorithm executes the task under any unknown distribution by measuring the distance between virtual and real targets. The second algorithm exhausts virtual version space under an arbitrary distribution. The third algorithm exhausts universal set under the uniform distribution. The fourth algorithm measures influence of variables under the uniform distribution. Knowing the number $r$ of relevant variables, the first algorithm runs in almost linear time for $r$. The second and the third ones use less membership queries than the first one, but runs in time exponential for $r$. The fourth one enumerates highly influential variables in quadratic time for $r$.

## 1 Introduction: Terminology and Strategy

We propose several algorithms with their own character for automatically finding relevant variables in the presence of many irrelevant ones. Recent application of such algorithms ranges from data mining in the genome analysis to information filtering in the network computing. In these applications, sample data consist of a huge volume of variables, although the target phenomenon may depend on only a few of them. In order for a machine to find such crucial variables, we study algorithms in PAC model with membership queries, and analyze their query and time complexities.

To learn an unknown Boolean function that depends on only a small number of the potential variables, the learner may (1) find a set of relevant variables and

---

\* Author supported in part by the EC through the Esprit Program EU BRA program under project 20244 (ALCOM-IT) and the EC Working Group EP27150 (NeuroColt II) and by the spanish DGES PB95-0787 (Koala).

(2) combine them into a hypothesis that approximates the target concept with an arbitrarily high accuracy. Most inductive learning algorithms do not separate these conceptually different tasks, but rather let them depend on each other. On the other hand, some AI learning papers separate them and execute (1) as a preprocess for (2) (see [5] for a survey). This paper pursues (1) for the learning goal.

Let us begin with fixing notion of *relevant variables*. We say that two Boolean instances are neighbor of each other if they have the same bit length and differs by exactly one bit.

**Definition 1.** *A variable $x$ is* relevant *to a function $f$ if there exist neighbor instanes $A$ and $A'$ such that $x(A) \neq x(A')$ and $f(A) \neq f(A')$.*

Let $\text{Rel}(r, n)$ be the class of Boolean functions with $n$ variables that depend on only $r$ of them, or equivalently, have at most $r$ relevant variables. In this paper, the target concept is an arbitrary function in $\text{Rel}(r, n)$. In other words, the learner is given the $n$ Boolean variables, say $x_1, \ldots, x_n$, and told that there are at most $r$ relevant variables to the target concept [1].

In this paper we work on *Probably Approximately Correct* (PAC) Learning introduced by Valiant [11], where the target concept $f$ and the target distribution $\mathcal{D}$ are postulated and hidden from the learner. The learner receives a sequence of examples $(A, f(A))$, $(B, f(B))$, $\ldots$ independently and randomly from $\mathcal{D}$. From these examples, the learner must build a hypothesis that can approximate the target concept by an arbitrary accuracy with respect to $\mathcal{D}$.

This paper sets a weaker goal for learning. For a Boolean function $h$ let $\text{rel}(h)$ denotes the set of relevant variables to $h$.

**Definition 2.** *A set $V$ of variables is called an $\alpha$-dominator, $0 \leq \alpha \leq 1$, if there exists a function $h$ such that $\text{rel}(h) \subseteq V$ and $\text{Prob}_A\{h(A) = f(A)\} \geq \alpha$, where $A$ is randomly chosen according to $\mathcal{D}$.*

A weaker goal of learning is to find an $(1 - \varepsilon)$-dominator. Our algorithms may use inner coin flips and achieve this weaker goal with probability $\geq 1 - \delta$ for arbitrary given constants $0 \leq \varepsilon, \delta \leq 1$.

Unfortunately, random examples are not enough as information resource for identifying relevant variables of a given Boolean concept, because:

– There can be computationally hard problems even though we can information-theoretically identify the function. For instance consider the class of conjunctions of an $(\log n)$-bit majority and an $(\log n)$-bit parity. This class (contained in $\text{Rel}(2 \log n, n)$) is believed to be hard to predict within polynomial even under the uniform distribution [3]. The problem there is that we may have enough information to identify the function (using a universal set) but it is computationally hard to discover the set of relevant variables.

---

[1] We can tune our algorithms up into adaptive versions for $r$ by guessing and doubling $r$, that is to execute the algorithms by guessing $r = 2^0, 2^1, 2^2, \ldots$ until they succeed.

- Moreover, due to reduction from set cover, it is NP-hard in general to discover a set of relevant variables on which one can build an accurate hypothesis [8].

We will thus allow algorithms to use more active query in addition with random examples, that are *membership queries* introduced by Angluin [1].

**Definition 3.** *A membership query for an instance $A$ about the target concept $f$ is a request for the value* $MQ_f(A) = f(A)$ *to the membership oracle* $MQ_f$.

In empirical test, reverse engineer or information search, however, membership queries are much more expensive than random examples. We will thus present econimical algorithms in Section 3 that spend at most $r \log n$ membership queries.

The algorithms in this paper follow a common learning strategy; Find witnesses for relevance and execute binary search on them. The algorithms differ in methods to discover witnesses for relevance.

**Definition 4.** *For an instance $A$ and a set $V$ of variables $A_V$ and $A^V$ are instances such that*

$$x(A_V) = \begin{cases} x(A) & \text{if } x \in V, \\ 0 & \text{otherwise.} \end{cases} \qquad x(A^V) = \begin{cases} 1 - x(A) & \text{if } x \in V, \\ x(A) & \text{otherwise.} \end{cases}$$

**Definition 5.** *A witness for relevance outside of $V$ about the target concept $f$ is a pair $(A, B)$ of instances $A$ and $B$ such that $A_V = B_V$ and $f(A) \neq f(B)$.*

Given a witness $(A, B)$ for relevance, binary search finds a relevant variable as follows. It flips half of the different bits between $A$ and $B$, and ask the membership query for the obtained instance $C$. If $f(A) \neq f(C)$ then it repeats the argument on a new witness $(A, C)$, otherwise on $(B, C)$. Either case reduces the number of different bits in the witnesses by half. This divide-and-query argument repeats until reaching to a variable $x$ such that $x(A) \neq x(B)$.

**Lemma 1.** *Given an arbitrary witness for relevance outside of $V$, the binary search outputs a relevant variable $x \notin V$ by using at most $\log n$ membership queries in $O(n \log n)$ time.*

The proof is folklore (see e.g. [7, Lemma 2.4]). Note that $\log n$ is a query complexity lower bound in finding one relevant variable from a given witness for relevance, hence $r \log n$ is a lower bound in finding $r$ relevant variables.

## 2 Measuring the Distance between Virtual and Real Targets

This section provides a distribution-free algorithm that runs in time almost linear to $r$. It measures the distance between virtual and real targets and if the distance is large then the algorithm discovers a new relevant variable.

**Definition 6.** *The virtual target $f_V$ on a set $V$ of variables about the target concept $f$ is a Boolean function $f_V$ with $\mathrm{rel}(f_V) \subseteq V$ such that $f_V(A_V) = f(A_V)$ holds for any instance $A$.*

In the mistake bound model with membership queries, Blum, Hellerstein and Littlestone [4] measures $\mathrm{Prob}_A\{f(A) = h_V(A)\}$ for a temporal hypothesis $h$ to find a new relevant variable that is not yet implemented in $h$. Here we measure $\mathrm{Prob}_A\{f(A) = f_V(A)\}$, the distance between $f$ and $f_V$. If it is large, then our algorithm finds a witness for relevance $(A, A_V)$ with high probability.

**Lemma 2.** *Let $m$ be any integer with $(1 - \varepsilon)^m \leq \delta$. Draw a sample $O$ of $m$ examples. If $V$ is not an $(1 - \varepsilon)$-dominator then $f(A) \neq f(A_V)$ happens for some $(A, f(A)) \in O$ with probability greater than $1 - \delta$.*

*Proof.* Suppose that $V$ is not an $(1 - \varepsilon)$-dominator. Then the distance between $f$ and $f_V$ is greater than $\varepsilon$, hence $f(A) = f(A_V)$ happens for each $(A, f(A)) \in O$ with probability $< (1 - \varepsilon)^m \leq \delta$.

Now we implement this lemma in an algorithm MsrDist and analyze its performance.

    Procedure MsrDist
        Input: Integers $n$, $r$ and $m_0$.
        Output: A set of relevant variables.
        Set $V := \emptyset$ and $m := 0$.
        Do until either $|V| = r$ or $m = m_0$
            Draw a random example $(A, f(A))$ and increment $m$ by 1.
            Let $\beta := \mathrm{MQ}_f(A_V)$.
            If $f(A) \neq \beta$ then Do
                Set $m := 0$.
                Execute the binary search on $(A, A_V)$ and put an obtained variable
                into $V$.
            EndDo
        EndDo
        Output $V$.
    EndProc

**Theorem 1.** *MsrDist finds an $(1 - \varepsilon)$-dominator (a set of relevant variables) with probability greater than $1 - \delta$. For some $m_0 = O(\varepsilon^{-1} \log(r/\delta))$, MsrDist uses at most $m_0 r$ random examples, at most $r(m_0 + \log n)$ membership queries and runs in $O(nr(m_0 + \log n))$ time.*

*Proof.* Fix an arbitrary $m_0 = O(\varepsilon^{-1} \log(r/\delta))$ such that $(1 - \varepsilon)^{m_0} \leq \delta/r$. Then, in view Lemma 2, in each stage of the Do loop in the procedure MsrDist where

$V$ is not an $(1-\varepsilon)$-dominator, each example $(A, f(A))$ may be a witness $(A, A_V)$ for relevance outside of $V$ with probability greater than $\delta/r$. Since MsrInf can draw $m_0$ examples in the stage, it will succeed in find a witness with probability greater than $1 - (1 - \frac{\varepsilon}{er})^{m_0} \geq 1 - \delta/r$. Since there are at most $r$ stages, due to the union bound, every stage will succeed with probability $\geq 1 - \delta/r \cdot r \geq 1 - \delta$, so with this probability MsrDist outputs an $(1 - \varepsilon)$-dominator.

## 3   Exhausting Virtual Version Spaces

This section presents two algorithms that saves membership queries than one in the previous section. One algorithm is distribution-free and exhausts virtual version spaces, while another works under the uniform distribution and exhausts an $r$-universal.

Intuitively, a version space is the set of hypotheses under consideration in inductive learning. Haussler [9] proposed to exhaust the version space by throwing the hypotheses away that are inconsistent with drawn examples until only accurate hypotheses may remain. In this section, for a set $V$ of variables,

**Definition 7.** *the virtual version space on $V$ is the set of Boolean functions $h$ with* $\mathrm{rel}(h) \subseteq V$.

Let $V$ be the set of already found relevant variables. Then virtual version spaces may expand at each moment that a new relevant variable is discovered and added to $V$. Unless $V$ is an $(1-\varepsilon)$-dominator, exhausting the virtual version space on $V$ is shown to provide a witness for relevance outside of $V$ with high probability.

**Lemma 3.** *Let $m$ be any integer such that $(1-\varepsilon)^m 2^{2^r} \leq \delta$. Draw a sample $O$ of $m$ random examples. If $V$ is not an $(1-\varepsilon)$-dominator then there exists a witness $(A, B)$ for relevance outside of $V$ with $(A, f(A)),(B, f(B)) \in O$ with probability at least $1 - \delta$.*

*Proof.* Suppose that $V$ is not an $(1 - \varepsilon)$-dominator. Then for every function $h$ in the virtual version space on $V$, $h(A) \neq f(A)$ holds with probability greater than $\varepsilon$, so $O$ is consistent with $h$ with probability $< (1 - \varepsilon)^m$. The union bound thus implies that $O$ does not provide any witness for relevance outside of $V$ with probability $< (1 - \varepsilon)^m 2^{2^r} \leq \delta$.

We now implement this lemma in an algorithm ExhVVS that finds an $(1 - \varepsilon)$-dominator. For each new example $(A, f(A))$, ExhVVS checks over the old examples $(B, f(B))$ in a stock that whether $(A, B)$ is a witness for relevance outside of $V$. If ExhVVS finds a new witness it discards all the old examples and make the stock empty.

Procedure ExhVVS

   Input: Integers $n$ and $r$.

   Output: A set of relevant variables.

   Set $O := \emptyset$, $V := \emptyset$, $s := 1$ and $m := 0$.

   Initialize $m_0 :=$ the minimum integer such that $(1 - \varepsilon)^{m_0} 2^2 \geq \delta/r$.

   Do until either $|V| = r$ or $m = m_0$

     Draw a random example $(A, f(A))$.

     For each $B \in O$ Do

       If $A_V = B_V$ and $f(A) \neq f(B)$ then Do

         Update $O := \emptyset$, $m := 0$ and $s := s + 1$.

         Update $m_0 :=$ the minimum integer such that $(1 - \varepsilon)^{m_0} 2^{2^s} \geq \delta/r$.

         Execute the binary search on $(A, B)$ and put an obtained variable into $V$.

       EndDo

     EndDo

     Put $(A, f(A))$ into $O$ and increment $m$ by 1.

   EndDo

   Output $V$.

EndProc

**Theorem 2.** *The procedure ExhVVS outputs an $(1 - \varepsilon)$-dominator (a set of relevant variables) with probability greater than $1 - \delta$. ExhVVS uses at most $m_0 = O(r2^r \log(1/\varepsilon) \log(r/\delta))$ random examples, $r \log n$ membership queries and runs in $O(n(m_0 + r \log n))$ time.*

*Proof.* If $|V| = s$ then ExhVVS draws $m_0$ random examples so that $(1 - \varepsilon)^{m_0} 2^{2^s} \geq \delta/r$. Therefore, due to Lemma 3, if $V$ is not an $(1 - \varepsilon)$-dominator then it derives a witness for relevance outside of $V$ with probability at least $\delta/r$. The remaining argument is the same with the proof of Theorem 1.

Under the uniform distribution, a modification of ExhVVS can find all the relevant variables by exhausting an $r$-universal set.

**Definition 8.** *A set $U$ of instances is called $r$-universal if every $r$-bits on every set of $r$ variables occurs in some instance $A$ in $U$.*

Damaschke [7] worked in the exact learning model with only membership queries and studied the numbers of (adaptive and non-adaptive) membership queries for exhausting $r$-universal set. Here we show that, under the uniform distribution, an enough number of random examples provides an $r$-universal set and that any of those sets is a sufficient source for witnesses for all relevant variables.

**Lemma 4.** *Let $m$ be any integer such that $(1 - 2^{-r})^m 2^r \binom{n}{r} \leq \delta$. Draw $m$ instances independently and randomly under the uniform distribution over the $n$-bit instance space. Then it forms an $r$-universal set with probability at least $1 - \delta$.*

*Proof.* We say that the sample hits an $r$-bits on a set of $r$ variables if an assignment $A$ of some example $(A, f(A))$ in the sample sets those variables to those bits. Then, due to probabilistic independence of examples, the sample does not hit a given $r$-bits with probability $(1 - 2^{-r})^m$. Since there are $2^r \binom{n}{r}$ possibility of such $r$-bits's, the union bound implies that the sample does not hit some $r$-bits with probability at most $(1 - 2^{-r})^m 2^r \binom{n}{r} \le \delta$. Or equivalently, the sample hits every $r$-bits with probability at least $1 - \delta$.

Let ExhUniv be a modification of ExhVVS that does not discard old examples at all; ExhUniv omits updating $O$ and $m_0$ in the lines 9 and 10 of the procedure ExhVVS.

**Theorem 3.** *Under the uniform distribution, ExhUniv finds all the relevant variables with probability at least $1 - \delta$ by at most $m_0 = O(r 2^r \log n \log(1/\delta))$ random examples and $r \log n$ membership queries in $O(n(m_0 + r \log n))$ time.*

*Proof.* Let $R$ be the set of relevant variables and let $s = |R| \le r$. Let $m_0$ satisfy $(1 - 2^{-s})^{m_0} 2^s \binom{n}{s} \le \delta$. Then, due to Lemma 4, the sample of size $m_0$ presents an $s$-universal set with probability $\ge 1 - \delta$. Such a sample induces every $s$-bits on $R$, so in particular ExhUniv discovers a witness $(A, B)$ for relevance of every variable $x \in R$ such that $A_R$ and $B_R$ are neighbors at $x$, hence $x$ itself by binary searching on $(A, B)$.

## 4    Measuring Influence of Variables

An algorithm in this section measures influence of variables to the target concept under the uniform distribution and outputs highly influential ones. Such an approach for learning has been taken in many AI and data mining research papers and achieves good empirical success (see [5, Section 2.4]). Based on this approach, we will design an algorithm that finds an $(1 - \varepsilon)$-dominator under the uniform distribution in time almost quadratic for $r$, the number of relevant variables.

**Definition 9.** *The influence $\mathrm{Inf}(x)$ of a variable $x$ is the number of instances $A$ as a fraction of the set of all instances such that $f(A) \ne f(A')$ for the neighbor instance $A'$ of $A$ at $x$.*

Therefore, $\mathrm{Inf}(x) = 0$ if and only if a variable $x$ is irrelevant, and $\mathrm{Inf}(x) = 1$ if and only if $f = x \oplus g$ for some function $g$ irrelevant with respect to $x$. To show existence of highly influential variables, Ben-Or and Linial [2] applied the edge-isoperimetric inequality (see [6, Section 16] for edge-isoperimetric inequalities).

**Lemma 5 (Edge Isoperimetric Inequality).** *For a given Boolean function $f(x_1, \ldots, x_n)$ choose $b \in \{0, 1\}$ and $1 \le k$ such that*

$$2^{-k-1} \le \mathrm{Prob}_A\{f(A) = b\} \le 2^{-k}$$

*under the uniform distribution on $A$. We then have $\sum_{i=1}^{n} \mathrm{Inf}_f(x_i) \ge k 2^{1-k}$.*

In order to implement this inequality in a learning algorithm, we need to relatize it on a given set $V$ of variables.

**Lemma 6.** *If $V$ is not an $(1 - \varepsilon)$-dominator then $\sum_{x \notin V} \mathrm{Inf}(x) > 2\varepsilon$.*

*Proof.* Let $h$ be a Bayes optimal predictor of $f$ on $V$. That is, (1) $\mathrm{rel}(h) \subseteq V$ and (2) $h(A) = 1$ if and only if $\mathrm{Prob}_B\{f(B) = 1 | B_V = A_V\} \geq 1/2$. We suppose $\sum_{x \notin V} \mathrm{Inf}(x) \leq 2\varepsilon$ and prove that $h$ approximates $f$ with accuracy $\geq 1 - \varepsilon$.

For any instance $A$ we let

$$p(A) = 1 - \max\{\mathrm{Prob}_B\{f(B) = 1 | B_V = A_V\}, \mathrm{Prob}_B\{f(B) = 0 | B_V = A_V\}\}.$$

Then expectation of $p(A)$ on $A$ is $E_A[p(A)] = \mathrm{Prob}_A\{h(A) \neq f(A)\}$, so it is enough to claim that $E_A[p(A)] \leq \varepsilon$.

For any instance $A$ let $f_{A,V}$ be the function that fixes the input-bits of $f$ on $V$ by $A$. Hence $\mathrm{rel}(f_{A,V}) \subseteq \mathrm{rel}(f) - V$. Lemma 5 then promises $2p(A) \leq \sum_{x \notin V} \mathrm{Inf}_{f_{A,V}}(x)$, so taking average on $A$ for both sides derives

$$2E_A[p(A)] \leq \sum_{x \notin V} \mathrm{Inf}_f(x) \leq 2\varepsilon,$$

so we obtain $E_A[p(A)] \leq \varepsilon$.

Uehara et. al. [10] apply the following lemma for finding relevant variables to fundamental Boolean functions (conjunctions, parities, etc).

**Lemma 7 (Uehara et. al. [10]).** *Let $R$ be any set of $r$ elements in the $n$ element set $X$. Choose a subset $W$ of $X$ with $|W| = n/r$ uniformly at random. Then $|V \cap W| = 1$ happens with probability $> 1/e$.*

Now, we present an algorithm that applies Lemma 6 and Lemma 7 and finds highly influential variables.

Procedure MsrInf

    Input: Integers $n$, $r$ and $m_0$.

    Output: A set of relevant variables.

    Set $X := \{x_1, \ldots, x_n\}$, $V := \emptyset$, $m := 0$, $n' := n$ and $r' := r$.

    Do until either $r' = 0$ or $m = m_0$

      Draw a random example $(A, f(A))$ and increment $m$ by 1.

      Choose a set of variables $W \subseteq X - V$ with $|W| = n'/r'$ uniformly at random.

      Let $\beta := \mathrm{MQ}_f(A^W)$.ppp

      If $f(A) \neq \beta$ then Do

          Update $m := 0$, $n' := n' - 1$ and $r' := r' - 1$.

          Execute the binary search on $(A, A^W)$, put the obtained variable in $V$ and remove the variable from $X$.

      EndDo

    EndDo

    Output $V$.

    EndProc

**Theorem 4.** *Under the uniform distribution, MsrInf finds an $(1-\varepsilon)$-dominator (a set of relevant variables) with probability greater than $1 - \delta$ by at most $m_0 = O((r/\varepsilon)\log(r/\delta))$ random examples and $r(m_0 + \log n)$ membership queries in $O(nr(m_0 + \log n))$ time.*

*Proof.* Fix an arbitrary $m_0 = O(\varepsilon^{-1}\log(r/\delta))$ such that $(1 - \frac{\varepsilon}{er})^{m_0} \le \delta/r$. Let $R$ be any set of $r$ variables containing all the relevant variables.

In view of Lemma 7, choosing $W$ as in the procedure, we have $|(R - V) \cap W| = 1$ with probability greater than $1/e$. Moreover, if it is so, $(R - V) \cap W = \{x\}$ happens equally likely for each $x \in R - V$. Therefore, drawing $A$ according to $\mathcal{D}$ and choosing $W$ as in the procedure, $f(A) \neq f(A^W)$ happens with probability greater than $\frac{1}{2er} \cdot \sum_{x \notin V} \mathrm{Inf}_f(x)$. Thus if $V$ is not an $(1 - \varepsilon)$-dominator then Lemma 6 promises $\sum_{x \notin V} \mathrm{Inf}(x) > 2\varepsilon$, so $(A, A^W)$ happens to be a witness for relevance outside of $V$ with probability greater than $\frac{\varepsilon}{er}$.

Therefore, in each stage of the Do loop, if $V$ is not an $(1 - \varepsilon)$-dominator then a witness for relevance is successfully found with probability greater than $1 - (1 - \frac{\varepsilon}{er})^{m_0} \ge 1 - \delta/r$. The remaining argument is the same with the proof of Theorem 1.

The procedure MsrInf enumerates variables in order of their influence to the target. For example, suppose that there are 100 relevant variables where only three of them have influence 0.1 and the other 97 have only 0.001. MseInf gets the three in precedence with the other 97 with probability $> (0.9)^3 = 0.729$.

## Acknowledgments

Osamu Watanabe contributed to this research from the beginning. We would like to thank him for motivation and many technical improvements. We would also like to thank Ryuhei Uehara for his helpful comments.

## References

[1] D. Angluin. Queries and concept learning. *Machine Learning*, 2:319, 1987.
[2] M. Ben-Or and N. Linial. Collective coin flipping. *Advances in Computing Research*, 5, 1989.
[3] A. Blum, M. Furst, M.l. Kearns, and R. J. Lipton. Cryptographic primitives based on hard learning problems. In *Proc. CRYPTO 93*, pages 278–291, 1994. LNCS 773.
[4] A. Blum, L. Hellerstein, and N. Littlestone. Learning in the presence of finitely or infinitely many irrelevant attributes. *Journal of Computer and System Sciences*, 50(1):32–40, 1995.
[5] A.L. Blum and P. Langrey. Selection of relevant features and examples. *Machine Learning*. to be appeared.
[6] B. Bollobas. *Combinatorics*. Cambridge Univ. Press, Cambridge, 1986.
[7] P. Damaschke. Adaptive versus nonadaptive attribute-efficient learning. In *Proceedings of the 30th Annual ACM Symposium on Theory of Computing (STOC-98)*, pages 590–596, 1998.

[8]  A. Dhagat and L. Hellerstein. PAC learning with irrelevant attributes. In *Proceedings of the 35th Annual Symposium on Foundations of Computer Science*, pages 64–74, 1994.

[9]  D. Haussler. Quantifying inductive bias: AI learning algorithms and Valiant's model. *Artificial Intelligence*, 36(2):177–221, 1988.

[10] R. Uehara, K. Tsuchida, and I. Wegener. Optimal attribute-efficient learning of disjunction, parity and threshold functions. In *Proceedings of the 3rd European Conference on Computational Learning Theory*, volume 1208 of *LNAI*, pages 171–184, 1997.

[11] L. G. Valiant. A theory of the learnable. *Communications of the ACM*, 27(11):1134–1142, 1985.

# General Linear Relations among Different Types of Predictive Complexity

Yuri Kalnishkan*

Department of Computer Science, Royal Holloway, University of London,
Egham, Surrey TW20 0EX, United Kingdom,
yura@dcs.rhbnc.ac.uk

**Abstract.** In this paper we introduce a general method that allows to prove tight linear inequalities between different types of predictive complexity and thus we generalise our previous results. The method relies upon probabilistic considerations and allows to describe (using geometrical terms) the sets of coefficients which correspond to true inequalities. We also apply this method to the square-loss and logarithmic complexity and describe their relations which were not covered by our previous research.

## 1 Introduction

This paper generalises the author's paper [4]. In [4] we proved tight inequalities between the square-loss and logarithmic complexities. The key point of that paper is a lower estimate on the logarithmic complexity, which follows from the coincidence of the logarithmic complexity and a variant of Kolmogorov complexity. That estimate could not be extended for other types of predictive complexity. The main theorem (Theorem 7) of [4] pointed out the "accidental" coincidence of two real-valued functions but [4] did not explain the deeper reasons beyond this fact.

In this paper we use a different approach to lower estimates of predictive complexity. It relies upon probabilistic considerations and may be applied to a broader class of games. The results of [4] become a particular case of more general statements and receive a more profound explanation.

As an application of the general method we establish linear relations between the square-loss and logarithmic complexity we have not covered in [4].

When giving the motivations for considering predictive complexity, we will briefly repeat some points from [4].

We work within an on-line learning model. In this model, a learning algorithm makes a prediction of a future event, than observes the actual event, and suffers loss due to the discrepancy between the prediction and the actual outcome. The total loss suffered by an algorithm over a sequence of several events can be regarded as the complexity of this sequence *with respect to* this algorithm. An

---

* Supported partially by EPSRC through the grant GR/M14937 ("Predictive complexity: recursion-theoretic variants") and by ORS Awards Scheme.

O. Watanabe, T. Yokomori (Eds.): ALT'99, LNAI 1720, pp. 323–334, 1999.

optimal or universal measure of complexity cannot be defined within the class of losses of algorithms, so we need to consider a broader class of "complexities", namely, the class of optimal superloss processes. In many reasonable cases, this class contains an optimal element, a function which provides us with the *intrinsic* measure of complexity of a sequence of events with respect to no particular learning strategy.

The concept of predictive complexity is a natural development of the theory of prediction with expert advice (see [1, 3, 5]) and it was introduced in the paper [7]. In the theory of prediction with expert advice we merge some given learning strategies. Roughly speaking, predictive complexity may be regarded as a mixture of all possible strategies and some "superstrategies".

The paper [10] introduces a method that allows to prove the existence of predictive complexity for many natural games. This method relies upon the Aggregating Algorithm (see [8]) and works for all so-called mixable games. It is still an open problem whether the mixability is a necessary condition for the existence of predictive complexity but, in this paper, we restrict ourselves to mixable games.

In Sect. 2 we give the precise definition of the environment our learning algorithms work in. A particular kind of environment (a particular game) is specified by choosing an outcome space, a hypothesis space, and a loss function. A loss function measures the loss suffered by a prediction algorithm in this environment and thus it is of interest to compare games with the same outcome space and the same hypothesis space but different loss functions. In this paper we compare the values of predictive complexity of strings w.r.t. different games and therefore we compare the inherent learnability of an object in different environments.

Our goal is to describe the set of pairs $(a, b)$ such that the inequality $a\mathcal{K}^1(x) + b|x| \geq^+ \mathcal{K}^2(x)$ holds for complexities $\mathcal{K}^1$ and $\mathcal{K}^2$ specified by mixable games $\mathfrak{G}_1$ and $\mathfrak{G}_2$. In Sect. 3 we formulate necessary and sufficient conditions for inequalities $a\mathcal{K}^1(x) + b|x| \geq^+ \mathcal{K}^2(x)$ and $a_1\mathcal{K}^1(x) + a_2\mathcal{K}^2(x) \leq^+ b|x|$ to hold. We establish both geometrical and probabilistic criteria. It is remarkable that both inequalities hold if and only if their counterparts hold "on the average".

In Sect. 4 we apply our results to relations between the square-loss and logarithmic complexity we have not investigated before.

## 2    Definitions

The notations in this paper are generally the same as in the paper [4] but some extra notations will also be introduced.

We will denote the binary alphabet $\{0, 1\}$ by **B** and finite binary strings by bold lowercase letters, e.g. $x, y$. The expression $|x|$ denotes the length of $x$ and **B**$^*$ denotes the set of all finite binary strings.

We use the following notations, typical for works on Kolmogorov complexity. We will write $f(x) \leq^+ g(x)$ for real-valued functions $f$ and $g$ if there is a constant $C \geq 0$ such that $f(x) \leq g(x) + C$ for all $x$ from the domain of these functions (the set $\mathbf{B}^*$ throughout this paper). We consider mostly logarithms to the base 2 and we denote $\log_2$ by log.

We begin with the definition of a game. A *game* $\mathfrak{G}$ is a triple $(\Omega, \Gamma, \lambda)$, where $\Omega$ is called an *outcome space*, $\Gamma$ stands for a *hypothesis space*, and $\lambda : \Omega \times \Gamma \to \mathbb{R} \cup \{+\infty\}$ is a *loss function*. We suppose that a definition of computability over $\Omega$ and $\Gamma$ is given and $\lambda$ is computable according to this definition.

Admitting the possibility of $\lambda(\omega, \gamma) = +\infty$ is essential (cf. [9]). We need this assumption to take the very interesting logarithmic game into consideration. The *continuity* of a function $f : M \to \mathbb{R} \cup \{+\infty\}$ in a point $x_0 \in M$ such that $f(x_0) = +\infty$ is the property $\lim_{x \to x_0, x \in M} f(x) = +\infty$ (the continuity in the extended topology).

Throughout this paper, we let $\Omega = \mathbf{B} = \{0, 1\}$ and $\Gamma = [0, 1]$. We will consider the following examples of games: the *square-loss* game with

$$\lambda(\omega, \gamma) = (\omega - \gamma)^2 \tag{1}$$

and the *logarithmic* game with

$$\lambda(\omega, \gamma) = \begin{cases} -\log(1 - \gamma) & \text{if } \omega = 0 \\ -\log \gamma & \text{if } \omega = 1 \end{cases}. \tag{2}$$

A prediction algorithm $\mathfrak{A}$ works according to the following protocol:

```
FOR t = 1, 2, ...
   (1) 𝔄 chooses a hypothesis γ_t ∈ Γ
   (2) 𝔄 observes the actual outcome ω_t ∈ Ω
   (3) 𝔄 suffers loss λ(ω_t, γ_t)
END FOR.
```

Over the first $T$ trials, $\mathfrak{A}$ suffers the total loss

$$\text{Loss}_{\mathfrak{A}}(\omega_1, \omega_2, \ldots, \omega_T) = \sum_{t=1}^{T} \lambda(\omega_t, \gamma_t) . \tag{3}$$

By definition, put $\text{Loss}_{\mathfrak{A}}(\Lambda) = 0$, where $\Lambda$ denotes the empty string. A function $L : \Omega^* \to \mathbb{R} \cup \{+\infty\}$ is called a *loss process* w.r.t. $\mathfrak{G}$ if it coincides with the loss $\text{Loss}_{\mathfrak{A}}$ of some algorithm $\mathfrak{A}$. Note that any loss process is computable.

We say that a pair $(s_0, s_1) \in [-\infty, +\infty]^2$ is a *superprediction* if there exists a hypothesis $\gamma \in \Gamma$ such that $s_0 \geq \lambda(0, \gamma)$ and $s_1 \geq \lambda(1, \gamma)$. If we consider the set $P = \{(p_0, p_1) \in [-\infty, +\infty]^2 \mid \exists \gamma \in \Gamma : p_0 = \lambda(0, \gamma) \text{ and } p_1 = \lambda(1, \gamma)\}$ (cf. the canonical form of a game in [8]), the set $S$ of all superpredictions is the set of points that lie "north-east" of $P$. We will loosely call $P$ the set of predictions. The set of predictions $P = \{(\gamma^2, (1 - \gamma)^2) \mid \gamma \in [0, 1]\}$ and the set of superpredictions $S$ for the square-loss game are shown on Fig. 1.

A function $L : \Omega^* \to \mathbb{R} \cup \{+\infty\}$ is called a *superloss process* w.r.t. $\mathfrak{G}$ if the following conditions hold:

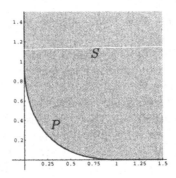

**Fig. 1.** The sets of predictions and superpredictions for the square-loss game.

- $L(\Lambda) = 0$,
- for any $x \in \Omega^*$, the pair $(L(x0) - L(x), L(x1) - L(x))$ is a superprediction w.r.t. $\mathfrak{G}$, and
- $L$ is semicomputable from above.

We will say that a superloss process $K$ is *universal* if it is minimal to within an additive constant in the class of all superloss processes. In other words, a superloss process $K$ is universal if for any other superloss process $L$ there exists a constant $C$ such that

$$\forall x \in \Omega^* : K(x) \le L(x) + C \ . \tag{4}$$

The difference between two universal superloss processes w.r.t. $\mathfrak{G}$ is bounded by a constant. If superloss processes w.r.t. $\mathfrak{G}$ exist we may pick one and denote it by $\mathcal{K}^{\mathfrak{G}}$. It follows from the definition that, for any $L$ which is a superloss process w.r.t. $\mathfrak{G}$ and any prediction algorithm $\mathfrak{A}$, we have

$$\mathcal{K}^{\mathfrak{G}}(x) \le^+ L(x) \ , \tag{5}$$

$$\mathcal{K}^{\mathfrak{G}}(x) \le^+ \mathrm{Loss}_{\mathfrak{A}}^{\mathfrak{G}}(x) \ , \tag{6}$$

where $\mathrm{Loss}^{\mathfrak{G}}$ denotes the loss w.r.t. $\mathfrak{G}$. One may call $\mathcal{K}^{\mathfrak{G}}$ the *complexity* w.r.t. $\mathfrak{G}$.

Note that universal processes are defined for concrete games only. Two games $\mathfrak{G}_1 = (\Omega, \Gamma, \lambda_1)$ and $\mathfrak{G}_2 = (\Omega, \Gamma, \lambda_2)$ with the same outcome and hypothesis spaces but different loss functions may have different sets of universal superloss processes (e.g. $\mathfrak{G}_1$ may have universal processes and $\mathfrak{G}_2$ may have not).

We now proceed to the definition of a mixable game. For any $A \subseteq [-\infty, +\infty]^2$ and any $(u, v) \in \mathbb{R}^2$, the *shift* $A + (u, v)$ is the set $\{(x + u, y + v) \mid (x, y) \in A\}$. For the sequel, we also need the definition of the expansion $aA = \{(ax, ay) \mid (x, y) \in A\}$, where $a \in \mathbb{R}$. For any $B \subseteq [-\infty, +\infty]^2$, the *A-closure* of $B$ is the set

$$\mathrm{cl}_A(B) = \bigcap_{(u,v)\in\mathbb{R}^2 \,:\, B \subseteq A+(u,v)} A + (u, v) \ . \tag{7}$$

We let

$$A_0 = \{(x, y) \in [-\infty, +\infty]^2 \mid x \geq 0 \text{ or } y \geq 0\} \ , \tag{8}$$
$$A^\beta = \{(x, y) \in [-\infty, +\infty]^2 \mid \beta^x + \beta^y \leq 1\} \ . \tag{9}$$

On Fig. 2 you can see the sets $A_0$ and $A^\beta$ for $\beta = 1/3$.

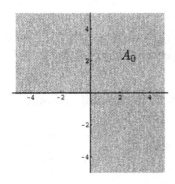
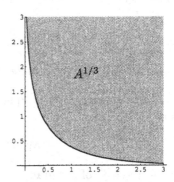

**Fig. 2.** The sets $A_0$ and $A^{1/3}$.

**Definition 1 ([8, 9]).** *A game $\mathfrak{G}$ is mixable if there exists $\beta \in (0, 1)$ such that for any straight line $l \subseteq \mathbb{R}^2$ passing through the origin the set $(\mathrm{cl}_{A^\beta} S \setminus \mathrm{cl}_{A_0} S) \cap l$ contains no more than one element, where $S$ is the set of superpredictions for $\mathfrak{G}$.*

**Proposition 2 ([8]).** *For any mixable game, there exists a universal superloss process.*

**Proposition 3 ([2, 7]).** *The logarithmic and the square-loss games are mixable and therefore the complexities $\mathcal{K}^{\log}$ and $\mathcal{K}^{\mathrm{sq}}$ exist.*

## 3   General Linear Inequalities

In this section we prove some general results on linear inequalities. Throughout this section $\mathfrak{G}_1$ and $\mathfrak{G}_2$ are any games with loss functions $\lambda_1$ and $\lambda_2$, sets of predictions $P_1$ and $P_2$, and sets of superpredictions $S_1$ and $S_2$, respectively. The closure and the boundary of $M \subseteq \mathbb{R}^2$ in the standard topology of $\mathbb{R}^2$ are denoted by $\overline{M}$ and $\partial M$, respectively.

## 3.1    Case $a\mathcal{K}^1(x) + b|x| \geq^+ \mathcal{K}^2(x)$.

The following theorem is the main result of the paper.

**Theorem 4.** *Suppose that the games $\mathfrak{G}_1$ and $\mathfrak{G}_2$ are mixable and specify the complexities $\mathcal{K}^1$ and $\mathcal{K}^2$; suppose that the loss function $\lambda_1(\omega, \gamma)$ is continuous in the second argument; then the following statements are equivalent:*

*(i) $\exists C > 0 \forall x \in \mathbf{B}^* : \mathcal{K}^1(x) + C \geq \mathcal{K}^2(x)$,*
*(ii) $P_1 \subseteq \overline{S_2}$,*
*(iii) $\forall p \in [0,1] \exists C > 0 \forall n \in \mathbb{N} : \mathbf{E}\mathcal{K}^1(\xi_1^{(p)} \ldots \xi_n^{(p)}) + C \geq \mathbf{E}\mathcal{K}^2(\xi_1^{(p)} \ldots \xi_n^{(p)})$,*
*    where $\xi_1^{(p)}, \ldots, \xi_n^{(p)}$ are results of $n$ independent Bernoulli trials with the probability of 1 being equal to $p$.*

Loosely speaking, the inequality $\mathcal{K}^1(x) \geq^+ \mathcal{K}^2(x)$ holds if and only if the graph

$$\{(\lambda_1(0,\gamma), \lambda_1(1,\gamma)) \mid \gamma \in [0,1]\} \tag{10}$$

lies "north-east" of the graph

$$\{(\lambda_2(0,\gamma), \lambda_2(1,\gamma)) \mid \gamma \in [0,1]\} . \tag{11}$$

*Proof.* The implication $(i) \Rightarrow (iii)$ is trivial.

Let us prove that $(ii) \Rightarrow (i)$. Suppose that $P_1 \subseteq \overline{S_2}$ and therefore $S_1 \subseteq \overline{S_2}$. Let $L$ be a superloss process w.r.t. $\mathfrak{G}_1$. It follows from the definition, that, for any $x \in \mathbb{B}^*$, we have $(L(x0) - L(x), L(x1) - L(x)) \in S_1 \subseteq \overline{S_2}$. One can easily check that $L(x) + (1 - \frac{1}{2^{|x|}})$ is a superloss process w.r.t. $\mathfrak{G}_2$. If we take $L = \mathcal{K}^1$ and apply (5) we will obtain $(i)$.

It remains to prove that $(iii) \Rightarrow (ii)$. Let us assume that condition $(ii)$ is violated i.e. there exists $\gamma^{(0)} \in [0,1]$ such that

$$(\lambda_1(0, \gamma^{(0)}), \lambda_1(1, \gamma^{(0)})) = (u_0, v_0) \notin \overline{S_2} . \tag{12}$$

Since $\lambda_1$ is continuous, without loss of generality we may assume that $\gamma^{(0)}$ is a computable number. We will now find $p_0 \in [0,1]$ such that

$$\mathbf{E}\mathcal{K}^2(\xi_1^{(p_0)} \ldots \xi_n^{(p_0)}) - \mathbf{E}\mathcal{K}^1(\xi_1^{(p_0)} \ldots \xi_n^{(p_0)}) = \Omega(n) . \tag{13}$$

We need the following lemmas.

**Lemma 5.** *Let $\mathfrak{G}$ be a mixable game; then the set of superpredictions for $\mathfrak{G}$ is convex.*

*Proof (of the lemma).*

Let $S$ be the set of superpredictions for $\mathfrak{G}$ and let $\beta \in (0,1)$ be the number from Definition 1. Consider two points $D, E \in S$ and the line segment $[D, E] \subseteq \mathbb{R}^2$. We will prove that $[D, E] \subseteq \mathbb{R}^2$.

If one of the points lies "north-east" of another i.e.

$$\{D, E\} = \{(x_1, y_1), (x_2, y_2)\} , \tag{14}$$

where $x_1 \geq x_2$ and $y_1 \geq y_2$), then there is nothing to prove. Now suppose that $D = (x_1, y_1)$, $E = (x_2, y_2)$, $x_1 < x_2$, and $y_1 > y_2$ (see Fig. 3). There exists a shift $A'$ of the set $A^\beta$ such that $D, E \in \partial A'$. Let us prove that the closed set $M$ bounded by the line segment $[D, E]$ and the segment of $\partial A'$ lying between $D$ and $E$ is a subset of $\mathrm{cl}_{A^\beta} S$.

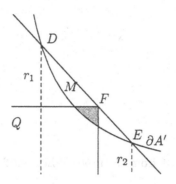

**Fig. 3.** The set $Q \cap M$ from the proof of Lemma 5 is coloured grey.

Consider a shift $A''$ of the set $A^\beta$ such that $D, E \in A''$. Trivially, two different shifts of $\partial A^\beta$ can have no more than one point in common. It follows from $D, E \in A''$ that $\partial A''$ intersects the rays $r_1 = \{(x_1, y) \mid y \leq y_1\}$ and $r_2 = \{(x_2, y) \mid y \leq y_2\}$. The continuity of $\partial A^\beta$ yields $M \subseteq A''$.

If there exists a point $F = (x_0, y_0) \in [D, E]$ such that $F \notin S$, then the whole quadrant $Q = \{(x, y) \mid x \leq x_0 \text{ and } y \leq y_0\}$ (see Fig. 3) has no common points with $S$ and the set $Q \cap M \subseteq (\mathrm{cl}_{A^\beta} S \setminus \mathrm{cl}_{A_0} S)$ violates the condition of Definition 1.

$\square$

**Lemma 6.** *Let $M \subseteq \mathbb{R}^2$ be a convex set closed in the standard topology of $\mathbb{R}^2$ and $(u_0, v_0) \notin M$. Suppose that for any $u, v \geq 0$ we have $M + (u, v) \subseteq M$. Then there exist $p_0 \in [0, 1]$ and $m_2 \in \mathbb{R}$ such that, for any $(u, v) \in M$, we have*

$$p_0 v + (1 - p_0)u \geq m_2 > m_1 = p_0 v_0 + (1 - p_0)u_0 . \tag{15}$$

*Proof (of the lemma).*

The lemma can be derived from the Separation Theorem for convex sets (see e.g. [6]) but we will give a self-contained proof. Let us denote $(u_0, v_0)$ by $D$. It follows from $M$ being closed, that there exists a point $E \in M$ which is closest to $D$. Clearly, all the points of $M$ lay on one side of the straight line $l$

which is perpendicular to $DE$ and passes through $E$ and $D$ lays on the other side (see Fig. 4). The straight line $l$ should come from the "north-west" to the "south-east" and therefore normalising its equation one may reduce it to the form $p_0 v + (1 - p_0)u = m_2$, where $p_0 \in [0, 1]$.

□

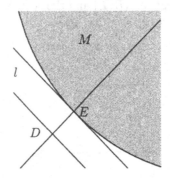

**Fig. 4.** The set $M$ from the proof of Lemma 6 is coloured grey.

**Lemma 7.** *Suppose that a game $\mathfrak{G}$ is mixable and the set $S$ of superpredictions for $\mathfrak{G}$ lies "north-east" of the straight line $pv + (1 - p)u = m$ i.e.*

$$\forall (u, v) \in S : \; pv + (1 - p)u \geq m \; , \tag{16}$$

*where $p \in [0, 1]$. If $\mathcal{K}$ is the complexity w.r.t. $\mathfrak{G}$, than*

$$\mathbf{E}\mathcal{K}(\xi_1^{(p)} \dots \xi_n^{(p)}) \geq mn \; . \tag{17}$$

*Proof (of the lemma).* Consider a superloss process $L$ and a string $\boldsymbol{x}$. The point $(L(\boldsymbol{x}0) - L(\boldsymbol{x}), L(\boldsymbol{x}1) - L(\boldsymbol{x})) = (s_1, s_2)$ is a superprediction. We have

$$\mathbf{E}(L(\boldsymbol{x}\xi^{(p)}) - L(\boldsymbol{x})) = p_0 s_2 + (1 - p_0)s_1 \; , \tag{18}$$

where $\xi^{(p)}$ is a result of one Bernoulli trial with the probability of 1 being equal to $p$.

□

**Lemma 8.** *Let $\mathfrak{G}$ be a mixable game with the loss function $\lambda$ and the complexity $\mathcal{K}$. Suppose that $\gamma^{(0)} \in [0, 1]$ is a computable number such that*

$$p_0 \lambda(1, \gamma^{(0)}) + (1 - p_0)\lambda(0, \gamma^{(0)}) = m \; , \tag{19}$$

*where $p_0 \in [0, 1]$; then there exists $C > 0$ such that*

$$\mathbf{E}\mathcal{K}(\xi_1^{(p_0)} \dots \xi_n^{(p_0)}) \leq mn + C \; .$$

*Proof (of the lemma).* The proof is by considering the strategy which makes the prediction $\gamma^{(0)}$ on each trial and applying (6).    □

The theorem follows.    □

For any game $\mathfrak{G}$ with the loss function $\lambda$, any positive real $a$, and any real $b$, one may consider the game $\mathfrak{G}_{a,b}$ with the loss function $\lambda_{a,b} = a\lambda + b$. Any $L(\boldsymbol{x})$ is a superloss process w.r.t. $\mathfrak{G}$ if and only if $aL(\boldsymbol{x}) + b|\boldsymbol{x}|$ is a superloss process w.r.t. $\mathfrak{G}_{a,b}$. This implies the following corollary.

**Corollary 9.** *Under the conditions of Theorem 4 the following statements are equivalent:*

(i) $\exists C > 0 \forall \boldsymbol{x} \in \mathbf{B}^* : a\mathcal{K}^1(\boldsymbol{x}) + b|\boldsymbol{x}| + C \geq \mathcal{K}^2(\boldsymbol{x})$

(ii) $aP_1 + (b, b) \subseteq \overline{S_2}$

(iii) $\forall p \in [0, 1] \exists C > 0 \forall n \in \mathbb{N} : a\mathbf{E}\mathcal{K}^1(\xi_1^{(p)} \ldots \xi_n^{(p)}) + bn + C \geq \mathbf{E}\mathcal{K}^2(\xi_1^{(p)} \ldots \xi_n^{(p)})$,
    *where $\xi_1^{(p)}, \ldots, \xi_n^{(p)}$ are results of $n$ independent Bernoulli trials with the probability of 1 being equal to $p$.*

It is natural to ask whether the extra term $b|\boldsymbol{x}|$ can be replaced by a smaller term. The next corollary follows from the proof of Theorem 4 and clarifies the situation.

**Corollary 10.** *Suppose that under the conditions of Theorem 4 the following statement holds:*
    *For any $p \in [0, 1]$ there exists a function $\alpha_p : \mathbb{N} \to \mathbb{R}$ such that $\alpha_p(n) = o(n)(n \to +\infty)$ and for any $n \in \mathbb{N}$ the inequality*

$$a\mathbf{E}\mathcal{K}^1(\xi_1^{(p)} \ldots \xi_n^{(p)}) + bn + \alpha_p(n) \geq \mathbf{E}\mathcal{K}^2(\xi_1^{(p)} \ldots \xi_n^{(p)}) \tag{20}$$

*holds, where $\xi_1^{(p)}, \ldots, \xi_n^{(p)}$ are results of $n$ independent Bernoulli trials with the probability of 1 being equal to $p$.*
    *Then the inequality*

$$a\mathcal{K}^1(\boldsymbol{x}) + b|\boldsymbol{x}| \geq^+ \mathcal{K}^2(\boldsymbol{x})$$

*holds.*

*Proof.* The corollary follows from (13)    □

**Corollary 11.** *If under the conditions of Theorem 4 there exists a function $f : \mathbb{N} \to \mathbb{R}$ such that $f(n) = o(n) (n \to +\infty)$ and, for any $\boldsymbol{x} \in \mathbf{B}^*$, the inequality*

$$a\mathcal{K}^1(\boldsymbol{x}) + b|\boldsymbol{x}| + f(|\boldsymbol{x}|) \geq \mathcal{K}^2(\boldsymbol{x}) \tag{21}$$

*holds, then the inequality*

$$a\mathcal{K}^1(\boldsymbol{x}) + b|\boldsymbol{x}| \geq^+ \mathcal{K}^2(\boldsymbol{x})$$

*holds.*

The next statement shows a property of the set of all pairs $(a, b)$ such that $a \geq 0$ and the inequality $a\mathcal{K}^1(x) + b|x| \geq^+ \mathcal{K}^2(x)$ holds.

**Corollary 12.** *Under the conditions of Theorem 4 the set*

$$\{(a, b) \mid a \geq 0 \text{and} \, \exists C > 0 \forall x \in \mathbf{B}^* : a\mathcal{K}^1(x) + b|x| + C \geq \mathcal{K}^2(x)\} \qquad (22)$$

*is closed in the topology of* $\mathbb{R}^2$.

*Proof.* The proof is by continuity of $\lambda_1$.     □

## 3.2   Case $a_1\mathcal{K}^1(x) + a_2\mathcal{K}^2(x) \leq^+ b|x|$.

In the previous subsection we considered nonnegative values of $a$. In this subsection we study the inequality $a\mathcal{K}^1(x) + b|x| \geq^+ \mathcal{K}^2(x)$ with negative $a$ or, in other words, the inequality $a_1\mathcal{K}^1(x) + a_2\mathcal{K}^2(x) \leq^+ b|x|$ with $a_1, a_2 \geq 0$.

**Theorem 13.** *Suppose that games $\mathfrak{G}_1$ and $\mathfrak{G}_2$ are mixable and, for any $\gamma \in [0,1]$, we have*

$$\lambda_1(0, \gamma) = \lambda_1(1, 1 - \gamma) , \qquad (23)$$
$$\lambda_2(0, \gamma) = \lambda_2(1, 1 - \gamma) , \qquad (24)$$

*where $\lambda_1$ and $\lambda_2$ are the loss functions. Then, for any $a_1, a_2 \geq 0$, the following statements are equivalent:*

*(i)* $\exists C > 0 \forall x \in \mathbf{B}^* : a_1\mathcal{K}^1(x) + a_2\mathcal{K}^2(x) \leq b|x| + C$,
*(ii)* $a_1\lambda_1(0, 1/2) + a_2\lambda_2(0, 1/2) \leq b$,
*(iii)* $\exists C > 0 \forall n \in \mathbb{N} : a_1\mathbf{E}\mathcal{K}^1(\xi_1^{(1/2)} \ldots \xi_n^{(1/2)}) + a_2\mathbf{E}\mathcal{K}^2(\xi_1^{(1/2)} \ldots \xi_n^{(1/2)}) \leq bn + C$,
     *where $\xi_1^{(1/2)}, \ldots, \xi_n^{(1/2)}$ are results of $n$ independent Bernoulli trials with the probability of 1 being equal to $1/2$.*

*Proof.* The proof is similar to the one of Theorem 4 but a little simpler.

**Lemma 14.** *Suppose that a game $\mathfrak{G}$ is mixable, $\lambda$ is its loss function, and $\mathcal{K}$ is the complexity w.r.t. $\mathfrak{G}$. If, for any $\gamma \in [0,1]$, we have $\lambda(0, \gamma) = \lambda(1, 1 - \gamma)$, then, for any $x \in \mathbf{B}^*$, we have*

$$\mathcal{K}(x) \leq^+ \lambda(0, 1/2)|x| . \qquad (25)$$

*Proof (of the lemma).* The proof is by considering the strategy which makes the prediction $1/2$ on each trial and applying (6).     □

Clearly, the sets of superpredictions $S_1$ and $S_2$ for $\mathfrak{G}_1$ and $\mathfrak{G}_2$ lay "northeast" of the straight lines $x/2 + y/2 = \lambda_1(0, 1/2)$ and $x/2 + y/2 = \lambda_2(0, 1/2)$, respectively. It follows from Lemma 7 that, for any $n \in \mathbb{N}$, the inequalities

$$\mathbf{E}\mathcal{K}^1(\xi_1^{(1/2)} \ldots \xi_n^{(1/2)}) \geq \lambda_1(0, 1/2)n , \qquad (26)$$
$$\mathbf{E}\mathcal{K}^2(\xi_1^{(1/2)} \ldots \xi_n^{(1/2)}) \geq \lambda_2(0, 1/2)n \qquad (27)$$

hold. The theorem follows.     □

## 4    Application to the Square-Loss and Logarithmic Complexity

In this section we will apply our general results to the square-loss and logarithmic games.

**Theorem 15.** *If $a \geq 0$, then the inequality*

$$a\mathcal{K}^{\log}(\boldsymbol{x}) + b|\boldsymbol{x}| \geq^+ \mathcal{K}^{\mathrm{sq}}(\boldsymbol{x}) \tag{28}$$

*holds if and only if $b \geq \max(\frac{1}{4} - a, 0)$.*

*Proof.* We apply Corollary 9.

Let $p \in [0, 1]$. To estimate the expectations, we need the values

$$E_p^{\mathrm{sq}} := \min_{0 \leq \gamma \leq 1} (p(1 - \gamma)^2 + (1 - p)\gamma^2) \tag{29}$$

$$= p(1 - p) \tag{30}$$

and

$$E_p^{\log} := \min_{0 \leq \gamma \leq 1} (-p \log \gamma - (1 - p) \log(1 - \gamma)) \tag{31}$$

$$= -p \log p - (1 - p) \log(1 - p) \ . \tag{32}$$

It follows from Lemmas 7 and 8 that there are $C_1, C_2 > 0$ such that, for any $p \in [0, 1]$ and for any $n \in \mathbb{N}$, we have

$$|\mathbf{E}\mathcal{K}^{\log}(\xi_1^{(p)} \ldots \xi_n^{(p)}) - E_p^{\log} n| \leq C_1 \ , \tag{33}$$

$$|\mathbf{E}\mathcal{K}^{\mathrm{sq}}(\xi_1^{(p)} \ldots \xi_n^{(p)}) - E_p^{\mathrm{sq}} n| \leq C_2 \ . \tag{34}$$

Therefore the inequality $a\mathcal{K}^{\log}(\mathbf{x}) + b|\mathbf{x}| \geq^+ \mathcal{K}^{\mathrm{sq}}(\mathbf{x})$ holds if and only if for any $p \in [0, 1]$ the inequality $aE_p^{\log} + b \geq E_p^{\mathrm{sq}}$ holds.

**Lemma 16.** *For any $a \geq 0$, we have*

$$\sup_{p \in [0,1]} (E_p^{\mathrm{sq}} - aE_p^{\log}) = \max(\frac{1}{4} - a, 0) \ . \tag{35}$$

The theorem follows.    □

The next theorem corresponds to Subsect. 3.2.

**Theorem 17.** *For any $a_1, a_2 > 0$ and any $b$ the inequality*

$$a_1\mathcal{K}^{\mathrm{sq}}(\boldsymbol{x}) + a_2\mathcal{K}^{\log}(\boldsymbol{x}) \leq^+ b|\boldsymbol{x}|$$

*holds for any $x \in \mathbf{B}^*$ if and only if $a_1/4 + a_2 \leq b$.*

*Proof.* The proof is by applying Theorem 13.    □

# 5   Acknowledgements

I would like to thank Prof. V. Vovk and Prof. A. Gammerman for providing guidance to this work. I am also grateful to Dr. A. Shen for helpful discussions.

# References

[1] N. Cesa-Bianchi, Y. Freund, D. Haussler, D. P. Helmbold, R. E. Schapire, and M. K. Warmuth. How to use expert advice. *Journal of the ACM*, (44):427–485, 1997.

[2] A. DeSantis, G. Markowski, and M. N. Weigman. Learning probabilistic prediction functions. In *Proceedings of the 1988 Workshop on Computational Learning Theory*, pages 312–328, 1988.

[3] D. Haussler, J. Kivinen, and M. K. Warmuth. Tight worst-case loss bounds for predicting with expert advise. Technical Report UCSC-CRL-94-36, University of California at Santa Cruz, revised December 1994.

[4] Y. Kalnishkan. Linear relations between square-loss and Kolmogorov complexity. In *Proceedings of the Twelfth Annual Conference on Computational Learning Theory*, pages 226–232. Association for Computing Machinery, 1999.

[5] N. Littlestone and M. K. Warmuth. The weighted majority algorithm. *Information and Computation*, 108:212–261, 1994.

[6] F. A. Valentine. *Convex Sets*. McGraw-Hill Book Company, 1964.

[7] V. Vovk. Probability theory for the Brier game. To appear in *Theoretical Computer Science*. Preliminary version in M. Li and A. Maruoka, editors, *Algorithmic Learning Theory*, vol. 1316 of *Lecture Notes in Computer Science*, pages 323–338.

[8] V. Vovk. Aggregating strategies. In M. Fulk and J. Case, editors, *Proceedings of the 3rd Annual Workshop on Computational Learning Theory*, pages 371–383, San Mateo, CA, 1990. Morgan Kaufmann.

[9] V. Vovk. A game of prediction with expert advice. *Journal of Computer and System Sciences*, (56):153–173, 1998.

[10] V. Vovk and C. J. H. C. Watkins. Universal portfolio selection. In *Proceedings of the 11th Annual Conference on Computational Learning Theory*, pages 12–23, 1998.

# Predicting Nearly as Well as the Best Pruning of a Planar Decision Graph

Eiji Takimoto[1]* and Manfred K. Warmuth[2]**

[1] Graduate School of Information Sciences, Tohoku University
Sendai, 980-8579, Japan.
[2] Computer Science Department, University of California, Santa Cruz
Santa Cruz, CA 95064, U.S.A.

**Abstract.** We design efficient on-line algorithms that predict nearly as well as the best pruning of a planar decision graph. We assume that the graph has no cycles. As in the previous work on decision trees, we implicitly maintain one weight for each of the prunings (exponentially many). The method works for a large class of algorithms that update its weights multiplicatively. It can also be used to design algorithms that predict nearly as well as the best convex combination of prunings.

## 1 Introduction

Decision trees are widely used in Machine Learning. Frequently a large tree is produced initially and then this tree is pruned for the purpose of obtaining a better predictor. A pruning is produced by deleting some nodes and with them all their successors. Although there are exponentially many prunings, a recent method developed in coding theory [WST95] and machine learning [Bun92] makes it possible to (implicitly) maintain one weight per pruning. In particular Helmbold and Schapire [HS97] use this method to design an elegant algorithm that is guaranteed to predict nearly as well as the best pruning of a decision tree. Pereira and Singer [PS97] modify this algorithm to the case of edge-based prunings instead of the node-based prunings defined above. Edge-based prunings are produced by cutting some edges of the original decision tree and then removing all nodes below the cuts. Both definitions are closely related. Edge-based prunings have been applied to statistical language modeling [PS97], where the out-degree of nodes in the tree may be very large.

In this paper we generalize the methods from decision trees to planar directed acyclic graphs (dags). Trees, upside-down trees and series-parallel dags are all special cases of planar dags. We define a notion of edge-based prunings of a planar dag. Again we find a way to efficiently maintain one weight for each of the exponentially many prunings.

In Fig. 1, the tree $T'$ represents a node-based pruning of the decision tree $T$. Each node in the original tree $T$ is assumed to have a prediction value in

---

* This work was done while the author visited University of California, Santa Cruz.
** Supported by NSF grant CCR 9700201

O. Watanabe, T. Yokomori (Eds.): ALT'99, LNAI 1720, pp. 335–346, 1999.

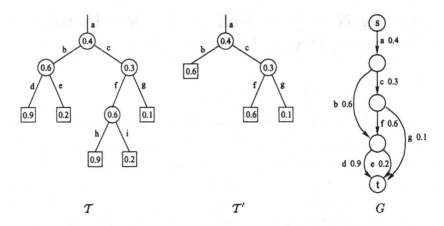

**Fig. 1.** An example of a decision tree, a pruning, and a decision dag

some prediction space $\hat{Y}$. Here, we assume $\hat{Y} = [0, 1]$. In the usual setting each instance (from some instance space) induces a path in the decision tree from the root to a leaf. The path is based on decisions done at the internal nodes. Thus w.l.o.g. our instances are paths in the original decision tree. For a given path, a tree predicts the value at the leaf at which the path ends. For example, for the path $\{a, c, f, i\}$, the original tree $\mathcal{T}$ predicts the value 0.2 and the pruning $\mathcal{T}'$ predicts 0.6.

In what follows, we consider the prediction values to be associated with the edges. In Fig. 1 the prediction value of each edge is given at its lower endpoint. For example, the edges $a$, $b$ and $c$ have prediction values 0.4, 0.6 and 0.3, respectively. Moreover, we think of a pruning as the set of edges that are incident to the leaves of the pruning. So, $\mathcal{T}$ and $\mathcal{T}'$ are represented by $\{d, e, g, h, i\}$ and $\{b, f, g\}$, respectively. Note that for any pruning $R$ and any path $P$, $R$ intersects $P$ at exactly one edge. That is, a pruning "cuts" each path at an edge. The pruning $R$ predicts on path $P$ with the prediction value of the edge that is cut.

The notion of pruning can easily be generalized to directed acyclic graphs. We define *decision dags* as dags with a special source and sink node where each edge is assumed to have a prediction value. A pruning $R$ of the decision dag is defined as a set of edges such that for any s-t path $P$, $R$ intersects $P$ with exactly one edge. Again the pruning $R$ predicts on the instance/path $P$ with the value of the edge that is cut. It is easily seen that the rightmost graph $G$ in Fig. 1 is a decision dag that is equivalent to $\mathcal{T}$.

We study learning in the on-line prediction model where the decision dag is given to the learner. At each trial $t = 1, 2, \ldots$, the learner receives a path $P_t$ and must produce a prediction $\hat{y}_t \in \hat{Y}$. Then an outcome $y_t$ in the outcome space $Y$ is observed (which can be thought of as the correct value of $P_t$). Finally, at the end of the trial the learner suffers loss $L(y_t, \hat{y}_t)$, where $L : Y \times \hat{Y} \to [0, \infty]$ is a fixed loss function. Since each pruning $R$ has a prediction value for $P_t$, the loss of $R$ at this trial is defined analogously. The goal of the learner is to make predictions so that its total loss $\sum_t L(y_t, \hat{y}_t)$ is not much worse than the total loss of the best pruning or that of the best mixture (convex combination) of prunings.

It is straightforward to apply any of a large family of on-line prediction algorithms to our problem. To this end, we just consider each pruning $R$ of $G$ as an *expert* that predicts as the pruning $R$ does on all paths. Then, we can make use of any on-line algorithm that maintains one weight per expert and forms its own prediction $\hat{y}_t$ by combining the predictions of the experts using the current weights (See for example: [Lit88, LW94, Vov90, Vov95, CBFH+97, KW97]). Many relative loss bounds have been proven for this setting bounding the additional total loss of the algorithm over the total loss of the best expert or best weighted combination of experts. However, this "direct" implementation of the on-line algorithms is inefficient because one weight/expert would be used for each pruning of the decision dag and the number of prunings is usually exponentially large. So the goal is to find efficient implementations of the direct algorithms so that the exponentially many weights are implicitly maintained. In the case of trees this is possible [HS97]. Other applications that simulate algorithms with exponentially many weights are given in [HPW99, MW98]. We now sketch how this can be done when the decision dag is planar.

Recall that each pruning and path intersect at one edge. Therefore in each trial the edges on the path determine the predictions of all the prunings as well as their losses. So in each trial the edges on the path also incur a loss and the total loss of a pruning is always the sum of the total losses of all of its edges. Under a very general setting the weight of a pruning is then a function of the weights of its edges. Thus the exponentially many weights of the prunings collapse to one weight per edge. It is obvious that if we can efficiently update the edge weights and compute the prediction of the direct algorithm from the edge weights, then we have an efficient algorithm that behaves exactly as the direct algorithm.

One of the most important family of on-line learning algorithms is the one that does multiplicative updates of its weights. For this family the weight $w_R$ of a pruning $R$ is always the product of the weights of its edges, i.e. $w_R = \prod_{e \in R} v_e$. The most important computation in determining the prediction and updating the weights is summing the current weights of all the prunings, i.e. $\sum_R \prod_{e \in R} v_e$. We do not know how to efficiently compute this sum for arbitrary decision dags. However, for planar decision dags, computing this sum is reduced to computing another sum for the dual planar dag. The prunings in the primal graph correspond to paths in the dual, and paths in the primal to prunings in the dual. Therefore the above sum is equivalent to $\sum_P \prod_{e \in P} v_e$, where $P$ ranges over all paths in the dual dag. Curiously enough, the same formula appears as the likelihood of a sequence of symbols in a Hidden Markov Model where the edge weights are the transition probabilities. So we can use the well known forward-backward algorithm for computing the above formula efficiently [LRS83].

The overall time per trial is linear in the number of edges of the decision dag. For the case where the dag is series-parallel, we can improve the time per trial to grow linearly in the size of the instance (a path in the dag).

Another approach for solving the on-line pruning problem is to use the *specialist* framework developed by Freund, Schapire, Singer and Warmuth [FSSW97]. Now each edge is considered to be a specialist. In trial $t$ only the edges on the path "awake" and all others are "asleep". The predictions of the awake edges are combined to form the prediction of the algorithm. The redeeming feature of their algorithm is that it works for arbitrary sets of prunings and paths over some set of edges with the property that any pruning and any path intersect at exactly one edge. They can show that their algorithm performs nearly as well as any mixture of specialists, that is, essentially as well as the best single pruning.

However, even in the case of decision trees the loss bound of their algorithm is quadratic in the size of the pruning. In contrast, the loss bound for the direct algorithm grows only linearly in the size of the pruning. Also when we use for example the EG algorithm [KW97] as our direct algorithm, then the direct algorithm (as well as its efficient simulation) predicts nearly as well as the best convex combination of prunings.

## 2    On-Line Pruning of a Decision Dag

A decision dag is a directed acyclic graph $G = (V, E)$ with a designated start node s and a terminal node t. We call s and t the source and the sink of $G$, respectively. An s-t path is a set of edges of $G$ that forms a path from the source to the sink. In the decision dag $G$, each edge $e \in E$ is assumed to have a predictor that, when given an instance (s-t path) that includes the edge $e$, makes a prediction from the *prediction space* $\hat{Y}$. In a typical setting, the predictions would be real numbers from $\hat{Y} = [0, 1]$. Although the predictor at edge $e$ may make different predictions whenever the path passes through $e$, we write its prediction as $\xi(e) \in \hat{Y}$.

A *pruning* $R$ of $G$ is a set of edges such that for any s-t path $P$, $R$ intersects $P$ with exactly one edge, i.e., $|R \cap P| = 1$. Let $e_{R \cap P}$ denote the edge at which $R$ and $P$ intersect. Because of the intersection property, a pruning $R$ can be thought of as a well-defined function from any instance $P$ to a prediction $\xi(e_{R \cap P}) \in \hat{Y}$. Let $\mathcal{P}(G)$ and $\mathcal{R}(G)$ denote the set of all paths and all prunings of $G$, respectively. For example, the decision dag $G$ in Fig. 1 has four prunings, i.e., $\mathcal{R}(G) = \{\{a\}, \{b, c\}, \{b, f, g\}, \{d, e, g\}\}$. Assume that we are given an instance $P = \{a, b, e\}$. Then, the pruning $R = \{b, f, g\}$ predicts 0.6 for this instance $P$, which is the prediction of the predictor at edge $b = e_{R \cap P}$.

We study learning in the on-line prediction model, where an algorithm is required not to actually produce prunings but to make predictions for a given instance sequence based on a given decision dag $G$. The goal is to make predictions that are competitive with those made by the best pruning of $G$ or with those by the best mixture of prunings of $G$. We will now state our learning model more precisely. A prediction algorithm $A$ is given a decision dag $G$ as its input. At each trial $t = 1, 2, \ldots$, algorithm $A$ receives an instance/path $P_t \in \mathcal{P}(G)$ and generates a prediction $\hat{y}_t \in \hat{Y}$. After that, an outcome $y_t \in Y$ is observed. $Y$ is a set called the *outcome space*. Typically, the outcome space $Y$ would be the same as $\hat{Y}$. At this trial, the algorithm $A$ suffers loss $L(y_t, \hat{y}_t)$, where $L : Y \times \hat{Y} \to [0, \infty]$ is a fixed *loss function*. For example the square loss is $L(y, \hat{y}) = (y - \hat{y})^2$ and the relative-entropic loss is given by $L(y, \hat{y}) = y \ln(y/\hat{y}) + (1 - y) \ln((1 - y)/(1 - \hat{y}))$. For any instance-outcome sequence $S = ((P_1, y_1), \ldots, (P_T, y_T)) \in (\mathcal{P}(G) \times Y)^*$, the cumulative loss of $A$ is defined as $L_A(S) = \sum_{t=1}^{T} L(y_t, \hat{y}_t)$. In what follows, the cumulative loss of $A$ is simply called the loss of $A$. Similarly, for a pruning $R$ of $G$, the loss of $R$ for $S$ is defined as

$$L_R(S) = \sum_{t=1}^{T} L(y_t, \xi(e_{R \cap P_t})) \ .$$

The performance of $A$ is measured in two ways. The first one is to compare the loss of $A$ to the loss of the best $R$. In other words, the goal of algorithm $A$ is to make predictions so that its loss $L_A(S)$ is close to $\min_{R \in \mathcal{R}(G)} L_R(S)$. The other goal (that is harder to achieve) is to compare the loss of $A$ to the loss of the best mixture of prunings. To be more precise, we introduce a mixture vector $u$ indexed by $R$ so that $u_R \geq 0$ for $R \in \mathcal{R}(G)$ and $\sum_R u_R = 1$. Then the goal of $A$ is to achieve a loss $L_A(S)$ that is close to $\min_u L_u(S)$, where

$$L_u(S) = \sum_{t=1}^{T} L(y_t, \sum_{R \in \mathcal{R}(G)} u_R \xi(e_{R \cap P_t})) \ .$$

Note that the former goal can be seen as the special case of the latter one where the mixture vector $u$ is restricted to unit vectors (i.e., $u_R = 1$ for some particular $R$).

## 3  Dual Problem for a Planar Decision Dag

In this section, we show that our problem of on-line pruning has an equivalent dual problem provided that the underlying graph $G$ is planar. The duality will be used to make our algorithms efficient. An s-t cut of $G$ is a minimal set of edges of $G$ such that its removal from $G$ results in a graph where s and t are disconnected. First we point out that a pruning of $G$ is an s-t cut of $G$ as well. The converse is not necessarily true. For instance, the set $\{a, e, f\}$ is an s-t cut of $G$ in Fig. 2 but it is not a pruning because a path $\{a, d, e\}$ intersects the cut with more than 1 edge. So, the set of prunings $\mathcal{R}(G)$ is a subset of all s-t cuts of $G$, and our problem can be seen as an on-line min-cut problem where cuts are restricted in $\mathcal{R}(G)$. To see this, let us consider the cumulative loss $\ell_e = \sum_{t:e \in P_t} L(y_t, \xi(e))$ at edge $e$ as the capacity of $e$. Then, the loss of a pruning $R$, $L_R(S) = \sum_t L(y_t, \xi(e_{R \cap P_t})) = \sum_{e \in R} \ell_e$, can be interpreted as the total capacity of the cut $R$. This implies that a pruning of minimum loss is a minimum capacity cut from $\mathcal{R}(G)$.

It is known in the literature that the (unrestricted) min-cut problem for an s-t planar graph can be reduced to the shortest path problem for its dual graph (see, e.g., [Hu69, Law70, Has81]). A slight modification of the reduction gives

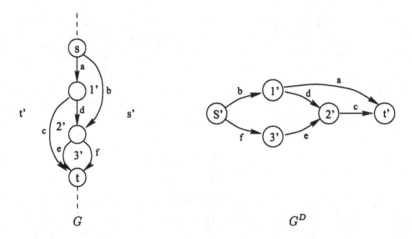

**Fig. 2.** A decision dag $G$ and its dual dag $G^D$.

us a dual problem for the best pruning (restricted min-cut) problem. Below we show how to construct the dual dag $G^D$ from a planar decision dag $G$ that is suitable for our purpose.

Assume we have a planar decision dag $G = (V, E)$ with source s and sink t. Since the graph $G$ is acyclic, we have a planar representation of $G$ so that the vertices in $V$ are placed on a vertical line with all edges downward. In this linear representation, the source s and the sink t are placed on the top and the bottom on the line, respectively (See Fig. 2). The vertical line (the dotted line) bisects the plane and defines two outer faces s' and t' of $G$. Let s' be the right face. The dual dag $G^D = (V^D, E^D)$ is constructed as follows. The set of vertices $V^D$ consists of all faces of $G$. Let $e \in E$ be an edge of $G$ which is common to the boundaries of two faces $f_r$ and $f_l$ in $G$. By virtue of the linear representation, we can let $f_r$ be the "right" face on $e$ and $f_l$ be the "left" face on $e$. Then, let $E^D$ include the edge $e' = (f_r, f_l)$ directed from $f_r$ to $f_l$. It is clear that the dual dag $G^D$ is a planar directed acyclic graph with source s' and sink t', and the dual of $G^D$ is $G$. The following proposition is crucial in this paper.

**Proposition 1.** *Let $G$ be a planar decision dag and $G^D$ be its dual dag. Then, there is a one-to-one correspondence between s-t paths $\mathcal{P}(G)$ in $G$ and prunings $\mathcal{R}(G^D)$ in $G^D$, and there is also a one-to-one correspondence between prunings $\mathcal{R}(G)$ in $G$ and s'-t' paths $\mathcal{P}(G^D)$ in $G^D$.*

Thus there is a natural dual problem associated with the on-line pruning problem. We now describe this dual on-line shortest path problem. An algorithm $A$ is given as input a decision dag $G$. At each trial $t = 1, 2, \ldots$, algorithm $A$ receives a pruning $R_t \in \mathcal{R}(G)$ as the instance and generates a prediction $\hat{y}_t \in \hat{Y}$. The loss of $A$, denoted $L_A(S)$, for an instance-outcome sequence $S = ((R_1, y_1), \ldots, (R_T, y_T)) \in (\mathcal{R}(G) \times Y)^*$ is defined as $L_A(S) = \sum_{t=1}^T L(y_t, \hat{y}_t)$. The class of predictors which the performance of $A$ is now compared to consists of all paths. For a path $P$ of $G$, the loss of $P$ for $S$ is defined as

$$L_P(S) = \sum_{t=1}^{T} L(y_t, \xi(e_{R_t \cap P})) \ .$$

Similarly, for a mixture vector $\boldsymbol{u}$ indexed by $P$ so that $u_P \geq 0$ for $P \in \mathcal{P}(G)$ and $\sum_P u_P = 1$, the loss of the $\boldsymbol{u}$-mixture of paths is defined as

$$L_{\boldsymbol{u}}(S) = \sum_{t=1}^{T} L\left(y_t, \sum_{P \in \mathcal{P}(G)} u_P \xi(e_{R_t \cap P})\right) \ .$$

The objective of $A$ is to make the loss as small as the loss of the best path $P$, i.e., $\min_P L_P(S)$, or the best mixture of paths, i.e., $\min_{\boldsymbol{u}} L_{\boldsymbol{u}}(S)$. It is natural to call this the on-line shortest path problem because if we consider the cumulative loss $\ell_e = \sum_{t:e \in R_t} L(y_t, \xi(e))$ at edge $e$ as the length of $e$, then the loss of $P$, $L_P(S) = \sum_{e \in P} \ell_e$, can be interpreted as the total length of $P$. It is clear from the duality that the on-line pruning problem for a decision dag $G$ is equivalent to the on-line shortest path problem for its dual dag $G^D$. In what follows, we consider only the on-line shortest path problem.

## 4    Inefficient Direct Algorithm

In this section, we show the direct implementation of the algorithms for the on-line shortest path problem. Namely, the algorithm considers each path $P$ of $G$ as an expert that makes a prediction $x_{t,P} = \xi(e_{R_t \cap P})$ for a given pruning $R_t$. Note that this direct implementation would be inefficient because the number of experts (the number of paths in this case) can be exponentially large.

In general, such direct algorithms have the following generic form: They maintain a weight $w_{t,P} \in [0,1]$ for each path $P \in \mathcal{P}(G)$; when given the predictions $x_{t,P} (= \xi(e_{R_t \cap P}))$ of all paths $P$, they combine these predictions based on the weights to make their own prediction $\hat{y}_t$, and then update the weights after the outcome $y_t$ is observed. In what follows, let $\boldsymbol{w}_t$ and $\boldsymbol{x}_t$ denote the weight and prediction vectors indexed by $P \in \mathcal{P}(G)$, respectively. Let $N$ be the number of experts, i.e., the cardinality of $\mathcal{P}(G)$. More precisely, the generic algorithm consists of two parts:

- a prediction function $\mathtt{pred} : \bigcup_N \left([0,1]^N \times \hat{Y}^N\right) \to \hat{Y}$ which maps the current weight and prediction vectors $(\boldsymbol{w}_t, \boldsymbol{x}_t)$ of experts to a prediction $\hat{y}_t$; and
- an update function $\mathtt{update} : \bigcup_N \left([0,1]^N \times \hat{Y}^N \times Y\right) \to [0,1]^N$ which maps $(\boldsymbol{w}_t, \boldsymbol{x}_t)$ and outcome $y_t$ to a new weight vector $\boldsymbol{w}_{t+1}$.

Using these two functions, the generic on-line algorithm behaves as follows: For each trial $t = 1, 2, \ldots$,

1. Observe predictions $\boldsymbol{x}_t$ from the experts.
2. Predict $\hat{y}_t = \mathtt{pred}(\boldsymbol{w}_t, \boldsymbol{x}_t)$.

3. Observe outcome $y_t$ and suffer loss $L(y_t, \hat{y}_t)$.
4. Calculate the new weight vector according to $w_{t+1} = \text{update}(w_t, x_t, y_t)$.

Vovk's Aggregating Algorithm (AA) [Vov90] is a seminal on-line algorithm of generic form and has the best possible loss bound for a very wide class of loss functions. It updates its weights as $w_{t+1} = \text{update}(w_t, x_t, y_t)$, where

$$w_{t+1,P} = w_{t,P} \exp(-L(y_t, x_{t,P})/c_L)$$

for any $P \in \mathcal{P}(G)$. Here $c_L$ is a constant that depends on the loss function $L$. Since AA uses a complicated prediction function, we only discuss a simplified algorithm called the Weighted Average Algorithm (WAA) [KW99]. The latter algorithm uses the same updates with a slightly worse constant $c_L$ and predicts with the weighted average based on the normalized weights:

$$\hat{y}_t = \text{pred}(w_t, x_t) = \sum_{P \in \mathcal{P}(G)} \bar{w}_{t,P} x_{t,P}, \text{ where } \bar{w}_{t,P} = w_{t,P} / \sum_{P'} w_{t,P'}.$$

The following theorem gives an upper bound on the loss of the WAA in terms of the loss of the best path.

**Theorem 1 ([KW99]).** *Assume $Y = \hat{Y} = [0,1]$. Let the loss function $L$ be monotone convex and twice differentiable with respect to the second argument. Then, for any instance-outcome sequence $S \in (\mathcal{R}(G) \times Y)^*$,*

$$L_{\text{WAA}}(S) \leq \min_{P \in \mathcal{P}(G)} \{L_P(S) + c_L \ln(1/\bar{w}_{1,P})\},$$

*where $\bar{w}_{1,P}$ is the normalized initial weight of $P$.*

We can obtain a more powerful bound in terms of the loss of the best mixture of paths using the exponentiated gradient (EG) algorithm due to Kivinen and Warmuth [KW97]. The EG algorithm uses the same prediction function pred as the WAA and uses the update function $w_{t+1} = \text{update}(w_t, x_t, y_t)$ so that for any $P \in \mathcal{P}(G)$,

$$w_{t+1,P} = w_{t,P} \exp\left(-\eta x_{t,P} \frac{\partial L(y_t, z)}{\partial z}\bigg|_{z=\hat{y}_t}\right).$$

Here $\eta$ is a positive learning rate. Kivinen and Warmuth show the following loss bound of the EG algorithm for the square loss function $L(y, \hat{y}) = (y - \hat{y})^2$. Note that, for the square loss, the update above becomes $w_{t+1,P} = w_{t,P} \exp(-2\eta(\hat{y}_t - y_t)x_{t,P})$.

**Theorem 2 ([KW97]).** *Assume $Y = \hat{Y} = [0,1]$. Let $L$ be the square loss function. Then, for any instance-outcome sequence $S \in (\mathcal{R}(G) \times Y)^*$ and for any probability vector $u \in [0,1]^N$ indexed by $P$,*

$$L_{\text{EG}}(S) \leq \frac{2}{2-\eta} L_u(S) + \frac{1}{\eta} \text{RE}(u\|\bar{w}_1),$$

*where $\text{RE}(u\|\bar{w}_1) = \sum_P u_P \ln(u_P/\bar{w}_{1,P})$ is the relative entropy between $u$ and the initial normalized weight vector $\bar{w}_1$.*

Now we give the two conditions on the direct algorithms that are required for our efficient implementation.

**Definition 1.** *Let $w \in [0,1]^N$ and $x \in \hat{Y}^N$ be a weight and a prediction vector. Let $\mathcal{P}_1 \cup \cdots \cup \mathcal{P}_k = \mathcal{P}(G)$ be a partition of $\mathcal{P}(G)$ such that $\mathcal{P}_i \cap \mathcal{P}_j = \emptyset$ for any $i \neq j$ and all paths in the same class have the same prediction. That is, for each class $\mathcal{P}_i$, there exists $x'_i \in \hat{Y}$ such that $x_P = x'_i$ for any $P \in \mathcal{P}_i$. In other words, $x' = (x'_1, \ldots, x'_k)$ and $w' = (w'_1, \ldots, w'_k)$, where $w'_i = \sum_{P \in \mathcal{P}_i} w_P$, can be seen as a projection of the original prediction vector $x$ and weight vector $w$ onto the partition $\{\mathcal{P}_1, \ldots, \mathcal{P}_k\}$. The prediction function* pred *is projection-preserving if* $\text{pred}(w, x) = \text{pred}(w', x')$ *for any $w$ and $x$.*

**Definition 2.** *The update function* update *is multiplicative if there exists a function $f : \hat{Y} \times \hat{Y} \times Y$ such that for any $w \in [0,1]^N$, $x \in \hat{Y}^N$ and $y \in Y$, the new weight $w' = \text{update}(w, x, y)$ is given by $w'_P = w_P f(x_P, \hat{y}, y)$ for any $P$, where $\hat{y} = \text{pred}(w, x)$.*

These conditions are natural. In fact, they are actually satisfied by the prediction and update functions used in many families of algorithms such as AA [Vov90], WAA [KW99], EG and EGU [KW97]. Note that the projection used may change from trial to trial.

## 5 Efficient Implementation of the Direct Algorithm

Now we give an efficient implementation of a direct algorithm that consists of a projection-preserving prediction function pred and a multiplicative update function update. Clearly, it is sufficient to show how to efficiently compute the functions pred and update. Obviously, we cannot explicitly maintain all of the weights $w_{t,P}$ as the direct algorithm does since there may be exponentially many paths $P$ in $G$. Instead, we maintain a weight $v_{t,e}$ for each edge $e$, which requires only a linear space. We will give indirect algorithms below for computing pred and update so that, the weights $v_{t,e}$ for edges implicitly represent the weights $w_{t,P}$ for all paths $P$ as follows:

$$w_{t,P} = \prod_{e \in P} v_{t,e} . \tag{1}$$

First we show an indirect algorithm for update which is simpler. Suppose that, given a pruning $R_t$ as instance, we have already calculated a prediction $\hat{y}_t$ and observe an outcome $y_t$. Then, the following update for the weight of the edges is equivalent to the update $w_{t+1} = \text{update}(w_t, x_t, y_t)$ of the weights of the paths. Recall that $w_t$ is a weight vector indexed by $P$ given by (1) and $x_t$ is a prediction vector given by $x_{t,P} = \xi(e_{R_t \cap P})$. Let $f$ be the function associated with our multiplicative update (see Definition 2). For any edge $e \in E$, the weight of $e$ is updated according to

$$v_{t+1,e} = \begin{cases} v_{t,e} f(\xi(e), \hat{y}_t, y_t) & \text{if } e \in R_t, \\ v_{t,e} & \text{otherwise.} \end{cases} \tag{2}$$

**Lemma 1.** *The update rule for edges given by (2) is equivalent to* update($w_t$, $x_t, y_t$).

*Proof.* It suffices to show that the relation (1) is preserved after updating. That is, $w_{t+1,P} = \prod_{e \in P} v_{t+1,e}$ for any $P \in \mathcal{P}(G)$. Let $e' = e_{R_t \cap P}$. Since update is multiplicative, we have

$$w_{t+1,P} = w_{t,P} f(x_{t,P}, \hat{y}_t, y_t) = \prod_{e \in P} v_{t,e} f(\xi(e'), \hat{y}_t, y_t)$$

$$= \left( \prod_{e \in P \setminus \{e'\}} v_{t,e} \right) \left( v_{t,e'} f(\xi(e'), \hat{y}_t, y_t) \right) = \prod_{e \in P} v_{t+1,e},$$

as required.                                                                    □

Next we show an indirect algorithm for pred. Let the given pruning be $R_t = \{e_1, \ldots, e_k\}$. For $1 \le i \le k$, let $\mathcal{P}_i = \{P \in \mathcal{P}(G) \mid e_i \in P\}$. Since $|R_t \cap P| = 1$ for any $P$, $\mathcal{P}_1 \cup \cdots \cup \mathcal{P}_k = \mathcal{P}(G)$ forms a partition of $\mathcal{P}(G)$ and clearly for any path $P \in \mathcal{P}_i$, we have $x_{t,P} = \xi(e_i)$. So,

$$x' = (\xi(e_1), \ldots, \xi(e_k)) \tag{3}$$

is a projected prediction vector of $x_t$. Therefore, if we have the corresponding projected weight vector $w'$, then by the projection-preserving property of pred we can obtain $\hat{y}_t$ by pred($w', x'$), which equals $\hat{y}_t = $ pred($w, x$). Now what we have to do is to efficiently compute the projected weights for $1 \le i \le k$:

$$w'_{t,i} = \sum_{P \in \mathcal{P}_i} w_{t,P} = \sum_{P : e_i \in P} w_{t,P} = \sum_{P : e_i \in P} \prod_{e \in P} v_{t,e} \ . \tag{4}$$

Surprisingly, the $\sum \prod$-form formula above is similar to the formula of the likelihood of a sequence of symbols in a Hidden Markov Model (HMM) with a particular state transition ($e_i$) [LRS83]. Thus we can compute (4) with the forward-backward algorithm. For node $u \in V$, let $\mathcal{P}_{s \to u}$ and $\mathcal{P}_{u \to t}$ be the set of paths from s to the node $u$ and the set of paths from the node $u$ to t, respectively. Define

$$\alpha(u) = \sum_{P \in \mathcal{P}_{s \to u}} \prod_{e \in P} v_{t,e} \quad \text{and} \quad \beta(u) = \sum_{P \in \mathcal{P}_{u \to t}} \prod_{e \in P} v_{t,e} \ .$$

Suppose that $e_i = (u_1, u_2)$. Then, the set of all paths in $\mathcal{P}(G)$ through $e_i$ is represented as $\{P_1 \cup \{e_i\} \cup P_2 \mid P_1 \in \mathcal{P}_{s \to u_1}, P_2 \in \mathcal{P}_{u_2 \to t}\}$, and therefore the formula (4) is given by

$$w'_{t,i} = \alpha(u_1) v_{t,e_i} \beta(u_2) \ . \tag{5}$$

We summarize this result as the following lemma.

**Lemma 2.** *Let $x'$ and $w'$ be given by (3) and (5), respectively. Then* pred($w', x'$) = pred($w, x$).

The forward-backward algorithm [LRS83] is an algorithm that efficiently computes $\alpha$ and $\beta$ by dynamic programming as follows: $\alpha(u) = 1$ if $u = \mathbf{s}$ and $\alpha(u) = \sum_{u' \in V:(u',u) \in E} \alpha(u') v_{t,(u',u)}$, otherwise. Similarly, $\beta(u) = 1$ if $u = \mathbf{t}$ and $\beta(u) = \sum_{u' \in V:(u,u') \in E} \beta(u') v_{t,(u,u')}$, otherwise. It is clear that both $\alpha$ and $\beta$ can be computed in time $O(|E|)$.

## 6    A More Efficient Algorithm for Series-Parallel Dags

In the case of decision trees, there is a very efficient algorithm with per trial time linear in the size of the instance (a path in the decision tree) [HS97]. We now give an algorithm with the same improved time per trial for series-parallel dags, which include decision trees.

A series-parallel dag $G(\mathbf{s},\mathbf{t})$ with source $\mathbf{s}$ and sink $\mathbf{t}$ is defined recursively as follows: An edge $(\mathbf{s},\mathbf{t})$ is a series-parallel dag; If $G_1(\mathbf{s}_1,\mathbf{t}_1),\ldots,G_k(\mathbf{s}_k,\mathbf{t}_k)$ are disjoint series-parallel dags, then the series connection $G(\mathbf{s},\mathbf{t}) = s(G_1,\ldots,G_k)$ of these dags, where $\mathbf{s} = \mathbf{s}_1$, $\mathbf{t}_i = \mathbf{s}_{i+1}$ for $1 \leq i \leq k-1$ and $\mathbf{t} = \mathbf{t}_k$, or the parallel connection $G(\mathbf{s},\mathbf{t}) = p(G_1,\ldots,G_k)$ of these dags, where $\mathbf{s} = \mathbf{s}_1 = \cdots = \mathbf{s}_k$ and $\mathbf{t} = \mathbf{t}_1 = \cdots = \mathbf{t}_k$, is a series-parallel dag. Note that a series-parallel dag has a parse tree, where each internal node represents a series or a parallel connection of the dags represented by its child nodes.

It suffices to show that the projected weights (4) can be calculated in time linear in the size of instance/pruning $R_t$. To do so the algorithm maintains one weight $v_{t,G}$ per one node $G$ of the parse tree so that

$$v_{t,G} = \sum_{P \in \mathcal{P}(G)} \prod_{e \in P} v_{t,e}$$

holds. Note that if $G$ consists of an single edge $e$, then $v_{t,G} = v_{t,e}$; if $G = s(G_1,\ldots,G_k)$, then $v_{t,G} = \prod_{i=1}^k v_{t,G_i}$; if $G = p(G_1,\ldots,G_k)$, then $v_{t,G} = \sum_{i=1}^k v_{t,G_i}$. Now (4), i.e., $W(G,e) = \sum_{P \in \mathcal{P}(G),e \in P} \prod_{e' \in P} v_{t,e'}$, is recursively computed as

$$W(G,e) = \begin{cases} v_{t,e} & \text{if } G \text{ consists of } e, \\ W(G_i,e) v_{t,G}/v_{t,G_i} & \text{if } G = s(G_1,\ldots,G_k) \text{ and } e \in G_i, \\ W(G_i,e) & \text{if } G = p(G_1,\ldots,G_k) \text{ and } e \in G_i. \end{cases}$$

The weights $v_{t,G}$ are also recursively updated as

$$v_{t+1,G} = \begin{cases} v_{t+1,e} & \text{if } G \text{ consists of } e, \\ v_{t+1,G_i} v_{t,G}/v_{t,G_i} & \text{if } G = s(G_1,\ldots,G_k) \text{ and } R_t \text{ is in } G_i, \\ \sum_{i=1}^k v_{t+1,G_i} & \text{if } G = p(G_1,\ldots,G_k). \end{cases}$$

It is not hard to see that the prediction and the update can be calculated in time linear in the size of $R_t$.

Note that the dual of a series-parallel dag is also a series-parallel dag that has the same parse tree with the series and the parallel connections exchanged. So we can solve the primal on-line pruning problem using the same parse tree.

## Acknowledgments

We would like to thank Hiroshi Nagamochi for calling our attention to the duality of planar graphs.

## References

[Bun92]     W. Buntine. Learning classification trees. *Statistics and Computing*, 2:63–73, 1992.

[CBFH+97]   N. Cesa-Bianchi, Y. Freund, D. Haussler, D. Helmbold, R. Schapire, and M. Warmuth. How to use expert advice. *Journal of the ACM*, 44(3):427–485, 1997.

[FSSW97]    Y. Freund, R. Schapire, Y. Singer, and M. Warmuth. Using and combining predictors that specialize. *29th STOC*, 334–343, 1997.

[Has81]     R. Hassin. Maximum flow in $(s, t)$ planar networks. *Information Processing Letters*, 13(3):107–107, 1981.

[HPW99]     D. Helmbold, S. Panizza, and M. Warmuth. Direct and indirect algorithm for on-line learning of disjunctions. *4th EuroCOLT*, 138–152, 1999.

[HS97]      D. Helmbold and R. Schapire. Predicting nearly as well as the best pruning of a decision tree. *Machine Learning*, 27(1):51–68, 1997.

[Hu69]      T. Hu. *Integer Programming and Network Flows*. Addison-Wesley, 1969.

[KW97]      J. Kivinen and M. Warmuth. Additive versus exponentiated gradient updates for linear prediction. *Information and Computation*, 132(1):1–64, 1997.

[KW99]      J. Kivinen and M. Warmuth. Averaging expert prediction. *4th EuroCOLT*, 153–167, 1999.

[Law70]     E. Lawler. *Combinatorial Optimization: Network and Matroids*. Hold, Rinehart and Winston, New York, 1970.

[Lit88]     N. Littlestone. Learning when irrelevant attributes abound: A new linear-threshold algorithm. *Machine Learning*, 2:285–318, 1988.

[LRS83]     S. Levinson, L. Rabiner, and M. Sondhi. An introduction to the application of the theory of probabilistic functions of a markov process to automatic speech recognition. *Bell System Technical Journal*, 62(4):1035–1074, 1983.

[LW94]      N. Littlestone and M. Warmuth. The weighted majority algorithm. *Information and Computation*, 108(2):212–261, 1994.

[MW98]      M. Maass and M. Warmuth. Efficient learning with virtual threshold gates. *Information and Computation*, 141(1):66–83, 1998.

[PS97]      F. Pereira and Y. Singer. An efficient extension to mixture techniques for prediction and decision trees. *10th COLT*, 114–121, 1997.

[Vov90]     V. Vovk. Aggregating strategies. *3rd COLT*, 371–383, 1990.

[Vov95]     V. Vovk. A game of prediction with expert advice. *8th COLT*, 51–60, 1995.

[WST95]     F. Willems, Y. Shtarkov, and T. Tjalkens. The context tree weighting method: basic properties. *IEEE Transactions on Information Theory*, 41(3):653–664, 1995.

# On Learning Unions of Pattern Languages and Tree Patterns

Sally A. Goldman[*1] and Stephen S. Kwek[2]

[1] Washington University, St. Louis MO 63130-4899, USA,
sg@cs.wustl.edu,
http://www.cs.wustl.edu/~sg
[2] Washington State University, Pullman WA 99164-1035, USA,
kwek@eecs.wsu.edu,
http://www.eecs.wsu.edu/~kwek

**Abstract.** We present efficient on-line algorithms for learning unions of a constant number of tree patterns, unions of a constant number of one-variable pattern languages, and unions of a constant number of pattern languages with fixed length substitutions. By fixed length substitutions we mean that each occurence of variable $x_i$ must be substituted by terminal strings of fixed length $l(x_i)$. We prove that if an arbitrary unions of pattern languages with fixed length substitutions can be learned efficiently then DNFs are efficiently learnable in the mistake bound model. Since we use a reduction to Winnow, our algorithms are robust against attribute noise. Furthermore, they can be modified to handle concept drift. Also, our approach is quite general and may be applicable to learning other pattern related classes. For example, we could learn a more general pattern language class in which a penalty (*i.e.* weight) is assigned to each violation of the rule that a terminal symbol cannot be changed or that a pair of variable symbols, of the same variable, must be substituted by the same terminal string. An instance is positive iff the penalty incurred for violating these rules is below a given tolerable threshold.

## 1 Introduction

A *pattern p* is a string in $(T \cup S)^*$ for sets $T$ of terminal symbols and $S$ of variable symbols. The number of terminal symbols could be infinite. For a pattern $p$, let $\mathcal{L}(p)$ denote the set of strings from $T^+$ that can be obtained by substituting non-empty strings from $T^+$ for the variables in $p$. We call $\mathcal{L}(p)$ the *pattern language* generated by $p$. The strings in $\mathcal{L}(p)$ are positive instances and the others are negative instances. For example, $p = 1x_10x_21x_3x_10x_2$ is a 3-variable pattern. The instance 11010111001101011 is in $\mathcal{L}(p)$ since it can be obtained by the substitutions $x_1 = 101, x_2 = 11, x_3 = 001$.

Pattern languages were first introduced by Angluin [4, 5]. Since then, they have been extensively investigated in the identification in the limit framework [44, 41, 40, 21, 31, 45, 20, 1, 16, 38, 46]. They have also been studied in the PAC

---

* Supported in part by NSF Grant CCR-9734940.

O. Watanabe, T. Yokomori (Eds.): ALT'99, LNAI 1720, pp. 347–363, 1999.
© Springer-Verlag Berlin Heidelberg 1999

learning [33, 24, 39] and exact learning [11, 19, 27, 32, 33] frameworks. They are applicable to text processing [36], automated data entry systems [41], case-based reasoning [22] and genome informatics [7, 8, 9, 13, 35, 42, 43].

Learning general pattern languages is a very difficult problem. In fact, even if the learner knows the target pattern, deciding whether a string can be generated by that pattern is NP-complete [4, 25]. Ko and Tzeng [26] showed that the consistency problem of pattern languages is $\Sigma_2^P$-complete. Schapire [39] proved a stronger result. He showed that pattern languages cannot be learned efficiently in the PAC-model assuming $P/poly \neq NP/poly$ regardless of the representation used by the learning algorithm. In the exact model, Angluin [6] proved that learning with membership and equivalence queries requires exponential time.

A natural approach in making pattern languages learnable is to restrict the number of occurrences of each variable symbol in the pattern to one [40] or at most some constant $k$ [33]. Another approach is to bound the number of variables by some constant (though there is no restriction on the number of times each variable symbol can be used). Kearns and Pitt [24] gave a polynomial-time PAC-learning algorithm for learning such $k$-variable patterns under the assumption that examples are drawn from a product distribution. However, for arbitrary distributions, the problem seems to be difficult even if $k = 2$ [4, 18]. We present an efficient algorithm that does not place any restrictions on $k$ or the number of times each variable symbol occurs (albeit at the cost of only allowing fixed length substitutions). Furthermore, we can also learn the union of a constant number of patterns even with attribute noise.

For $k = 1$, Angluin [4] presented a learner that produces a descriptive pattern in $O(l^4 \log l)$ update time, where $l$ is the length of all the examples seen so far. A pattern $p$ is said to be *descriptive* if given a sample $S$ that can be generated by $p$, no other pattern that generates $S$ can generate a proper subset of the language generated by $p$. Erlebach *et. al.* [16] gave a more efficient algorithm that outputs a descriptive pattern in expected total learning time $O(|p|^2 \log |p|)$ where $|p|$ is the length of the target pattern $p$. Recently, Reischuk and Zeugmann [38] proved that if the sample $S$ is drawn from some fixed distribution satisfying certain benign restrictions and the learner is not required to output a descriptive pattern, then one can learn one-variable patterns with expected total time linear in the length of the pattern while converging within a constant number of rounds.

In their paper, Reischuk and Zeugmann [38] suggested several research directions in learning one-variable patterns. First, they pointed out that even with two variables (i.e. $k = 2$) the situation becomes considerably more complicated and will require additional tools. One open problem they suggested is to construct efficient algorithms for learning unions of constant number of one-variable pattern languages. In Section 5, we present an efficient algorithm to learn the union of $L$ one-variable pattern languages in the mistake bound model. Our algorithm tolerates attribute errors but requires the learner be given one positive example, which does not contain attribute noise, for each pattern. The number of *attribute errors* of a labeled string $\langle s, y \rangle$, with respect to a target pattern, is the number of (terminal) symbols of $s$ that have to be changed so that the classification of the resulting string by the target pattern is consistent with $y$. The update time is polynomial in the length of the noise-free positive example of each pattern, and the current instance that we want to classify. However, it is exponential in $L$. When $L = 1$ our algorithm is less efficient than Reischuck and Zeugmann algorithm. However, our analysis is a worst-case analysis which does not assume the sample is drawn from a fixed distribution. It also tolerates concept drift.

A concept class that closely resembles pattern languages is the class of tree patterns. A *tree pattern* $p$ is a rooted tree where the internal nodes are labeled using a set $T$ of terminal symbols while the leaves may be labeled using $T$ or a set $S$ of variable symbols. An instance $t$ is a *"ground"* tree if all the nodes are labeled by terminal symbols. An instance $t$ is in the language $\mathcal{L}(p)$ generated by a tree pattern $p$ if $t$ can be obtained from $p$ by substituting the leaves labeled with the same variable symbol by the same ground tree. Those tree patterns where the siblings are distinguishable from each other are referred to as *ordered* and otherwise as *unordered*. A union of ordered (resp. unordered) tree patterns is called an *ordered forest* (resp. *unordered forests*). In this paper, we consider only ordered trees and forests. For recent results on learning unordered forests see Amoth, Cull and Tadepalli [3].

The study of tree patterns is motivated by natural language processing [15] and symbolic integration [34] where instances are represented as parse trees and expressions [34], respectively. Tree patterns are also closely related to logic program representations [10, 23]. Using the exact learning model with membership and equivalence queries, Arimura, Ishizaka and Shinohara [11] showed that ordered forests with bounded number of trees can be learned efficiently. Subsequently, Amoth, Cull and Tadepalli [2] showed that ordered forests with an infinite alphabet are exactly learnable using equivalence and membership queries. They also showed that ordered trees are exactly learnable with only equivalence queries. We give an efficient algorithm to learn unions of a constant number of ordered tree patterns (in the mistake bound model *without* membership queries) in the presence of attribute noise. The number of *attribute errors* of a labeled ground tree $\langle t, y \rangle$, with respect to a target pattern, is the number of (terminal) symbols in the nodes of $t$ that have to be changed so that the classification of the resulting tree by the target tree pattern is consistent with $y$. Our algorithm does not require any restrictions on the alphabet size for the terminal symbols or on the number of children per node.

## 2    Our Results

In this paper, we present algorithms to learn unions of pattern languages and tree patterns. We obtain all of our algorithms by reductions of the following flavor. We introduce two sets of boolean attributes. One set is to ensure that the terminal symbols have not been changed. The other set is for ensuring all variable symbols are substituted properly. The target concept is then represented as a conjunction of a relatively small number of these attributes. More specifically, the number of *relevant* attributes depends only on the number of patterns in the target union, the number of variables in the patterns and the number of occurrences of the variable symbols in the patterns. We achieve this goal while keeping the total number of attributes polynomial in the length of the examples (which could be arbitrarily longer than the number of variable symbols). Furthermore, since the target concept is represented as a conjunction of boolean attributes, we can employ Winnow to obtain a small mistake bound and to handle attribute noise. Finally, since a disjunction of a constant number of terms can be reduced to a conjunction (with size exponential in the number of terms) we can use our technique to learn unions of a constant number of patterns. This approach seems to be quite general and was employed to learn geometric patterns [17]. It is possibly applicable to learning other pattern related concept classes as well.

In Section 4, we apply our technique to learn a union of a constant number of pattern languages with the only restriction being that there are fixed length substitutions. A pattern language $\mathcal{L}(p)$ is said to have *fixed length substitutions* if each variable $x_i$ can only be substituted by terminal strings of constant length $l(x_i)$. The constant $l(x_i)$ depends only on $x_i$ and can be different for different variables. Trivially, this means that all strings in $\mathcal{L}(p)$ must be of the same length. The resulting algorithm learns a union of pattern languages $\mathcal{L}(p_1)$, ..., $\mathcal{L}(p_L)$ with fixed length substitutions using polynomial time (for $L$ constant) for each prediction and with a worst-case mistake bound of

$$O\left(\left(\prod_{i=1}^{L}(2V_i - k_i + 1)\right)\left(\sum_{i=1}^{L}\log n_i\right) + \sum_{j=1}^{T}\prod_{i=1}^{L}\min\left(2A_j, 2V_i - k_i + 1\right)\right)$$

where $k_i$ is the number of variables in $p_i$, $V_i$ is the total number of occurrences of variable symbols in $p_i$, $A_j$ is the worst-case number of attribute errors in trial $j$, and $n_i$ is the length of the given positive example for $p_i$ (which must have no attribute errors). Note that the mistake bound only has a logarithmic dependence on the length of the examples. In addition, we could assign a penalty (*i.e.* weight) to each violation of the rule that a terminal symbol cannot be changed. The weights can be different for different terminal symbols. Similarly, we can also assign a penalty to each violation of the rule that a pair of variable symbols, of the same variable, must be substituted by the same terminal string. If the penalty incurred by an instance for violating these rules is below a given tolerable threshold then it is in the target concept $\mathcal{L}'(p)$ generated by $p$. If the penalty is above the threshold then it is not in $\mathcal{L}'(p)$. Since Winnow can learn linear threshold functions, the algorithms we present here can be extended tot this more general class of pattern languages.

Contrasting this positive result, we prove that if unions of an arbitrary number of such patterns can be learned efficiently in the mistake bound model then DNFs can be learned efficiently in the mistake bound model. Whether or not DNF formulas can be efficiently learned is one of the more challenging open problems. The problem remains open even for the easier PAC learning model.

Next, in Section 5, we present an algorithm to learn $\mathcal{L}(p_1) \cup \cdots \cup \mathcal{L}(p_L)$ where each $p_i$ is a one-variable pattern. Our algorithm makes each prediction in polynomial time (for constant $L$) and has a worst-case mistake bound of

$$O\left(\left(\prod_{i=1}^{L} 2V_i\right)\left(\sum_{i=1}^{L} \log n_i\right) + \sum_{j=1}^{T}\prod_{i=1}^{L} \min\left(2A_j, 2V_i\right)\right)$$

where $V_i$ is the number of occurrences of the variable symbol in $p_i$, $A_j$ is the worst-case number of attribute errors in trial $j$, $n_i$ is the length of the first positive example for $p_i$ (which must have no attribute errors) and $m$ is the length of the example to be classified.

In Section 6, we apply our technique to obtain an algorithm to learn ordered forests composed of trees patterns $p_1, ..., p_L$. Our algorithm makes each prediction in polynomial time (for constant $L$) and has worst-case mistake bound

$$O\left(\left(\prod_{i=1}^{L} |p_i|\right)\left(\sum_{i=1}^{L} \log n_i\right) + \sum_{j=1}^{T}\prod_{i=1}^{L} \min\left(2A_j, |p_i|\right)\right)$$

where $A_j$ is the worst-case number of attribute errors in trial $j$, and $n_i$ is the length of the first positive example for $p_i$ (which must have no attribute errors). As in the case of pattern languages with fixed length substitutions, it has been shown that in the exact learning model with equivalence queries only, efficient learnability of ordered forests implies efficient learnability of DNFs [2]. Thus, it seems unlikely that unions of arbitrary number of ordered tree patterns can be learned in the mistake bound model.

In all of our algorithms, the requirement that the learner is initially given a noise free positive example for each pattern or tree pattern in the target can be relaxed. One way is to sample the instance space for positive labeled instances. If the attribute noise rate is low then with high probability, we can obtain one noise-free positive example for each (tree) pattern unless the positive instances for a particular (tree) pattern do not occur frequently. In the latter, we can ignore that (tree) pattern. We can then run our algorithms for each $L$-subset of these positive examples and use the weighted majority algorithm [30] of Littlestone and Warmuth to "filter out" the optimum algorithm.

## 3   Preliminaries

In concept learning, each instance in an instance space $\mathcal{X}$ is labeled according to some target concept $f$. The target concept is assumed to be some concept class $\mathcal{C}$. The model used here is the *on-line* (a.k.a. *mistake-bound*) learning model [28, 6]. In this model, learning proceeds in a, possibly infinite, sequence of trials. In each trial, the learner is presented with an instance $X_t$ from some domain $\mathcal{X}$. The learner is required to make, in polynomial time, a prediction on the classification of $X_t$. In return, the learner receives the desired output $f(X_t)$ as feedback.

A mistake is made if the prediction does not match the desired output. The learner's objective is to minimize the total number of mistakes.

An important result in this model is Littlestone's algorithm Winnow for learning small conjunctions (or disjunctions) of boolean attributes when there is a large number $n$ of irrelevant attributes. Winnow maintains a linear threshold functions $\sum_{i=1}^{n} w_i x_i \geq \theta$ where $w_i$ is a weight that is associated with the boolean attribute $x_i$. Initially, all the weights are equal to 1. Upon receiving an input $\langle v_1, \cdots, v_n \rangle$, the algorithm predicts true if the sum $\sum_{i=1}^{n} w_i v_i$ is greater than the fixed threshold $\theta$ and false otherwise. Typically, the threshold is set to $n$.

If the prediction is wrong then the weights are updated as follows. Suppose the algorithm predicts false but the instance is in the target concept. Winnow *promotes* the weight $w_i$, for each attribute $x_i$ in the instance that is set to 1, by multiplying $w_i$ by some constant update factor $\alpha$ for $\alpha > 1$ (typically, we set $\alpha = 2$). Otherwise, the algorithm must have predicted true but the instance is not in the target concept. In this case, for each literal $x_i$ in the instance that is set to 1, Winnow *demotes* the weight $w_i$ by dividing it by $\alpha$.

The number of attribute errors of a labeled example $\langle X_t, y_t \rangle$, with respect to the target disjunction, is the number of attributes of $X_t$ that have to be changed so that the classification of the resulting example by the target is consistent with $y_t$. In the presence of attribute noise, Littlestone offers the following performance guarantee for Winnow.

**Theorem 1.** *[29] Suppose, the target concept is a k-conjunction (or k-disjunction) and makes at most A attribute errors. Then Winnow makes at most* $O(A + k \log(N))$ *mistakes on any sequence of trials.*

Auer and Warmuth [12] suggested a version of Winnow which tolerates concept drift. Here the target disjunction may drift (change slowly) in time. The idea is that when a weight is sufficiently small, we do not demote it any further. We restrict our discussion in this paper to the original version of Winnow but remark that we could use the drift-tolerant version of Winnow to yield results that tolerates shifts (details omitted).

## 4 Learning Unions of Pattern Languages with Fixed Length Substitutions

Although general pattern languages are difficult to learn, we prove the following theorem which states that if the target concept is a union of $L$ (a constant number of) pattern languages that have fixed length substitutions then we can learn it efficiently in the on-line model with the presence of attribute noise. We note that for the case of a single pattern with fixed length substitutions without any attribute noise, one can use a direct application of the halving algorithm [14, 28] to obtain an algorithm with a polynomial mistake bound. Along with the restrictions mentioned above, when directly using the halving algorithm exponential time is required to make each prediction. The algorithm we present handles a union of a constant number of patterns, is robust against attribute noise, and each prediction is made in polynomial time.

We first prove our result for the case where the target is a single pattern with no attribute noise. Then, we generalize our result to unions of patterns in the presence of attribute noise.

**Lemma 2.** *Suppose the target concept is the pattern language $\mathcal{L}(p)$ with fixed length substitutions. Further, suppose that $p$ is composed of variables $x_1, \ldots, x_k$ with $V$ total occurrences of the variable symbols in $p$. Then the target concept can be efficiently learned in the mistake bound model with $O\left((2V - k + 1)\log n\right)$ mistakes in the worst case. The time complexity per trial is $O\left(n^3\right)$ where $n$ is the length of the first (positive) counterexample.*

*Proof.* Our algorithm obtains its first positive counterexample by predicting negative until it gets a positive counterexample $s_0$. Let $n$ be the length of $s_0$. Since all substitutions of the same variable in the target have the same length, we know that if an instance has length different from $n$ then it is a negative instance. Thus, without loss of generality, we assume all the instances are exactly of length $n$. We denote the substring of a string $s$ that begins at position $i$ and ends at position $j$ by $s[i, j]$ and the $i$th symbol of $s$ is denoted by $s[i]$. To make a prediction on an instance $s$, we transform $s$ to a new instance with the following sets of boolean attributes:

- $X[i, j, l], 1 \leq i < j \leq n, 1 \leq l \leq n - j + 1$. Each variable $X[i, j, l]$ is set to 1 if and only if the two substrings $s[i, i + l - 1]$ and $s[j, j + l - 1]$ are identical.
- $C[i, j], 1 \leq i \leq j \leq n$. The variable $C[i, j]$ is set to 1 if and only if the substrings $s[i, j]$ and $s_0[i, j]$ are the same.

We note that our reduction is a refinement of a more direct reduction that uses $O(n^2)$ variables (versus the $O(n^3)$ variables used above) for the case where the length of the substitutions must always be one. The following claim shows that by introducing the $\frac{n^3}{6} + o(n^3)$ variables of the form $X[i, j, l]$, the target concept can be represented as a conjunction where the number of relevant variables is independent of $n$ (versus having a linear dependence on $n$). By applying Winnow to learn this conjunction, we obtain a mistake bound with a logarithmic dependence on $n$ versus a linear dependence on $n$.

*Claim.* The target $k$-variable pattern $p$ can be expressed in the transformed instance space as a conjunction of $2V - k + 1$ attributes. Here, $V$ is the total number of occurrences of the variable symbols in $p$.

*Proof.* Since the substitutions of the same variable $x$ must be of the same length $l(x)$, the substitution of a particular variable symbol in all positive instances must appear in the same locations. That is, for the variable symbol $x$ to appear in a particular location in $p$, its substitution in a positive instance must appear in position $i$ to $i + l(x) - 1$ for some fixed $i$. The substitutions for a variable $x$ that appears in two distinct positions $i$ and $j$ are the same iff $X[i, j, l(x)] = 1$.

Consider a particular variable, say $x_i$. Suppose that $x_i$ appears in a positive instance at positions $j_1 < \ldots < j_{\alpha_i}$. Then for an instance to be positive, the $(\alpha_i - 1)$ transformed variables $X[j_1, j_2, l(x_i)], \ldots, X[j_{\alpha_i-1}, j_{\alpha_i}, l(x_i)]$ must all be set to 1. Conversely, if one of these transformed variables are set to 0 then the instance must be negative.

Further, suppose $s_0[i, j]$ is a substring of $s_0$ that corresponds to a maximal substring in $p$ consisting of only terminal symbols. In other words, all symbols in $s_0[i, j]$ are terminal symbols in $p$, but $s_0[i - 1]$ and $s_0[j + 1]$ are symbols obtained from substituting a variable with a string of terminal symbols. Notice again that the substitution of a variable symbol must appear at a specific location and be of the same length. Therefore, for an instance $s$ to be positive, the substring $s[i, j]$ and $s_0[i, j]$ must be the same. The latter means that $C[i, j]$ must be set to 1. Conversely, if for some $s_0[i, j]$ that corresponds to a maximal substring in $p$ consisting of only terminal symbols, the substring $s[i, j]$ of some instance $s$ does not match $s_0[i, j]$ (i.e. $C[i, j] = 0$) then $s$ must be negative. There are at most $V + 1$ of the $C[i, j]$'s that are positive (since each one, except the last, must end with one of the $V$ variables).

A positive instance $s$ is positive if and only if (1) all the variables of the same variable symbol are substituted by the same strings of terminal symbols and (2) none of the substrings in $p$ consisting of terminal symbols only are substituted. The above discussion implies that (1) and (2) can be ensured by checking at most $\sum_{i=1}^{k}(\alpha_i - 1) = V - k$ variables $X[i, j, l]$'s and $V + 1$ variables $C[i, j]$'s are all 1s, respectively.    □

Consider the pattern $p = x_1 1 x_3 01 x_2 001 x_1 x_2 11 x_1$ with $l(x_1) = 3, l(x_2) = 4, l(x_3) = 2$ as an example. The proof of the above claim says that it can be represented as the conjunction

$$(C[4, 4] \wedge C[7, 8] \wedge C[13, 15] \wedge C[23, 24]) \bigwedge (X[1, 16, 3] \wedge X[16, 25, 3]) \bigwedge X[9, 19, 4]$$

The variable $x_1$ must appear at position 1, 16 and 25. Thus, the target conjunction must contain the variable $X[1, 16, 3]$ and $X[16, 25, 3]$. The substring $s[4, 4]$ of any positive instance $s$ must always be the same as $s_0[4, 4]$ and is the string "1". Thus, $C[4, 4]$ must be present. The presence of other attributes can be similarly explained.

From the above claim we know that there are at most $2V - k + 1$ *relevant* attributes. Combined with the fact that there are $O(n^3)$ boolean attributes, we obtain the desired mistake bound of Lemma 2 by applying Winnow. (Since Winnow learns a disjunction of boolean attributes, we apply Winnow to learn the negation of the target concept which is represented as a disjunction of the negations of the attributes.) A straightforward implementation of the above idea would have time complexity of $O(n^4)$ per trial. To reduce the time complexity, for each distinct pair of $i$ and $j$, $1 \leq i < j \leq n$, the learner first finds the longest common substring of the string that begins at position $i$ and the string that begins at position $j$. Say the common substring is of length $l'$. Then the learner sets all variables $X[i, j, l], 1 \leq l \leq l'$ to 1 and $X[i, j, l], l > l'$ to 0. The

$C[i, j]$'s can be evaluated in a similar way. This implementation reduces the time complexity to $O(n^3)$ per trial. This completes the proof of Lemma 2. $\qquad\square$

We now extend this result for the case of a union of a constant number of patterns with fixed length substitutions under attribute noise.

**Theorem 3.** *Suppose the target concept is a union of pattern languages $\mathcal{L}(p_1)$, ..., $\mathcal{L}(p_L)$ with fixed length substitutions. Further, suppose that for $1 \le i \le L$, $p_i$ has $k_i$ variables and $V_i$ total occurrences of variable symbols. Then the target concept can be efficiently learned in the mistake bound model. The number of mistakes made after $T$ trials is bounded by*

$$O\left(\left(\prod_{i=1}^{L}(2V_i - k_i + 1)\right)\left(\sum_{i=1}^{L}\log n_i\right) + \sum_{j=1}^{T}\prod_{i=1}^{L}\min\left(2A_j, 2V_i - k_i + 1\right)\right)$$

*in the worst case. The time complexity per trial is $O\left((n_1...n_L)^3\right)$. We assume that initially the learner is given a noise-free positive example, of length $n_i$, for each pattern $p_i$. Here, $A_i$ is the number of attribute errors in the $i^{\text{th}}$ trial. (For this bound to be meaningful, we assume $A_i$ is zero in most of the trials.)*

*Proof.* First we consider the case where the target is a union of $L$ patterns satisfying the condition of Theorem 3, but with no attribute noise. In this case, each pattern $p_i$ can be represented as a conjunction $C_i$ of $2V_i - k_i + 1$ attributes. The target is a disjunction $\hat{f}$ of the $C_i$'s. Thus, its complement can be represented as a $\prod_{i=1}^{L}(2V_i - k_i + 1)$-term DNF which we denote by $f'$. The term in $\hat{f}$ must contain exactly one literal from the set of transformed attributes corresponding to a pattern $p_i$, $i = 1, ..., L$. Since there are at most $O(n_i^3)$ attributes for each pattern $p_i$, there are at most $O((n_1...n_L)^3)$ possible terms to consider. Each such candidate term can be treated as a new attribute. Applying Winnow would then give us the desired mistake bound. Further, as before, the transformed attributes corresponding to the pattern $p_i$ can be computed in $O(n_i^3)$ time. Thus, the time complexity to update the $O((n_1...n_L)^3)$ attributes is $O((n_1...n_L)^3)$.

Finally, we introduce attribute errors. Suppose $A_j$ symbol errors occur at trial $j$. Each symbol error can result in at most two relevant attributes of $C_i$ being complemented. There are at most $2V_i - k_i + 1$ literals in $C_i$. Thus, at most $\min(2A_j, 2V_i - k_i + 1)$ of the attributes in $C_i$ are complemented. This implies that at most $\prod_{i=1}^{L}\min(2A_j, 2V_i - k_i + 1)$ attributes in $f'$ are complemented. This gives us the second term in the mistake bound that is due to attribute errors. $\qquad\square$

The next theorem suggests that it appears necessary to bound the number of patterns in the target for it be efficiently learnable.

**Theorem 4.** *In the mistake bound model, if unions of arbitrary number of pattern languages with fixed length substitution restriction can be learned efficiently, then DNFs can be learned efficiently.*

*Proof.* Suppose the learner is asked to learn a DNF $f$ in the mistake bound model. Without loss of generality, we can assume $f$ is monotone and there are $n$

variables $x_1, ..., x_n$. Let $\{0,1\}$ and $\{\alpha_1, ..., \alpha_n\}$ be sets of terminal and variable symbols, respectively. Each term $t$ in $f$ can be represented as a pattern $p(t)$ with $n$ characters. The $i^{\text{th}}$ character is set to 1 if the literal $x_i$ is in term $t$ and $\alpha_i$ otherwise. We represent an instance $x$ as an $n$-bit vector (string). If we restrict $l(\alpha_i) = 1$ for all $\alpha_i$'s then clearly, $t(x) = 1$ iff $x \in \mathcal{L}(p(t))$. This is a polynomial-time prediction preserving reduction [37], which completes the proof.     □

## 5    Learning Unions of One-Variable Pattern Languages

We now consider the case of one-variable patterns without the fixed length substitution requirement. As in the last section, we first prove our result for the case where the target is a single pattern with no attribute noise. Then, we apply the same technique to generalize this result to unions of patterns in the presence of attribute noise.

**Lemma 5.** *Suppose the target concept is a one-variable pattern $p$ with $V$ occurrences of the variable symbol. Then the target concept can be efficiently learned in the mistake bound model with $O(V \log n)$ mistakes in the worst case. The time complexity per trial is $O(n^4 mV) = O(n^5 m)$ where $n$ is the length of the first (positive) counterexample and $m$ is the length of the example to be classified.*

*Proof.* The learner guesses negative until obtaining a positive counterexample $s_0$. Denote the length of $s_0$ by $n$, and the starting position[1] of the $i^{\text{th}}$ (counting from the leftmost end of the pattern) substitution of the variable $x$ by $\alpha_i$. For a moment, we assume the learner is told the number of occurrences $V$ of the variable symbols in the target, and length $\ell$ of the substituted terminal string.

Suppose the learner is asked to classify a given unlabeled instance $s$ of length $m$. If the difference in length of $s_0$ and $s$ is not divisible by $V$ then we can conclude immediately that $s$ must be classified negative. Henceforth, we assume the difference between the lengths of $s_0$ and $s$ is divisible by $V$. If $s$ is positive then the substitution of $x$ in $s$ has length $\ell' = \ell + \frac{m-n}{V}$. The $i^{\text{th}}$ substitution of $x$ in $s$ must begin at location $\alpha'_i = \alpha_i + (i-1)\frac{m-n}{V}$ and the substitution for the variable $x$ is the substring $s[\alpha'_i, \alpha'_i + \ell' - 1]$. In other words, to see if all substitutions of $x$ in $s$ are the same, we simply check for all $i = 2, ..., V$, whether $s[\alpha'_{i-1}, \alpha'_{i-1} + \ell' - 1] = s[\alpha'_i, \alpha'_i + \ell' - 1]$. If this is not so then we can immediately conclude that $s \notin \mathcal{L}(p)$.

Unfortunately, we do not know the $\alpha_i$'s. To circumvent this problem, we introduce new attributes $X[\beta, \gamma, i], 2 \le \beta < \gamma \le n, 1 \le i \le V$ such that $X[\beta, \gamma, i]$ is set to true if and only if the substring $s[\beta + (i-1)\frac{m-n}{V}, \beta + (i-1)\frac{m-n}{V} + \ell' - 1]$ is the same as $s[\gamma + i\frac{m-n}{V}, \gamma + i\frac{m-n}{V} + \ell' - 1]$. Clearly, if all substitutions of $x$ in $s$ are the same then the $(V-1)$-conjunction

$$C_X = X[\alpha_1, \alpha_2, 2] \wedge \ldots \wedge X[\alpha_{i-1}, \alpha_i, i] \wedge \ldots \wedge X[\alpha_{V-1}, \alpha_V, V]$$

is satisfied, and vice versa.

---

[1] These positions are not known to the learner.

To classify an instance correctly as positive, we also need to ensure that the terminal symbols in $p$ remain the same. Let $\alpha_0 = -\ell$ and $\alpha_{V+1} = n$. Then clearly, the $i^{\text{th}}$ substring of terminal symbols between the $i^{\text{th}}$ variable symbol and $i + 1^{\text{st}}$ variable symbol is the string $s_0[\alpha_i + \ell, \alpha_{i+1} - 1]$ (which is defined to be the empty string if $\alpha_i + \ell > \alpha_{i+1} - 1$). If none of the terminal symbols in this maximal substring of terminal symbols is changed in $s$ then it must appear in $s[\alpha_i' + \ell', \alpha_{i+1}' - 1]$. In other words, to check if none of the terminal symbols in the target has been replaced, it is sufficient and necessary to verify that

$$s[\alpha_i' + \ell', \alpha_{i+1}' - 1] = s_0[\alpha_i + \ell, \alpha_{i+1} - 1] \ \forall i = 0, ..., V \tag{1}$$

As before, since we do not know where the $\alpha_i$'s are, we introduce new attributes $C[i, B, E], 0 \leq i \leq V, 1 \leq B \leq E \leq n$. We set $C[i, B, E]$ to 1 when $s[B + i\frac{m-n}{V}, E + i\frac{m-n}{V}] = s_0[B, E]$. It is easy to verify that saying Equation 1 is satisfied is the same as saying the conjunction $C_T$ (shown below) is satisfied.

$$C_T = \bigwedge_{i=0}^{V} C[i, \alpha_i + \ell, \alpha_{i+1} - 1]$$

Therefore, the target pattern $p$ can be represented as a conjunction $C_T \wedge C_X$ of $2V$ boolean attributes. There are $O(n^2V)$ possible attributes to consider. Thus by running Winnow to learn $C_T \wedge C_X$ guarantees at most $O(2V(\log n + \log V)) = O(2V \log n)$ mistakes are made (since $V \leq n$).

The question remains in guessing $\ell$ and $V$ correctly. Well there are only $O(n^2)$ such guesses. We can run one copy of the above algorithm for each guess and run weighted majority algorithm [30] on these algorithms. The mistake bound is $O(\log(n^2) + 2V \log n) = O(V \log n)$ with running time $O(n^4mV) = O(n^5m)$. $\quad\square$

Lemma 5 can be extended to learn unions of one-variable pattern languages in the presence of attribute noise (except for the first counterexample which must be noise free). The bound obtained is shown in the next theorem.

**Theorem 6.** *Suppose the target concept $p$ is a union of one-variable pattern languages $\mathcal{L}(p_1), ..., \mathcal{L}(p_L)$. Further, suppose the number of occurrences of the variable symbol in $p_i$ is $V_i$. Then $p$ can be efficiently learned in the mistake bound model. The number of mistakes made after $T$ trials is bounded by*

$$O\left(\left(\prod_{i=1}^{L} 2V_i\right)\left(\sum_{i=1}^{L} \log n_i\right) + \sum_{t=1}^{T}\prod_{i=1}^{L} 2\min\left(A_j, V_i\right)\right)$$

*in the worst case. The time complexity per trial is $O\left(m(n_1...n_L)^4 \sum_{i=1}^{L} V_i\right) = O\left(m(n_1...n_L)^5\right)$. Here,*

- *We assume that initially the learner is given a noise-free positive example, of length $n_i$, for each pattern $p_i$.*
- *$m$ is the length of the unlabeled example to be classified in the $T + 1^{\text{st}}$ trial.*

- $A_i$ is the number of attribute errors in the $i^{th}$ trial. (For this bound to be meaningful, we assume that $A_i$ is zero in most of the trials.)

*Proof.* (Sketch) We obtain this result by extending Lemma 5 to unions of languages with attribute noise using the same technique as that used in extending Lemma 2 to Theorem 3.                                               □

## 6  Learning Ordered Forests

We have demonstrated how the problem of learning unions of pattern languages can be reduced to learning conjunctions of boolean attributes. Next, we apply this idea to learning ordered forests with bounded number of trees. No restrictions are needed on the number of children per node or the alphabet size for the terminal symbols.

**Theorem 7.** *Ordered forests composed of trees patterns $p_1, ..., p_L$ can be efficiently learned in the on-line model. The number of mistakes made after $T$ trials is bounded by*

$$O\left(\left(\prod_{i=1}^{L} |p_i|\right)\left(\sum_{i=1}^{L} \log n_i\right) + \sum_{j=1}^{T}\prod_{i=1}^{L} \min\left(2A_j, |p_i|\right)\right)$$

*in the worst case. The time complexity per trial is $O\left((n_1...n_L)^3\right)$. Here,*

- *We assume that initially the learner is given a noise-free positive example, of length $n_i$, for each tree pattern $p_i$.*
- *$A_j$ is the number of attribute errors in the $(j)$th trial. (For this bound to be meaningful, we assume that $A_j$ is zero in most of the trials.)*                □

*Proof.* (Sketch) We present only the proof for the case of learning a single ordered tree pattern. The extension of the proof to the case of learning ordered forests in the presence of attribute errors is like that used to prove Theorem 3.

Suppose $t$ is a tree and $u$ is a node in $t$. Let $\text{path}_t(u)$ denote the labeled path obtained by traversing from the root of $t$ to $u$. Given two distinct trees $t$ and $t'$, we say $\text{path}_t(u) = \text{path}_{t'}(u')$ if and only if the sequences of the node labels (except for the last) and the branches taken as we traversed from the root of $t$ to $u$ and from the root of $t'$ to $u'$ are the same. As before, we simply keep predicting negative until we get a positive counterexample $t_0$. Let $n$ denote the number of nodes in $t_0$.

To make a prediction on an instance $t$, we transform $t$ to a new instance with the following set of $O(n^2)$ attributes (See Figure 1 for an illustration).

- For each vertex $u_0$ in $t_0$, we introduce a new attribute $C[u_0]$. This attribute is set to 1 if and only if $\text{path}_{t_0}(u_0) = \text{path}_t(u)$ for some node $u$ in $t$, and the labels of the nodes $u$ in $t$ and $u_0$ in $t_0$ are the same.

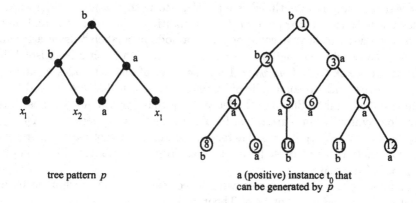

tree pattern $p$

a (positive) instance $t_0$ that
can be generated by $p$

**Fig. 1.** The figure on the left shows a tree pattern $p$. The figure on the right is a tree instance $t_0$ that can be generated by $p$. If $t_0$ is the first counterexample obtained then the conjunctive representation of $p$ is $C[1] \land C[2] \land C[3] \land C[6] \land X[4, 7]$.

- For each distinct pair of nodes $u_0$ and $v_0$ in $t_0$, we introduce a new attribute $X[u_0, v_0]$. $X[u_0, v_0]$ is set to 1 if and only if there are two distinct nodes $u$ and $v$ in $t$ that satisfies:

  1. $\text{path}_{t_0}(u_0) = \text{path}_t(u)$ and $\text{path}_{t_0}(v_0) = \text{path}_t(v)$
  2. The two subtrees in $t$ that are rooted at $u$ and $v$ are identical. (Since the siblings are distinguishable, we can check that the subtrees are identical in linear time).

Let $t'$ be the new instance with $\binom{n}{2}$ boolean attributes obtained by the above transformation.

*Claim.* The target tree pattern $p$ can be represented as a conjunction $f$ of at most $|p|$ of the new boolean attributes such that given an instance $t$, the transformed instance $t'$ is classified positive by $f$ iff $t$ is classified as positive by $p$.

*Proof.* To verify an instance $t$ is in $\mathcal{L}(p)$, it is necessary and sufficient to ensure the following two conditions are satisfied.

1. For each node $\hat{u}$ in $p$ that is labeled by a terminal symbol, there is a corresponding node $u$ in $t$ such that $\text{path}_p(\hat{u}) = \text{path}_t(u)$ and both $\hat{u}$ and $u$ have the same terminal label.
2. For each pair of distinct leaves $\hat{u}$ and $\hat{v}$ in $p$ labeled by the same variable, there are two nodes $u$ and $v$ in $t$ such that $\text{path}_p(\hat{u}) = \text{path}_t(u)$ and $\text{path}_p(\hat{v}) = \text{path}_t(v)$. Furthermore, the subtrees in $t$ rooted at $u$ and $v$ are identical. That is, the substitutions in $t$ for $\hat{u}$ and $\hat{v}$ are the same.

Clearly, $\text{path}_p(\hat{u}) = \text{path}_t(u)$ is equivalent to $\text{path}_{t_0}(u_0) = \text{path}_t(u)$ for the nodes $u_0$ in $t_0$ that corresponds $\hat{u}$ in $p$. Condition 1 is satisfied if and only if for each node $u_0$ in $t_0$ that corresponds to a node in $p$ labeled using a terminal symbol, the attribute $C[u_0]$ is set to 1. To ensure Condition 2 is satisfied, it is sufficient to check that $X[u_0, v_0] = 1$ for each pair of distinct nodes $u_0$ and $v_0$ in $t_0$ that corresponds to some pair of distinct leaves in $p$ that are labeled by the same variable symbol. Suppose the leaves in $t_0$ that corresponds to substituting a variable symbol $x_i$ in $p$ are $l_1, ..., l_k$. Then it suffices to check that $X[l_1, l_2] = X[l_3, l_4] = ... = X[l_{k-1}, l_k] = 1$. Therefore, the target concept can be represented as a conjunctions of at most $|p|$ of the transformed attributes. This completes the proof of the claim.                                                                                    □

Combining the above Lemma with Theorem 1 and the technique used in Theorem 3 completes the proof of Theorem 7.                                                   □

Amoth, Cull and Tadepalli [2] have shown that DNF and the class of ordered forests with bounded[2] label alphabet size and bounded number of children per node are equivalent. Hence, it seems unlikely that unions of arbitrary number of tree patterns can be learned in the mistake bound model.

## 7   Conclusion

In this paper, we demonstrated how learning unions of pattern languages and pattern-related concept can be reduced to learning disjunctions of boolean attributes. In particular, we presented efficient on-line algorithms for learning unions of a constant number of tree patterns, unions of a constant number of one-variable pattern languages, and unions of a constant number of pattern languages with fixed length substitutions. All of our algorithms are robust against attribute noise and can be modified to handle concept drift. Further, our mistake bounds only have a logarithmic dependence on the length of the examples. The requirement that the learner be given a noise-free example for each pattern can be removed by sampling as discussed in Section 1.

There are several interesting future directions suggested by this work. As we have discussed, we could generalize the class of pattern languages by assigning a penalty (i.e. weight) to each violation of the rule that a terminal symbol cannot be changed. The weights can be different for different terminal symbols. Similarly, we can also assign a penalty to each violation of the rule that a pair of variable symbols, of the same variable, must be substituted by the same terminal string. If the penalty incurred by an instance for violating these rules is below a given tolerable threshold then it is in the target concept $\mathcal{L}'(p)$ generated by $p$. If the penalty is above the threshold then it is not in $\mathcal{L}'(p)$. It would be very interesting to explore applications for this extension and compare our approach to those currently in use.

---

[2] They showed that ordered forests can be learned using subset queries and equivalence queries. Further, if the alphabet size or number of children per node is unbounded, then subset queries can be simulated using membership queries by using a unique label or a subtree to stand for each variable.

In this paper, we solved one of the open problems suggested by Reischuk and Zeugmann [38]. Namely, we gave an efficient algorithm to learn unions of a constant number of one-variable pattern languages. We also were able to learn a unions constant number of pattern languages (with no restriction on the number of variables) when we restricted the substitutions to fixed length substitutions. A challenging open problem from Reischuk and Zeugmann that we did not resolve here is learning the class of 2-variable pattern languages (in the mistake bound model). While, additional tools will be needed to solve this problem, we feel that the technique proposed here may be applicable for this problem.

# References

[1] Andris Ambainis, Sanjay Jain, and Arun Sharma. Ordinal mind change complexity of language identification. In *Computational Learning Theory: Eurocolt '97*, pages 301–315. Springer-Verlag, 1997.

[2] Thomas R. Amoth, Paul Cull, and Prasad Tadepalli. Exact learning of tree patterns from queries and counterexamples. In *Proc. 11th Annu. Conf. on Comput. Learning Theory*, pages 175–186. ACM Press, New York, NY, 1998.

[3] Thomas R. Amoth, Paul Cull, and Prasad Tadepalli. Exact learning of unordered tree patterns from queries. In *Proc. 12th Annu. Conf. on Comput. Learning Theory*, pages 323–332. ACM Press, New York, NY, 1999.

[4] D. Angluin. Finding patterns common to a set of strings. *J. of Comput. Syst. Sci.*, 21:46–62, 1980.

[5] D. Angluin. Inductive inference of formal languages from positive data. *Inform. Control*, 45(2):117–135, May 1980.

[6] D. Angluin. Queries and concept learning. *Machine Learning*, 2(4):319–342, April 1988.

[7] S. Arikawa, S. Kuhara, S. Miyano, Y. Mukouchi, A. Shinohara, and T. Shinohara. A machine discovery from amino acid sequences by decision trees over regular patterns. In *Intern. Conference on Fifth Generation Computer Systems*, 1992.

[8] S. Arikawa, S. Miyano, A. Shinohara, T. Shinohara, and A.Yamamota. Algorithmic learning theory with elementary formal systems. In *IEICE Trans. Inf. and Syst.*, volume E75-D No 4, pages 405–414, 1992.

[9] S. Arikawa, A. Shinohara, S. Miyano, and A. Shinohara. More about learning elementary formal systems. In *Nonmonotonic and Inductive Logic, Lecture Notes in Artificial Intelligence*, volume 659, pages 107–117. Springer-Verlag, 1991.

[10] H. Arimura, H. Ishizaka, T. Shinohara, and S. Otsuki. A generalization of the least general generalization. In *Machine Learning*, volume 13, pages 59–85. Oxford Univ. Press, 1994.

[11] Hiroki Arimura, Hiroki Ishizaka, and Takeshi Shinohara. Learning unions of tree patterns using queries. In *Proc. 6th Int. Workshop on Algorithmic Learning Theory*, pages 66–79. Springer-Verlag, 1995.

[12] Peter Auer and Manfred Warmuth. Tracking the best disjunction. In *Proceedings of the 36th Annual Symposium on Foundations of Computer Science*, pages 312–321. IEEE Computer Society Press, Los Alamitos, CA, 1995.

[13] A. Bairoch. Prosite: A dictionary of sites and patterns in proteins. In *Nucleic Acid Research*, volume 19, pages 2241–2245, 1991.

[14] J. M. Barzdin and R. V. Frievald. On the prediction of general recursive functions. *Soviet Math. Doklady*, 13:1224–1228, 1972.

[15] C. Cardie. Empirical methods in information extraction. In *AI Magazine*, volume 18, pages 65–80, 1997.

[16] Thomas Erlebach, Peter Rossmanith, Hans Stadtherr, Angelika Steger, and Thomas Zeugmann. Learning one-variable pattern languages very efficiently on average, in parallel, and by asking queries. In *Algorithmic Learning Theory: ALT '97*, pages 260–276. Springer-Verlag, 1997.

[17] Sally A. Goldman, Stephen S. Kwek, and Stephen D. Scott. Agnostic learning of geometric patterns. In *Proc. 10th Annu. Conf. on Comput. Learning Theory*, pages 325–333. ACM Press, New York, NY, 1997.

[18] C. Hua and K. Ko. A note on the pattern-finding problem. Technical Report UH-CS-84-4, Department of Computer Science, University of Houston, 1984.

[19] O. H. Ibarra and T. Jiang. Learning regular languages from counterexamples. In *Proc. 1st Annu. Workshop on Comput. Learning Theory*, pages 371–385, San Mateo, CA, 1988. Morgan Kaufmann.

[20] Sanjay Jain and Arun Sharma. Elementary formal systems, intrinsic complexity, and procrastination. In *Proc. 9th Annu. Conf. on Comput. Learning Theory*, pages 181–192. ACM Press, New York, NY, 1996.

[21] K. P. Jantke. Polynomial-time inference of general pattern languages. In *Proceedings of the Symposium of Theoretical Aspects of Computer Science; Lecture Notes in Computer Science*, volume 166, pages 314–325. Springer, 1984.

[22] K. P. Jantke and S. Lange. Case-based representation and learning of pattern languages. In *Proc. 4th Internat. Workshop on Algorithmic Learning Theory*, pages 87–100. Springer-Verlag, 1993. Lecture Notes in Artificial Intelligence 744.

[23] C. Page Jr. and A. Frisch. Generalization and learnability: A study of constrained atoms. In *Inductive Logic Programming*, pages 29–61, 1992.

[24] M. Kearns and L. Pitt. A polynomial-time algorithm for learning $k$-variable pattern languages from examples. In *Proc. 2nd Annu. Workshop on Comput. Learning Theory*, pages 57–71, San Mateo, CA, 1989. Morgan Kaufmann.

[25] K. Ko, A. Marron, and W. Tzeng. Learnig string patterns and tree patterns from examples. abstract. In *State University of New York Stony Brook*, 1989.

[26] K. Ko and W. Tzeng. Three $\Sigma_2^p$-complete problems in computational learning theory. *Computational Complexity*, 1(3):269–310, 1991.

[27] S. Lange and R. Wiehagen. Polynomial time inference of arbitrary pattern languages. *New Generation Computing*, 8:361–370, 1991.

[28] N. Littlestone. Learning when irrelevant attributes abound: A new linear-threshold algorithm. *Machine Learning*, 2:285–318, 1988.

[29] N. Littlestone. Redundant noisy attributes, attribute errors, and linear threshold learning using Winnow. In *Proc. 4th Annu. Workshop on Comput. Learning Theory*, pages 147–156, San Mateo, CA, 1991. Morgan Kaufmann.

[30] N. Littlestone and M. K. Warmuth. The weighted majority algorithm. *Information and Computation*, 108(2):212–261, 1994.

[31] A. Marron. Learning pattern languages from a single initial example and from queries. In *Proc. 1st Annu. Workshop on Comput. Learning Theory*, pages 345–358, San Mateo, CA, 1988. Morgan Kaufmann.

[32] Satoshi Matsumoto and Ayumi Shinohara. Learning pattern languages using queries. In *Computational Learning Theory: Eurocolt '97*, pages 185–197. Springer-Verlag, 1997.

[33] Andrew R. Mitchell. Learnability of a subclass of extended pattern languages. In *Proc. 11th Annu. Conf. on Comput. Learning Theory*, pages 64–71. ACM Press, New York, NY, 1998.

[34] T. Mitchell, P. Utgoff, and R. Banerji. Learning by experimentation: Acquiring and refining problem solving heuristics. In *R. Michalski, J. Carbonell, T. Mitchell eds., Machine Learning*, pages 163–190. Palo Alto, CA: Tioga, 1983.

[35] S. Miyano, A. Shinohara, and T. Shinohara. Which classes of elementary formal systems are polynomial-time learnable? In *Proc. 2nd Int. Workshop on Algorithmic Learning Theory*, pages 139–150. IOS Press, 1992.

[36] R. Nix. Editing by example. In *Proc. 11th ACM Symposium on Principles of Programming Languages*, pages 186–195. ACM Press, 1984.

[37] L. Pitt and M. K. Warmuth. Prediction preserving reducibility. *J. of Comput. Syst. Sci.*, 41(3):430–467, December 1990. Special issue of the for the *Third Annual Conference of Structure in Complexity Theory* (Washington, DC., June 88).

[38] Rüdiger Reischuk and Thomas Zeugmann. Learning one-variable pattern languages in linear average time. In *Proc. 11th Annu. Conf. on Comput. Learning Theory*, pages 198–208. ACM Press, New York, NY, 1998.

[39] R. E. Schapire. Pattern languages are not learnable. In *Proc. 3rd Annu. Workshop on Comput. Learning Theory*, pages 122–129, San Mateo, CA, 1990. Morgan Kaufmann.

[40] T. Shinohara. Polynomial time inference of extended regular pattern languages. In *RIMS Symposia on Software Science and Engineering, Kyoto, Japan*, pages 115–127. Springer Verlag, 1982. Lecture Notes in Computer Science 147.

[41] T. Shinohara. Polynomial time inference of pattern languages and its applications. Proceedings, 7th IBM Symp. on Math. Foundations of Computer Science, 1982.

[42] E. Tateishi, O. Maruyama, and S. Miyano. Extracting motifs from positive and negative sequence data. In *Proc. 13th Symposium on Theoretical Aspects of Computer Science, Lecture Notes in Computer Science 1046*, pages 219–230, 1996.

[43] E. Tateishi and S. Miyano. A greedy strategy for finding motifs from positive and negative examples. In *Proc. First Pacific Symposium on Biocomputing*, pages 599–613. World Scientific Press, 1996.

[44] R. Wiehagen and T. Zeugmann. Ingnoring data may be the only way to learn efficiently. *Journal of Experimental and Artificial Intelligence*, 6:131–144, 1994.

[45] K. Wright. Identification of unions of languages drawn from an identifiable class. In *Proc. 2nd Annu. Workshop on Comput. Learning Theory*, pages 328–333. Morgan Kaufmann, 1989. (See also the correction by Motoki, Shinohara and Wright in the Proceedings of the Fourth Annual Workshop on Computational Learning Theory, page 375, 1991).

[46] T. Zeugmann. Lange and Wiehagen's pattern language learning algorithm: An average-case analysis with respect to its total learning time. Technical Report RIFIS-TR-CS-111, RIFIS, Kyushu University 33, 1995.

# Author Index

Balcázar, José L., 77
Bshouty, Nader H., 206

Castro, Jorge, 77
Cheung, Dennis, 231

Dalmau, Víctor, 301
De Comité, Francesco, 219
Denis, François, 219
Domingo, Carlos, 241

Eiron, Nadav, 206
Evgeniou, Theodoros, 106

Fukumizu, Kenji, 51

Gilleron, Rémi, 219
Goldman, Sally A., 347
Grieser, Gunter, 118
Guijarro, David, 77, 313

Haraguchi, Makoto, 194
Hermo, Montserrat, 291
Hirata, Kouichi, 157

Kalnishkan, Yuri, 323
Kushilevitz, Eyal, 206
Kwek, Stephen S., 347

Lange, Steffen, 118
Lavín, Víctor, 291
Letouzey, Fabien, 219

Mitchell, Andrew, 93
Morik, Katharina, 1
Morita, Nobuhiro, 194

Nessel, Jochen, 264
Nock, Richard, 182

Okubo, Yoshiaki, 194

Pontil, Massimiliano, 106, 252

Rifkin, Ryan, 252
Rossmanith, Peter, 132

Sasaki, Yutaka, 169
Schapire, Robert E., 13
Scheffer, Tobias, 93
Sharma, Arun, 93
Simon, Hans-Ulrich, 77
Stephan, Frank, 93, 276

Takimoto, Eiji, 335
Tarui, Jun, 313
Tsukiji, Tatsuie, 313

Verri, Alessandro, 252

Warmuth, Manfred K., 335
Watanabe, Sumio, 39
Watson, Phil, 145
Wiedermann, Jiří, 63

Yamanishi, Kenji, 26

Zeugmann, Thomas, 276

# Lecture Notes in Artificial Intelligence (LNAI)

Vol. 1599: T. Ishida (Ed.), Multiagent Platforms. Proceedings, 1998. VIII, 187 pages. 1999.

Vol. 1600: M. J. Wooldridge, M. Veloso (Eds.), Artificial Intelligence Today. VIII, 489 pages. 1999.

Vol. 1604: M. Asada, H. Kitano (Eds.), RoboCup-98: Robot Soccer World Cup II. XI, 509 pages. 1999.

Vol. 1609: Z. W. Ras, A. Skowron (Eds.), Foundations of Intelligent Systems. Proceedings, 1999. XII, 676 pages. 1999.

Vol. 1611: I. Imam, Y. Kodratoff, A. El-Dessouki, M. Ali (Eds.), Multiple Approaches to Intelligent Systems. Proceedings, 1999. XIX, 899 pages. 1999.

Vol. 1612: R. Bergmann, S. Breen, M. Göker, M. Manago, S. Wess, Developing Industrial Case-Based Reasoning Applications. XX, 188 pages. 1999.

Vol. 1617: N.V. Murray (Ed.), Automated Reasoning with Analytic Tableaux and Related Methods. Proceedings, 1999. X, 325 pages. 1999.

Vol. 1620: W. Horn, Y. Shahar, G. Lindberg, S. Andreassen, J. Wyatt (Eds.), Artificial Intelligence in Medicine. Proceedings, 1999. XIII, 454 pages. 1999.

Vol. 1621: D. Fensel, R. Studer (Eds.), Knowledge Acquisition Modeling and Management. Proceedings, 1999. XI, 404 pages. 1999.

Vol. 1623: T. Reinartz, Focusing Solutions for Data Mining. XV, 309 pages. 1999.

Vol. 1630: M. M. Huntbach, G. A. Ringwood, Agent-Oriented Programming. XIV, 386 pages. 1999.

Vol. 1632: H. Ganzinger (Ed.), Automated Deduction – CADE-16. Proceedings, 1999. XIV, 429 pages. 1999.

Vol. 1634: S. Džeroski, P. Flach (Eds.), Inductive Logic Programming. Proceedings, 1999. VIII, 303 pages. 1999.

Vol. 1637: J.P. Walser, Integer Optimization by Local Search. XIX, 137 pages. 1999.

Vol. 1638: A. Hunter, S. Parsons (Eds.), Symbolic and Quantitative Approaches to Reasoning and Uncertainty. Proceedings, 1999. IX, 397 pages. 1999.

Vol. 1640: W. Tepfenhart, W. Cyre (Eds.), Conceptual Structures: Standards and Practices. Proceedings, 1999. XII, 515 pages. 1999.

Vol. 1647: F.J. Garijo, M. Boman (Eds.), Multi-Agent System Engineering. Proceedings, 1999. X, 233 pages. 1999.

Vol. 1650: K.-D. Althoff, R. Bergmann, L.K. Branting (Eds.), Case-Based Reasoning Research and Development. Proceedings, 1999. XII, 598 pages. 1999.

Vol. 1652: M. Klusch, O.M. Shehory, G. Weiss (Eds.), Cooperative Information Agents III. Proceedings, 1999. XI, 404 pages. 1999.

Vol. 1669: X.-S. Gao, D. Wang, L. Yang (Eds.), Automated Deduction in Geometry. Proceedings, 1998. VII, 287 pages. 1999.

Vol. 1674: D. Floreano, J.-D. Nicoud, F. Mondada (Eds.), Advances in Artificial Life. Proceedings, 1999. XVI, 737 pages. 1999.

Vol. 1688: P. Bouquet, L. Serafini, P. Brézillon, M. Benerecetti, F. Castellani (Eds.), Modeling and Using Context. Proceedings, 1999. XII, 528 pages. 1999.

Vol. 1692: V. Matoušek, P. Mautner, J. Ocelíková, P. Sojka (Eds.), Text, Speech, and Dialogue. Proceedings, 1999. XI, 396 pages. 1999.

Vol. 1695: P. Barahona, J.J. Alferes (Eds.), Progress in Artificial Intelligence. Proceedings, 1999. XI, 385 pages. 1999.

Vol. 1699: S. Albayrak (Ed.), Intelligent Agents for Telecommunication Applications. Proceedings, 1999. IX, 191 pages. 1999.

Vol. 1701: W. Burgard, T. Christaller, A.B. Cremers (Eds.), KI-99: Advances in Artificial Intelligence. Proceedings, 1999. XI, 311 pages. 1999.

Vol. 1704: Jan M. Żytkow, J. Rauch (Eds.), Principles of Data Mining and Knowledge Discovery. Proceedings, 1999. XIV, 593 pages. 1999.

Vol. 1705: H. Ganzinger, D. McAllester, A. Voronkov (Eds.), Logic for Programming and Automated Reasoning. Proceedings, 1999. XII, 397 pages. 1999.

Vol. 1711: N. Zhong, A. Skowron, S. Ohsuga (Eds.), New Directions in Rough Sets, Data Mining, and Granular-Soft Computing. Proceedings, 1999. XIV, 558 pages. 1999.

Vol. 1712: H. Boley, A Tight, Practical Integration of Relations and Functions. XI, 169 pages. 1999.

Vol. 1714: M.T. Pazienza (Eds.), Information Extraction. IX, 165 pages. 1999.

Vol. 1715: P. Perner, M. Petrou (Eds.), Machine Learning and Data Mining in Pattern Recognition. Proceedings, 1999. VIII, 217 pages. 1999.

Vol. 1720: O. Watanabe, T. Yokomori (Eds.), Algorithmic Learning Theory. Proceedings, 1999. XI, 365 pages. 1999.

Vol. 1721: S. Arikawa, K. Furukawa (Eds.), Discovery Science. Proceedings, 1999. XI, 374 pages. 1999.

Vol. 1730: M. Gelfond, N. Leone, G. Pfeifer (Eds.), Logic Programming and Nonmonotonic Reasoning. Proceedings, 1999. XI, 391 pages. 1999.

Vol. 1735: J.W. Amtrup, Incremental Speech Translation. XV, 200 pages. 1999.

# Lecture Notes in Computer Science

Vol. 1701: W. Burgard, T. Christaller, A.B. Cremers (Eds.), KI-99: Advances in Artificial Intelligence. Proceedings, 1999. XI, 311 pages. 1999. (Subseries LNAI).

Vol. 1702: G. Nadathur (Ed.), Principles and Practice of Declarative Programming. Proceedings, 1999. X, 434 pages. 1999.

Vol. 1703: L. Pierre, T. Kropf (Eds.), Correct Hardware Design and Verification Methods. Proceedings, 1999. XI, 366 pages. 1999.

Vol. 1704: Jan M. Żytkow, J. Rauch (Eds.), Principles of Data Mining and Knowledge Discovery. Proceedings, 1999. XIV, 593 pages. 1999. (Subseries LNAI).

Vol. 1705: H. Ganzinger, D. McAllester, A. Voronkov (Eds.), Logic for Programming and Automated Reasoning. Proceedings, 1999. XII, 397 pages. 1999. (Subseries LNAI).

Vol. 1706: J. Hatcliff, T. Æ. Mogensen, P. Thiemann (Eds.), Partial Evaluation Practice and Theory. 1998. IX, 433 pages. 1999.

Vol. 1707: H.-W. Gellersen (Ed.), Handheld and Ubiquitous Computing. Proceedings, 1999. XII, 390 pages. 1999.

Vol. 1708: J.M. Wing, J. Woodcock, J. Davies (Eds.), FM'99 – Formal Methods. Proceedings Vol. I, 1999. XVIII, 937 pages. 1999.

Vol. 1709: J.M. Wing, J. Woodcock, J. Davies (Eds.), FM'99 – Formal Methods. Proceedings Vol. II, 1999. XVIII, 937 pages. 1999.

Vol. 1710: E.-R. Olderog, B. Steffen (Eds.), Correct System Design. XIV, 417 pages. 1999.

Vol. 1711: N. Zhong, A. Skowron, S. Ohsuga (Eds.), New Directions in Rough Sets, Data Mining, and Granular-Soft Computing. Proceedings, 1999. XIV, 558 pages. 1999. (Subseries LNAI).

Vol. 1712: H. Boley, A Tight, Practical Integration of Relations and Functions. XI, 169 pages. 1999. (Subseries LNAI).

Vol. 1713: J. Jaffar (Ed.), Principles and Practice of Constraint Programming – CP'99. Proceedings, 1999. XII, 493 pages. 1999.

Vol. 1714: M.T. Pazienza (Eds.), Information Extraction. IX, 165 pages. 1999. (Subseries LNAI).

Vol. 1715: P. Perner, M. Petrou (Eds.), Machine Learning and Data Mining in Pattern Recognition. Proceedings, 1999. VIII, 217 pages. 1999. (Subseries LNAI).

Vol. 1716: K.Y. Lam, E. Okamoto, C. Xing (Eds.), Advances in Cryptology – ASIACRYPT'99. Proceedings, 1999. XI, 414 pages. 1999.

Vol. 1717: Ç. K. Koç, C. Paar (Eds.), Cryptographic Hardware and Embedded Systems. Proceedings, 1999. XI, 353 pages. 1999.

Vol. 1718: M. Diaz, P. Owezarski, P. Sénac (Eds.), Interactive Distributed Multimedia Systems and Telecommunication Services. Proceedings, 1999. XI, 386 pages. 1999.

Vol. 1719: M. Fossorier, H. Imai, S. Lin, A. Poli (Eds.), Applied Algebra, Algebraic Algorithms and Error-Correcting Codes. Proceedings, 1999. XIII, 510 pages. 1999.

Vol. 1720: O. Watanabe, T. Yokomori (Eds.), Algorithmic Learning Theory. Proceedings, 1999. XI, 365 pages. 1999. (Subseries LNAI).

Vol. 1721: S. Arikawa, K. Furukawa (Eds.), Discovery Science. Proceedings, 1999. XI, 374 pages. 1999. (Subseries LNAI).

Vol. 1722: A. Middeldorp, T. Sato (Eds.), Functional and Logic Programming. Proceedings, 1999. X, 369 pages. 1999.

Vol. 1723: R. France, B. Rumpe (Eds.), «UML»'99 – The Unified Modeling Language. XVII, 724 pages. 1999.

Vol. 1725: J. Pavelka, G. Tel, M. Bartošek (Eds.), SOFSEM'99: Theory and Practice of Informatics. Proceedings, 1999. XIII, 498 pages. 1999.

Vol. 1726: V. Varadharajan, Y. Mu (Eds.), Information and Communication Security. Proceedings, 1999. XI, 325 pages. 1999.

Vol. 1727: P.P. Chen, D.W. Embley, J. Kouloumdjian, S.W. Liddle, J.F. Roddick (Eds.), Advances in Conceptual Modeling. Proceedings, 1999. XI, 389 pages. 1999.

Vol. 1728: J. Akoka, M. Bouzeghoub, I. Comyn-Wattiau, E. Métais (Eds.), Conceptual Modeling – ER '99. Proceedings, 1999. XIV, 540 pages. 1999.

Vol. 1729: M. Mambo, Y. Zheng (Eds.), Information Security. Proceedings, 1999. IX, 277 pages. 1999.

Vol. 1734: H. Hellwagner, A. Reinefeld (Eds.), Scalable Coherent Interface – SCI. XXI, 490 pages. 1999.

Vol. 1564: M. Vazirgiannis, Interactive Multimedia Documents. XIII, 161 pages. 1999.

Vol. 1591: D.J. Duke, I. Herman, S. Marshall, PREMO: A Framework for Multimedia Middleware. XII, 254 pages. 1999.

Vol. 1665: P. Widmayer, G. Neyer, S. Eidenbenz (Eds.), Graph-Theoretic Concepts in Computer Science. Proceedings, 1999. XI, 414 pages. 1999.

Vol. 1730: M. Gelfond, N. Leone, G. Pfeifer (Eds.), Logic Programming and Nonmonotonic Reasoning. Proceedings, 1999. XI, 391 pages. 1999. (Subseries LNAI).

Vol. 1735: J.W. Amtrup, Incremental Speech Translation. XV, 200 pages. 1999. (Subseries LNAI).

Vol. 1736: L. Rizzo, S. Fdida (Eds.): Networked Group Communication. Proeceedings, 1999. XIII, 339 pages. 1999.